Alaska's
No.1 Guide

The History and Journals of
Andrew Berg
1869 - 1939

Catherine Cassidy

Catherine Cassidy
Gary Titus

Spruce Tree Publishing

FRONT COVER
Image of Andrew Berg over an 1895 map of Alaska, photo inset (circa 1920s) shows Hank Lucas on the far left standing in front of an Alaska Guides' cache located up the Funny River near the north end of the MoosehornTrail. The man on the right holding a pipe is Duncan Little.

REAR COVER
Upper right photo of Kenai Mountains taken from the benchland between Tustumena Lake and Skilak Lake. Andrew Berg's homestead cabin in 1938, (photo courtesy of Smithsonian Fish and Wildlife Service Records Group) this cabin has been restored and relocated to the Kenai National Wildlife Refuge Visitor Center in Soldotna, Alaska. Lower right photo of Andrew Berg with unidentified dog on the ice on Tustumena Lake (photo courtesy of Fabian Carey Collection, Accession no. 75-209-24N, Archives and Manuscripts, Alaska and Polar Regions Dept. UAF).

Printed in the U.S.A.

Library of Congress Control Number 2003103271

ISBN 0-9720144-0-3

Spruce Tree Publishing
35555 Spur Hwy. PMB 265
Soldotna, AK 99669
www.sprucetreepub.com

AUTHORS' NOTE

In the course of pursuing our individual interests in local history we encountered many kindred spirits. This book reflects our desire to participate in the process of sharing the wealth of resources about the history of the Kenai Peninsula which have surfaced to date.

Andrew Berg's biography was initially conceived as a small project. It quickly grew far beyond our expectations. First we decided to include Berg's entire journal rather than excerpts so as not to lose the flow and rhythm of his daily entries. Then the friends and neighbors who appeared in Berg's journal required inclusion and the rich context of his era demanded more and more space. New sources of materials and photographs came to light during our work and will continue to emerge, perhaps fueling revised editions and additional books.

We hope that Alaska's No.1 Guide and other local history publications generate interest in our past and the preservation of resources. Other journals were kept and may be tucked away and forgotten along with precious old photographs, letters and documents. These materials have great value in the context of your community's history. When you find them, share them with historical societies or libraries.

We also hope to encourage respect for archaeological and historical sites. There is much we still have to learn about our past, from 50 to 9,000 years ago. Human artifacts left in the places where they were created or used are vital tools in the documentation of cultural identities and experiences. If you come across historic sites or artifacts in your wanderings in the Kenai National Wildlife Refuge and other public lands, look, photograph and report your find, but leave the pieces of the puzzle in place for those who are working to develop a better understanding of those who came before us.

Every journey has a beginning. Here is a first look at the setting for much of Andrew Berg's story. Looking southeast across Tustumena Lake toward Tustumena Glacier and the Kenai Mountains. Photo by Joe Secora, circa 1939, courtesy of Ella and John Secora.

ACKNOWLEDGMENTS

Any history project is inherently a collaboration. We acknowledge and thank the following people without whom this book could not have been created.

Lorraine and Ray Blake, for preserving and sharing Andrew Berg's journal over the years.

These generous contributors of photographs, materials and reminiscences:

Dolly Cole Christl	Cheryl Cline	Marion Cole
Betty A. Crocker	Art Frisbee	Wanda M. Griffin
Benjamin Jackinsky	Ed Jackinsky	Rocky Johnson
Joan McLane Lahndt	Lori Landstrom	Dave Letzring
Norman Lowell	Linda McLane	Stan McLane
Lars Näs	Edward Ness	Susan & Joe Perletti
George Pollard	Terry Rude	Ella Hermansen Secora
Zeke Shadura	Clare Swan	Jim Taylor
Allen Try	Irene Ness Wilcox	

Erik Huebsch, editor and publisher, for his wholehearted commitment to the project and involvement in every aspect from research to design.

Dave Kenagy, Nancy Hewitt and Jeffrey Hewitt for their contributions of professional and technical expertise in graphics and design.

Editors and proofreaders Candace Ward, Walter Ward and James Munson, for their guidance and attention to detail.

Mona Painter, Cooper Landing historian, for first inspiring Gary's interest in researching local history.

The staff of the Kenai Community Library, especially Emily DeForest, Linda McNair and Julie Niederhauser, who not only provided sources and leads but also nudged Gary in the direction of local history.

Don Barber, Gary's longtime hiking partner, for sharing countless miles and numerous bear encounters while retracing the steps of the old-timers and locating historic sites.

Author and artist Susan Woodward Springer for inspiring us with her beautiful book *Seldovia, Alaska.*

The archives, collections and helpful staff members at:
Consortium Library, University of Alaska Anchorage; Alaska Room, Loussac Library, City of Anchorage; National Archives - Pacific Alaska Region, Anchorage; Cañon City, Colorado Municipal Library and Museum; Anchorage Museum of History and Art; E.E. Rasmusen Library, University of Alaska Fairbanks; Museum of Vertebrate Zoology, University of California at Berkeley; Denver Museum of Natural History; National Museum of Natural History; Smithsonian Institute.

Alaska's No.1 Guide

Contents

Gold, salmon and moose would attract Euro-Americans to Alaska's Kenai Peninsula in the last part of the nineteenth century. Tustumena Lake and Mt. Redoubt volcano are in the background of this picture shot in the late 1920s. Photo by Slim Crocker, courtesy of Betty A. Crocker.

CHAPTER 1

INTRODUCTION

Every life is a story. The plots are similar: we are born; we live; and we die. But events mingle with individual characteristics to create unique adventures and perspectives. Some stories are made more compelling by circumstances and some by the telling. Andrew Berg's story has both powerful particulars and engaging narrators.

Berg came to Alaska's Kenai Peninsula in 1888. A young Finnish immigrant seeking wildlife and wilderness, he found both in great abundance. At that time Alaska was lagging a good hundred years behind most of America in social and industrial development. Things would change very little in Andrew's lifetime.

Berg was the first big game guide in southcentral Alaska. As civilization crept into the Territory he became the first licensed guide and held guide license "No. 1" for over 20 years. Like many early Alaskans, Andrew was also a trapper, fisherman and miner. At times he worked as a game warden and a fish warden. All of these activities generated articles and correspondence about Berg and by him. In addition, he kept a daily journal for many years. The various documents are gathered here to take us on a journey back in time.

Some of Andrew Berg's actions and adventures may be considered incredible and we tend to accord a sort of high status to the "mountain man" image, but he was, ultimately, just a man. And he was a man of his time with very ordinary prejudices and self-serving principles. Our intent is not to portray a hero but simply present his story in the extraordinary context of his time and place on America's last frontier.

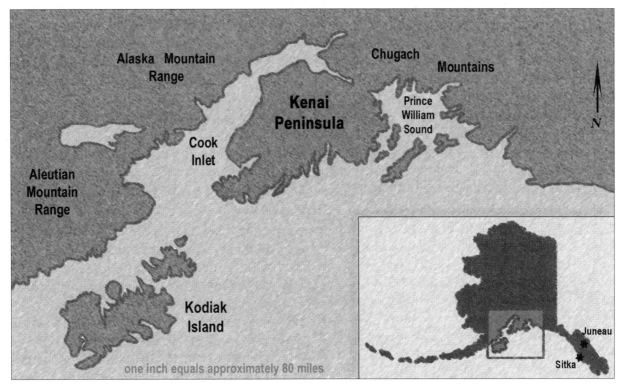

When Alaska was purchased by America in 1867, Sitka remained the seat of government. Juneau was designated the capital in 1900 although government offices didn't move for some years.

Amidst the steam-powered flood of European immigrants to America in 1887 was sixteen year old Andrew Berg. Poverty in Russian-controlled Finland encouraged emigration at that time. At least three of Andrew's eleven siblings also left their homeland. Andrew's younger brother Emil would follow him to America in 1901 to avoid Russian military service.

Andrew was born "Anders Berg" on October 16, 1869. His father, Johan Eriksson Berg, was a well educated man for the time and place, having had two years of agricultural college. He and his wife, Lovisa Johansdotter Skytt, taught their children to read and write Swedish, their native tongue (Sweden had controlled Finland for many centuries until the early 1800s). They lived on a small farm in Kantlax, Nykarleby on the Gulf of Bothnia. Fishing and hunting augmented the family's farming but there was very little opportunity for young men. Andrew's uncle Erik Berg and his wife Brita had recently emigrated to America when it was decided that Andrew would go.

Three months shy of his seventeenth birthday he sailed from Finland, with two other boys from Kantlax, bound for England. His father had asked him to write home of his journey to help them decide if any of his siblings should follow him to America. Andrew wrote of his departure: "I almost trembled with fear before the long trip."[1] He also described harrowing experiences with stormy sailing weather and seasickness. The boys spent over a month sailing to Hull in England and then had to find their way to Liverpool by train. Fortunately, they met an Englishman also traveling to Liverpool and were able to follow him at transfer points.

At Liverpool they bought 3rd class passage to New York City on the steamer *St. Andreas*. Their accommodations consisted of large holds equipped with wooden sleeping shelves. They had to supply their own eating utensils as well as bedding. A total of 400 emigrants were on board when they left England and another 100 joined them in Ireland. They experienced a fifteen day Atlantic crossing in stormy weather and were diverted to Quebec due to a cholera outbreak in New York.

By the time they reached North America it was late September. The boys made their way west, by train to Chicago and then by steamboat over Lake Michigan to Michigan City, Indiana where 20 sawmills were consuming the virgin forests. The sawmills wouldn't hire them but, not surprisingly, they were able to get work as lumberjacks. Many sawyers were needed to keep all

Andrew Berg's parents, Johan Berg and Lovisa Skytt, in Finland. The children are unidentified. Photo courtesy of Lars Näs.

of those mills fed. Berg wrote to his parents that he had been regretting leaving his home but now life was starting to be brighter. He described working "in the wild forest together with indians and many wild animals".[2] From childhood Andrew had exhibited a strong interest in hunting. His desire to find big game soon led him further west. His next letter home was from Kenai, Alaska in 1888.

Andrew wound up in Alaska, via San Francisco, as an employee of a salmon cannery.[3] He was likely in the company of his uncle Erik, who made his home in San Francisco but spent summers working in Alaska.

Andrew's westward migration brought him to Alaska's Kenai Peninsula and there he found his dream – big game animals beyond count and seemingly endless wilderness in which there were no rules, no regulations, no private property and very few people. He also found a landscape and climate strikingly similar to that in his Finnish homeland.

Southcentral Alaska possesses dramatic, breathtaking beauty. Tectonic collisions have created mountain ranges which tower five thousand to ten thousand feet over verdant sea shores. Ongoing tectonic movement keeps volcanoes active in this northern sector of the Pacific Ring of Fire. Millions of years of erosion and periodic glaciation have produced vast sedimentary basins, deltas and rounded foothills below rocky peaks. Ice fields and glaciers still adorn the mountain tops and valleys.

The Kenai Mountains form the bulk of the more than 15,000 square miles comprising the Kenai Peninsula. This mountain range curves around the eastern and southern sides of the Peninsula, dropping precipitously into the

deep, green waters of Prince William Sound and the Gulf of Alaska. The land comes to a point at the southwest corner where Cook Inlet opens northward from the Gulf. The western side of the Peninsula presents a friendlier scene of hills and dales rolling inland from sandy bluffs along the shore. This terrain is the result of glacial deposits left by ice sheets which flowed out of both the Kenai Mountains to the east and the Alaska Mountain Range to the northwest. These "lowlands" bear significant similarity to Finland in topography, climate, flora and fauna. This is where Berg would settle, splitting his time between the coast and the interior.

Ocean currents warm the outer, southern coastline of the Peninsula and produce temperate rain forests of towering Sitka spruce and hemlock. Inland, spruce forests are dotted with lakes and interwoven with stands of birch,

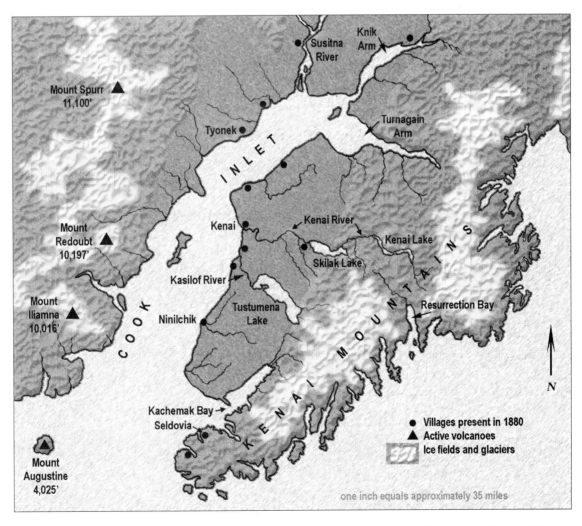

Kenai Peninsula and Cook Inlet map indicating general topography and many of the communities which existed in 1880. Contemporary names and spellings are used. Many variations will be seen in the documents transcribed here. For example, Cook Inlet and Kasilof were "Cook's Inlet" and "Kussiloff" well into the twentieth century.

aspen and cottonwood. Expanses of tundra-like bog open up grand vistas. Glaciers carved out three tremendous lakes below the mountains. Water flows in crystal clear streams and silty glacial rivers into these lakes and out to the sea. Glacial meltwater still supplies most of the water for the flow of the two major rivers, the Kenai and the Kasilof.

Knowledge of the earliest people here is still in the process of discovery. The upper and lower parts of the Peninsula were inhabited by different cultures during various periods over the last nine to ten thousand years. The residents of the Kenai lowlands at the time of the first European invasion were Dena'ina Indians, members of the Athabaskan language group. The Dena'ina have been in the area since around A.D. 1000.[4]

Russians came into the Cook Inlet region in the late 1780s. Through the dissemination of disease, economic servitude and religious conversion, the Dena'ina on the Kenai Peninsula, dubbed "Kenaitze" by the Russians, were subjugated and nearly decimated. By 1867, when America purchased Alaska, perhaps ten percent of the original population remained.[5]

The 1880 census listed thirteen villages on the entire Kenai Peninsula with a total enumeration of 519 people. Three people out of this number were listed as "White," meaning Euro-American. Another 155 persons were described as "Creole," meaning of mixed Alaska Native and Russian descent. Ten of the communities were located in the Kenai lowlands and all but one of them was on the coast of Cook Inlet, the virtual highway for this region. The village of Kenai (population - 44) was a dominant community in the area at this time. Two of the three Euro-Americans on the Peninsula were in Kenai where competing trading companies had outposts. Kenai was the center of the Russian Orthodox Diocese encompassing the Peninsula, though no priest was in residence in 1880. Territorial government was over 800 miles away in Sitka. Washington, D.C. may as well have been on the moon.

Residents led subsistence life styles augmented by fur trading. Resources were abundant. Caribou, moose, brown bear, black bear, wolf, fox, coyote, lynx, Dall sheep, mountain goat, wolverine, beaver, otter, porcupine, marmot, mink, marten, muskrat, and weasel were available to the hunter and trapper. Skin boats and wooden skiffs provided access to rivers, lakes and the sea for harvesting waterfowl, fish and sea mammals.

The annual return of spawning salmon to Cook Inlet's rivers and streams was another source of bounty and also provided the impetus for the first significant American ingress into this region.

The trading companies dabbled in salting salmon in barrels, but canning salmon was the industrial trend which was working its way up the Pacific coast. The first cannery came to Cook Inlet in 1882. Salmon return to most of the tributaries of Cook Inlet with the largest concentrations in the Kenai and Kasilof rivers. The San Francisco-based Alaska Packing Company chose to build a cannery by the mouth of the Kasilof River, perhaps because no town existed there to interfere. Canneries built in remote areas were towns in and of themselves although only for a few months out of the year.

That first spring the locals must have been astonished to see a virtual city rise up out of the mud and sand dunes on the bank of the Kasilof River. Quickly constructed were processing facilities, warehouses, bunkhouses, messhall, hospital, company store, offices and an extensive wharf reaching out into the river. All of the building materials, equipment, supplies and personnel required for construction and operation were brought by sailing ship from San Francisco.

The monumental job of building this complex in the wilderness was compounded by the local tides. Cook Inlet's length and shallow depth produce the second largest tidal fluctuations in North America. At the extremes, tidal surges can roar up and down the Inlet at over 10 knots, rising and falling over 30 feet in six hour cycles. The extent of the tidal fluctuations vary daily depending on the phase of the moon and other factors. Low tide may expose hundreds of yards of muddy beach. High tide can completely cover the beach and lap up against the bluffs. Tributaries flowing into Cook Inlet may appear to be navigable rivers at high tide and simple creeks at low tide.

The sailing schooners and barks ferrying materials to Cook Inlet could not navigate even the area's largest rivers. They would anchor well offshore and the cargo, everything from huge steam boilers to nails, would be laboriously transferred to small boats for transport to the building site. Even this process had to be carefully coordinated around the tide changes because the beaches exposed at low tide are covered with deep, sticky mud. Once a wharf was built the whole process was greatly

This picture of the Kasilof Cannery was taken in 1890 by the superintendent of the plant, Harry M. Wetherbee. The wharf is on the left, the tide is out. You can see the scale of the operation and the expanse of mud exposed on the river bank at low tide. Photo courtesy of the H.M. Wetherbee Collection, Accession number 866-164, Archives, Alaska and Polar Regions Department, University of Alaska Fairbanks

facilitated but work still had to be judiciously timed as boats could only get to the dock at certain tide stages.

The fishing and cannery operations were extremely labor intensive. Thirty to forty fishermen including many Scandinavian immigrants fished the Inlet in rowboats. They caught salmon using 300 foot long linen gillnets which they pulled into the boats by hand. Chinese immigrants canned the fish, beginning with cutting out and assembling cans from flat sheets of tin. At season's end, in late August, the tens of thousands of cases of canned salmon were transported out to the tall ship and carried back south.

The cannery provided seasonal work, housing, health care, a company store and the company debt that went along with the store. The majority of the workers came and went with the sailing ships but locals were also employed. A few of the imported workers, particularly Scandinavian immigrants who were not intimidated by the prospect of an Alaskan winter, stayed over. The cannery had a watchman who also staffed the company store, selling nonperishable staples stocked the previous summer. From October through March, no boats would come to Cook Inlet.

Winter closes in quickly. The sun loses its warmth in September and snow usually arrives in October. Average winter snowfall is sixty inches and the winter temperatures average fifteen degrees Fahrenheit. In December, the daylight decreases to little more than five hours a day. Temperatures may drop to extremes of thirty degrees below zero and colder. Hearty people accustomed to the climate could find plenty of resources for survival. The Kenai and Kasilof River systems provided access into the interior of the Peninsula. On the water, or on the ice once it froze, people used these routes to hunting, trapping and prospecting areas.

The Kenai River system, including Skilak Lake and Kenai Lake, almost transects the Peninsula. It provides a travel corridor from Cook Inlet to within 18 miles of the Peninsula's eastern coast. The Kasilof River runs seventeen miles between Cook Inlet and Tustumena Lake. Tustumena Lake stretches eastward another 24 miles through the lowlands and ends against the mountains. No permanent human settlements existed on Tustumena Lake when Berg arrived. In this vast expanse of water, woods and wildlife Andrew would generally spend at least half the year – the cold half.

It was common for the early Euro-Americans to split their time between summer fishing jobs on the coast and trapping cabins in the interior in the winter. It was a tough life-style and many would only endure it for a short time. Andrew Berg lived it for over fifty years.

Berg's first two decades in Alaska are documented by a miscellany of articles and correspondence. International trophy hunters wrote of their guided hunts with Berg on the Kenai Peninsula. Andrew exchanged letters with clients and government officials. Newspaper articles describe events and life-styles.

From 1921 through 1938, Berg tells his own story through journals he kept at his home at Tustumena Lake. His daily entries tell a tale of self reliance: the constant effort required to maintain warmth and sustenance; the ingenuity and patience involved in making and repairing everything from mittens to outboard engines; and the forbearance demonstrated in the face of injury and illness. These qualities are predictable in someone who chose to live in the wilderness.

The surprising element in his writing is his description of the greater community on the lake. We get acquainted with his neighbors who think nothing of hiking ten miles for a visit and a game of cards. Area residents and other characters come and go and through their stories we get snapshots of life on the western Kenai Peninsula.

Settlers trickled into the area over the course of Berg's lifetime. Some, like Andrew, were looking for unfettered living on the edge of wilderness. Others came with big dreams and expectations but realized only frustration and disappointment. Climate, geography and economic factors conspired to keep this corner of Alaska isolated from the rest of the world. The people who made their lives here were ultimately sustained by the salmon and the game. The animals and fish were sustained in turn by various conservation efforts which are also part of our story.

This photo shows a crew scooping live salmon out of a fish trap into a barge. Fishing technology made a great leap in efficiency in 1885 when the first fish trap was built in Cook Inlet. Traps were built along the beaches to take advantage of the salmon's tendency to swim along the shoreline. The structures could trap up to 20,000 salmon and hold them alive until the cannery boat came to collect them. Constructed of driven piling, poles, wire fencing and cord webbing, they had to be built and dismantled every year because Cook Inlet's winter ice would destroy them. Cutting timber for fish traps was a winter occupation for many Peninsula men. Photo courtesy of McLane Collection.

CHAPTER 2
1890 - 1899

The 1890s began quietly enough in southcentral Alaska. Gold rushes on the Peninsula and points north during the latter half of the decade would drastically change the scene.

Early in the decade prospectors were just starting to create mining districts in this part of the territory and coal was being dug around Kachemak Bay. The Alaska Commercial Company and the Northern Alaska Commercial Company were both trading in Cook Inlet. The competition between them drove fur prices relatively high.[1]

Furs and fishing occupied Andrew Berg during his first years in Alaska. An early reference to Berg is found in an *Alaska Sportsman* article about another old-timer:

Chris Spillum first met Andrew in the late 1890's. Chris was strolling along the beach at Seldovia one day, when a schooner came sailing into the bay. The crew and some of the passengers came ashore to try their land legs, and among them was Andrew. Andrew and Chris began to chat... [Berg] was living at Kenai, where he had built a cabin in 1893. For a living he trapped furs in the winter and fished for the Alaska Packers Association during the summer.[2]

So Berg chose the village of Kenai for his home base. Here, the young immigrant was exposed to a society we would hardly recognize. Barely a handful of non-Native men lived there all year. During the summer influx, the canneries segregated the European, Native and Asian-Americans. For the first half of the 1890s, the Dena'ina in the village of Kenai were threatened with violence and supplied with liquor during the long winter months by the storekeeper working for the Alaska Commercial Company. The government did nothing in spite of complaints from the community. A high ranking representative of the Russian Orthodox Church finally

A Dena'ina family around 1890. The building style is largely traditional. Their summer clothing appears entirely western. Note the "bidarka" frame stored upside down on the rack. Photo courtesy of the H.M. Wetherbee Collection, Accession number 866-26, Archives, Alaska and Polar Regions Department, University of Alaska Fairbanks.

persuaded the Company to remove the offending individual.[3]

The Indians spoke Dena'ina and Russian but little English exacerbating the discrimination against them. Attitudes wouldn't change for many decades and legal protections

would improve only gradually with the coming of more Euro-Americans to the region.

Prospectors were crawling all over the Peninsula during the 1890s and finally struck pay dirt in 1895. Sailing and steam vessels of all sizes and descriptions headed north to the Kenai Peninsula in March of 1896. As many as 3,000 people came to Cook Inlet that year. The center of the rush was on the northern side of the Peninsula where the towns of Hope and Sunrise sprang into existence. Typically, there were far more miners than the potential claims could support and most moved on to the Yukon and points north. On the Peninsula there was enough accessible gold to keep things going on a small scale for a decade.

A significant effect of the mining activity in central and western Alaska was the development of a transportation infrastructure. "Infrastructure" is used rather loosely here, meaning seasonal steamer service from west coast cities, intra-Alaska freight and passenger boats, a few trails and the tentative beginnings of a railroad. For much of the territory, including Cook Inlet, ships and boats continued to operate only from late spring through early autumn due to weather and ice conditions.

Boom and Bust Salmon

The commercial salmon industry in Alaska would prove to have a persistent boom-and-bust style. The 1880s were boom years. Between 1878 and 1891, thirty-seven canneries were built in Alaska. Three of them were in Cook Inlet, two in the mouth of the Kasilof River and one in the Kenai River. A resulting glut in the market for canned salmon caused a major shakedown in the industry. By 1893, only the original Kasilof cannery was operating in Cook Inlet after twenty-nine of the Alaskan canneries consolidated into the "Alaska Packers Association." [4]

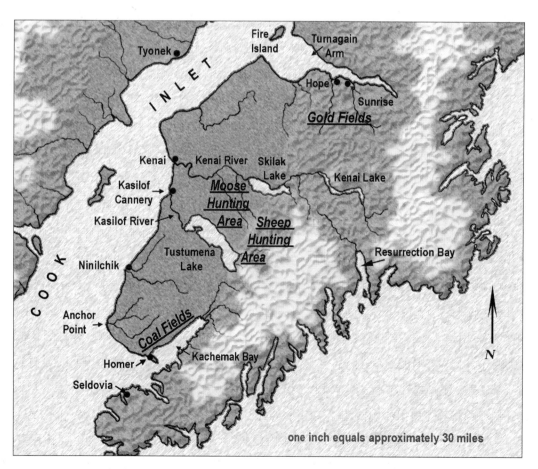

one inch equals approximately 30 miles

New communities on the Peninsula included Homer, Hope and Sunrise. Homer would be abandoned for a time and then start again.

Gold, coal and hunting brought prospectors, con artists, settlers and world travelers to Cook Inlet in this decade.

In addition to fishing and trapping, Andrew Berg was hunting, prospecting and exploring. In his travels he encountered massive trophy moose. Moose antlers started streaming out of Cook Inlet during this period.[5] Berg and others had found a new commodity and their pursuit of cash for trophies initiated the novel industry of big game hunting which was aided by the increasing transportation services.

One set of Berg's antlers ended up in the hands of W.F. Sheard, a dealer in trophy game mounts in Tacoma, Washington. Sheard had a photo of the seventy-three and one quarter inch antlers published in the March 6, 1897 issue of Forest and Stream.[6] This photo piqued the interest of Dall DeWeese, a wealthy fruit grower and entrepreneur from Colorado with a passion for hunting and wildlife. He saw the photo of the trophy antlers and set out to find the source.

DeWeese was the first person known to travel to the Kenai Peninsula for the express purpose of hunting. He wrote magazine articles of his adventures and his words illustrate the challenges of travel and hunting in Alaska at this period:

Head of Kusiloff River, Cook's Inlet, Alaska. Moose Camp, September 9th, 1897... When I left home June 2d, I had my head set on "Cook's Inlet," but had arranged to meet Mr. A. J. Stone at Seattle and talk over the probability of a hunt with him up the Stickee [Stickine] River. We met on time and on July 8 we boarded the steamer "Queen" and started for Alaska... I decided to go on my route as originally planned, for I could see so much more of Alaska and get into a locality where there might be more of a variety of game than existed in the upper Stickeen country. Another reason was that while I was at Seattle I visited Tacoma and learned that the big moose head whose picture I showed you last winter in Forest and Stream of March 6th had come from Cook's inlet instead of the Yukon and you know it was big moose I was after... I left Fort Wrangel on a little steamer "Alaska" and reached Juneau, the 13th. There I found everybody mad with the Klondike fever, and hundreds arriving on every boat. A mining company wanted me to make a trip over the then "supposed to be completed White Pass Trail," and report on its condition. I also thought it might be possible to find some game over the divide and if not I still had till

August 6th before I could sail for Cook's Inlet, as the boats for that direction made but monthly trips. I soon arranged affairs and went up to Skaguay, one hundred and ten miles. The next day I started with the first pack outfit of twenty-one horses that crossed White Pass... When at the summit of the pass, day closed at 10 p.m. and dawn at 3 a.m. it was a rough hard trip, but I enjoyed every foot of it. There were plenty of caribou and white goat, but I did not care for either of these specimens, for you know I killed all the caribou I want last fall on my hunt in northeast New Brunswick. I then made a swing to the head of chilkoot and reached Sitka August 4th on the "City of Topeka." My supplies were soon on board the Dora, and on the morning of the 6th we were headed for Cook's Inlet, some eight hundred miles to the westward... The Dora landed us at Homer on the 11th where the little steamer "Parry" lay in wait to take passengers and freight to Turn-again Arm... We reached Tyoonok the second day, and I had now learned from the fur buyer of that country that a Mr. Berg had killed that big moose mentioned in Forest and Stream and that he was working at a fish cannery at the mouth of Kusiloff River, some sixty to seventy miles across and down the inlet. I took a boat and crossed over to the mouth of Turn-again Arm, the most terrible waters of the world – tide forty-feet, which comes in with a roll (bore) eight to twelve feet high. On reaching Kusiloff I found Mr. Berg and soon decided from his talk that he was a good hunter and knew where the moose lived as well as bear and white mountain sheep. He is twenty-six years old, six feet tall, one hundred and ninety-eight pounds weight and is one of the strongest men I ever met. He said he would go with me if he could get off from the cannery. I went to the superintendent, Capt. Wetherbee, who very kindly arranged for his release.[7]

"Capt. Wetherbee" was Harry M. Wetherbee, superintendent of the cannery for many years and virtual grocer, banker, mayor and magistrate of the area during the fishing season.[9] Later, Wetherbee would add outfitting services for hunters to his mercantile business.

DeWeese continued his account with an evocative description of traveling up the Kasilof River and enjoying his hunt:

The S.S. Dora, 112 feet long, was built in 1880 by the Alaska Commercial Co. for the San Francisco-Bering Sea freight and passenger service. Later based in Seattle, she would make eleven round trips a year, taking a month off for annual maintenance. Her long service ended in 1920 after she became stranded in shallow water in British Columbia.[8]   Photo courtesy of Jim Taylor.

THE ALASKAN   Sitka, Alaska
October 16, 1897

Saturday, Oct. 10, 1897. Among the passengers who came down on the "Dora" was Mr. Dall Deweese, a prominent real estate man of Canon City Colorado. Mr. Deweese is a thorough sportsman and has established a reputation among his associates in Colorado, of which any huntsman might be proud. He left his home in the Rockies about four months ago. On reaching Sitka he took passage on the "Dora" for Cook Inlet, where he engaged a canoe and Indians to help pack the provisions and guns to Kusiloff River. Arriving there he sent the Indians back, merely retaining one white man, to assist in getting the specimens down the river. Among the rocks and glaciers he succeeded in killing eight white mountain sheep. Encouraged by this he proceeded to Kusiloff lake, a long, hard trip, but he was well rewarded for his trouble, for in the spruce and birchwood he espied three splendid moose, and with a few well directed shots soon brought them down. Two of them are the largest ever killed in this country. Magnificent heads, large and massive, each set of antlers having thirty-two points, one having a spread of sixty-five inches and the other sixty-nine....he had seen the tracks of a bear and he must follow the trail, securing two large bears, one Alaskan brown bear, measuring ten feet, seven inches. Even the Alaskans who are used to big game, expressed great surprise on seeing the fine specimens brought down by Mr. Deweese. He is thoroughly satisfied that Alaska is the happy "hunting ground" for the sportsman who is not afraid of hard work and we will be pleased to welcome him back to the far northwest some future time.

[A great fluff piece for the first hunt, although later writers would learn to mention the name (and prowess) of the guide. This article has the geography confused, reflecting the absence of maps in the territory.]

On August 17th, we had supplies and my outfit in a good boat and with this man [Berg] and three Indians we started up the river. They had to pull the boat with a line and water was ice cold running from the mountain glaciers. The mosquitoes and sand flies were in countless millions, and never in my life have I endured such punishment. Our eyes were swollen almost shut. Our faces and hands were so bitten and swollen that the pain was terrible. The mosquitoes are gentlemen compared to the sand flies and gnats. It was well that I had taken a good supply of netting and carboized vaseline. We had been wading along the banks of the swift river, which is about one hundred yards wide and four to six feet deep, pulling the boat for three days, crossing the stream many times on account of the overhanging trees that obstructed our way. At times the poor Indians would go in up to their necks, while the sand flies continuously sapped the life out of us and it was all I could to steer the boat. Yet we call this sport, and once when the Indian said, "White man d— fool to this," I thought him about right. But I had a purpose and determined that it would take something bigger than a mosquito or sand fly to knock me out. When I return with my trophies these Indians will say that "I'm a Big Ty-ee,"   We had now reached the foot of Lake Tust-u-me-na, which is fifty-two miles long and about fourteen miles wide. [DeWeese estimated the lake at about double its actual size] We had a fair breeze and a good sail, and ran the lake in one day. I let the Indians rest up a day and sent them packing their bi-dar-ka, which we had towed up with us. I went twenty miles in this on the lake going across and they are treacherous boats indeed... We made our permanent camp at the head of the lake, three miles from the foot of the mountains and near the base of an enormous glacier (no name) [Tustumena] the scenery is grand and indescribable...we killed two sheep same night and in five days had ten fine old rams heads, eight from my own gun....[11]

The hunt was a great success. DeWeese killed eight Dall sheep, two bears and three bull moose with antler spreads ranging from 58-69 inches. (Dall sheep, or *Ovis dalli*, were named for William H. Dall, not Dall DeWeese.) He wrote and published articles about this hunt in at least three journals in the following months.

Cannery Work

A federal survey of the salmon fisheries in Alaska was conducted during this time and the report describes the operation of the Kasilof cannery in 1897. Berg presumably numbered among the 35 "white" fishermen employed to operate the eight fish traps and 15 small fishing boats. They would start building the fish traps in April or May, fish from late May through mid-August, disassemble the traps and then load the season's catch on board the ship which would carry it back to San Francisco. For this work Berg received room and board, $30 a month and 3/4 cent per case of salmon. The cannery packed 32,532 cases that year adding $244 to a fisherman's seasonal wages.[10]

The word was out and Andrew Berg's guiding career and the trophy hunting industry were launched in 1898.

DeWeese returned to the Kenai the following year to hunt and photograph wildlife. In the meantime he had negotiated an agreement with the Smithsonian Institute to collect specimens. The required work entailed taking precise measurements of the animals and preserving the skins and bones for shipment back east. He again engaged Berg as his guide. DeWeese wrote additional articles about his second trip. While his prose style is exaggerated, his writing gives great detail on the experience of hunting the Kenai Peninsula.

I returned to Alaska again last fall (1898) to procure specimens of large mammals for the Smithsonian Institute. On this trip I had provided myself with cameras suitable to photograph some of this wild game in their native haunts, which would give me more pleasure than shooting the animals. Never before had the Ovis dalli been caught in the sportsman's camera.

After a six weeks trip of four thousand miles, August ninth found me in camp (with two packers, one white man and one Indian) on the Kenai Mountains, at timber-line, some ninety miles back of Cook's Inlet. At the start I had three white men and five Indians in my party to assist me in getting my outfit up the rapids of the Kussiloff River and to the head of Lake Tuslumena...

Mr. Berg, who was with me in 1897, also started with me, but the first night out from salt water he was taken with rheumatism in the limbs so severely that it was necessary for him to stay in the boat. His condition grew worse from day to day, and on reaching the lake I made camp for him, and detailed Mr. Singer to remain with him and do everything possible for his comfort while I pushed on to the mountains. I kept two packers constantly on the trail between this camp and my line of camps to the summit of the range, so that I could get supplies, send meat down, and learn the condition of my unfortunate companion.

...The home of the Ovis Dalli *in this section of Alaska is on the high range where its frowning sides break into deep gashy canons and*

precipitous walls to a mighty nameless glacier [Tustumena] from ten to twenty miles long.

I had now made a side camp above timber-line... We had nothing to burn but a scrubby willow brush which we pulled up by the roots. The weather was very changeable at this altitude; rain, heavy fog and spitting snow, with an occasional day of sunshine, and cold, frosty nights...[12]

DeWeese does not mention Berg again in this particular article but we know that Andrew recovered enough to rejoin the party from another piece DeWeese wrote about this same hunt:

All this is easy to write, but no person, save the hunter who has gone through it, can form the

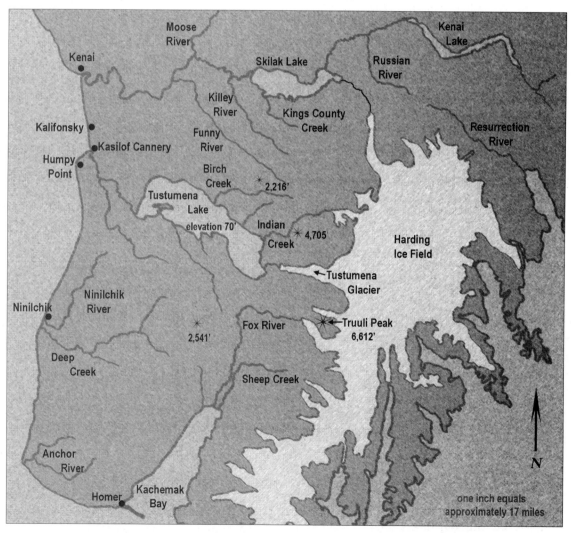

The central peninsula in this decade. Truuli Peak, at 6,612 feet, is the highest point in the Kenai Mountains. Tree line is around 2,500 feet. Tustumena Lake was often called Kasilof or Kussiloff Lake in old documents.

remotest idea of the hard work necessary to get picked specimens of moose from the wilds of Alaska. Think of the days we spent in getting up that rapid river with mosquitoes sapping our very life-blood day and night, the nights without sleep, hastily prepared food with no chance to eat it; yet all this is easy, for after you have done it and made your camps in the moose country you have not yet got your moose. It must be remembered that moose are scarce, even where they are plentiful, as compared with other large game, and his wary nature and instincts are pitted against you if you stalk them. I killed these by the "still hunt" without "call" or tracking snow. I killed one the first day, but it took me over two weeks to get the other three. There were days of continuous rain that soaked you through, no matter what your clothing may be. The grass is

The high country of the Kenai Mountains in late summer. This view looks east from the bench between Tustumena and Skilak lakes. "Twin Lakes" are nestled in the valley. Photo by Joseph P. Mazzoni, courtesy of U.S. Fish and Wildlife Service.

Dall DeWeese posed in front of Tustumena Glacier. Photo courtesy of DeWeese Collection, Accession number 3686, Local History Center, Cañon City Public Library, Cañon, City CO.

waist-high through which you drag yourself, then over marshy flats, sinking in half way to your knees, then over broken hill or down timber to the slopes of spruce and birchwood where you expect to find his mooseship, he may not be there: then on to another favorable looking place, and noiselessly you pick your way taking care not to break a twig: that not the slightest sound escapes your ear or any object or motion passes your sight, and that your route is such that you are on the lee side of your quarry, for, once you are on the weather side, he will soon put miles between you, and you see nothing but fresh tracks, You have now wandered far from camp and circle for a return route: you have had no dinner, and reach camp after dark, find everything wet and cold, and alone for the night. But all this is sport and easy for tomorrow you have the same experience,

Dall DeWeese with a boat load of trophies. Note the furled sail on the mast amidst the antlers. A line of hanging hides is on shore on the right. Photo courtesy of DeWeese Collection, Accession number 3685, Local History Center, Cañon City Public Library, Cañon City, CO.

DeWeese mentioned in his story that the boat was too small to carry their gear down the river. The men apparently built a raft to accommodate some baggage. In this photo Dall and his raft are beached by the cannery at the mouth of the Kasilof River. Photo courtesy of DeWeese Collection, Accession number 3687, Local History Center, Cañon City Public Library, Cañon City, CO.

only that you have stalked your moose and after "sizing him up" through your field glasses you find his crown is smaller than you want to take. You steal out of his sight and hearing, and you may see another one that day and you may not, and so on for a week...

On the 26th we had everything packed out to the lake and ready for our boat, which was too small to carry all my outfit farther than across the lake to the head of the rapids in the river – about forty-five miles. Next morning was cold, with a westerly drift in the sky, although calm on the lake. Our boat was 18 feet long, 5-foot beam, with good lines. My outfit sunk her rail to within eight inches of the water. There were now but four in my party, as I had dispatched the Indians in their bidarka some ten days previously.

At 9 o'clock a. m. my two men were pulling hard at the oars: at 1 o'clock a fair wind sprung up: we set sail and headed for the foot of the lake, while the wind grew stronger and stronger: at 3 o'clock we were out in the middle and ten miles from the shore: the white caps began chasing each other, and we really began to be alarmed. I held the sail rope and Berg the helm: we saw we were in for it and we simply attended to business and said nothing. A high sea was now rolling and breaking over the rails on both sides, while

Tustumena Lake

Tustumena Lake is twenty-four miles long, four to six miles wide and notorious for foul conditions. Southeast winds frequently roar down out of the mountains with no warning. Relatively straight shorelines provide little shelter for boaters when the wind starts kicking up waves. Over 900 feet deep in places and fed by glacial meltwater, the lake is always life-threateningly cold, never getting much above 50 degrees. Tons of glacial silt flow into the lake from the meltwater of Tustumena Glacier. The fine silt, or "flour", stays suspended in the water and turns the lake an opaque gray, the same color as the sky on an overcast day. Except during rare moments when the water is flat calm and the sun is shining, this vast lake is awe-inspiring and intimidating.

The lake's name comes from the Dena'ina name "Dusdubena," meaning "peninsula lake".[12]

we were plowing through the water at a terrible speed.[13]

DeWeese ended his article right there. The reader is left to assume that they arrived safely as the author was alive to write about the adventure.

In hunting camp. DeWeese is on the right and Berg is to his left. DeWeese's headdress of netting was a mosquito deterrent. Photo courtesy of DeWeese Collection, Accession number 3682, Local History Center, Cañon City Public Library, Cañon City, CO.

By 1898 other hunters had discovered the Kenai moose and miners were swarming over the peninsula looking for another big strike. One result was increased hunting pressure on the game populations. Fur prices fell in 1897 giving locals more incentive to trade in big game trophies and meat rather than pelts. DeWeese noticed a decrease in game animals during his second visit to Alaska and shared his observation with the Sitka newspaper:

I have hunted in all of the Southern and Eastern states and in the Rocky Mountains said Mr. DeWeese, but never have I seen such hunting as I have had during the last two summers on the Kenai Peninsula. It has been and is a hunter's paradise, but bids fair to soon undergo a change. The game is the largest of its several kinds. The mighty moose, herds of caribou in the interior

uplands and great droves of mountain sheep are there in plenty. But the number is slowly decreasing...

I want to make a plea for its preservation. Since the Indians found a market for furs by trading them for almost nothing to the white miner or trapper, a ruthless slaughter has been going on. The whites have joined in it to a certain extent, but not nearly so extensively as they will next year. The Indians are getting reckless for in the trail of a hunting party one can see many dead sheep at the bottom of a gully or on the sides of cliffs where they have been shot and left because it would be a difficult job to get them up or down. The moose are also perishing in great quantities. One reason for the Government protection of this

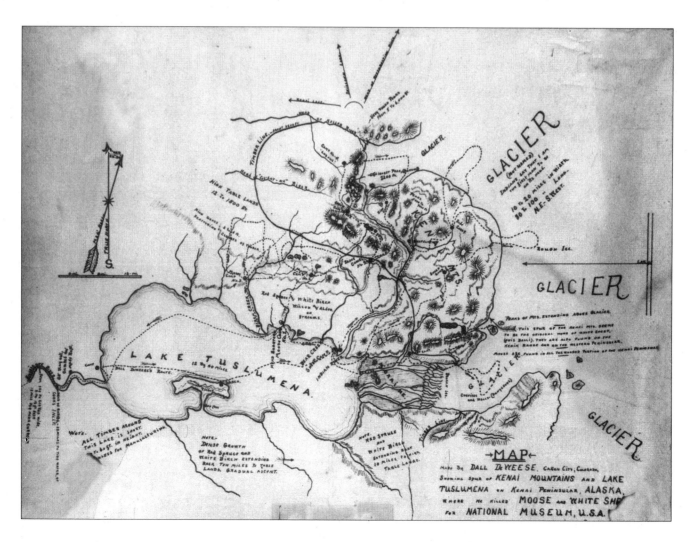

While on his hunting trip in 1898, Dall DeWeese created this map which he gave to the Smithsonian. Map courtesy of the National Museum of Natural History, Division of Mammals, Washington, D.C.

game is that without it the Indians will become government charges. Reservation will have to be provided and Indian agents appointed. A steamer will be kept busy carrying supplies to the Indians for with the game gone, they will starve... [15]

This article is the first known call for conservation and game regulations on the Peninsula. DeWeese had typical values and attitudes of a man of his class and time. He combined a genuine love of wildlife with his own interest in seeing it preserved for trophy hunting. His perspective was influenced by the recent decimation of the buffalo herds and the devastating consequences for the Plains Indians.

It is interesting to contemplate the influence which DeWeese and the other wealthy trophy hunters would have had on Andrew Berg. Long evenings were spent around campfires with much opportunity for conversation. When Berg began guiding he was a young immigrant who had spent his first adult years in the wilds of Alaska. By 1900 he had learned to read and write English and had become a naturalized citizen. [16] From his diary we sense that, while he was by no means an intellectual, he was an avid reader and interested in abstract ideas. Upper class sportsmen from America and Europe would expose him to their own perspectives on topics ranging from game regulations to politics.

Berg's intellectual horizons may have been broadened by his hunting clients but his physical reality remained primitive. Around this time Andrew accidently shot himself. No professional medical care existed on the Kenai Peninsula except seasonally at the cannery. Berg gave an account of the incident to a newspaper reporter decades later and the following version of the story was printed:

...Mr. Berg shot himself accidentally in the wrist while near Kenai, and in order to save his life a party of his friends there hastily bound the wounded member, and setting out in face of a storm with him made a wild trip over the waves in a sail boat from Kenai to Kodiak, to get the services of a doctor. With the tides and fierce gale favoring them they covered the approximate 200 miles in a bitter night trip, and got there in time to get surgical attention which resulted in saving his life... [17]

Kings County Mining Company

The various Alaskan gold rushes generated some outrageous adventures and fiascoes. Fools rushed in but even those who tried to plan a careful expedition often met with disaster when confronted with Alaskan conditions. In the spring of 1898 a group of entrepreneurs from Kings County, New York chartered the Kings County Mining Company and planned an assault on the Yukon gold fields. Some of their party left New York with supplies by schooner and headed for the west coast by way of Cape Horn. Other members of the company crossed the continent by train, joining the vessel in San Francisco. Reaching Kodiak in October, they were too late to continue north to the Yukon. The company decided to try their luck in the Kenai Peninsula gold fields at Sunrise.

Apparently intimidated by the prospect of navigating Cook Inlet, their ship's captain convinced the group that Sunrise was easily reached overland from Kachemak Bay. On October 16, 1898 the members of the company were dropped off on the north side of Kachemak Bay with their mountains of supplies. Accounts conflict but there may have been as many as sixty people, including some women and children. They headed north cutting a trail and ferrying their belongings with packboards and handmade wheelbarrows. Besides a large quantity of foodstuffs, such as casks of flour and bacon, they had all of their mining equipment including pans, picks, shovels and sledges.

Their route took them up the Fox River to Tustumena Lake. They ascended Birch Creek to the Tustumena-Skilak bench and then down to Skilak Lake ending up by the mouth of became known as Kings County Creek. At this location they built cabins and settled in. In the spring they dissolved their charter, built boats to carry them down river to Kenai, and dispersed, never having mined at all. At least two men of the company were not discouraged by the experience and stayed on the Peninsula.

For many years afterward trappers using their trail found caches of equipment and food which the hapless group had abandoned along the way. [19]

Another version of Andrew's injury was recounted by Kasilof resident Harry Gerberg:

Sometime in the late 1890's he had an accident with his shotgun down here at the mouth of the river and he blasted part of his left hand off. Well they had heard, the people around here then, that there was a doctor in Kodiak. Course this was long before there was an Anchorage and possibly Seward too. So old Victor Holmes undertook to take Andrew over to Kodiak in a flat bottom dory. No outboard motors in those days. He was rowing and had a small stick for a mast and a sail if the wind was favorable. Now that's a long, long ways from here to Kodiak. I would not want to make it with anything [boats] we have owned, really. Anyway they got to Kodiak and found there was no doctor there but there was a first aid man and he couldn't do anything I guess but damage Andrew's hand. Andrew himself told me about this trip and he said if he haven't of got over there, he just left the thing alone, he would've been better off. That hand was completely crippled but still he made it up and down this river with his dory to his home up at the head of the lake without any help from anyone.[18]

Victor Holm was another Finnish immigrant who had settled in Kasilof. The men did not sail all the way back to Cook Inlet in their small boat. Another ship carried them back to Seldovia. Chris Spillum's version of his "late 1890's" encounter with Berg as he disembarked from a schooner in Seldovia included the following details:

Andrew was wearing his left arm in a sling, and he explained to Chris that he had shot himself accidentally in the hand. He had just come from Kodiak, where Dr. Dickerson, the only doctor in that part of Alaska at the time, had amputated two of his fingers.[20]

Surprisingly, this disabling injury had no apparent affect on his daily life. Hunting, trapping, boating and building would continue unabated. None of his hunting clients would deem it worth mentioning in descriptions of their guide.

Dall DeWeese returned for six weeks in 1899 with his wife, Emma. On this trip they arranged to meet Andrew Berg and two more men in Homer in late May. They traveled by small boat up to the head of Kachemak Bay, pulled the boat loaded with provisions up Sheep Creek as far as they could go and then hiked over to Tustumena Lake. Berg had another boat waiting there and they proceeded across the lake and then climbed up to sheep hunting country.[21] It was presumably on this trip that a small lake above Indian Creek was named for Emma. They finished up their adventure in early July and Berg may have returned to the cannery or guided other hunters.

During their hunting trip Berg and the DeWeeses probably encountered miners staking claims around Indian Creek. Twelve claims were filed in 1899, mostly around the headwaters of the north fork of the creek. These claims ended up belonging to the Aurora Mining Company (which also had a large operation in Kachemak Bay) but never produced anything of note. Another mining outfit would soon make a genuine effort at Indian Creek in the new century.

Most of the photos of Andrew Berg show his injured hand in this position. It appears that he cannot open his fingers, and some may end at the second knuckle. How much use of his thumb he retained is unknown. Photo courtesy of McLane Collection.

CHAPTER 3

1900 - 1909

With the arrival of the twentieth century the territory remained a backwater. Alaska was attractive only to hearty souls drawn to the allure of wilderness or those seeking to exploit natural resources for quick gain.

In the 1900 census, Andrew Berg described his occupation as a miner and hunter. In October of 1901 Andrew, his recently arrived brother Emil, and two other men filed claims on 80 acres of placer ground along Indian Creek on the north shore of Tustumena Lake. Fifty-one other placer claims had already been located and filed along the lower reaches of the creek. These claims and a claim for miner's water rights for the outlet of Emma Lake were filed in May. In July the claims were consolidated under the Northwestern Development and Mining Company (NWD&M Company) which issued $50,000 of bonds to fund the enterprise. In October, the NWD&M Company also filed claim on 40 acres on the lake shore just west of Indian Creek, the proposed site of their work camp and lumber mill.[1]

It is not clear what, if any, relationship Andrew Berg had with the NWD&M Co. He may have worked for the company. He may have been a bond holder. The only certainty is that they had a relationship of proximity. Berg built a cabin for himself on land included within the company's claim (see exhibit on next page).

Meanwhile, Dall Deweese returned for his fourth and final trip to Alaska in 1901. He wrote no more magazine articles, perhaps because his conservation concerns strengthened during the visit. Rather than promoting hunting, he turned to promoting hunting regulations in Alaska with a letter to President Theodore Roosevelt. DeWeese expressed his greatest concern for the Dall sheep population. Besides the observable decline in numbers, he had undoubtedly also learned of the mining company's intended plans at Indian Creek, the base of the best sheep hunting grounds. At the same time, he was not successful influencing Andrew Berg on game conservation. Andrew and Emil Berg were making quite a dent in the bull moose population shipping out twelve trophy heads to dealers during the following winter.[2]

DeWeese's letter among others was disseminated to Congress while Alaska's first game laws were

Early Gold Mining on the Kenai Peninsula

Gold occurs in rock of volcanic origin. Deposits in the Kenai Mountains were generally found in quartz veins. The gold ore in these veins could be mined directly. When a promising vein was located, it was followed through the rock by excavating tunnels and the ore was removed manually or mechanically. This could involve one man with a pick and shovel or large companies with machinery, drills and explosives. This type of mining is variously referred to as "hardrock," "lode" or "quartz" mining.

"Placer" mining takes advantage of erosion. When gold-bearing ores are exposed and eroded from their rocky niches, they work their way down watersheds, like other sediments. But gold is heavier than most minerals and it settles and accumulates in predictable ways in stream and river beds. This is the situation where the quintessential gold pan comes into play. But the gold pan was merely a prospecting tool here. To mine placer gold, large quantities of gravel had to be moved and processed to extract the "pay dirt." A small operation would run gravel and water through a rocking sluice box, using gravity to separate the heavy gold from the other sediments. Larger operations used giant sluice boxes, called "long toms" or "flumes." These required lots of water and labor. (See photo on page 287.)

Northwest Development & Mining Company placer claims along Indian Creek in the Big Horn Mining District.

The arrow indicates the approximate location of the cabin Berg built in 1902.

The claim on the lake shore above the arrow was the site of the company mill and camp. A road was cleared from the camp to the creek, as marked on the map.

Indian Creek has changed course since the map was drawn and the mouth of the stream is currently further away from the cabin site, toward the south.

The map and records are from the Seward Recording Office, Seward, AK.

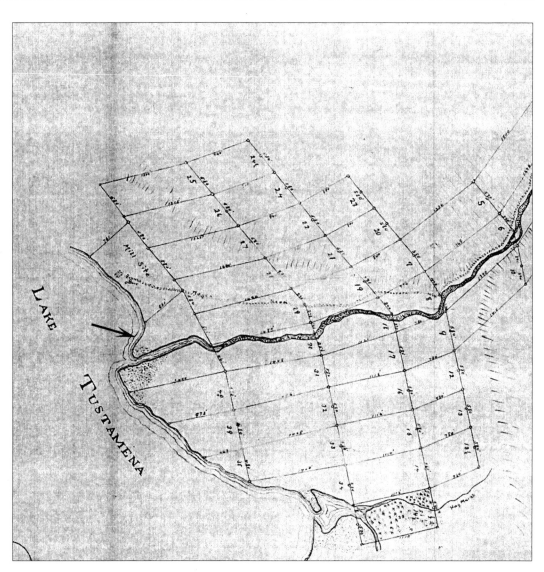

Records of Office of United States Commissioner and Ex-Officio Recorder at Valdez, Alaska, Volume A, book 59. Mortgages. July 15, 1901

This Indenture, made this 15th day of July, 1901, between the Northwestern Development and Mining Company, of the state of Washington, incorporated under the laws of said state, with its principal office in the city of Seattle in said State, the party of the first part, and Ira A. Nadeau of said city of Seattle, said state, trustee for the bond holder hereinafter mentioned, the party of the second part. Whereas: the said corporation, the Northwestern Development and Mining Company, having established a mining department and issued therein and for the purpose of operating its Fifty-one gold placer claims and water right located in the Big Horn Mining District of Alaska, a series of five hundred bonds of one hundred dollars each, being of the aggregate amount of fifty thousand dollars...for the use of said party of the first part in the operation of its said gold placer claims...described as follows, to-wit: [claim names]

New Jersey, Minnesota, Pueblo, Denver, Indiana, Mississippi, Secretary Dakota, Wyoming, Maine, Massachusetts, Maryland, Skagway, Louisiana, Kansas, Michigan, Iowa, Kentucky, Portland, Utah, Texas, New York, Missouri, Montana,

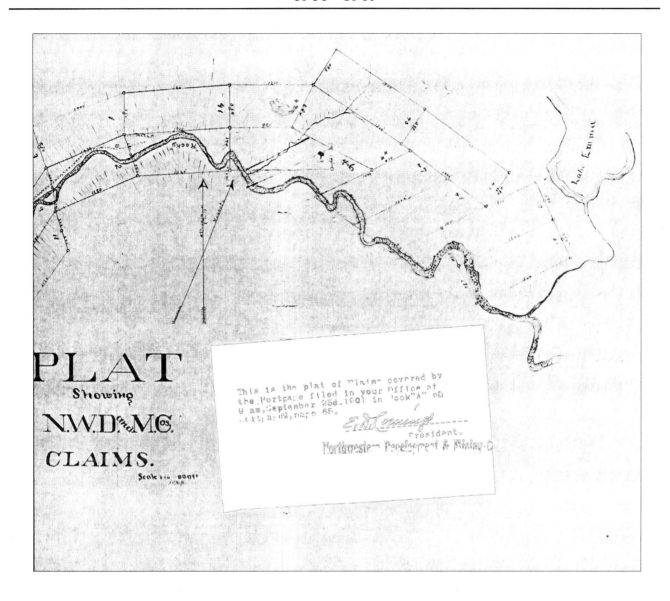

Florida, Nebraska, New Mexico, Siwash, New Hampshire, Illinois, Idaho, Georgia, Colorado, California, Delaware, Arizona, Alabama, Tacoma, Arkansas, Connecticut, Washington W., Virginia, Wisconsin, Denver, Carolina, President, Indian, Vermont, Tennessee, Juneau.

Together with all and singular the rights, privileges and appurtenances thereunto belonging, as to each and all of said gold and placer claims and water right. To have and to hold the said fifty-one gold placer claims and water right, with the appurtenances, unto the said Ira A. Nadeau, trustee as aforesaid, and to his heirs and assigns, to and for the only proper use and behoove of the holders of the aforesaid bonds, their heirs and assigns forever. In witness whereof, the said, the Northwestern Development and mining Company of the State of Washington, has caused to be hereunto affixed its common or corporate seal at its office in the city of Seattle, State of Washington, and the president of said corporation by virtue of the authority invested in him had hereto affixed his signature, and the secretary of said company had duly attested the execution hereof, the day and year first above written. Edward D. Comings. President of the Northwestern Development and Mining Company. J. G. Ellis, Secretary.

In witness, whereof, I have hereunto set my hand and seal this 15th day of July 1901. I. A. Nadeau.

Canon City, Colo., December 1, 1901.

The President:

This is a subject that appeals to every "true-blue sportsman," every lover of animal life, and all those who see beauty in nature, embracing forests, plains, and mountains throughout our entire country, and while the woods, plains, and mountains are naturally beautiful, we all agree that they are much more grand and lifelike when the wild animals and birds are present. There are now several organizations doing work toward the preservation of wild animal and bird life. There is much yet for us to do – resolve is to act, let us be up and at it.

For twenty years of my life I have taken my fall outing, embracing the greater part of North America. I have made trips in recent years to various parts of our mountains, where I hunted eighteen to twenty years ago, and it is appalling to note how rapidly the wild animals are disappearing. While I am but 43 years of age, I have seen in this short period the extermination of our buffalo; at the time of my first trip west there were millions...

During my four seasons' hunting in Alaska, my observations from past experience foreshadows that without stringent laws and their rigid enforcement the big game of Alaska is doomed to as rapid an extermination as it was upon the plains and mountains of Colorado. I will narrate one instance: when in the Kenai Mountains, Alaska, on the 23rd day of August, 1897 (from my diary), Mr. Berg and myself, while sitting together on the mountain side with the aid of a field glass, counted 500 wild white sheep all within a radius of 6 to 8 miles, 10 here, 6 there, then 20 and 30 in another locality. Can a true hunter or a lover of nature imagine a more beautiful sight? Look! Here and there were grand old towering mountains, all snow capped, some furrowed with gaping canyons, some separated with a mighty glacier, others with a gradual slope, carpeted with nutritious grass, upon which these beautiful denizens of the snowy mountains of the north loitered about in groups, either feeding or resting.

I was in these same mountains again in 1898, my wife accompanying me there in 1899. I wanted her to see what had at that time never before been a woman's pleasure. I was in these same mountains again this (1901), and there is no question about the Ovis dalli decreasing in numbers; it is perceptible. If mineral should be discovered in these mountains, and with no laws to protect this animal, they would be exterminated in a very short time. In 1899 when passing through a section where a "so-called sportsman" had been hunting, four carcasses were lying on one small hill, nothing having been touched, the heads of horns being too small and the work of skinning and preserving too great to suit his-I was going to say his "sport"-ship, but will make it his "devil" ship.

In 1899 myself, wife and party killed four sheep, two of which were killed by my wife. We could have killed a hundred. This season (1901) we killed but one, as we needed it for meat, also one bull caribou...

Make a non-resident license law, requiring every sportsman going to hunt and hunting in Alaska to pay $50 for that privilege, and that this sum allows him to take out of the Territory only one specimen of each species killed by him. The same law to provide a license fee of $100 which would give the sportsman or hunter taking out that license the right to kill and transport two specimens of each species of animal killed by him, and that he is not allowed to take out more than this quota....make a law that prohibits sportsmen or other persons from employing natives or other men for killing big game animals or birds, for in doing so most of the meat is wasted and the heads shipped and sold....

Let us all act now and use our influence to have some measures appertaining hereto properly brought before the coming session of Congress with the earnest appeal for their enactment. I have talked several times with Hon. J. G. Brady, governor of Alaska, regarding this subject, and he urged me to formulate some practical measures and he would give it his support.

Yours, fraternally, Dall DeWeese, Canon City, Colo.

developed.[3] Enacted in 1902, the regulations set hunting seasons and bag limits for deer, moose, caribou, sheep, mountain goats, bears, sea lions, walrus and game birds. Restrictions were also placed on the sale and export of these animals. Alaska Natives were exempted from the regulations when hunting for food or clothing, as were "miners, explorers, or travelers on a journey when in need of food..."[4] Violations were misdemeanors punishable by up to $200 in fines and 3 months in jail. The duty of enforcement was assigned to marshals, customs collectors and officers of revenue cutters. These enforcers were few and far between. But, nevertheless, the rules were changed and selling trophies was no longer a legitimate source of income for residents of the territory.

In 1902, for the first time, local happenings were documented by a newspaper. The *Alaska Prospector* began weekly publication in Valdez and covered the Cook Inlet region through its Kenai correspondent, George S. Mears.

Mears was the Postmaster in Kenai. He was also connected with Harry Wetherbee in a mercantile venture. His correspondence had a distinct chamber-of-commerce tone, full of great details:

Cook Inlet News. Kenai, Alaska, June 10. From the Mines, Canneries and Summer resorts. Moose are plentiful. We are having very beautiful weather at present, although this spring has been colder than usual. Snow and ice has all disappeared from this neighborhood although the snow appears to be plentiful on the other side of the Inlet. Quite a few hunting parties have gone over to Snug Harbor and vicinity for bear and beaver. Some of them are from British Columbia and others are from here but they all use Kenai as their starting point. ....The Northwest Mining and Development Co. on Indian River, a tributary of Kussiloff lake have quite a gang men and expect to have their plant working in July. They ought to do well having a sawmill now in operation and a gasoline launch on the lake to do the towing etc. The King salmon are running very well now, the traps for the different canneries are about finished and they have already canned several hundred cases. Talk about your summer resorts in California why if one of those fagged out, brain weary city men after spending a week on Cooks Inlet especially

in Kenai was not cured it would be beyond human belief. The weather lately has been beautiful we have had it as hot as 76 in the shade but always a little breeze enough to keep off the mosquitoes... J. T. Cornforth, general manager of the Northwest Mining and Development Co. came in on the Tonquin accompanied by Warner E. Smith, a civil engineer formerly of Illamina and six or seven more men for the plant on Kussiloff Lake. Their saw mill has been running quite a while having now about 40,000 feet of lumber for fluming Indian River. They expect to start their hydraulic plant 1st of August....The two canneries at Kussiloff and Kenai are doing finely...[5]

Cook Inlet Letter. Kenai, July 4th. As usual we had a shower of rain this morning to dampen everything in readiness for the display of fireworks and shooting of firecrackers. The American colors are flying all over town and at high noon we fired the national salute of 21 guns. .....The hunting parties from the other side of the inlet have been rather successful. F. F. Paget of Victoria, B. C., has just returned from a two months hunt for bear in the neighborhood of Snug Harbor and Chinitna Bay with five very fine brown bears. Col. C. Cane, of the Home Militia, London, Eng., is still over there in company with Mr. Little of Victoria, B. C. .....

Mears is misspelled in this ad for outfitting in the Alaska Prospector *on October 2, 1902.*

Among the social events. I might mention that Mrs. H. M. Weatherbee, wife of Supt. Weatherbee of the Alaska Packers Association at Kussiloff, gave a "pink tea" last week to some ladies visiting from Kenai.[6]

Correspondence. Kenai, July 14, 1902. The run of "red fish" has just commenced, and the rivers and inlet are virtually alive with them, jumping all over. All the canneries are doing well. I do not think any of them ought to fall short of their expected pack. .... The Northwestern Mining and Development Co. at Kussiloff Lake have about thirty men working at present and expect to have the water ready to turn into the flume about the 1st of August.[7]

Kenai notes. Special Correspondence to the Prospector. Kenai Aug. 15. ...It has been an exceptional year for fish. The canneries in the Inlet have every can and case filled and could have used many more. In 1893 and 1898 they had similar runs of fish, and now in 1902, so it seems they come in larger numbers every five years. H. N. Wetherbee, superintendent of the Alaska Packers Association at Kussiloff expects to have his ship the Centennial, loaded by the 24th of this month, and ....Mr. Weatherbee has packed 42,000 cases ... The news about the game law having passed, has been interpreted to the Indians and there has been a dearth of fresh meat ever since. They have been employing their time since the fishing closed in picking berries, which seem to be very fine this year.... I have no fresh news of the three hunting parties that went to the lakes, but expect to have by the time the next mail leaves. G. S. M.[8]

Colonel Claude Cane (mentioned in the July fourth letter on the previous page) went on to Tustumena Lake for moose hunting. In his book, *Summer and Fall in Western Alaska*, he described the progress of the NWD&M Company at Indian Creek later in the season:

The mining company of which I have already spoken had erected a small saw-mill, and had already made about a couple of miles of road along the river, up to where their claim-a gravel bank, in which they expected to find gold in paying quantities-was located. There were eight of them altogether, including Mr. Ellis, the manager, who was most hospitable incline, and they possessed a small naphtha [gasoline] launch, which lay at anchor off the camp. This launch, and the machinery for the mill, had taken seventeen Indians twenty-nine days to tow up the river. The storm of the day before had filled and sunk a scow containing all the piping they had brought up for their hydraulic machinery, and they would have to wait until the lake got low in the winter before they could recover it.[9]

The lumber mill, powered by a large steam boiler, generated the materials for constructing the flume and buildings. The "piping" that sank with the scow was in the form of flat sheet metal which was shaped and riveted on site into pipe up to a foot in diameter. This was used mainly for running water to the flume. The sinking of the scow apparently prevented the outfit from operating the flume this year, so 1902 would pass with no gold production.

Andrew Berg may have helped move all the equipment up to Indian Creek. This same year he built his cabin on the shore of Tustumena Lake by the mining operations. Colonel Cane was not overly impressed with the building but praised Andrew's hunting prowess:

Besides the mining outfit, two brothers - Russian Finns - had built a shack, in which to live and hunt round the borders of the lake. The elder of the brothers, Andrew Berg, is the best hunter on the Kenai Peninsula, and, though entirely self-taught, is most successful at calling moose, He accompanied Mr. A.S. Reed in 1900, when that gentleman got the magnificent heads which now adorn the walls of the Union Club at Victoria BC certainly the finest six moose heads ever collected by an amateur, the largest nearly 75 inches in spread...[10]

Alaska Prospector articles in September and October mention six different hunting parties having been on the Kenai Peninsula, including Baron Gustav Von Plesser of Munich. The newspaper made much of the Baron's retinue which included a Major W.E. Lennox as "guide and manager." But Lennox was no Andrew Berg and a later article written upon the Baron's departure quipped that the party had "only done fairly well in securing moose and sheep, but was very successful with porcupine..."[11]

There is no evidence that Berg guided any hunts this year. Sources aren't conclusive, but it may be an indication that he was fully occupied with mining. Most of the NWD&M Company men left Alaska for the winter. A few stayed on to move supplies to camp after freeze-up and salvage their sunken piping. Their scow wasn't the only freight casualty, they also lost a dory and its cargo in the river during the summer. Moving supplies on sleds over the frozen river and lake seemed sensible, but they would experience an even greater loss during the winter operation.

Tustumena Lake usually doesn't freeze over before January. On December 11, company men James Chase and A.L. Weaver were making their way to the mining camp from Kasilof in a canoe when it overturned in the lake. Chase drowned and Weaver barely made it to shore. That Weaver survived is surprising, they must not have been far from their destination when they went into the frigid water. We don't know if Chase's body was ever found, but a memorial marker was erected for him on the lake shore. Thirty years later, Andrew Berg still maintained the wooden monument.

1903 brought few changes to the western Peninsula. The NWD&M Company started washing gravel for gold. Kenai's cannery burned down at the height of the fishing season. (Coal-fired steam boilers, wooden buildings and the pressure of getting perishable fish into cans proved a combustible combination.) George Mears continued his dispatches of news and Cook Inlet public relations in the *Alaska Prospector*.

Chase's monument in 1939. Chase was a Freemason. The inscription reads "Brother; James G. Chase; Rob Morris Lodge, AF+AM; Denver, Colo.; Drowned Dec. 11 1902." Carved in a different style are the words "Friend Protect This Spot." We believe Andrew Berg added that inscription in 1933. Photo by Joe Secora, courtesy of Ella and John Secora.

Andrew Berg's "Home" cabin on Tustumena Lake, built in 1902. The roof is covered with small flat sheets of canning tin. Photo courtesy of the Anchorage Museum of History and Art, Accession number B91-9-101B.

ALASKA PROSPECTOR Valdez, Alaska March 19, 1903

DROWNING OF CHASE   Particulars of Accident at Kussiloff Lake. Kenai Items. Kenai, Feb. 28. On Dec. 14, last; John (sic) G. Chase was drowned in Kussiloff Lake, while crossing with A. L. Weaver in a Peterborough canoe, which capsized in a sudden squall. Mr. Chase was formerly from Denver, Colo. And until the summer of 1901, was paymaster for the P. C. S. S. Co. at Seattle, where he had made many friends. He resigned his position there to accept a more lucrative one with the Northwestern Mining and Development Co. on Kussiloff Lake. He had been down to Seattle last fall and returned on the October trip of the Santa Ana to take charge of the company's works during the winter. He and A. L. Weaver, his assistant, had been down towards Kussiloff getting the freight in readiness for sledding, and on their way to the mine. It was blowing a pretty stiff breeze, but not enough to occasion any alarm, when a sudden squall from the glacier at the head of the lake struck them, and before they realized it, they were in the water. Both managed to reach the upturned canoe and sit astride of it, but the wind increasing, the seas would turn the frail craft and throw them into the water, it being so cold and everything freezing, they could not retain their hold on the slippery bottom of the boat. After standing it for about half an hour Chase called to Weaver that he could hold out no longer. Weaver started to go to his assistance at once, but before he could reach him, Chase was gone, and it was all Weaver could do to return to the boat, although he is a strong swimmer. Weaver managed to reach shore in another half hour with his clothes frozen stiff, and that is about all he remembers distinctly, until he found himself being rubbed by some men who happened to be at camp. He had a very narrow escape from freezing to death and even now has by no means recovered from the exposure. Mr. Chase left many sorrowing friends in this part of the country, as his geniality and courteous manner had endeared him to all whom he had met. He was a member of the Masons; was unmarried, and had an only sister in Johnstown, N. Y. To whom we extend our heartfelt sympathies. G. S. M.

Kenai, May 3. [1903] ...The Kussiloff and Kenai canneries boats and ships have all arrived, been unloaded and towed away to their summer anchorage. The pile drivers have started in to build the traps for ensnaring of the unwary salmon... Mr. C. C. Acton and Mr. Woods who arrived on the April Santa Ana on their way to Kussiloff Lake in the interest of the N. W. Mg. And Dev. Co. have reached their destination and have quite a crew of men and expect quite a force to arrive with Mr. J. D. Cornforth who is expected on the next boat. The spring stock for Mr. Weatherbee's stores at Kenai and Kussiloff arrived on the ship Centennial, and never was such a complete stock of everything ever seen in this Inlet before.[12]

Kenai May 14th. Like the tail of a comet, which can be seen long after the head has disappeared from view so the presence of Judge Hildreth can be felt in this town, after his honor has departed for Sunrise. The natives who had ever tasted a drink of whiskey and I think that includes the whole population made themselves very scarce when the news came that the Judge had arrived...[13]

Kenai, June 3rd. The river is full of large king salmon....Both the canneries of the A. P. A. At Kusilof, and the P. P. & N. Co. at this place put up their initial case of salmon for this season the same day, May 29th... J. T. Cornforth is still at Kusilof lake, pushing ahead the work on the property of the N. W. Mg. & Dev. Co.... At 3:20 a.m. yesterday we were very much shaken up by one of the severest earth tremblers that has been experienced for years...[14]

Kenai, June 15. .... Mr. Clinton Gurnee of San Francisco, formerly of the Surveyor general's office, at Sitka, and now surveyor for the A. P. A. Has been in this neighborhood for the past two weeks. Besides running lines for the company he has performed quite a little work for private parties, and quite a number of there residents have had their ground staked, including the Russian church; and the new fences give this place quite a citified appearance....The N. W. Mg. & Dev. Co., at Kussiloff lake started in to sluice last week, but I have received no official returns as yet of their clean up.[15]

Kenai, July 17th. On Monday, the 6th Judge Hildreth arrived here in his private yacht, the

Mink, accompanied by Marshal Sexton and Mr. T. Jeter. A short performance was given in the school house on the evening of the 7th where doses of justice were dispensed for the sums of $10 and costs, in two cases of assault and battery, which was nearly occasioning a national controversy between the Russian Finns and Swedes...[16]

Kenai, Alaska, Aug. 28. ...There are five hunting parties on the Kussilof and Kenai Lakes getting their camps in readiness for the opening of the moose and sheep season. From the records which some of them bring from other hunting grounds, there ought surely be some fine trophies brought out this fall. The majority of them are Englishmen, there being only two Americans in the eight who are hunting. ....The report from N W M & D Co. continue to be good both having their plants running full blast... Mr. H. M. Wetherbee, the superintendent of the A. P. A. at Kusilof expect to leave for San Francisco on the 26th having put up the record pack for the Inlet 45,600 cases. G. S. M.[17]

The new game regulations began an unending process of reinterpretation and change. Subsistence needs, special interests, conservation concerns and regulatory ambiguity would keep them in constant flux. In 1903 they underwent a rendering by Washington bureaucrats which, according to a disapproving editorial in the *Alaska Prospector*, exempted Alaska Natives from all the restrictions of seasons, bag limits and shipping of carcasses and furs. The writer complained that "this will leave a loophole for hunters who will be able to take a native along with them and shoot to their hearts content."[18] Another change this year was the presence of a Territorial Marshal on the Kenai Peninsula during much of the summer and hunting seasons.

U.S. Deputy Marshal Sexton was a zealous enforcer who did not hesitate to interpret ambiguities in the law. His judgment and grasp of the law appear questionable, but he did apply his interpretation evenly to all whom he encountered, regardless of ethnicity or station. He nabbed Andrew Berg on suspicion of operating a still on his property at Tustumena Lake. George Mears reported the event with some skepticism:

Kenai, Alaska, Sept. 16.[1903] Quite a number of American and English hunting parties are up at Kenai and Kussiloff lakes, and I expect they will all return with good trophies..... Marshal Sexton has been here again on his way to Kussiloff lake ostensibly to enforce the game law and bag some of the English hunters. But when he returned he was accompanied by Andrew Berg and a distilling outfit. I believe he charges Berg with making whisky although Berg was at Kenai arranging about a hunting party when the Marshal got to the lake, but a barrel and a long,

The village of Kenai around Mears' time. Photo by Tom Odale, courtesy of Simonson Collection, Accession no. B91.9.90, The Anchorage Museum of History and Art.

thin tin pipe with a bowl seems to be perfectly satisfactory evidence to the Marshal...[19]

Unfortunately, further accounts of the alleged still and Andrew's conviction or exoneration have not been found. Marshal Sexton did go back to bag some English hunters. A British Army Captain, C.R.E. Radclyffe, had acquired a permit (from the Bureau of Biological Survey, USDA) for collecting big game specimens for the British Museum. Marshal Sexton arrested Radclyffe and two other members of his party for killing Dall sheep prior to the opening of the legal season. Once they got to Judge Hildreth in Kenai, Marshal Sexton discovered that Radclyffe's permit entitled him to shoot bear, sheep and moose at any time. The collecting permit had been issued in Washington, D.C. and Radclyffe had the understanding that the permit applied to all members of the hunting party. The Marshal and the Judge interpreted it otherwise and prosecuted the other two members of the hunt not named on the permit for shooting sheep out of season.[20]

Marshal Sexton brewed up another controversy when he arrested an American, C.S. Bonham, who was collecting specimens for himself and for the Colorado Museum of Natural History. The offense was possession of more specimens than his permits allowed, though the permits appear to have been vaguely worded and general regulations allowed him to possess additional purchased specimens. A jury trial in Seldovia acquitted the accused but Marshal Sexton was not satisfied. He attempted to have Marshals in Valdez and Juneau intercept Bonham on his journey south, seize his specimens and rearrest him. Bonham made it home and a flurry of letters between Colorado, Washington and Alaska eventually resulted in the return of his specimens the following June.[21] Not surprisingly, very few collecting permits were issued in 1904 and the game regulations were further modified.

Records indicate that only one nonresident hunter braved the regulatory hazards to hunt on the Kenai Peninsula in 1904. But future business for Andrew Berg was enhanced by the publication this year of Captain Radclyffe's *Big Game Shooting in Alaska,* an account of his 1903 hunting trip. Berg had not guided Radclyffe but he still garnered acclaim in this account of Radclyffe's hunt:

Kussiloff lake is thirty miles long, and on the third evening after leaving Kussiloff we reached the farthest end. Here there is the headquarters of a mining company, and also the cabin of a man called Andrew Berg, who is the most celebrated hunter on the Kenai Peninsula. We had previously met him at Kussiloff, and he kindly offered me the use of his cabin, of which we availed ourselves, as it was then empty. The cabin contained a number of trophies of the chase, and many curious and ingenious appliances made by Berg himself for use in his various occupations.[22]

We heard that two American sportsmen had engaged the brothers Berg and were then hunting somewhere near us. On September 25 I met one of the party, who informed me that his name was Mr. Forbes, and that he had been lucky enough to kill a moose two days before which had a head measuring 74 inches.[23]

On the same day I met Mr. Hasard, the other American sportsman who was hunting with the Bergs not far from our camp. He said that they had temporarily lost the services of Andrew Berg, since the Deputy U.S. Marshal of the district had discovered an illicit whisky still at Berg's cabin and had arrested the owner and taken him to Kenai. The younger Berg, by name Emile seemed to me a particularly smart-looking fellow... Emile Berg admitted to me that he was only a novice when compared with his brother Andrew as a hunter, but Mr. Hasard said that he had seen him call up a bull moose quite close to them, in a similar manner to that in which his brother calls them. My natives, and other people who have hunted formerly with Andrew Berg, declare that they have repeatedly seen him call-up bull moose by imitating the challenge call of another bull...

Both the brothers Berg have the reputation also of being able to judge the size of any head on sight to within an inch or two of its actual measurements... I maintain that to any in need of a hunter when after moose, the services of such men as these two brothers are invaluable at any reasonable price. "The proof of the pudding is in the eating," and every season sportsmen who have employed Berg have come out with record heads of the year obtained on the Kenai Peninsula.[24]

Andrew turned again to his mining interests in 1904. He filed an affidavit of annual labor for the four claims at

Indian Creek. Maintaining the legal right to a claim required an "assessment", really an investment, of at least $100 in a year. Berg reported 400 dollars worth of improvements consisting of "wing dams, sawing lumber and labor expended." [25] This was the only affidavit of annual labor found for these claims.

George Mears continued to be a source of news of the NWD&M Company as well as other Cook Inlet happenings in the *Alaska Prospector*:

Kenai, May 16 [1904] *...there was more fur caught last winter and more in town this spring than any year since the balmy days of the A. C. Co. station here.... The Alaska Packers superintendent at Kussiloff has quite a number of pile drivers out on the beach getting the traps ready for the fishing season. As the cannery at this place will not be rebuilt this year and the cannery at Tyonic has been sold to the S. P. A. Mr. Wetherbee will virtually have the whole inlet to himself this year...* [26]

Kenai, June 18. ....Mr. L. N. Wood, general manager of the Northwestern Dev. & Mining Co., is here for a few days waiting for the mail boat. He has quite a number of men working on Kussiloff lake and they started the pipe on the 7th instant, and from the present outlook expect to do quite well this season.... the cannery of the A. P. Ass'n at Kussiloff has been canning for the past two weeks and although there are plenty of fish there does not seem to be as large a run of the king salmon as last year. G. S. M. [27]

Kenai, Oct. 20. The mining companies have about shut down for this season and quite a number of the owners, managers and workers have left on the last two steamers L. W. Wood, manager for the Northwestern Mining and Development Co. and J. B. Pike, foreman, left for their homes in Colo. They had a fairly good season but the weather was not encouraging to hydraulic work this summer. [28]

This routine report of a fairly good season is the last we hear of the Northwest Development and Mining Company. Like so many other ventures of that type, the return on investment didn't materialize as expected and the effort fizzled. We don't know if any company man even returned to the Peninsula because George Mears's final report from Kenai was written in January of 1905:

Kenai Jan. 8. .....The American school is doing very well having an attendance of ten. If there was only some way of stopping the opposition of the Russian priest there is no doubt but there would be an attendance of about thirty....... Moose are becoming quite plentiful and tame.... It seems a shame that the department will not issue to sportsmen permit for a moose and a few sheep when they are so plentiful, as they not alone advertise the county but help the natives to live as each hunting party employs two or more men. As it is now the native men have to roam around looking for work and the only kind that offers good pay is with pick and shovel and that is a little out of their element whereas with hunting parties they are at home. We all hope that the restrictions on permits will be removed for next season, I do not favor permits being granted to curio hunters under salary from museums and institutes but genuine sportsmen who are able to pay a few thousand dollars for a hunting trip and appreciate a good moose head specimen and two or three mountain sheep ought not to be restricted.... G. S. M. [29]

Surprisingly, Mears did not mention William A. Langille's visit to Kenai. Langille was appointed the first federal Forest Officer for Alaska in 1902. His reconnaissance survey of the territory brought him to the Kenai Peninsula in September and October of 1904. Langille probably encountered George in Kenai as he echoes Mears's position on the benefit of trophy hunters to the local economy in his own reports. In Langille's analysis, both commercial timber and agriculture had only marginal potential on the Peninsula but the area had unique value as a wildlife and hunting preserve. Like DeWeese and others, Langille perceived looming conservation problems. Even with the low population density at this time the hunting pressure appeared unsustainable. He recommended establishing a Kenai Forest Reserve within which game preserves for moose and sheep could be created. [30]

With few hunters and the end of the NWD&M Company, the west-central Peninsula was mighty quiet. The Kasilof cannery burned down in 1905 and was rebuilt the following spring, providing a little excitement and extra wages. George Mears drowned in Cook Inlet in September 1905 after falling overboard from the *S.S. Tyonek* near Fire Island. [31] Other parts of the Kenai Peninsula were experiencing greater changes at this time.

Gold was still drawing people to Alaska's interior and Cook Inlet provided access to the shortest overland route to the Yentna and McKinley mining districts via the Susitna River. Seldovia, enjoying ice-free water all year, emerged as a significant port for this traffic. A local merchant built the first deepwater dock there in 1906. Seward was the other Kenai Peninsula port for gold seekers. Resurrection Bay, also ice-free, was chosen by private entrepreneurs as the southern terminus of a railroad line intended to penetrate Alaska's mineral-rich interior. The town of Seward was founded in 1903. Track was laid as far as Turnagain Arm by 1909 when the project stalled. Seward and its rail connection to Kenai Lake provided another route for hunters traveling to the Peninsula.

One of the hunters who came in 1906 was Californian Annie Montague Alexander. A paleontologist by training, she had an abiding interest in all animals. Her trip to Alaska helped inspire her to propose and fund a natural history museum for the University of California at Berkeley. The Museum of Vertebrate Zoology was established in 1908. The Museum's specimen database reveals that Andrew Berg provided numerous specimens collected between 1906 and 1909. A brown bear skull, skin and skeleton acquired in 1906 listed both Andrew and Annie as the collectors. During the subsequent four

years Andrew Berg provided specimens of seven brown bears, one moose and two lynx. Three of the bears came from the Crescent River on the west side of Cook Inlet. The rest came from Tustumena, variously referred to as Lake Tustumena, Kusilof Lake and Kussiloff Lake.[32]

Emil Berg is listed in the data base as the collector of river otters acquired in 1907 and 1908. The source listed was the Moose River, a tributary of the Kenai River, indicating Emil was based in Kenai in the winter. Andrew and Emil had a falling out at some point and went their separate ways. In their later years Emil would build a place on Tustumena Lake close to Andrew's and they regained a cordial relationship.

William Langille's work in southcentral Alaska came to fruition in 1907 with the designation of the Chugach National Forest. The boundaries of the Forest were expanded in 1909 to include most of the Kenai Peninsula.[33] Over the next twenty-five years the boundaries of the National Forest on the Kenai would change, retreating from the lowlands into the mountains.

A significant revision of the Alaska Game Laws was enacted in 1908. For the first time, nonresidents were required to obtain hunting licenses. They were further

Changes during this decade included the railroad and the inclusion of most of the peninsula within the Chugach National Forest.

Prospectors were active throughout the mountains between Hope and Seward and north of Turnagain Arm.

Placer mining was also yielding some gold from the beaches around Anchor Point.

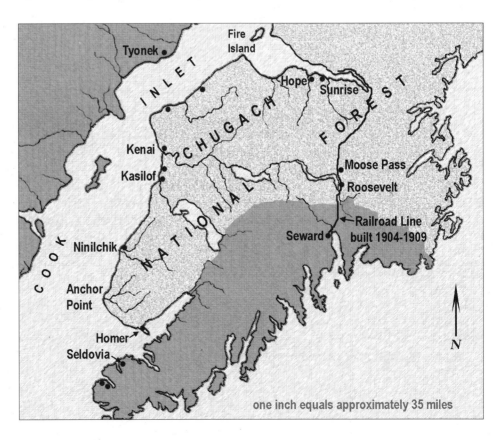

one inch equals approximately 35 miles

required to hire a registered guide in order to hunt on the Kenai Peninsula. This may have been partly the result of Langille's survey. When he reported his conservation concerns, one of the problems he described was trophy hunters killing many animals and retaining only the best specimens.[34] Requiring the use of registered guides would reduce that behavior. That this restriction applied only to the Kenai is a reflection of the world class hunting found there and possibly a recognition of the vulnerability of wildlife populations in this geographically isolated area.

Caribou on the Kenai Peninsula were nearly extinct at this time. A combination of irresponsible hunting practices and environmental factors – particularly widespread wildfires which generated forage more favorable to moose – led to the disappearance of caribou here. This occurred in spite of their protection under game law beginning in 1903.

Wolves disappeared by 1910. Andrew Berg had a hand in eliminating the wolves. He also reported that the Kings

An example of Berg's correspondence with Annie Alexander. "Creson River" is the Crescent River. Letter courtesy of the Archives, Museum of Vertebrate Zoology, University of California at Berkeley.

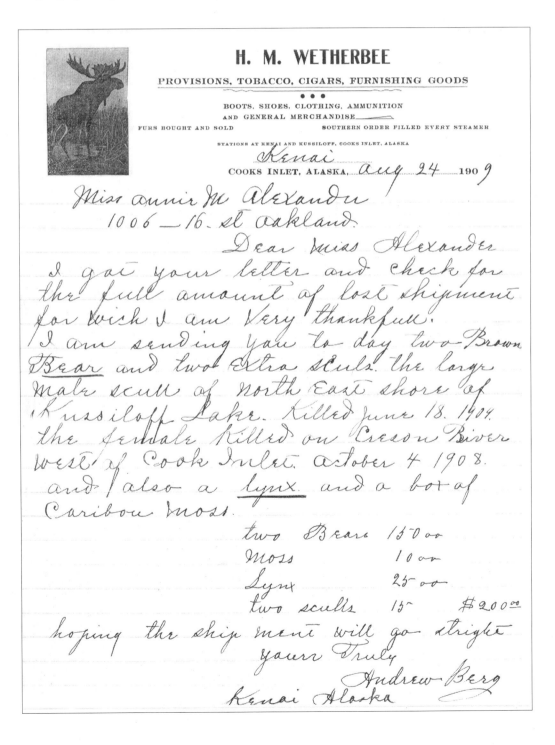

County Mining Company spread poison as they trekked their way from Homer to Skilak Lake in 1898.[35]

Wolves eventually made their way back onto the Peninsula from the mainland and reestablished a population. Caribou were reintroduced to the Peninsula by humans long after Andrew's lifetime.

The 1908 regulation requiring registered guides necessitated a licensing process. Any American citizen or Alaska Native was eligible as long as they were "of good character" and filed an affidavit that they would obey game laws and regulations and report any violations.[36] The Governor of the Alaska Territory was authorized to employ game wardens for enforcement and to set further regulations and rates of compensation for guides.

When the territory began the licensing process, Andrew Berg received Alaska Guide License No.1.

Bull caribou. Photo by Jon Nickles, courtesy of U.S. Fish and Wildlife Service.

This is a picture which Andrew Berg sent back to his family in Finland. Andrew is holding the rifle. Emil Berg is the second man from the left in the back row, "Russian Pete" Kalning is at the left end of the back row and Martin Hermansen is at the left end of the front row. The men are probably at a cannery. Photo courtesy of Ella and John Secora.

CHAPTER 4

1910 - 1919

In 1910, Alaska Governor Walter E. Clark issued detailed regulations for the licensing and compensation for guides and packers. His regulations began by defining "first class" guides as "white citizens of the United States" and "second class" guides as "men of mixed blood leading a civilized life, Indians, Eskimos or Aleuts, all herein referred to as natives." First class guides paid $25 for their two year license and second class guides paid $7.50. All guides were directed to charge no less than $5 and no more than $10 per day for their services. Packers were to register their names and addresses and receive $2.50 per day. Guides and packers were also charged with the following obligations:

Licensed Guides shall be required to report verbally or in writing to the nearest Game Warden at least once in each month or as often as their return from hunting trips will permit, any information as to the presence, absence or habits of game as observed by them in the localities which they visited; and any other information obtained or possessed by them reactive to game or the operation of the law and regulations.

It shall be the duty of every Guide and Packer to report to the nearest Game Warden or any other officer charged with the enforcement of the game law, at the earliest possible moment, any and all infractions of the Game Law or Regulations which may have come within his observation or knowledge. [1]

This latest modification of the game laws generated much correspondence between Andrew Berg and the authorities. Berg's communications give the impression that he favored the changes and would have preferred greater enforcement powers. It also appears that the guides' obligation to report violations was taken very seriously, even to the extent of reporting the absence of violations. Letters from the Territorial Governors' Correspondence archives are reproduced here verbatim. The only changes made are the addition of spaces between apparent sentences where punctuation was lacking.

Feb.24, 1910 Kenai Cook Inlet Alaska
Governor Clark Juneau Alaska.
Dear Sir, While I was out hunting last September I found several moose killed and left lying in the woods. I pretty sure in my mind who killed those moose. I am a licens guide but the afidavit that I tok give me only power to report a violation of the law so I could not put the party under arest those men who was there when I found the moose had native guides and they are not riliable as guides in the first place they think that a man trying to infors the law their animy and I doubt if they understand the natur of the oat [oath] they have taken I was guide for Mr. Fred Caykindall of New York City I have heard from parties that those men have done sych tings before but this is the first time I have found any direct evidence of any such work as I got guides licence that reads until revoked I would like to know if I have or not the power to put a man under arest the way I interpet the game law I have the power but I am told here that I have not.
Yours Truly Andrew Berg
Kenai Cook Inlet Alaska [2]

Bureaucracy loomed large for Berg in 1910. He was also having trouble with one of his shipments to, presumably, Annie Alexander in California.

SEWARD WEEKLY GATEWAY

February 19, 1910

Well Known Guide in Seward

Andrew Berg, probably the best hunter and guide within the confines of Alaska, reached Seward from Kenai on Cook Inlet, yesterday afternoon. While a resident of Kenai peninsula for the past twenty years, this is Berg's first visit to Seward. It is said of Berg that when he goes moose hunting he has a call which brings the animals to him. He is a man of prodigious strength and endurance, and woodcraft is an open book to him.

[Berg would have traveled to Seward by dog sled via the Kenai River system. By mid-February the river and lakes were normally frozen and provided a relatively level trail to the southeast end of Kenai Lake. From there, the trail ran along the railroad tracks to town. The trip from Kenai to Seward could be made in as little as two days under ideal conditions.[3]]

Kenai Cook Inlet
March 1st 1910
Governor W. E. Clark Juneau Alaska
Dear Sir.

I wrote som time back to you regardin a shipment of speciemens for scientific purpos wich was stopped at Ketchican and also an afidavid regarding same   I sendt this shipment to same party who I adressed former shipment to when I shipped under speicies shipping permit from Washington   that permit went out with prior shipment   now cant you relixe the shipment or let me know wath to do about it   the shipment consist of two brown bear and two extra sculs I killed on Kenai peninsula where I dont think it right to protect brown or black bears as they destroy a lot of young moose and mountain sheep   I have been here twenty years and had lots of chanse to look into condition of game   I tok a hand in destroing wolfs and from that time on moose have been increasing and still continue to do so   but at precent the worst enemy the moose got is the bear and mountain sheep the eagle who pick up a great number of lams [lambs] in early spring   the gam [laws] have been complied with fairly well ther is no open violation of the law   I wrote somting in my

An early photo of Seward, likely taken in this decade. Seward's population had gone from zero to 534 between the 1900 and 1910 censuses. Steamships like the one at the dock here provided the only link with America. Photo courtesy of Carpenter Collection, No. 349, Library of Congress Prints and Photographs Division.

*former letter regarding killing of moose and
letting them lay without even cutting them   that
same party is comming up again and they will be
loking for native guides probably the same ones
is was out with them before   now wath can be
done to make those men obey the law   the
natives do not value their oath or it would be
easy matter to get sufiscent evidens   could you
not put the man under oath when he gets the
shipping licens or put som man in the ground
during hunting season   are I as licen guide
inpowered to put a man under arest who I find
violating the law   Hoping somting can be done
to look after those tings*
*I am very respectful yours Truly Andrew Berg
Lisens guide Kenai Cook Inlet Alaska*[4]

Berg displays the prevailing attitude that game
conservation included eradicating predators. Even bald
eagles would eventually have a territorial bounty placed
on them when their predation was perceived to impact
the salmon stocks which were a significant source of
tax revenue for the territory.

In the previous letter Berg also reiterates his law-and-
order stand on game regulations. We don't know if this
reflected his respect for all laws or just those which could
affect his livelihood. We do know that the licensed guides
were not given the power to arrest law breakers.

On September third Berg wrote his report to the Governor
on "Interlocked Moose Horns Club" letterhead (see
exhibit on next page). The club was a combination social
and sporting organization which connected trophy hunters
with guides and packers. Peter F. Vian was the originator
and manager of the club. Vian was also a territorial
game warden.

William Hunter, a resident of Kenai and hunting guide,
wrote a lengthy letter to Governor Clark in October 1910
complaining about the club. He accused Peter Vian and
the Interlocked Moose Horns Club of numerous
transgressions including operating a "blind pig" or illegal
liquor sales operation, stealing hunting parties from
nonmember guides, blackballing longtime guide Phillip
Wilson because he was half Native and discriminating
against the Natives in general. Hunter wrote that he
and other men had resigned their memberships and he
suggested to the Governor that "if there were a licensed
saloon and a commissioner and a marshal [in Kenai]
there would be more harmony in the place."[5]

> ## SEWARD WEEKLY GATEWAY
> ### July 16, 1910
>
> ### Original Club in Kenai Village
>
> The little settlement of Kenai on Cook Inlet, has an
> organization which has on its membership roll princes
> and potentates from the old country besides noted
> persons in the United States. It is called the Interlocked
> Moose Horn Club, and its object is the protection of
> the game on the Kenai peninsula the entertainment of
> big game hunters who may, in their travels stop at Kenai
> and for social purposes generally. The president of the
> club is Peter F. Vian, the well known trader.....
>
> [Interlocked moose horns are antlers of two bull
> moose which have become locked together during a
> rutting battle. The entrapment results in the death of
> the animals and the antlers may be found long after, still
> uniting the skeletal remains of the moose.]

The Governor apparently confronted Game Warden Vian
with the accusations. The archives revealed a
subsequent letter from Vian denying all charges and
impugning Hunter's character. Hunter was playing a
risky game because the game warden had the power to
block his application for a guide license. The licensing
regulations added new dimensions of politics and
personalities to the guiding business.

Andrew Berg is inferred to have been a member of the
Interlocked Moose Horns Club. Some of his letters
written in 1910 and 1911 were on Club letterhead.
According to local legend, Berg built the cabin which
housed the club headquarters.

He also wrote the following odd letter to Governor Clark,
in apparent defense of Vian and the Interlocked Moose
Horns Club. This one was not on Club letterhead:

*Kenai Alaska
Dec 28 1910*
*I the undersigned lizence guide do hereby
certifi that no one had anyting to do with me
Andrew Berg or the man who I guided this fall it
was strickly him and I and the hiring of packers
I will state that I have had my choise as to who I
wanted and hiring of them*
Andrew Berg Lizence Guide Kenai [6]

Andrew wrote two more letters on this same day, having just returned to town.

Kenai Alaska
Dec. 28 1910
In regard to pot hunters I dont know of any and if I should at any time find out it is my duty to report it I have sworen to do. Andrew Berg Lizence guide Subscribed and Sworn to before me this 28 day of December 1910
[witnessed:] P.F.Vian Notary public District of Alaska Residing at Kenai.[7]

Mr. Vian
Dec.28 1910
As I have not given my report since in early October regarding any violation of game laws the reason for not doing so was my crossing Cook inlet with Mr. Slaughter to get Brown Bears then getting to Seldovia and walking up from Homer finding noting that is in conflict with the game law nor any violation since I got back.
Andrew Berg Lizence Guide [8]

Andrew Berg to W.E. Clark, Governor, Sept. 5, 1910, General Correspondence of the Governor of the Territorial Government of Alaska, 1909-1958; Archives and Manuscripts Department, Consortium Library, University of Alaska Anchorage.

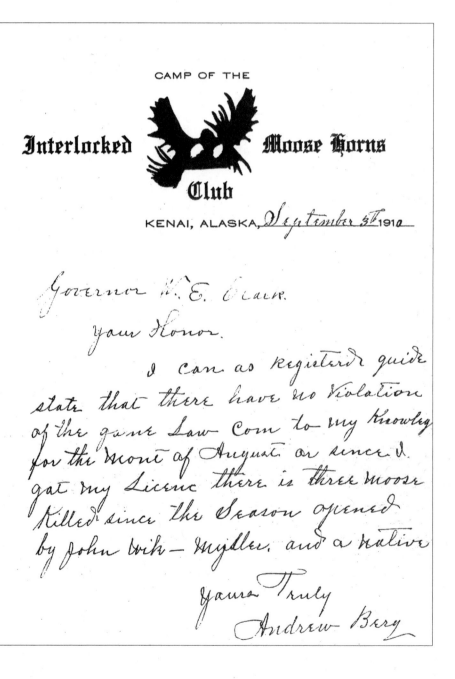

Note his reference to "walking up from Homer." This jaunt was over 80 miles long following the shore of Cook Inlet. At an optimum pace of four miles an hour that was over twenty hours of walking. But there were also numerous river crossings involved and in places the beach was impassable at high tide. Berg would have found hospitality on his way in the small settlements along the coast. In addition to the other communities there were now a few permanent residents in Kasilof and around Anchor Point.

With all of the report writing going on, it seems surprising that the previous letter is the only one which makes reference to an actual hunting trip. A third-hand account of Berg's bear hunt with Mr. Slaughter on the west side of Cook Inlet was found in the January, 1946 issue of the *Alaska Sportsman* magazine:

"Brownie in the Dark" by Katherine Bayou

Chris [Spillum] *tells me of one time when he was working for Dan Morris and his wife, who were running Seldovia House the town's one hotel. Dan had a wealthy and important guest whom Chris knew only as Mr. Slaughter, from Chicago, Chris spent most of his evenings in the hotel lobby, and once he and Mr. Slaughter fell into a conversation. Mr. Slaughter told Chris about his*

big game hunts for tigers and elephants, and mentioned that he had been at Kenai several times hunting with Andrew Berg. Chris warmed at the name of his friend. "You know Berg?" asked Slaughter. "You bet I do," answered Chris who, like any sourdough, was as much at home talking to a millionaire of the Chicago Stock Exchange as he would be talking to the old-timer in the cabin next door. "Well, never again will I go hunting with Andrew Berg!" declared Slaughter. Chris was surprised, since Andrew was reputed to be one of the best guides, and listened with interest to the man's story. It seems they were camped at Snug Harbor, hunting Brown Bears. Just before nightfall, Andrew took his powerful binoculars and searched the surrounding mountains. Then, after dark, he told Mr. Slaughter to come along, leaving all his cigarettes and cigars behind. Andrew was a strict guide, and never allowed his hunters to have tobacco along when he took them out not that he objected to smoking, but because the game could smell the tobacco and make a getaway. Slaughter hadn't the slightest idea Andrew would plan to go after a Brownie in the dark, and he protested. "I'm your guide," Andrew told him, "and I've guaranteed you a bear. So come on. We're going

This is the building purported to have been built by Andrew Berg and used as the headquarters of the Interlocked Moose Horn Club. Kenai's Russian Orthodox Church is in the background. Photo by Tom Odale, courtesy of Simonson Collection, Accession no. B91.9.90, Anchorage Museum of History and Art.

after your bear right now." They climbed and crawled through the thick alders. After a long time Andrew whispered, "easy now, easy. We're getting close to the bear now." "How do you know?" Mr. Slaughter whispered back. "Because I can smell him. And this is the spot where he should be if he bedded down in the alders for the night." Slaughter told Chris he hoped fervently there wouldn't be any bear that he considered himself a brave enough hunter, but going after a Brownie in the dark was more daring than he cared to be. But sure enough, as they got closer they could hear the hoarse breathing of a bear. It must have been on the alert; for there would be a dead silence for a time, then a horrible rasping sound as if the bear had held its breath as long as possible, then let it out with a mighty wheeze. They spent almost an hour creeping up on the bear in the dark. Slaughter said he was trembling so hard from fear that he began to worry lest he wouldn't be able to shoot straight when the time came. Finally they could barely make out a huge, dark form. Andrew studied the situation carefully. "Easy now," he whispered. "See the outline of his back?" "Yes," Slaughter whispered with a shudder. "You can't see the sights on your gun, but shoot at that outline. Point as near as you can to it." Slaughter mustered his nerve. There was nothing to do but shoot, now! It wouldn't do to get panicky and run, then the bear would probably kill them both. He pointed the gun, but it took all the strength of will he possessed to keep from breaking down. He squeezed the trigger. The gun went off with a deafening roar. Then silence. "You got him!" yelled Andy. But Slaughter's knees had turned to jelly. "Maybe" he whispered. "Sure you did," laughed Andy. "Sure as hell! I can't hear even a breath out of him!" They stood in the darkness for some time, waiting for a sound from the bear. At last Andrew went to the still, dark form, his gun ready for the slightest move. Chris says sometimes bears play dead and let the hunter come up to them, then take their last revenge! "He's stone dead!" Andrew's voice rang out "not even a kick out of the brute!" He poked the bear in the mouth with the gun. Slaughter came up and wanted to put another bullet into the carcass to make sure, but Andrew wouldn't let him. They hiked back to

SEWARD WEEKLY GATEWAY
August 20, 1910

Aug. 20, Game Hunters Flock to Kenai ... Prince Ghika of Romania, and Captain Radclyffe, of the British army, will hunt in the Kenai country, instead of on Kodiak island. Andrew Berg will be their head guide.

October 22, 1910

The [SS] Portland took all the big game hunters who scoured the Kenai Peninsula in search of trophies during the past two months, save a Mr. Slaughter, a Philadelphia millionaire, who, with Andrew Berg as guide, is still in the region of Kisilof Lake.

camp, planning to come up the next day for the trophy. Slaughter's nerves quieted down, and before long he was laughing and joking with Andrew. Back at camp, the cook had steaming coffee ready, they sat around talking for awhile, then slept for the rest of the night. Next morning they went back for the bear. And what a bear it turned out to be! It hadn't moved a muscle after being shot, for its back was broken. When the hide was skinned out and stretched, it measured twelve feet from nose to tail! "But," Slaughter told Chris, "never again!" Some day Andrew will sneak in on the wrong bear. You mark my words, a bear will get him yet!" [9]

In the same article the author told this suspiciously legend-like bear story from her own recollection:

"I've had many long, pleasant chats with an old, old man from Kenai who had known Andrew Berg well, and had been a guide himself at about the same time Andrew was. "I understand Andrew Berg was quite a fellow," I said to him one day, "Come on, tell me a tale about him." Without batting an eye, the old man told me this. "Andrew used to go hunting all by himself at times just for the fun of it . He'd tie a piece of bacon to a rope, and knot the other end of the rope around his leg. Then he'd wrap up in his heavy overcoat and lie down to sleep. Pretty soon an old Brownie would come along sniffing around for something

to eat. He'd find the bacon, and take a bite. That would jerk the rope and wake Andrew. Then Andrew would pull the rope toward him, and the bear would follow the bacon. When the bear got up close, Andrew would shoot it. Then he'd come back to Kenai and tell us all about it. He got some mighty big bears that way!" [10]

Whether the details are fact or fiction, the story is surely consistent with Berg's attitude toward bears. Andrew was back in Kenai at the end of January where he penned the following letters.

Kenai Alaska Jan 30 1911
Honorable Walter E Clark Governor of Alaska
Dear Sir.   Regarding the violation of the game law only one violation came to my notice so far a man by the name of Charles March in company with Carl Petterson killed a moose after season closed. Mr March reported same to me stating that he was out of meat
Yours Truly
Andrew Berg Guide Kenai Alaska [11]

Kenai Alaska Jan 30 1911
Honorable Walter E. Clark
*   I herby recomend John Wik for Lizenze guide and he wish to obtain lizenz but only got his intention papers   he was just about to start for Seward when news reached us that term of court be trancefered to aprill tenth and he will try and be there then if posible   he is a man that been here for nine years and reliable   I wish you   would let him know wath can be done regarding the matter*
yours truly
Andrew Berg Kenai Lizence Guide [12]

Berg may have been in town putting together another mining consortium. On February 7, 1911 he filed seven placer mining claims. Eight other men were listed on the filings, the only familiar name being Peter Vian. The locations were on Indian Creek and had the same names of claims formerly belonging to the Northwest Development & Mining Company (annual assessments hadn't been performed or filed so the previous claims were null). One year later, on February 16, 1912, Andrew filed for three additional placer claims around the mouth of the Anchor River near Anchor Point. His co-filers included a couple of the same men from the Indian Creek claims, but not Peter Vian. Emil Berg signed on for this

venture as well as two other relatives of the Bergs – Gust Ness and John Wik. (Ness and Andrew's father had the same grandmother, Wik's connection is unknown, he was listed as a relation in Emil Berg's obituary.)

On the same date Andrew filed a claim for a "Trade site" on the Kasilof River:

Berg, Andrew   Trade site   Feb. 16, 1912
1R, 75   Kussiloff River.

Trade Site. The undersigned a citizen of the United States and above the age of 21 years in compliance with the acts of Congress and the revised statues of the United States do hereby locate and claim 20 acres of lands for the purposes of trade, etc. Said land being situated on Kussiloff River about one and one half miles from the mouth. Notice posted at wath is known as Bergs landing running Northeast 1320 feet, hence southeast 600 feet, hence southwest 1320 feet, hence northwest 660 feet to place of beginning corners marked by stakes numbered 2-3-4. Located this 9th day of February 1912. Andrew Berg Locator. Filed for record at 10:30 a.m. February 16, 1912 by Chas Peterson. [13]

Local knowledge of the spot "known as Bergs landing" is lost but it may have been in the area of a low bank on the south side of the Kasilof. Victor Holm and Gust Ness both had cabins close to this place. Steep bluffs or estuarine wetlands line most of the lower river.

Berg's intention here is a mystery. Further documentation regarding either the trade site or the various placer claims has not been found. Clearly, he was in an ambitious phase in his life and he may have been reacting to relatively prosperous times in Cook Inlet. Big game hunters were showing up in force and the salmon industry had begun another boom. New canneries went up at Kenai in 1910 and 1912 and Seldovia opened its first cannery in 1911. Perhaps Andrew was anticipating a population influx and decided to preemptively stake the best claims and prepare a trading post site for the big game hunting traffic and prospective Kasilof residents. Speculation aside, he was surely a busy man.

Berg was guiding, mining, trapping, fishing and cutting fish trap poles for the canneries. Census data lists him as an employee of the Kasilof cannery in May of 1910. His name is included in Forest Service timber sale records

Andrew Berg in a skiff with clients or friends and the ubiquitous moose horns. Photo courtesy of McLane Collection.

for April, 1913.[15] He also continued his sideline of selling specimens:

July 28 1912
Walter E Clark Governor of Alaska
Dear Sir I had a letter from Vitoria Memorial musium Ottawa asking me to send them a scull of a Alaska brown Bear   they wrote me that they have communicated with you in regards to getting a special shipping permit   I wish you would send me the permit is soon is possible I have just recived the card for Licens guide.
Your truly Andrew Berg Kenai Alaska [16]

The frequent guide reports stop in 1912. They may have been discontinued or not preserved. At some point between 1912 and 1913 Peter Vian resigned or lost his Game Warden position and the nearest game warden was in Seward. Regulations, wardens and reports notwithstanding, the future of the Peninsula's game remained a concern to some. Moose were becoming scarce on the east side of the Kenai Mountains where hunting pressure from Seward was intense. This was exacerbated when the federal government took over Seward's defunct railroad line in 1914 and started new construction.

The number of trophy hunters coming to the area would decrease at the outbreak of World War I. The ongoing problem facing the game was Alaska's increasing population and great distance from the nearest source

Hon. Walter E. Clark. Governor of Alaska.
Juneau Alaska.
Kenai May 1st 1912.

Sir: I herewith tend you my report for the month of April, I am please to report that the game Law in all respect have been upheld in my district. Enclose find check for $40.00 dollars for the renewal of Andrew Berg Commission first-class guide, Inokenty Shangay, Pitka Bakoff, commissions second class guides.
      Name of guides holding badges, Andrew Berg No. 1, Math Yuth No. 2, W. J. McKeon No. 3, Geo. Kuppler No. 4, H. G. Singer No. 5, Dimidoff Mamala No. 6, F. W. Johanson No. 7, Pitka Bakoff No. 8, Inokenty Shangay No. 9, John Wik No. 10.
      Philip Wilson, Emil Berg Gust Ness, Feodor Chickalush, these four have not been supplied with badges yet.

Most Respectfully, P. F. Vian [14]

[William Hunter's name is absent from Vian's list.]

of fresh food. Market hunters selling moose meat to roadhouses, canneries and other buyers were a significant threat.

On the west side of the mountains, Andrew Berg was observing additional problems. In 1913 he counted some 200 moose carcasses, mostly cows, apparent victims of

SEWARD WEEKLY GATEWAY
August 16, 1913

Law Violations Will Result In Game Preserve

How would you like to see the Kenai peninsula, or the greater part of it, thrown into a game preserve in which the animal life therein would be immune from slaughter the entire year round, with penal servitude facing a violation of the regulation creating it?

We are nearer on the verge of such a consummation than most people here-abouts realize, and it is up to the men in the hills, or largely so, whether or not it shall come to pass.

Those who have the power to make such a regulation are not unaware that the Kenai peninsula is the great game country of Alaska. They are also fully alive to the fact that there has been a wanton destruction of this wild game. They know as well as we who gain a livelihood by trapping or hunting for the market; that these persons have a wholesome contempt for the wardens of game and miss no opportunity to harass and hinder their work of preservation.

The wild game of the Kenai peninsula is a great resource to the prospectors, miners, and operators engaged in mining. It affords a wholesome and adequate meat supply to the mining element. The game law was enacted primarily to conserve this splendid food supply to the men who are engaged in the legitimate development of this country. The law does not affect such men: rather, it is for their protection.

It is therefore up to the mining element to aid in the enforcement of the game laws. Self interest would seem to dictate such a course... Instead of harassing the game wardens, assist them to put a stop to the needless slaughter of game.

disease.[17] In spite of the die-off, Berg worried about available forage the following winter and the ever-present issue of enforcement. In the following series of correspondence we see his minor question resolved, but not his major concern.

January 29, 1914
Governor of Alaska Juneau Alaska,
Sir; I have inquires from parti of hunters man and wife wishing to engage only one guide as they be hunting togather   I have heard it

done at Seward (but how)   I also wish to call your atention to the fact that we got no game warden at Kenai wich is the game centre on Kenai penn. while at Seward is two within 30 miles of ich other on same road   could not one be transfered here as a new apointment made   I heard that a lot of moose was shot out of season last spring and sold to Libbys cannry at Kenai and posibly the same condition will repeat this spring   moose is getting to many for food rabit have girdled most of vilow bush and dead moose will be plenty in spring. Personal I dont aprov of more then one hunter hunting with one guide.
Yours Respectfully Andrew Berg Licens Guide Kenai Peninsula Kenai Alaska [18]

March 11, 1914.
Mr. Andrew Berg, Kenai Alaska
Dear Sir: I write to acknowledge the receipt of your letter of January 29th in which you ask if a man and wife hunting together should employ more than one guide. In reply I have to advise you that I find that in 1911 a ruling was made by this office in response to a similar inquiry from Game Warden Shea that where two or more persons hunted together so that one guide could easily keep them under his eyes, they might be permitted to hunt with one guide but if they did not agree to do this, they would have to employ two or more guides. In the matter of a man and wife hunting together, I believe discrimination should be made and that one guide would probably serve for both provided they actually hunted together. In the case of men, however, I believe the rule should be enforced that each man should have one or more guides. In regard to your suggestion that a game warden should be stationed at Kenai, that place being the center of the game country. I have to say that the appropriation available for the protection of game does not permit of the employment of additional game wardens in that section. I shall however take up the matter with game warden J.A. Baughman and if game warden Ericson can render better service by being transferred from Roosevelt to Kenai, I shall order the transfer to be make. Respectfully yours, Governor [19]

*Pheoll Manufacturing Co.
3021 Carroll Ave. Chicago
July 21, 1914
Governor of Alaska
Dear Sir   My wife Louise KeKowen Phelps and
myself are going on a hunting trip in the Kenai
Peninsula, Alaska this coming fall... My wife
and myself will always hunt together and will
only require one guide.   I have secured Andrew
Berg of Kenai to act in that capacity We will
come in from Kenai. I trust this is all the
information you require. Thanking you in
advance for fixing me up, I remain, yours very
truly, Mason Phelps* [20]

*November 11, 1914
Territory of Alaska Game Warden's Office,
Hon J F A Strong
Juneau Alaska
My Dear Sir: Leaving on the S. S. Maripose are
Mr Mason Phelps and wife, who have just
returned from a hunting trip at Kenai. They
killed three moose, two sheep, one brown bear
and one black bear, and are very well pleased
indeed with their hunt and with their party
consisting of Andrew Berg Guide and Tom Odale
and Billy Carlson as packers. ... two of the
moose were killed by Mrs. Louise Dekoven*

*Andrew Berg to J.F.
Strong, Governor,
August 1, 1914,
General
Correspondence of the
Governor of the
Territorial
Government of Alaska,
1909-1958; Archives
and Manuscripts
Department,
Consortium Library,
University of Alaska
Anchorage.*

Phelps and one by Mr Mason Phelps.
Yours very truly J.A. Baughman   Game Warden[21]

Game Warden Baughman did much of his work interviewing departing hunters on the dock in Seward as they all passed through there. Baughman would get to the west side of the Peninsula occasionally and check in with the locals. One of his most interesting reports came from information he obtained from Berg:

March 31, 1915
Report from Game Warden's Office, Seward,
J.A.Baughman...There is a ford on the Kussloff
River where the moose go to cross where the
water is very swift, and according to Andrew
Berg and others living there, about any place
from fifty to one hundred and fifty moose get
drowned every winter. This danger to the
animals could be obviated by placing a barb
wire fence on each side for a distance of four
miles and putting in a foot bridge some where in
the center for the moose to use in crossing. [22]

As always, Andrew was looking for ways to protect moose. But whoever conceived the fence and footbridge plan surely hadn't had any previous experience fencing wild game. Moose go over or through most fences, utterly failing to grasp the intent. It would have made a great local legend but there is no evidence that anyone beyond Warden Baughman thought the idea was worth pursuing.

After the 1915 hunting season, Berg tried again to influence the bureaucracy and improve enforcement:

Kenai Alaska Nov 22nd 1915
Mr. J.F.A. Strong Governor of Alaska
Juneau Alaska
Dear Sir I got your letter of Oct 22th
the guides instrution in regard to
packers and thier compensation   you
can not get any good man out here to go
packing at less then $5.00 per day unles
you get natives and then any sportman
would not want to have his equipment
smell like bunch of smoked salmon
besides they not being reliable as to
finding thier way. Now as regards game
wardens we hear of those but se them

only ones or two times in hunting season that it
be praclikle imposible to register packers here.
When most of people are in transit   unles we get
a game warden stationed here where he aucto be
as this is the center of pinninsula gam country
I wrote you befar in regards having mr Erikson
moved from Rosevelt to Kenai or apoint some
warden for Kenai   I talked with game warden
Boughman in regards to moving Erikson
Boughman stated that Erikson made som excuses
prinsiple one that he was sparking som girl at
least so I under stand him   Erikson is OK as a
game warden only misplased   Another ting
would be probibit all selling of meat at all time
as those who go out and shoot game for market
early open season still have to live and will kill
more game during winter   How about
nonresidents or sportsmen coming here shooting
down the limit of moose and taking out one out
of four moose   are they paying lizens for those
they leve to rot in the woods or only for those
they ship   I have heard of fellows shooting and
not taking any out but I know of two men this

A fine example of a trophy bull moose shot by Slim Crocker's
camera in the late 1920s. Photo courtesy of Betty A. Crocker.

fall who shot four and tok one would it not be better for them and guids that they had permits with them so a guide could tell if they where alowed to shoot or not and said permit be acompanied with a guides report of trip on thier return
Your truly Andrew Berg Kenai Alaska [23]

Roosevelt (later renamed "Lawing") was located 23 miles north of Seward along the railroad and it does seem odd that two game wardens would be stationed so close together. If Warden Erikson was indeed "sparking som girl," he could be forgiven for resisting a transfer. Single women on the Kenai Peninsula were rarer than ptarmigan teeth.

Andrew Berg Oath of Office, Guide License, August 19, 1916, General Correspondence of the Governor of the Territorial Government of Alaska, 1909-1958; Archives and Manuscripts Department, Consortium Library, University of Alaska Anchorage.

Andrew's recommendation to the Governor that packers' rates be raised to $5.00 a day was not incorporated into the revised regulations which came out in 1916. The maximum daily compensation for packers was raised from $2.50 to $3.50. The licensed guide's reporting requirements were revised as follows:

It shall be the duty of every guide and packer to report to the nearest game warden, or any other officer charged with the enforcement of the game law, at the earliest possible moment any and all infractions of the law or the regulations thereunder which may have come within his observation or knowledge.

Whenever a guide is employed by any personal party, such guide shall, at the expiration of the period of time for which he is employed, make a written statement to the nearest game warden in the district, stating the number of days he was employed, the number of persons guided, their names, residence, and the number of each kind of game killed; and if nonresident the number of their license.

Guides' reports were not preserved but the information requested is found in a few of Warden Baughman's surviving reports. There are almost no game reports in the archives of the Governors' Correspondence for 1917 and 1918 during America's participation in World War I.

Young men left the territory to join the war effort. Residents who remained had to cope with the worldwide influenza epidemic of 1917 and 1918. The "Spanish flu" dealt another terrible blow to the Dena'ina. It spread out to remote villages where people had the least immunity. The devastating result was a decrease in the Dena'ina population on the Kenai Peninsula from 680 in 1915 to 450 in 1920.[24] Many of the smaller communities were abandoned in the years following the epidemic as survivors moved to larger villages.

With the end of war in 1919 came the reappearance of game reports in the archives. Warden Baughman made an interesting reference to Andrew in one his reports: "Jan. 31, 1919... I also have a report from an old guide, Andrew Berg of Kenai into the effect that the brown bear killed a great many moose in that section last fall."[25] When he referred to Berg as "an old guide" did he mean old man or longtime guide? Andrew Berg would turn fifty this year but showed no signs of slowing down. During his winters at Tustumena Lake he maintained

many miles of traplines and made periodic trips to Kenai, traveling with a small dog team or on foot. As described in his journals, his traplines were scattered widely around the lake and beyond.

Trapping was Andrew's primary winter occupation. From the following letters it appears that he was encountering competition, game violations, or both:

May 3, 1919
Thomas Riggs, Jr Governor of Alaska
Juneau Alaska
Dear Sir. I wish to call your atention to a lot of aliens who go out here for the winter hunting and trapping, and aparently disregarding the game law Our game wardens we dont see oftner then once each year Would like to know if these aliens are intitled to hunt and trapp through the country Andrew Berg Kenai Alaska [26]

May 14
Dr. J. A. Baughman.
Game Warden, Seward, Alaska.
Dear Doctor Baughman: ...I am in receipt of a letter from Mr. Andrew Berg, one of the licensed guides for the Peninsula, drawing my attention to the hunting and trapping near Kenai conducted by, as he states, a number of aliens. Perhaps it would be well to investigate this alleged condition..... Thomas Riggs Jr. [27]

July 8th 1919 report to Governor Thos Riggs Jr. Governor of Alaska from game warden J. A. Baughman ...arrived at Forelands at 3:30 PM and interviewed Andrew Berg as to the report made to you on Aliens hunting and trapping. I found that these Aliens were all residents of Alaska, consequently no violations had been committed, as all of the accused had lived in Alaska for a number of years. Mr. Berg states that sheep are in fine condition, and estimates that there are at least 2000 sheep on that range. This report was verified by his brother Emil Berg who was formerly a guide, and later on June 3rd by one Windy Wagner, who to spent the winter there. Both Berg and Wagner report that quite a few moose had been killed by brown bear last fall, but few died of natural causes during the winter months as the snow did not crust nor was it as deep as in other sections. [28]

Berg was old enough and had been around long enough to be both possessive about his trapping areas and impatient with amateurs. In Baughman's report it appears that the game warden interviewed the supposed aliens in Kenai. But there were also people encroaching on Tustumena Lake from the south – Seldovia and Kachemak Bay. The practice of fox farming had begun around Seldovia in 1915. A common method of starting a farm without investing much capital was to collect foxes in the wild for breeding stock. At least two Seldovia men, Chris Spillum and Dan Morris, went to Tustumena around this time with the intention of collecting live foxes. They ended up building a cabin and spending a few winters trapping there instead.[29]

The trophy hunters returned after the war. There are records indicating at least ten hunting parties were on the Peninsula for the 1919 season. One of Baughman's reports from the Seward dock accounts for Andrew's time:

November 6 Report from Game Warden's office, Seward, J.A. Baughman:

On November 1st on the S S Northwestern Mr H C Cutting of New York City and Mr Walcott of Boston N Y, Walcotts license was No 61, and Cuttings License was No 62 and permit no 515 for the U S Biological Survey.

They hunted 57 days with Walter Lodge as for Mr Cutting and Andrew Berg guiding Mr Walcott. They had Tom Tracy as Cook with E Anderson, J Norman, Russian Pete and Tom Martin as packers. They report a very pleasant and successful trip and pleased with guides and packers.[30]

Fifty-seven days at the guides' rate of $5 to $10 a day could finance plenty of beans, flour, canned milk and kerosene for the winter.

Early Anchorage showing its roots. Started as a camp for railroad construction workers in 1914, Anchorage would quickly grow beyond anyone's expectations. Between 1914 and 1920 its population went from zero to 1,856. Photo courtesy of Carpenter Collection, no. 641, Library of Congress Prints and Photographs Division.

After ten years of pointing out the need for increased enforcement of game regulations on the western side of the Peninsula, Andrew Berg finally got the power himself. Apparently the necessary appropriations were made for another game warden and the Governor called upon Warden Baughman to find the man for the job:

June 17, 1920
Baughman, Game Warden Seward
      Please recommend game warden for Cook Inlet and alaska Peninsula for appointment July First, salary hundred fifty with expense allowance. Should have endorsement local committee.
Riggs, Governor.[1]

June 30, 1920
Thomas Riggs Jr Governor of Alaska
Dear Sir. I will recomend Mr. Andrew Berg of Kenai who will see that the law is obeyed in every way. And as Kenai and Katchamack bay need a warden very bad, it would be the wisest thing to appoint a man who lives in the vacinity and as Mr Berg has been a hunter and trapper for the last twenty years and has all ways been faithful in reporting irregularities in that section. While I do not know just what his politicts are he will be indorsed by the local committee.
Respecfully yours
J A Baughman Game Warden [2]

From Berg's earlier letters to the Governor requesting the authority for licensed guides to make arrests, we can infer that he was quite willing to be an enforcer. The following game warden report illustrates the variety of issues with which Berg had to contend. He was also expected to enforce Prohibition which began in January of 1920.

Game warden J.A. Baughman report to Governor Thomas Riggs Jr. July 1,1920.
      Andrew Berg (Guide of Kenai) reports a man by the name of Guthburg sold moose at Anchorage last fall. Also that Arvid Wickand, Hugo Holm killed a beaver about June the seventh 1920. And that Hugo Holm has run foxes into there holes or dens, and blocked them up and starved them to go into the traps. He starved one nineteen days it was a silver one evidently starved to death, as it did not show up in twenty six days and one he dug after he had plugged the hole for twenty days, it was blind and would only go backwards. Otto Nest helped him to dig it out, that was on the twentieth of March. Henry Gotberg is supposed to have sold a moose at Kenai about Xmas and this spring he come down Kassiloff lake and had two sheep and part of an other carcass, and he was supposed to bring some to the watchman at Libby Cannery. This man Gotbeg was bragging to Albert Thompson Charley March and Bill Carson about selling moose at Anchorage. I gave this letter of Bergs to Warden Martin at Anchorage when I came through, with instructions for him to make these arrests as soon as the fishing season was over, as it would inconvenient the witnesses to much to do so at once.[3]

Now Andrew would be able to deal with this sort of malfeasance directly. Of course, he was also required to cope with the increased paperwork of reports and expense accounting. From the following series of correspondences it appears that Berg's first task as Warden was guiding some of the Governor's friends on a hunt.

September 15 [1920]
Mr. G.W. Folta
Secretary to the governor

Dear Sir
    I entered the duties of game warden July
15th Did not have a chance to take oath of
office until Aug 27th did not get back home
until last night inclosed pleas find oath of office
        yours truly
Andrew Berg Game Warden

Letter and oath, 1920, General Correspondence of the
Governor of the Territorial Government of Alaska, 1909-
1958; Archives and Manuscripts Department, Consortium
Library, University of Alaska Anchorage.

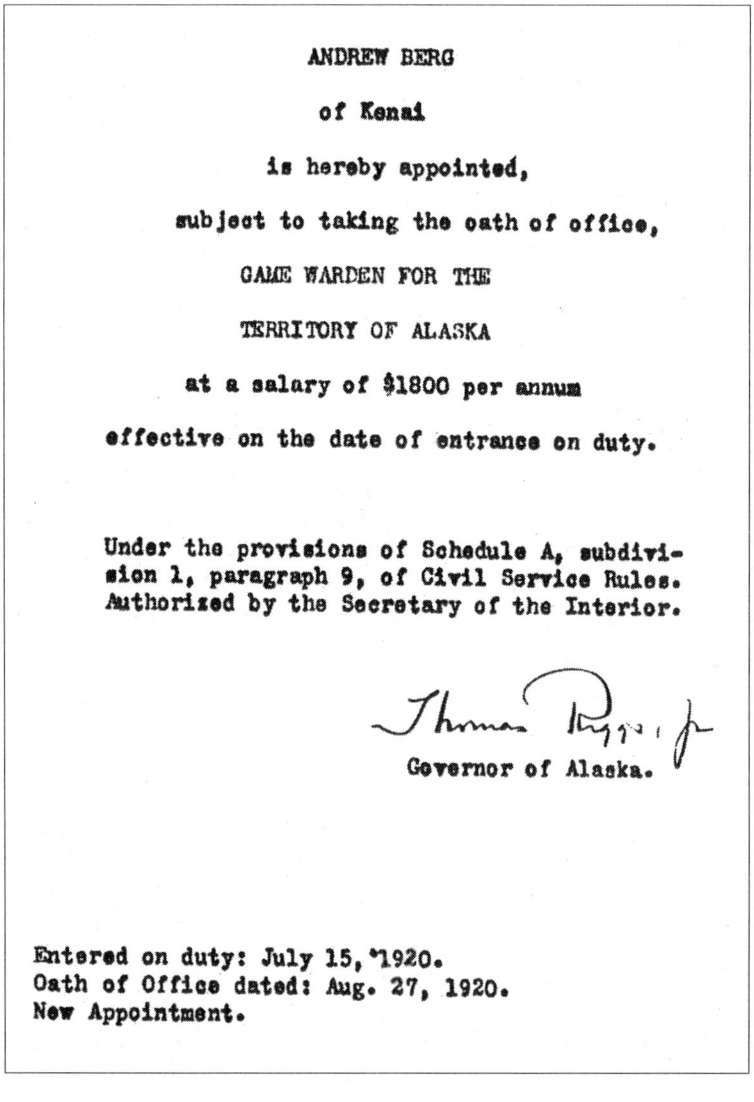

ANDREW BERG

of Kenai

is hereby appointed,

subject to taking the oath of office,

GAME WARDEN FOR THE

TERRITORY OF ALASKA

at a salary of $1800 per annum

effective on the date of entrance on duty.

Under the provisions of Schedule A, subdivi-
sion 1, paragraph 9, of Civil Service Rules.
Authorized by the Secretary of the Interior.

Thomas Riggs, Jr.
Governor of Alaska.

Entered on duty: July 15, 1920.
Oath of Office dated: Aug. 27, 1920.
New Appointment.

Sept 1st,   Report from Game Warden's office,
Seward, J.A. Baughman
    On Aug. 30th Mr. Coudert and Sons
arrived and left on Sept. 1st for lower lake
they had Andrew Berg as Game Warden and C.
Wagner as guide. Leo Aunheiser and F.
Jackobs as packers and H. Solburg as Cook.[4]

Berg reported on the hunting trip:

Sept 30,   The Governor of Alaska
Dear Sir: Since making the last return to your
office I wish to make the following report.

Aug.26, Left Kenai for Anchorage.
Aug.27, Arrived at Anchorage, in the morning.
Aug. 28, Waiting at Anchorage for train to
Seward.
Aug.29, Left Anchorage for Seward arriving
    there in the evening. [It was easier to boat
    to Anchorage and ride the train to Seward
    than to travel overland between Kenai and
    Seward]
Aug.30 & 31, Remained at Seward. Fitting
out for trip.
Sept.1, Left on morning train for upper
Kenai Lake with Mr. Coudert's party. Left
with party in motor boat for the landing
on the upper river. Arrived same evening.
Sept 2, Left with party in dories for down
river. Arrived on Lake Skillack on same
evening.
Sept.3, Packed in to Canyon Creek.
Sept. 4, out with party hunting bear.
Sept. 5, out with party hunting bear.
Sept. 6, started for sheep country, but
turned back on account of storm.
Sept. 7 Again started for sheep country
killing one ram about nine years old.
Fairly good specimen about 13 inches.
Saw about 100 sheep this day. Left half of
party in camp in sheep country, the other
part shifted to the moose country, with
myself
Sept. 8, Killed one moose a bull about nine
years old. Antlers 59 inches. Saw 12 to
15 moose that day.
Sept 9, Out hunting for bear. Saw one
black bear.

Sept.10,   Spent in cleaning preparing the trophies and other half of party hunting moose. They killed one bull about 55 inches.
Sept.11,   Packed the trophies to Kelly [Killey] River.
Sept.12,   Broke camp and returned to Skillack Lake.
Sept.13, Three packers returned to Kelly River for trophies there. Shifted outfit to lake.
Sept.14,   Broke camp and came down river to Kenai with party.
Sept.15,   Met another hunting party coming out in charge of Bill Kyser and Henry Lucas they arrived at Kenai same evening.
Sept.16,   At home in Kenai and remained there until the 30th.

Not knowing whether the trip with the Coudert party was official business or not, I paid my own expenses. I have not used any of the travelling expense money during the month. Found no Violations on this trip or since and none have been reported to me. The moose and sheep are in fine condition in fact are looking the best that I have noticed for years.

Have been making investigations in the matter of suppressing liquor traffic among the natives around Kenai, but have reported no violations. starting for a trip to the Lake Kussiloff country and on through to the head of Kachamack Bay to be gone about three weeks. This is for the purpose of watching the hunters and observing how they handle the game.
Very respectfully yours.
Andrew Berg Game Warden [5]

Game Warden J.A. Baughman also mentioned the hunt in his regular report:

Sept. 30, 1920.
The Coudert family left on last boat with 3 moose and 3 sheep. They also killed 3 black bear. Were well pleased with their hunt.
Wagoner & Berg guides [6]

Andrew's following letter addresses the issue of the long mail delays which added an element of frustration to official communications. The Governor's office would occasionally resort to telegrams.

October 30
Hon Thomas Riggs, Jr. Governor of Alaska. Dear Sir; I received your letter Aug. 29th two days ago   It is mailed at Anchorage Sept 26th the letter is in regards to our contemplated trip thru the game country of Kenai   Sory you could not come as we hade a fine trip only to short time to see much of the country. You ask my opinion as to the amount of game on Kenai Penn   We gat probably 2000 moose and the same amount of sheep. Bears on strong increes. You have I presume seen Mr. Coudart and have heard all about our hunting, we did all that could posible be done considering the short time
Yours Respectfully
Andrew Berg Game Warden [7]

Andrew also sent a detailed report of his "trip thru the game country of Kenai" (see exhibit on next page). In his entry for October twenty-fifth he mentioned fox farms. The first fox farms were started in Kasilof this year, the practice having worked its way up the coast from Seldovia.

During this last trip to Tustumena Lake Andrew also recorded his activities in his journal at "Home Camp," the cabin he had built in 1902 near Indian Creek. The journal entries reproduced in this book come out of two legal sized notebooks found in the 1950s.

The first entry is for October 1, 1920. There is no way of knowing if it is a continuation of previous diary-keeping or the start of a new habit. Entries are handwritten in Berg's rather elegant script. (Examples of original entries begin in Chapter 7). Guests at Andrew's cabin also wrote in his journals. Most of these entries are included. As with the letters and reports, the text is transcribed here verbatim except for the addition of spaces between apparent sentences.

These diary entries for October can be compared to the same days in his official report:

Happy to be Home Camp When it is raining & snowing

Oct 1th 1920   Left Kenai and ran down to Kussiloff and up as far as Standerfords

Oct 2th   Lined up river to Victors

COPY   COPY
                                        Kenai, Alaska,
                                        October 31st, 1920.

The Governor of Alaska,
        Juneau, Alaska.

Dear Sir:

        Since making the last return to your office I wish to make the
following report:

Oct. 1st - I left Kenai for Kussiloff on my way into the game country.
  " 2nd   - Interviewed a party of hunters; got up river as far as Victor's
            Cabin.
  " 3rd   - Lined the boat up to head of rapids, found a dead moose that
            was drowned, could not find any bullet marks on it.
  " 4th   - Traveling by motor up the lake, hunted up a party of Indians
            who were drying moose meat.
  " 5th   - Interviewed packers from the sportsmen's parties for who
            Lodge and Lean of Seward were guides.
  " 6th   - Hunted up some Indians who were curing some mountain sheep.
  " 7th   - Was up the mountain to find a bunch of Indians; interviewed
            the Indians and found where a bear had killed a young moose.
  " 8th &
       9th & 10th- Took a walk across the table land to Kenai country, saw
            a lot of game killed, two black bear from camp meat.
  " 11th - Stayed in camp all day and got in late last night.
  " 12th - Met Sigwald Hanson and Axel Vitbro who have been hunting south
            of us.
  " 13th - Was out to the camp of Ray Curtis who was working assessment.
  " 14th - Was out to the head of bear creek country.
  " 15th - Got back from Bear Creek, saw a lot of game in that section.
  " 16th - Went across the lake for a trip across country to Kaschekmak.
  " 17th - Snow and rain, went a ways into the country, had to turn back.
  " 18th - Went back across the lake to our main camp.
  " 19th - Had visitors so we all turned to and fixed up the camp.
            That is my old cabin that I expect to have use of in winter.
  " 20th - Took a trip up South Fork, found where a brown bear had
            killed a bull moose recently-the back of moose broken and legs
            torn loose from carcass, the bear got away.
  " 21st - Stayed in camp making ready to go back to Kenai.
  " 22nd - Was up on the mountains, got a ram; sheep looking fine.
  " 23rd - Starting down the lake, got to Birch-wood for the night.
  " 24th - Went down the lake and through the river to Kussiloff.
  " 25th - Stayed at Kussiloff looking over the fox farms.
  " 26th - Got back to Kenai and stayed at headquarters to end of the
            month.   I have not found any violations, but believe that I
            have saved a lot of animals by being through the grounds,
            both moose and mountain sheep are in a fine condition.   It
            is hard to tell when I can get a report out from now, as we
            have no regular out-going mail from October to January, so
            we have to depend on travelers for accommodation mail, even
            our election returns have to be sent out that way.
                    Respectfully yours,   (Sgd) ANDREW BERG, Game W.

*Andrew Berg report to Governor, Oct. 31, 1920; General Correspondence of the Governor of the Territorial
Government of Alaska, 1909-1958; Archives and Manuscripts Department, Consortium Library, UAA.*

Lined up to Bull Run found one dead bull floting above moose horn rapids.

Oct 4   traveling by motor   visit camp of Indians who was drying moose meat   saw packers from lodge and some parties of sportsman   came upon a party of indians at old saw mill who was curing sheep meat.

Oct 5   was up sout fork met five Indians coming out with sheep saw two bears found where a brown bear had killed young moose.

Oct 6   Stay in camp making bread

Oct 7   wind & rain

Oct 8   out to get camp meat shot a black bear cleaned and stritched the bear skins Sigwald came from Devils bay. Ray Curtis came up from Kussiloff.

Oct. 10   was up to head of bear creek saw several moose one bear track one wolferine that got wet wading thru snow

11th   was at home making ready to go acrost country to Caschak bay. Loking like snow did not go. Axel and Sigwald came over

12th   started to snow and blow did not go was out on glaser flats Ray Curtis came down from mine and went to bear creek

13th   blowing a storm   at home all day   Sigwald found a bear track on Emma trail

14th   up south fork   folowed bear to his hole

15th   at home taking moss for reparing cabbin the rest was out on mountain hunting sheep

16th   was out over glacier and got som meat

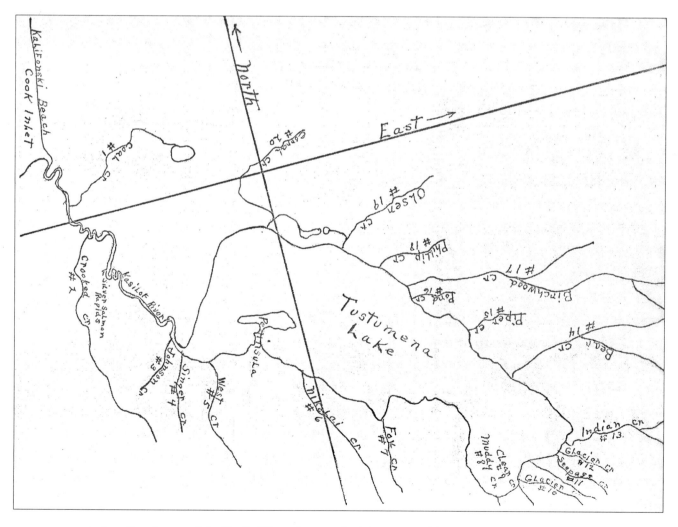

Andrew Berg's map of the Kasilof River drainage.[8]   More maps of this area are in the next chapter.

Lining a boat up the Kasilof River sometime in the 1920's. With a group, one member would stay in the boat to keep it off the bank while the others pulled from shore. At this time outboard motors were available but were not powerful enough to overcome much river current. Photo courtesy of McLane Collection.

17th   *Sunday atending religious service*

18th   *at home making bread*

19th   *started to fix up camp*

20th   *finnis the house work*

Berg's territory as game warden included all of Cook Inlet so he continued on his rounds in spite of shortening hours of daylight and wintery conditions. Boating on Cook Inlet in November is a very cold proposition. The dory he was using was likely equipped with only a small outboard motor. It was not powerful enough to propel the boat up the rapids of the Kasilof River nor was it strong enough to buck the tidal flow in Cook Inlet. Berg's movement described in the following report would have been carefully coordinated with the tide. In his travels he still relied on the hospitality of residents along the way.

November 30th
Hon Thomas Riggs Jr, Governor of Alaska
Dear Sir. Since making my last report I wish to make the following report.
Nov 5th, starting on a trip along the Inlet gat to Kussiloff.

Nov 6th, Went down the coast to clam gulsh [gulch] a point between Nilchick and Kussiloff Tok a trip acrost country to the foothills gat back to Inlet on the twelft.
Nov 13, ran down to Nilchick stopped at the water falls on my way where I saw a party of hunters.
Nov 14, went to Anchorpoint
Nov 15, Stay at Anchorpoint loking over som fox farmers.
Nov 16, Gat of the becht thru a havy surf [Got off the beach through a heavy surf] ran to seldovia.
Nov 17,18, 19,& 20, stay seldovea, interwewd a lot of people who get their meat from kashekmak bay moose sems to be far in and hard to get.
Nov 21, Left Seldovia going up the bay gat to yokan Iland [Yukon Island],
Nov 22, After seing the fox farmers on the islands i came to homer.
Nov 23, Stay over and saw a lot of people who settled down to farming raising cattle fox scunk and belgium hare.
Nov 24, Came up as far as Anchore point.
Nov 25, gat back to nelchick here they was

*selabrating the thanks given [Thanksgiving] by
being intoxicated   just wat they was drinking I
did not find out.*
*Nov 26, Still at nilchick found two of nativs having
two red fox in captivety that they have taken in
close season*
*Nov 27, I ordered them to turn them loose. I came
from nilchick to Kussiloff.*
*Nov 28, gat bac to Kenai finding the place
looking like a winter   that is snow have fallen
since i left, but there is hardly any ice to be seen
in the inlet, There is quite of liquire used here not
so much by natives as by white men, I saw marshel
Herington at Seldovia, he said that he was
coming down to Kenai soon.*
Respectfully yours
Andrew Berg Game Warden [9]

Communication delays were exacerbated in winter. Once
shipping on Cook Inlet stopped for the season then the
most direct route from the western Peninsula to an ice-
free port for mail and goods was overland to Seward. A
mail contract was normally given out for monthly delivery
from Seward by dogsled.

At some point during the winter, the following two letters
made their way to Andrew from Juneau. Written on the
same day in the same place, they have vastly different
messages. The Governor congratulates Berg as an
exemplary man, warden and guide. The Secretary to
the Governor takes him to task for his improper
bookkeeping.

December 1, 1920
Mr. Andrew Berg, Game Warden, Kenai Alaska.
*Dear Mr. Berg: I have your letter of October
30th   Certainly you cannot complain of getting
mail too frequently, if a letter of mine of August
29th has only just reached you. Mr. Coudert
and his sons came back singing your praises.
They have the highest regard for you, not only
as a warden and a guide but, also, as a man. I
thank you for your estimate of the game.*
Very truly yours   Governor [10]

December 1, 1920
Mr. Andrew Berg
*Dear Sir: Your expense voucher for October
has just been received, but an examination of it
shows many defects which I have corrected to
the extent possible, and will try to get it passed*
*by the auditor, without returning it to you, by
explaining to him the circumstances. Enclosed
is a model for your guidance in the future,
which shows the common and approved
manner in which to prepare expense vouchers.
Note carefully the following points: A. The
voucher should not be numbered. B. On the
line opposite the word "appropriation" should
appear the following: "protection of game in
Alaska, 1921," as since July 1, the fiscal year
is 1921, and therefore all expenses incurred
after that date are chargeable to and payable
from the appropriation for 1921 only. C. You
are allowed actual expenses not exceeding $5
a day, and not a per diem.... D. Unit prices are
not shown in every instance on the bill from
Dawson & Berg, as in the case of the following
items: 50 lbs flour....$4.50   In the case of such
an item as "1 can syrup," the quantity in
pounds, ounces, pints or quarts should be
shown. All indefinite and obscure terms such
as "kegs, box, bottle, can, bunch, carton,"
should always be avoided. This bill is not
receipted or stamped as paid. Unless bills
show on their face that they have been paid,
they cannot be claimed as an item of expense
for reimbursement. The instructions sent you
state that, in the case of a firm, bills must be
stamped with the name of the firm, followed by
the signature of a member of the firm or an
employee who is authorized to receipt bills and
your certificate on the bill to the effect that the
supplies enumerated in the bill were used by
you while absent on official business.... As I
have said, the voucher has been corrected as
far as possible and sent in to the auditor for
the Interior Department with an explanation as
to its defects, with the recommendation that it
be passed in this case in its present form.
Obviously an exception cannot again be made
in the case of any future voucher.*
Very truly yours, G. Folta
Secretary to the Governor and S. D. A. [11]

Poor Andrew joined the ranks of the many who have
opted into law enforcement or other public service in a
genuine desire to do good, only to be confronted with the
horrible reality of fiscal accountability. He made a
gracious reply acknowledging his strengths and
weaknesses:

Kenai Alaska
January 8 th 1921
Mr. G. Folta Secretary to the Governor
Dear Sir. I gat your sample voucher, showing how to fill out the same properly. For wich i thank you. Sorry to have made sych a mess of it, and still you have by this time another just as bad wich shows that office work is out of my line of busines if it was just to get a brown Bear out of alders i would know wat to do. I wants some copies of game circulars I find a lot of people who live out in the country who have not seen a copy of the Game laws I am down to the last Copy.
Respectfully Andrew Berg Game Warden.[12]

Events in the following story about Andrew probably took place this winter as Berg is quoted referring to himself as a game warden. It is a second hand story printed in 1945, so the details may be questionable, but it gives a sense of Andrew's personality and style.

Many years ago, when Dan Morris lived in Seldovia and he and Chris Spillum were fairly young men, they decided to go into partnership and start a fox farm. They planned to go to Kasilof Lake, up Kenai Peninsula a way, it was called Tustumena Lake then, but now almost everyone calls it Kasilof Lake, to trap silver foxes and bring them back to a little island near Seldovia for their breeding stock. But when they got to Kasilof Lake they liked the scenery so well that they decided to build a cabin and stay there. Not far from their cabin lived Andrew Berg, a well known hunter and guide. Andy was a good natured sourdough, and the three spent many jolly evenings in each others cabins. Shortly after Chris's experience with the [being treed by] moose, he was telling Andy about it. Andy laughed, and kidded Chris about a couple of moose having him up a tree. Andy had a team of malamute that Chris says were about the biggest he's ever seen. He had a home in Kenai, and used to drive back and forth often. When Andy rode, he really went in style! He had the seat of a car on his sled, and Chris says he looked like a nobleman sitting on his cushions and riding away. But Andy's language was far from high class. Chris says he would crack his whip and shout

all sorts of unprintable things! About two weeks after Chris's sojourn in the tree, he and Dan invited Andy over for supper. Dan was cooking, while Chris and Andy were talking politics. That's one thing about sourdoughs be they educated or ignorant intelligent or not, they'll always discuss politics with great enthusiasm. "Listen," Chris said suddenly, "I think your dogs are loose, Andy. Hear that barking up in the hills?" Andy started cussing. "I'll get those blankety-blank dogs back here! And I'll be back by the time supper's ready." Andy followed the trail up the trap line, and found his dogs holding a moose cow and calf at bay. The moose were fighting mad, and when they saw Andy coming, they charged him. Of course he hadn't brought his gun, and the only thing he could do was climb the nearest cottonwood tree. At first he thought the moose would leave soon, but these were even more stubborn then the two that had treed Chris. They stayed under that cottonwood tree for three hours! It was dark, and Andy got cold. He was angry too, just as angry as Chris had been. But I think it served him right, true people have to learn by experience but Andy, at least, could have learned by Chris's experience. Meanwhile Dan and Chris were wondering what had happened. Supper was ready and waiting, and they were hungry. "Think we should go look for him?" Dan asked. "I hate to go out in the dark," Chris mused. "Bet a moose had him up a tree. It would serve him right, after the laugh he got out of it when I was treed." After a long time they decided they'd better go out after Andy, whether it was dark or not. Just as they were ready to leave, Andy came stamping in. He was tired, hungry, and angry through and through, Andy who was usually jolly! "Say," he yelled, "I'm the game warden around here. I want every damn moose in sight killed! I don't care if there's not a moose left in all Alaska!" They finally calmed him down a little, but Chris couldn't resist teasing. "Now you can see it's no laughing matter to be treed by a moose in weather like this," Chris kidded. "Laughing matter!" Andy stormed, "who the hells laughing!" Then he had to grin when he remembered how he'd laughed at Chris's experience...[13]

CHAPTER 6
1921

Berg starts out the new year with game warden reports from Kenai. He succinctly describes the difficulty of winter travel in this roadless land. River crossings along the coast were unpredictable because tidal action in the river mouths would interrupt ice formation.

Game Wardens Office, Kenai
January 2th, 1921
Hon Thomas Riggs Jr. Governor of Alaska.
Dear Sir. Since making my last report I wish to submit the following,
Dec. 7th, tok a trip with my dog team on nikishy trail gat back the same day, was out as far as anybody been that way
Dec. 11th was out again with dog team loking over moose country very few moose down from the hills so it is hard for the people to get their meat, gat back to head quaters [Kenai] the thirteent, stay at head quaters to the 26th the rivers just freazing and trails unbroken so it is hard to go anywhere,
Dec. 26th after much truble i gat thru mush ice by boat to south side of Kenai river, landed the boat and went on with dog team finding lots of moose in this country was out in the country to the 30th gat to the cannery, went out the 31th killed a moose,
Jan. 1th tryed to get back to Kenai but found myself froze in that is unable to use the boat, went back to cannery january 2th came over the ice but had to go long way up river to get across. I have not found any violation of the game law since I entered duties as game warden, I had word that there was moose being fed to Foxes but upon investigation could not find any evidense to that effect, I have not carried any expence acount this mont as I have been among people who would not charge anyting for the acomodition. I have been doing

by best to keep the natives from being intoxicated but still I find one now and then.
Respectfully submitted,
Andrew Berg Game Warden[1]

Feb. 1, 1921
Honorable Thomas Riggs Jr. Governor of Alaska
Dear Sir: Since last report, i have been at headquaters thru all of january, oving to the traveling condition, We have had a lot of snow fall with short changies to cold weather so that no one have been traveling I would come to the end of the trail in three or four miles, out side of traveling the natives still celabrate the russian church holidays and those extend to about the nineteent of January, Moose seems to hold their own oving to the fact that the larger snow falls acurd along the coast so it will keep the animals at the foot hills, An unusual amount of ptarmigans are reported from Nilchik Kussiloff and lower penninsula. Respectfully yours, Andrew Berg Game Warden Kenai Alaska[2]

In February Berg gets back up to Tustumena and records his activities in both his journal and his warden reports.

Journal:

February 22 Came up from lonsom bay today was all night at Abes house saw a lot of moose out on ice Abraham was not at home he have gone in to Devils Bay

Feb 23rd Starting to blow from the mountains turning mild was up on the roof fixing som plates that have blown loose [the roof was sheathed with small sheets of canning tin] the man from the Cliff House came over this evening the morning I found a young moose that have

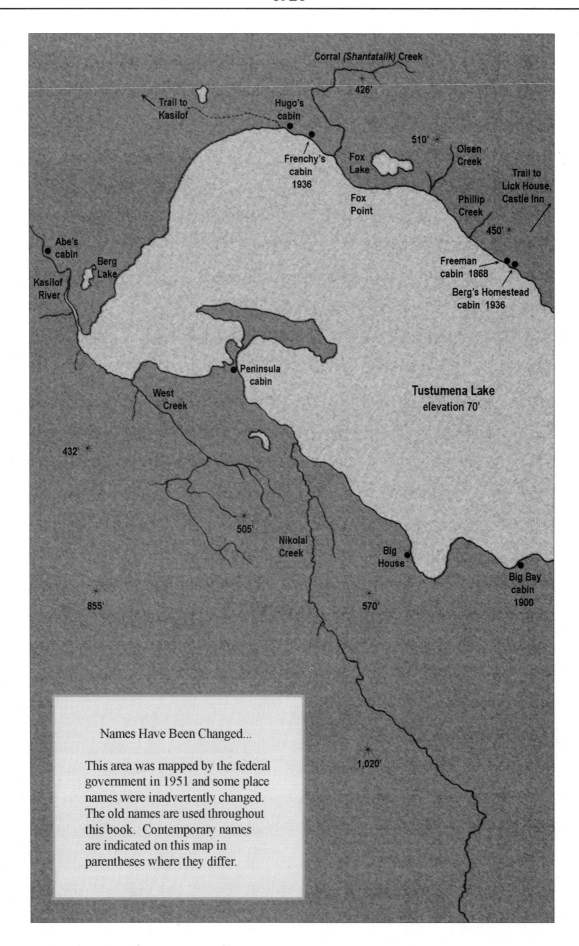

Corral *(Shantatalik)* Creek

426'

Trail to
Kasilof

Hugo's
cabin

Frenchy's
cabin
1936

Fox
Lake

510'

Olsen
Creek

Fox
Point

Phillip
Creek

Trail to
Lick House,
Castle Inn

450'

Abe's
cabin

Berg
Lake

Freeman
cabin 1868

Berg's Homestead
cabin 1936

Kasilof
River

Peninsula
cabin

West
Creek

Tustumena Lake
elevation 70'

432'

505'

Nikolai
Creek

Big
House

Big Bay
cabin
1900

855'

570'

Names Have Been Changed...

This area was mapped by the federal
government in 1951 and some place
names were inadvertently changed.
The old names are used throughout
this book. Contemporary names
are indicated on this map in
parentheses where they differ.

1,020'

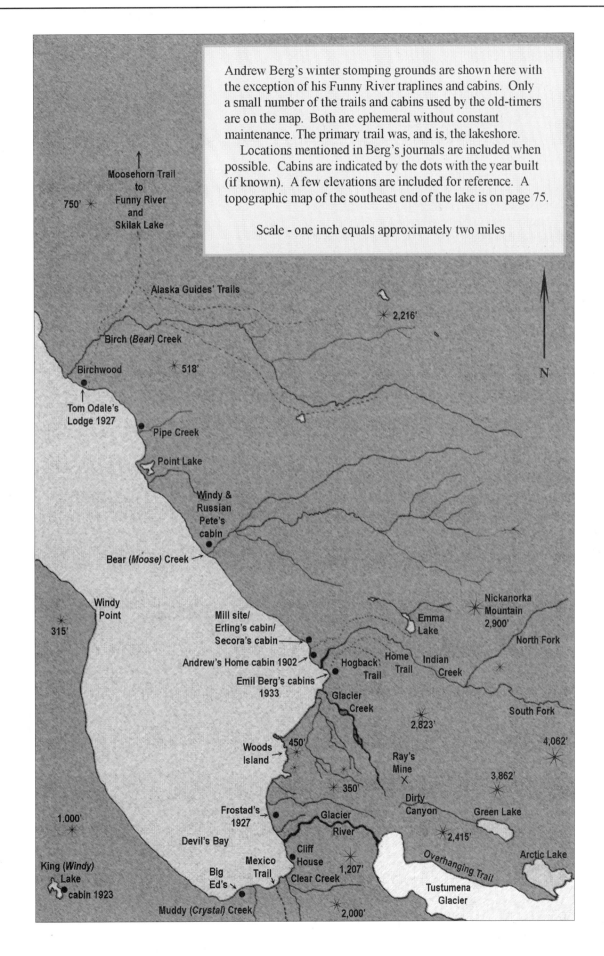

Andrew Berg's winter stomping grounds are shown here with the exception of his Funny River traplines and cabins. Only a small number of the trails and cabins used by the old-timers are on the map. Both are ephemeral without constant maintenance. The primary trail was, and is, the lakeshore.

Locations mentioned in Berg's journals are included when possible. Cabins are indicated by the dots with the year built (if known). A few elevations are included for reference. A topographic map of the southeast end of the lake is on page 75.

Scale - one inch equals approximately two miles

Moosehorn Trail to Funny River and Skilak Lake

750'

Alaska Guides' Trails

2,216'

Birch (Bear) Creek

Birchwood

518'

Tom Odale's Lodge 1927

Pipe Creek

Point Lake

Windy & Russian Pete's cabin

Bear (Moose) Creek

N

Windy Point

315'

Mill site/ Erling's cabin/ Secora's cabin

Emma Lake

Nickanorka Mountain 2,900'

North Fork

Andrew's Home cabin 1902

Hogback Trail

Home Trail

Indian Creek

Emil Berg's cabins 1933

Glacier Creek

2,823'

South Fork

4,062'

Woods Island

450'

Ray's Mine

3,862'

350'

Frostad's 1927

Glacier River

Dirty Canyon

Green Lake

1,000'

Devil's Bay

2,415'

Arctic Lake

King (Windy) Lake cabin 1923

Mexico Trail

Cliff House

1,207'

Overhanging Trail

Big Ed's

Clear Creek

Tustumena Glacier

Muddy (Crystal) Creek

2,000'

died during the night about 100 feet from the cabbin   raining tonight

Feb 24th   South eastly storm   mild raining   snow is melting fast   The boys was over this evening from the mill   Lake is getting black loking   turning to glare ice   fixed end of the bunk   all that I can give my self credit for as a days work unless reading is work

"The boys" may have been Dan Morris and Chris Spillum. The "mill" refers to the Northwest Development and Mining Company's mill site. The abandoned buildings and machinery were a source of building materials for lake residents.

Feb 25th   Still mild   som rain   snow to soft to go anywhere   has been at home all day reading a novel title "The Chasm"   was out trying scating but ice to soft

Feb 26   was at home all day reading a novel titled The chasm   Book handled the socialistic question but are seriusly overdrawn in United States and Russia   the boys was down to Bear Creek   came up with Ray Curtis sled   tok it to Devils Bay intending to haul out their boat while ice is good

February 27th   Still to mild to go any place thermometer at 40 this morning   Stay home making a pair of dog moccasins blowing hard in squalls with rain   regular spring weather   a moose came right up to the cabbin   tok a walk this evening to the glaser flats   a squall came up and drove me back

Feb 28th   Went up the creek thru the cannon saw a big lot of moose and some sheep   ice is poor tru the cannon that I thought have to turn

Kasilof in the early 1920s. A few more people lived here than are indicated.

The residents were Andrew's friends and neighbors. Berg passed through the community regularly and the Kasilof folks (and many from Kenai) went to Tustumena to hunt moose and sheep.

Several Kasilof residents were starting fox farms at this time. They would also go to Tustumena seeking porcupines and bears for fox feed.

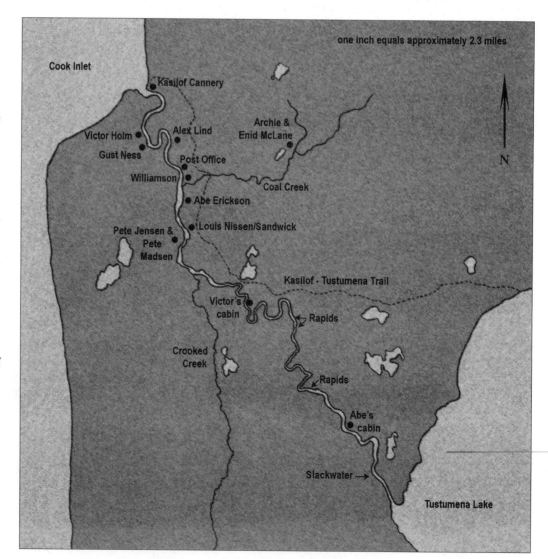

back but finally I got up went to pay a bear a visit found his hole last fall but he was not at home the boys was here this evening brought the dory over from the cliff house

March 1st Starting home Andrew

Game Warden Report:

March 6, 1921
Hon Tomas Riggs, Jr. Governor of Alaska.
Dear Sir; Since making the last report I wish to submit the folloving, On the tent of February, or the day after the mail left for Seward. I went to Kussiloff at a vilage called Colifonsky I found that the indians have just killed a moose, but upon examining thier food suply I decided that they needed it moose was plenty about the vilage at this time i saw about twenty moose the same day.
[February] 11&12 I stay at the cannery with the watchman as it was storming and blowing snow thru any tiny crack.
13— I went up the river to where some boys are living stay here for five days, tramping thru country loking over game, and here is certainly some moose, you could see them with in twenty yards of the cabbins, comming to feed of the

birch tops that they cut for fire wood, moose seem to be in good condition.
19—I went up the river saw moose all day,
20—gat up to lower end of lake moose are scarce on acount of snow and better feed on the inlet,
21—about half way up the lake saw six moose this day,
22—gat to head of lake soft snow all the way, had to snow shoe a head of the dogs to breck trail.
23—found a moose dead cut it open found lung truble, (influensa) traveled thru this country until march first on that date i found a moose that have been out on the lake when the snow melted of [off] the ice. and when it froze up and gat slick it could not get to shore I put it on the sled and houled it to shore, it was a three year old cow, not badly hurt,
23—gat down to Kussiloff stay over one day.
25—arived to Kenai mild raining came part of the way with the boat the first boating this season. no violation have come to my notice or being reported. Liquer quistion is not good last night i saw a lot of men drunk mostly wite men.
Respectfully submitted
Andrew Berg Game Warden Kenai Alaska[3]

This year the first Post Office opened in Kasilof in this small building on the north side of the river. The campers may be hunters on their way up river to Tustumena. Photo courtesy of the McLane Collection.

The preceding report piqued the curiosity of the folks in Juneau, prompting the following replies from the Governor and his secretary:

Thomas Riggs Jr. Governor of Alaska
March 23, 1921
Mr. Andrew Berg, Game Warden Kenai Alaska.
Dear Mr. Berg: I have your report of March 6. Two items have interested me greatly. The first, the dead moose which you cut open and found to have died from lung trouble; and secondly, the cow moose which you put on a sled and hauled to shore. Let me congratulate you upon your fine attitude toward game and the interest shown therein. In connection with violations of the liquor law, you are a special agent for the suppression of liquor traffic and are authorized to arrest men found drunk or to seize any illicitly sold liquor. I trust that you can take some steps toward clearing up the condition around Kenai. Very truly yours   Governor[4]

March 23, 1921
Mr. Andrew Berg, Kenai Alaska
Dear Mr. Berg: We were much interested in your remarks about the dead moose which you found during February, and the one that was marooned out on the lake. We should, however, like to know just what your autopsy disclosed that lead you to believe that the moose died of influenza, as the assertion that a moose, or in fact, any animal, should be susceptible to this disease, has not been made before, to our knowledge. We should also like to know how you were able to get the moose upon the sled which you hauled to shore. You are to be commended on your ability to do this, and you have evinced the proper interest in seeking to ascertain the cause of death of the moose found. Yours very truly, G.W. Folta
Secretary to the Governor[5]

Berg had time to send off another report before the previous letters, with their inquiries, made their way to him.

April 2, 1921
The Governor of Alaska.
Dear Sir; Since making the last return to your office i wish to make the following report

March 6th I gat home from five days trip along the coast   heard that was a lot of moose falling of the bluffs. but I found only two young calfs who have ventured to close to the edge and lost thier footing. Stay at headquarters until 17th   a report came to me that a moose was shot along the trail leading north from this place   I hunted it up but could not find any signs that it have been shot, the birds have been picking it that it was hard to determine if it was shot or not, but I found no bones scared by bullet. Since then I have been at headquarters, the moose is on a move from the coast towards the hills   the main heard [herd] was to the inlet about Kussiloff and ten miles south from there   all reports indicate that they are in good condition No expence used this mont, Liquire question seemes to have improved some,
Respectfully yours Berg Game Warden[6]

Andrew appears to be avoiding the mire of expense reports by reporting no expenses. He does not hesitate to respond to the questions about his moose-craft:

May 14, 1921
Mr G.W. Folta Secretary to the Governor.
Dear Sir; Your letter of March 23th to hand. In Regards to the dead moose that I found during the mont of february, that I said my have died of influenza   was examining the lungs for tuberculosis but found no trace of it, from the congested state of the lungs and the fact that the animal was in a good condition, so it must have [died] sudenly, made me think that it my have had som such deceise [disease].
*   As to putting a moose on the sled this was not the first time that I have brouht moose to shore that have been maroond on Kussiloff lake, when the ice get slick. It is simple anough to put them on the sled, in this instance I first unloaded my sled put out about 10 feet of line that hitched the dogs to   then when the moose was falling and getting up again, I showed [shoved] the sled aganst its front leggs and it fell over on to the sled   I jumped on to its weathers [withers] and hold it, it was kicking but could not get any foot hold while lying flat on its side, I just shouted to the dogs and to shore we went.*
Yours truly Andrew Berg Kenai[7]

Andrew didn't deem this moose rescue story worth recording in his own journal but he played it up well for the bureaucrats. A rumor about moose being used as fox feed had sent him on another trip to Kachemak Bay:

May 14, 1921
The Governor of Alaska
Dear Sir; Since making the last return to your office i wish to make the following report.
Apr 18, I went down to Kussiloff.
Apr 19, was up the river among the fox farmers.
Apr 20, went down the coast to Corea were som fishermen was at work constructing a fish trap.
[Corea was a place on the Cook Inlet beach north of Ninilchik where the cannery ship *Corea* went aground in 1890]
Apr 21, ran down to Nilchick.
Apr 22, went down the inlet as far as bluff point, gat to rough to land   stay in the dory all night,
Apr 23, gat ashore at the lagone. stay here two days visiting the fox farms   am making this trip on acount of report made to me by R.E. Bogart commisioner at Seldovia, to the efect that the fox farmers are feeding moose to fox.
Apr 26, left the lagoon ran around Homer into coal bay. found lots new setlers, both argriculture and fox farmers.
Apr 27, went up the bay as far as Mc Niel canyon found som young moose that have fallen of the bluffs   all of them shoving markings of being hurt by snow crust, before they fell.
Apr 28, ran up to the head of the bay   stay here two days climbing the hills, whenever I heard a raven crow i went to see wath he had found   one cow moose and several yearlings dead from the general hard time in spring, but noting that culd lay to violation of the game law, saw 7 a 8 moose each day loking fine
May 1, came down the bay about 15 miles stay here 2

days looking through the country, agriculture lund looks fine but the people are sadly in nead of roads and comunication.
May 4, came round homer to the west side of the spitt, when a wind sprung up wich held me for two days.
May 7, gat of from shore and up as far as bluff point but found wind to strong to round the point had to go ashore.
May 8, gat to dimond creek where som miners are operating.
May 9, went up as far as anchor point   here I saw several fox farmers
May 10, came on up to Nilchick stay over one day   gat the first king salmon for this season, people here busey making fishing gear ready.
May 12, gat home to Kenai, and after carefully loking thru the country have found no viloation.
Yours truly, Andrew Berg Game Warden.
P. S. the liquire trafic seams to have been stopped intirely.[8]

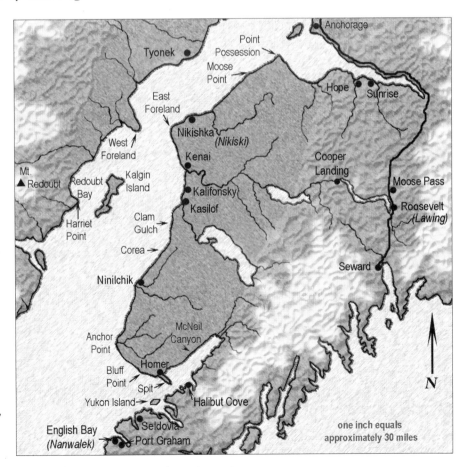

The Peninsula in the 1920s. Landmarks of Berg's travels as game warden are indicated. Where contemporary names are different, they are added in parentheses.

After fishing season started, Berg made a trip to the west side of Cook Inlet. Traveling alone in his wooden dory, he crossed 30 miles of open ocean on his return to Kenai.

June 30, 1921
Governor of Alaska.
Dear Sir; Since making the last return to your office i wish make the following report.
June 4th, Left Kenai going down the coast by way of Kussiloff, visiting the fishing camps and fox ranchers, gat back june 8th,
10, Started up the inlet, gat to moose point.
11, was out in the woods, saw tracks of lot of young moose.
12, visited some fish camps along the shore.
13, went by boat as far as point posession and loked over that country, gat back again to moose point june 14th,
15, walked along the beach to a smole [small] cannery, and back
16, went with boat to a creek about ten miles away,
17, was up this creek loking for som men suposed to be camping here but did not locate them,
18, came along the coast to east fore land, stopping at all the landings.
19, crossed the inlet to west foreland,
20, found lot of gillnet fishermen aroun the foreland,
21, walking up the coast saw wath I think was a sea otter.
22, motoring down the coast to big river found some men hunting hear [hair] seal.
23, went down to redoubt bay saw som big bears.
24, ran around point hariet to west point gat blowing that i had to go to kalgin island for shelter.
25, still blowing ran to the north end of island,
26, went down to a fish camp east side of the island found a man with five red fox pups, i ordered them truned loose
27, gat back to head quarters,
If the man with the fox pups still have them when i come should I conficate them or make him turn them loose he gat a fox ranch started and want a change in the breed, to arrest him would only be

going to expence, if he ask fore a jury trial they be sure to turn him loose.
Respectfully submitted.
Andrew Berg Game Warden.[9]

Berg's employment contract ran until July fifteenth. The following report is a summary of his year in service.

July 8, 1920
Governor of Alaska
Dear Sir: Since I was appointed game warden and entered duties on July 15th 1920 I have not made any arrests, and there have not been a charge made, that would warrant a arrest. I have heard rumors of violations and traveled quite a lot to acquire the facts and as I am well aquainted with both the game condition, and the people, I have been traveling thru country where I think I have done the most good in saving the game, principle moose and sheep.
It was reported to me that a lot of moose was starving to death but upon investigation I found that most of the moose was hurt by falling or hurt by snow crost. This was in Cachekmack bay. The percentage of dead moose was considerably less than it have been for many years. I have cut oppens som of the dead carcases in som cases I foun lung truble but in most cases I found the blader filled with urine of a black color and to a larg amount the bladder almost brecking.
I find that the moose are increasing on the west side of cook Inlet where there was not a track to be found a few years ago   I found frish tracks as far south as redoubt bay   this I tok notice of on my trip in the mont of June.
The bears are increasing on Kenai Peninsula to such an extrem that I hear of them killing moose every few days   to day a man by the name of John Wik came from Kussiloff he told me that he found a moose killed by bears three days ago.
The liquor appeard to be in abundance during the early part of the year but after we made one of the pool halls shut up and the parties arrested and convicted two of them to six monts and one by a fine of one hundred dollar. Everyting have been quite untill the last few days. But lately I have seen som men effected by liquore

Respectfully Submitted
Andrew Berg Game Warden Kenai[10]

The archives did not reveal any correspondence related to the renewal of Berg's annual contract as a game warden. His contract year ended July fifteenth. Andrew continued working past that date. On July twelfth he set out on another patrol after hearing about a cow moose killed near Homer. Meanwhile, the same poaching incident was reported to the Governor.

Homer via Seldovia, Alaska, July 13, 1921.
To The Honorable, The Governor of Alaska, Juneau, Alaska.
Dear Sir: A Mr. Snooks, recently of Anchorage, now with a bunch from there looking for locations on the north side of Kachemak Bay, went out on the 22nd inst, and killed a cow moose that was nurseing her young. With two witnesses I went out yesterday and found the entrails, hide and udder with the milk in it, but could see nothing of the calf. I brought home the hide and udder, the latter is suitable marked by witnesses and salted down. Mr. Snooks made his brags in the presence of myself and witnesses that he is practically immune from arrest by local authorities, and that he has a permit secured from or through Secretary of Labor Davis to secure two moose calves to be shipped to Mooseheart, Ind. On account of his brags I thought it well to write you as well as to notify Deputy Marshall Harrington at Seldovia. I regret to feel compelled to enter this complaint, but hardly think that I would be exhibiting the marks of a good citizen to refrain reporting the matter, as in the interests of the people and game of Alaska, it would seen to me that such killings should be put a stop to nipping it in the bud, I am Yours respectfully W. W. Cadle[11]

[Telegram] *U. S. Naval Radio Service.*
Juneau, July 16, 1921.
Andrew Berg, Kenai, via Anchorage.
Proceed to Homer immediately and investigate killing of cow moose by a Mr. Snook on June twenty-second. Complaint made by W. W. Cadle who you should interview. Report results.
Bone, Governor.[12]

Kenai Alaska. July 31, 1921.
Scott C. Bone Governor of Alaska.
Dear Sir: Since making my last return to your office, I wish to submit the following. Was at headquarters up to July 12th On July 11 th i met a man by the name of Perry he reported that a cow moose has been killed near his place at Homer Just got your wire about the same case yesterday.
July 12th. Got as far as Kussiloff went up the river to the rapids.
July 13th. Went down to Nelchik an old Russian settlement stay here two days on account of bad weather.
July 16th Ran down to Anchor Point saw several settlers.
July 17th Gat down to Homer (left my boat here)
July 18th Walked up to Fritz Creek about 7 miles where the cow moose was killed saw W. W. Cadle and Mr. And Mrs. Pops (?) who was with Mr Cadle when discovering the cow moose from thier statement they followed the party who was packing the meat by tracks and when they could not follow the track farther they found the hide of the moose in a patch of trees
July 19th Was at Homer interveying the settlers
July 20th Went down to Yukon Island heard the U.S. Deputy Marshall have gone to Homer spit
July 21th Meet Marshall Harrington who have been loking up the same case
July 22th Was out to Mr. Harrington place
July 23th I and Mr. Harrington went down to Colderts
July 24th Mr Snooks and his party declared that Mr. Snooks could not have killed the moose after carefull investigation by me and Mr. Harrington we decided that there was no chance of conviction
July 25 th gat to Dimond Creek
July 26 Back to Ninilchik no sign of violations here
July 27 was in to Corea head found an old fishing camp here I found traces of meat being used but the cannery have burned since I left Kenai and the fisherman gone
July 28 Gat to Kussiloff tok a walk up flats along river
July 29 Gat back to head quarters
Respectfully Submitted
Andrew Berg Game Warden Kenai[13]

August 15th, 1921.
Mr. Andrew Berg, Game Warden, Kenai.
Dear Sir: Your report for July has just been received, by which it is noted you went to Homer to investigate the killing of the cow moose about which this office wired you some time ago. It is not clear from your report just what the obstacles were in the way of arresting some one for this violation with a view to securing a conviction. Evidently those who packed the meat out would know something about it.
Yours very truly,
Secretary to the Governor.[14]

That was the final correspondence found between the Governor's office and Game Warden Berg. His term as game warden was over but the reasons are a mystery. Andrew may have been laid off, or voluntarily retired. There is no evidence that another warden was appointed to replace him for several years. The position may have been discontinued for lack of funds or Berg may have become disgusted with the intricacies of expense accounting and working according to someone else's schedule.

Andrew made no entries in his Tustumena journal until October tenth but many other people enjoyed his cabin and recorded their adventures in his book during the hunting season. The first group was composed of twelve Seldovia residents who left this account:

"Dunnings Dizzy Dozen"

Aug 23 1921   Left Seldovia Aug. 18th at 3:30 p.m. Stopped at Ninilchik 1 1/2 hours and arrived at Kussiloff 6 A.M. After resting until 2 P.M. we took on the pilot (Mr. Gordon Jones) who conducted us safely to the Williamson's fox ranch. From here we were taken in tow by L. Nissen and partner who towed us up river as far as their place. From here the lining began and after proceeding a mile and half we made camp. The next morning it was raining so we stayed in camp until it cleared up when we took the trail and river again. Made camp two nights along the river then we arrived here [Andrew's cabin] *4 P.M. Aug. 23   The river was high and the lining in some places hard with our two dories and their loads   Got some ducks and the first meal in this cabin was a regular feed. The men who had been on the line and had been in water above their*

waists most of the way to the lake. The weather was hot on the lake but we pulled [rowed] from about two miles down the river. Cloudy day but all started for the glacier but Mr. Olssen who staid to bake bread. Three came back home after chasing a black bear into the hills and seven went on to hunt sheep. In camp we washed

Aug. 24th   Sun shining beautifully   Sheep hunters did not return   We walked up to the mine on the other side of river also up to the mill   saw nothing alive.

Thursday Aug. 25th   Hunters returned at 11:30 with one fine big sheep, head and all. And say we had some sheep hunt too. After leaving the folks who returned home we proceeded on to the glacier where we spent 2 hours in crossing its face (Alpine tourists had nothing on us). We built a fire drien ourselves, had supper and then climbed the mountain until dusk, stopped and built a camp for the night. At four the next morning we sighted a sheep on a cliff far above and spent 4 hours of the greatest mountain climbing on record in sneaking on to him. At eight o'clock a. m. Aug. 24 in rounding a point of rock I, (A.L. Petersen) came upon him lying down and with one shot from my trusty fowling piece sent a bullet through his cranium, and the meat was ours. He was a very large fine ram, we found him to be very heavy before we got him out. We hunted some more that day and camped on the mountain again. Left for home at 6 a.m. the next morning. Had some fine, but wet and cold experience in crossing the glacier stream. Arrived here at 11:30 a.m.

Aug. 26.   Leaving for Birchwood today. Dunnings Dizzy dozen: Mrs. A Petersen, Miss E. Stryker, Mrs. Stryker, Mr. Charles Olssen, Agnes Olssen, Lawrence Dunning, Ralph Dunning, Archie Mclane

Members of the party not included in the above list were Allan Petersen, Gordon Jones, Archie Keller and a Mr. Keller. Miss Enid Stryker and Archie McLane were married the following year and moved to Kasilof to start a fox farm and a family. Enid's sister and brother-in-law, Jettie and Allan Petersen, also tried fox farming in Kasilof for a time.

The next two parties at Andrew's cabin were not locals. The first group departed Berg's cabin the same day as the second group arrived, but in this vast landscape they never saw each other. Andrew made an occasional entry complaining about visitors leaving messes and burning up his firewood. With all of these people traipsing through his home it's a wonder he didn't lock it up.

"The Indianaplis Indiance Minnick & Howard Long Party" Aug 30 1921

Howard Long, a guide based in Seward, was guiding Ira Minnick of Indianapolis, Indiana. Also in the party were a cook and two packers. Ira Minnick is the apparent author of these entries.

On Aug 25 We left Lakeview Alaska arrived Kussiloff Aug 27 in the AM Came on up the river with high tide as far as Jone's fox farm. Account of rain laid over there until after noon of Aug 28. The [illegible] up ended evening of Aug 29. where we spent the night in Chas Nest cabin. Landed in his cabin PM of Aug. 30th We saw many ducks & spruce hen but as the law was not yet open we kept our rusty trusty guns in the case. At 8 am Aug.31th we started for the sheep hills

Sept 11 When we lift here Aug 31 they said we were going to the sheep hills I call them mountains as the tops of them are above the clouds and I had to climb to the very top. One day we went up a slide that was so steep the seat of my pants was ahead of my face all the time and when we got to the top we found the moon hung up on some rocks so we had to kick it off so that we could make the last jump on the mountain top. On Sept 1st with my rusty trusty rifle I killed a sheep Sept. 2 in camp all day resting and cleaning up the scalp. Sept. 3rd I killed a sheep with my rusty trusty rifle. Sept 4th. Sunday in camp all day Sept. 5th I killed with my rusty trusty rifle a very large mean furocious bad Black Bear that night Long and I Siwashed it in some alders Rain and some sweet night it was. Sep 6th We got skunked slipped up on a nice bunch of rocks after about 2 1/2 hours of slipping On the way home we looked back and saw a very bad bear but what care we as we were on our way home and then too we were afraid of the bear as he looked to be a very

bad one From a couple of miles distance he looked as if he might have teeth. Sep 7th in camp all day. Sep 8th With my rusty trusty rifle I killed another sheep thus ending the sheep hunt. It was a very windy and cold day on the mountain top. Sep 9th in camp all day. Sep 10th Tom, Bill, and I came down to this camp while Howard & Lee went after the sheep meat you will see that in 5 days hunting 3 sheep and 1 Bad Bear fell for my rusty trusty rifle. Sep 9-10- 11th More days of very high wind with some rain

Sept. 12, 4 PM The Totem Party Fred Godwin, Shorty

Left Cordova Sept 3rd Latouche 4th, Seldovia 6th, A.P.A. cannery 7th lined and row bucking tide to 1 mile above Jones fox farm. Next a.m. at 8.30 fell in with John Nest and party lined to his cabin on 8th stayed all night hunted lake shore to cabin on point hunted lake shore next day to old cabin on next point never saw a single moose track that p.m. Shorty saw a mean looking big black bear on the beach he sneaked up on him like a scout and planted two 8 m.m. bullets thru him left next morning for glacier Slept all night on glacier flats went up to glacier saw a big black bear but couldn't shoot him as I could not get across glacier stream went back to beach my ass draging my tracks out got a good dinner then started for cabins have got here to late to see party from Lake View stove was warm.

Friday 13th went goat hunting saw some big fresh goat tracks but no goats saw 2 moose and a big bull swimming a lake it was 800 yds. and a little 22.H.P. was sure out of luck saw 2 more moose almost a mountain top coming out of a bunch of cotton woods 250 yds. away shot the bull along side the head first shot second shot somewhere in back fired 2 more shots at him but the cow just farted at me and went over the mts a helling about that time I was getting pretty dam disgusted and swore vangence on the moose family started home and out jumped a big bull across a ridge hill bent for election. I [illegible] up my short barrel 22 h.p. and sent one well aimed shot just missing his heart and braking his spinal colom killing him instantly

14th. pack 3 loads of meat to camp Oh Hell! but is hard work to be poor

Tues. Sept. 18   Axel & I just dropped in to have a look and see if you and John Johnson had arrived.   Left Cliff House this AM at 9 and here at 11 am   This is the first sunshine we have had since leaving Kenai.   Nothing but fog & rain. On our way home.   Sincley Young

Andrew returned to Home Camp in time to do some hunting. This winter he had a trapping partner named John Johnson. Johnson was an American name adopted by some members of the Ness family when they immigrated, so John may have been related to Andrew.

The men lived together in Andrew's cabin. The structure consisted of a seventeen foot by seventeen foot log cabin with three windows and a low ceiling. The roof extended ten feet beyond the cabin, on the door end. This unheated space was framed in on three sides and sided with rough-cut lumber, probably from the old mill. Attic space above the cabin was accessible from the partially enclosed porch and was used for storage and extra bunk space. It was tight quarters for two men. They spent most daylight hours out doors. In mid-December that was less than 6 hours a day. Travel to Berg's outlying traplines and cabins gave them additional solitude.

Berg's journal entries begin again in October:

Oct. 10th. was up to head of Bear creek   saw several moose and bear track and wolferine tracks   got wet wading thru snow

11th. Was at home making ready to go across country to [illegible] bay. Loking like snow did not go. Axel & Sig Wold came over

12th. Started to snow & blow   did not go   was out on glacier flats   Ray Curtis came down from mine & went on to Bear Creek

Ray Curtis was hard rock mining near Indian Creek. The 1910 Census listed him as an employee of the Kasilof cannery. Curtis was born in Iowa in 1880.

13th   Blowing a storm   at home all day   Sig Wold found a bear track on Emma Trail

14th   Up south fork   folowed bear to his hole

15th. At home   Taking moss for repairing cabbin the rest were out on mountain hunting sheep

The log cabins Andrew built were typically chinked between the logs with locally abundant sphagnum moss.

16th. Was out over gacier flats   gat som meat

17th. Sunday atending religous service

18th. At home making bread

19th. Started to fix up camp

20th. Finnis the house work

25th   Left Kenai for Kussiloff late in the after noon   had a fine run to Kussiloff   stopped with Karl

26th. Left the cannery about 9 a.m.   ran up to John Wiks for dinner and on to Victors cabbin by night

John Wik was starting the 'Happy Home Silver Fox Ranch' in Kasilof at this time.[15] Victor Holm lived on the Kasilof River a mile and a half upstream from the mouth. He also had a small cabin about six miles upriver.

27th. Got to foot of moose horn   lost one of my mittins during day and lose time getting it

28th. Started about nine o clock   lined the boat above the rapids   set up the outboard motor and ran on up to this cabbin   got here about five p.m   found that we have lost our trouth net

Berg routinely rigged a small gillnet to catch fish around the mouth of Indian Creek. The usual catch was lake trout or Dolly Varden char with an occasional salmon or whitefish. When the lake froze, the outflowing creek often remained ice free allowing the fisherman to work the net all winter.

29th. Started out to get som meat   Paul Wilson & I   got sheep & was back here about 4 p.m.

Paul Wilson was a contemporary of Berg's who lived in Kenai with his family.

30th. Started down lake 20 to nine   got to Hugos cabbin eleven forty five   left twenty minutes of one   got back to Hugos 7 p.m.   met John lund & [illegible] West

31th.   Started on my way home at 7 a.m.   got home after four   Sig & Sigwal came off a sheep hunt this evening

Tuesday Nov 1th   John Johnson & I Stay home all day repairing the cellar and storing our vedgetables for winter   repairing roof & Gable end.   Sig & Sigwald was up on the mountains came home with one sheep wet to the skin   Have been trying som short cuts in coming down the hill.   Gave the place some unrepeatable names

Wednesday 2th   I stay home all day making bread & putting line & leads on the trout net and put it out   the boys did not get home to way after dark heavy loaded with sheep meat

Thursday 3th   Johnson, Sig & Sigwald went after som meat that they left yesterday.   I tok my big rifle and went out loking for bear.   I went by way of Lake Emma   climbed along south wall of nicanorka mts. to north fork   came acrost mts.   saw one bear   shot & he fell but got up and away

Friday 4th   This morning Sig & Sigwald started down the lake to stop at Friman Camp for a moose hunt   we have been at home all day fixing up and washing clothes   Ed was over about dinner time

"Friman Camp" was the lakeshore site of a cabin probably built by William Freeman. The cabin logs have been dated to 1867 or 1868. Census data from 1900 lists William Freeman as an employee of the Kasilof cannery. It also indicates that he emigrated to the United States from Finland in 1865. He died in 1906 according to a grave marker in a small cemetery near the mouth of the Kasilof River.

Saturday 5th   Was up early this being the coldest morning so far   stay home all day doing smole tings around the cabbin   was out and felled a tree acrost the creek for Ed   Johnson tok a walk towards Bear Creek   the Indian River is making ice   I was nearly acrost on ice but came back on acount of overflow

Sunday 6th,   Took the dogs with pack sacks along   left half after eight   went up Lake Emma trail over the mountain to Kasky   got there after two   found the cabbin in bad shape   Porcupine have taken charge with sign of both bear & wolferine as helpers and som squirrels to clean the china

The remains of Freeman's cabin are up on the bank in this photo from the 1950s.

George Pollard is on the beach in the foreground and provided the photo.

Monday 7th,   After hearing the wind all night it looks fairly good this morning   loking out of the cabbin door I counted sixty sheep   about four hundred yards north I meet a young ram comming up to me   I shouted but he did not mind that   he started after one of my dogs and I hit him on the side of the head with my cane   at that he ran about thirty feet jumped on a rock and stod there as long as I could see him   went over the mountain to take up som fox traps that I had over the hils for five years   saw where a lot of ravens was having a danc   went to investigate and found a dead sheep who a wolferine have taken posession of   I fired three shots   the third shot rolled the wolferine over and down in a cannon towards me out of sight   I was shooting acrost cannon of watch creek   when I got near enough to see him again he saw me at the same time   a snow twister hit me so I could not shoot but could see the animal get away leaving a blody trail   I saw about 150 sheep & Fifty moose   got down after dark having had eight and a half hours good hard walk

Tuesday 8th,   Not feeling good   decided to stay home and it have been raining all day with a voley of wind off the mts. now and again   Walked acrost creek on ice   no snow in the hills to talk of   put a foot bridge acrost first stream   fixed straps to my spyglass   set out net

Wednesday 9th   We got a spring morning   warm with som puffs of wind coming off the mts. that feel warm to the face   the creek broke oppen   I have been working on a skiff that I got under repairs   fixed up som yeast   will try to get the old lady to make som fresh bread

Thursday 10th   Got up early this morning built fire & cook breckfast   tok a nap   set batter for making bread   after that I got working on the schiff   I was doing the carpenter work between times I was loking after the bread.   Molding it to loafs & set it to rise and baking   Johnson was caching & cooking up som trout with potatoes   We only got the net out one night in four   to much trash

Friday 11th,   this morning it loked so much like snow that I hurried to take my clotches in   Wheeled the wood in to the shade   I put the finishing tutches on the schiff   We had a heavy earthquake   Launched the boat and tried it out in setting our net   I had a walk   shot a couple of rabbits for dog feed   Irish [a dog] *would not eat rabbits*

Dog food was not purchased at this place and time. Porcupine, rabbit, fish and the carcasses of animals caught in traps were common dog fare.

Saturday 12th,   Fixed everything for battle road and started to a bear den that I know of   went up Lake Emma trail   tok up the creek bed leading to the den   after all when we got there the bear have not been there for somtime   I shot at it when I found the hole it dropped at the crack of the gun but got up and away thru alders   I may have hit it good anough to kill   Ed was down from south fork he said that the earthquake made it interesting for awhile   boulders was comming off the hill like great guns bombarding   he have also been up to wath he tought was a bear den but it was not a bear at all.

Ed Roth was another unmarried fisherman and trapper in his late thirties. Census data shows he had immigrated from Germany in 1896.   Of large stature, he was often

Ed Roth in a picture taken in the 1930s.
Photo courtesy of Ella and John Secora.

referred to as "Big Ed." Andrew referred to him as "Black Ed" when he was mad at him.

Sunday 13th got up early fished net and did not get a fish first time I got scunk We had breakfast and started up Eds trail put a bridg acrost the Indian Cannon went up loking for sheep but something have drove them back so we did not get any saw about 100

Monday 14th Caught eight trout this morning heated water and had a bath changing under weare John was out on the home trail cleaning out brush & wind falls afternoon I went to help tok the saw & cut out the heavy stuff at three I pulled up to glaser flats shot nine rabbits for dog feed

Tuesday 15th Started this day by washing som clotches limbered up som traps tok them out to glaser flats buildt a bridge over one of the creeks choppin trail along trapline set out som traps for lynx but had no bait along so we had to let them go without bait to [until] we come this way next time Wether foggy still mild

Wednesday 16th was out on glaser flats set out a few lynx traps & baited those we set out yesterday caught a rabbit in one of them saw tracks of som mink

Thursday 17th Got up about six loking out tick & cloudy but decided to go up the mountains after going thru the lower cloud found fine weather above saw som sheep all ewes & lams finely we found som rams shot one and in skinning Johnson stabbed the knife in to his leg got home late

Friday 18th Was at home to noon fixing tings around the house helped Johonson to dress & bandage his leg swolin som otherwise looks all right stopped bleeding entirely shortly after lunch I tok one of my dogs and som traps went on the glaser spit found som holes that look like mink holes set som traps near them did not get home to after dark coming

home thru a lot of alders saw lots of rabbits but it was already to dark to see shoot

Saturday 19th Stay in bed to seven a clock got up & cooked breakfast and set batter for making bread about noon I went up Indian River and set out six traps for mink & one for lynx this evernin while I was baking Ed came he have been in the mountains for a week he have caught one weasel

Sunday 20th Started acrost to Devils Bay stay all night at Cliff House found Alex at home

Alex Lind was born Jonas Alexander Nylander in Sweden in 1866. He had emigrated in 1902, settled in Kasilof in 1920 and soon took up fox farming.[16]

Monday 21th Got up at five started on mexico trail when it was still dark found trail bad full of windfalls set out three mink traps got to mexico after six hours of walk

Tuesday 22th Was at home chopping house logs

Wednesday 23th Working at house logs and splitting & peeling

Thursday 24th, Put the logs on old cabbin and covered [He was repairing his trapping cabin on Mexico trail, see photo on page 142.]

Named for its location near sheer cliffs descending into Devil's Bay, Cliff House is believed to have been built by Gust Ness. Photo courtesy of Norman Lowell.

Friday 25th   Put up the ridge pole and lay the roof on one side of cabbin when I heard a bear growling   tok my rifle and started after the bear found the place where he have stod loking at me working

Saturday 26th   Started early to go back to the lake   caught one mink   got to Cliff House about three o clock   found Alex Lind at home & Tony Martin comming a few minuts later

Tony Martin trapped around Sheep Creek towards Kachemak Bay. Seldovia was his summer residence.[17]

Sunday 27th, Slept late this morning   after breckfast Alex Lind came with me to my place. Blowing   found Johnson out   he came in shortly he came in with a mink that is the third after I left & one weasel

Monday 28th   This morning I and Alex Lind went over the glaser flats   he going to Cliff House along his trap line after I loking over my traps got one mink and two weasels   shot som rabbits was out on little penninsula   got dog chain

Tuesday 29th   Started about noon went to Bear Creek. I tok a walk up the creek and set out four traps for mink

Wednesday 30th   I went up Bear Creek set out 7 traps   went on to Windys upper cabbin   Johnson pulled [rowed] to Friman camp

Thursday Dec 1   I went over table land crossing the head of Trout Creek   comming down on west side to Birch Creek   set ten traps on lower birch got to Friman camp late   Johnson have killed a moose this day

At this time moose season was open from the first of September through the end of December. Hunting season for mountain goats and sheep opened August 20 and closed December 31.

Friday 2th   I tok 19 traps went down lake shore set out 5 in Philip Creek & 14 in Olson Creek Johnson was packing meat all day

Saturday 3th   I tok nine traps set som in Birch Creek som on lake shore. Johnson stay home & chopping wood. Blowing a cold south western

Sunday 4th   Johnson set out early to lok over the traps I set on Olson and Philip Creek   I made him a map of trap line   I went up lake shore as far as Emil Ness cabbin   set out a few more traps   Caught one mink   Johnson came in with two mink and one weasel having lost one mink   trap and all

Monday 5th   Loading everything in the skiff Johnson pulled along lake shore   I and my dogs walked loking over all traps in rich [reach]   got one weasel at Birch wood   got to Bear Creek at one o clock had a hurried lunch   I went up creek over trap line   got three mink   got here about five o clock after a walk of about twenty miles

Tuesday 6th   Stay at home all day making bread skinned & striched [stretched] six mink & four ermin   had a bath & washed clotches   Johnson was out on glaser spit met Alex Lind   came home with one weasel   Big Ed came off the hill

Wednesday 7th   Started in good time this morning walked down to Bear Creek   tok fifteen of the traps at Wagners house and set them for mink up Bear Creek   had tea at Wagners   I tok a walk up Indian river   after we got home saw Ed tearing up drift wood on the beach swearing at the place for it being hard to get dry wood

Charles "Windy" Wagner also split his time between Kenai and Tustumena Lake. He stayed in a cabin at Bear Creek when at the lake.

Thursday 8th   Was out on glaser flat to day loking over the trap line   did not get anyting shot a couple of rabbits   crossed the glaser stream on ice below first island   mild light wind up the lake

Friday 9th   Turning mild this morning   was up creek   was going to set a few fox traps but started rainning so I just tok a walk around the edge of flat to see wath I could find   saw a few rabbits came home at two just in time to get out of a shower of rain   John have been home all day

Saturday 10th   Was intending to go down to Birchwood but on account of havy rain squals we decided to go to Lake Emma   we set out 12 traps eight for lynx & four for mink   got into a snow storm   the first this season this evening it is raining to beat the band

Sunday 11th   at home keeping sunday by fixing our trout net making a knife handle & repairing som underwear   we are having quite a wind from south with snow sleet plastering everyting while getting coler in the evening with increase of wind velosity

Monday 12th   Found a nice lot of new snow this morning   tok a bunch of steel traps up on the flats and set on blanket set for fox   was up to mouth of dirty Cannon trying to find a porcupine for bait   saw one up on the mountain but it was to far to climb for it   came home thru the island trying to locate som mink lines.

Tuesday 13th   Went to Bear Creek to look over our traps   caught one mink & two ermins   rather mild

Wednesday 14th   Stay all day at Bear Creek   I tok a walk thru the country and came in good & wet

Thursday 15th   Blowing this morning but clearing   started on the hill   heard the surf getting less   I went back hurried launched the boat and went to Birchwood   got one weasel on way down

Friday 16th   Tok a walk to Philip & Olson Creek got one mink & three weasels

Saturday 17th   Was up Birch wood   caught one mink & two ermins

"Weasel" and "ermine" are seasonal names for the same animal. Brown in the summer, the weasel is called an ermine when its fur changes to white during the winter months.

Sunday 18th   Came home   got one ermin at Birch wood & two at Bear Creek   Tony came over from Devils Bay   Ed was home with a sprained ankle

On the glacier flats looking northwest towards Andrew's Home cabin. Photo by Joe Secora circa 1939, courtesy of Ella and John Secora.

Monday 19th   got out of bed four o clock this morning buildt fire & started to skin weasels   by six I had eight of them on the stricher [stretcher] had breakfast   set batter for making bread   John brought in another frozen weasel to tend to & he stared over our trap line to Lake Emma   I pack home water heated it up & had a bath   changed underwear   scrubbed the floor   now it was time to have coffee then working dow [dough] into loaves   at half after two I started to bake then John came in   had one mink   between tending & changing pans (I had three pans) twelf two pound loaves.   I went out & shifted our trout net   got one lake trout   move at half past five I am just trough with the bread, have the last pan still in the oven then as soon as the mink thaw I will skin   Tony have been busy all day reading a novel

Tuesday 20th   We went up on the glaser flats this morning   Tony & I going thru the island met Alex Lind   he was coming down to see us   he has a frostbitten fot and a sore finger   trying to get som medecine   Johnson was out along our trap line   Tony went to Devils Bay   I and Alex was up to look over a set of fox traps   going home we met Johnson coming up   we all walked home   John got one weasel

Wednesday 21th   Started before day on my way to Kussiloff   got down to Hugos when it was yet sun light

Hugo's cabin was a convenient stopping place between Kasilof and the eastern end of the lake. Hugo Holm, Victor's brother, may have been the builder or most recent occupant of the cabin. Hugo had gotten on the wrong side of the law the previous year (see the July 1, 1920 game warden report on page 47). He did not settle permanently on the Kenai Peninsula.

Thursday 22th,   Walked thru country to John Wiks place

Friday 23th   Visited from house to house in Kussiloff   got Gust Ness to go with me to Kenai stopped at the cannery for the night

Saturday 24th   Walked over the tundra to Kenai found a canvas canoe & paddled acrost among the ice

Sunday 25th   Celabrated X mas with dinner at Carl Pettersons house

Carl Petterson was one of the Kings County miners who stayed on the Kenai Peninsula after the mining consortium fell apart. Born in Sweden, he had emigrated in 1898 in his mid-twenties. He married Matrona Demidoff and raised their family in Kenai.[18]

Monday 26th   was at two Birthday Parties Mr Obrien 70 and Alice Petterson 17   had a fine time at both places

27th Tuesday   Blowing a gail of wind from the north   decided not to go anyway till the weather let up

Wednesday 28th   Snow shoing from Kenai to Kussiloff may be fun for som but when you have to go up river three or four miles & brecking in a foot of loose snow making about eighteen miles it feels to me like hard work

Thursday 29th   Came from the cannery   stay all night at John Wiks

Friday 30th   came acrost country to hugos place after about twelf mile of hard walk

Saturday 31th   Came from Hugos went up Olson Creek to look over the trap line   caught one mink   noting in Philip Creek

Allan Petersen's Account of Walking to Kenai

In the winter of 1922 and 1923 we [Allan and Jettie] were living in Kasilof where we were trying to get into the fox business. We had our foxes in some pens down there. We spent the winter and it was getting up around Christmas time. We got our mail here in Kenai and what shopping we had to do we did in Kenai. That was about 16 miles from where we lived to Kenai. Louis Nissen, who is another old-timer here in Kenai, he and I elected to make the trip. We took our packboards on our backs, our snowshoes and took off. We walked up the beach. We had our ice creepers along and used them on the ice. We hiked the beach as far as Libby's cannery and then we crossed the river on the ice at Libby's and walked around by the old Northwestern Cannery and into Kenai. We got there in the afternoon.

We didn't do much that day but visited. That night we stayed with a bachelor who lived all by himself. We had a nice evening and the next morning he cooked us a big stack of sourdough hotcakes. Then we started out to do our shopping. We went to the old post office which at that time was a little log cabin right on the bluff. We got the mail for everybody down at Kasilof then went to the store to shop for them. We had a pretty good pack which we put on our backs and started out. We had to walk around the old Northwest Cannery and across the flat and cross on the ice at Libby's. An old watchman by the name of Anderson asked us to have coffee with him. We rested and then got our packs and started off down the beach. It was kinda late that evening when we got back but we didn't mind. We rather enjoyed it.[19]

CHAPTER 7

1922

Sunday January 1st 1922
Was up Birch Wood snowing all day

Monday 2th   Came home from Friman camp wading thru snow all the way making a rather long tramp of it

Tuesday 3th at home all day   snowing   fished the net and got six nice trouts   atending the sewing circle is about the sum of my days work John has also been at home doing laundry work

Wednesday 4th   John got on his snowshoes & walked along the beach to Bear Creek   going up the creek to look over som mink traps   I have been home making bread   warmed up som water had a bath   weather still unsettled   wind dancing around to all points of the compass with snow

Thursday 5th   I was at home all day   Johnson came from Bear Creek towards evening   he had two mink & two ermine   clearing up in the evening   thermometer went down to one above zero   the coldest evening so far this winter

Friday 6th   Turned mild this morning   loking like snow   I went on glaser flats   it started to snow and heavy wind   I saw several moose & lots of Ptarmigans & a bunch of mallards

Saturday 7th   Snowing all day   been at home sewing a knife scabbard and set new webb in my snowshoes

Sunday 8th   John started over to visit Alex Lind who is stopping at the Cliff House in Devils Bay

blowing quite strong from the south   I stay home all day fixing up tings about the house

Monday 9th   at home again to day sewing at a piece of seal skin moccasins & roasting a leg of mountain sheep   fished the net & got seven trouts John came back from Devils Bay he found Alex getting better his toes all healed up but the felon still hurting his little finger   Alex have not seen or heard anyting from Tony Martin & Big Ed but was going over to find out how they are & take som letters to Eds

Tuesday 10th   I and Johnson started down lake shore   he stopped at Bear Creek & I went on to camp Friman below Birchwood   som puffs of wind coming off the hill   turning milder

Wednesday 11th   Rain and sleet this morning but I am going down to Philip & Olson Creek caught two mink   one on each stream

Thursday 12th   New snow about two inches   a gale of wind down the lake   could hardly walk along the lake shore facing the wind   I went up Birch Creek   got one mink and one weasel

Friday 13th   Lake lieing calm like a pan of milk fine wether far going home   had a fine walk had to use snowshoe at times but most places good walking   just enough snow to keep the cobble from rolling

The water level of glacier-fed Tustumena Lake undergoes significant seasonal changes. Highest water levels are in late summer with levels as much as ten feet lower in the winter. Winter conditions expose wide expanses of beach, often covered with cobble sized stones.

Saturday 14th   John tok a walk down to Bear Creek against a cold northerly wind and I was up on the glaser flats loking over the lynx traps no signs of lynx yet   John got one weasel on Bear Creek

Sunday 15th   I be home making bread   Yeast is working fine wich is the main thing   made an extra big lot of bread   enough to last us two weeks   had a bath & washed som clotches so it have kept me busi all day   wether is warm   a fog hanging over the lake   Thermonmeter at 28

Laundry and bathing would have easily kept him busy all day. Water had to be hauled and heated on the wood stove. Heavy woolen clothing had to be agitated, rinsed, wrung and hung. Fortunately, Andrew's lifestyle precluded the need for ironing.

Monday 16th   Was down the beach to get som firewood   Tony & Alex Lind came over from Devils Bay   weather fine calm

Tuesday 17th To day we went over to Devils Bay with two boats intending to go up on the Mexico trail   stay all night with Alex Lind   put out the net

Wednesday 18th   Started out late   called at Freds to see Tony and Ed. Tony was home but Ed was out visiting wesils   Tony had two foxes one black one cross. Five mink & som weasels   then we pulled down to King Country trail   Set out eleven traps for lynx   saw a lot of tracks of ermin but no sighn of lynx   was in about four miles

Thursday 19th   to day the bay have started to freeze over so we decided to get home before we got froze in   John came in the dory cutting thru ice & the boat   I walked over the glaser flats came over one of our trap lines   saw som tracks of game but did not catch anyting

Friday 20th   Have been at home all day hewing out some peises for making a bob sled and in

the afternoon I was splitting up som fire wood Lake on point of closing   thin skim of ice as far as you can see but thermometer went up to thirtytwo and this evening a wind have sprung up and I hear the ice moving   John was out to Lake Emma got one weasel

Saturday 21th   Quite mild this morning   John started down to Birchwood and I went down as far as Bear Creek   loking over our traps   found som of them sprung but no game of any kind   Ice entirely gone wind blowing up the lake and hiling the ice on the shore   Thermometer at about 34 this afternoon

Sunday 22th   Stay at home making bread   raining loking like a regular spring day   light breese up the lake

Monday 23th A bit of new snow this morning   not feeling good   Just lazy I think is wath ails me everyting wet out so I did not go anywhere

Tuesday 24th   Was going out on the flats but targeting my smole gun and found her foul   after I got it clean it was to late to go   John came home had two mink and three weasels   Alex Lind came   he is on his way out to Kussiloff

Wednesday 25th   Alex Lind started down the lake this morning with his dory & outfit trying to get down to Hugos   I was up to the glazer and tok a good walk over country   came home tired

Thursday 26th Was over to Devils Bay saw Tony acrost the bay   John was to Lake Emma and up on the hill along Nicanorka trail   caught one weasel on the lake

The Nicanorka trail went to Nicanorka mountains, a rounded foothill just above Emma Lake. "Nickanorka" was a surname belonging to families in Kenai and around Cook Inlet.

Friday 27th   John told me that he saw thermometer down to zero at four o clock this moring   when I got out to fish the net it was eight above   I have been home all day reading som periodicals that I brought from Devils Bay John was out for a walk about two hours   I have been trying to soak out som hide to make myself a pair of moccasin

Saturday 28th   Got out this morning to fish the net   found it in an ice pack so after having brackfast we went out got the net and three nice big trout   stay home all day sewing a pair of moccasins Thermometer one below   ice over the lake as far as we can see

Sunday 29th During the night I herd som cats paws of wind wich increased this morning, found us with a gale of wind that shook the cabbin At day light we could see no ice anywhere Thermometer up to thirty   wind strong "southeast"   have been working dressing lumber for bob sled

Monday 30th   This morning nice & calm John went to Birchwood 1 to Bear Creek loking over som mink sets   caught one ermin

Tuesday 31th Was up early   fished the net & caught four nice big trout   went up on glaser flats got caught in a storm   lost my cap and got some nasty falls when the wind squalls caught me   got home about four o clock   A moose stod right at the door when I came home

Wednesday The 1 Day of February   At home all day making bread   Mild thermometer registering forty above zero   Som wind but not very strong

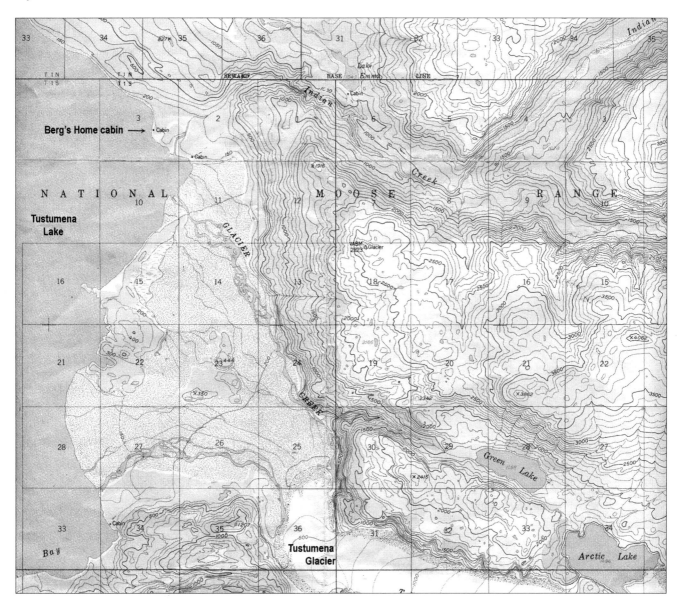

An illustration of the vertical terrain around the glacier and Indian Creek. Kenai A-2 Quadrangle, Alaska, 1951, USGS 360 Series Topographic.

got seven trouts real beuties   got som nice light bread

Thursday 2th   Have been home all day working at a bob sled   John came home from Birchwood, have not caught much   A little new snow fell during the night   heavy surf this morning   my net blowed to shore but it was that warm it did not freze to the beach

Friday 3th John went to Lake Emma   I tok the dory & pulled acrost to Devils Bay   fine weather som ice in the bay so I had to land the dory about three hundred yards up the beach

Saturday 4th   Stay at Cliff House all night   got up early tok the boat and pulled to Mexico trail went up along our trap line & set out thirteen more traps   saw a lot of new lynx tracks   got back to Freds house stay all night   Big Ed came out of Fox River had two minks two weasels & one lynx

Sunday 5th   A gail of north western is blowing so I had to leave dory & walk   Ice brecking in Devils Bay   had to climb two of the cliffs   wind quite cold on the glaser flats   lots of moose

Monday 6th   Blowing a gale of north westerly wind so we decided to stay home & replenish our wood supply. I put som fixtures on the bobsled and hauled in couple of loads of dry wood   sawed wood   there was regular ocean surf breaking on the beach

Tuesday 7th   The coldest morning we had this winter   3 below just waiting for the sun to come up and warm up the atmosphere when in comes Sig & Sigwald   brought som mail   John was up to Lake Emma caught one weasel

Wednesday 8th   This morning John started down to Birchwood   I tok five traps went up on glaser flats to set for wolverine   caught one wolverine in a mink trap   som ice was making but a wind up lake drove the ice pack to shore   Saw one sheep

Thursday 9th Was up to Ray's mine   saw one extra big ram   came down centre of flats loking for ptarmigens did not find any   got home abouth four

Friday 10th   At home all day making bread and cleaning up around the house   Lake have been quite [quiet] all day forming a skin of ice although the thermometer was up to thirty   it have mad ice a half inch thick that is slowly moving in shore

Saturday 11th   John came home today having seen Sigwald and Sig at Bear Creek   he brought in two weasels   Lost two weasels & one mink got away on Birch creek   I have been home all day fixing som tings around cabbin   mended som underweare washed clotches & scrubbed the floor   was out & set the net this evernin

Sunday 12th   Was up on the flats this morning caught one porcupine one squirrel one rabbit one magpie & one eagle   saw lots of moose   counted 74 from one stand   saw over one hundred in a space about two sections   Sigwald Hansen & Sig Lindgreen came up from Bear Creek   we all had a hair cutting match   Split som wood & started a Saw Horse

Monday 13th   Snowing   started in fixing my scates and it tok me nearly all day   John was to Lake Emma   no game

Tuesday 14th   Stay home to about noon then went to the Cliff house   got quite cold in the evening

Wednesday 15th   Got on my scates and ran over to Mexico trail   found som tracks of lynx but did not get any   Dogs ran after moose while I was in and had a cup of tea with Tony & Big Ed

Thursday 16th   Was out early hunting a dogs pack that one of my dogs lost   Tony found it about noon   I started home about one o clock Met Ed on the flats

Friday 17th   Sig & Sigwald came from Bear creek folowing carefully along the shore Sigwald broke through the ice two days ago and had a cold bath   Sig went with John up to lake Emma   Sigwald went on the flats with the dog team   I stay hom had a bath washed clotches & made yeast

Saturday 18th   Have been home all day making bread   John had a walk up glaser flats baiting som traps this evening   I walked up Indian River saw where a land otter have been working shifted one mink trap farther up the creek where were som fresh mink tracks   the otter is still on Indian River as I could not find any tracks leading from the river   I was out on ice about a mile but the ice is treacherous   where there is snow the ice is thin   som places open water

Sunday 19th   John started to Birchwood   I got on my scates to visit Bear Creek   Met Sig & Sig came back home   fixed up som traps   went up on flats and set them for otter   after I got home at dusk tok a walk up creek

Monday 20th Thick & foggy this morning   Sig came from Devils bay, going to Bear creek after a load of meat   I trying to fasten the meat grinder broke the foot of it and gave myself quite a job fixing it up   Was up Indian River shifted trap was to second bridge   otter moved to flats

Tuesday 21th Started late   went up on flats caught an otter   Met Sig & Sigwald, walked along with them to foot of glaser   when I came home I found Johnson at work building fire having just arived from Birchwood Creek   No sucses

"Washingtons Birth Day"

Wednesday 22th Was at home to noon   made a cake   About two o clock I went over to the Clif House   stay all night with Sig & Sig

Thursday 23th Rather mild to go anywhere but I started out on Mexico trail   did not get anyting a lynx have stepped on one trap but the trap being foul did not spring and a mink got out of a smole trap on middle creek

Friday 24th I am home from Cliff House today was out to island after wood   John was to Lake Emma   has three weasels

Saturday 25th   At home all day not feeling good had a walk out on the flats this eve got treed by a moose   John was sawing & splitting wood all day

Sunday 26th   At home making bread   John was out on the flats for Ptarmingan shoot   got no ptarmingan but one weasel   Sig & Sigwald came from Devils Bay and went down to Bear Creek

Monday 27th John started to Birchwood   I stay at home   had a bath & washed clotches

Tuesday the last day of February   Warm with strong wind   termometer up to 60   Got three beautifull trout this morning   It is to wet to go anywhere but I tok a walk up the Indian river John came back this afternoon   had a hard day coming up again the wind

March 1 Wednesday   Started on my way to Kenai at 8 a.m.   got to Hugos at twelf   found a sled track leading towards Kenai   followed it to six o clock and was at Kussiloff

Thursday 2th   Got a sled from Peterson and got to Kenai just in time to stop Paul Wilson from starting up with a telegram   waiting for mail & bad weather I stay at Kenai to the elevent having blown and snowed for several days   We started to Kussiloff with six dog team.

Sunday 12th   went thru a blistering snow storm to Gust Ness   stay there 13 & 14th   15th was out breacking trail.

Thursday 16th   Alex Lind & I left Kussiloff bound for Hugo's & had a devils owntime getting to the lake   breaking thru loose snow & rabbit stubble   was no easee going   got to Hugos late but felt fine after a good feed

Friday 17th   Came up from Hugos   met John at Birchwood on his way down to look for me   he then went to run the traplines on Olson & Birch & I got home about three o clock

Saturday 18th   Started over Mexico trail   brought som mail to Tony Martin   Tok in the trap line had one lynx and shot it with a 22 pistol   hit it in the mouth   it made a jump broke loose and got away

Sunday 19th   Stay home making bread   John came home towards evening   I cut holes in ice and set out our trout net

Monday 20th   tok a walk up glaser flats to day came down the south side   had a look on sunny sloops to see if any bears was out did not find any   saw about sixty moose on the flats and near Rays mine I distinctly smelled sheep   but I did not go up to investigate as I had only a 32 automatic pistol and probbably would have to shoot at long distance   but if I found bear tracks I likely found him in the hole   filed a saw after I got home

Tuesday 21th   was out today chopping som birch wood & tramping trails for hauling it home wood to dry during summer for future use

Wednesday 22th   was out this fornoon hauling home wood   got it all in by noon   went out again and chopped a few more loads   John was out and got a porcupine for dog feed   I fished & shifted the trout net   got no fish

Thursday 23th   this morning I filed the crosscut saw & after sun got good and warm we went and hauled home five loads of wood   got through by one o clock   In afternoon we sawed up what we hauled today

Friday 24th   this morning I fixed my snowshoes harnessed my dogs and I tok a side trip to Devils bay   Johnson was splitting wood after I got back   I sawed som this eve   we got one rick five by twenty feet

A "rick" is a unit of measurement for wood. Technically, a rick is the equivalent of a single row of firewood four feet high by eight feet long. Berg appears to use the term for rows.

Saturday 25th   working at sawing & splitting wood   have all sawed that we got home   be problbly enough   weather wich have been clear & cold for ten days turned cloudy this morning & som warmer   Greb werdna ["Andrew Berg" reversed]

Sunday 26th   I harnnessed the dogs and tok a trip up on flats to bring in som wolferine traps John was finishing splitting wood   we was short one stick to fill the rick went out and got that sawed and split it   I hauled the traps and put them away. We got 18 steel traps 16 dubble spring & 38 smole traps   72 in all at this place

Monday 27th   at home making bread & fixing ting to put away for summer   making ready to leave

Tuesday 28th   was over to Devils bay to get my dory

Wednesday 29th   Starting down going as far as Birchwood   have a few mink traps to take in

Berg had two boats. One was a large dory he used on the lake, river and Cook Inlet. The second was a smaller skiff he kept at his Home cabin on Tustumena Lake. The lake typically is frozen from January to May. At some point prior to the lake freezing Andrew would leave his big dory in Kasilof. When he walked out in the spring, the boat was there ready for him.

Berg probably spent this summer fishing. He also continued his role of protecting moose. In a June letter to Game Warden George Cotter in Seward, Andrew complained of two Kasilof men capturing moose calves which died in captivity.[1] Related documentation reveals a permit was issued for the capture of moose calves. The calves were held in captivity at the Kasilof Cannery where at least eight died before a reliable diet was developed for them.[2] Cotter reported that the permit was issued by the fur warden at Tyonek for ten moose calves to be taken and apparently shipped out to the national headquarters of the Moose Lodge. In his report to the Governor, Cotter assesses Andrew's complaint in this way: "Berg is a self-important Russian and may possibly be trying to stir up a little neighborly ruction at not having been given the work of capturing moose. I do not see him in the light of a revolted citizen rushing to protect the game..."[3]

Given what we know about Andrew, it is easy to see him revolted at this treatment of moose. Cotter may not have been familiar with Berg, or he may have been too familiar. Cotter had reason to resent successful guides and ex-game wardens. In 1919 George Cotter was employed as one of two guides on a trophy hunt. After spending sixty days with him, the two hunters described Cotter as "...the most incompetent man we have ever seen in a responsible position."[4] Game Warden J.A. Baughman stripped him of his license and reported to the Governor that Cotter "will never act as guide again."[5] George Cotter was appointed game warden by a new governor two years later.

Berg made a trip to Tustumena Lake in late summer to prepare a base camp for a hunting party he was guiding:

August 14th

We left Kenai August 10th got as far as Kussiloff on ebb   tok flood up to John Wiks place   stay all night

11th Started up river and just got out in a rain storm   got up to Victors cabbin wet to the skin

12th stay all day at Victors on acount of rain

13th got up to cape harm

14th Lined for two hours then put on evinrude ran to lake   had lunch   came over to Freeman camp   pitched tent unloaded our provision and stored in tent   got in to boat and came up here got here 6:30   mowed the grass out of trail Andrew

Around this same time Game Warden Cotter was experiencing paperwork problems. Andrew's hunting party had applied for a permit listing him as their intended guide but Cotter's records indicated that Berg was not currently holding a license. The investigation begins with an August twelfth letter from Cotter to the (new) Secretary to the Governor:

August 12, 1922
Dear Mr Hardings
Will you be so good as to look up for me the date of issue of the guide's license of Andrew Berg? He has been engaged by E.J.Brandeis for a September hunt, and I find I have his name in my book and nothing under it, The only check I had, last October, does not list him, but I think it was merely an oversight as he is such an old timer guide that he would have asked for his license properly. It takes five weeks or more to get a reply from him, otherwise I would not trouble you...
Sincerely Yours George Cotter Game Warden[6]

Mr. Harding was unable to find record of Berg renewing his license, prompting Cotter to confront Andrew with the bad news:

September 7, 1922
Mr Andrew Berg Kenai, Alaska
Dear Sir; The Governor's office writes me that your license as guide expired April 26th 1921, and that there is no record of your having applied for a license renewal after that date...

Please notify me immediately upon receipt of this, whether some mistake has been made and you were granted a renewal which was possibly not recorded. Otherwise you cannot act as a guide upon Kenai Peninsula, until a license is granted to you, application being made through myself in the usual manner. Also in the latter circumstances that you have no license kindly return by mail to me badge number one, which is listed as being held by you. Yours very Truly Game Warden[7]

Andrew replies calmly with only a touch of sarcasm:

September 12, 1922
Mr George Cotter. Game Warden Seward.
Dear Sir; My licenses Card was issued by [Governor] Scott C. Bone Oct 27 1921. My commision expires Oct 26th 1923 I have been out on a hunting tripp with E.J. Brandeis. Our packers was Mr John Wik, Mr Pete Kalning, Mr John Fritz, cook Mr Krist Jensen. My licens have never been run out since first issued under

five differnt Governors exept from April 26 1921 to Oct 27 1921 at the time I was game warden. so you can readily see that the error are from the governors office   if you in the mean time find me incompetent to act as guide or in other words to satisfy some of my friends, i will turn it in with out rerets [regrets].
Yours Truly Andrew Berg Registered Guide[8]

Cotter forwarded this information to Secretary Harding in Juneau who dug deeper into the file cabinet. According to Harding's next letter, the previous secretary had vacated the office right around the time of Berg's last license renewal and left things in a muddle. Harding never found any record of the license renewal but he found Andrew's letter requesting the license and twenty dollars unaccounted for in the "game and guide license accounts." The Secretary concludes that "...the situation remains that a guide fee was received and turned in by [former secretary] Folta about the time Berg claims he was appointed guide and as he says he had the certificate, I suppose he is a regular guide at the present time and will be such until October, 1923."[9]

Exactly two months after beginning his investigation Cotter closed it with a final letter back to Harding. Two months is not bad for resolving a problem involving people and records spread out between Kenai, Seward and Juneau. Cotter's last letter reveals more about his own character than Berg's:

October 12, 1922
Mr L.L. Harding Juneau, Alaska
Dear Mr. Harding; Re yours of Oct 5th about the statue [status] *of Andrew Berg; I wrote him very cautiously in reply to his report that he had his guide's card to the effect that as he had furnished the date, the Governors office would probably be able, under business on that date, be able to locate the error, etc. I don't much mind Berg's tender feeling getting a slight jolt, as his ego can stand it. I am not satisfied with his too brief account of his hunt with E.J. Brandeis in September, and have requested that he furnish further details as to the number of hunters, what they got where and when, etc. A report has come along that the wife of Brandeis also hunted, and if so, as she had no license, Berg allowed it. I dont of course know that he did, but his answer will give me a line and if it too brief again I will land on him... which leaves us so we needn't*

apolgize to him as he can be kept busy explaining.
Sincerely yours George Cotter Game Warden[10]

Andrew may have been spared the "explaining" as he retreated to Tustumena Lake for the winter. John Johnson joined him again as trapping partner.

October 11th   Wednesday came from peninsula was over to camp Freeman to get up som tings left last fall

Thursday 12th   We have been busy all day putting away stores fixing yeast and putting tings to order two o clock the rain stopped I tok my gun and tok a walk but started raining   got good and wet

Friday 13th   Stay at home all day baking bread fixed a brace put in a foot bridge & washed my clotches   John was sewing pack socks for the dogs   Krist Alex & Erik was up on Nicanorka mountain each bringing in a sheep

Saturday 14th All hands at home. Erik making bread the rest was just loafing around doing odd tings cleaning guns shooting som   Raining quite steady I started ones to go up the side hill looking for bear but the rain drove me back   started strong wind this evening

Sunday 15th Great Bear Day to be

It was a bear hunt allright but no bears could any one find   although five hunters was out the wind was so high that it was nearly imposibly to stand up where the wind had a chance to hit one I and Krist was up south forks to the junction of south and north fork [Indian Creek] *then back over the hils to new trail   saw lot of ptarmigans and they was nearly white*

Krist (Christian) Jensen was a thirty-six year old Danish immigrant. He had come to America in 1904 but just recently moved to Alaska in September of this year. Christian joined his older brother Pete who had been in Kasilof since 1916.[11] Both men would live out most of their lives in this small community on the river. Pete Jensen and fellow Dane Pete Madsen had started the Swallow Nest Silver Fox Ranch in Kasilof in 1921.

Monday 16th this morning Erik Isackson & Alex Lind went over to Devils Bay on their first leg to

Kussiloff   I and Krist Jenson went with boat to woods island & walked up to foot of glaser and up on Devils mountain hunting for bear   got as far as the turn of crazymans cannon   following the cannon to Nymans trail saw a lot of sheep acrost cannon and one was right in our way but we did not want any sheep   did not get home until seven o clock after putting in a day of eleven hours of hard travel   heard the evinrude from Bear Creek just as we was getting home

Tuesday 17th   tok a walk to the fork of Bear creek and on up the creek to pick fork   saw a lot of moose   one fine head with a spread of 68 inch   John Johnson have been painting our schiff and doing house work   we had the door oppen and just now in walks a porcupine   I spoke to him and he gently walked out again

Wednesday 18th   Started down to Friman camp on our way to funny River to build a cabbin

Thursday 19th   Came up to Camp valey view tok tents and gear out to timber back of moose lick nob and pitched camp

Friday 20th   Worked all day getting log and started to put up cabbin

Saturday 21th   Not feeling well and did not do much to the cabbin

Sunday 22th   Was at work again at cabbin finished the walls

Monday 23th   John was out this morning and got a moose   Krist and I splitting & putting on seeling [ceiling].

Tuesday 24th   Put up ridgepole & started cutting scoops for water roof

The exact dimensions of this cabin are unknown but most of Berg's trapline cabins were around nine feet to a side. He used a common construction design of installing a low ceiling of split poles with moss laid above for insulation. Then the "water roof" was put up to shed water and the gable ends were left open. The "scoops" Berg mentions were spruce logs which he split in half and then scooped, or hollowed out along their length. These were laid overlapping each other like long roofing tiles. (Andrew describes the scoops in more detail on February 6, 1935.)

Wednesday 25th   Finished water roof   put in stove & windows

Thursday 26th   Tok a walk over Funny River valley   raining & snowing all day   moved in to new cabbin   calling it Lick House

Friday 27th   Left Lick house in a snow storm got down to Friman at dusk

Christian Jensen at brother Pete's farm in Kasilof. Photo courtesy of Susan and Joe Perletti.

Saturday 28th Came home from Freeman called in at Bear Creek saw Wagner

Sunday 29th At home all day I have been making bread John doing som cooking anyway it was not fit weather to be out snowing in fornoon turning to rain in afternoon strong wind blowing

Monday 30th have been at home all day shifting our wood in to the entry and doing odds & ends got ten trout this morning snowing & raining all day. Made a knif for Krist Jenson.

Tuesday 31th Stay home all day tok out dubble windows washing the single windows & painting windowcases Krist & I made a house for Irish & cleaned our front yard John tok a walk up Indian

Wednesday November 1th We have all been at home today I sewed a smole sail for our sciff John have been running a laundry Krist rumaging thru my reading matter nibbling at little of everyting towards evening I pulled to glaser flats to find a stick for mast sprit & boom finnis those & had a bath

Thursday 2th Blowing a gale of wind from the glaser was out fishing the net but did not but two trout the wind having fouled the net John tok a walk to Bear Creek Sig lindgrin heard that Yung & sixteen HP Pete is snowed in at Wagners Cabbin [illegible] afternoon trying timber far splitting

Friday 3th Loking rainy this moring so we decided not to go after sheep but Krist & I went to the island & cut a trail thru to the flats worked in a drisling rain and came home about one o clock ringing wet John was at home fixing sights on his gun

Saturday 4th Still the weather is looking ugly som snow falling this morning Krist & I had a walk up the flats wind quite cold shot eight rabbits on our way home John have also been out and killed som rabits Clearing tonight

Sunday 5th was up early this morning to go on the mountain after sheep but wind sprung up and it started to rain I went up creek building a cribb for a bridge John went up Lake Emma trail Krist came and helped me with the bridge but it got to wet all of us was home by two o clock

Monday 6th pulled out to Brewery trail & walked to glaser Krist & John went up overhanging trail and I went out on the glaser after I got out about four hundred yards I saw one sheep close down & a lot moving up glaser got the nearest sheep the other fellows came down no sheep

Tuesday 7th was at home all day making bread & washing clotches John & Krist was up over the home trail loking for sheep did not see any but found lots of tracks weather fine frezing som the creeks making anchor ice

Wednesday 8th got up early Krist & I was up to glaser saw one sheep hunted to him and got within 25 feet of the sheep wind was blowing quite strong and just as I exposed myself to shoot a voley struck me so hard that I could not shoot the sheep got away John was at home

Thursday 9th Raining hard this morning Fixing my evinrude. H. S. Young & Sig Lindren came

Dall sheep. Both rams and ewes have horns.
Photo courtesy of FreeStockPhotos.com.

over from Bear Creek & stay to two o clock then started back to Bear Creek   Krist & I went out & buildt a cribbin for a bridge

Friday the 10th   Started in good time this morning after sheep   John went the short way to overhanging trail and got there first   brought home a sheep   Krist & I was up dirty cannon got one sheep and was back home between two & three o clock   John got in at four

Saturday 11th   Went from kusiloff to Kenai

12 Sunday — Walking from house to house

13   waited for Gust & Emil to com from Anchorage bundled up my furs & shipped them to Prauty's Son's   New York

Abe Erickson, whom Berg refers to variously as Ebb, Ebbe, Abb and Abraham.   Erickson was another Finn who had emigrated to the U.S. in 1882.[12] He started the Riverside Silver Fox Ranch on the north side of the Kasilof River in 1921. Abe had a cabin further up the river and another one on Tustumena Lake. Photo courtesy of Dolly Cole Christl.

Tuesday 14th   Left Kenai noon got to Kussiloff Stay all night with Emil Ness

Wednesday 15th   Tok a little schiff & pulled up to Ebbe   had dinner   walked up to Petersons found all the ladys there   went to John Wiks with som mail & back to Ebbe

Thursday 16th   Left Ebbs just after day breck got to lake eleven & to Birchwood or Friman cabbin at 2:30   stay all night   saw hundred of moose

Friday 17th Came up from Friman called in at Bear Creek they had two mink & one weasel caught to early

18 Saturday   was up Lake Emma trail   set out 14 traps the first lot set out this season   saw one mink track   snow hard   Rabbit tracks every where

Sunday 19th   at home all day not feeling good having chills   cant hardly keep warm even in bed   John was up creek set six traps

Monday 20th   Last night the Indian River shot & caried away my new bridge and the south abuttment   blowing and cold   was up on the river bar splitting shakes

Tuesday the 21th   Was out on glaser flats & set out 25 traps for mink weasel & lynx   shot a dozen rabbits coming home   flats in good condition to walk   most of the smole streamlets are froze

Wednesday the 22th   I have been at home all day making bread and doing some other tings about the house   cooking some head cheese that will take me well into the night to finnis John was up Indian & glaser flats   got two ermin

Thursday the 23th   Started in to snow last night snowing untill this morning when it begun to rain cutting away nearly all the snow   was home all day fixing a pair of snowshoes   John got a weasel up stream   I got one by the door

Friday the 24th   Mild weather   John went to glaser flats   I stay home finishing up snowshoes then take a walk up creek   split a bundle of shakes   tok up som traps but mised one & went *back at dusk to hunt it up   snow is disapearing fast   icy & mean walking just now*

Saturday the 25th   Soft & rainy weather   strong wind at home   fixed a saw handle   made a cartrige pouch   ground som axes   towards evening I set out six steel traps   Johnson caught a mink on Indian

Sunday the 26th   Was out at breck of day fishing net   got only six trout but just enough to breckfast I pulled out to woods island   cut trail thru som alders   set out four traps caught one mink & two weasels   Johnson on Lake Emma got one mink & two weasels

Monday the 27th   After breckfast I put som water to heat on the stove and tok a walk up creek   got one weasel in the last trap on Indian River   tok a walk along lake shore got back at elven asorted som steel traps   washed clotches scrubbed the floor   was out for a pray [pry pole] to rise the corner of cabbin   tok up the net Johnson got two weasels on glaser flats

Tuesday the 28th   Went down to Camp Friman set out six traps for lynx

29th Wednesday   I was out Birchwood   set out 16 traps   John set a lot on Philip & Olson Creek

Thursday the 30th   I was down to the creek S.E. from Friman caut noting   tok som traps up on Lick House trail   John was down to Olson Creek

December 1th   was up to smole streamlet got one weasel   started up Lick House trail caut two more   set out som traps

2th Saturday   was down south branch Funny River   set out 9 traps

3th Sunday   walked down south fork abouth two miles   cut north east acrost country to midle fork   set out som traps

4th Monday   Came down to Friman

5th Tuesday   I was down to P & O creek got one mink & two ermine   John was up Birch got two ermine & one mink

6th Wednesday,   Came home from Freeman   caut one ermine & to more at home cabbin   John got

two mink & one ermine up Indian   so we got 4 mink 13 ermine on trip

7th Thursday   Stritched 4 mink & 8 ermine this morning then I went out on glaser flats got one mink & five ermine   John up Lake Emma trail got one mink & three ermine

8th Friday   Stay home making bread   fixed up a work bench & repairing som old clotches   John tok a walk on the flats hunting som traps that I over loked last trip   noting captured

9th Saturday   Going to Devils Bay I walked over the flats   got three ermine   set out ten traps in Clear Creek and Nyman coast

10th Sunday   Was up Mexico trail   set out eleven traps   had to turn early the dogs ran away

Peter "Russian Pete" Kalning was partnered with Windy Wagner this winter. Andrew called him "sixteen horse power Pete" in his December thirteenth entry. Berg enjoyed conjuring nicknames. In this case we have to wonder if Berg was referring to the man's physical strength or the size of outboard engine he used. According to census data Kalning emigrated from Russia in 1900. Photo courtesy of McLane Collection.

11th Monday   Set out 12 traps   got in to Beaver camp saw som sign of game

12th Tuesday   got up early went out and dragged for our trout net   got net & one trout large enough for breckfast   I went to pick traps got one mink   John after wood & up Clear Creek got mink   John rowed home & run trapline got five ermine & rabbit

Wednesday 13th   I stay home all day making a saw frame and filing and sharpening a saw for Friman camp below Birchwood   about noon sixteen horse power Pete came up from Bear Creek to see John who was up lake Emma trail loking over som traps   He had one mink & four ermine when he came   that put us upstakes [even] with Pete & Wagner in mink & Three ermine to the good   I tok a little walk along the beach caut 2 ermine

Thursday 14th   John started down lake to camp Freeman & Lick House on Funny River   tok Irish along   I not feeling good, stay home all day

cooking up som head cheese and tending som furs   to night I am heating water for a bath cloudy loking like snow

Friday 15th   washed some clotches this morning then tok a walk over the trapline on the flats   set out four traps for lynx on the hogback and mts side   got three ermine   had a devils own time getting acrost streams comming home

Saturday 16th   Pulled over to Devils Bay   had a fine day   got to Chas Nymans cabbin 1 hour and fifty minutes   caut one ermine and two on clear creek

Sunday 17th   tok a bunch of traps started for dans camp   found Eds trail leading up ahead of me so I set five more traps for mink on Clear Cr & four from creek to cliff & six traps for lynx towards Nymans   got one ermine

Monday 18th   started early along Mexico trail set out seven traps   no game moved   caut one ermin

Charles "Windy" Wagner was one of the gang on Tustumena Lake in the winter for many years. He moved to the Kenai Peninsula around 1905 and was a licensed guide. He was better known for practical jokes and hospitality than for veracity. In 1912, Game Warden Tolman wrote to the Governor's office:

September 13
Mr. Shorthill
Dear Sir; I wish to write you in reference to the appointment of Wagner as guide, there were some things that I did not care to mention in the cable-gram, as I did not think it necessary to make an official record of it.
It is my idea that in appointing new guides that the standard should be raised and in his case it would certainly not be, his personal character and his associates are not good, he is ignorant and exceedingly vulgar and I do not think he could be depended upon to enforce the game laws with any party he should be out with, as I have no doubt that a few dollars extra would be sufficient for him to over look any infringement.
He should be chuck full of truth, for it is only by accident that he lets any out of him. He is known here as "Windy Wagner"...[13]

Photo courtesy of Dolly Cole Christl.

Tuesday 19th   Came home from Devils Bay loked over our traps on flats got three ermine got home just befor snow started to fall

Wednesday 20th   Got up early on acount of setting batter for making bread   after I had breckfast I went up the creek to look over the traps   the second trap are under the flow and I dont know the place   got one weasel at bridge somting got away from last trap   was back here before eleven   worked down the dough then hurried to look at six traps by the mill   when I came back I had dough everwhere   I had the tub hanging from the beams & the stuff spilled itself over stove and all it could reach. I feelt like cursing but I decided it would'nt help any & here was none to hear (No fun in it if you cant cus som one)

Thursday 21th   Soft almost raining   at home fixing som utensels   Towards evening I tok a walk up creek found the missing trap & caut three ermine   was out on mill shore but did not git anyting in that line

Friday 22th   was up to Lake Emma   ran into a wolferine but had no gun   got two ermine John came home he had 38 ermine & one mink   still mild   feel like we are going to have som snow

Saturday 23th   Had a walk on the flats but the weather was bad   som nasty valys with rain and sleet   anyway I got over the trap line only got two ermine   shot six Rabits to bait traps both lynx and mink traps

Sunday 24th   Just one of the finest days   warm as a spring day   I walked down to Bear Creek to see Pete and Wagner they was both out   John was up Indian got one ermine

Monday 25th   John went down the beach to Birchwood   I went acrost the flats to Devils Bay Caut a mink & three ermine   Walking somting fears [fierce]   slick as a bottle   had som nasty falls but was still in tact when I got there

Tuesday 26th   got out of bed quarter of six and by half after seven I was on my way up Mexico trail   been raining thru this country so that all the traps was frozen springing all   had a time to get them to snap after beating the ice off them

Lynx tramped down pan on one but no go   got one ermine last flat   eagle in a lynx set   mink got out of last trap burrowed under som grass dog pointed him I dug him out shot him   Big Edd he said he was going to Kussiloff with furs has 80 ermine & two mink.

Wednesday 27th   Sawed a stick of wood   piled the tings in a boat   tok in the net got four trout pulled home in two hours   cooked up som fish & potatoes   tok a walk down beach   look over som traps

Thursday 28th   At home cooked up a big kettle of beans & stewed som apples   Raisins & cranberry that is   after I tok a walk started to go out on the flats but the alders was so full of snow so I tryed to go up to Lake Emma but just at the time I got to the hill a wind sprung up & snow was flying so bad I went back home   got one ermine on Indian

Friday 29th   was up to Lake Emma   the hill was bad   three of the traps sprung   no sign of game up on the hill but along Indian River lynx have been out in several places   Lynx   pulled trap out of chute at shingle camp   got one ermine Emma Creek

Saturday 30th   tok a walk up glaser flats   bad walking   had a nasty fall going of the hog back to lake   saw several lynx tracks but not at any traps they could get in   quite of moose on the flats   saw a dozen in one bunch   got two ermine

Sunday 31th   At home making bread & certainly made a lot of it   I have bread everywhere   just a fine day for staying indoors   snowing and cold wind about eight above zero   I am expecting Devils Bay to freze over most any time as there was ice drifting there when I left   I pulled home tok me over two hours   I followed right close to shore all way   brought the saw & net   got lot of trout towards Chas Nymans   Happy New Year

CHAPTER 8

1923

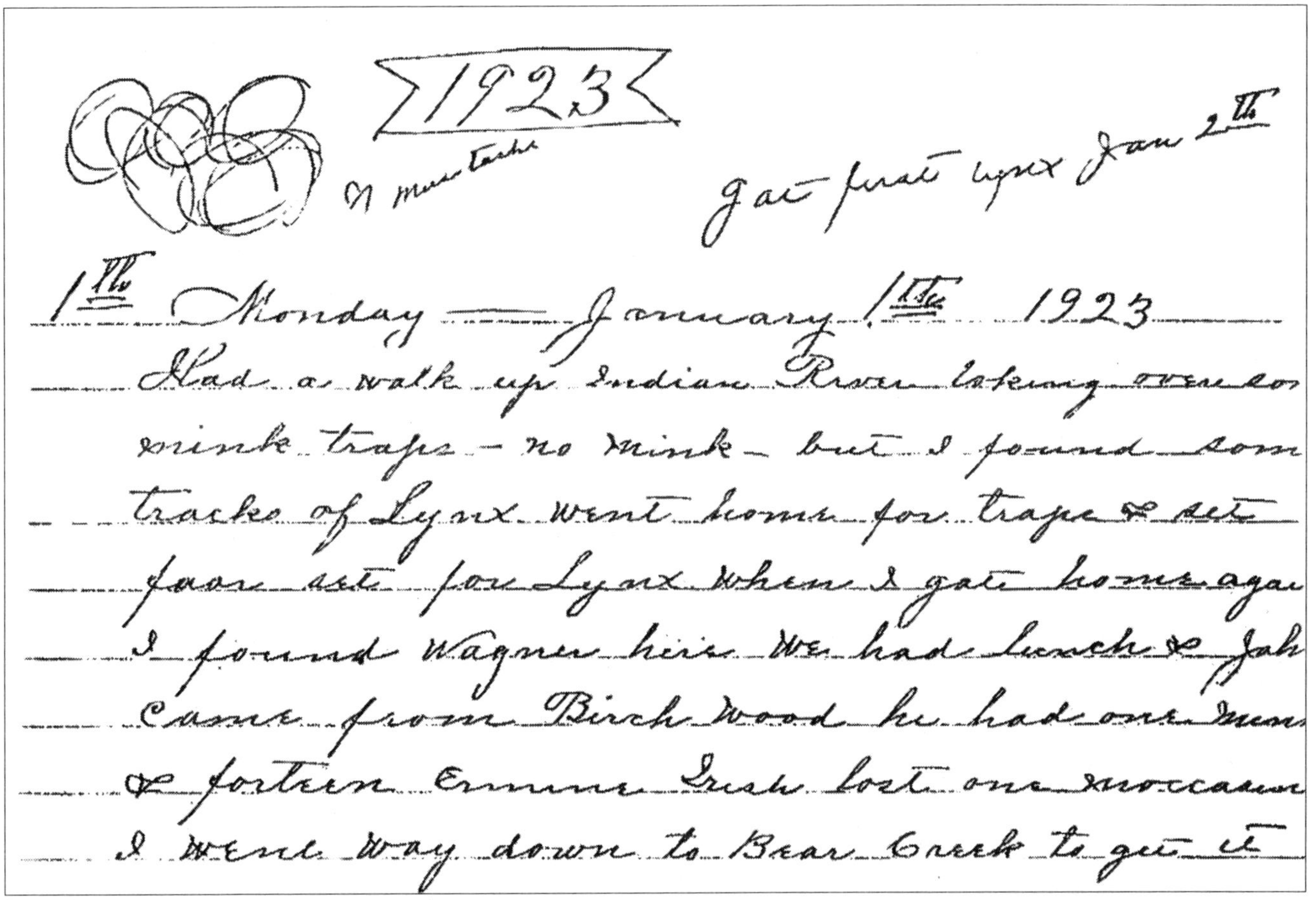

[handwritten journal entry]

1923

A mustache

got first lynx Jan 2th

1st Monday — January 1st 1923
Had a walk up Indian River taking the on mink traps — no mink — but I found som tracks of Lynx went home for trape & set foor set for Lynx when I got home agai I found Wagner here We had lunch & Joh came from Birch Wood he had one mun & fortien Ermine Irish lost one moccasin I went way down to Bear Creek to get it

Tuesday 2th   Late last night I was gainting a saw & cut acrost my right tumb half ways into the tumb nail   it is feeling num but not hurting very much   Filed the saw today   in the afternoon was up creek got a lynx   John was on the flats got a ermine

Wednesday 3th   Started out to set som traps but when I toke hold of the ax handle I found that my thumb was to sore to do any chopping so I came home again   worked at setting a saw and reading Saturday Evening Post   John was up to Lake Emma came home with one ermine   there is hardly any game around

Thursday 4th   was out on glaser flats got one weasel   John was up creek & by the mill

Friday 5th   Stay home all day fixing up som underwear   had a sort of bath   reading Saturday Evening Post two years old   Scimmings of ice over the lake   getting colder about six above this evening   John went down to Lick House

Saturday 6th   was intending to go to Cliff House this morning but it got foggy so I decided to stay over one more day and let the ice get stronger   2 above this morning   16 H.P.Kalning came from Bear Creek   exchange reading material and get *a couple plugs of tobaco   he came with me up Indian river   one ermine*

Sunday 7th   Started out on ice but to young had to take shore and the rim ice was hardly strong enough so I tok the trap line over flats inside woods   I found noting in any trap on the flats   after I got Cliff House heated I went up Clear Creek got one mink   put on my scates ran over to Eds but he was not home

Monday 8th   to cold to skate the ice frosty good walking   went out on Mexico trail got one ermine coming back to lake I found Ed coming from Kussiloff   he brought me som mail

Tuesday 9th   went and set six lynx traps on lake shore   foot of Mexico trail saw Ed   looked thru Clear Creek shifted one trap from Clif to Cliff House got one ermine   Nyman coast ran scates all way but at gold penin I got on weak ice   tuned back went acrost neck on hand and knees   set the net

Wednesday 10th   tok a walk up creek loking over som traps   got noting   got on my skates tok a run down to Bear Creek with som mail   met John coming from Birchwood   he had one mink & Nine ermine

Thursday 11th   I was out on glaser flats along mountain to Dirty Cannon set out six lynx sets got one lynx & one ermine   John was to Lake Emma he had one mink & one ermine Cold 10 below this morning   turning mild   hear the roar in Mts

Friday 12th   Snowing all night   tryed the skates but the snow was to deep so I walked to island loking over som traps   did not catch anyting John got two ermine

Saturday 13th   Have been at home all day making bread & while waiting for bread to rise made a smole plane   John was up to Lake Emma running trap line

Sunday 14th   Chopped som green birch   hitched up our dogs for the first time   Hauled home the logs   sawed & split   ran the trap line near home

Monday 15th   Nineteen below zero this morning John started down to Birchwood   I intended to

go to Devils Bay but cold feet & came back decided not to go until the weather moderates

Tuesday 16th   At home all day   weather to cold to travel   fished the net & got three trout   Its about all I can do to keep warm with fire burning in the stove

Wednesday 17th   Weather moderating today just going to Cliff House   walking mean

Thursday 18th   Quite mild this morning   was out on Mexico trail   Lot of lynx sign but I cant get them to go near the traps

Friday 19th   Raining all last night forming a bad crost   still raining in showers   Ice is sinking watering thru snow in many places   got three ermine   tanned the net & set it out

Saturday 20th   Packed home water from creek had a bath   tok a walk up creek   got two ermine Scrubbed floor   washing clotches   Fished the net did not get a fish

Sunday 21th   At home all day   rather cold this morning   got two trouts   changing to warmer about middle of day   started hunting for somting to make moccasins from

Monday 22th   Blowing a gail of wind   Wagner was over   John came home had eight ermines Wagner ready to start down

Tuesday 23   weather soft rainy   at home all day   make bread & sewing a pair of moccasins John tok a walk up Indian River brought one ermine

Wednesday 24th   Snowing to beat the band this morning   I started out on the glaser flats got one lynx & two ermine   John after finish washing clotches went up to Lake Emma got four ermines

Thursday 25th   Started down to Kenai   I met Windy at Bear Creek his dogs have run away he asked me to wait and he go with me

Friday 26th   Stay all day at Bear Creek   towards evening Pete Kalning came in with Wagners dogs

Saturday 27th   We started down lake got to Hugos   caught one lynx at Birchwood

Sunday 28th   Snowing and thick   went crost country to Kussiloff

Monday 29th   Snowshoed all the way to Kenai snow soft and heavy going

Tuesday 30th   Stay at Kenai

31th Wednesday   Still at Kenai   snowing & blowing

Thursday February 1   Still loking thick and snowing but we came to Kussiloff

Friday 2th   a southerly gale blowing with rain

Saturday 3th   Still raining and snowing   no weather to be out in

Sunday 4th   Started out this morning but got to heavy   left sled abrest silver S   tramped trail to pass   went back to Lapland

Monday 5th   was up Kussiloff visiting fox farmers

Tuesday 6th staying in Lapland   Rain and snow melting

Wednesday 7th   Left Kussiloff   was at Hugos one o clock   turning mild   lot of snow on lower end of lake

Thursday 8th Frezing during the night   started early snowshoing up lake to fox point got better going and a mile further got onto patches of clear ice   made good time   got to Bear Creek noon ran home on skates   John was down to visit Pete   have five lynx and about 20 ermines hanging in store room

Friday 9th   At home all day   had a bath changed clotches   Baking bread and doing work John was up to mountain got one ermine on glaser flats and one on Indian   Wether fine   lake clear as glass

Saturday 10th   Went to Cliff House   at Nyman coast got two lynx   fine traveling

Sunday 11th   Got up this morning with cramps stay in bed all day   Ed Roth came in on his way to glaser flats

Monday 12th   Rode up as far as Mexico trail and straight home   stritched the skins   cooked up som rice & mess of beans

Tuesday 13th   Was at home to noon   took a walk up creek   when I got back I found John home   He brought five ermine   I saw lot of moose up creek but no fur of any kind. (got three trout morning)

A little bit of "Lapland," Berg's nickname for Kasilof with all of its Scandinavian residents. This is a view from the frozen Kasilof River looking up at the Swallow Nest Silver Fox Ranch, taken in the 1920's. The ranch belonged to Pete Jensen and Pete Madsen. Fox pens are along the hilltop in the left half of the picture. Photo courtesy of Susan and Joe Perletti.

Wednesday 14th   have been home all day mending tings   John was up to lake Emma got one lynx & one ermine

Thursday 15th   tok dog team & rode over to Cliff House   while I was up on Clear creek dogs got lose and ran home

Friday 16th   started 8 oclock sharp going up Mexico trail looking over trap line   got to last trap 11:45, back to Cliff house at 3 - Five hours using snowshoes   John brought the dogs rode right home   got five ermine

Saturday 17th   was up on the mountains for a piese of meat   climbing bad   glasers slipery rock icy and treacherous snow   soft one step hard & slippy next   Saw lot of moose   was within one hundred feet of 22 on an icy space at foot of glaser   would have made fine picture had I carried a camera

Sunday 18th   Hitched up the dogs went to woods island and hauled home two loads of dry spruce after I fixed my snow shoes and tok a good long nap   John sawed up som wood & cooking a pot of stew

Monday 19th   John tok French [dog] and went down the lake to Friman   Lick House and Funny River trap lines   I have been home making enough bread to last at least two weeks

Tuesday 20th   Heated water had a bath   tok a walk up creek loking over traps   George Hirshey came up with couple of Siwashes [Natives]   Skated down to Bear Creek   got late stay all night   Wagner at home

George Hirshey was a 48 year old New Yorker who came to Alaska seeking gold.[1] His home base was Kenai.

Wednesday 21th   Came from Bear Creek got home nine thirty   went to lake Emma   after I got back filed saw & sawed a few blocks   Hirshey was over for a while

Thursday 22th   Leagal holyday in United States tok a walk up glaser flats went to a ways above Dirty Cannon

Tuesday 27th   Stay home all day   Blowing a nasty wind with snow drifting (Reading class)

Wednesday 28th   Thermometer down to zero this morning   about ten o clock we went up Nicanorka trail and cut a few shingle bolts   Cold all day

Berg was making spruce shingles or shakes for roofing his Home cabin. The process began with logs cut into blocks the length of the desired shake. The blocks were split into wedges or "bolts." Shakes were then split off the bolts with a tool called a "froe."

Thursday March 1   John had to start down without dogs as the dog have got lose during the night   just after John left one of the dog came home   I tok him & went up glaser flats   found the other dog   Caught two ermine   found a old set of sheep horns

Friday 2th   Got two trout   enough for a substantial breckfast   snowing and some wind After cleaning up breckfast dishes I boiled some hops & started new yeast then I put pack sadles on the dogs and went up Indian river thru cannon found Hirsey working on my old grounds climbed out of cannon to lake Emma   run the trapline but did not catch any fur animal

Hirshey was prospecting on Berg's old placer claims.

Saturday 3   Stay home all day making bread about noon the dogs got loose and ran out chasing   At five when I was thru with my work I tok a walk along the lake shore found the tracks of dogs going that way   I went down to Bear creek found both Pete & Wagner home   stay until moon got up   came home about ten o clock

Sunday 4th   was up early fished the net and got two of the nicest kind of trout one extra large Tok a walk up creek   tryed to split som shingles but to cold had to quit   Clouding but cold

Monday 5th   was at home all fore noon fixing my mits and making a new bunker on my wood sled   An Indian came from Hirshey camp up the cannon   John got home while I tok a tramp up Indian river

Tuesday March 6th   going to Camp Freeman by way of Alex Linds cabbin   Windy point found

Alex gone down march first   could barely see his tracks   got to Freeman two o clock

Wednesday 7th   Snowed during the night to give me heavy going   about three inches of soft sandy snow   sled pulled like on a grindstone   Met a Siwash at Birch point going to Kussiloff he had one of his snowshoes broken and his dogs would not lead   I stopped at Bear Creek about two hours

Thursday 8th   Raining & blowing to beat the band   John went up on glaser to kill a moose he found the day before with a broken leg   I stay home all day made a couple of drow [drawer] *pulls and reading a copy of American magazine that I have overlooked*

Friday 9th   Still blowing but it is that much colder that wath is coming down is snow in place of rain but it melts as soon is it hits the ground   I have been up the creek splitting shakes   I tryed som shingle bolts of spruce but they would not split   But this afternoon I tryed out som Aspen and think that I will find som of them that will runn good

Saturday 10th Up the river splitting shakes got a nice lot found a tree that split good Wagner have been over while we was away brought home a book

Sunday 11th   Blowing a cold northerly wind was out cutting down a dozen birch trees & hauled home seven   Big Ed came over from Devils Bay stod a little while & went back

Monday 12th   Quite cold this morning hitched up dogs and hauled in a few loads of birch   at the second last load I got a catch in my back in bending down without lifting   sticth over right hip and back   I can move about by going slow and being careful   John tok in traps from Emma

Tuesday 13th   at home making bread and nursing a sore back   John was up glaser flats after a load of dog feed

Wednesday 14th   Turning mild & blowing yet I went to Cliff House and down lake shore to take in a string of traps   had trouble with my dogs Lynx tracks plenty   no other game exepting Big Ed and his dog   I saw them at long distance

slised my hand with cleaver   John at home trying to get our wood pile started

Thursday 15th   I stay home all day   towards evening I went over to Cliff House   John have been busy all day sawing fire wood

Friday 16th   Started early tok all my belongings from the Cliff House to foot of Mexico trail   lift everyting at the sled exept dog and thier pack sacks   tok in a lot of traps   left 23 steel & one little gint   got two mink & one ermine

Saturday 17th   Started down lake   called in at Bear Creek   Saw Wagner & Pete   they was ready to go out but waited on acount of weather

Sunday 18th,   Stay in Camp Friman all day (Snowing)

Monday 19th   Was up Birchwood tok in all traps hard snowshoing   wet & sticky

Tuesday 20th   Went up to Lick House   had hard hunt to find all my traps   Hewed down one wall in the cabbin this evening [flattened the interior surface of logs with an ax]

Wednesday 21th   Was over and tok in all traps on both branches of Funny River   got two mink 1 ermine

Thursday 22th   Came off the hill to Camp Friman was down to Olson Creek and tok in the traps got one mink 1 ermine

Friday 23th   Cold   started home early snowshoes to lake point   was in to Bear Creek got som potatoes & one dozen carnation milk Total For season Ermine-221 Mink-26 Lynx-10

Fur values could vary considerably depending on the quality and condition of a pelt. The average prices paid in Alaska this year were $19 for lynx, $8 for mink and 90 cents for ermine.[2] At these prices, Berg's trapping catch would have brought him $596.90.

Saturday 24th   Have been home all day making bread & ripped som birch timber for making a sled   John was out colecting the last traps so we got them all in excepting five that we lost   I was

out a few minutes ago and fished the net   got
one nice trout

*Sunday 25th Was up early this morning   had
breckfast and was out sawing down timber for
wood before seven o clock   Mild fine day   filed
the saw*

*Monday 26th   Was out this morning at half
after six starting to haul home green birch for
fire wood and was finis at ten thirty   John started
to saw and & I went up Indian river and split
som shingle bolts to shakes   got back here after
four*

*Tuesday 27th   Went out this morning to the
island & sawed down two dry spruce & hauled
them home   in the afternoon I was hauling home
two loads of shakes   John was on the wood pile
lot of snow in the woods yet but it is getting soft
later in the day*

*Wednesday 28th   Was up the creek this morning
cutting a couple of larg spruce for shingle bolts
that took us to noon   I hooked up the dogs and
hauled home a load of shingles   John chopped
som wood and cooked up a pot of stew   I was
out and tryed splitting   two wolfererine came by*

*Thursday 29th   Everyting frozen hard   we split
wood to about ten o clock   I had a walk thru
hills loking for a tree that would make shingles
was out & split som*

Masons whos picture apear on postage stamps

*Georg Washington
Benjamin Franklin
Andrew Jackson
William McKinley
James A Garfeild
Theodor Rosevelt
W. G. Harding
Henry Clay
Alexander Hamilton
John Marshal
Livingston
Charles A Lindberg*

*How easy it is from day to day to shun the little
task that means so much in a friendly way though
why we do not ask while not unwilling we push it
aside and answer with a smile I'll do that sometime*

*but not to day I do that after while   Thirteen
masons*

*we have trod the [illegible] Sacred pathway We
have trod the sacred pathway of Ancient Scottish
rite   we have lerned the royal secret gazed upon
its shining light   may it ever guide upward till
were placed beneath the sod to a greater
understanding with our brother and with god
Mr Greb*

*Werdna
ianek Greb Werdna
ianek Kenai
ianek ianek
Verdna Greb Werdna
Greb Werdna
ianek
Kenai Alaska*

Andrew was a Freemason, there were Masonic Lodges
in Seward and Anchorage. The men involved in the
Northwest Development & Mining Company were
Freemasons and may have prompted Berg's membership.

*Friday 30th   was out this morning splitting &
ricking wood while it was cold anough to split
easy   about noon I tok a walk up creek   trying
to split shakes out of som block I have quit ones
but no go   John have been sawing wood all day
Nearly finis*

*Saturday 31th   Finis sawing & splitting wood
today about noon   I then went to millvilla [the
old mill site] to scrape togather som lumber for
sheeting under shakes   getting cloudy*

*Sunday April 1   Fine warm morning   tok a
walk up to mountain side loking for trees that
would make shingles   located som and came bak
home   about noon we went out felled a tree and
split two bolts   broke my watch crystal*

*Monday 2th   Went out early this morning
hauled home two loads of shakes in the fornone
or to one o clock   after lunch we went out and
split enough for one good load and quit splitting
(Got anough.)*

*Tuesday 3th   Hauled home a load of shakes
this morning on the frost & two loads of lumber
then I went out & cut timber for making two step*

ladders after that we fixed up and started to lay the roof fine weather calm & clear.

The men installed the new roof over the old. Boards which they had scavenged from the old mill site were nailed horizontally in rows across the tin roof. Then the fresh shakes were fitted and fastened to the planks.

Wednesday 4th Been busy all day nailing at the roof and getting along fine got one side finis over cabbin and started on the other side leaving the shed to the last

Thursday 5th Been on the roof all day laying shakes Clouded up during the night and turned warmer snow is disapearing

Friday 6th Frozety this morning so we fixed an addition to our wood shade [shed] Fixing up tings around the place was out on lake shore picked up a log brought it home for a pray [pry] pole to rise the house next fall After ten o clock finis the roof fixed yeast set out trout net and by that time it was five o clock

Saturday 7th Been busy clining up tings for summer I had a bath changed clotches made bread and washed up all the old clotches I could find John scrubbed out the cabbin while I hauled home the boat and we hoisted him overhead in the outeroom got everyting in order and ready to leave in morning

Sunday 8th A heavy south westerly storm brock out during the night and when I tryed to fish my net I snagged & we had to bring the boat out had breckfast & then had to rise the boat again we got our tings loaded on the sled and by that time it was after nine we went along fine got to Camp Freeman after twelf sawed som wood and cooked luncheon and I was on the point of taking a stroll along the lake shore when I happeded to think of my glasses I hitched the dogs & came here on the runn fifteen miles about two hours and fifteen minutes wind strong a head I had to lay flat on the sled to easy the recistance

Monday 9th Starting for Kenai with wether permitting we should get there in three or four days

Berg's Home cabin with shakes on the roof. The pole structure on the left edge of the photo was probably related to his well which he mentions frequently in his journal. Photo courtesy of Dolly Cole Christl.

Game Warden Walter Culver spent time on the western Peninsula in February and March. His main purpose was to gather information about the moose.[3] There was a reported shortage of moose feed at this time. Snowshoe hares were at one of their cyclical population peaks. The hares, universally called rabbits, were believed to compete with moose for winter forage. Culver spent time in Kenai and Kasilof and attended a meeting of the Anchorage Rod and Gun Club. His report acknowledged the rabbit problem but also pointed to the ongoing market hunting of moose as a threat and a waste. Typically, market hunters salvaged only the hindquarters of the animals they killed.

Culver also wrote up his observations of the fox farming in this area. Six farms were now operating in Kasilof and one outside of Kenai. Most of them were just starting up. The farmers reported that their intense trapping of the rabbits in the area for fox food didn't seem to be making a dent in the population.

Culver made observations about other animals as well. Lynx numbers were up, in synchronization with the rabbits. Fox were scarce due to a good market for pelts and live animals during the previous eight years. Because fox numbers were down, weasels were abundant. Mink, beaver and land otters were rare, probably as a result of trapping pressure. Andrew's winter take of 221 ermine, 10 lynx and 26 mink supported the report although the mink were more plentiful in his area. The flush economy and fashions of the 1920s would keep fur prices high for trappers and fur farmers.

1920 and 1921 were poor years for salmon fishing in Cook Inlet. In 1922 the salmon runs started rebounding. The original Kasilof cannery operated for the last time in 1923. In this ever-changing industry the old plant had been superceded by more modern facilities in Kenai and Seldovia. During the 1923 salmon season, Andrew Berg and Charles LaMatyr shared a federally issued fishing permit on the east shore of Cook Inlet.[4] They may have been fishing with gillnets anchored in place along the beach or operating a small fish trap.

Andrew either had no hunters to guide this season or had a short hunt. He returned to Tustumena before hunting season was half over.

September 24th   Came up from Birchwood   had an exeptional fine trip   got the evenrude so that it works fine   started to rain after we got here   lake exeptional high

25 Tuesday   was up on the mountain got one large ram   was back home at 3:20 o clock   Salted down meat   set yeast making ready to make bread tomorrow   had a bad atack of reumatism

26th Wednesday   At home all day   I not filing good   was in bed most all day   toward evening I got feeling better   Blowing hard most all day the yeast did not work good so we had to let go making bread to next day

27th Thursday   At home all day   Krist making bread and I working at my evinrude   changing tings to suit and painted the machine white so I named him the white wing   got one more ting to fix   the comutator spring is lose

28th Friday   Weather loking treatening out   we decided to take a hunt   went up home trail crossed over to Dirty cannon to pass at lower end of lake   saw som sheep in slide rock but did not want to pack meat up the cliff so we did not go near them   we then decided to go Tonys cabin on south fork but ran in to sheep in a snowstorm got som meat   got hom at dark.

29th Saturday   At home doing adds & ends Keeping busy   salted som meat   weather unsettled looks like rain in devils bay

30th Sunday   Thru raining this morning gave us a chance to get started up South fork near Tonys cabbin   Saw a black bear   I climbed up but I had to go above them to shoot   I found that there was two when I got closer   Killed one with first shot but the other jumped into alders and got away

1 Monday October   Having stayed over night at Tonys cabbin went up thru cutting gorge and over mountain to where we had a sheep cashed brought it in   with fair size horns and the bear hide gave us fair loads

2th Tuesday   Raining & wet   fished the net and got a dozen nice trout   Nailed the bearskin to the wall   cleaned out the big dorey   tok the white King (envinrude) and tryed it out on a run to Cliff House   saw Doctor Flanders & his friend they was busy fixing up the house

According to George Cotter's game warden reports from September and December of this year, Dr. John A.

Flanders was a shell-shocked veteran of World War I who came to Alaska from Chicago to recuperate. He was the company doctor at the Kasilof cannery during the summer of 1923. Cotter believed that Flanders had money and intended to build a hunting lodge on Tustumena Lake.[5]

3th Wednesday was up early but did not go anywhere working at putting new gable end to cabbin and putting in window did not get quite finnis got only three trouts this morning creek swelled from rain and carried out a lot of leafs sinking the net

4th Thursday Raining & blowing stay home all day put in a window in the attic cleaned up & put down som boards to walk on & set up a cot to sleep on if we have visitors Cut away som grass around cabbin Indian river have rised full to the bank caut a lot of ancient silver salmon to day

5th Friday Making a roof joint 2 o clock going to Wagners Blowing hard so we just set up a little sail and ran down in short time found Wagner to his neck in grease fleshing bears

6th Saturday Urban & Wagner was going to see the doctor so I tok them up to my place & after we had lunch we all went to Cliff house found doctor & his friend cutting the stern of dory to fit evinrude Stay to lunch came home Wagner & Urban started walking to Bear creek

Urban was probably Urban Petterson, Carl Petterson's teenaged son from Kenai.

Sunday 7th Raining went up to foot of glaser and half mile up over ice to wet to go up mountain came home about two o clock

8th Monday at home making bread Raining and mean weathre

9th Tuesday Going to Cliff house (did not go) in afternoon when we was ready to start a nasty head wind sprung up so we waited for it to calm down Then Doctor Flanders came I was with him to mill still blowing & at last minute it treaten to rain so we gave up trip for tonight

10th Wednesday Went to Devils bay went up by Dan's cabbin crossing foot hills to Fox river wall climbing higher came back thru sheep country saw four sheep two moose few signs of bear but no bear got to lake late

11th Thursday Rainy we set sail and moved down lake shore two miles put up tent and pitched camp I tok a look up hill where we intended cutting trail came in wet

12th Friday Was out chopping trail started to rain had to come in Had the hardest rainstorm I ever saw

13th Saturday Wind moderated but still rainy tok a walk to King lake tok a lot of moss got back late tired Chopped out a lot of trees that have fallin cross our trail

14th Sunday came home found Indian river have changed her bed heavy drifts forming floting islands hundreds yard in diameter drifting on the lake

15th Monday Got up late fished the net and got one trout the reason is that a lot of hooknosed silver salmon had the net twisted so the net could not catch a trout Pulled to the flats and went up overhanging trail Cut the trail clean saw som fresh signs of bear but just as we got up saw one lone ram and two moose got a pease of meat

Tuesday 16th On our way to Kenai got back here Nov 4th

Sunday November 4th Came from Ebbs cabbin on the penninsula came from lower end of penninsula to this place in 3 hours & 45 minutes the little evinrude is good

Monday the 5th Stay at home making bread Brick & Paul was up Mts loking for sheep but it started to blow so they came home early bringing in one porcupine & got five trout waiting for a hot skilet in the morning

6th Tuesday Starting early after eight March & Paul went up overhanging trail after they left I tok the skif went to mouth of Dirty cannon cut som alders saw som sheep got home just before dark waited for three hours before they came [they] have killed five sheep and got lost on the glaser flats creeping trough alders for a couple of hours

7th Wednesday   Brick & Paul started out this morning to pack in meat & did not get home to after dark   Saw one bear track yesterday & one to day   I have been home had a bath & washed clotches & cleaned up tings around the house

8th Thursday   This morning Paul & Brick started up overhanging trail to get som meat just after I tok a tramp trough alders along woods island loking for bear but saw no signs   so I went to foot of glaser just then I thought a private war have started I heard nine shots   I shot one shot got one ram

9th Friday   Stay home all day   John Johnson came up from Bear creek   I put the machine on the little sciff and tok John half ways to Bear creek   Paul & Brick was up on mountains to get the last of thier sheep meat

Apparently John Johnson was living in the cabin at Bear Creek this winter.

10th Saturday   going to Birchwood   tok my skiff on the dory with Paul & Brick and thier meat & dunage as far as Birch creek   there we put a shore & they made tea and fixed up a tarpauline for sail   it was by now a splendid breece   fair I was padling along to Friman Camp   when I got there I saw the sail at Penninsula

Paul and Brick took Andrew's big dory down to Kasilof for the winter.

11th Sunday   Blowing a cold northerly wind   I went to the Lick House but was almost froze   got there about noon   found that a bear have broken in the window and smashed ting in general   I had a extra window aloft   I put that in and went back to Friman   saw lot of moose

12th Monday   Blowing hard in valys with rain and snow   I tok a walk to Philips creek hunting for som traps found one   got back to camp wet had som dinner tok a rest   wether cleared   I started to go home   before I got ready up came another squall that put going out of question

13th Tuesday   Was up early ready to go home but it was raining so I had to wait to quarter to nine   still raining but not so heavy   got home in two & one half hour after stopping twice   put Johns pack sadle in at Bear creek

14th Wednesday   At home all day not feeling good the only ting to my credit today is getting my little 22 pistol to work & was out & shot 3 rabbits they seems to be plenty in the heavy drifts in the old chanel of Indian river   I was hunting for a crook to frame a new sawblade in but did not find the right   started to rain so I tok a napp

15th Thursday   had a miserable day of it   sick at my stomak   stay in all day   started to read a book titled "The Chasm" but I have been even to sick to read so I got only half trough the book fished the net this morning and got four trout

Abe's cabin on the peninsula which Andrew mentioned on November 4. This picture was taken some decades later. Photo courtesy of Allen Tri.

16th Friday   Have been home all day   feeling better but not ambitius to do any work   weather have been fine that is the lake have been smooth with light cloud & hazy fog from the mountain   I tryed several different ting to do but found noting I could do   shot som rabbits for dog feed   I saved the skins for lynx flags but will set no traps to Dec 1

A "flag" is hung prominently near a baited trap to attract lynx to the vicinity.

17th Saturday   Fixing up my winter mitts to make them last to I have time to make new ones   about eleven o clock here come sixteen hors power pete with Sig John & Windy   had a load of sheep Fixed frame for saw & tok a walk up cannon lord wath a mess   cuts made 150 feet deep

18th Sunday   At home tok the fot of evinrude apart   found the trues bearing badly worn   was going to try & babbit it but just then sixtin horse power pete came   talked me into shim   it did not work   heard evinrude from devils bay   gave pete 2 gals oil

19th Monday   was late getting up   started to put up tings to take along   finding it would be to late to get over & camp set up I decided to go up Indian River to see the work the flood have been doing   it was simply majestic   tok me 3 hours to go up & back   shot 4 rabbits- dog feed

20th Tuesday   Blowing quite of gale but got up to glaser flats and on to Cliff House   met Ed & Myers who have been after som moose meat   stay at Cliff House all night

21th Wednesday   Feeling bum but weather being nice I moved to King lake trail & set up tent set net & fixed camp

22th Thursday   Tok up chopping where Krist and I quit   foggy but I could hear evinrude at Cliff House   Got thru fine   found a naturly drow [natural draw]   *it tok me right to the lake*

23th Friday   I tok a pack & packed the dogs and walked in to the lake   built a lean to for construction camp

Berg is preparing to build another trapping cabin.

24th Saturday   Som snow fell during the night & I had to have my saw set before I tok it on the hill so I went to Cliff House   found no one at home tok saw set   met Jack Ed came down from south fork   cold hands

25th Sunday   Got out of bed 5:30 this morning but before I had breckfast ready it was 7:00   after cleaning breckfast dishes it was daylight   I set batter for making bread & as a little snow fell during night I hiked out to see wath animal might be around   saw only one lynx track   got home saw Ed on his way to Devils Bay   tok a walk to mouth of Indian river   saw one mink track   set out four traps   betwin time I watched my baking the first this season

26th Monday   Was late getting out of bedd heard the surf on the beach so I slept to daylight lost part of my evinrude (terminal on spark plug) hunted the house   finely along trail to beach I found it   Set out ten traps for mink   shot five rabbits for dog feed on my way home   Cooked up a big feed & tok a good long sleep

27th Tuesday   Tok fifteen traps up lake Emma trail   set ten for lynx & five for mink   saw no tracks of either lynx or mink   Cold wind

28th Wednesday   Tok twenty one trap pulled to glaser flats   set out twelf for lynx & nine for ermine & mink   saw no signs of any animals but it was not hardly snow enough to show tracks no moose any where

29th Thursday   Started over to Devils Bay started to blow and had to stay over night celabrating (thanksgiven)

30th Friday   Blowing a gale of wind   stay at Cliff House   had a game of cribb & started to read the Wind Of Chance by Rex Beach

1th Dec Saturday   started down to tent on lake shore   set out 7 lynx traps

2th Sunday   Packed in bedding to King Lake & set six lynx traps

3th Monday   tok in stove shovel and other junk stay all night

4th Tuesday   Started working on cabbin   put in two rounds & cut four more logs

5th Wednesday   Ran up one of my old trap lines & set out 12 traps   went down to lake Tustemina & pulled to Cliff House

6th Thursday   Snowing   left 2 o clock got home in good time   found Krist & Pete just arived from below

7th Friday   Loked over som traps on glaser flats tok along eight mink traps went to the flats with Krist Jensen & Pete Madsen who was going out for sheep   I went along the first creek thru the islands intended to set som traps but no sign of game so I did not put out any traps   ran over the traps I have out   Got one ermin & one mink got home early   was out shot som rabit for dog feed   (Going towards six sheep hunter out)

8th Saturday   Going to Lake Emma be back about one   [This was a message for anyone dropping by while he was gone.]   Traveling fine but did not get back to 20 to 2:00   was delayed by skinning a lynx   been stritching & cleaning the game & repairing my old snowshoes   the boys came off the Mts   still no sheep on acount of snow squall

9th Sunday   Found about two feet of new snow this morning   trying out the snow shoes but could not go anywhere the snow being to lose   shot a porcupine & two rabbits

10th Monday   started to go to Birchwood got only to Bear Creek when a wind sprung up   stay all night Pete   Krist   John & myself   John Johnson just came home having killed a moose at Pipe Creek

11th Tuesday   Going down with three boats   I to Freeman after having somting to eat   I set out 11 traps at Birchwood   Krist & Pete came and had the house warm

12th   Wednesday   was down to Philip & Olsen Creek set 16 traps   saw a lot of moose   got home tired   Pete & Krist have hunted moose but found only cows & calfs so they had no meat

13th Thursday   I went to Lick House   set out som traps on my way

14th Friday   was down Funny River   set out 15 traps saw lots of moose but no fur signs

15th Saturday   Came to Freeman set five lynx sets as I came along   Got down early   tok a walk to Philip Creek no game   Krist Jenson & Pete Madsen have gone to Penninsula

16th Sunday   Blowing a westerly wind   hard to get off the beach so I left dogs to walk to where I could pick them up   they ran away   I got the machine going but below Bear Creek I lost pumps valve & plug so I rowed to Bear Creek   had lunch & pulled on home   got here after dark made new pieses for machine   by 7:30 I had her ship shape again

17th Monday   got sick last night   sort of chills put on bedding to I swetted   still chilling   tok som physed so I been home all day reading a book by Zane Grey "The Riders Of The Purple Sage"   Even tonight I got a dull headache

18th Tuesday   8 Above this morning the coldest I have seen this winter   Was out on glaser flats could hardly keep my feet warm in rubber packs everyting snowed under   no game   saw two lynx tracks

19th Wednesday   going to Lake Emma be back about one   had a tough trip brecking new trail trough a foot of new snow going up the steep hilside   got no game   couple of traps sprung som was to deep to spring   Came down fine coasting all the way down   saw two lynx tracks

20th Thursday   started to Birchwood to hunt my dogs   stopped at Bear Creek yelled but no one was home   met John on Pipe Creek   found dogs at Friman

21th Friday   Loked over traps at Birchwood & hunted for pack sack & pistol Frency have lost

22th Saturday   tok a walk to olson & Philip Creek no sign of fur

23th Sunday   Intended to start home but decided to take an other hunt for missing pack sack & 22 calibre pistol without results

24th Monday   This morning found every ting deadly still   lake was skimming over with ice about eight I could pull along shore but it closed in had to leve boat & walk   walked to Bear Creek stay all night with John & Wagner who thought it was 23th

Tuesday 25th Xmas   came home from Wagners Ice abreast of mill   mean going   westerly wind breacking up the ice   22 above   felt a little dribble of snow this morning   Wagner fix up two sets of harnes started to train the pups

26th Wednesday   Mild snowing this morning Stay home all day was out & shot som rabbits for dog feed   saw one moose   broke in and got my feet wet   set new fot webb in snowshoe

27th Thursday   was out on glaser flats set two Lynx traps   saw lots of moose   shot at one wounded it but it milled in with the bunch & I could not find it & did not want to hit a new one so I came home

28th Friday   I think the lake tok the count last night   it was ten above zero this morning but deathly calm   I did not see any water as far as I could see   to day been home doing the family laundry

29th Saturday   was slow with home work this morning   hanged out som clotches & towles that I boiled last night   11:30 went up on flats   shot a moose   heard six shots from som one   after butchering my moose I went to see who it was found snowshoe track   no man in sight

30th Sunday   Sleep late   while having breckfast Jack Laxinen & Windy came with word that Dr Flanders was sick & to bring his partner   I got on my scates & ran to Cliff House   Jack got home to late to go anywhere   stay all night

31th Monday   got up early chopped his net out of ice   lake broke   cam home over glaser flats had lunch   I went back to Cliff House   had tough time getting there again   heavy storm rain & sleet

Doctor Flanders was not only sick, he had been on quite an adventure according to Game Warden Cotter:

January 1, 1924
Hon. Scot C. Bone   Governor of Alaska
Juneau, Alaska
Dear Sir;
Following is my report as Game Warden for the Seward and Anchorage districts, for the month of December, 1923...
[December] 18th ...[I] returned Seward 2 p.m. and learned that Dr. John A. Flanders...had been taken from [S.S.] Northwestern coming from Seldovia, very ill, found that N wester's captain had called for "the Marshall to take this dope and put him in the jail." Got busy and explained what shell shock is to the Marshall's office, as otherwise I think Dr. Flanders, who had already while too sick to function, during a relapse, paid out large sums and probably been robbed of more, would have suffered greatly from the ignorance

The small cabin on the lake shore at Pipe Creek. This structure is approximately 12 feet by 15 feet, the builder is unknown. Photo by G. Titus

of those who saw him unable to stand alone. Spent rest of day quieting him. He is a fine influence in the Kasilof country, which is full of big game being interests and helping with game protection. Last summer was doctor for the Alaska Packers cannery at Kasilof, doing some wonderful operations on injured personal I saw result of his work.

19th ...Afternoon and night, [I] took care of Dr. Flanders and by phone located a 15 dog team in Anchorage, arranging for it to come to mile 23 on 22nd freight train, meeting him there...

20th Weather clear. At headquarters. To train to help Dr. Flanders aboard; had found a reliable helper to care for him and aid with team. By phone sent word ahead and down Kenai River about care for him, and will have Guides Nelson and Lucas break trail ahead of

team from Skilak Lake to his home to make sure of his safe arrival. This would be a very severe trip for a well man; he must be carried on sled....

George Cotter Game Warden Seward [6]

This is a tantalizingly brief version of an intriguing story. We can only wonder why Flanders was on the S.S. Northwestern and how long it took George Nelson and Hank Lucas to mush from Skilak to Cliff House. Berg's diary provides no further details.

This winter the Alaska Road Commission improved the trail from Kenai to Kenai Lake. The trail work was performed in winter because this was a winter trail, crossing wetlands, streams and lakes which were impassable in other seasons. The dogsled trail was widened and provided with three shelter cabins equipped with stoves and utensils.[7]

A recent photo of the country traveled by Dr. Flanders and his Samaritan crew. Spruce trees are much more abundant now than they were in 1923. Photo by G. Titus

CHAPTER 9

1924

January 1th 1924.
Tuesday! stay in all day finished reading
the mad monk of Russia & started to read
Richard Carvel by Vinston Churchill
Raining all day

2th Wednesday working to two o clock to get boat out & pulled to my tent got two lynx on lake shore

3th Thursday Stay at tent all day bad weather

4th Friday Brok trail to upper camp still soft

5th Saturday Ran trap line got one mink Came back to lake & pulled to Cliff House stay all night got there after dark

6th Sunday tok dory & engine from Cliff House & ran home head wind & choppy sea got home about one been busy cooking & cleaning & striction skins

7th Monday Started late to go over trap on glaser flats all traps out of order drifted in or sprung no sign of game exepting moose Set two traps for mink

8th Tuesday was up to Lake Emma set three traps for lynx & replaced one that I broke the spring in one of teeth traps got two lynx saw one fresh track

9th Wednesday Stay home making bread had a sort of bath changed clotches & scrubbed the floor Weather about 18 above

10th Thursday Just as I was going up to flats to get som meat I heard an evenrude and here was the Doctor & Jack coming up with my boat had lunch & tok a trip on glaser flats tok in the hocks and a load of ribs came home & went thru my mail again got my glasses but one of them was chipped

11th Friday Was making ready to go down lake when a heavy wind & rain came off hill had to stay while dressing my sore finger out came a peice of bone Thermometer stands at 43 above

12th Saturday started about 9:00 on my way to Birchwood with dorey & evinrude saw Wagner at Bear Creek did not stop went on thru to Freeman put tings ashore & hiked to Philip & Olson Creek got back to Freeman after dark set out trout net

13th Sunday Started out early on my way to Lick House before I came to Cow Cannon I caught a lynx   packed it back to camp skinned it and started out again   in swamp betwin valey junction & horsepower hill a lynx have taken trap clog & all dragging it a long way   had quite hunt finding it   got to Lick House 1:30 hiked down Funny River running trap line   no game here   got back to Lick House at dark

14th Monday Started before daylight coming down to Freeman   set out one mink trap for lynx got to lake about 10:30   to strong southeaster to go home so I tok a hike up Birch Creek   the whole country is flooded with ice   set no traps here

15th Tuesday Lake just beautifull smote not a riffle anywhere got in sciff & ran up to Bear Creek stopped & had lunch with Wagner brought him his [illegible] got a bunch of reading matter got home early   stritched & cleaned the lynx

16th Wednesday Tok six teeth traps & set them up on the spur of Nikanorka Mts for lynx & wolferine   coming hom I got one lynx on Lake Emma got in way after dark saw no signs of lynx & wolferine

17th Thursday New snow this morning but still warm   no ice making   tok a walk on glaser flats   dirty alders full of snow   noting in traps saw one lynx track

18th Friday Stay home all day feeling lazy   som wind in Devils Bay   this evening it started to snow   10 above zero

19th Saturday Repairing som traps   was going up glaser flats but found over flow so I tok a walk up Indina River   found som lynx tracks came home & got som traps set out five for lynx to night heavy gale   10 above   light snowfall all day

20th Sunday Tok a hike up glaser flats chopped a road thru som alders that been mean when loaded with snow   no sign of game   saw only one moose Was to meat cashe   brought home a peice of meat   fried up a bushel of doughnuts   still cooking moose shank to somting like head cheese 10 PM

In the winter Andrew would cook up large batches of doughnuts and store them in a sack hanging from a tree.[1]

21th Monday   4 below this morning   I started to go up on the hill but meet a strong wind so I turned back   nearly got my face froze   saw one lynx track on Indian River

22th Tuesday zero this morning   I was up to Nicanorka Mts running trap line   never saw a track of any kind fur bearing animal   quite cold when I got out in open where wind hit me   quite tonight   looks as the lake my freze tonight

23th Wednesday Been at home all day lazy   have not done a ting excepting reading som stories form Elks magazine   rather cold   4 below this morning   Lake still oppen exepting for a field a front my landing   feels still tonight so we got another chance

[Entry by Jack Harning] *24th Thursday* Stayed in to thaw out a little shortly after 3 o clock   the ice towards Cliff House is bad along the islands and this side   one open streak as far as I could see about where the glacer stream should be on the flats   two big open places forming a V out from the bay between the islands   broke in twice trying to get by the rocks but had a pole along Looks to me like you were at Bear Creek and the ice looks good along the shore so I am going too Jack Harning

Its eight PM now and my clothes are not all dry yet so Im going to roost awhile   she's making more ice   6 above to night and calm   nobody here yet septin me my dog and I   Jack

Jack was staying with Dr. Flanders at Cliff House.

25th   Got up as far as Bear Creek

26th Saturday Came home from Bear Creek I & Jack Harning   scating fine had a fine run   9 below zero at Bear Creek this morning

27th Sunday Ran down to Bear Creek on scates with som letters then on to Cliff House   found Doctor fine   out splitting wood & swinging the axe like an old logger

28th Monday   was up Mexico trail to Ratt Lake and back to Cliff having decided during the day to go to Kenai so I have to make forced marches got one mink

29th Tuesday   Came from Cliff House got som tings to take along   went to Bear Creek   waited there for John to come in   Mayers came over from Devils Bay   stay all night

30th Wednesday   John & I started for Kussiloff scating to lower end of lake   got to Abbes fox ranch about three PM

31th Thursday   this day looked tough to go anywhere so John decided to stay at Kussiloff untill weather cleared   I started at day breack got to Kenai noon   Gust Ness overtook me on Califonsky flats

February 1th Friday   Came from Kenai to Abrams Johnson have moved acrost the river to visit Emil Ness Brother   I and Gust Ness left Kenai   Emil left us at timber crossing to go to head of Goat Creek Valey where he have a cabbin running a trap line

Emil Ness was Gust's younger brother. Four Ness brothers were on the Kenai Peninsula at various times. Only Gust spent his life there.[2] Around this time Gust and Mary Demidoff Johansen were married.

2th Saturday   Came from Kussiloff to Birchwood met Crist Jenson at sand bluffs   was up Olson Creek   no game

3th Sunday   Went up Lick House trail running trap line   got one lynx   came to Bear Creek stay for lunch   Wagner was busy making bread doughnuts and chocolate cake   you my belife [may believe] me I did disfigure a lot of his doughnuts

4th Monday   At home all day   making bread cooking up a lot of meat & cakes   a stew   after first repairing the stove that was coming to peases & repairing a twenty five calibre pistol & putting a new bead   had to hammer out triger point & templat

5th Tuesday   8 below zero this moring   I stay home to twenty minutes of twelf   started on my scated to Devils Bay with a letter for Ed also a letter for Dr F all Cliff House   came back over glaser flats   saw tracks of moose sheep lynx mink & caught one ermine   there have been several large rams off the hill

6th Wednesday   Was up Lake Emma line atacked by a cow moose shot it with 32 pistol to make it quit   bleeding badly but still going   got no game   Coming hom on Indian River I shot a calf with broken back   saw lot of tracks (Asorted)

Abe Erickson's fox farm on the bank of the Kasilof River. Rabbit carcasses are hanging on the rack and covering much of the ground. Photo courtesy of McLane Collection.

7th Thursday   At home all day   Emil Ness   Doctor & Jack came over   Doctor went to Bear Creek   Emil & Jack stay with me   wether turning mild 5 above zero

8th Friday   Emil   Jack & I stay here   Dr Flanders & Wagner came up from Bear Creek   Wagners dogs ran away   also Irish & Doctors browny the two last named came back so Doctor Emil & Jack started for Cliff House   Wagner & I went to glaser stream to set out my net   after we got back tok a walk up Indian River hunting dogs shot som rabits found two young dogs just at dark later old dog came

9th Saturday   Wagner went home this morning I hitched my dogs went up on flats to get home a load of moose meat   Fished the net at mouth of glaser stream got three nice trout   got home at noon ran my trapline on flats   set out two traps at slough   (no sign)

10th Sunday   Snow fell during the night but about noon it let up   I started to King Lake   got there late   getting cold

11th Monday   Dogs ran away during night   I ran trapline   packed out to lake   found irish at tent   went to Cliff House   tok sick   relap of Ptomain poisoning   tok treatmint

12th Tuesday   Doctor & Myers started for Kenai after giving me orders to keep quite & take medicine for one week

13th   Wednesday

14th   Thursday

15th   Friday   Stay at Cliff House

16th   Saturday

17th   Sunday

18th Monday   Jack & I got on scates   ran to glaser stream where I had out [net]   got five fish

19th Tuesday   I came home today   Jack cam with me   we set the two nets yesterday but ice was bad so we did not get them out good   got only two trout

20th Wednesday   Tok a walk out on glaser flats running my trap line got noting exept eagles squirrels porkupine & rabbits   Saw one moose fished the nets got only one trout   Jack came over from Cliff House   brought my glasses   mild

21th Thursday   Jack Herney stay with me last night   this fornoon we got on our scates ran down to Bear Creek   John Johnson have brought my mail from Kenai   John was to Birchwood   We ran back had lunch & walked to glaser stream to fish our nets   got no fish   Jack went to Cliff House

22th Friday   got up late this morning & was reading for som time   Then I decided to go and fish the net before breckfast   just as I started out Jack Harney came from Cliff House   turned around & had brecfast   started to rain about noon   We fished the net got two trout   Towards evening Jack went to Bear Creek   I blacksmithed a knif   had a bath   gets in to clean underwere & scrubbed the floor

23th Saturday   Was out fishing nets no fish caught in rain squall got soaking wet before I got in   had to change clotches   had breckfast tok a nap   Raining & blowing   finnished knife Jack came from Bear Creek helped me grind the knife

24th Sunday   got up late   still rain & sleet Jack was turning the grindstone for me while I was sharpening several knifs & axes   Cleared up had fine sun shin   went to glaser stream fished the nets   I got one trout   Jack tok his net and went to Cliff House   After I got home I washed som underwere   Started reading a novel

25th Monday   (Earthquake mid night) Storming & raining the worst I have seen for a long time I was up to flats to look after the net but had to go thru timber in order to stand up against the wind   got no fish   changed the net & blow over ice back home   been busy reading a novel (The Spenders)

26th Tuesday   At home baking bread and doing odds & ends at the sam time   Johnson came up from Bear Creek   brought Doctor scates along John stay here quite som time giving me the news from Kenai

27th Wednesday was over Lake Emma trail lot of new snow at timberline Going out a moose ran over a steep bank fel on to ice could not get up still there when I got back try to help it on its feet culd not get it up cut its troat skinned it left hind leg broken stifle joint dislocated broken hip Jack Harney came in from Bear Creek went home to Cliff House

28th Thursday got on my skated ran over to Cliff House stod there som time & ran over to see Ed & Myers about getting som potatoes that they got to spare when they are going out Went out King Lake trail got one lynx came back to Cliff House stay all night had a game of solo and som musik

29th Friday Doctor I and Jack came here on skates was in on islands loking up som bear holes locating mining claim had lunch Went up Indian River to cannon [canyon] *I set out two wolferine traps Doctor & Jack went back to Cliff House*

March 1th Saturday Being up all night got som sleep to wards six oclock didnt get up to after eight stay in all day got wind off hill with rain feeling weak stomak still rumbling made som lye to take hair off moose hide had to postpone trip to Birchwood on acount of stomack troble (had earth quake this morning easy time)

2th Sunday went down to Birchwood mild but ran the skates most of the way Left dogs at Camp Friman ran down to Olson Creek and loked over Philip Creek on my way back just after I got back here came Gust Ness going after the Doctor his wife suffering with appendictas

3th Monday Started 8 o clock for Lick House was up there at 11 am had lunch went down Funny River got one lynx in last trap and foot of mink broke loose last cold weather stay all night at Lick House found note from Dr at Camp Friman was there 10:15 am on way to Kussiloff Jack went with him

4th Tuesday Came from Lick House walowing thru six inches of new snow all you come in contact with sticking to your snowshoes rested at Freman came to Bear Creek in nasty snow squalls saw roaring gimlet [ice boat] *deserted*

off lake point Found John & Wagner at home stopped & had lunch got two cans of butter just managed to get home before next squall been busy reading a novel The Spenders

5th Wednesday At home all day not well started fixing my net am very slow at mending smole mash [small mesh] *nets the size for trout Weather mild high wind in squalls but no rain or snow Cooked about two bushels doughnuts but they came out as usualy (no good)*

6th Thursday Finished the net went to glaser stream to set it there is now a larg oppening but water in the creek are muddy Was loking around for som birch to make wood fixed trail for hauling tok in som traps Fine weather saw new moon to day

7th Friday was up to flats fished the net no fish got home & lay reading befor I had brecfast John came from Kussiloff having stayed all night at Bear Creek dismantled the roaring gimblet he was packing sail & rope stay here only few minutes got on his skates & ran to Cliff House I went out sawed up som drift birches but quit as the wood was not good Tok up a dozen traps got one ermine had a bad fall bruised hip & elbow went up on Indian River cut three birches tok them to lake

Evidence suggests that the roaring gimlet or gimblet was an ice boat. Ice boats had been used on the lake before. In 1903 when George Mears was writing up Kenai news for the *Alaskan Prospector* he reported that three men "crossed Kussiloff lake in an ice boat, and as the wind was favorable and the lake glare ice, they made a trip in twelve minutes that usually takes three hours and a half to walk." [3]

8th Saturday was up to fish net no fish for breckfast harnes dogs starting to haul home wood got in five loads went out chopped four more logs hauled them to lake shore then set out net by time I got home it was dark

9th Sunday was out early this morning just as I had the dogs hooked to sleds a hail storm sprung up and made hauling heavy but I got my wood home just the same About noon Jack came from Cliff House he brought me three fish he went down to Bear Creek

10th Monday   at home all day   John Johnson & Jack Harney came from Bear Creek about ten o clock   stay here to about three then went over to Cliff House skating   heavy squals coming off the hills with som rain

11th Tuesday   was out & got three trout this morning   after that I have been home all day unable to walk any distance   been in bed nearly all day

12th Wednesday Stay home all day   Dr Flanders & Gust Ness came from Kussiloff to day   made the trip in six hours   Johnson came from Cliff House   ran my trap line   came in with a lynx & report one trap missing

13th Thursday   Doctor & Gust Ness went to Cliff House   I went up on flats   tok in trap line got one mink   was up Indian shot som rabbits for dog feed   Doctor & Gust came back about dusk   weather mild   Ice are getting pore   Gust broke in

14th Friday   was out fishing net this morning got two trouts   Gust started for Kussiloff   I had a trip on glaser flats   brought in a moose hide not feeling good

15th Saturday   Was up to mouth of Dirty Cannon after a piese of meat   found where a big ram fell off cliff   left hanging by horns in a crevis   saw five sheep all rams   one on the upper island was out for rabbit for dog feed   tok in traps

16th Sunday   At home not feeling good   in after noon tok a walk to flats to fish the net   got three trout   tok a walk up Indian River to cannon brought in six traps   shot som rabbits for dog feed   Rain this morning with heavy wind   warm during day   to night 42 above

17th Monday   At home making bread   still warm was out getting porcupine & rabbit for dog feed Dr was out & packed in som meat (cat missing)

18th Tuesday   Doing noting wort talking about exept it be cooking & eating   fine weather   a little colder last night so that ice felt fine   John came over on scates just to bring the skates to me but I got him to take them down again to save him from walking   Wind in north (cat came back)

19th Wednesday   Been in bed nearly all day not feeling good   weather changed from north to east   this evening I hear a rumbling in the mountains so we my expect a storm   was out fished the net   got two golden trout

20th Thursday   At home   the storm is on lake broke this fornoon   heavy wind   my wood shed blow down   heavy sea run   open water as far as we can see   Perhaps Bear Creek   was out and got som dog feed   I am still cripled so I cant go anywhere

21th Friday   went out after breckfast I and Dr to get Doctors boat from islands   got back about eleven o clock   tok a rest   filed cross   hitched dogs & was up Indian River for meat & picked up a load of lumber coming down

22th Saturday   A little colder this morning and I feeling a bit better so I tok a hike up Emma trail tok in all trap   Cashed 16 at cash & left one at head of Emma Creek   brought home eighteen had two lynx that have been in traps for long time

23th Sunday   went down with boat to edge ice walked along beach to Bear Creek   John home he came with me   picked out drift lumber along the lake

24th Monday   At home   snow on ground this morning   dispatched Irish to the happy hunting grounds   cut som logs for wood shed   got two trout in morning & one at noon   snow melted away but we got a drisly rain

25th Tuesday   got only one trout this morning working at laying foundition & floor for wood shed   was down the coast for som lumber & spikes I broke out of an old penstock   Triten to rain all day   this eve we had som

A penstock was a sluice or gate used in the water system at the old mining site.

26th Wednesday Started to Birchwood   Dr came along as far as Bear Creek   I went down to Friman   tok in all traps along lake shore   went down to Olson & Philip Creek

27th Thursday   Started early was up to Lick House and back again by one o clock   cleaned out cabbin and put away traps   this morning being the coldest experiense I had this winter fasing a strong northerly wind   Ice building in my mustache & eyebrows I could hardly see   got a lynx

28th Friday   Came from Friman   good going young ice   strong enough to walk on that was open two days ago   got to Bear Creek befor ten o clock   found John busy splitting wood   got a can of zeroline Pete left me   started sawing wood

29th Saturday   At home making bread   made a good lot   sixteen two or three pan loaves   sawed a few blocks of wood & rise som of the frame of wood shade   cloudy   a floe of ice came to this side   almost landed but then the wind quith

30th Sunday   Found that we had a new winter this morning   ground covered with new snow coming down   was lot more of the same   stayed in to middle of day then sun came out & I was out working at wood shade for about two hours lot of ice came up   look likes winter

31th Monday   Light snow fall but warm   just monkeying with wood shade   John Johnson came from Bear Creek   Jack Harney from Devils Bay was here a few minutes loking for flatfoots snowing heavy this evening

April 1 Tuesday   At home all day reading a novel The Sailor   Snow lay all day that it was to wet to do anyting outside

2th Wednesday   Working on the shade   Dr came back from Bear Creek   wind sprung up from Devils Bay with snow   ice drifted in piling highter on shore   just time to save net & boat

3th Thursday   Finnis wood shade   cleaned up about the place   Dr shifted wood to new shade I sawed som spruce   Wind strong from north east ice drifting towards Windy Point

4th Friday   Cold this morning   split som birch got two ricks in wood shade (chapel)   put in new floor upstairs   climbed up on first bench with binaculars looking far oppening in ice to get acrost to King Lake   no chance   blowing from all points of compas   Dr was up to dirty cannon   I sawed up two birch trees to split in morning if frozen

5th Saturday   was out this morning splitting wood & sawing   worked up to one o clock   sawed & split a rick into stove wood 5 x 9 feet   Dr was up loking for sheep came home with cold feet   have fallen in creek & got wet   weather changed to a snow storm this afternoon   gale of wind blowing thermometer down to twelf

6th Sunday   At home   changing my gumboots to a pair of shoe packs   tough sewing   it looked more like winter this morning than anytime   this ice have drifted in and the heave pressure ridges makes it look like an arktic sceane   blowing a cold wind   thermometer about ten   no oppen water to be seen anywhere

7th Monday   Thermometer down to two this morning at sunrise   was sawing wood   weather turning warmer   was down lake shore shooting rabbit for dog feed   climbed the hill so I could look over the ice   reading som trash by Ruddard Kiplin

8th Tuesday   Cold this morning but by noon it changed   wind comming off the hill and turn mild   blowing hard for a spell but it quit this evening   wind is comming up the lake   Sawed som wood   got the last log on the saw

9th Wednesday   Finis the wood pile this morning & I think that I got enough wood to last me all winter   wind came off mountains and drove the ice away so we are in open water exept from this point to below old mill   fixed stem of schiff this evening

10th Thursday   At home all day not feeling good found an old novel read it   Weather calm & warmer with light mist   feeling like a spring day had a boon fire distroying the rubbish

11th Friday   Awok this morning to find that we had a brand new winter with about five inches of snow   tok a walk to foothils loking for bear tracks   no sight   ice came in from Devils Bay (Locked in)

12th Saturday   At home all day trying to make bread but yeast was slow that it tok to nearly night befor I started baking   Blow from Devils Bay

13th Sunday   Hauled the boat over cakes of ice to open water   pulled out a way but wind was quite strong   som ice drifting but a fair day messing around with ting about cabbin

Back to Kenai and salmon fishing for the summer. Berg's house in Kenai was centrally located near the Orthodox Church, next to Carl Petterson's home.[4] When the days grew short again Andrew headed inland.

1924   Left Kenai for lake Tustemina

October 3th Friday   Came down to Kussiloff

Saturday 4th   Started early got up to Victors cabbin

Sunday 5th   Pulled up by tow line to foot of moose horn rapids

Monday 6th   Towed to head of moose horn saw Alex Lind & John Landman coming up with two boats   went by motor to penninsula   wind to strong went back to trail point   followed shore to Camp Friman   saw moose   got shot at bear (found two strangers at Friman)

Tuesday 7th   Came home   fine weather   got home early   Met the strangers below Bear Creek they was loking for Emil Ness cabbin   told them where to find cabbin

Wednesday 8th   was up over home trail   rain snowing & blowing on the hills

Thursday 9th   was up to foot of glaser looking for bear   saw one sheep no bear

Friday 10th   Raining   stay in camp all day putting away provisions   cut grass out of trail made new sight for my 22 pistol   Clearing towards evening   snow down low in hills   had heavy lightning & tunder during last night with big fall of hail

[Cole writes:] *October 11th 1924*

RL Cole   H I Stager   departed for Birch Creek after having a very successful sheep hunt Guided by the giniel guide and hunter Andrew Berg

Roy L. Cole was Master of the U.S.F.S. "Teal," in charge of salmon management in Cook Inlet for the Bureau of

Fisheries. The Bureau was responsible for enforcing of regulations and monitoring spawning escapements (counting the salmon which "escaped capture" on their return journey to their spawning grounds). Cole would hire Berg to work as a temporary employee of the Bureau of Fisheries in 1925.[5]

Friday 17th Oct 1924   Started from Kenai at low water   ran again the tide   got to Gust Ness place in three hours   found Alex Demidoff there helping Gust with fox corrals   left a package with Gust for Ed Roth   saw Mc Lean at Magous place

Saturday 18th   Stay with Gust fornoon helping with wiring corralls   Gust & Alex came with me to Abrams   I stay there all night

Sunday 19th   walked overland to lake   saw Sandmann at Hugos   11:30 walked to Birchwood pups ran back to Hugos   I went right back after them   stay at Hugos all night

Monday 20th   Chas Sandman & I walked to Camp Friman had lunch   he went up to Emil Ness cabbin   I tok a hunt for bear   both of us back to Friman by night

"Chas Sandman" is probably Kasilof resident Charles Sands. A fifty year old Finn who emigrated in 1891, Sands was a salmon fisherman.[6]

Tuesday 21th   Left Friman for this place about noon   got here in good time   machine running fine   had lunch   set out net   saw tracks of wath we expected was the doctors parti on the beach and up here

Wednesday 22th   In camp all day   was going to Devils Bay to see Dr Flanders but it started to snow then we heard an evinrude   Dr sent a siwash & a nig with a load of junk from Cliff House   I made yeast   been at home reading new agr   had a walk up creek saw a track of mink and lynx

Thursday 23th   Started to blow last night from the glaser but quit som time after dark   mild   feel like rain   set bread and fixing tings about the place   about one Sandman came over with Doc & his outfit   machine broke down Dr was in loking for repair parts   starting to rain with som wind from north

Fox pens at Jensen and Madsen's. The wire fencing had to be run several feet underground to prevent the animals from digging out. Separate enclosures and houses were required for each breeding pair. The investment of time and materials was substantial. Photos courtesy of Susan and Joe Perletti.

Friday 24th   Caught 7 trout this morning   Chas Sand went down lake going to Hugos cabbin   I had a hunt to find my tools so I got late started to make a stove in afternoon   Crist Jensen came from Penninsula this evening   Doc brought home my scythe   cooked som dog feed

Saturday 25th   was out early going up wall of Dirty Cannon   bear tracks a plenty   just as we was at mouth of cannon Dr party came   going to overhanging trail heard lots of shooting   we got one sheep   wounded one bear   Carlson was in reported Dr missing   brown siwash came thru dirty cannon had to shoot to keep bears from devouring him (that wath he said)

Sunday 26th   was out the whole gang hunting for Flanders   went to glaser where he was last seen   found no trace of him   in going home found him waiting at the boat   we came in our boat have not seen him   Carlson said he acted irration could give no acount of where he been   got them to heat water for use in hiperdermik   (working at painting dory)

Monday 27th   went up Indian River crossed at new breck   pup [illegible] came after us   tried to chase him back but was to far out   foun sheep track after crossing the river the second time saw lot of sheep   first lot 63 all ewes & lams exepting one   after saw a flock string out   must have been near one hundred   came in over Nicanorka Mts

Tuesday 28th   started early up the glaser flats to go on mountain for a sheep hunt   found a ram crossing from Rays mine   killed it about 8:30 am   got home at 10:30   rigged up a whip for emptying the well but had to give it up after taking out about 300 gallons   we caud only draw 30 gallons a minute culd not lower water in well any

Wednesday 29th   Crist Jensen started down this morning   I help him load his tings then I painted my dory   Carlson came in he is home loking after Doctor Si & Nig on Nicanorka hunting sheep I started to go to Rays mine noon but could not get acrost Indian without geting wet so I came home   washing clotches & cooking tok me to dark

Thursday 30th   Stay home all day rendering som lard and doing odd tings   chopped open a bit of trail leading to river bottom of old chanell Carlson came in having been up Emma Trail all day   saw som one coming up coast from Bear Creek think it was one of the boys from Birchwood looked dog feed

Friday 31th Tok boat down to lake shore this morning but was not feeling good so I lay reading awhile   wind from north   sailed up to glaser flats   turned the dory bottom up after making everyting snug   expecting a storm of mts got only a moderate breeze sailing both ways feeling sick headache & reumatism every joint & muscle making itself heard from

November 1th Saturday   Lay in bed nearly all day sick as a dog   headach   one of my tonsils inflamed & tender as a boil   Fred came over about noon had som troble in getting acrost the creeks   Carlson & Brown siwash was over to Cliff House for last load of junk   I hear the Dr are still taking a shot ones in a while

Sunday 2th   Fred Sandel left this morning after we had an argerment about politicks   he have changed from socialism to comunist but apearently dont know or at least cant tell wath is the meaning of either form of govermenent   he left about 10 am   I was tinkering with a stove saw a boat coming up   heard an evinrude cooked up a feed for dogs

Monday 3th   At home all day   not to well yet to do noting so I stay at home   have a dry cough sounding deep in the lungs   weather just fine the dope party have som spare member they have been out som where   I have heard their shoot ever since dark   som one lost again   have not seen any of them for days

Tuesday 4th   Have not done a ting to day   not feeling well   would go and see the doctor but he [illegible] in such condition that the boys say there have takin turns at watching him   got my mail to day   eliction day   from Birch boys

Wednesday 5th   Got up about day brick   had breckfast and started to make a holster for my new pistol   Carlson and a niger came for Dr sled   they have decided to start down   had som truble about getting the amount he wanted to take in their dory   Carlson said they have not found his rifle   he still insists that he left it with the mining inspector   somting radically wrong with the man & his actions

Thursday 6th   At home all day putting up som suplies to take along to King Lake   about noon I saw a dory coming up lake   it was Brown siwash coming for another lot of Drs trash engine went dead on him & he had to pull

thermonmeter at 20 this morning   the coldest so far   dont feel good yet

This is the last we hear of Doctor Flanders. Apparently the wilderness therapy was not effective for his post traumatic stress syndrome.

Friday 7th   going in on Mexico Trail if weather permits   after I got to landing I found that I left my tent so ran down to Freds   found Ed there thawing ice out of his dory

Saturday 8th   I left Freds just little before Ed   he started to penninula   I got to my landing fixed pack for myself & dog   went to King Lake   fixed camp   found both of my agate kettles leaking

Sunday 9th   Working at my cabbin got only three logs in place

Monday 10th   Tok a walk over old trap line picked up six traps   came to my landing loaded up again   got back to camp put in two logs to cabbin

Tuesday 11   worked in four logs   had to spend rest of day before I found porcupine & rabbits for dog feed

Wednes 12   Got side walls high anough

Thursday 13   Put up one end log   ridge poles starting to splitt covering for roof

Friday 14   finnis roofing   was down to old King cashe to get som spikes

Saturday 15th   taking moss covering   broke trough frost shoveling ground   filled in loose & set up stove

Sunday 16th   Raining but I moved into new residence but had to sleep on ground the night

Monday 17th   Was down to landing   tok in lumber   made a bunk also brought in lamp & oil so I had it good & comfortable

Tuesday 18th   was in as far as Rat Lake   found two muskrats frozen to ice   probbably killed by eagles or hawks   also found beaver building onto new house but no sighns of lynx   found salmon up in smole creeks where I never saw them shot a mallard found it full of salmon eggs

Wednesday 19th   Came from King Lake cabbin saw two tracks of lynx   got evinrude started fine was home at two o clock   found som books left by Fred   think as they are radicals boosting som unthinkably ting for precedental [presidential] election

Thursday 20th   Have been home all day doing noting but feasting at several big trouts this morning & having had non crost [across] the lake I was hungrey for trout   started yeast   loked like a snow storm over glaser this morn   it turned out to be fine weather

Friday 21th   At home making bread & reading and fine weather for the job   I found it rainning in big squalls   somtime it got so dark that I could hardly see anyting   wind south east in upper skys but somtimes coming up lake

Saturday 22th At home   atack of rumatism & lasynes   been reading the Manchester Guardian about aceptance of Daws plan & London conference   also the late meeting of League of Nation   the truble in Ittaly and Marocko Rainning great gobs

Sunday 23th   Loking better this morning   went up Emma trail set out 17 traps   twef far lynx   5 for mink   saw two tracks one of lynx & one of mink   At dark Freds bitch came all wet   I went Indian River shouted but got no answer she must have run away

Monday 24th   I chained Fred Sandels bitch this morning when I went up on the flats with som traps   when I got back she was taken loose   he evidently have come after her   I set out 17 traps 10 lynx sets & 7 mink sets   fogg in mountains hanging low   feel like snow

Tuesday 25th   Raining to beat the band this morning so I decided to stay around home Started to fix my well   timber it higher & make a cover so I was over to old mill site & found som old 2x6 rafters wich I cut up to make well comming   found a drygoods box for cover   it tok me until dark to finis the job

Wednesday 26th   storming from the hils with heavy rain   had to stay home fixed a stove & tok evinrude apart   put in som new pieses   the house have been shaking as if it had chills

1994 photo of the remains of Berg's King Lake cabin. The building was approximately 9 feet by 9 feet inside. That was plenty of space for the necessities of stove and bunk, and easy to heat. The construction and corner notch are crude compared to his Home cabin. Photo by G. Titus.

This close-up of Berg's Home cabin shows his meticulous dovetail notch joining the hewed logs at the corners. Photo by G. Titus.

Thursday 27th   Still blowing and rain   fixed to go out to set som traps but started to rain so heavy I had to give it up   waited to after twelf loked a little better   I went up Indian set 4 lynx traps & six mink sets   clearing som this evening but wind still continuse

Friday 28th   have been home all day   got thinking about my evinrude tok it apart did not find anyting wrong   got five trout

Saturday 29th   Blowing in volys yet this morning so I am going up to Lake Emma   found the lake rising   nearly all my traps in disorder one blown into the lake got porcupines squirrels & rabbits and one weasel   set out two traps for lynx   weather fine this evening   putting tings togather to go to Birchwood or Camp Friman

Sunday 30th   went to Camp Friman   saw Cydon and an other man at lake point   one man at Emil Ness cabbin

December 1th Was down at Camp Friman – Birchwood went down lake shore to Philips & Olson Creeks   set out 20 traps   ran into somones trap line   blowing a strong northerly wind   met a young fellow coming from Kenai

Tuesday 2th   Went up to Lick House set out fifteen traps   weather fine   saw several moose

Wednesday 3   Came back to lake chopped trail part of way   set out thirteen traps & four aditional along lake shore   total seventy

Thursday 4th   Went up Birch Creek to Trout Creek tok in a stove and bedding but cabbin to far gone to be used this winter

Friday 5th   Came back to lake   traveling fine set out four traps   chopped wood   shot som rabbit for dog feed

Saturday 6th   Set out six traps this [illegible] started home half after twelf   foggy   saw Fred Sandels boat at Bear Creek

Sunday 7th   Was up to Lake Emma   got three porcupines three squirrels one lynx & toe of a mink   saw several moose   mild foggy

Monday 8th   was up on the glaser flats   got a lot of porcupine and trash but only one mink it being partly destroyed   set out one trap at Dowsons old cabbin got back early   washed clotches snowing for first time this winter   cant hardly keep meat

Tuesday 9th   At home all day   snowing   the ground is all white   som wind from the south started to make a pair of mitts but been feeling drowsy so I slept most of the time   clouds brecking saw moon just now

Wednesday 10th   At home building bread & sewed a pair of seal skin mitts preparing for cold weather   still snowing som so we got good track snow but I think it be hard walking   my go Emma trail or for sheep tomorrow

Thursday 11th   was up on the flats ran trap line saw tracks of one mink & one weasel   was to Rays cabbin & also into the mine   no sign of anyone being in there all fall   thermometer down to zero this evening at six   up two degrees by ten set out the net   I think we got a change of wether

Friday 12th   4 below this morning   went over trail of 95 to cannon then up to bear den trail down to Lake Emma   set out ten traps for lynx mink have tramped down two traps at Emma   7 below this eve

Saturday 13th   Have been home all day not doing anyting wort mentioning   to cold to go out with the boat and I got every ting in order when I can go over land   it is only two below but wind is quite strong making it apear much colder

Sunday 14th   getting a little warmer   10 above this evening after she have stayed about zero all day   hardly any wind just a ligt surf   started to sew som moccaisins but the sheep shanks started slip so I gave it up   my try boating to morrow

Monday 15th   Started acrost lake a little sloppy got over by one o clock   got to King Lake cabbin by three o clock   got a lynx just befor I got to cabbin   dragged it in skinned it & got the dogs eat it

Tuesday 16th   was over to Ratt Lake   set out six traps   got one lynx & one mink   snowing

Wednesday 17th   Came down from King Lake to Tustemina   set out 12 traps on lake shore & 4 along my trail   had four more traps but got so tired that I had to quit

Thursday 18th   Started from King Lakes early set out the four traps I had left   got to lake got the evinrude running ran down to Freds he was at home   stopped long enough to ask how he was getting on   he said he was ok

Friday 19th   got up early this morning but after fishing the net I cooked trout with potatoes and had such feast that I got sleepy   lay down & had a nap of two hours   tok a walk to glaser flats   no sign of game   snow is getting to deep to walk without snoshoes

Saturday 20th   was debating with my self whether to go down to Birchwood or not for fear of getting froze in but concluded to go as I dont remember a winter without a mild spell about three days before Crist mass   foggy that I had to run along shore   got into ice had to land about a mile above cabbin   later the fogg lifted and I went back and pulled around the ice field and got there allright

Sunday 21th   tok schiff and pulled down to Olson Creek   got one mink & two ermine   Met Windy Wagner he was on his way to Kenai loaded with furs and fresh trout for bait   ice as far as I can see up the lake

Monday 22th   Lake loking like it mean to close   hardly any water to be seen any where   got one lynx one mink one ermine   set out one more trap in Funny River

Tuesday 23th   Mild this morning but deadly still calm   when I got down to lake lot of ice but quite larg opening westward   nice and mild   shifted two lynx traps

Wednesday 24th   This morning at day breck I found the drift ice packed in for half mile   outside every ting looked clear   I put my tings in the boat   worked out thru the broken ice pack outside I found quite swell running but not very much wind below Bear Creek   I saw a green horn trying to work a dog team at Bear Creek stopped the machine & talked to Axel Vitbro   got home fine

Thursday 25th   Birth day of the jew who was practicle repeating the prophesies & practice of Crisna of India!   mild   almost raining this morning but later turned to snow   still somting coming down this evening   have been in all day reading old books   stritched two mink & three weasels   heavey wether makes one sleepy and I had my share of it to day   got six large trout this morning   two of them with potatoes for brecfast

Friday 26th   Ran the trap line over hillroad to upper level   tok ninty five trail to bear den canyon   folowing bear den trail to Lake Emma saw couple lynx tracks and one mink track   never couth a fur of any kind

Saturday 27th   Feeling drowsy & sleepy this morn got up late   went up glaser flats got one lynx reset som of the traps   no tracks of any game to be seen   everyting covered

*The view from King Lake looking east
to the mountains. Photo by G. Titus.*

Sunday 28th Went up on the glaser flats this morning   it was that foggy I could not see anywhere   finely got to Rays point   it tinned [thinned] out som   I saw a larg ram in the slide over the mine   killed it   after I got it dressed I cached it in the tunel of the mine   ice was making this evening   I could see tinny crytals but now I hear surf on the beach

Monday 29th   At home making bread   got up early so as to get ting started in time   all exept the old stove was working rather badly so it tok a long time to get trough baking   I also washed a lot of pillow slips and [illegible]   it have keept me busey all day   I got sixteen loaves of bread weather mild about 20 above   still lake are skinning over it is deatly calm

Tuesday 30th   Ice as far as I can see at daybreck but I hear a noise down the lake and feel a light northerly wind   tok a walk on glaser flats to get som dog feed   shot several rabits and brought home a lynx carkas that I am cooking now for the dogs   all ice broken with heavy surf on beach

Wednesday 31th   was to mild to go to Lake Emma so I tok a walk over glaser flats to visit the boys at Chas Nymans cabbin   found nobody home tok me 1 hour 45 minutes to go over   after I got back I put the harnes on the dogs for the first leson   ice practilcle all gone

New ice on the lake cannot withstand much wind. Here it has been broken up and blown onto the beach in front of Birchwood. Photo by Lori Landstrom.

Chapter 10

1925

> *January 1925*
>
> *Thursday the 1th* going up to Laker Emma be back by two oclock tok a good long walk up 95 trail coming back by Laker Emma shifted two traps set out one new set. Never saw a track of anyting the whole trip rather mild feet getting wet 25° above zero still making Ice afully still Hoisted the water out of the well after I got home it was getting Raely.

Friday 2th   Stay home all day reading som old trash of periodicals and sleeping betimes snowing ligthly wether warm about 28   quite as a grave tok a walk trying to get som dog feed but didnt get a shot   had a bath   lost my sleep had to get up again   have forgotten the diary   it is now 1 a.m.

Saturday 3th   going acrost with boat if I can for ice   got acrost fine had to run in & out to advoid ice floes   ran close in at Nyman Coast talked to Ole (I think thats is his name)   ran down to Freds stay all night   Fred is going to Bear Creek

Sunday 4th   Going along the beach to my trail from Freds I got a lynx   traveling mean   lot of lose snow   got to King Lake Cabbin early   fixing som furniture   everyting bright & clean   quite cold

Monday 5th   was up the line to Rat Lake   set out four more traps   got no game   couldn't ever get anyting to bait mink traps with   clouding up

Tuesday 6th   Came back to Freds   snowing found Fred at home   had som mail   Xmas greeting from Youngs was all they brought me

Wednesday 7th   Snowing & a skin of ice closed us in this morning at Freds so it looked like I my have a time of getting home but directly the ice started to move   left me a narow lead   I tok it and got to Nyman shore   got home wind changed & ice closed in had to make a landing quarter mile south

Thursday 8th   Snowing steady but the snow is so fine that it is not amount of much on the ground tok a walk up glaser flats but all the traps was in good condition exept one it had a rabbit   tried to find som rabbits or porcupine for dog feed did not see a single one quite   snowing this eve (20 above)

Friday 9th   tok a walk out to Lake Emma snowshoed it all the way saw one mink track & one old lynx track   caught one ermin   the loose snow makes walking heavy

Saturday 10th   Stay home all day reading and generaly lazy feeling   sleepy and drowsy cant make up my mind to go down the lake as I would have to walk   to much ice for boating and a lot of new snow along the beach where I would have to snowshoe among lot of boulders & driftwood and the lake is ready to freze over   I think tonight will do the trick   thermometer have been hanging between 20 and 30   to night so far she is down to four above at 7 oclock P. M.

Sunday 11th   at home making a pair of moccasins   about noon a man came up from Birchwood by the name Jonas   was out got som porcupine for dog feed   wether turning mild   I can hear ice drifting

Monday 12th   Tok a walk up glaser flats to Rays mine where I had som meat chached in the drift   som animal and birds have been away in that black hole and destroied my meat   Mr Thomas came with me to the mine   was going to Nymans Coast to visit som boys

Tuesday 13th   At home   som wind to day but not enough to breck the ice that was making yesterday   I walked over young ice along shore this evening but it just sag under your feet   I can see oppen water out of Bear Cr   15 above last night but she are down to 4   6AM

Wednesday 14th   I heard the wind this morning so I expeted the ice to wash up but the wind was from the north east so it left a bridge from Woods Island to the first point towards Bear Creek   had the net at mouth of Indian River got two trout walked on ice part of the way this eve when I got a porcupine for dog feed   fine snow coming down making the ice treacherous

Thursday 15th   At home all day   snow drifting and snow coming down making it one of the uglist days I have had this winter   was out on ice but it is sagging when you step on it   was out and tok in the net got six large trout   tok a walk up Indian as far as Lake Emma trail shot a porcupine   wind coming down the river with drifting snow that I could hardly stand up in it

Friday 16th   weather permitting I will start for Camp Friman & Lick house   got down below Bear Creek the ice was that poor I turned back stay with Axel at Bear Creek   Windy out along line

Saturday 17th   went to Camp Friman chopped up a lot of wood   could walk on ice in bights but at each point I was forced to go up on the beach and wade thru the loose snow   about Birchwood I saw the slim biscuit shooter coming up on a pair of snowshoes   6 below at Bear Creek this morning

The "slim biscuit shooter" is another of Berg's whimsical nicknames. It refers to nineteen year old Ardith "Slim" Crocker who was spending his first winter in Alaska at Tustumena Lake. The young man moved on after his

Slim Crocker with a fine trophy. Photo courtesy of Betty A. Crocker.

winter adventure but returned in 1927 and spent many years in Kasilof.[1]

Sunday 18th   Walked down to Philips & Olson Creek   ran a line of twenty traps got only one ermine

Monday 19th   Went to Lick House got one lynx early   hanged it up   next creek caught a mink froze in ice   an overflow had started and I had to chop out mink trap and all   struck water & nearly ruined the mink getting it out

Tuesday 20th   went from Lick House down in to Funny River   got two frozen lynx   packed them way down to Friman so I could taw out all three at one time

Wednesday 21th   Started a roring fire 7 am to taw the lynx wich I found still hard as rock   tok me to 11:30 for I was redy to start home   struck wick ice   got to Bear Creek a little after two they told me that it have been 20 below several days   Martin (of Nyman) was at Bear Creek

Thursday 22th   Cold this morning   I tok a long hike over the hill   started late after eleven got swetty climbing and lot of loose snow   sun was back of Mts when I was at Lake Emma   little draft of wind I nearly froze my face 15 below after I got home   saw tracks of one lynx & cub and one mink track   several traps foul

Friday 23th   was up on glaser flats all traps just as I left them   saw tracks of a wolferine the first I seen this winter   wether still continuing cold 17 below this morning 15 below right now 9 pm

Saturday 24th   20 below this morning   tings cold in the house but my yeast and flour is cold that the batter I fix was very slow starting   Fred cam over to borrow an axe rip saw & plane he is going to build a sled   got the bread finis after nine   had a bath & changed clotches

Sunday 25th At home all day rather cold to be out 20 below this morning feeling lazy washed my underware   lay down to have a sleep afternoon harnes my dogs   tok a run to Bear Creek saw Axel Wagner was up hill   they have 25 or 26 below at Bear Creek   just loked at thermometer 16 below

Monday 26th   16 below this morning   I waited to sun warmed tings up a bit them went acrost the lake   tramped in to King Lake cabbin   saw a couple of lynx tracks but noting but trash in my traps owls porcupine rabits squirrils   went out shot three porcupines for dog feed   sawed up som wood   getting dark and cold by this time the logs in cabbin wall was snapping like pistol shots

Tuesday 27th   Milder this morning but still feeling cold with a light north west breeze cutting thru a fellow   ran the upper line   got back early intinding to go home but it turned cold again so I decided to stay   lynx have sprung two of my traps just left a few hair

Wednesday 28th   Started home   got to Tustumina 10:30 am   had ten traps to run   got a lynx in the last trap   got home one o clock   everting in cabbin froze up   am busy to put tings up for a trip to Kenai   4 below

Thursday 29th   Starting for Kenai went as far as Hugos digout   Sandman was away

Friday 30th   snowshoed thru to Abs Fox Ranch

Saturday 31th   went along Wiliamsons trail   met som boys from Nelchik who brought a man that have shot his hand to Doctor

[In Kenai] February Sunday 1th   Pesticating a jew to be paid my price and sold him my furs

Fur prices were down this year. Average payments were $17 for lynx, $7 for mink and 80 cents for ermine. Lynx had averaged $22 the previous year.[2]

Monday 2th   Writing letters   answering som hunters who want to come to look for som speiciements of big game

Tuesday 3th   Found out that Game Warden was expected to bring som mail (first class) so I decided to wait to he comes

Wednesday 4th   Game warden came late this evening   I got several important letters

Thursday 5th   writing all day   met Otto Shroder & his chum Ernest Lindeman who just arrived from San Francisco

Friday 6th   went to Kussiloff had lunch with Victor   met the fur buyer that bought my furs on his way back from Nelchik   stay all night at Abbs

Saturday 7th   Stay all night at Sandman   lost my knife   was at Hugos at two oclock

Sunday 8th   I came up to Friman   running my trap line at Olson Creek got one lynx lost one trap in overflow   Sandman went to Kussiloff to find my knife

Monday 9th   went to Lick House   bitter cold couth one mink at cannon crossing

Tuesday 10th   came to Friman   turning mild was down early chopped som wood and filed the saw

Wednesday 11th Came home from Friman   hard walking snowshoed first part but it was getting to wet   stopped in at Bear Creek saw Axel & Martin from Nyman coast   Wagner was coming in just as I was leaving but I was on my way had no chance to speak

Thursday 12th At home all day   tok a walk to glaser flats but foun to much water on ice so I came back home Ole came from Bear Creek weather warm to warm to use snowshoe

Friday 13th After my visitor left I fixed up and went to glaser flats   found most of my traps out of order caught one lynx & one ermine   tok the wolferine trap out of Rays drift back to otter cliff tramped wood trail after I got home

Saturday 14th   Started up Indian this morning and tok Lake Emma trail   had a hard day of it snowshoes handled badly   most of traps out of order   saw a couple of lynx tracks got noting that have been my luck with that line all winter used to be my best

Sunday 15th At home all day   got my scates ran to woods island trying to find som porkies for dog feed   found none   ran back to Dowsons cabbin   shot two got one

Monday 16th Are having a lazey spell have felt drowsy and sleepy all day   freezening feel cold although I got it warm in the cabbin   I expect a change of weather likely a storm   light shok of

earth quake last night north & south motion   was out loking for porcupine did not find any

Tuesday 17th   This morning I found one of my pups missing   waited couple of hours thinking he was around lake shore digging up dried fish then went to look at the only trap I thought he posibly could be caught in   not there   comming back I found him in a mink trap   he have put his paw in to dig out bait   stay home rest of day putting new webb in my old snowshoes

Wednesday 18th   going to Freds be back 21th went as far as glaser flat nyman coast   heard there that Ed was at Freds so I stay all night with Ole & Martin   they have just got two more lynx so they had 8th lynx 7 mink 7 ermine

Thursday 19th Called at Freds on my way to King Lake   Fred had truble with a sled he was building   stay but few minutes

Friday 20th   was over my traps to Rat Lake saw one lynx and lot of tracks   couth none   several of my traps froze down

March Sunday 1th   Found a brand new winter this morning   was all hocked up to go to Camp Friman but thought that the traveling be to heavy so I stay hom   Krist Jenson & Slim came up quite snowing   only got about four inches

Monday 2th The boys went over to Nyman house so I made ready and started to Freeman   called in at Ness cabbin   saw Thomas   had a cup of coffe

Tuesday 3th   was down to Olson & Philip Creek caught one lynx & one ermine   all my traps on Philip Creek lost in overflow   left four traps & knif for Sanman at Big Lake

Wednesday 4th   was up to Funny River & back no game lots of moose saw about thirty

Thursday 5th   Came home from Friman to day met Thomas at Bear Creek saw Olle at a distance he was puching a sled ahead of him from Emils Cabbin just to have somting to take thier junk out on

Friday 6th   Soft snow falling almost rain   at home all day washing clotches and tending the furs   all I have been doing exepting eating wich I do continusly when at home

Saturday 7th   Tok in the Lake Emma line to day all exepting one trap   I must have been dreaming when I came by cache   11 traps at beaver mond 9 at cache point   6 at sumit   two at first set   one on fallin birch (total 29)   got one lynx one ermine at Emma outlet   Fished the net got tree trouts

Sunday 8th Had a walk out on glaser flats loking over my traps got noting saw one track of lynx coming back I fished my net and not a ting did I get so I came home cooked som ting for dog feed and started reading a story in Argosy wich tok me thru seven copys of weekly alstory Argosy

Monday 9th   Blowing a gale   mild   water pouring off the roof   was out to net got trout for brecfast   lay around reading   finaly ground my axe   went out and chopped & sawed down three larg birches for a starter to fill my wood shed to meet next   winters cold

Tuesday 10th   Still at home just having a lazy spell   fished   got three trout   mild & wet

Wednesday 11th   warm foggy   no chance of going anywhere to day so I put in new foot webb in my old snowshoes   Mr Thomas came up from Birchwood bringing me som reading matter   fogg cleared this evening look like better weather to run trap line

Thursday 12th   Still mild but I fixed to go acrost to King Lake but just as I got started I found that two men was coming this way so I turned around & waited   Thomas who was going to visit Krist in west bay did the same   it was Ole & Martin from Nyman coast   Thomas started later but Ole & Martin stay all night

Friday 13th   I went with the boys when they went home and got to King Cabbin about two o clock tok a hike down outlet no signs of game

Saturday 14th   Started about six am to Rat Lake running my trap line saw no sign of anyting to I got to beaver medows then I found a smole trap with a lynx toe in it   next two traps had a squirrel & rabit   then I had only seven traps left on Rat Lake as I came to the lake I had a lynx and so one in each of the four traps on north side of lake   skinned them & hurried home   Ole came off Moris trail with one lynx & legs of cross fox I came here about 4:30 PM

Sunday 15th   stay home all day making som lynx stritchers and strictching the lynx I brought home yesterday   fished the net and got two large lake trout

Monday 16th fixed my sleds and hauled in three birch trees that I had cut   I did not use the dogs I hauled the loads by the neck   chopped three more birches snow falling

Tuesday 17th   Have been home all day making bread & reading som story books   new snow on the ground & hardly tawed any   to day I did not even fish the net

Wednesday 18th   A lot of new snow this moring was out after a load of green birch but it pulled too heavy so I did not haul any more   fished the net but noting there   tok a hike up the Indian River   snowshoed all the way   saw no tracks of game   had a light earthquake last night

Thursday 19th Have done noting again to day weather bad   som snow falling with volys of wind hitting somtime up the lake somtime off the mountains   caught two larg trout weather quite warm in the middle of the day

Friday 20th   New snow falling in morning cleared about noon   hitched up the pups to see how they act on wood trail   hauled in three loads got four trout   tok in som traps on the foot of glaser flats & lake shore

Saturday 21th Snowing good lot this morning so I stay home reading to about one o clock tramped up on glaser flats took in all traps exepting one froze in   was quite warm this afternoon snow melting   hauled in one load to make trail good

Sunday 22th   Hauled in seven loads of wood today & cut som more for to haul in the morning walked out to the net caught 4 large trout   fried one smothered in onion (good)

Monday 23th Hauled in seven loads of birch timber this forenoon   started to snow & got mild it was almost rain before night

Tuesday 24th   was out this morning choped five loads of birch & had it all home by noon   got six nice trout   heated water had a bath washed up a lot of clotches

Wednesday 25th   Going to birchwood be back 28th   snowing to beat the band   fell about six inches of snow   tok in long shore traps   got one ermine

Thursday 26th   Tok in traps from Olson Creek pound & lake & along lake shore   lost two on Olson Creek & four on Philip Creek   got one ermine

Friday 27th   Went up to Funny River & back tok in the traps   caught one mink   lost one lynx found dead moose

Saturday 28th   Came home from Birchwood started to blow up lake cold   got here by noon looks like som more new snow

Sunday 29th   At home all day started to make my self a new knife & had a unhandy peice to make it from besids heating in stove as slow work   then it tok som time to cut the horn for handle   about three hours boiling to get it soft enough to drive Cut som wood

Monday 30th   was intending to go to King Lake but it started snowing & grew to a regular blizard so I stay indors all day reading until evening   tok my net and went to mouth of Indian River to set the net   to my surprize I found it frozen after being oppen all later part of winter

Tuesday 31th   was out early this morning to take in last string of traps   got two lynx so that closed season catch   lynx 21   it was a fine crost and good traveling all fornoon but later it got ofully heavy   the new snow sticking to snow shoes but I plowed trough to I got finnis

Berg's twenty-one lynx were worth $357 at the average price of $17.

April Wednesday 1th   Got out early to take advantage of running on the crost   dragging traps to caches and making tings snug for summer traveling far & fast riched home before one o clock   got the skins on stritchers & fixed tings in cabbin   cooked som dog feed

Thursday 2th   Stay home all day feeling lazy have not done a ting wort mention exept eating I certainly can do that after one of those acrost country runs

Friday 3th Hauled home three loads of birch set out the net   had to breck ice to get it in at river mout

Saturday 4th At home making bread   had quite of snow fall to day   noon flakes as big as my hand

Sunday 5th   Filed up my saw this morning & started to saw & split my wood for next winter finis nearly one rick   weather warm cloudy

Monday 6th   Raining and snowing this morning I was out fishing the net befor breckfast got one trout   about noon weather let up a little so I was out and sawed one stick but it started to snow and by five o clock it came down that heavy that it got that dark in the cabbin that I could hardly see to read !!

Tuesday 7th   Raining & snowing   not feeling good lay a bed to after eight   went and trying saw som wood but I no sooner get there then another squall comes along and I had to quit

Wednesday 8th   Still bad weather and only fit to be indors for a man not feeling well   tok a walk to mouth of Indian River to set out the net   saw two mallards   weather changing

Thursday 9th   was out this morning got a trout hauled my boat home   I found new snow this morning but weather been fine during the day

Friday 10th   Sawed wood all day and put in good hard day so I got about half of next winters wood sawed split and ricked

Saturday 11th Started in early intending to make a long day of it   by ten o clock it was blowing so hard that I had to quit   went out to the net could hardly stand up

Sunday 12th   Did not go to work to about ten o clock   was not hury and still I finis more then one rick of wood   I got the same amount finis that I had alltogater last year   was out to set net the ice is getting rotten at flats   saw two mallards two day ago   buterflye yesterday

Monday 13th   Was out this morning to get a couple of loads of dry spruce wood the snow is just going and I had hard work to get the loads off the lake   got finis about noon and called it a day   had a little nap & sawed som stove wood Fished the net and got two trouts

Tuesday 14th   Sawed up another rick of wood fine weather warm & nice   was out fishing and got three big trouts   clouding towards evening   I thought that I smelled tobaco smoke to day

Wednesday 15th   Have a brand new winter when I got up this morning   I found nearly a foot of new snow and still snowing but later in the day it got to warm so that by evening about half of the snow have melted away   shot one of the largest bald eagels I have seen

Thursday 16th   More snow this morning so I decided it was a day of lasure   all I did was putting a new cover on a robe   having a quilting bee   waded out to the net   the new snow riched to the brand of knee of my gum boot

Friday 17th   At home again to day just laying reading som litterary digest and an elk magazen later tok a yale lock to pieces to make a new key

and fix broken parts that some one smashed in breacking in

Saturday 18th   Still at home & doing noting   I still got som wood to cut but made up my mind that I would not bother with it to the new snow melted

Sunday 19th   Clear and frosty & a new musik when I got out after breckfast   I heard sea gulls making noyse anough to carry from glaser flats to here   when I was out fishing the net I saw lots of them   som ducks came a few days ago   have been getting three trout each morning for several day   sawed som wood so I got only couple sticks left

Monday 20th   Blowing a gail this morning so I stay in bed as long as there was any sleep left got to reading som light story dept   on to about four the wind let up I got out & finnis the wood pile   was out this eve to set the net   Frency left behind   is not home yet   nearly bed time

Tuesday 21th   Had a bath   changed clotches made a quilt out of discarded swetters & four suits of heavy underware   made a fine warm quilt only heavy

Wednesday 22th   Started this morning to clean up and put tings away for winter   tok the sciff in

A trophy of a different kind shot in the 1920's. All predators were considered vermin in Berg's time. This bald eagle is in immature plumage, the men are unidentified. Photo courtesy of Wanda M. Griffin

& hanged it over head in shedd   started raking up the yard but a snow storm drove me indors

Tursday 23th   Doing ods & ends all day   starting to pick out wath I want down with me   fixed a old sled   scrubbed the floor   could start tomorrow but weather an still treatening and it well take a while to put my tings togather   set out the net   fixed som tan   put down a moose hide to tan   it should be finis by fall if the mixture is right

Friday 24th   Froze nice this morning for traveling but I was not ready to go so I been putting tings to order today so as to be able to leve early tomorrow   I think I got every ting in shape to leve for summer

Saturday 25th   Will probbly start down to day !

Andrew was employed part-time by the U.S. Bureau of Fisheries this summer. He may have performed stream escapement surveys after he finished commercial fishing.[3]

Further changes in Alaska's game laws were enacted this year. For many years the territory had been trying to wrest control of game management from the federal government. Finally, Congress passed a measure establishing the Alaska Game Commission. Four of the five members of this board were to be residents of the territory while the fifth represented the U.S. Bureau of Biological Survey.[4] The first regulation promulgated by the Commission was the requirement that any nonresident hire a licensed guide for hunting anywhere in the territory, not just on the Kenai Peninsula.

The popularity of hunting trips to Alaska reflected the prosperity of the times during the latter 1920s. One entrepreneur in Anchorage, Gus Gelles, started making big plans for marketing Tustumena Lake for the next hunting season. After scouting the Peninsula, he selected Birchwood as the future site for his "Alaska Glacier Tours" base camp for sheep and moose hunting in 1926.[5]

Meanwhile, plenty of hunters were enjoying Tustumena Lake this year. At least three parties there took advantage of Andrew Berg's absentee hospitality:

Sunday Aug 30   The following has been occupying this cabin since tuesday on sheep hunt P. O. Beaulien Winner S. D. Bill Kaiser and Mel Horner Seward   Mr Kellar and Archie from Seldovea   Beaulien kille 2 rams near mout of north fork   the other south   Many thanks for use of cabin & couvenien   now leaving for Friman Camp for moose

Thurs Sept 3   The following party has been at your cabin hunting sheep on south fork   got three sheep and one black bear   Mr & Mrs Brands from Johnstown Penn, Al Peil, Jack Lean, Frank Revell, and Alex Bolan of Seward Alaska

Monday Sept 14   Party of nine which included Major Byron Capt Stewart Lieut Pence Lient Caldwell Lieut Byron Sgt Schmitz Sgt Johnston and Fred Judd (Guide) all of Anchorage and Mr Hal G Evarts (Author) of Hutchinson Kansas arrived here thursday the 10th and camped outside but left things in cabin   On Friday morning Mr Evarts Judd Caldwell & Pence went up Indian Creek about nine miles to cabin and siwashed until monday getting four nice rams   as Mr Berg has mentioned in his diary the porcupines have taken possession of cabin so we built lean to   used all the rice and some beans and all of coffee as two of party got caught

Gus Gelles incorporated air travel into his outfitting business and worked with Russ Merrill's Anchorage Air Transport Inc. This photo shows Merrill taxiing on Tustumena Lake. Photo courtesy of Wanda M. Griffin.

on mountain one night which caught us out longer than anticipated   there is left in cabin there sugar   flour about three pounds of beans and about a pound of bacon   in returned for the rice and bean we used we left four army blankets tied in bundle to top rafter also a coffee pot   thanks   Merl Lavory

Andrew was probably guiding hunters this fall as he did not return to Tustumena Lake until November.

Tuesday Nov 10th Tuesday   Left Kussiloff saturday 7th   got to penninsula 8th   blowing a gale ninth stay over   got here noon 10th in fine shape everyting o.k.

Wednesday 11th   Was out helping Gust to get engine started   Gust Ness & Alex Demidoff started down was going as far as Birchwood or Friman to get rabbit or porcupine for fox   moose if posible for them self   but was ancsios to get home as quick as posible   been repairing sight on my 22 pistol and cleaned & targeted my big rifle   was out getting rabits for dog feed

Thursday 12th   tok a good long walk up Indian River to see if posible bears be out   walked in about nine miles to cabbin and back out   tok me from 25 minutes after eight to four o clock and for the first hike I think I am doing alright for an old codger going on fifty seven   Fished the net got 7 trout   cooked two for my self the rest went in the dogs kettle   heated water had a bath & changed clotches   feeling fit for an other trip

Friday 13th   At home making bread   a light new snow have fell during the night so tings looks a little more wintery   having a nasty cold & feeling drowsy   got sixtin loaves raisin bread

Saturday 14th   Snowing this morning   I am figting a bad cold that I contracted coming up & on my tramp in mountains   had a tuch of flu this summar and this feels somting simlar   Sharpened a couple of saws and put som tings away   had a good long nap this afternoon

Sunday 15th   At home all day   washing clotches reading a story in the cosmopolitan   working with som hides I had in tan that the porcupine nearly destroied   was fishing net got a bucket full of fish   lake trout & dolly vardens   cooked

up a four gallon kettle full for dogs   still fighting a nasty cold

Monday 16th   At home reading som stories in Cosmopolitan   snowing and nasty out and I have dicided to stay in to I get over the cold   it have settled on my lungs that my cough sounds like a vayse from the lifes other side   had to turn my boat over in the lake to taw the snow out of it got a big lot of trout

Tuesday 17th   A lot of snow fell during the night had to get out about four this morning   heard the wind roaring in the trees & heavy surf on lake shore   my boat was turned over but not tied didnt kick up any heavy storm but a heavy swells from south   just fine weather to stay in cabbin still lot of new reading weather

Wednesday 18th   Still snowing & nasty   tok up my net   have been working for three hours taking spruce twigs out of it   the heavy swells rolled it up that it was hard as a cable and full of trash coughin less to day but not well by any means dont want to go out any wheres to the wether is settled as I feeling good   anyway the season fur lynx are not oppen & here is no mink   I was after the game warden early this fall to get lizence for trapping he said he had no blank then but would be sure to get me the lizence before season opened & he would leave blanks with the stores at Kenai   he neglected to do so I am expecting him anytime   anyway I sendt two dollar with Gust Ness & Alex Demidoff as I had to get up the river on acount of it getting late

Thursday 19th   At home doing noting   the wind changed to south east and som milder but snowing extra heavy at times   still feeling sick but not coughing as much   to rough to set out the net   I can hear the heavy surf now & the wind howling in the trees

Friday 20th   An other day gone with noting acomplished exepting the dogs dragging away part of a moose hide I had in tan all summer been raining to day so that it cleaned the trees and the snow have fallen to nearly noting (Lake is way high)

Saturday 21th   Sun was out for an hour or two to day   I tok the dogs along & went to mouth of

Indian River   shot three rabbits for dog feed crost on snow making lot of racket   hard walking feeling tired   short winded   coughing

Sunday 22th   Colder this morning   working around house   north corner settled   wedged it up & chinked lower rounds   pulled up to glaser flats had a tramp around first island   saw several fox tracks   got eight big trout did not get a rabbit saw som but to dark

Monday 23th   Was up earlier than usual this morning   tok a tramp over glaser flats to Rays mine to see if sheep my posible be down   got snowing so I could not see   com back thru lower islands to Elbow creek   saw som tracks of lynx & fox no tracks of smole game

Tuesday 24th   Found a lot of new snow have fallen during the night   trees hanging full of snow so I have been home again all day doing smole little ting   washed a suit of underware puttied up the window   calking the corners of house   cooked up a big kettle full of trout for the dogs   was out loking for rabbit but got none frost on the windows first time this morning

Wednesday 25th   Another fine day to stay indors snowing & trees just loaded with fresh snow   a regular santa claus weather & I am getting tired of staying indors   got a bucket full of lake trout

Thursday 26th   Was up Lake Emma trail to day sawing out som windfalls   walking is very heavy saw one lynx track   but a lot more rabbits then last year   weather quite & still mild   expect more snow

Friday 27th   Was up early this morning to go to Lake Emma   after I had breckfast and it begin to show daylight I found a lot of new snow have fell during the night & I heard wind in the mountains   got blowing heavy   turned to raining by this eve   snow is melting fast

Saturday 28th   Was out on glaser flats   set out the first traps   put out seventeen   saw only one mink track   had to do a lot of choppin   just as I got to oppen flat a rain squall came and I got wet   a lot of snow even now after it have melted a lot

Sunday 29th   Started to go to Lake Emma but the snow was to deep   I turned back 12 o clock saw no game exepting rabbits   got an empty oil can full of trout this eve   24 nice big fellows

30th Monday   Snowing again this morning so that give me one more day in this mont doing noting

December 1th Tuesday   A little cooler this morning here   was som frost on the windows   I got trough with breckfast   dishes cleaned & cabbin swept som   after eight tok my snowshoes & started on Emma trail   thought I saw a boat on lake not sure   snow deep made fine snowshoing   set out nineteen traps   got home at dusk   tok in net got only four trout

2th Wednesday   Was up glaser flats   saw tracks of Olle Frostead   crossed the stream but she was bad with anchor ice   set out four traps   blowing up lake this evening

Ole Frostad was a twenty-four year old Norwegian immigrant who was spending his first year in Alaska. He resided in Kenai when not at Tustumena Lake.

3 Thursday   At home all day fixing tings so that I can get away if weather permits   made a battery box   mixed oil   putting up provisions   had a bath   washed a chang of underware swetter & towls   been busy all day

4th Friday   Starting to Birchwood   on my way down I saw Wagner who told me that he had som mail for me also som mantles for gas lamp and a trout net from Erik   had no time to stop

Saturday 5   Blowing a gail north east and cold but I went down to Olson & Philip Creek   set out 14 traps   found six I lost last spring   very little sign of game exepting moose

On December fifth the *Seward Phoenix Log* published a "Prosperity Edition." The Alaska Railroad had been completed to Fairbanks in 1923 and Seward was prospering as the "Gateway to the Interior."[6] Seafood processing, fox farming, big game hunting, tourism, gold mining and service industries were all contributing to the growth of the town. The newspaper extolled all of the progress to date and predicted great things to come.

Seward Phoenix Log

1925 Prosperity Edition

December 5, 1925

Sportsman From All Over The World
Hunt Peninsula

From the British Isles, India, Germany, Austria-Hungary, France, Belgium, Russia and Australia, and from practically every state in the Union sportsmen have come to Alaska and procured big game trophies on Kenai Peninsula, which had been termed as the big-game incubator of Alaska. Seward is the port of entry of the Kenai Peninsula.

...In later years Andrew Berg, resident of this district, claims to have procured the record moose trophy, when he found a dead moose with a spread of horns measuring 84 inches...In 1904 Andrew Berg, and an Indian boy, discovered near Kenai Lake the skulls of two bull-moose with the antlers interlocked. The heads are now a part of the "combat collection" in the Head and Horns house of Bronx Zoological Park, New York City.

One article described a proposed road which would connect Seward with the "westward districts" of the Kenai Peninsula.[7] The Seward Chamber of Commerce had already endorsed the concept and a "Special Committee" was at work petitioning the Bureau of Public Roads Department for construction. The suggested route was to run up the Resurrection River valley to the head of the Russian River, down the Russian to the Kenai River, along the existing trail to Kenai and down the coast to Homer. Dairy farms, pulp mills, power plants and coal mines were projected to pop up along the route.

With hindsight we can see this was a pipe dream of a prosperous time. It would be over ten years before a road between Seward and Hope was completed and decades before the westward districts would be connected. The dream would persist in the meantime.

Sunday 6th   Went up to Lick House   set out 20 traps   got there in good time   found everyting in good shape

Monday 7th   tok a long hike down Funny River set sixteen traps   came back tired

Tuesday 8   set three traps then came to Freeman Camp   went along shore to swimming pounds   set out ten traps

Wednesday 9th   went up Cow Cannon   tok up east fork went to little lake   set out 12 traps   got home to Friman after dark   snowing all day

Thursday 10th   Set the last trap near Friman blowing of the hill   snowing   gathered my tings to the boat   got every ting in was som time getting egine started   came fine   stopped in at Bear Creek had coffe with Wagner   heard the news got my mail & ting   by the time I was ready to go the engine had froze that I had to take it in to cabbin taw it out   came home fine

Friday 11th   Coolest day so far this winter   2 abov zero this morning & som westerly wind been in house all day   was going to Emma but had to fix yeast   tok me to long so it got late working at fixing my moccasins   was out got a porcupine for dog feed   this evening I am mending som mitts

Saturday 12th   Have been home all day making bread   anyway no weather fit to be out in   four below this morning & hanging about zero all day snowing & wind in squalls   My lungs on the bum   was putting on iodine against plurisy this evening but I think it is an attack of flu trying to go into pneomonia

Sunday 13th   Been in bed nearly all day my left lung hurting when I cough   put on idoine again to night as far as I could reach   I shure have my chest collored indian style   the biggest snow fall I seen for many years   tok a tramp up Indian River one mile

Iodine appears to have been Berg's all-purpose health remedy. He utilized it as a topical treatment for everything from torn ligaments to "plurisy."

Monday 14th   Feeling som better to day but laying down most of the time   weather mild was out setting the net   snow so deep I could hardly find the skiff   22 abov this evening   I think another painting of idoine will give me wind anough to climb hill to Lake Emma

Tuesday 15   At home   was out fishing got 12 trout   still feeling bum   towards evening Olle came from Nyman coast reporting heavy traveling creeks on flats still oppen

Wednesday 16th   This morning I started up Lake Emma trail   found traveling lighter then I expected   made the trip easy   got two lynx   Olle left same time I did for Bear Creek   I got back befor dark   fished net got lot of fish

Thursday 17th   tok to long to taw out the frozen lynx   so I had no time to go up on flats   so after I had lynx on stritcher pulled down to drift jam to try to get som rabbits for dog feed & lynx flaggs got none

Friday 18th   got up late this morning but after I had breckfast I turned the lynx I had on stritcher tok boat & pulled up to glaser flats   ran the line got one lynx   came from island back   saw six moose to day   snow quite heavy to walk in

Saturday 19th   Was up early this morning intent on fixing tings during the day to be in shape to crost the lake next morning   fixed a lot of lynx flags   turned mild   raining   shoved boat out swamped it   capsised it to get it free of ice washed clotches   scrubbed floor   tok in trout net

Sunday 20th   Mild raining and some wind   stay home all day   most all day surf at landing have been to high to go away with loaded skiff   I was out trying snow shoes but it was altogater to wet to go anywheres exepting just tramping trails

Monday 21th   was all fixed to go acrost the lake when I saw Olle Frostad coming up from Bear Creek   so I waited thinking of giving him a ride to his place but he said that he would walk and look after his traps on the flats   I got acrost   set tent   put up stove   set out six traps on lakeshore it got dark

Tuesday 22th   went up King trail   wet heavy walking   set out 7 traps   found cabbin all white with frost   bedding damp   tings nasty

Wednesday 23th   started up Mexico trail   snow to wet to go any place   came back   set out 11 traps around King Lake   sawed up a lot of wood started to rain   snow backing up waters started to leak   had a nice time trying to keep dry   had to sleep on the floor   chinks in wall at bunk got leaking

Thursday 24th   Froze up a little so I tok a chance of getting back   set out three traps coming out and set 6 more on lakeshore   put tings in dorey & came home   have broken my spectakles so I got only one glass   makes it bad to do anyting

Friday 25th   was out early this morning found that it was raining so it made it a day for staying home   lay down to read finaly fell a sleep   when I woke up it was making day   put on my gumboots waded out got two laketrout   blowing & snowing in spells   about one o clock Olle came over on his way to Bear Creek   fished net   got a dozen or more trout for dogs & sure doing good to our self in line of eats so we celebrate christmass

Saturday 26th   Olle went to Bear Creek this morning   I got in schiff & pulled up to glaser spit   had to go around placse & over hills in islands to advoid getting wet   saw a lot of moose but not a single rabbit to be found any where fished net & got four trout

Sunday 27th   Blowing & raining   stay in house all day   tok a walk this evening up to Wagon road   set out one trap   feeling dopy

Monday 28th   Was over Lake Emma trail   got one lynx & one ermine   was up there without snowshoes   saw som grouse   shot one   Lake Emma floded over   no sign to be seen of game

Tuesday 29th   Had a fine run to Camp Friman after packing tings to cabbin & cutting wood it was getting dark   set the trout net   lake like a mill pound

Wednesday 30th   Went up to Lick House   got four lynx & one mink   weather warm a drisly rain all day   got in about two o clock   shot two porkies for dogs   they looked so nice that I cooked hams & shoulders of one for my self and it certaily was fine

Thursday 31th   Went down Funny River   got two lynx one mink & weasel   packed ting to Lick House   skinned the two lynx   put the junk in pack for me and the big dog   got down to Friman dog tired & so was I

CHAPTER 11

1926

Friday 1th January 1926.
Raining & snowing to beat the Band
Stay in most all day. toward evening
tok a walk toward Birch wood put out
net got eight big Lake trout each
Time I fished

Saturday 2th   was down to Olson & Philip Creek got one lynx   three mink   two ermine   got one mink on lakeshore

Sunday 3th   was up Cow Cannon to Birch Creek wall   got four lynx   set out twelf traps

Monday 4th   Piled junk in schiff came home fine weather   a regular summer day   got busy strictched 3 mink 3 lynx 2 ermine

Tuesday 5th   was still raining this morning but after it got daylight it stopped   fished net   got ten nice trout lake   so rough that I could not go out with the boat so I had to haul it in   been busy making stritchers & stritching Lynx   but I got eleven on the boards now but say it keeps me hurrying   made five new boards & most of lumber had to be split from trees   sea gulls came back today thinking it spring

Wednesday 6th   Started yeast this morning & commenced to turn som lynx then I decided to go out and get dog feed   Meet Ole Frostad so I came back home   he brought me a lynx from glaser flats   Sea guls shure tok this long spell

for spring   they are along there nesting grounds turned & hang out the rest of lynx   set out net by that time it was dark   still mild   about 44   no snow

Thursday 7th   Hard labor all day building bread it is now after six & still have one pan to bake got only two trout this morning   just wondering if the guls have somting to do with it   still mild

Friday 8th   was up to Lake Emma the second time this winter without using snowshoes   got one lynx & two minks   loked like a snow storm this morning on the mountains but did not materialise yet   still warm but not wet   got 8 trout

Saturday 9th   was cleaning & stritching the minks this morning   blowing a gale   went up on flats had a nasty fall   got one lynx did not go to island skinned a couple porcupines for dog feed raining   rough   I did not fish the net

Sunday 10th   Got up late   being lazy   feeling like snow   cleared up som   sun shining   got a bucket full of trout   cooked two for myself the rest I cooked for dogs   stritched the lynx I brought in yesterday   made som snowshoe strings during after noon I set fire to dead grass it went good just then it started to rain   now I am just through washing som clotches

Monday 11th   At home again another day   this morning the skys was clear but som catspaws came off the hills   the ground covered with about two inches of snow   turning mild again   38 abov this evening   the air feels heavy

Tuesday 12th   Ran over to tent   south shore   set out six traps on lake shore   after setting the net it was getting dark   noting in the traps on lake shore exepting owls and such trash

Wednesday 13th   Went acrost ridge to King Lake got 3 lynx   the net was full of the nicest kinds of trouts   mild but fine going

Thursday 14th   Was up to Rat Lake   set out sixteen traps   mild   getting my feet wet

Ole Frostad in a domestic moment. The picture was probably taken in the 1930s in Kenai where Ole was raising his family. Photo courtesy of Ella and John Secora.

Friday 15th   Started early from King Lake   got to big lake Tustumina just after day breck   ran in by way of Devils Bay   nobody home anyplace got one lynx this morning   to early to se shoot was home about noon   Ole Frostad came up from Bear Creek

Saturday 16th   tok a walk on glaser flats trying to get to Ray Curtis mine but was cut off by creek rising on acount of anchor ice   lost mink by eagle   saw two moose   Ole went with my sciff to Nyman Coast

Sunday 17th   was in bed to daylight after reading som cheap trash to after midnight   tok in net got three trout   after bredkfast went up Lake Emma trail   got four lynx   Ole came back about elevin

Monday 18th   Have been at home all day   didnt wake up to almost day   Ole Frostad went over glaser flats to Nymans Coast   I tok four lynx off stritchers & put on four more   fixed my old mitts & plated my old briches   would have sent them Tiffanys had it been more convinient   wether still holding nice & warm   calm to night with near first quarter of moon showing thru a fleesy sky

Tuesday 19th   weather permitting going to Camp Friman

[Ole wrote:] *Friday 22th   Took a look in to your place   going over to Bear Creek   was over to Ed Roth yesterday he did not bring any news   hardly sayed that R A Grus got one year for to start with   looked at your traps on the islands   took some rudebakers from the cellar   Ole Frostad*

[The following four entries made by Berg after his return to cabin: Tuesday 19th] *Going down lake stopped in at Bear Creek with som provision for Ole Frostad   fine day   machine running fine just below Birchwood I got a lynx on lake shore*

Wednesday 20th   Was down to Philip & Olson creek   got one mink & one ermine   two mink have chewed out   in one trap under a stump was a nice big mink   I culd not hit him so I poked at him with the ax handle   got him lose from trap and he got away

Thursday 21th   Started to Lick House in a nasty snow storm   got three lynx   one mink   went on *down Funny River got one lynx and one mink*

Friday 22th Came down to No 3 creek set a trap for mink cut acrost country to old trail got two lynx saw som tracks

Saturday 23th Just as I was comming away from Friman I saw the dog team with Tom Odale Al Hardy game warden I ran down with dory to meet them stopped in at Friman and I got my trapping lizens came on home set out net and got the lynx on stritchers (now nine my bed time)

Tom Odale had come to the Kenai Peninsula around the turn of the century to join his brother in gold mining. He subsequently worked on railroad construction and then had a shipping business transporting freight and passengers around Cook Inlet on a succession of boats. Guiding was one of his many occupations.

Al Hardy had originally moved to Anchorage for the railroad construction. He worked off and on as a hunting guide and game warden on the Peninsula. In 1926 he and his wife, Alice, moved permanently to Kasilof and started a fox farm.

Sunday 24th Raining to beat the band this morning and I got anough to do to tend the furs I have on hand my lungs have bothered me som last two days turned the fur this evening still raining I can see the rain running down the window panes thermometer at 44 outside heavy wind off the glaser

Monday 25th Raining but getting tired of staying home so I split up an old oilskin tok away the outer covering leaving only lining that makes it light and still of service against rain pulled out to flats tok a walk along hogback got one ermine saw a lot of moose feeding in willows coming home got into squall that almost liffed the sciff out of water this evening the wind went down som but I can hear a puff now & then hitting trees

Tuesday 26th Tok a hike up to Lake Emma the only ting caught was a wolferine it draged the clog for about a mile then got the trap lose from clog so there went my strong trap wolferine with chain draggin warm as a summer day Emma had about 6 inch of water on the ice the ground

is tawed out that you can feel the ground setting thru the frost as you step

Wednesday 27th At home all day cleaning up had a bath & doing som laundry work was going to Bear Creek this eve but was afraid catching cold so I stay home wanted to see Frostad to let him know that I canseled the trip to Kenai pending arival of Windy as he my bring mail & I probbably miss him on the road (Summer weather)

Thursday 28th Bad weather stay home Ole came over from Bear Creek he expected that I start to Kenai but the way I am feeling and wet weather I dont dare to takle it anyway I am expecting Wagner and he my bring my mail so I well wait his comming Rain storm out to night again so it feel fine to have shelter

Friday 29th was at home to about noon Ole Frostad went over flats to Nyman I got junk &

Alice and Al Hardy after a successful sheep hunt. Photo courtesy of Dolly Cole Christl.

dogs in sciff when I though it smoote a nough to cross   went toward Windy Point south shore trying to get north end of my line on lake shore Black Ed have set som traps amitating [imitating] my sets so closely that I had to land before I could tell if it was my set or not   somplases setting in betwin my traps   he had one trap withn one hundred feet of my tent   caught my pup Irish in that   the only ting he caught this winter as far as I know   I got one lynx and a toe of the other

Saturday 30th   Started out early to go to King Lake   within 200 yards from my tent I got a lynx that got in during the night   tok it back to camp skinned it started anew   traps all ok to King Lake   went up to Rat Lake   no lynx   had out four mink traps   have had mink in all but three   got away   got only one

Sunday 31th   came in by way of Devils Bay stopped for luncheon at Nyman Coast   Ole was at home   came by Eds he was away   wath I brought in now makes it just one lynx each day for January 1926

February Monday 1th   was slow to get ready to go out   intended to go Lake Emma route but decided that it was to lat so I tok the skiff went to glaser flats   never saw any place so deserted two mallards was in one stream   the beach have tawd out & I saw leves of wild onions two inches long that rabbits have missed   rabbits certainly have a fine time cutting the green onions

Tuesday 2th   At home watching bread grow   Ole Frostad came over on his way to Bear Creek weather still mild   about 28   it sure been hard to have to stay home on a day like this but it dont help to try to save the soul when you have to have bread

Wednesday 3th   was out to Lake Emma   not a sign of lynx   saw several moose   got one mink Emma Creek   came down B Creek   no ting to be seen of game   no track snow   creek open nearly all the way   was over to mill site got a pipe for well pump

Thursday 4th   At home all day & sure hade a job unscrewing 2 & half gas pipe with out wrenches   tok me all day making a foot valve & conecting niples to get the right lengh   fell little

new snow this morn   now it is clear with south easterly wind

Friday 5th   Tok a run down to wher I was told som meat was cached   found it brought home three peases   It was just noon when I got here tinkered with the machine som   put on a hunk of meat to roast   this is the first winter that I had to use wheelborow to cary tings to and from landing

Saturday 6th   Started down to Camp Friman som swell coming from west   ran down to Bear Creek stoped machine and talked to Ole   did not go ashore   went down the shore with a light fair wind to lake point   there wind hauled to east getting stronger so I ran close to shore   at Birch Point had fair wind a gain away below swing to north east   got to within 500 yards of Friman   a gale brok off shore   machin hit a rock and stoped sprays coming over in sheets   tok machine of try to work in with oars but no chance   oars full of ice   all this time I was carried to sea   my only chance lay in getting machine started & an oful job   everyting icy   talk about Providence as I trow the wheel over the machine started barking with slivers of ice flying off fly wheel   now I had to edg towards Birch Point to quarter the chop that have kicked up   I finely got a shore and even wet as I was I was happy to feel the gravel under my feet again   was not very wet exept my knees   I had to stay on my knees steering with one hand and bailing with the other   the reason I was not wet I had on a lot of clotches to keep warm with my Parky over all   the first sprays froze is it hit the parkey make it stiff & water tight as a boars hide but say I had one sweet time getting out of it all   this tings puts togather is wath we call spark

Sunday 7th   tok a walk to Olson & Philip Creek got one mink   several traps sprung   tok two lynx   set out from beach & set then up Olson shifted one mink set to other creek branch

Monday 8th   was up Cow Cannon way   set out 8th traps for lynx   shifted two   no sign of game snow glasy hard

Tuesday 9th   went up to Lickhouse & down Funny River   got two mink one lynx

Wednesday 10 Came back to Freman early   tok a walk down to Philip Creek   not a sign of a ting althoug there is half inch new snow

Thursday 11th   was ready to com home and started to put tings in boat but not likeing the looks of the sky I decided to stay over another day and good ting to   in a half hour a gale from north   tok a walk up cow cannon   set 5 mink traps

Friday 12th   Started early   fine weather but looked treatening   heavy clouds bedding under the sun indicating bad weather   got home about eleven   an hour later a gale blowing off the glaser

Saturday 13th   Lay in bed to after seven this morning   fished the net got four trout   cooked one nice big fellow with potatoes & it was so dog gone good that I finis the whole mess but it made me drousy & I had to have a fifteen minuts nap before I could do anyting   tended the furs I brought   mixed som gasaline   tok a walk loking for porcupines   found none   a young moose is camping about thirty yards from cabbin & I have a fine chance to learn the pups not to chase moose

Sunday 14th   Going to Lake Emma be back one or two o clock   was back by 12n   had lunch & rested one hour   having caught noting on Emma line I decided to try glaser flats   left here 1:15   bad crosing on Indian River   got back here by 5 pm   got two lynx   skinned them   caught one mink   lost wolverine   went off with one of my good traps again   just finis stritching & cleaning the furs and it is bed time

Monday 15th   One o clock just back from Ole's place   when I got close to his house I found his tracks leading this way   tok it for granted that he was on his way to Bear Creek so I rushed in to his house grabbed the bottle of iodine that I came to get hurried back thinking to catch him here but he must have gone som place els   tok me 1 hour 30 min coming back want to go to lake shore & King Lake

line but weather have looked treatening for several days

Tuesday 16th   Expected Ole to day   tok a walk on flats this morning was back by eleven   after luncheon I was running the steam laundry   I supose thats wath you would call it   I was rubbing the clotches and steaming to beat the band when I was out working the clotches wringer   just at dusk I heard a lynx yelling & I had four traps left in the shed   I went out on old creek bed & set traps ones by moonlight   me setting traps after I heard the lynx is somting like the woman who forgot to put the yeast in the dough trew it in the oven where the bread was baking   Have also been trying to sew som canvas into a pack sack for one of the young dogs   sure have a time to get the butt end of nidle [needle] hit the pawm [palm]

[Ole writes:] *Wednesday 18th 17 changing dates was only going acrost a mistake I left out fifteen Called in going to Bear Creek did not notice you had been over before this morning when I saw the dog tracks   I was up glacier flat that day you was over   got three lynxs   three minks and two weasel   after I saw you at Bear Creek   I see you have changed the date but not the days Ole Frostad*

Frostad's cabin on the glacier flats. This building was destroyed by a flood of the Glacier River in the 1940s. Photo courtesy of McLane Collection.

Wednesday 17th   Left late   going acrost fine weather   landed 20 min to 12   tok a walk north along shoreline had a lynx in the last trap   Ed have been feeding it   it was then laying on a pile of porky meat & the lynx was good & fat   then I ran south end of line but noting in it   3 o clock I was ready to crost the ridge   got to cabin about five   got one lynx each side of cabbin with in two hundred yards   (I was good and tired)

Thursday 18th   Frosty this morning   it does feel nice to feel it sharp at the ears ones in a while was on my way early hiking west to Rat Lake got three mink on the way over & shot som rabbits for dog feed & lynx flags   got two lynx on the lake that just been caught   huried back   stopped at cabin long anough to warm up a plate of soup wash dishes   put tings in order   shouldered the pack and crosed the ridge got to big lake 2 pm built a brush fire to taw out pump & hose for evinrude   came home fine   lake smote as glass did not dare set out trout net saw som nedles of ice floating   it is not cold but dead calm   anyting below frezing will run ice   water well cooled have been working for two hours putting five lynx on boards   I still got three mink but they are still frozen so they will have to stay to morning

Friday 19th   After breckfast I skinned the three mink & washed the pelts then went up to Lake Emma   caught noting   all exepting two traps was good   in one lynx set was a foot of porcupine in the other was a snow drift   the mink trap at inlet saw a couple of lynx tracks

Saturday 20th   Clearing up of the fog that have been hanging since yesterday   tok a walk up glaser flats   Indian River are rising in anchor ice that I had a job to get over   finely got acrost on Ole's bridge   no game exepting moose   In coming back the stream was still higer   the stream spreading on lake shore   I managed to run acrost between the seas as it was huge swell running but no wind   after I got home here comes a gale from the west   every sea topping   20 above

Sunday 21th   At home all day   wind radging high   getting cooler   wind going down   the westerly skye loked at sun set as if it had a thin coating of idoine a sure sign of falling temperture it is going down towards zero so it still give us a

chance of seeing ice   finis the pack sack I started that is about all I can give me self credit for to day

Monday 22th   At home celebrating our national holiday   a nasty cold wind out from south   about ten abov zero but it is cutting cold   made new foot well in my snowshoes & tok about half hours tramp thru the woods   shot four rabbits for the dogs   rabbits are getting scarce but those that is left are in good condition   (tired of staying home have to move)

Tuesday 23th   Will take a walk to Friman Camp if noting turns up to interfere   got to Friman ok nasty head wind

Wednesday 24th   was down to Olson & Philip Creek got two mink   was out evening shooting rabbit for dogs   found a dead moose calf the first this season

Thursday 25th   went up to Lick House   got two lynx one mink   went down to Funny River caught noting   saw the ugliest ting I remember having seen   on the ninth I had a porcupine in one of the traps   hit it with a stick to both eyes   blodshot out of one eye blod was pouring   trew it alongside of trail to tak home for dog feed but felowed a lynx and came to camp an other way   that porcy have came to and wandered around stone blind for two weeks   I could see somting was wrong hunted it up & put it out of missery   makes me sick just to think of it

Friday 26th   Came back to lake early   tok a walk up Cow Cannon   all traps standing fine but no game anywhere in this place   saw only two frish lynx tracks but lots moose

Saturday 27th   Have been blowing a gale all night that the moss was coming out of walls started home   fair wind carring me on   got to Bear Creek one   stoped and made coffe   started to snow   beach got slippery the little snow made it bad

March 1th Monday   I have been a day behind I think from the time I came up   this would be my last of february but as the fellows I have met have convinced me that I am wrong   so I have done anough work to day to give myself credit with *two days work and so we call this march 1th   after breckfast I set so yeast   stritched & cleaned three mink pelts that I washed last night   them put pack sacks on the dogs & started to Lake Emma a light snow falling making walking bad   slipery on steep hilside   got one lynx on the summit comance to show sign of spring this one is rubbed a little   skinned it   hanged the pelt & carkas untill my return   got no more game after reabaiting & fixing the lot   came back packed the pelt & carcas on the dogs   had to follow hilside way below in order to get down on acount of new snow   had lunch about three thirty chopped up the lynx & started it cooking for dog feed with som pearled barley   put pump in well pumped for about one hour to get the roily water off the bottom   tok walk out killed a porcupine dragged it home skinned it & fed the dogs for to night   the lynx be dog pudding for tomorrow when I get the pelt turned wel call it a day & a start on the new month   the old one was poor got only eleven or twef lynx but several mink*

Tuesday 2th   At home watching bread grow & I got a stack that surely well last but I fear it won't mad it out of hard wheat well sweetened & shot full of sedles raisins   I just set here tasting it and it take half a loaf

Wednesday 3th   Was mild with high wind blowing off the glaser with a little rain but feeling like taking a walk   I went up on glaser flats   going up the hog back at head of my sets I crossed to islands got one lynx in the last trap   just as I was skinning it up comes Ole   I went along with him to his place   had luncheon & my hair cut wich was the main reason for going over   got back home just befor dark   Ole got 22 lynx 49 mink now but was talking of starting to take up traps he also told me Ed had 4 lynx 6 mink wich is a wonder   he generaly gets nodings [nothing]

Thursday 4th   At home all day   nasty weather raining & wind from all points of the compas   one voley came up the lake that pulled your hair   put the lynx pelt on stritcher   pumped out well banded one oar blade   put a brand new leg under toilet   fished the net & got six nice trout

Friday 5th   At home all day   sawed out som trees that have drifted in at landing   the lake is

the lowest that I ever saw it   went out this morning to see where I can get birches handy to fill the woodshed   here is not a particle of snow so sleding is out of question   I my be able to raft it home   saw it at the beach & pack it up   got sixteen fish   among the trout was one white fish & one steelhead   first steelhead I seen for a long while   just had a bath & feel brand new again

Saturday 6th   Finaly found a day that suited to go acrost   went acrost fine   had a lynx in the last trap north end   going along beach with dorey to tent   walking to other end of line & back got to tent 2 pm   went acrost ridge to King Lake two inch water on lake   got one lynx

Sunday 7th   was out hiking by six   was up to Rat lake   got one lynx   tok in 14 traps   fine traveling early   light crost   went by cabbin coming to lake met Ed at my tent   quite of wind sprung up north easter   hevy surf on beach decided to stay over night   tok a walk to end of Eds line   pups jumped a moose for half mile & got a splendid dressing down

The back of Andrew's outhouse showing the "legs" which needed periodic replacement. Photo by G. Titus.

Monday 8th   After raining & blowing all night the heavy surf went down som so I decided to start home   there was a question how I could keep the sciff off shore long anough to get the machine on and fill the tank   got out but came near being trown in again just as I got the machine going a valy struck me & spray coming over nicely got so rough in a few minutes that I could not land with out swamping but quartering into it for about four miles to Ed Roths place I have shelter for heavy sea   got there by bailing & getting wet   Ed stod on the beach & saw that I was wet to the skin   a white man would have asked a fellow in to dry   not he   got here about noon ran into good weather exepting for light rain & it is a little to early in the season to set out in rain when a man got a tuch of pneomonia

Tuesday 9th   At home all day taring down the spare bunk & rebuilding it   tok me to noon   high wind yet from south east   caught a cold again settled on my lungs   they feel congested   big display of eurora borialis   whole northern sky is lit up   I sopose the next storm be from that quarter   was thinking of taking a trip to Kussiloff

Wednesday 10th   At home   Ole came from Bear Creek at noon   have taken up all his traps on that run   he got 24 lynx & two lines still to take in   I bundled up 51 lynx to day   intending to bring that bundle out   start to morrow if weather is fine   scrubbed the floor & done quite a lot of sleeping

Thursday 11th   Was making ready to start down the lake this morning when loking out of the window I found it snowing   I waited for it to clear up but kept drissling all day so I put in a full time sleeping & reading

Friday 12th   It was blowing & raining at half after five so I went back to bed & slept to eight got up & after breckfast tok a look at the weather & saw it was moderating   put my tings in sciff & started down at ten o clock   heavy head wind at Friman but got by   got to Hugos about three cut & hewed out a pair of sled runners

"Big Ed" Roth's cabin in 1983. The cabin and door were relatively short, even by local standards. Photo courtesy of Jim Taylor.

Saturday 13th   was up at daybreck to work at building sled   finis sled & started over land for Kussiloff   naked ground nearly all the way exepting on smole lakes was in ice   got to Abs fox ranch at five   all in and so was the dogs

Sunday 14th   Left Abs about 8 o clock   got to lake 11:30   pulled my sciff to Hugos   raining so I stay there the day

Apparently Berg made the trip to Kasilof to transport his bundled furs before the spring thaw.

Monday 15th   Left early   pulled up the lake shore   a beutiful day   smoth as a looking glass & wanted to save gasoline   stopped at Olson Creek   tok in all the traps   stoped at Philip Cr left four mink traps frozen down   got two mink

Tuesday 16th   Started up Lick House trail but it got to wet had to quit   got one mink   sprung a lot of traps   tok in shore line exepting to mink traps   my shoe packs starting to leak

Wednesday 17th   Came home fine trip   machine working like a clock   was here noon   make lunch   had a nap   stritched & cleaned three mink pelts   was out shot three rabbits for the dogs

Thursday 18th   At home   raining & high wind not fit to go out in not even to please on's mother in law   had the hardest rain fall I seen since last fall at Seward when you could have rode a sciff down the guter each side of that steap main street

Friday 19th   At home all day done noting worh mentioning   still stormy & wet   tok in a few traps off Indian River & shot som rabbit for the dogs   I will have to hurry to get in the trap befor season closes

Saturday 20th   Tok the trap off glaser flats noting have disturbed them   lost two traps there during the season   one by wolferine & one probbably by high water during flood

Sunday 21th   Here we are at home all day & it looks like a brand new winter   I have been worying about getting wood home for next winter but the way it looks to night I think that I and the dogs be busy to morrow

Monday 22th   I was out early cut six birch trees sawed them in short lengths so the dogs could haul them in the snow   did not amount to much half inch   one trip with bob sled & it was naked grass but I managed to get home wath I cud by nine o clock   an hour later & the snow gone

Tuesday 23th   Tok in Lake Emma line   caught one wolferine in a mink trap   one mink & two lynx still in fine condition as good as in middle of season   wind sprung up in the after noon but died down to night

Wednesday 24th   At home watching bread & cutting up som tin cans   gasoline & petrolium tins for finising roof of King lake Cabbin   I have to get there as soon as weather alows but the wind is dansing to all points of compass on acount of equanoctial storms

Thursday 25th   Was stormy this morning so I tok a walk towards Bear Creek to find out if Wagner had any rubber cement   found none   coming home the lake was just having lots of fun   the wind was strongest at south side   the wind on this side coming from north east the other coming down glaser from south east forming a rip down the lake   the sprais flying high in the sun loked good   raining to night with wind lower

Friday 26th   Blowing a nasty gale & I am not feling any to good but am anxius to get acrost the lake to get in the last traps exepting a few I had to leve at Friman

Saturday 27th   Here is another day gone & noting done to day   have been the worst weather so far trees falling & anyting loose as tossed about in the wind   yes it rain to especialy this afternoon (getting tired   to much rest)

Sunday 28th   The wind let up this morning so I started but by the time I got tings in the boat it started up again   I had tough time keeping along the shore at glaser flats   got to Nymans soaking wet from sprays   from here to my tent it went fine tok in the traps on lake shore

Monday 29th   Fine this morning   was out early was at King Lake by 11 am   went beong   tok in the rest of traps   got a mink & lynx in the last two traps   when I got back to cabbin it started to snow and I had to stay in to evening   just at dark it let up   I went out & chopped a ridge pole for new roof on cabbin

Tuesday 30th   Was out early cutting & splitting roofing stuff & worked at my best as I had fine weather & by night I had new roof on the cabbin tok a walk to outlet of lake   all kinds of ducks

Wednesday 31th   Got up at four   made breckfast and hurried along on the crost [crust]   came to lake about 7   built a fire to warm up machine when I tok down tent & packed up tings to cary to load the boat   water smote   had a fine run got here about half after eight

Berg's "crost" is the crust on top of the snow. Warming daytime temperatures melt the top of the snow layer. It refreezes at night, forming an icy layer which softens during the day.

April 1th Thursday   went down to Friman to get in a few traps I had left out & been out several days   put som chinks in Friman Cabbin & repairing the roof at Lick House

Monday 5th   Left Lick House this morning early in order to use the crost dogs ran moose I got them stop   Irish would not mind so I killed him with a 22 pistol & mad an o full mess of it   22 short to weak to go thru his scull   had to shoot at his heart to kill him   was out at Friman by eleven   put tings to order & came on home (seasons catch 55 lynx 31 mink 1 wolferine)

Fur prices were up a bit this year. Average payments were $20 for lynx, $12 for mink and $15 for wolverine.[1] At these prices Berg made $1,487 on his season's catch.

Tuesday 6th   working to day sawing wood   my first wood cutting for this year   sawed up all I have home   I probbably will have to pack a lot if I want to put in my lot in birch wood   thats wat I like to have

Wednesday 7th   was out early splitting wood frosty   splitting good   split one rick   sawed one stick   was out and got a porcupine for the dogs   tok in the shallow net   put out the deep one   fixing yeast ready to start bakery

Thursday 8th   At home making bread   when I had a few minutes to spare I have been out cutting down hamocks & stump around the place   cut down a large birch & sawed up four blocks   got som realy nice bread

Friday 9th   Not feeling good   ruiematism is making my old joints grone like an old bogy   som change in weater   sawing & packing home som blocks of green birch   started raining this afternoon so I got a much neaded rest   strong south easter to night   last night there was light earth quake

Saturday 10th   Packed home som green birch by the neck   just got four ricks put up so it will have to do   if I can only make my visitors act like white men in stead of siwashes & leve my wood pile be for winter   wath it is intended for

Sunday 11th   Have been putting tings to order overhauling tings & putting away for summer washed som under clotches   lifted north corner of house   pulled to glaser flats   shot a rabbit for the dogs   been busy all day & cant see that I done anyting

Monday 12th   Intended to go and get som game pictures to day but it clouded up so it spoild that idea   so it left me home with noting perticular to do just fussing around cabbin   sleeping most of time

Tuesday 13th   Foggy in mountains so I stay home all day   scrubbed the floor & when that was done I found an story book   tok a trip with Nick

Carter   after counterfitters got killed about seven times   com out ok

Wednesday 14th   Clearing som this morning   tok a hike to foot of glaser   saw about fifty sheep did not go up as I had only one spool of films with me   went through islands   found one ram down   just as I got to where I could get a picture wind changed & I got left   come home   was out & got rabbit for dogs & planted som potatoes saw som yellow flowers a bloming on the hilside som plases green grass was six inches long

Thursday 15th   At home all day been picking out tings I auto take with me   rain & storm south easter   my chest feeling bum   waiting fine weather

Friday 16th   I was nearly sure I would sail to day as I generaly starts friday but raining & storming   I have a cold and it settled on my chest & I am afraid to change to salt sea unles I have fine weather

Saturday 17th   It has been a fairly good day allthough it have been raining lightly   but I have made up my mind to find a nice day to travel if I can got everyting in order as near as I can see waged [wedged] up the south corner of cabbin would have taken out banking but all my shovels are cached along creeks & smole [small] cabbins

"Banking" probably refers to dirt banked up against the lower logs of the cabin, he may have removed it during summer months to reduce rotting.

Sunday 18th   Still raining

Monday 19th   Good morning   making ready to go

The following entry made in June appears to be an account of a brown bear hunt guided by Andrew for a Mr. Brown. Brown bear season was open from September 1 through June 20. The men were squeezing the hunt in at the last minute.

June 1926   Sunday 13th   Left Kenai early morning   came with skiff to portage   walked up to slak rock   went up creek trying to find Emils Cabbin at Coal Creek divide   got tired out & siwashed it that night about half a mile from cabbin   found it in morning   roof fallen in

Monday 14th   After leaving Emils place we walked along ridge betwin Coal Creek & stream falling in to slack rock   cirkling Coal Creek Lake north & east struck a cours for lake   got to Hugos tired out   jumped som bears this morning

Tuesday 15th   Left Hugos late in morning   got to Friman cooked a mess of bean & rested to about 9 o clock evening   started up Birch Creek saw som game moose lynx   jumped one big brown bear but alders to thick   got up to Windys noon 16th   getting som pictures of moose

Wednesday 16th   Rested the remander of day at Windys   ofully hot

Thursday 17th   Started over edge of table land to head of Bear Creek   jumped a bear but in alders again   left him in head of Bear Creek found a bear feeding   Mr Brown got five shots bear got away   cam on to lake   had lunch at Windys lower cabin   thermometer registered 82 in shade   walked on to here but had to soak our shoepacks in the lake every few hundred yards or scald our feet   butter melted in a can in Mr Browns pack sack that it was running like oil

Friday 18th   Had quite of rest exepting for getting up & killing three porcupines to keep them from cutting the floor out of my shed caught six big trout cooked up three for breckfast mowing hay   mending our torn garments etc was out in evening targeting Mr Browns gun found it shooting eigteen inches low in hundred & twenty five yards so we found wath was saving the bear

Saturday 19th   Got up late   got three trouts one the biggest I seen on the lake estimated 6 or 7 lbs finnis cutting hay after repairing scythe thermometer over eighty in shade   tok a walk up old river chanel to see if old foot bridge was still there   finis the day by playing som solitary

Sunday 20th   Intended to go early on a bear hunt but didn't get away to five twenty   went up Emma trail to timberline of Nikanorka mountain walked around the mountain to first branch of Bear Creek   went up to sadle of north fork found & killed brown bear   tok pictures of som sheep

weather still hot   saw smoke rising from forest fire som where in big bend country

Monday 21th Starting for Kenai 8 P.M.

The bear hunters headed back at eight p.m. on June twenty-first. They did not have to worry about running out of daylight. The sun is above the horizon for twenty-one hours at the summer solstice.

By now, the prosperous roar of the 1920s could be heard even in Kasilof, Alaska. Fox farmers had developed successful husbandry techniques. The good market for their furs was augmented by a demand for live breeding pairs. Gus Gelles's Alaska Glacier Tours Association (AGTA) had many bookings for the 1926 season and was bringing an entirely new level of opulence to the Alaskan hunting scene.

The business was designed to provide full service for hunters and tourists in Alaska from the moment they stepped off a steamship in Seward or Seldovia. Birchwood at Tustumena was the primary destination for clients this year. While airplane travel to and from Tustumena was possible, most guests traveled by boat. Gelles had invested in a tunnel river boat with an inboard motor, the *AGTA II*, which was the first boat on the Kasilof River which could ascend the rapids under its own power. The new boat cut the river ascent time from 2 days to six hours. Descending the 17 miles of river took the power boat little over an hour.[2]

Accommodations at camp were deluxe. Wall tents were equipped with stoves, rugs, dressing tables, spring beds, mattresses and bed linen. Photographic expeditions and glacier hikes were available. A sample dinner menu included "Cream of oyster soup, cold slaw, sweet and sour pickles, brook trout, tenderloin of moose a la hamburg with onion dressing, served with wild cranberry sauce; boiled ham and cabbage, sweet potatoes, white potatoes, creamed peas, mushrooms fried in butter, Tustumena frijoles, white and raisin bread, hot baking powder biscuits, strawberries, coconut banana layer cake, sugar cookies, doughnuts, molasses drop cakes, creamed Swiss cheese, tea and coffee."[3] Fifteen men were employed as guides, packers and cooks.

Gelles had powerful public relations partnerships with the *Anchorage Daily Times* and the *Seward Daily Gateway*. Numerous articles touted the coming and going of fifteen clients this season. Most of the hunters

The AGTA II ascending rapids on the Kasilof River. "AGTA" was an acronym for the Alaska Glacier Tours Association. Note the pitcher pump to the left of the driver, it was likely the bilge pump. Photo courtesy of the McLane Collection.

were quoted in exuberant praise of the new company before they left the Territory:

Although I have been on hunting trips in Canada, New Brunswick, Mexico, Colorado, Wyoming, Arizona and Florida, I have never been on a trip that will even compare with the one on the Kenai peninsula, from which I have just returned conducted by the Alaska Glacier Tours association enthusiastically declared Harvey F. Noble of Palm Beach, Fla.[4]

The public relations effort went beyond soliciting hunters. Local support for this private company was overtly promoted in this newspaper article:

A large part of the earnings of the company is spent in Anchorage for supplies. More money is being distributed in this community by the organization than any other industry except the railroad and canneries, officials of the organization state. The enterprise is virtually a new industry in this section. The association has no stock to sell. But is asking the support of the community, for an increase in business will also be an aid to the community because of the greater amount of money that will be spent here. That the organization will have a good future is forecast by the business developed during this its first year.[5]

The promotional tone in the newspaper articles is reminiscent of George Mears' reports from Kenai over

Anchorage Daily Times
August 13, 1926

Tours Association has First Party

Men to Take Movies and Hunt Large Game on Tustumena Lands

The first hunting party to be conducted by the Alaska Glacier Tours association arrived in Anchorage yesterday and will leave on the boat Agta for the Tustumena country, via Kenai, tomorrow morning. Members of the party are S. A. Thompson, Frank Hitchcock and Donald W. Brown, Jr. Of New York City, and A. H. Nichol of Fort Steel, B. C. The party will be guided by Alex Liska, Fred Judd and Andrew Berg. The party will remain in the Tustumena country for a month, spending its time, at first taking moving pictures of game. When the season opens the men will hunt moose, sheep and bear. The next party to be conducted by the association is scheduled to arrive at Seward tomorrow. A number of other parties have been booked for this season, the first for the organization. Members of the association believe that prospects for a successful season are bright.

20 years earlier. The difference was that the latest cheerleading was coming out of Anchorage. The village of Kenai had already been left far behind by Anchorage and Seldovia as a port on Cook Inlet. Now Anchorage was becoming the central hub for trophy hunting as well.

Seward Daily Gateway
September 9, 1926

Two Hundred Per Cent Silver Fox Increase In Kussilof District

Foxes in region are valued at approximately $250,000. Many of farmers had increases exceeding 200 per cent. Ample rabbits, porcupines, and fish keep feed larder well supplied. Weather conditions ideal for raising pups. Activities of region described by Louis Nissen, now in the city.... A rough estimate of the value of the silver fox in the Kussilof district is placed by Mr. Nissen at about $250,000. The value of the breeders run from $1,000, to $3,000 a pair. Mr. Nissen together with John Sandwick conduct but one of the many farms in the region for according to him every one is absolutely modern in every respect and all are continually adding to their improvements both in building and fox raising equipment. Mr. Nissen has been down in the Kussilof country for the last seven years but may relinquish his interest to his partner and sometime around Christmas plans leaving for the States where he may locate in the silver fox business. From eight pair of silvers they now have 38 pups.

Mr. And Mrs. Al Hardy former game warden for this district and who it is stated may re-enter the service this fall and assume charge of the Kussilof region bought two pairs from the Williamson fox ranch and it is believed both pairs produced litters. The Hardy's have completed this summer the construction of a fine log home as well as added many improvements to their ranch. Ericksen and West have raised a hundred fox from 20 pair a remarkable increase in a short period of time. Jensen and Madsen, from 11 pairs produced 55 pups well over a 200 per cent increase. Archie McLean raised 28 pups from six pairs of silvers. Gus Ness got 30 pups from seven pair. It was estimated that the Williamson ranch has about 90 pups. The number of pairs is not known.

Porcupines and rabbits have been very plentiful and there has been ample fish, all of which has been gathered in quantities for fox feed. The mild spring which settled over the region has continued all through the summer making for the best of conditions for the propagation of pups. Mail is received twice a month in the summertime but only once in the winter months, via Moose Pass down the Kenai, Paul Wilson has the winter contract for hauling the mail.

Fox pens at the Williamson's ranch by Coal Creek on the Kasilof River. Photo courtesy of McLane Collection.

Roy Cole, Andrew's boss with the Bureau of Fisheries, was back at Tustumena this fall. Cole and his guest left entries in Berg's journal:

Sept 3rd 1926   Called at Andrew's the day after the big sheep hunt from Cliff House   going after the moose this day & tomorrow   having a great time   sorry I can't stay long   Lawrence Richey asst to Mr Hoover Dept of Commerce Washington DC

Sept 3rd 1926   Here with Mr Richey investigating the salmon spawning grounds   excellent seeding is noted on all streams   visited 30 days earlier would be a better time for getting data on spawning areas   R.L. Cole, U.S. Bureau of Fisheries

Richey may have been Cole's supervisor. The Bureau of Fisheries was within the Department of Commerce.

According to an August 13 article in the *Anchorage Daily Times*, Andrew Berg worked with the Association this year, but not through the entire hunting season. He gathered up his winter supplies and returned to his Home cabin by mid-October.

October 13th   Came up from Jenson & Madsen fox ranch to Camp Friman   had a fine day machine walking right thru with fifteen hundred pound in dory

Thursday 14th   Came up from Freeman   stopped in at Glaser Tour Camp met Alex Liskie [Liska] and Tom Odale   have been busey putting tings

away   set out the net   dug up my potatoes   put a sight on a gun

Alex Liska and Tom Odale were both guiding for the Association. AGTA had big plans for improving Birchwood camp, as two more articles in the *Anchorage Daily Times* attested. Liska and Odale were to spend the winter in construction of a log lodge, smokehouse, ice house and foundations and frameworks for additional wall tents.[6]

Friday 15th   was out loking for bear but no one did we see   saw seven moose   one fairly good head   got 14 trout this morning   most of them dol varden

Saturday 16th   At home making bread   was out this morning shot four grouse with a twenty two stevens pistol   while I was watching the bread I sewed a pack sack of seal skin   made a place upstairs for lizzy to sleep in   Lizzy is my young cat and I have to train her to stay out doors & to take care of herself when I am out

Sunday 17th   was out on sheep mts today   saw at least 85 sheep nearly all ewes & lambs   saw a few rams at long distance   came home without meat   saw the bigest lot of swans I ever saw any one day   counted eighty this evening but saw a larger bunch in the morning   weather beutiful

Monday 18th   Finis sewing my pack sack   had Robert shooting target   got pived when he missed & refused to practice   cooked som tan   tanned

Pete Jensen's house at the fox farm. Photo courtesy of Susan and Joe Perletti.

the trout nets & a bunch of traps   turning mild
got twelf trout this morning

*Tuesday 19th   Raining this morning   tok
another nap and lay in bed to 7 oclock   Robert
got up and buildt fire   the first time   after rain
let up I was making a stove of a joint of hydraylik
pipe for Lick House*

Wednesday 20th   Went down to Friman

Thursday 21   Went to Lick House

*Friday 22   Thru Funny River basin to Sterlines
old camp   saw 50 moose*

Saturday 23   Started building cabbin

Sunday 24th

Monday 25th   Finis cabbin

Berg dubbed his newest cabin "Castle Inn." He may
have been indulging in irony. Like his King Lake cabin,
Castle Inn was about nine feet to a side.

26 Tuesday   Came down to lake shore

27   Stay at Freeman hunting moose

28 Thursday   Came down to Kussiloff

30th   Home to Kenai

*November   Saturday 13   Left Kenai came to
Kussiloff   stay with Gust Ness all night*

*Sunday 14   Gust Ness came with me
to Moose Horn   tok the big boat back
I came on to Hugos   found Sandman
and a stranger by the name of Smith
there*

*15th Monday   New snow this morning
I came to Birch wood   raining (half
snow)   stay all night   had a concert
at glaser tour camp*

*16 Tuesday   Mr Hardy McLean
Bartlet went up sheep hunting early
I came home about noon cooked up
a big kettle of beans expecting sheep
hunters back   heard a machine but
no hunters*

*Wednesday 17th   Had a nasty cold leaving Kenai
and added to it coming up that I have been in
bed nearly all day   aguing all over from base of
head to my feet   heavy south easter all day*

*Thursday 18th   Still on the sick list but feeling
better but couffing up som sticky slime   choking
similar to whoping cough   strong wind yet this
morning but to night calmed down   only som
rain   I have been reading som trash of old books*

*Friday 19th   At home all day still coughing   tok
a walk got a copple grouse   a stranger by name
of Smith came up half after two   change in
weather calm & clear   expect som frost by
morning   saw a muskrat in slough right home*

*Saturday 20th   Was up to Lake Emma set out a
few lynx traps   came early but would not go
around the lake as it was still oppen & wet
shoreline   Bob Smith left this morning bound for
Cliff House   quite frozty last night   som of it did
not taw even during the day*

*Sunday 21th   My ink was getting so lumpy I
tried to boil it   spilled most of it   the rest got
rather thick   tinned it out with some denatured
alcohol   got it better but not good   have been
home all day making bread and I got a stack
that will last me a month without assistance   foggy
& forzty all day   my cold still holding on to
[illegible] that I am afraid to take any longer trip*

The remains of Castle Inn in the
1990s. Photo by G. Titus

Monday 22th   Foggy this morning   stay in bed to day lighs   after brickfast picked out ten strong traps   set the out over hog back trail   cut alders for about half mile   saw several rabbits   killed two   no sign of other game   lake still upon glaser flats   came home after dark   set out trout net still cold   only fog from vapor rising off lake

Tuesday 23th   At home   noting doing   change in weather   clouding up turning mild   reumatism is treating me rough at every change in weather put som tings up to take acrost to mexico should I decide to go in the morning   got to have a bath to night   my cold still on

Wednesday 24th   got away from here late   ran acrost to south side   set up my tent   set out fifteen traps on lake shore and trail to King Lake   found lake frozen   ice clear   saw several rats [muskrats]

Thursday 25th   Tok a walk to Mexico   first time in three years   found it in bad shape   door torn down   window smashed   everyting in cabbin turned inside out & upside down exept the bedding hanging in sealing   one quilt and blanket was good but the other quilt wrapped outside bundle all torn

Friday 26th   Came back to King Lake set out som traps on Rat Lake   chopped and blased trail saw no game of anykind   there is no snow just som frost   I think I heard a fox barking at me on upper bench   got in at dusk

Saturday 27th   Left King Lake about 9 am   set som traps   chopped out som windfalls   set six traps on lakeshore & came home thru the tickest kind of fogg   found the cliff at island & came along shore the rest of way

Sunday 28th   At home all day   was intending to go up to Lake Emma but did not feel like traveling   my lungs feels plumb full and I am coughing so I had som work on my evinrude   tok it apart   soldered up a leaky tank   set out four traps for lynx on old chanal shot couple rabbits

Monday 29th   Was at home until eleven thirty then went to Lake Emma

to set a few traps I had cached   got three lynx on my way over   set out fourteen traps   got dark befor I got down off the hill   wether fine   frosty foggy on lake

Tuesday 30th   Went to glaser flats to set out som mink traps   the first I set this season   cought one lynx   quite cold   the creeks are rising in anchor ice   no tracks to be seen any place   no snow   did not see a rabbit   thermometer registered 8 abov this morning   did not go out to sun was over mountains

December   Wednesday 1th   Can hardly hold the pen to right   late last night I was out in the shed to get in an other lynx stritcher I knocked down the adze and cut my hand badly   Brothers Frostad came in on thier way to Bear Creek   they dressed and bandaged my sores so it feels better   they reported zero weather at Nysman Coast

Since he could hardly hold his pen, he must have injured his right hand. With two bad hands it is understandable that he could use some help dressing his wound. The "Brothers Frostad" are Ole and his younger brother Erling. Erling had moved to Alaska the previous May and was enjoying his first winter at Tustumena Lake.

Thursday 2th   Fifteen abov zero this morning   a decided change in weather   was out and pulled in the trout net   got a nice pan full of trout   four about 16 inches long   the boys came up from

The remains of Berg's Mexico Cabin.
Photo courtesy of Dave Letzring.

Bear Creek Wagner have com up so he be taking care of his own trapline my hand have not hurt much to day

Friday 3th Tok a walk up to Lake Emma got one mink weather changed cloudy stormy with a few flakes of snow falling hand feeling good

Saturday 4th Was out on glaser flats met one rain squall saw one good size bull moose got one mink set out two traps by cabbin after I got home weather mild & melting at noon

Sunday 5th At home all day tok the bandage off my hand and put on a new one had a job acomplishing the bandage the cuts are doing fine Raining out so I did not go anywheres thermometer up to 40 to night put in a day reading

Monday 6th Went acrost to south side of lake started to rain got wet befor I got to my tent caught one lynx on lake shore hiked acrost to King Lake got there just at dark

Tuesday 7th Went over to Rat Lake set out one mink trap going had one lynx on Rat Lake caught a mink in trap I set in morning set out two more mink traps & replased one lynx trap that somting got away with

Wednesday 8th After storming all night I started home at day breck got lake hurried my tings in skiff pulled along lake shore overlooking six traps I had towards Devils Bay got one lynx started machine and ran along to Nymans where Frostad boys are stopping one was home stopped in and had lunch Ole came in as I was ready to go

Thursday 9th At home all day keeping house snowing all last night and all day but it is to warm to make any snow to amount to anyting heated water had a bath made such splashing over the floor that I scrubbed out the cabbin too it looks cleaner

Friday 10th Started out eleven 25 went up to Lake Emma light snow fall nearly all trap was out of order snow on Emma about 8 inches sinking when I got home found Mr Lisker up having heard that I was hurt

Mr. Lisker was Alex Liska. One of his hunting clients described him as a Hungarian who wore a green eyeshade, spoke nine languages, subscribed to two Italian newspapers and was as strong as a horse.[7] In later years Alex ran newspaper ads for chiropractic services in Anchorage.

Saturday 11th Was up early making ready to go but waited until sun up and it got warmer was in at Bear Creek saw Windy left Mr Lisker at Lake Point to run his trap line ran down to Friman Ice making could hardly get in landed my junk ran back to Birch wood stay all night

Sunday 12th Walked down to Friman went up to Trail Lake on acrost to main trail set out twenty traps

Monday 13th Was down to Philip & Olson Creek set out twenty six traps came acrost end of smole lake end of Sands line

Tuesday 14th To windy to go to Lick House set out a few along beach & cow canyon got in early went on visit to Mr Liskie and have my hand dressed walked back to Friman in moonlight

Wednesday 15th Heavy loaded went to Lick House set out few traps in Funny

Thursday 16th Went on thru to Serline Camp tok one five hours of hard hiking made new door for cabbin

Friday 17th Went down Funny som distance set out traps for mink & lynx 28 in all

Saturday 18th Started back tok along eight traps set for mink in middle stream stopped at Lick House 45 min for lunch afraid of weather no snowshoes

Sunday 19th Blowing a gail south wind with lot of snow cant start home so I tok a hike to Philip & Olson Creek got two lynx one mink lost one

Monday 20th Came home early saw Tom Odale at Birch Wood & Windy at Bear tok a walk up creek while house warming got a lynx set net heating water for laundry

Tuesday 21th   Cold   eight abov this morning waited to after eleven befor I went to glaser flats got one mink at Dowsons Slough   all my traps exepting two stod just as I left them   saw a fox track on flats   ice is making crystals   floating in smoth places

Wednesday 22th   Lay in bed to daylight was making   after making breckfast & washing up I had a mink to skin stritch & clean   snowing quite heavy   I got thinking if I go out to Lake Emma to day I may make it without snow shoes   of I went 10:30   got a lynx in second trap   got one more on top of hill   got home at dark   have been busey since working with furs

Thursday 23th   At home making bread   light snow falling all day   towards evening it cleared so I could see Redoubt as thru a fogg   weather about 20 abov zero   was expecting taw but I guess this is as near as we will com to it

Friday 24th   At home all day without acomplishing anyting   started to sew a pair of seal skin mitts but not feeling good so I got along porly   main reason is Saturday Evening Post new reading matter I got from Tom Odal at Birch Wood the twentiet

Saturday 25th   Still snowing lightly   saw a mink track yesterday morning going towards flats

caught in 3th trap   creek floding   sewing at my mits & fixing Christ mass feast   not feeling good to much eats

Sunday 26th   Started late on to sheep hills   got on to a track on the flats leading to islands   saw a big ram cirkling island couple of time   it got away   met young Frostad

Monday 27th   Started over about nine   got into quite squall   got som tings icy   lost one lynx on lake shore & one on ridge   got one lynx & one mink on King Lake

Tuesday 28th   went up to Rat Lake   got one lynx

Wednesday 29th   Came home by way of Nyman Coast   young Frostad came over with me   saw a lynx sitting along side of one of my mink traps Frostad shot at it   it got away

Thursday 30th   was up to Lake Emma   got ermine in last trap

Friday 31th   Snowing this morning but I decided to take a walk up glaser flats   so I and young Frostad walked up to Dirty Cannon   I got in to a blizard comming back   had to leve sciff at Dowson Slough

Looking up into Dirty Canyon from the glacier flats. Photo by Joe Secora, circa 1939, courtesy of Ella and John Secora.

CHAPTER 12

1927

January 1927!

Saturday 1th At home all day not doing much of anyling cooked up a big mess of Beans fixing som old clothes sky full of Mare tails but no wind mild thermometer standing at about 18° abou

Sunday 2th Was at home to noon than tok a couple of traps set them out for lynx at mouth of Indian and Dowsons Cabbin Brought the skiff home it was getting to icy & heavy so I tok it home to get the ice tawed had a job getting it in to cabbin

Monday 3th 2 abov zero this morning have been home all day mending my snowshoes put the boat out but from the way it looks now I my not have to use it again this winter deathly calm to night

Tuesday 4th A blizard blowing up lake this morning about 10 am switched to east turned mild but churned the lake to foam had a bath & been washing up still blowing

Wednesday 5th wind still strong no chance of trying to go anywheres with a dorey rain & snow squalls most snow have disapeared have been indoores all day going to Camp Friman when ever I get a chance

Thursday 6th Fine as silk lake as a pane of glass went down to Friman & walked back to Birch to see the boys Hardy came up this evening with dog team walked back to Friman got one mink

Friday 7th went to Olson & Philip Creek got one lynx & one ermine

Saturday 8th went by way of Trail Lake to Lick House got two mink on No 3 heavy traveling

Sunday 9th went down to Castle inn got two mink on south one on middle & one on north fork ran the line on Funny got to cabbin way after dark plum tired out

Monday 10th Came stright thru to Friman stopped at Lick House for lunch my snowshoe strings broke & put me in for hard going hurt my hand got one mink & one ermine

Tuesday 11th Came home to day stopped in at Birch & got a dog for Wagner stopped at Bear

Creek deliverin the dog   saw Wagner just ariving at Birch when I was about a mile on my way

Wednesday 12th   Was turning & working with furs this morning   about 12 n I went up to Lake Emma   got one lynx & one ermine   a wolferine have sprung two traps   no catch   weather have stod warm for ten days   calm to day   fog was hanging over lake

Thursday 13th   Tok a walk out on glaser flats got two lynx & one mink   lost one trap by wolferine   foggy mild   fog so thick that days are very short   had a bath and after I got thru with furs I had som laundry work to do

Friday 14th   At home repairing my snow shoes tok a walk toward evening saw about thirty malards that have come in   we have had a regular summer weather   no wonder it is deciving the birds   scrubbed the floor & cleaned up tings

Saturday 15th   Going south if calm   was snowing this morning so I did not go   stay home reading som unimportant trash

Sunday 16th   Went acrost   south west swell making it slappy so I ran under islands   a light mountain breeze smothed it down som   saw Ole Frostad at Nyman & later met his brother coming from Dan's   he had a lynx making thier tally 8th

Monday 17th   Went to head of line   got one mink the only ting for the trip   coldest day I feelt this winter

Tuesday 18th   Not so cold this morning clouding up from the south   came out when I got to big lake   I found it iced over as far as I could see no chance of getting boat unles a blow sprung up so I walked by way of Devils Bay   met smith & had lunch at Frostad boys   they just brought in the nineth lynx   went over my traps   got home at dark

Wednesday 19th   Tok a walk down towards Bear Creek   set out five mink sets & five lynx sets   got to where Wagner had som mink traps   I guess he have one mink frozen down   I pulled at chain thinking it was only trap fell in but found som bones in trap   walked on ice part of ways   fog setting in quite thick   looks like a milder spell

Thursday 20   Let my yeast get to warm & nearly killed it   make som bread today but not good yeast working to slow   snowing all day not hevy but anouth to keep the ice from making   she be bad dangerous to travel on unles it get heavy anough to sink (seep through)

Friday 21th   Going to Lake Emma back by one got noting on my whole trip   all mink traps sprung on Lake Emma   did not see a lynx track & very few of any game

[Ole wrote:] Saturday 22th   Over on a visit nobody home so I am going over to Wagners intend to be back to morrow   Ole Frostead

Was up in Dirty Cannon intending to set som traps for the wolferine that got away with my trap but the cannon was to dirty to get thru   so I set out four traps in my line on flats   got only one trouth

Sunday 23th   Been busy all day washing clotches fixing snowshoes   fished net got three trouths Ole did not com back   tok a walk & scate down to point   ice getting stronger   will start to Birch Wood in morning

Monday 24th   Went on to Birch Wood   stopped at Bear Creek listening to Wagner set off som pent up hot air having Ole Frostad I & Windys partner to listen   was at glaser tours camp went on to Friman   scat back & stay all night

Tuesday 25th   Went on to Olson Creek   caught one lynx & one mink   scated to Camp to hear Windy splice tings

Wednesday 26th   Just as I was having breckfast Windy & Tom Odale came bye on there way for Kussiloff   I went up to Lick House   got one lynx & one mink on way up

Thursday 27th   Went acrost Funny basin to Castle Inn   got one mink

Friday 28th   Came on thru to Friman ran up to Birch Wood stay all night in Tom Odales new house with Mr Liskie & Mr Bartlet   found out that the Game Wardens have gone by

Saturday 29th   Ran on down to Olson   set out eleven more traps for mink & lynx   went to Hugo I came back & stay with Mr Liskie

Sunday 30th   Came home   stopped at Bear for lunch   ice getting som stronger but not good still cracking under the snow   clouding up   been cold at Birch Wood

Monday 31th   Had a walk up glaser flats   no sign of any game   saw two bunches of malards   Wagners partner was over to get som reading matter & som onions

February Tuesday 1th   was up to Lake Emma got one lynx & one mink   after I got back home I went to Glaser Flats   set trout net in mouth of stream   there was fifteen mallards when I came there   thermometer sinking   only three abov zero at six p.m.

Wednesday 2th   At home all day   cold this morning   the coldest morning of the season   8 below zero   was out fishing got two trouth   Ole Frostad came over

Thursday 3th   Stay home trying to work at making a pair of moccasince   started to snow and to night we have quite of a snow fall   weather is warm   fished the net & got only one trout   looks like winter

Friday 4th   We have this morning nearly one foot of new snow laying loose & flaky that one steps right to the bottom   Ole went home this P.M.   I was out fished net   got four nice trout finnis my moccasince and sure got the best ones

on the lake   just having water warm for a bath saw new moon about one hour ago

Saturday 5th   Was home to about noon washing up my clotches   then put on my new moccasince waded to the net   fished it and got one lake trout & two doly vardens   walked on up flats to my traps   no signs of any game

Sunday 6th   Started acrost this morning   after I got out about two miles it started to rain   snow was getting wet so I came back   resewed one of my moccasince   loking like bad weather was comming so I decided to start yeast   stay home & bake when tings get to humming if it be a howling northeaster   tok a walk dusk of evening down lake shore to som traps   lost my knife while setting som mink traps   water are already coming up in some places wetting thru the snow   got one silver salmon

Monday 7th   Set bread   as soon as I had breckfast waded down & found my knife   raining but not storming as hard as I expected   lake showing black   I was afraid one time to day that the ice was brecking   got thur with bread making about 7 p.m.   got 12 loaves 2 lb each   the finest yet so far   did not fish the net   the wind was to strong to go there

Tuesday 8th   Was out early to try & fish the net water on ice frozen in places so I had to along

Mentioned in Berg's journal on January 28th, Tom Odale's "new house," on the left, was a two-story, 1500 square foot log lodge. Photo courtesy of Dolly Cole Christl.

the lake shore   when I got there the sand have washed over the net so I could not get it in   after breckfast I went to Lake Emma   got one lynx & one mink   got back 3 p.m.   put on my gum boots tok a sluice fork & went to get the net   lost about 12 feet of it   got the rest with seven nice trouth

A sluice fork is a rake-type tool used in placer mining.

Wednesday 9th   Heavy storm to day   thermomter ran up to 48 abov   rain in spels   have been afraid of icebrecking   it is loos from the shore by swells forming from pressur of wind coming off mountain   been in house all day repairing som old clotches reading play in solitary   getting tired of staying in the House

Monday 14   Starting to Friman Camp weather permitting   went down in fine shape   met Mr Liskie   he invited me to come and stay over the night so I ran down to Olson Creek looking over my trap line & back to Birchwood   stay all night in

Tuesday 15th   Went up to Lick House against a gail of wind   got one ermine

Wednesday 16th   Went on down to Castle Inn got two mink in route   got there about two o clock made a bunk & started the stove going with a fire   went along my trap line   got one mink and one lynx

Thursday 17th   Got up early skinned the three minks   got on my way eight thirty   got to Birchwood at dark   turning mild starting to snow very strang wind all afternoon

Friday 18th   Came on home this noon   ran the skates to lake point   after that the ice was getting rough   was in at Bear Creek   had a cup of coffe with Wagners partner   ice was wetting through along cracks

Saturday 19th   Have been home all day tending the furs I brought in   tok a walk to glaser flats to try to get the net out   brock thru the ice and got my feet wet   got home without frezing

Sunday 20th   Going to Lake Emma be back about one o clock   was to Emma snowing al the way   saw two lynx tracks   coming back I went along ridge   came to lake a mile below   somone have come up and gone over to Devils Bay   I got one ermine   set the net this evening by chopping ice & splitting loos feilds at mouth of glaser stream

Monday 21th   At home al day exepting a trip out to fish the net   got one big trout   a gail of wind blowing from west   Windys partner came from Devils Bay he had Windies dogs but in the drifting loos snow they could not do much   Tom Odale came from Kenai with Wagner on his return trip from Anchorage

Berg in his trekking gear. Imagine him gliding across the lake on ice skates. Photo courtesy of Fabian Carey Collection, Accession no. 75-209-24N, Archives and Manuscripts, Alaska and Polar Regions Dept., University of Alaska Fairbanks.

Tuesday 22th   Cold   2 abov zero this mornings went up glaser flats   tok that trap line in   after I got home I went out & got a porcupine for dog feed   later tok in som trap near home   that is how I celebrated our national holiday

Wednesday 23th   Snowing to beat the band this morning   I waited to it cleared & tok my net along to Bear Creek   shortly after I got there came young Frostad   I came back alone   heating up   themometer stand at 13 abov this eve   will have to start early in morning to go to south side in order to rush in my traps befor season closes

Thursday 24th   Started out in a bad snow storm got so thick out from shore that it was hard to keep the course but I finally was able to reach the further shore   heavy walking   nearly eight inches of loos snow   got to trail went on acrost the ridge   was wet when I got to cabbin   made fire stay half hour changed clotches had a bite of lunch   went on to end of line tok in all the traps   got one lynx   snowing all night

Friday 25th   Had a tough time getting home   got an other lynx on lake shore   frozen & had to pack it about eight miles   snow is melting on lake   waded thru water & snow sluch several inches deep & wind high that when I got home I was about all in (dead tired)

Saturday 26th   Have been home all day   got the frozen lynx tawed out & skinned   tok the other of the stritcher   this afternoon picked a malard duck & stewed it   weather still unsetled   cloudy & warm

Sunday 27th   Going to Birch Wood if I posibly can get thru on acount of wet snow   started early got close to Bear Creek as Wagner & partner started on thier way to Kussiloff   I set my net at Bear Creek to get som fish to take on my trip & told Wagner that I be ther 27th   that snide went & fished my net just befor I got there   I overtok him at Birch Wood & bawled him out

Monday 28 th   Was down to Olson & Philip creek tok in traps   saw lot of lynx tracks caught noting went to glaser tour camp   stay all night

Tuesday 1 March   Went on up main line springing traps   stay at Lick House   repaired door of cabbin

Wednesday 2th   Went on thru to Castle Inn   took up all the traps & put tings to order for summer got 29 traps   3 on No 3   8 on No 2   14 on No 1 creek   54 [total]

Thursday 3th   Blowing a gail   snow is drifting badly but I started down to Lick House   got thru almost frozen   after resting for two hours I came on to lake   got to Friman at twenty to Seven

Friday 4th   Cold this morning when I left Friman my moccasinc where frozen stiff befor I got to glaser camp   saw Tom Odale Bartlet & Mr Liski Mr Liski is leaving to morrow for Anchorage Tom will accompany him as far as Kenai   one lynx   five mink   Total catch 29 lynx 32 mink 7 ermine

A nice payday of around $1,300 for trapper Berg this year. Average prices had climbed to $29.47 for lynx, $14.52 for mink and $1.85 for ermine.[1]

Saturday 5th   A nasty storm on   I have been in cabbin all day tending the few furs I brought in I still got a few traps on Emma trail but I cant get there as long as this gail keeps up   I can hardly get the cabbin warm anough with stove going full blast   I fixed the nedle valve for Tom from johnson motor belonging to Glaser Tour outfit my windows cary ice all day

Sunday 6th   Storm quit but it is still cold   been home nearly all day   toward evening I tok a walk to glaser flats   hard walking lot of loos snow later have hammered out a nice of steel for peepsight on my pistol

Monday 7th   I was going up to Emma but it was rather cold early & by the time it moderated it started to snow   so I have been home tinkering with som smole tings but most time I spent reading two copys of Cosmopolitan Tom gave me

Tuesday 8th   Started out to day but an attack of muscular reumation got me that bad that it tok me hours to get off the creek   half mile   now my legs are as sore as a boil   I aplied sloans liniment and it gave some relive   I am just going to try foot bath

Wednesday 9th   Going to lake Emma be back about two   was up to Lake Emma   cashed [cached] the traps & tok in all flags   saw several track of lynx & wolferine   my legs have not bothered me much   snowshoes all the way   was up to glaser stream with net

Thursday 10th   Ten below this morning the coldest I seen this winter   tok a walk over to Frostads   they have left the third   tok som lard & my book   put my oars upstairs   fished no fish   saw fox

Friday 11th   At home all day   made me self a new lamp as I am getting short of gasoline   went out fishing   got four nice trouts   I fried one for lunch & sure it was good   Mr Smith came on a visit   warmer to day but towards eve it gettin clear & cold

Saturday 12th   At home making bread   was out fishing   cold wind blowing from north   turned to snow   had som light snow falling   shot target & cleaned big rifle   mad sixteen loaves of bread expect to stay to I get it masticated if in the mean time I can muster up curage to fill woodshed

Sunday 13th   Smith started down to Birch Wood to se if he be able to get som tobaco   it seems strange to me that a man would walk that far to get som leves of vegetation to burn   I got two trout   cut & hauled home several loads of birch timber for wood   was out & got a porcupine to feed scott & lizzie (the dog & cat)

Monday 14th   Snowing this morning so I got one of curent history and put in my time studing wath have transpired in the several contrys during month of Jan 26   was out clearing a wood trail

Tuesday 15th   Was out this morning & hauled in two birch trees   turning mild   walked out to glaser stream got one trout   just is I was cooking up my catch Smith came up from Birchwood informing me that Tom Odale was not back yet who went with Mr Liskie to Kenai

Wednesday 16th   Soft snow falling almost rain to wet to atemt to do any ting so I going thru my last years collection of Current History & find som articles that I past over without reading them

cought two of the nicest golden trouts   ice on lake is buckled up in preasure ridges & likes   in betwen full of water

Thursday 17th   Still snowing but was out cutting wood   Smith was hauling it   got to wet so we quit at eleven o clock had a rest   after luncheon went out fished net   got only one white fish   was out hunting porcupine found none   shot six squirrels (weather brecking)

Friday 18th   Hauled home the last of wood this morning   at least I think I got anough   Smith went to Devils Bay this morning   I brought up & fixed saw horse   altered handle on saw   fished net (weather rain)

Saturday 19th   Thawing this morning   strong wind   filed my saw   was out & sawed a stick but it was alltogather to wet to be out so I heated water & had a bath & general cleanup   the rest of time I put in at sleeping & reading

Sunday 20th   Sawed & split one rick of wood but the way I cut in to my wood pile I think I will have to get home som more timber   fished the net but no fish   the net was foul   washed som clotches & scrubbed the floor so I done a whole weeks work to day

Monday 21th   Put in another rick of wood to day but my arm is that sore & aguing that if weather is fine I will go acrost lake to haul my boat tent bedding & machine home   would wait for clear ice but fears it might go to snowing again

Tuesday 22th   Had an earth quake last night wich made this old cabbin squeek   to much wind to go after the boat   sawed som wood droped a block of wood on my foot it is quite sore this evening but the arm feel better   split out one nice block   adzed it down for a meal board   warm to day

Wednesday 23th   Sawed up all timber I had home but not anough   I well have to get in the harnes again   got four nice trout this after noon   tok up net to give it a chance to dry out

Thursday 24th   Snowin & wet this morning   sit watching it thru the window   it got little better & went out cut thre birch trees   hauled home four loads   it got to wet to be out   Smith came in   he

have started with all his junk on an ice jack   left
dory a mile or so on ice   going towards big house
with rest of duffel   ran in to soft snow left
everyting   walked to big house got sled   hauled
loft to Bear Creek   tok sled to where he left dorey
hauled it to where he started   he went to Bear
Creek to day towing by neck the borrowed sled
I sawed & filled the fourth rick this evening

Friday 25th   I went acrost   got dory evinrude
bedding oil tent winter cloting one dozen xxx 3
steel traps flags tools axes etc   good traveling
ice in patches & shell ice   the rest hard snow
drift but when I got everyting on sled it was hevy
to start   was traveling 20 miles & with load   I
dont know who was most tired I or the dog   but
I think I was worst

Saturday 26th   At home all day resting up after
yesterday hike   snowing all fornoon   was out to
net & got three nice trouts   this evening I started
sawing wood for the last rick   sawed a couple
logs I had home   comensing to put my ting
togather for taking with me when I go to Kenai

Sunday 27th   Was out choping down & bucking
up som birch to finis my wood contract   houled
home & sawed about half of it to stove wood
started snowing about noon & been at it ever
since but it is very fine & dont amount to anyting
on the ground

Monday 28th   Indoors all day   having a regular
winter day out to day   snowing & strong wind
making it a regular blizard   have been bundling
up my furs ready for travel & shipment   I am just
going to have a bath

Tuesday 29th   Windows all icy this morning   with
a lot of new snow it looks as much like a winter
day as any we had this year   At home building a
washstand   tok me to two o clock to finis then I
got home som wood & hiked out to set the net
by that time it was 7 p.m.

Wednesday 30th   Had a rolling good earth quake
at 10 last night   had a tub of water standing on
floor   it splashed water out of it & the way the
walls was creaking you would think you was on
ships board & dishes & cans sure did rattle
scrubbed the floor the last time season   hauled
the dory in the shed & hanged it over head   got

only one trout   shot at som rabbit but it was
getting dark did not get any   lot of loos snow
but I am getting tired of laying around so I think
I will go down

Thursday 31th   Was out early sawed & split the
last wood to fill five ricks   after that I have been
busy putting tings away for summer   emptied the
well   tok home my trout net   got one large trout
shot a rabbit for the dog

April 1th Friday   Starting to go to Kenai if the
weather permit

In the spring of 1927 Tom Odale killed an enormous brown
bear on the lake. The hide was hung on the back wall of
the Kasilof Post Office, as seen here. The hide measured 11
feet, 10 inches and the animal was estimated to have
weighed 1,800 pounds. It was impressive enough that the
Alaska Glacier Tours Association mentioned it in their
brochure. Photo courtesy of Wanda M. Griffin.

Andrew's cabin was put to good use in June by bear and porcupine hunters. The gutted and skinned porcupines went back to Kasilof to feed foxes.

June 1927   Thursday 2nd   Arrived with a fair wind and Pete and Elmer on the "Jonson Bar" Left the Pete and Pete fox ranch on sunday May 28 and lined up river   arrived at Peninsula cabin at 12 p.m. had dinner and the morning and evening was the first day

On monday took dory across peninsula and anchored it   then went to big house   wind come up   Brown went up creek to look for bear signs got 4 porkeys there   At 8 p.m. left for Eds cabin in Devils Bay   Was forced ashore at point by glacier wind   made camp on the beach and the morning and evening was the second day

On Tuesday Brown went up canon by Cliff House   saw only one bear track in snow on top of mt   someone had been on top with dog   saw few sheep tracks to much snow   cold wind on top arrived Camp about 6:30 p.m.   Pete and Elmer killed 26 porkys and the morning and evening was the third day

Wednesday was spent in camp and porky hunting   46 were killed   made a trip to Cliff House to hunt in evening   Game Warden had been there but was gone when we arrived bagged a few more along the hill   Saw a bull moose on the beach   And the morning and evening was the fourth day

On Thursday put a new plank on bottom of dory   got ready to leave at 12 am but wind come up   repaired evenrude   left at 1:00 p.m.   engine trouble at glacier sand   went ashore and got some gull fruit [eggs]   Pete & Elmer had to back to the Johnson Bar   arrived at Home Cabin at 4:20 p.m.   Elmer climbed cotton wood to get porky picture   Killed 6 more around cabin   Pete got bolts from boiler to repair evenrude [see photo]   Put out two nets   Weather cold and cloudy and the morning and evening was the fifth day

Friday 3rd   Pete rebuilt his put put and went over in the flat by overhang trail and completed the quota of porkys   Elmer and I went up on the mt   missed the right canyon by one On this canyon Elmer saw a small brown bear by a log   he rushed across the canyon and up through alders to head him off   When he got close the log got up   I saw the log and the small

bear go over the hill together   We went on to the top   we also saw 8 sheep at bottom in the flat saw about 100 on top   bands of 8 to 10   Elmer tried to get picture   I saw 3 over prceipill only 10 ft away but had no camera   We came down the big canyon   It was fill with snow in many places and was solid enough to holed us up   only one browny had gone up this spring   The alders have not come to leaf yet   few flowers were seen arrived in camp at 7:30 p.m. and the morning and evening was the sixth day

Saturday 4th   Pete was up at 4   cot 1 fish and on the seventh day we departed from all the things we had done   W Brown

June 16 1927   Pete Matson and J Elmer arrived here 12:30 from Divel's bay   had 37 porques Williamson & Luybin beat us to it by one day they stopped in Big Ed's cabin   we in Ole's place shot 41 porques first day   second day we got 22 and we meant to leave in the evening the 17 but glacer wind came up   it blew all night and the next day the 18   but I think well make it this eve the books and magazine were a life save for killing time   thanks Pete & Elmer

July 5th   Prospected around here for two weeks but found nothing worth while so we leave today

The Northwest Development and Mining Company's abandoned steam boiler was a valuable source of spare parts. Photo by G. Titus.

for dvuca bay   thanks for use of comfortable cabın   Chas Schneider Carl Johnson John Gillispie

Thursday Sept 22nd   Ocar Andrew Al blair and myself visited your hospitable camp for two nights we went to the glacer for bear   we went not succesful   The water was fine but there was no salmon   bears were in the big hills   I hope I shall have the pleasure of meeting you some day

to thank you for the use of your cabin and also the pleasure of your aquaintance   sencely — Cottam of New Orleans La

H. Tom Cottam of New Orleans was hunting as a client of the Alaska Glacier Tours Association. Andrew Berg spent his summer working for the Bureau of Fisheries and may well have been guiding in September when Mr. Cottam was visiting. The following letter is the last

Odale's bear is mentioned in the Kenai Peninsula section of the right-hand page. Brochure courtesy of Wanda M. Griffin.

known reference to Berg acting as a professional hunting guide.

July 7, 1927
Mr. H.W. Terhune Executive Officer
Alaska Game Commission Juneau Alaska.
Dear Mr Terhune: When Mr. Church and I were in Juneau, last fall we were told that the commission would issue a special permit to Tony Martin, to guide for us only. We engaged Tony to look after the Tustamena end of the trip because he knows that country thoroughly and we found him so reliable and trustworthy last year. Andy Berg and Chas Wagner both said they would have licenses, and be with us, but it seems impossible to reach them by correspondence, and I am informed that they are under contract with the Fish Commission until Sept. 1. As I am sailing from Seattle August 3, and will want to get some sheep hunting with my party of six, beginning Aug. 20 and a second party of our friends on the Westward will arrive before the 1 of Sept. ... I am willing to furnish you with a bond and take the full responsibility for satisfactory service to our people on the part of Harry Lewis and Tony Martin of Seldovia, Paul and Philip Wilson, Andy Berg and Chas Wagner of Kenai, if you will allow them to go out with our party not as full licensed guides but under special permit for our party only...[2]

Andrew Berg quietly faded out of the professional guiding arena this year as AGTA was rapidly expanding operations. Hunts were conducted in Kodiak, on the west side of Cook Inlet, in the Chickaloon area (northeast of Anchorage) and in the Rainy Pass area (northwest of Anchorage) as well as Tustumena. Rising star guide Andy Simons was hired as a field manager. Airplanes were used increasingly to transport hunters between Anchorage and the remote camp locations. Supplies and bulky items like moose racks still moved by boat and pack horse.

Two of AGTA's clients this season included Van Campen Heilner, an editor of *Field & Stream,* and Captain W. H. Fawcett, a successful magazine publisher and marketing genius (his magazine titles included *Whiz Bang, True Confessions, Screen Secrets,* and *Golfer*). These two men convinced AGTA's management that they should change the company's name to the Alaska Guides Association, Inc.[3]

Berg's journal entries continued when he headed back to the lake in late October.

October 1927 20th Thursday Left Kenai ran down to Kusiloff stopped at Erik Isaksons Cabbin for the night (feasted on duck)

Erik Isakson was yet another Finn who had emigrated in 1902 at the age of twenty-two.[4] He lived on the north

Alaska Glacier Tours Association's lake skiff loaded up with trophies. Photo courtesy of McLane Collection.

A typical AGTA camp after the hunt. Several hunters accumulated this collection of 3 bears, 5 moose and 8 sheep. Photo courtesy of Wanda M. Griffin.

side of the Kasilof River between the cannery and Alex Lind's place.

21 th Friday Went late foornoon to Abbs mixed som oil started up river about three o clock got to Victors Cabbin in one hour & eight minnutes

22 th Saturday Left Victors Cabbin ran up the river all the way started to snow & was real dirty machine broke down 3 miles below Birch Wood pulled [rowed] in to camp got there about fifteen minuts of four

23 th Sunday Stay here taking machine down found one of cylinders cracked putting that half of machine out of action

24th Monday Ran up here on one lung had good time came from Glaser Tours Camp in one hour 45 minutes found lot of frish bears tracks both brown & black fine weather mild

Tuesday 25th Up early started out to look for bear weather still & fine did not find any bears saw lot of tracks got to foot of mts saw a lot of sheep shot one about 400 feet from

glaser flats got back home 1:30 Erik put lines on my new net starting to blow from the hill

Wednesday 26th At home all day snowing to beat the band Erik has been mending trouth net all day put sinkers under little net set it out fishing walked out to creek but found no tracks of bears put my smole schiff out & swamped it turned the other over in the lake to get snow out of it cooking & eating

Thursday 27th Was out this morning up the Indian River to look for bears saw no sign went up glaser flats & over to Erling Frostad Erik found tracks of bears Pete Madsen Louis Madsen Chris Madsen came up

Friday 28th Snowing this morning went up loking for bear jumped three bears Erik killed a ram getting lot of trout turning cold

Saturday 29th Tok a walk to Dirty Cannon Louis Madsen & Pete Sandson went up over hanging trail got four sheep Erling Frostad came over going to Kenai

November the 1st   Leaving here to day for Big House   Wagner Frostad Goldstein and Ward stayed here last night   went over to Frostad this morning   Thanking you for your kindness

Chris Jensen   Pete Madsen   Louis Madsen

Som letters in front page for Earling Frostads

Am afraid to go to Friman on acount of cold   the skiff are liable to ice under   just trying to doctor my pen point

Saturday 5   Started from Kenai came with Gust Ness in gas boat Sea Otter   stay all night at Issaks camp

Sunday 6   Walked up to Ab's fox ranch & had a tramp to big hill lake   came acrost to visit McLane   stay to dinner

Monday 7   Started acrost country to Tustemina fine traveling   jumped a brown bear   got to Hugos 1 p.m.   les then four hours from McLanes icy on lake

Tuesday 8   Went to look for the bear   heard Wagners machine as I was tracking the bear   quit the track when I saw he was off on a long hike

Wednesday 9   Waited to about ten o clock to let it warm up then got my donage in schiff and started home   stopped at Birch Wood in Toms cabbin for lunch and to pick up Lizzy   saw a lynx on the lake shore as I came along so we got one chance

Thursday 10   At home all day putting tings away found my flash light tampered with so I am without serch light   it is strange that som people cant see a ting without taking it apart to see wath makes it work   it was in good order Oct 30th   a lot of men stay here to Nov 1th   still cold   it took all day to warm the cabbin   set the net

Friday 11   Started about ten to look for sheep just as I came around cliff abov Rays Mine I saw two rams quite high their body's partly covered by the cliff   tok a shot at the one I saw the most of   saw a bunch of hair rise as I shot   one jumped on a cliff but I did not shoot   climbing up I found the one I shot on his feet going   have to shot him again   a fine big fellow four years

The remains of "Big House," one of the few cabins on the south side of the lake. Photo courtesy of Allen Tri.

old   saw frish bear track   got back home at 3 p.m. bringing it all home skin & all

Saturday 12   At home making bread   cleaned the stove   fixed damper so is to give the old ting a chance to perform & it certainly done fine   I got about forty pounds of the nicest kind of bread with four pounds of raisins in it & done to a cake brown all around   so I am readly to go when season oppence to set traps   weather foggy to day   a mite warmer

Sunday 13   Slept to late this morning   been in all day fixing up som tings   set the net grinding my traveling axes   rendered som sheep talow cooking & eating to I am getting in my own way fogg hanging over the lake & frost in trees over Devils Bay side   I cooked a big kettle ful of old silver salmon for Schott

Monday 14   Started out this morning to string out som traps to make them quick set when season oppens   saw all kinds of tracks even sheep   have been down to creek   one mink track one wolferine track and several lynx tracks   making

Al Hardy appears to have had a very lucky hunt here with a moose killed close to the boat. The hard part would have been getting the carcass into the skiff. The dog peering over the gunwale looks ready to assist. Photo courtesy of McLane Collection.

to much noys [noise] to see any game   I saw som work of muskrat

Tuesday 15   Erling Frostad came over & got his mail   I went up on glaser flats set out 12 traps for lynx   saw lot of bear tracks along the flats Erling report Hardy up at his place on a sheep hunt   started at noon to go setting traps   got back home just getting dark

Wednesday 16   Season oppens on lynx   was out early set out 17 traps   shot a rabit the first one this season   saw one ermine it was swering at me when I was crossing culvert on the Indian river mining trail   som sheep was out on ice on Indian River   a wolferine on there tracks

Thursday 17   Probbably will cross the lake if weather permit   I woke with a cough & hedague so I stay home all day   weather cold 8 abov this morning   rather cold to sit in boat & not feeling well   shot som squirrels that have begin pesticats around here

Friday 18   Started about eleven   crossed to south shore   set out eight traps for lynx   got too late going to King Lake so I came back to Frostads   stay over night   Dark when I got there

Saturday 19   Started out at daylight   got the machine started ran for five minutes stopped   I

pulled back fixed the points & it ran fine   set five more traps along south shore & ten more acrost to King Lake   snow abov my knees at summit   tough wallowing   no snow shoes   got to my cabbin tired   some one stole my lamp & smashed window   nice mess to get into but all this tings put togather is wath they call sport

Sunday 20   Been snowing all night & it was up to me to get out of there or stay & make my self snowshoes   set out five traps as I left cabbin broke my ax handle so I waded along my tracks of yesterday wich I could hardly follow   ran into a bear track   was not interested my only wepon being a 22 stevens pistol   bear was a big "browny"   got to Mr Frostads in good time   lake rough

Monday 21   Was making redy to go this morning Erling busey to write letters to take to Glaser Tours Camp when I go to Freeman   wind quite strong   I was hurrying to get acrost before it got to rough   as it was I had tings in bow of boat covered with ice   got here eleven tirty   got my tings out of boat & up to cabbin   cooked lunch and was on my way to glaser flats by one ran the line of twelf traps got two lynx   killed & skinned them and got back here just at dark

Tuesday 22   Surf was rough last night   cause for me not getting any trout   started late going over my trap line to lake Emma   got two lynx back here by sunset traveling on snow shoes the first time this winter   set net this evening   getting cold

Wednesday 23   A cold nasty wind blowing up the lake   got three nice trouth this morning   tok a walk down lake shore   wind cutting like a knife   got noting   no tracks of any animals   turned som lynx skins on stritchers   having water warm for a bath but the cold wind makes me afraid of catching cold

Thursday 24   Abov zero & a northerly wind blowing   am anxsious to get to Friman but no chance of me going boating in this weather   a boat would ice under in short time   was up on flats set two traps   going thru island saw one lynx track   had a bath after I got home   washing som underwere

Friday 25   At home all day   intended to go to Lake Emma but when I heard the wind howling on the hill I concluded to stay by the stove   It has been about zero most all day & this evening the wind riched here and blowing hard from the north

Saturday 26   10 below this morning   I bundeld on a lot of cloting & climbed to Lake Emma   an intirely useles trip as all traps was in good shape exepting one where I cought a squirrel   wind was beastly cold where it hit me fair   got back at sun set

Sunday 27   8 below zero this morning but everyting clear not a cloud to be seen   stay home reading a lot of cheap trash   towards evening Earling Frostad came over   have made himself a couple of new knife that he wanted ground and this is the nearest grind stone   he was thinking of going to see if Wagner have come up to Bear Creek

Monday 28   6 below this morning   waited to after it warmed up then I & Erling walked down to Bear Creek to see if Wagner have com up   he was up but was out somwheres probably the upper cabbin on Birch Wood   saw tracks of one lynx one mink & one animal of the weasel family white smole without black tip in tail   cant find anyone knowing the name for it

Tuesday 29   9 below zero this morning   waited to noon still at zero   Erling was going home & I went up on glaser flats so we went in company to the end of my last set   I came back over hog back   no sign of any game   two below when I got home but we are close to som change   there is moisture in the air and it is clouding up som from the south   som fine dust of snow started to fall & the way I looked when I got in you think it was forty below   my face was all iced up mustach one solid lump of ice but it is on acount of moisture in the air

Wednesday 30   Snowing to beat the band this morning   thermometer registering two abov zero stay home loking into winter from a safe distance been mending up tings and put togather what I my need on a trip out   mixing oil for machine and oil for lamps   cooked up a kettle full of stew to have ready in case I get down late   it looks cold to go out boating in snowstorm but I have been here now a week waiting for the weather to moderate so I could go down there and get som traps set out

Thursday 1 December   Started late on my way to Friman in order to let it warm up by the sun as it is getting cold to sit in the boat   at Bear Creek I saw Wagner   stopped the machine & shouted hello   at Birch I over tok Ray & Slim   sent Erlins letters

Friday 2   Went to Olson & Philip Creek set out 24 traps   wallowing thru without snowshoes had a extra hard day of it

Saturday 3   Set ten traps along lake shore   it was raining nearly all day   shot som rabbits for lynx flags & mink bait   the rest of day I put in reading

Sunday 4   Too mild to go out anywhere so I stay home cutting wood   foggy   tok the schiff to cabbin that I have had down to the point on acount of ice   set the net

Monday 5   On my way to Lick House setting traps as I went   snow got very deep & loose before I got there   found that a bear have broken in smashed the door & chewed my table to splinters   made him self a nice bed in one corner

Tuesday 6   Went down Funny River set som traps walking very heavy   saw no tracks of any fur animals & not many of moose   got the cabbin fixed up so it is quite comfortable   thought that I smelled tobaco smoke so plain that I shouted if a body was near

Wednesday 7   Came down from Lick House   dug up som traps that I passed on my way up   got out early went along beach to bait som mink traps set two lynx traps with Sunday comicle section as flags   found that Tom Odale have com up on the 6th

Thursday 8   Got six nice trout this morning & after I had everyting cleaned up I put my tings in the boat & started home   saw noting of Tom   I guess he was out setting traps   At Lake Point I saw Windy on the beach going towards BirchWood

Friday 9   Soft [illegible] of snow almost rain about eleven I decided to go on glaser flats got one lynx in last trap   no tracks of any more   it was raining when I got back but getting towards evening its getting cooler   after I had somting to eat I stritched the pelt them started to work at my snowshoes   set in new foot webb then my gas lamp went bad   tok me a whole hour to take it apart & put it to work again   now it is ten o clock   I got water ready for a bath and then to bed

Saturday 10   After I had breckfast I begin at taking my evinrude apart to see how badly I had it damaged   It fell off the sled load when I came up from Friman two days ago   found noting so badly broken but that I think it will run   several parts was badly bent   after I had the machine ok I scrubbed out the cabbin   then I saw that I had nearly two hours of day left so I tok a walk up Indian for a mile where I have four traps for lynx   got one   washed som clotches striched the pelt   cooked a kettle of dog feed & my super so I will put on the hatch & call it a day

Sunday 11   Was late getting started   wind off mts so I hoged [hugged] the islands   found walking good on lake shore but crossing summit I found deep new snow   got to King Lake cabbin at dark   got three lynx

Monday 12   Was going in to Rat Lake but walking is rather heavy & bitterly cold   shoe pacs are no foot gear when it is cold so I started home   set one trap & flaged several   lost one trap   lost so mych time hunting it that I got home in dark   caut one lynx   tok it home & skinned it & got all four on the boards   it is nine o clock

Tuesday 13   Turning mild   stay home all day about noon Erling Frostad came up from Wagners where he have been on a visit   lost his mitt on the beach had to go back nearly to Bear Creek I tok a walk a way up Indian River   set a trap for mink   saw no signs of any animals exept moose

Wednesday 14   Heavy wind all night   raining towards morning   mild   water running off roof last night   got up about five o clock about day breck   Erling Frostad started home & I went to Lake Emma running trap line   did not get a single ting   got back early   snowing   set trout net

Thursday 15   At home watching bread   got two trout for breckfast   set the batter & it kept me busey all day baking but I got anough to last me a month   clouded up & started to blow   to night it is melting snow   I can hear the water dripping off the roof

Friday 16   Storming and raining whole day   I was down to the boat this evening to clean the ice out of it   found all clear   tok a walk up the creek but it was to wet   loos snow & water   have not acomplished a ting to day worth the notice & noting much that I could do

Saturday 17   Still mild but have not been raining much to day   tok a walk up on the glaser flats had to walk around pools where water left standing from melted snow   went up thru Islands & came back over hogback along my trap line but no game in any   saw tracks of one lynx and one mink   got home at two since then I been reading Saturday Evening Post

Sunday 18   At home   found new snow covering the ground this morning & more coming down was intending to go to mountains to get a sheep before season closed but knowing that the flats was icy & this new snow would make bad traveling I decided to stay home and proced to ruin my eyes by reading   set out the net & had a walk up Indian just at dusk

Monday 19   Here I had another holday done noting but reading   wind still blowing & jus a little snow fall   feeling lazy & tired   started to make a pair of moccasins but not getting anyting done   my right shoulder agu whenever we got rainy or dirty weather   got five nice trouth

Tuesday 20   At home   was intending to go to mountains but it have been falling snow at intervals all day so I got sewing at my moccasins and that kept me nearly all day   cloudy & I had to light the lamp at half after three

Wednesday 21   Went to mountains this morning to look for sheep   when I got to where I expected to find sheep the fogg closed down that I had to abandon the sheep hunt   have been tending the cullinary job   just got water hot for bath

Thursday 22   Have been home all day repairing stove for Friman & putting tings up to take along when I go down   weather have been quite dull cloudy   a little snow falling this evening   washed som clotches   reading

Friday 23   Did not get away this morning on acount of heavy sea running with strong wind from the south west   tok a walk down lake shore towards Bear Creek and after I got home I went upcreek   no tracks of any game

Saturday 24   Went down to Friman   fine weather light headwind   when I got there I found tracks of Tom & Wagner going to Kenai   tok a walk up lake shore got one mink and a toe of a lynx in no 1 1/2 trap   no ice in the lake just a little shore ice

Sunday 25   Blowing a gale of wind   tok a walk to Olson & Philip Creeks got one lynx & lost one most of traps out of order   I had a long blistering cold day figting my way over Olson pas without snow shoes

Monday 26   Went up to Lick House   fine traveling   rather cold   got up about noon   no game on this run

Tuesday 27   Was down Funny River got two mink and one ermine   came by Lick House and down to Friman   was afraid of frezing in   wether getting cold

Wednesday 28   Thought that I was froze in this morning but I was making ready to go home a wind sprung up from south west & broke up the ice   I had quite time getting thru at that running into some hevy plases but did not breck anyting in machine

Thursday 29   Have been busey all day tending the pelts   lot of cleaning to do on them   fished net got only three trout   set som snares for rabbit was up creek to look over som traps   put new foot webb in one of my snow shoes besides cooking   just got water warm for bath

Friday 30   Foggy this morning & cold but thought it my last chance of using the boat so I started to south shore following glaser flats so as to find my way   got to Devils Bay   there I ran into ice   had a time getting to shore   tok the boat up   stacked my outfit   walked on over to King Lake   got one little lynx   walking fine   at cabbin after I got fire going I set 3 traps

Saturday 31   Started on my way back at daybreck got to lake shore early   went to hunt for a trap I lost but no sign of it could I find so I set out four more traps   no tracks to be seen   the lake shore icy   fell in the icy beach & sprained my left wrist   got to Earling Frostads about one o clock   lake frozen but not strong anough to walk   had to climb the clifs

CHAPTER 13

1928

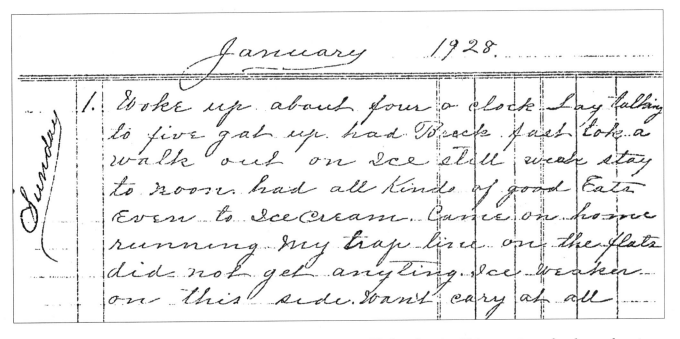

January   1928.

Sunday

1. Woke up about four o'clock Lay talking
to five got up had Breck fast toke a
walk out on Ice still weak stay
to noon. had all kinds of good Eats
Even to Ice Cream. Came on home
running my trap line on the flats
did not get anyting. Ice weaker
on this side. wan't cary at all

Monday 2   Have been home all day   was going to scate to Bear Creek to see if Wagner have got back   ran about a mile & found the ice so poor so I turned back as I did not feel like taking a bath to day   have been doing odds & ends around the house   was to mouth of Indian to set net   the only open water I know   turning mild this eve   strong south easter   the ice be probably gone in morning

Tuesday 3   Started to blow during night & broke up our nice ice field   was out to mouth of Indian River to haul my net   got seven nice big trout after I got thru brecfast & put tings to order I went up to Lake Emma   meet a ewe sheep on sumit it came up to twenty feet loked like it expected me to run   only when I hit the dog with my can to keep him back did it jump down the slide rock   I got five lynx   bigest catch so far two of them have got caught last night during the storm   the thirth one the night before   the other two have been in long

Wednesday 4   This morning after house keeping was done I skinned two of the lynx that was froze last night   put them on stritchers then tok som traps went up on flats   set three sets   comming home I got one lynx   tok up the net   to much trout cought sixteen

Thursday 5   Tok a walk to Bear Creek this morning   found tracks of somone persumable Tom Odale   tok som tan back   on coming home boiled & tanned two trout nets   heated water had a bath washed som clotches   weather mild raining just now

Friday 6   Blowing and almost to wet to go any place but I dont feel satisfied to stay home so I tok a walk over hill to Lake Emma   slipery & hard climbing   I made the trip in just over three hours   saw no game or signs of game   wind quit   still warm 34

Tustumena glacier in the late 1920s. This meltwater lake in front of the glacier would have been frozen when Erling took his walk described by Andrew on January seventh. Photo courtesy of Wanda M. Griffin.

Saturday 7   At eleven am I decided to go to Erling Frostads   got there just ahead of him   he just had a walk to foot of glaser for exercise   flats free of snow but icy south of islands

Sunday 8   Got on my skates started down south shore   shifted my schiff covering machine running down I had a nasty axident   ran into soft ice stubbed left skate wich trow me in a squatting position on my right heel to save a bad fall   I jumped up but put to much strain on the leg   stripped a part of tendon and got my self crippled   managed to get back to Frostads started to doctor up   Frostad putting on iodine

Monday 9   Had som sleep but leg sore & heavy aguing in evening but got quite to morning comens to show purple this morning but after fourth application of iodine it looks blackish brown   stiff after being in sitting position I can hardly strighten   the leg cord full of lumps

Tuesday 10   Limped home to day   tok me a long time but am here & not so sore as you would think had fine footin   ice covered with frost so it was not to slippery   put no iodine on to day feeling to much like the skin was comming apart

Wednesday 11   When I came home yesterday a moose stod by my wood shade & she was here all day to day picking up leaves & grass   ones to day when I came out the dog was sitting on the trail within twenty feet of one another loking like they was trying to figer out the best way to mak friends   went to mouth of Indian River to set the net   coming back I went up river to where I had som trap   had som rabbits snares out but the birds so far got ahead of me

Thursday 12   Had a new winter this morning & it was still snowing   my leg is sore and aguing was out and tok in my net got only one trouth Erling Frostad came shortly after noon   cloudy but having quit snowing this evening

Friday 13   Been in the house all day   my leg have given me much troble so sore that I cant sit still for a moment   have aplied hot compres but not succeeded to bring the swelling down   this evening there sprung up a nasty easterly storm squalls just shaking the house

Saturday 14   Saturday stay in to noon   tok a walk up to som rabit snares   after wards we hunted up som poles making a rig to set out the net   finely set the net   wether fine   during night a wind sprung up with snow sleet

Sunday 15   Had three trouts this morning   my leg afully painful   Erling was down to Bear Creek   som one been there with dog team   could not tell who

Monday 16   Still in bed   luckly I had nearly a year of Curant History unread   it comes in handy now   Erling went up creek to bring me home a lynx (so he said) but came without anyting (unexperience)

Tuesday 17   Erling started just after breckfast up glaser flats to run his trap line and on to his cabbin intending to come back here by night if posibly and bring som iodine   am getting short of it   Erling got back just before dark   caught one lynx

Wednesday 18   Had a most misserable night painted with a new cot of iodine and it was ever so much stronger   the skin was hanging in ribbons this morning   clouded up in forenoon & started to snow   turned mild & is raining this evening   hobbled up creek   saw a hawk lift a sawbill duck out of creek   started to eat it alife I shot with a 22 pistol   hurt the hawk that it let go duck dove under ice edge

Thursday 19   At home watching bread   weather mild   melted snow stands in big pools but it cleared up in midle of day   towards evening a cloud came up from south   thermometer rised to 35   my leg bothers me som but I have been on my feet nearly all day

Friday 20   Started in company with Erling Frostad upon the glaser flats   Erling was going to his cabbin thru lower islands where he have a trap line   I went without snow shoes and got into the worst kinds of walking   crost nearly holding then brecking thru giving my sore leg som affully [illegible]   I lost one wolferine at head of line & caught a lynx last trap coming home

Saturday 21   Was up to Lake Emma   foun deep loose snow   was sinking inches with my snow shoes   so this was the second and an extra heavy day on my bum leg   got three lynx   two dead

that I had to pack home frozen   weather foggy 16 abov just now

Sunday 22   My leg feeling sore so I decided to stay home   after breckfast I lay down had one hours good sleep   got up & had a feeling som one was coming   limped to landing where I saw Wagners team with Mr Cook out buying furs stay to lunch   went on to Erling Frostads

Monday 23   Waited to noon   Mr Cook & Windy came from Frostads   I sold wath furs I had   after lunch we started for Wagners at Bear Creek   I went alone on to Birch wood   found Tom Odale home   stay all night as I left my pack with Mr Cook

Tuesday 24   Waited to noon for my pack   went on to Friman looking over traps on the beach no sign of game

Wednesday 25   Just as I was having breckfast I saw Cook Windy & Tom going down   I went after to Olson Creek   came within a mile of Tom had a hard day   packed four frozen lynx to Frimans   lost two mink   eagle tok one trap clog & all

Four frozen lynx could have weighed more than sixty pounds. Assuming he had other gear in his pack, Berg may have easily been packing eighty pounds.

Thursday 26   Started for Lickhouse   found deep new snow & saw I could not mak it with my sore leg   started back after going to near the summit   saw only one mink track & lots of moose no sign of lynx

Friday 27   Started from Friman befor nine stopped at Toms about two minutes to leve wet stone   saw dark fox out on ice at lake point fox tracks along whole beach   one lynx this side of Bear Creek   tok me four hours & twenty minutes to limp home from Friman

Saturday 28   Was upon glaser flats trying to follow wolferine that tok my traps but to much snow have fallen had to quit   wind so strong I could hardly stand on open flats   sprung som traps   the beginning of the end

Sunday 29   Started up flats but went thru islands following Erlings line   found one lynx in his *trap   killed it skinned it hanged the skin in his cabbin   went on to my cabbin on King Lake met Erling at Muddy Creek coming from Fox River flats   got one lynx*

Monday 30   Came back from King Lake   tok in traps west end of lake shore line   got to Erlings tired   stay all night   played som pinocle

Tuesday 31   Came home from Erlings   went on up to Lake Emma   tok up traps as I came over flats   got one lynx on Indian & three more over summit

Wednesday 1 February   Was down lake shore tok in all traps towards Bear Creek   got one lynx   putting tings togather to take along on my trip to Friman   if wether holds good I well go in the morning

Thursday 2   Started down to Friman   saw Tom Odales tracks going up Bear Creek   at Birch wood found tracks of Hardys team hauling porcupines & moose meat

Friday 3   Went up over the ridge to Lick House repaired the door & fixed tings so I can leave tings in order for the summer   had one hundred pounds of flour there for several years   this winter the mice got at it so I trew the last fifty pound out to stop them from fouling shak

Saturday 4   Went down Funny River tok in all traps   got one mink & came on down to Friman & tok a walk along lake shore & tok in all traps no sign of any game so I am taking in mink traps as well as lynx trap

Sunday 5   Was down to Olson & Philip Creek tok in the last traps   cashed them   got a lynx on Philip Creek   put tings in shape at Friman and came on to Toms   stay all night

Monday 6   Came on home with bad walking after pasing Bear Creek I got into strong head wind   I could hardly stand up in it   Tom started to lower line on coal creek lake   He had two lynx at Birchwood   had one on the second   caut one when I was there

Tuesday 7   Was up on the glaser flats hunting a wolferine that got away with my trap clog & all but could not find any sighn of him

Wednesday 8   At home all day   not feeling good have been reading the last copy I got up here of Current History   set out net and got a nice mess of trout   been making yeast

Thursday 9   At home making bread

Friday 10   Started to south side to finis that line got som mink traps on King Creek   found Erling home   stay over night   he started to teach me pinocle   I did not make much showing

Saturday 11   Started out in a gail of wind but walking fairly good   I got to King Cabbin in good time   fixed the window the bear smashed for me   was down to creek tok in all traps   made a chair

Sunday 12   Coming back I was gathering in all traps and gear   by the time I got to my schiff I had load   sixtin steel traps with a lot of other junk

Monday 13   Raining & blowing   ice brecking a field of about two miles in Devils bay   we finely got it started so we could put out our trout nets tok a walk to my schiff   got six porcupines for dog feed

Tuesday 14   Came home without getting a single ting exepting getting wet   the flats is glare ice with deep pools of water   cleaned out the well after I got home

Wednesday 15   Raining & blowing   afraid snow will go before I have time to haul home my winters wood   was out tramping trail   caught four trout

Thursday 16   Blowing that the house is shaking raining snowing   this evening the most beutiful sunset I ever saw   (five nice trout)

Friday 17   Was out on flats to get in som traps just as I got home I heard an evenrude   Erling bringing my schif & machine   try dogs on track but turned out no good

Saturday 18   Erling started home this morning & I went up to Lake Emma to take up som mink traps   the country is dead for game   just got three more traps out then through

Sunday 19   Tok a walk down the beach to pick up two mink traps that I left out   got a mink in one of them   after I got back I cooked up a kettle of dog feed   tok one of my nets to mouth of Indian River to get trout

Monday 20   Got only two trout but mouth of stream are splitting up   it is really a poor place for fish   not feeling good   tutch of reumatism probbably a change of weather   was going to file up my saws but lost my files

Tuesday 21   A storm raging to day   mild   I am afraid it will take all the snow befor I get my wood home   was out to start cutting   to wet had to quit   tok home my net   got only two again

Wednesday 22   Was out cutting som timber for fire wood   did not think of it as a legal holiday to I got in at noon

Thursday 23   Was up early this morning starting to make bread   blowing and raining so that the snow are almost gone   did not get a trout this morning but set the net again to night

Friday 24   Still warm   40 abov zero   clearing up about four o clock but clouded up again   just raving because I cant get my wood home   snow is disapearing fast   over fifty abov and this is no Sewards Ice Box and we have not had hardly ice anough the whole winter to make an ice cream   was sitting by the stove hamaring out a peice of steel making a knife   cought four trout this morning

Saturday 25   Still to wet to do anyting about getting home wood   blowing hard in squalls about noon we had a regular snow storm   trees ground & all white in half hour   then the sun burst out of clouds & snow melted off the trees in about five minuts   went out cut two pair bob sled runners & by the time I was thru it was evening

Sunday 26   Went out this morning to hunt a tree that would make a fish pole   got one fourly three feet long draged it home & started sawing got dark   set fire to long dead grass and it certainly ran in the gail its blowing

Monday 27   Still mild with a squall of wind ever so often   have been cleaning up around the

place   firing som bunches of grass the escaped fire yesterday   cooked up a big kettle of trout for dog feed   then I was finnishing ripping the fish pole that I was working on yesterday   about three o clock Erling Frostad came over the flats thru wind so strong that he could hardly stand up

Tuesday 28   Calm & fine weather   warm thermometer up to 48 during to day   snow all gone so there be no chance of sleding wood unles som snow falls   cleaning up around the place put up a target & had som target practis & did the worst shooting I ever did   Erling tok my schiff & pulled over to get som stuff & came back shortly after three o clock

Wednesday 29   Somwath cooler this morning so we decided to haul home som firewood or rather birch logs for fire wood   I started hauling while Frostad was building up the trail   it went better then I expected   we got hom all I had cut & sawed up som   then after lunch we shot a couple shots at target but no good yet   need more practice   had just a summer day   saw the first seagull to day   weather more like May then February

Thursday 1 March   Found a regular summer weather this morning   light rain shortly afternoon   have been sawing & splitting wood most of the day   got about one & a half rick or a little better   about one third of what I want to have to do me next winter

Friday 2   Have been working like hired men all day   cut & packed home a lot of birch and this evening sawed a half rick   a drizly rain at noon gave us a couple of hours rest   went out with sciff to clear the net & got four trout

Saturday 3   Got a nice lot of trout this morning been raining during the night   cut up wath wood we had home wich made over three ricks then we cut up som birch we had in old slough   smole anough that we culd pack them home   Erling went to hunt meal for dog & cats   got one rabbit & one porcupine

Sunday 4   Frosty this morning   saw som drift ice coming from down the lake   went out and tok in the net   working hard to four oclock &

finis our wood pile   wind is from north west feeling cool   burned the dry grass east of cabbin

Monday 5   Was out this morning hunting wilow for to repair old sled to take me down   tok me to noon to get sled redy   had a bath   washing clotches & getting tings ready for leaving

Andrew was employed again by the Bureau of Fisheries this summer. In July he and Captain Cole brought a biologist up to Tustumena who recorded his impressions of the lake in Berg's journal:

July 20 1928   Left APA cannery at mouth of river yesterday morning about 4 am with Andrew Berg and Capt Roy Cole of the USFS "Teal"   came up to lake in Andrews skiff with a Johnson outboard which baulked like hell all the way to the lake   Had an army mule skinned a mile and just like an army mule it smiled sweetly and pulled along the way it was intended to pull as soon as we got out of heavy going and into the lake   Had breakfast at "Victors" cabin on the way up river and got into the lake about 1:30 pm   Water of the lake very milky from glacial water entering at head   Limoloyg [limnology] of this lake ought to be interesting as it is quite a different lake from any I know of that have been studied   Water is cold   53 F at surface below peninsula and 48 F at surface near head about one mile from where one mouth of the glacial river empties   Transpearancy then one foot   Heat budget must be low and poor permetion of light would limit photosynthies and therby production of phytoplankton and hence of zooplankton   Very few salmon seen in river and none so far in the lake except for 3 males (ONerka) [Oncorhynchus nerka, a.k.a. sockeye] which Andrew caught in his trout gill net last night ·   Very few good streams for spawning and I imagine that rich spawn largely along shore   Examined stream at head of lake this morning and will go on down lake this pm and back to mouth of the river tommorow   Willis H Risk   (USBF)

Mr. Risk was certainly correct in his assessment of the limited productivity of the lake due to the glacial silt. But there were more suitable spawning streams than he realized and the salmon had not yet shown up in force. Berg and Cole returned a month later to count salmon in the streams.

Aug 14   Came trugh rapids in 3 hours 12 minutes including time of filling tank four times & mixing oil ones   had lunch at lower point of pinninsula ran to Nikolai Creek   walked up about three miles examining salmon escapment   found quite a number of salmon (Red) but not near wath the stream could carry   saw one nice brown bear of the grizly kind cam up to big house stay all night

15   Came up to Muddy Creek   found som fish but they extended only a short distance up cleared the stream the beter let the fish get up went to Clear Creek   had lunch   walked up stream as far as fish culd go up   Counted eight hundred fish killed by bears   looked trough spawning bed at Nyman Coast   got here by night

16   Started early went up Clear stream on glaser flats   the best spawning grounds seen so far weather fine   in after noon went up Indian River found som red salmon in this stream also   when we got to camp found Wiliamson & Ames here

17   Friday   was down to Bear Creek loking this stream over   saw quite of lot of fish & three

This is the mouth of the "Clear stream on glaser flats" Cole mentioned on August sixteenth. Thousands of red salmon are lurking just below the reflective surface of the water here, pausing before swimming further up the creek to spawn. Photo by C. Cassidy.

Alaska brown bear. Adult bears, on a seasonal diet of salmon, can range from 500 to 1,400 pounds. Eyewitness accounts report that "up close, they are a lot bigger." Photo by Jon Nickles, courtesy of U.S. Fish and Wildlife Service.

ANCHORAGE DAILY TIMES   August 24, 1928

BROWNIES ATTACK BUREAU OFFICIALS IN KENAI REGION

Captain Cole and Andrew Berg have narrow escape from death. One of the most thrilling bear stories ever related in Anchorage was brought to the city this week by Charles L. Cadwallader, fur and game warden who returned on the Discoverer from an official trip down the inlet as far as Kusilof. The story was told to him by Captain Roy L. Cole of the Bureau of Fisheries patrol boat Teal, shortly after that official and Andrew Berg had made their escape from five huge brownies in the Tustumena lake district. The escape was such a narrow one that the captain's hair was still on end as he related the experience to Mr. Cadwallader.

Captain Cole and Berg were making a survey of fish conditions on Birch creek, which flows into Tustumena lake at the old base camp of the Alaska Glacier Tours association They had made their way up the stream to the edge of the timber and were picking their way through the low willows when they were set upon by five brown bears, the largest either of the men had ever seen. Neither of the men was armed and the bears were so close to them and so apparently bent on their destruction, that there seemed small hope of escape. A short distance away there stood a lone tree, a safe refuge for one of them if it could be reached ahead of the bears, and Captain Cole, being the one selected by the bears for the chase, made a run for the

lonely sentinel of the forest with the big brownie close behind, almost within striking distance.

In the meantime Berg, thus far unobserved by the leader of the attack, had backed into a clump of willows scarcely high enough to hide him and was crouching there when the captain raced by him, headed for the tree. When the bear came opposite the willows he caught the scent of Berg and halted for an instant for a glance around. He did not tarry long but it was sufficient time for the captain to reach the tree. While the bear stood close to Berg, sniffing and looking about, almost certain to discover him, Captain Cole drew his attention again by breaking away some dead limbs to permit his ascent of the tree. Leaving Berg, the brownie made a rush for the captain and made vicious swipes at him as he clung perilously to the upper branches with his raised feet just beyond reach. After wearying of the attempt to dislodge the captain from his perch and apparently having forgotten that there was easier prey close by in the willows, the old warrior and his four companions wandered off.

Captain Cole believes in the protection of game but he knows four brownies that are not deserving of the safeguards which the government has placed upon them. His experience has suggested to him that there is such a thing as too much protection.

bears two black one brown   going to Birchwood if wind let up   went on down to Birch Wood stay all night in Tom Odales cabin   I was wandering around in evening calling my cat but got no answer

18   Early morning started out to examine Birch Creek   went up stream for about two miles   found some 14 life salmon in stream and tousands laying dead on bars tossed up by bears and indication was the most of the dead salmon was under developed when killed   just as we got to the opening where 1923 flood tore out the timber we beheld two larg brown bears in about two hundred yards distance   so they saw us they charged as a mad dog would   I yelled to Capt Cole "run"   at that we both raced down along the creek   I relised at ones that I had no buisnes in that race so I jumped to the creek bank into a patch of young alder sprouts   I no soner had time to conceal myself than the bear ran by me at the speed of a race horse   he evedently know that he was being tricked   stopped with a bellow of rage & started back up stream to look for me pasing by me at aproximately eight feet following center of creek bed that was about six feet wide at this point   pasing me again going by about nine feet   climbing the creek bank on same side of creek I was standing   letting out a growl at every step   going there fortth around the bunch of alders I was hiding in   getting to sea of me he rised his head loking stright at me of a distance about eight feet   here I thought that my time have come when Capt Cole who in a hurry was strugling up a dry spruce broke a limb off the tree   the bear let out an aful roar charged the noise and hit the tree   from the way the top of it was swinging I was afraid hed breack it down just then I ran up stream making good time nearly ran into five more but saw som snags of cotton wood about eight feet high   got up on them when Capt Cole shouted inquiring about my well being   I answered ok   I asked him to look around and see if the two murderous beast was still aroud   he said he could not see into the alder ticketts but told me to look back of me as there was five more   of those I only saw four   I shot one of them with a 22 calibere stevens pistol the only gun we had among us   we withdrew from the battle as gracefully as we could   that is

sneaking down an old chanel making the least noise   alway I had my focus on the nearest tree that would be easy to clim   we got away

The remarkable element of this story is that the two men were carrying only one .22 caliber pistol between them. Bears gather around salmon streams in August. Birch Creek (now called Bear Creek) splashes and winds through steep banks and dense underbrush making it all too easy to surprise a bear, or five.

Berg did not stay at Tustumena after the bear encounter, he may have gone on to the Kenai River for stream counts. Fox farmer Pete Madsen and Ed Zettle came to Tustumena for porcupines and a sheep hunt and left the following entry in Andrew's journal:

[August] 23   Left Big Hill at 11:00 am for lake arrived at Peninsula cabin at 3:00 pm   stayed there till next day on account of heavy glacier wind

24, 25   Left peninsula at 2:00 pm for Devils Bay glacier wind came up so we stopped at Big House and had coffee   left there at 5 pm and arrived at Fred's cabin at 8 o clock   stayed there until next morning and then came over to Andrews cabin

26   Walked up to Lake Emma hunting porkies poor hunting   saw no bear so far

Aug 27   1928   Left camp at 5 am for the overhanging trail   had our three sheep by 9:30 saw three nice black bear also

28   Went up overhanging trail and brought the last of our meat down   Saw two more nice black bear today

29   Finished packing out meat across glacier flats and cut some wood and got ready to go home Peter Madsen & Edward E Zettle

Madsen may have been scouting bears for the next hunting trip recorded in the journal:

Sept 14 to Sept 16   W G Hansen Alfred Gustafson Sacramento California   Ed Jesson Anchorage Alaska   Peter Madsen & M. L. Cole   Kasilof Alaska   3 black bear & 1 brownie

M.L. Cole was Milton Cole, a fox farmer with no relation to Captain Roy Cole. Milton and his father, Perry, had previously farmed foxes in New York State. Perry Cole first came to Alaska as an inspector for the American National Fox Breeders Association. The availability of fox feed (rabbits, porcupines and fish) convinced him that prospects were good for farming in Kasilof and he started a fox ranch in 1928.[1] Cole brought an entourage of family and associates, a herd of angora goats, a Kohler generator and big plans.[2] He intended to syndicate his fur ranch in Kasilof.[3] To this end, Perry was interested in promoting both the fur business and Kasilof. At his instigation, talk began of establishing a territorial school and building a road.

Perry Cole imported goats to provide a dependable source of fox food when natural supplies were fluctuating. Rabbits were the favored food for the captive foxes but their population was in a downswing at this time. Porcupines were not as easy to come by and salmon were only seasonally available. The other Kasilof fox farmers adapted by building a cooperative cold storage plant at Abe Erickson's place. Skinned carcasses and fish could be stacked in the freezer like cordwood during times of abundance. A diesel generator provided the power. The building of the plant was a newsworthy event and was duly reported in the *Anchorage Daily Times*.[4]

Ed Zettle, Perry Cole's son-in-law, showing off some fine log work. Photo courtesy of Dolly Cole Christl.

ANCHORAGE DAILY TIMES
September 10, 1928

Raising Of Foxes Growing Industry In Kusilof Region

The fact that nearly all the prize winning silver foxes at last week's fair came from Kusilof shows the advance of this growing Alaskan industry in that vicinity. Archie McLane, who arrived in town last week to show his and the Abram Erickson fox entries at the fair, was among the first fox breeders to engage in the industry at Kusilof. This little settlement of the Kenai Peninsula is situated at the mouth of the Kusilof River, a meandering little stream that carries the glacial waters of Lake Tustumena through a woody wilderness and empties into Cook Inlet. Here the Kusilof Packing Co. once canned salmon, but now the fox raising industry is the sole enterprise of the district. Within an area of only three square miles there are no less than seven fox ranches, with an eighth, that of Perry Cole, an eastern fur farmer, now in the process of construction and calculated to be in operation soon on a large scale...

The fox breeders have experienced general good fortune and are very successful, in the opinion of McLane, but in the last year, owing to the scarcity of rabbits, chief food of the foxes, the production of pelts has met with a decrease of from 50 to 75 per cent.

ANCHORAGE DAILY TIMES
September 15, 1928

Fox Farmers of Kasilof Section Install Storage

Co-operative cold storage established to keep fox food fresh. For several years the fur farmers of Kusilof have been confronted with the problem of keep fox food in a fresh condition during the warm summer months. Often it has been the case that game was very scarce in the immediate vicinity and the farmers were compelled to go out quite a distance from the village to obtain rabbits and other meat for the consumption of the foxes with the result that's a big part of it would spoil before it was entirely consumed. This problem is now being solved by Abram Erickson, a fox breeder who has lived at Kusilof for over eight years. Realizing the need of having fresh provisions at hand at all times, he conceived the plan of building a cold storage plant which will be operated on the cooperative method.

My Pioneer Days   Marion S. Cole

[In June of 1928, a young woman in New York state dropped out of high school to travel to Alaska with her fiance's family. Decades later, Marion S. Cole wrote down the highlights of her few years spent in Kasilof. Milton Cole was her fiance. He had been sent ahead with his brother-in-law, Ed Zettle, to begin live trapping foxes and gathering building materials for the Cole's new farm. The rest of his family, and another family named Brown, came the following summer. They made their way from New York to Alaska by car and ship. Milton rendezvoused with them in Ketchikan where he and Marion were married. We take up Marion's story when they reached Anchorage by train from Seward:]

We spent two days there before boarding a gas boat, the Discoverer, down Cook Inlet to Kasilof. The boat was loaded with supplies and it took a long time to unload it by hand. We stayed with Al and Alice Hardy until the men got the tents put up on the homestead which was about four miles up the river.

The tents were made of two by four boards on the floor and walls with canvas tops. There was lots of land and wide open spaces with millions of mosquitoes. The first look I got of it made me wish I was back home in New York... We had a tent for the Browns, one for the Coles, the cook tent and our little tent which was soaked with rain most of the time as it had no wood floors or walls. We lived in the tents until October 20th. By then the men folks had the walls of the [log] house half up and half of the roof on. The fourteen of us had to move into the half of the house while the tents were torn down to sheet the other half of the roof. What an experience for a new bride.

Moose were so plentiful that they scratched their backs on the corners of our house. If the doors were open they would stick their heads in. That was pretty scary to us.

Mrs. Cole, Mrs. Brown and I took turns cooking. Mrs. Brown and I used one bedroom as a school and taught the school age children as there was not a teacher available. The Territorial Government paid us about $250 each for the whole year.

[The Coles had four other children with them: Dorothy, age 22; Comer, age 15; Lucille, age 12; and Burton, age 3. There were at least two other families with children in Kasilof, the McLanes and the Sandwicks, but none of their children had reached school age. More excerpts from Marion's memoir are included later in the book.]

The Cole's homestead in Kasilof. A small lake sits just down the hill in the foreground. There is a fence around the buildings in this scene, so moose can no longer scratch their backs on the corners of the house or poke their noses indoors. Photo courtesy of the McLane Collection.

Also reported in the *Times* was the installation of a generator and electric ice box at the Kasilof home of Al and Alice Hardy.[5]

The Hardys had moved to Kasilof from the metropolis of Anchorage and brought their desire for urban amenities with them. By this time Al Hardy had spearheaded the installation of a crank telephone system, stringing lines on trees and poles to connect seven farms and the boat dock on the river.[6] The instantaneous communication must have seemed close to miraculous. Invitations and emergencies were handled without the long distance legwork. But misunderstandings were a cost of this modern convenience when people couldn't resist eavesdropping on the community-wide party line.

Fox farming was doing well but not so well that the farmers wouldn't take other jobs on the side. Al Hardy was a head guide for the Alaska Guides Association business this year.[7] The company shrank its name to "Alaska Guides Inc." and was still rapidly expanding state-wide. Birchwood on Tustumena Lake was just one of their base camps. Some of their parties were taken by car or rail from Seward to Kenai Lake and then by boat to the south shore of Skilak Lake. Here the hunters were met with pack trains of horses, thirty-four of which had been imported in July from Montana. A new boat mastered the obstacle presented by the rapids of the Kenai River canyon. Designed by Andy Simons and Tom Odale for both river and lake travel, the vessel was equipped with a 30 horsepower engine.[8]

Tustumena Lake was still a draw for locals, including Anchorage residents whose names show up occasionally in Berg's journal. Heinie Berger, owner of the motorship

Discoverer and his agent, C. F. Peterson, advertised Tustumena as a hunting destination in the *Anchorage Daily Times*. They had arrangements with people in Kasilof for providing the additional transportation and other services these hunters might require, although Alaska residents did not have to use registered guides.

Hunting trips were just a sideline for the *M.S. Discoverer.* Heinie Berger was a German immigrant who had purchased the Discoverer in 1927 after successfully operating a transportation service out of Seward with a smaller boat. With his new vessel he expanded his service to Cook Inlet.[9] Providing a vital link in sustaining communities and remote home sites, boat operators like Berger carried passengers and an unimaginable array of freight.

Anchorage Daily Times, September 25, 1928

The M.S. Discoverer *at anchor on the outer coast of the Kenai Peninsula. Freight might include groceries, building supplies, live animals or pianos. Passenger accommodations were spartan at best. Photo courtesy of McLane collection.*

Another owner and captain was Tom Perry. Based in Seldovia, his sixty-five foot *M.S. Princess Pat* worked just within Cook Inlet and made two trips a month to Anchorage.[10]

Andrew Berg took a load of winter supplies to Tustumena in September and enjoyed a hunt. He was accompanied by twenty-two year old Urban Petterson. Urban wrote the following three entries in Berg's journal:

Sept 23   Left Pete & Pete and made the cabin about 7 o clock same night   lost our jonson about a half a mile from cabin   pulled in the rest of the way   fairly tough pulling   everything ok in cabin

Sept 24   Left cabin around six a.m. for sheep hunting   on the way spoted a bear and killed him   dressed him out   a little further ran on another one   shot at him and Andrew hit him   he showed us what he could do in the line of a bear dance   He double up and whirled like a butterfly   We saw some sheep but to far   came back by the home trail   brought some meat and the skin in

Sept 25   Put away the winter's provisions and left this cabin for Birchwood   —Urban Petterson

Andrew took up his own pen when he returned in October:

October 10 Wednesday   Started from Kenai   Evenrude broke down had to row all way   got to Kussiloff evening bringing lot of provision for old man Berg

Tuesday 11   Waited at the Kussiloff cannery until the water got over flats   pulled to Chas Sands place   got his Johnson motor & som provision that he was sending up to Hugos cabbin   stopped in at Williamsons & Pete & Petes   ran up to Victors slough   walked back to Mr Cole fox ranch with som mail   set up tent where we had boat   camped all night

Friday 12   Started up river 8:45   ran through in fine style but ran into a nasty gale off trail point   got to Hugos wet & cold   found Sid Sandstom & Mr Jarwell camped here   stay with them all night

Saturday 13   Rather damp otherwise calm weather   left Hugos stopped at Friman & at

Toms Cabbin   had lunch at Toms   found Lizzy Pitsudsky & brought her with us   put our tings away & tok a bear hunt up Indian

Sunday 14   Was home to about ten a.m.   ground our axe and knifs   started up Indian to put in a bridge at upper box cannon   finis the bridge came back hom north side of stream by way of Lake Emma   got hom just as it was getting dark after we had supper & rested up I set out the net for trout   cloudy and drizling rain

Monday 15   Was up early this morning intending to go after mountain sheep but found mountain covered in fog & raining   got two trout for brecfast   Mr Cook was out with my 22 caliber pistol & got 3 squirels   I was mending my net put the potatoes in cellar & tok a walk up glaser flats   came home at dusk

Tuesday 16   Got a late start   walked up glaser flats   tok mouth of Dirty Cannon trail   saw two sheep   killed one & brought it in   got in after dark

F.W. "Billy" Williamson and Victor Holm.
Photo courtesy of McLane Collection.

Wednesday 17 Got away at fair time this morning went up Emma Trail went around Nicanarka Mountain saw two moose one good head sighted a couple hundred mountain sheep got up to four killed one packed it acrost our new bridge I got tired out left packs stumbled in 8:30 coming the last two miles after dark

Thursday 18 Started yeast this morning rainning and nasty weather but could not live meat in woods so we went to bring it in got it home but gat wet trough so much that Mr Cook did not put on his gum boots in crossing Indian River as he said he would not get any wetter if he came acrost without boots was home early set trout net

Friday 19 At home making bread blowed hard during the night & this morning we got snow down to foothils was out making tings in order should the snow fall by turning over dory etc saw a larg flock of swans light in the lake

Andrew left the lake for a couple of weeks and other hunters made use of his cabin:

Oct 24 We are leaving for Kenai this date have enjoyed my trip & hunt very much thanks too the courtesy of Andrew Berg George R Lesske

The following six entries were made by Ray Ferbrache, origins unknown.

Nov 6 Monday Pete Matson John Sandwick & Elmer Stohl arrived here at Andrews cabin at 10 am when they got here they seen that someone else was here so they taken a walk up south fork looking for a few porcupines and there met Al Hardy & Milton Cole comming down with two sheep They got 6 porcupines and called it a day

Tuesday 7 The next day they went part way with Al & Milton up Indian River Al had told Pete John & Elmer that there were lots of sheep up that way They left Al & Milton just this side of Andrews bridge then on up the mountain to the top of Nicknori mountain with out even seeing any sheep Then back to the cabin at 6 p.m. with out even a thing

Wednesday 8 Left the cabin at 6 a.m. for the overhanging trail and up to the sheep mountains

John got 2 sheep Pete got one & Elmer one then back to Andrews at about 6 pm there they found the cabin good & warm with the coffee pot on the stove as I had came up here about 11 am with Earling & Ole Frostead from the where we had stayed over night with Chris Jensen Earling Ole & I had left Kenai on the 6 of Nov we stayed at Victors Cabin that night up the river the next day Nov 7

Friday 9 Pete Matson John Sandwick Elmer Stohl and my self Ray Ferbrache left here at 6:15 for the over hanging trail and up to the sheep mountains Elmer got another sheep while I hunted all over the mountains and only seen two but they were too far off and did not get a shot While Pete & John were packing there out to the trail We got those four down and packed them out to the lake then home at 6 p.m.

Saturday 10 We four went back up the over hanging trail again and about three miles back up on the mountain I got 2 sheep Pete Elmer & John helped me to pack them out in and to save time then down the trail and as it was giting late we left them at the glaser then down to the cabin had a fine supper of sheep meat Elmer was the cook

Sunday 11 Armistess day we left here for the glacer and brought back the last of the sheep While on the way back John developed a tooth so as soon as we got back to the cabin we performed a slight operation on him by tying a piece of snare wire on it and after looseing it with a pair of plyers I pulled it out Much to his relief While writing this Pete & John are out cutting wood and Elmer is cooking dinner Just as we started in to eat Andrew came in he had just came up from Kenai Thanks Andrew for the use of your cabin and things And we hope that we have left it in shipshape Ray M Ferbrache John Sandwick Peter Madsen Elmer Stohl

John Sandwick and his wife Jennie, both Norwegian immigrants, had bought Louis Nissen's Riverview Fur Farm in 1926. Elmer Stohl was a young, second generation Finn born in California. He and his widowed father, Abel, were living at Abe Erickson's.[11]

A Kasilof gathering at the Hardy's. Left to right are Tom Odale, Pete Jensen, Archie McLane, Al Hardy, John Sandwick, James Stryker, Alice Hardy, Bertha Stryker, Enid McLane, Jettie Petersen and Jennie Sandwick. The children include Stan, Jettie and Joan McLane and Shirley and John Sandwick, Jr. The Strykers and Jettie Petersen were visiting Kasilof from Seldovia at this time. Photo courtesy of the McLane Collection.

After Andrew's return on November eleventh, he records his activities since leaving Kenai:

Wednesday 7   Started from Kenai bringing Mrs Cooke to Mrs Williamsons for a visit   ran up to Post Office met Mr Williamson coming to meet us   stay all night at cannery

Thursday 8   Was down to Humpy point to get som piling as fire wood for the old man   stay up to after midnight to hear Japanese singing over the radio

Friday 9   Came up river to Ebs   stay all night Abraham being alone home   the boys up on the lake hunting

Saturday 10   Started 8 am   met Mrs Sandwik at thier fox ranch   walked over big hill   saw old man Cole & som boys   got to lake 12 n   shortly after met young Cole coming down with 3 [illegible]   stay at Hugos all night

Sunday 11   Had truble to get evenrude started came home on one gallon of oil in les than four hours   found Ray John Elmer & Pete here redy to go   Williamson & two campanion came off sheep mountains this evening so we put in Armistice Day   Andrew Berg

Monday 12   At home   started to make a stove but it got snowing so it got to nasty to work outside so I quit   Williamson & one man started to sheep hills   had to com back on acount of snow   the thirth man went to Bear Creek to pack out som moose meat

Tuesday 13   Got a nice mess of trout this morning have been home all day making bread & working at stove at times   Williamson started for the hills this morning   fine weather up to noon when it clouded up   turning milder

Wednesday 14   Was up to Lake Emma cutting out wind falls clearing trail   put out twenty nine traps   did not see any tracks of game animal or fur bearer exepting one black bear   Williamson was over to Erlings to get his Johnson

Thursday 15   Fine loking morning   Williamson & party started for sheep mountains   I was up glaser flats setting som traps & cutting alders about noon it tickened up & begin to snow putting home the wind got so strong I put ashore on old chanel

Andrew's guests wrote an entry expressing gratitude in his journal when they departed:

Friday 16   Finished packing out this a.m. and are leaving for Camp Freeman this p.m.   have had tough weather but got 3 nice sheep anyway have enjoyed the coutese [courtesy] and cooking of Andrew Berg whom we have been staying with here   Carl Newcomb Anchorage   F W Willimson

Berg continues the entry for November 16:

After everybody left to day I am alone the first night since I came up   working at stove but did not get it finnis   after the party came back from Bear Creek to get somting they forgot I found a garment hanging in the hallway   Raining again to night   was just out feeling off the line atached to my trout net   feel noting like trout kicking

Saturday 17   Have been at home all day batling with reumiatiss   the weather is the worst   raining & snowing at times with heavy wind   I been feeling so pore that I ocupied the bed nearly all day   tryed to finis the stove but had to quit   this after noon I put in reading a Comopolitan   I got three dolyvarden trout this morning   now I am boiling the net to clean it

Sunday 18   Have been busy all day from one ting to an other   finished the stove   repaired the evinrude   warmed water had a bath   got into clean underware & feel 100% alright weather warm but raining with pufs of wind off mountain   toward evening I gathered up corage to scrub the floor   putting tings up for a trip to Birch Wood

Monday 19   was aiming to start this morning for Friman but some showers in the morning detained me to do that   it is to late bring the boat home from the old channel   have been putting in my

time reading som old periodical   weather turned out fine in afternoon (mild)

Tuesday 20   Snow covering the ground this morning with strong westerly wind kicking up quite a sea   still snowing in spells   was out cutting a trail in the forenoon to a walk up Indian River later but saw no signs of game   bushes too dirty with snow to go into timber   got three trout

Wednesday 21   Starting for Friman   in going by Toms camp saw sombody there   rather rough all the way   came down & landed fine   set out trout net   rather long evening as I had forgot my glasses   all I could do was to repeat ting I have committed to memory to get time to pass

Thursday 22   Tok a walk down to Olson Creek set out a lot of lynx traps   found that I had better taken my snowshoes   snow is quite deep with good strong crost   no game track

Friday 23   Snowing and blowing   stay home packing in som wood allthoug it no weather to be out in   packed home quite a stack of dry wood and sawed up som green birch

Saturday 24   Went up Lick House trail to near the summit   set out 13 traps wading trough loose snow   got in just at dark tired   the old shak felt as comfy as any mansion could do

Sunday 25   Chinking up cabbin & cleaning my trout net when Tom and Slim came along   going down to cork som fellows that buildt at Hugos they told me of som mail at Toms for Frostad   I walked down to get it   set eight traps

Monday 26   Was down to Olson Creek set out eight traps   saw a track of mink   the other animal track I saw was one on snowshoes going up Olson Creek just east of lake

Tuesday 27   Swell roling in at Friman that I was afraid to start home   finely got off beach after loosing my mit & pull over   got home but had a time sitting and bailing all time   sprays coming over regular   got here everyting was wet

Wednesday 28   Got a bucket full of trout this morning and have been feasting on them all day doing noting but reading & listen to the howling wind outside   I sure felt glad I got home yesterday   here was a lot of snow   when I came this morning it was all gone   to night it turned cold & got the ground covered with new snow

Thursday 29   Wind have gone down som this morning but we have everyting covered with snow   even my shed   the south wester drifted in a lot of snow   Pulled out to glaser flats & set out 7 mink traps   mink season oppens December first   heard a machine running in Devils Bay so I hurried home thinking I would have visitors being thanks given

Friday 30   At home making bread   weather foggy looks like it would start snowing all day but only som fine dust came down

Saturday 1 December   This morning I heated water   had a bath   just then Frostad boys came over   we had lunch then I fixed a couple of steel traps   had super   Played two games of pinocle I washed som clotches & so we call it a day   mild out   snow melting

Sunday 2   A gale of wind blowing so it is no chance to go anywhere with a boat   Ole Frostad working at mending my trout net   Erling out loking for a homstead & working at ods & ends in afternoon the wind let up in spells so then boys started home   I set out net   now 8:30   the wind is whistling thru the trees

Monday 3   Raining   tok in net full of trout weather to dirty to do anyting out   stay in house all day   in cloudy weather light are so poor that I can hardly see with out a lamp   wind quit this evening but still cloudy & warm

Tuesday 4   Had a fine day   was up on glaser flats set out five mink traps   caught one ermin & one lynx   the first catch this season   frosty this morning   turned cloudy

Wednesday 5   my dog have run off this morning I thinking he would be back & soon found that it was to late for me to go up to Lake Emma after waiting

Thursday 6   I guess my dog is left for good was going out this morning but then it started snowing so I stay home hoping the dog would

com back   have been in all day reading som cheap trash   set the net

Friday 7   Was up Lake Emma trail   had to reset a good many of the traps   got one lynx   one have pulled out   not cout by the toes but probbly hock   used snowshoes for a short distance the first time this winter   had to relase [re-lace] them this evening   got only one trout this morning so I set it again this evening

Saturday 8   Started acrost   got to snowing so bad that I could not see anyting   when it lifted I was nearly acrost the lake holding good cours Set out six traps for lynx & five for mink   Run to Frostads got there at dark   the boys have gone same morning   stay all night

Sunday 9   Started at daybreck   set out six more traps   landed boat cached machine & gear under a spruce   went acrost ridge to King Lake got there at half past two   lot of new snow

Monday 10   Stay in camp all day   snowing & blowing   got out in afternoon   brought home and cutup som fire wood   still snowing

Tuesday 11   Was out set som traps but nasty to do   timber hanging full of snow and it all seems to want to fall in your neck   set out eleven   I dont know why   no tracks

Wednesday 12   Started home this morning   quite cold   my mustach was full of ice before I was a mile from camp   snow so deep that I could not se my tracks in coming in   set eight traps on the ridge   got home fine   rather cold in the boat this evening the dog came home just at dark snowing & blowing a gale again this evening

Thursday 13   Slept to almost daylight this morning   setting reading   new snow being to wet to walk in   just when I decided to clean up dishes after breckfast in comes Erling Frostad on his way to Bear Creek   after he went I tok a walk up Indian River   saw lot of moose tracks but no animals   after I got back set out trout net Erling came back   after super we had a game of domy lole

Friday 14   Weather loked tretening this morning but turned out to be a fine day but it was late when it cleared so we stay home   I cut me a pair *of pull overs out of a bear skin then we played a game of Solo   Erling started home late in afternoon   stormy this evening*

Saturday 15   Been at home all day trying to finish a pair of bear hide mitts but on acount of the rainstorm raging outside I have not been able to do much as reumatism & rain storm seimes to have som connection

Sunday 16   At home   storm during the night was the strongest yet   rain [illegible] against the house with such forse that it wetted thru   finished my mitts   had a bath   washed clotches

Monday 17   Went to Friman   stopped at Birchwood saw Tom & Slim   they just packed in frish meat   Tom tryed to tell me it was a month old and that crows have nearly eat it up but I think he was trying to fool me as I saw frish blood running out of a box   not very old I think

Tuesday 18   Stay in camp al day   raining & blowing   manged to get out betwen squalls to saw up a stick of wood

Wednesday 19   Fine day   warm just a light breze   went to Olson & Philip Creek walked out on creek broke thru snowshoes and all got my feet wet   caught one ermine & one lynx

Thursday 20   After I had breckfast sitting reading in come Ole Frostad on his way to Kenai   Slim and Tom came up shortly after going to Hugos or Corral creek   I went up to Lick House   started raining   got one ermine & mink

Friday 21   Went down into Funny River set som traps   started snowing   hurried back & came on down to Camp Friman

Saturday 22   Walked along beach to Toms where I had my dory   buildt a fire at Toms slip to dry off machine & warm plugs   got started & ran into one rain squall after the other   wind was so strong that I thought I would have to go ashore but I hanged on bailing steady   at Bear Creek it started raining so heavy that it killed the wind   got home

Sunday 23   Snow & rain this morning   after I got lines put in shape I waited a while   it cleared & loked as if it was to be fine   I went up to flats wher there came a voley off mountains with such roar wind I had to get in timber for shelter   since then it kept it up all day

Monday 24   Heard wind blowing this morning so I did not get out of bed to daylight   after I had breckfast and put tings to order it was afternoon   I tok the skiff pulled to flats   ran the trap line   coming back of hogback I got a lynx in the last trap   got home just as it was getting dark   found two moose standing close to house when I cam home   one is here now   I just heard it few minuts ago   skinned & stritched the lynx   put out net & been reading several pages of the Three Musketeres   how I celebrate x mass

Slim Crocker found an old skull with unusual antlers. (The palm of the antler on the right is bifurcated.) Andrew mentioned seeing Slim in November and December. Crocker had returned to Kasilof in 1927. This year he acquired guide badge number 75 and joined the Alaska Guides.[12] Photo courtesy of Betty A. Crocker.

Tuesday 25   At home celabrating christmass   did not know just how to go about it but have heard that cleanlines is next to godlenes so I heated water and had a bath   made a cake for my self & cooked a nice fat lynx for my dog Schotte   just at dusk Erling came visiting   weather mild with light drisling snow

Wednesday 26   Have been home all day   Erling & I started this morning playing domy solo so kept it up to noon   than I prepared som lunch after that Erling started to make redy to go home went to lake shore with him to watch him get started   afterwards I mended my snow shoes heated up a smole hunting axe hammered it out retempered it put it on handle ground it

Thursday 27   Was up on glacer flats   found som sheep down   killed one old ram at the island did som bad shootin being so foggy that it was dificult to find the game thru the sight   tok it all home including hide exepting head & feet

Friday 28   Intended to go up to Lake Emma but befor I got everyting in shape it was to late to go anywhere   got a lot of trout   had them in a dish pan in the shade   heard a noys   looking out I saw a ermine eating them   I started to set som

traps   while I stod there it came back and got caught

Saturday 29   Was up to Lake Emma got two lynx good going after I got up but treacherous   hill icy under with loose snow covering   just as I was skinning the first lynx I heard a lot of shooting towards the glaser by a havey calibre rifle   thermometer at 12 abov 6 am

Sunday 30   At home all day watching bread made 16 larg loaves   betwin times been mending up a pair of pants   nasty weather   heavy northerly wind   lake being feather white from breacking sea   quite cold in morning

Monday 31   Going to Visit Erling   went over after waiting at fornoon   heard a machin running thinking it might be Erling coming foggy in Devils Bay could see noting   finely I went over found the place deserted   Erlings boat at Clear Creek so it was somone else I heard tok a walk to Clifhouse   to late to go to King Lake so I stay all night celebrating new year eve

My Pioneer Days   Marion Cole

(continued)

We ordered Christmas gifts from Sears Roebuck in Seattle only to learn there would be only first class mail delivered until late the next April. We had to make our own gifts with what we had. Believe me or not they turned out great.

Christmas Day everyone was to gather at the McLane home. As there were no roads we had to snowshoe. Even though I grew up in upper snowy New York, I had never worn snowshoes. I was pregnant and took many falls over logs and willow brush before we reached McLanes which was about four miles from our homestead. I don't remember where we all slept but we spent the night there.

CHAPTER 14

1929

January 1929.

i Tuesday 1. As it would likely be warm all day, I decided to start for my cabin on King Lake, machine running fine got to my second trap on south coast I had a lynx. tok it into the schiff drued along to my landing place landed the ouitfit skinned the lynx got my pack west acrost ridge got one lynx came to cabbin at 2.30 p.m. had a cup of coffe went to end of line no more game. Lost one mink just missed a Lynx

Wednesday 2 Left for home   ran another string of traps got one lynx   made a fire to warm machine   quite choppy & cold wind   the sprays building ice on the schiff   got home in good time   finnis cleaning skins & ready for bed 10:30 p.m.

Thursday 3 Blowing up lake a nasty wind   went thru timber to mouth of Indian River walking before wind   went thru island over seing my trap line   saw som sighn of game but no catch this eve is a regular blizard   sea to high to set the net

Friday 4 During night wind hauled around to south east   when I got up this morning it was raining   thermometer stod at 38 so I had to make it a day of rest   mending som underwear

had a bath   changed clotches   mopped the floor & set out the net   blowing hard this evening

Saturday 5 That warm and wet that I was undecided if I could use snowshoes on the ridg or not   anyway I started about eleven o clock the hillside was tawed so that lose ground slipping on frozen ground made hard going   on top fine going   water on ice on Lake Emma got one wolferine   back here at 3:50 p.m.

Sunday 6 Was intending to go to Friman to day but wind sprung up with heavy swell so I decided to wait   was cleaning up tings I found I had eight traps here   I tok them   pulled to glaser flats and set them out for fox   tok a walk up hogback   when I got back home I found my mail   Ole had com while I was gone   I dont se *how I missed him   acording to his note he have just left   all ok at Kenai*

Monday 7   Started to Friman 11:30   fine weather a regular summer day   thermometer at 35   lake as smooth as a mill pond   got there in less than two hours and a half   tok a walk up the beach to som traps I had   all I caught was one old horn owl

Tuesday 8   Was down to Olson Creek   meet Tom Odale coming from Corral Creek   started raining   lynx was to a couple of traps but squirrels got there first   did not get furs of any kind

Wednesday 9   Went up to Lick House   good traveling below but on the ridge I had a lot of loos snow to walk thru   got only one ermine on my way up   set up new stove pipes & cut anough wood for trip

Thursday 10   Mild   a drizly rain   did not like to go anywhere but decided to try rather than go thru a lot of new snow in case it would turn colder heavy going but all down hill brecking new trail caught three mink in Funny River and lost one lynx trap by a wolferine   snow very wet   hurried back fixed tings in shape and started right down to Friman   was heavy snowshoeing   had to stop every few minutes to clean snow off the snowshoes   got one ermine   came in good and tired

Friday 11   Have been raining and blowing all night   nearly all snow have disapeared   hevy swell this morning   by ten o clock the swell was flattening so I got in the sciff and came home in fine stye   saw one man at Glaser Tours Camp to far to tell who it was

Saturday 12   Tok a walk into glacer flats   found most of my trap out of order   it must have been blowing hard the few days I was away   stumps and tings been rolling along glaser morain   saw a lot of moose   two cows with calf   one had two the first calfs I seen this season   mild   som fine snow coming down this evening 11 p.m.

Sunday 13   have not done anyting to give myself credit for   it have been a nice calm day   inclined to be somwhat foggy under the mountains   have

had a feeling that somone was coming so I have been listening for exaust every few minute

Monday 14   Went over to Frostad boys to bring over a pair of skies   just as I was leaving there the high tention wire broke and I had to return take the thing apart to fix it   when I was ready to start again Erling decided to go along   we ran along my trap line   crossed the ridge to King Lake   fine traveling   got no game of any sort

Tuesday 15   Was intending to go to Rat Lake to have a look over the country but it started raining so we came back crossing the ridge about a mile south   stay at Frostads all night   raining all night

Wednesday 16   Came home early   started to blow from the south   ran along edge of glaser flats loking after my trap   got home about eleven tok my machine apart   not running good and tank leaking

Thursday 17   Was out fishing the net this morning but not a single trout did I get so after breckfast I cut up som meat and cooked up a big kettle of stew   reading so I spent the whole day   weather still mild   just about frezing point

Friday 18   Foggy this morning with a light breze off the mountain   I walked up to Lake Emma climbing the hill was hard icy   I went in without snowsshoes   made it   just broke thru at few places   no game   came down back of millsite crost good in side hill   saw tracks of 1 lynx one fox & one wolferene

Saturday 19   Started to walk to glaser flats but was unable to get acrost Indian River   cam back put out the sciff   tok machine and ran to flats warm regular summer day   left the machine lay on beach it did not freeze up   foggy towards evening

Sunday 20   At home making bread   weather quite warm   thin fog coming down covering smoth plases but not anough to be noticed on naked grass land   This evening when I was at my landing setting the net I cleared som rocks & piled them clear of landing   rocks have not frozen to the beach all winter

Monday 21 Fixed up a work bench outside and planed up enough lumber to widen out my bed tok me nearly all day   this morning set the net again   this evening tok a walk up old bed of river   got close to a moose

Tuesday 22 At home all day and not acomplished much of any ting   8 degre abov this morning lake laying that smoth that ice was forming all over   if it had been 10 or 15 colder it sure would have laid it   water is well chilled it dont take much to freeze it   tok a walk up to som fox traps no game   28 abov this evening   will wait one more day to see if I go by boat or walk   changed the scent for woferine on home lines

Wednesday 23 Raining during the night and this morning everyting as slick as a glass botle Erling Frostad came over we grined a knif for him   I put new webb in my snowshoes   setting playing Solo to near midnight   heavy swell on beach   wind changing to north   still raining almost imposible to stand up

Thursday 24 Weather cleared up with a westerly storm   Erling left going up to Dirty Cannon to look after som wolferine sets and try to get som pictures of mountain sheep   I have acomplished noting exept gathering togather tings I need to Birchwood   Mixin oil and such

Friday 25 Went down to Friman   sloppy head wind off Bear Creek   had to play monkey sea to keep from taking toppers over the stern   Ran in to fine weather below   by the time I got there it was dead smoth   tok a walk up beach   tok in wath lynx set I had   the start of taking in

Saturday 26 Before got out of bed this morning Tom Odale came in at Friman on his way to Kussiloff   went to Olson Creek tok up all lynx sets in that line   got two ermine   getting poor picking with furs so it is time to quit   fine traveling & no snowshoes

Sunday 27 Went to Lick House   crost holding without snowshoes but glased that it made it mean walking to I got near to summit then I had to

---

My Pioneer Days   Marion Cole
(continued)

About the middle of January, when an airplane landed on our lake in front of our house with first class mail and passengers, Mr. Cole went to Anchorage on business. Before he returned, Milton became seriously ill. Mr. Hardy came with his dog team to take him out to the railroad so he could go to the hospital in Anchorage. It was a four day trip by dog team. The next day the plane came to bring Mr. Cole home and learned the news about Milton. The pilot, Russell Merrill, said he would fly over the trail where he thought they might be, land on a river or lake to pick Milton up and take him to the hospital. Mr. Cole said that I should go with him. I hustled a few clothes into a suitcase and we were on our way.

We landed in Kenai, a little native village about fourteen miles away, to leave mail and supplies. Usually we got our mail once a month by dog team. The pilot said I should stay there to save weight in landing. He would pick up Milton then return for me. I was to rush out to the airport as soon as I heard a plane. At that time Kenai had only a couple hundred natives, about five hundred dogs, the U.S. Marshal and family and the storekeeper and his family. I had met the storekeepers wife so I went to her home and was graciously welcomed. There was no plane that day or night. We listened on the radio for a message but none came. We could get radio only after dark. The next morning about eleven we heard a plane and rushed out to the airport. It was the pilot to pick me up. He had picked up Milton the day before and decided he wouldn't have enough gasoline to come back for me.

I knew nobody in Anchorage but Milton had gotten acquainted with Mr. and Mrs. Axe. She was at the hospital to meet me and take me home with her. That evening she was to go to Seward on the train to see some friends off who were leaving for the "Outside". I stayed in her home alone. About midnight I was awakened by someone banging on the front door. I jumped out of bed and ran to the door to find a policeman there. He said they wanted me at the hospital as soon as possible. I hurried so fast I think I forgot to thank him. When we got there Milton was in surgery for adhesions. I was so nervous and upset they gave me a shot and put me in bed. The doctor was afraid I would have a miscarriage. The next morning Milt asked for me and was feeling much better. After about three weeks we returned to Kasilof by plane.

start wearing snowshoes   no game   moose had to go to lake shore on acount of crost   saw signs of wolferine and fox

Monday 28   Went a long ways into Funny Basin took me over seven hours befor I was back to Lick House tired and hungry and the dog was in just as bad shape with sore feet cut by sharp crost

Tuesday 29   Came down to lake shore by one o clock   ice as far as I could see   heavy fogg just then Tom came up the beach had som mail for Frostad boys   stoped in left me the mail had som lunch

Wednesday 30   Lots of ice as far as I could see still foggy   did not atemt to take boat out   walked along the beach called in at Toms   he was occupied at gobbin solder on a cast iron pump handle that was broken (som job)   saw Slim towards Emil Nesses place   looked quite clear from ice here   got home about two

Thursday 31   Was at home cleaning up having a shave and etc   well in fornoon I started to take the mail to Frostad boys   had a time getting acrost Indian River   fine walking on the glaser flats   was a lot of moose   found the boys at home putting a floor in shade room   coming back tok in as many traps as dog could pack got here at dark

Friday 1 February   Wake up this morning with sore troat an congestion on my left lung   stay home all day painting chest with iodine and trying to care for troat   I think I am getting the best of eftiction

Saturday 2   At home to noon watching ice making so I could go on it to south side but it is turning mild so I am afraid I got no chance   afternoon I walked out to glaser flats   tok in the last traps wind making noise in mountains   fog clearing will have a storm

Sunday 3   Stormy this morning with weather turned mild   no ice in sight   intendid to go on the hill but with the icy trails and wet snow there be no chance of getting up   towards evening it started to snow and came quite a lot   I set out net again as ice is gone

Monday 4   Erling Frostad came just after I had breckfast on his way to bring mail to Tom & Slim who are going acrost country to Anchorage   mild light fog   inclined to be wet   have been home all day   my throat still sore   got three trout

"Going acrost country to Anchorage" means dog sledding to Lawing or Moose Pass to catch the train.

Tuesday 5   Was up to Lake Emma   packed all traps   14 at cach point and 14 at summit   raining and blowing   got back at two   bad climbing coming back of hill   Erling came back

Wednesday 6   Have been home listening to the storm and playing Solo   was out fornoon but was drove home by rain   went out again at dusk got a porky for the dog   set out net   still windy my left lung is feeling very sore

Thursday 7   Erling Frostad and I walked over to there place   found Ole at home   the only piese of ice at this end of lake was brecking up stay all night   had a game of pinocle this evening

Friday 8   Erling started me on my way by bringing me down about four miles with dory and evinrude I went to my cabbin at King Lake   put tings in shape to leve it untill next winter

Saturday 9   Came back it started to rain so I was afraid to stay over   met Erling and crossed Devils Bay with him   had lunch at there place met Ole half way home comming from Bear Creek talked him into comming back to my place

Sunday 10   Blowing and raining this morning so we decided to waste this day on solo   played three games   about four p.m. calmed down   sun broke thru   Ole went home   I started to wash clotches

Monday 11   Raining again this morning so I hunted up som rags that needed washing and here I been all day doing the old ladys work

Tuesday 12   At home all day   washed som clotches   boiled out a lot of hankerchif   raining steady and quitily all day   warm feeling like a day in may   inclined to be moist   got three doly varden and four makinaw trout

Mackinaw is another name for lake trout.

Wednesday 13   Frostad boys came over   cutting house logs   played three games of solo   to night raining   thermometer been at 46 all day

Thursday 14   Fine weather   tok a walk on glaser flats   tok in the last traps set for mink no game   after I came home I tok a walk to where the boys is chopping house logs

Friday 15   At home all day tinkering my snowshoes   warmed water had a bath   no trouth this morning   the first miss for a long time Ole cut top off the big cotton wood for me

Saturday 16   Went with the boys as far as Bear Creek in boat then walked the rest of way to Friman   tok in traps

Sunday 17   Raining   stay in cabbin all day

Monday 18   Continued rain with heavy wind

Tuesday 19   Fine weather this morning   went to Olson Creek   tok no snowshoes   had tough going   snow getting soft

Wednesday 20   Snappy cold   went to Lick House lot of new snow over summit   total catch   lynx 9 mink 5   ermine 14   wolferine

Berg's catch was down but prices were very high this year, he probably made at least $700. Average payments were $61.10 for lynx, $20.70 for mink, $1.74 for ermine and $19.95 for wolverine.[1] These amounts reflect a 300 percent increase since 1922.

Thursday 21   Was down into middle creek of Funny River   had a regular winter day   got cold feet

Friday 22   Snowing   turning milder   going back to lake   all thru with traps for season started to blow   was in snow storm all way down see noting but drifting snow

Saturday 23   Storm continue today with lot of snow and a regular gale   stay in cabbin reading all the old periodicals I could fine

Sunday 24   Wind changed to south by west decided to walk home and leave my boat for an other trip   had tough going   to strong head wind had to go thru woods nearly all the way lake was running the hevyest sea I seen on it

found the boys at my cabbin   weather to bad to be out

Monday 25   An other winter day   been busy fixin tings   put a new handle on ax   sharpened the saw and making ready to refill the wood shed in case I be up here again next winter   boys was out in fornoon getting som logs yarded but it got to bad so they had to quit   since then we been playing Solo and reding

Tuesday 26   Started to day in a snowstorm to cut and bring home green birch for next winter wood the boys came to help with dog team and all hands working hard we had nearly all I wanted by noon after noon we yarded logs

Wednesday 27   The Frostad boys went home this morning   I was getting home som more wood logs when it started to rain and I thinking that I have anough home quit   had lunch and after resting som I heated water and had a bath

Thursday 28   Was out early fishing   got seven makninaw trout   after breckfast rumaging in wood shade dropped a block of wood on my foot that laid me up for the day   not much diffent anyway as it was raining to beat puget sound all day

Friday 1 March   Have been hom all day my foot swolen and bruise   have been painting with idoine to take out the sornes   in afternoon limped out to glaser flats to bring two bots I had left out there   quit raining   getting coler

Saturday 2   Snowing this morning   when it got light anough to see out the spruce have got old during night   each was silvery   got only two trout   have been in all day   my foot feeling stif but sornes is leaving

Sunday 3   An other day of noting acomplished stormy and snow   lake have been feather white with brecking swels   could not even get the net out this evening   to heavy swells   been reading morals & dogma and find it quite of study

Monday 4   The coldest morning that I have noticed was to day   thermometer at 2 abov   it was making ice on the windows   have been in the cabbin   hewed som on the wall & leveled up the floor

Tuesday 5   At home   snow and som wind   6 abov this morning   while I was out to lok at thermometer I met a regular blizard   the shed drifted ful of snow   got only one trout (doly varden)

Wednesday 6   Snowing with light breze at ten abov zero   tok a walk over flats to Frostads place to get a hammer   I brok mine yesterday just as I was nearing thier place I saw them leaving   I hailed them   they came over here on their first leg on trip to Kenai   I walked back had quite a time to get acrost Indian River overflow nasty   got three Makinaw trout

Thursday 7   Thermometer down to six abov this morning   Erling was up befor day fishing net and making breckfast   got two trout   after sun got up was making ready to leve but waited to ten o clock to let it get warmer   after they left I put a handle in my splitting axe and repared an emery wheel

Friday 8   A thin field of ice lay acrost my net this morning but lukily I got it in without damage thermometer was down to zero the coldest I have seen it this winter   started yeast making ready for a days baking   been in all day   my foot is swelled up so I soaked it in warm water to reduse it

Saturday 9   Have been busy all day watching bread and got a nice lot to show for my days work   a lot of ice drifting a way out on the lake I had not out the net last night but this evening I set it tho I take a chance losing it

Sunday 10   A fine snow coming down all day not much but anough to be nasty to be out in got no trout second time this morning   was out towards evening with the dog to get porcupine but none been out far several days   getting tired of being in

Monday 11   Started to saw som wood to day but had to quit   have been waiting for good weather to work in   just about one hour after I started a wind sprung up and you could not stand up in drifting snow   blowing all day

Tuesday 12   Have actualy started to saw wood the day was the best for somtime   sawed quit a lot for a start   timber is frozen and saw slow tok a walk out loking for porcupines   did not find any

Wednesday 13   Went to take in the net found it fast in ice   tramping thru with gumboots I finaly got it loos but no fish so after breckfast I put net in tub with water to thaw the ice   was out got som wilow bark   tanned it [the net]   same time shifted rick of dry wood to make room for next winter stock   filed croscut saw   cut two largest logs   cooked dog feed   this evening came a snow storm about six o clock

Berg's gillnet was made of linen. It had to be treated to prevent rot. Commercial nets were periodically soaked in "bluestone," a copper-based preservative. Willow bark was used in leather tanning. Berg obviously thought it would help his nets as well as hides. (If he knew then what we know now, he would have dunked his nets in iodine and doctored himself with the salicylic acid of the willow bark.)

Thursday 14   Have not acomplished much to day   split som twisted birch   set a kink in my back and weather still is contrary   som wind from south set in a lot of drift ice that it looks like winter in ernest

Friday 15   Weather changed to south east with strong wind   turned mild   ice in lake intirely gone   started to split som wood but rain and snow drov me in here   I been a week and have not a rick of wood

Saturday 16   Mild   quit raining   split wath wood I had sawed   ricked it and sawed a couple more sticks to fill the rick so I got one rick finis any way   strong wind   snow disapearing fast making it wet   set out the net this evening to get som trout

Sunday 17   Storming during the night that I was afraid of loosing my net   heavy sea was running but the net have only drifted a little and had six nice trout in it   I filed the saw and sawed a couple sticks but the wind is to strong had to quit

Monday 18   South easterly wind still continues with light rain   not much but anough to get wet bein out in it   repaired a pair of shoepacks heated water had a bath and feeling more lazy than usualy

Tuesday 19   Had a fine day and I got in about four hours on the wood pile   had som tough sticks to split so four hours is plenty unles I want to get sore not being used to manual labor and besides I had som clotches to wash   thawed snow to get soft water to wash in

Wednesday 20   Got up early this morning expected to do wonders at the wood pile   when I got thru with breckfast and dishes cleaned it started to rain   just a mist to begin with but getting more right along   finely wind & snow so I put in another day not acomplishing anyting

Thursday 21   Had som new snow this morning so I went out and hauled in two loads of green birch   sawed and split and ricked mor than half a rick   set out trout net   tok dog & cat was well pleased but the dog refused frish meat in form of rabbit   I got one rabbit   they are very scarce

Friday 22   This morning a regular summer day fished the net   got a nice lot of trout   cooked up two for breckfast   one doly varden & one makinaw   after setting cabbin in shape washing dishes sweeping out and feeding schot and lizze pileudski I ventured out to saw som wood and the first stick I cut up was so twisted and tough that I thought I would have to split it with a ripe saw   got only scant half rick to day

Saturday 23   Found a brand new winter when I got up this morning   so much snow have fallen and drifted in that I had troble of pulling the net ashore and then without a fish   went out cut som green birch   hauled home fair loads then it started to snow so heavy and snow getting that wet I had to get in

Sunday 24   Sawed split and finished a good half rick so I got three ricks finis   snow covered everyting this morning but sun is getting that strong it nearly all melted during the day   was out porcupine hunting this evening   got one got a trout for my breckfast

Monday 25   I tok a walk thru the hilside to find if any bear have begun to come out as there was anough new snow left for good track snow   went

clean to Bear Creek without finding any sign or a track

Tuesday 26   Not feling good   been in cabbin nearly whole day reading som old books but most of time I spent asleep   can do that fine   heavy storm off north east   saw snow drifting on mountains at daybreck   set out the net but had a time getting it out thru the surf   cooked up som dog feed

Wednesday 27   Had a little frost on the window this morning   lake loking nice and smoth   got just one trout for breckfast but anough   it was a makinaw fair size so I was taking my time about clearing away dishes   at ten started cutting wood three hours   was out toward evening hunting saw log

Thursday 28   Have been in all day making bread it have been a very beutiful day   cold in morning but skys clear as a bell   calm lake laying as smoth as a pan of glass   was out eve hunting saw log but got a porcupine

Friday 29   At home cleaning up   washed som clotches   scrubbed the floor   cooked up a kettle of dog feed   have kept my self busy all day and cant see wath I been doing   weather nice and calm   regular summer day

Saturday 30   Was feeling good and sasy all day change in weather   cloud rising   towards evening I saw a few hail stones dropping   fixing up som old wearing apearals   in rumaging thru I found one copy of New Age Magazen   tok me som time to go thru that   sawed a few sticks of wood   towards evening set the net again   got only one makinaw this morning   I hear the surf on lake shore sounds heavy

Sunday 31   Got up early this morning   the wind have gone down considerably but surf still running   nearly half of the net was rolled up but it had not came ashore   I hauled it in and got one dolly varden trout so I got my breckfast just the same   I am so used to have my breckfast of frish trout that if I dont get them I feel like I went without breckfast   been working at the wood hard   finis wath I had home but have to pack in a couple sticks to fill last rick   blowing a south westerly storm   the hardest I ever saw from that quarter

Monday 1 April   Storming all night and cold making beach glased wher sea and spray washed upon the shore   not doing much of anyting spliced my fish pole   tok a walk up Indian   saw one porky but he was so smole I did not take him cold anough to pinch my ears

Tuesday 2   This morning when I went fishing the beach line was frozen down that hard I had to go back home to get a steel bar to get it loos been busy all day from one ting to an other and done noting wort mentioning   towards evening I tok a walk to glaser flats to find out if any bears have come out   came back along foothils to one mile up Indian River   saw signs of game   but no bears

Wednesday 3   Cold   about 10 abov with strong wind up the lake   I got couple of trout and cooked som potatoes to go with them and it makes a right tasty breckfast   stay in to after noon when the wind let up I wheeled home a lot of gravel to fix around the well

Thursday 4   Had a good hike to day   got thinking there aucto be som bears showing   went up glaser flats along foot of mountain al the way to Rays Mine   went in to Rays cabbin found tings in bad shape there   the door tore down saw a lot of sheep   old rams   found two dead rams   probably wounded   packed in the largest head   after I got home I cleaned out the well had to climb in and out for every boket of dirt and water I tok   water was low so I got it fairly clean

Friday 5   Have a nice new winter this morning everyting white and snow still falling   look to nasty to go into and having noting pressing to do I decided to stay right home   made a waxend and sewed a knife scabbard for my new knife weather turned out fine in afternoon   cleared up but to cold to taw much   its frezing to night

Saturday 6   Put som tings up to take along walked down beach to Camp Friman to get my sciff   befor I got to Birchwood I heard two rifle shots in side of glaser tours camp   tok a walk in to timber found tracks of a man   turned around

came to Toms   found him just got in   said he shot twice at a raven

Sunday 7   Hauled my boat over ice one hundred and seventy yds   packed my tings in   started my machine and was home by twelf o clock   tok a walk up Indian to cannon loking for porkies had my big rifle along expecting to find a bear started to snow again this evening

Monday 8   New snow on ground this morning but warm so snow started melting   got one trout fishing poor   had to cut som wood to day   nearly out of last years wood   then it started to snow in ernest   heavy flakes falling   this evening the spruce are loaded down with christmas decoration   tok a walk in got a porcupine for the dog   have been putting away traps   stacked emty boxes   cleaning out shed for summer sorting out tings to take with me when I go out

Tuesday 9   The first realy warm day we had for somtine   snow is disapearing fast   by to night is hardly any snow left that fell yesterday clouding up again that I had no sun this afternoon   have been monkeing around from one ting to another not acomplished much of anyting

Wednesday 10   Another snow storm this morning blowing hard from south   Heated water and tok a bath   washed up som clotches   finely heated water and scrubed the floor   Cleared towards eve   tok a walk up creek and along fothil to old mill   got two porcupines   got a lot of trout this morning

Thursday 11   Had a realy fine day   lake as smot as a pane of glass   have been home making bread   tok a pair of old bobsleds apart to take along to Penninsula so is to be able to cross to head of river   I expect it to be frozen   was out towards evening to get som vilows for my bobs getting ready to start down next coming fine day

Friday 12   Have been busy all day rebuilding a pair of bobsleds   after I got finnis with them I had the dog pul them along the beach to scour the runners   feel like rain this eve

Saturday 13   New snow this morning but it went away as soon as the sun got up   by noon we had the nicest kind of a day   I was near starting down but it was rather late in the day   now I got everyting in shape to leve for the summer   furs and war bag packed ready to go

Sunday 14 April   Starting for Kussiloff weather permitting

1929 was the peak of another boom in the salmon industry. Twenty-three canneries operated in Cook Inlet this year harvesting salmon from 106 fish traps.[2] Many of the canneries were small operations without much equipment. Small outfits, often family-run, tended to come and go. Fluctuations in fish populations and market trends made stability exceptional, even among the large canneries.

Cook Inlet's open season for fishing sockeye or red salmon was June fifth through August first. New regulations this year increased the weekly closure period from thirty-six hours to forty-eight hours.[3] Fishing was prohibited from six a.m. Saturday through six a.m. Monday in order to ensure that enough salmon would escape up the rivers to spawn.

During the summer of 1929, Andrew was one of six stream guards, or fish wardens, employed by the Bureau of Fisheries in Cook Inlet. During the fishing season their main occupation was monitoring the closed period. Patrolling in boats, they would check for illegal nets and make sure traps were rigged open to allow salmon to pass through. Ninilchik resident Ed Jackinsky has memories of Andrew Berg when he was working as a fish warden. Ed knew the sound of Berg's outboard and could hear him coming from miles away as his rounds brought him along the east side of Cook Inlet. Andrew would occasionally stay the night at the Jackinsky's fox farm in Ninilchik.[4]

After fishing season the stream guards would perform the escapement counts in various areas. The Bureau of Fisheries report for 1929 included the following excerpt regarding salmon escapement in Cook Inlet:

While there were small numbers earlier in all parts of the district, the main run of red salmon struck at Salamato Beach on July 17 and continued for 5 days – 48 hours of which was in the weekly closed period, permitting a satisfactory escapement into Kenai and Kasilof Rivers. Later, an investigation of the spawning grounds tributary to Tustemena Lake at the head of

Kasilof River showed that all streams had been bountifully seeded. The spawning beds at the head of Bishops Creek and Swanson's Creek were also visited and were reported to be well seeded. Streams tributary to Kachemak Bay, Seldovia Bay, and other lower Cook Inlet areas showed an average escapement of pinks.[5]

Some fox farmers spent summers working in the fishing industry, leaving their families to tend the daily needs of the foxes. Billy Williamson apparently was not compelled to make extra cash from fishing. He visited Tustumena Lake in July, leaving the following entry in Andrew's journal:

Monday July 29   Mrs Williamson and I arrived last saturday evening   Mrs first trip to the lake Had wonderful weather all the way up and while here   Hunted porkies up Indian River Lake Emma trail and glacial flat   fair success   Enjoyed the hospitality of your cabin which could only have been more appreciated had you been present leaving here 8:30 P.M. for home   FW Williamson

Mickey Williamson was well known for taming foxes. Photo courtesy of McLane Collection.

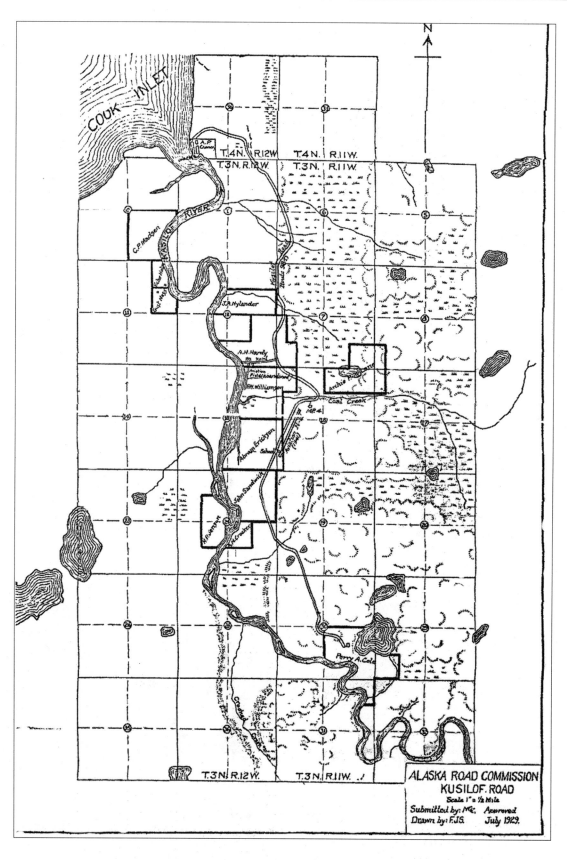

Only patented homesteads or homesites are shown on the Road Commission's map of Kasilof. There were additional residences in the community not indicated on the map, such as Erik Isakson's home on the first bend upriver from the cannery. The site labeled J.A. Nylander was Alex Lind's. Map courtesy of the McLane Collection.

The Williamsons had decided this year to move their fox ranch to Lawing on Kenai Lake where they had access to the railroad and the bright lights of Seward and Anchorage. Kasilof proved to be too isolated in the winter for this family.[6] There was talk about establishing regular winter boat service from Seldovia to Kasilof but Cook Inlet's ice would prevail over people's progressive intentions. For most residents of Kasilof, Kenai and Ninilchik, winter's icy solitude was penetrated only by emergency dog sled rides to the railroad or air flights to Anchorage.

Roads continued to be an issue on the Peninsula and in the Territory. The federal government was making some investment in Alaska's infrastructure at this time. Somehow Kasilof managed to qualify for a bit of the road building funds. Perry Cole's political sophistication may have had some influence. A seven mile stretch of road was built from the cannery site at the mouth of the Kasilof River over swamps, creeks and hills all the way to the Cole's homestead. Begun in 1929, construction would not be finished until 1930.

The isolation which plagued homesteaders and farmers was the joy of hunters and served to protect the wildlife. Hunting parties continued to benefit from Andrew Berg's open-door hospitality.

August 21   Pete Matsen   Ed Lovedale and John Sand arrived here the 19 August and staid here two days   Weather was not very favorable for hunting but fairly successful leaving here the 21

The traditional mode of transportation in Kasilof. Six miles of the lower river are affected by tidal changes, adding to the challenge of travel. Photo courtesy of McLane Collection.

st for home   leaving cabin nice and clean   Thanks to the courtesy of Andrew Berg

[Andrew writes:] *Friday 20 September   Came up from Kussiloff yesterday   found Alex Lind accuping cabbin   he came in with a black bear to day we was all out on mountain   got one sheep   saw one bear but let the bear get away*

Saturday 21   Have been home working at a steel range   Alex Lind & Ralf Petterson went up to Tonys Cabbin on south fork to stay over night in order to have a bear hunt   August Juntonen was out since morning to look for bears but found only moose & acording to description they was all record breckers   Cooked up a mutton stew that was to queens taste and good anough for Kings

Ralph Petterson was the 19 year old son of Carl and Matrona Petterson. Ralph got his first fishing job on a trap when he was 16 years old and would fish every summer for the next 63 years.[8]

Sunday 22   Was up early intending to go out for a walk   just as we was ready to go it started to rain so I decided to stay home and put in the range   after we finis Gunnar & August went up on hill   I stay home repairing my shoe packs   Alex and Ralf came down from South Fork wet to the skin   August brought in two porcupine (he called them sup)

Monday 23   Started out this morning to take a look over glaser flats to see if any sheep would be down but the wind sprung up so we had to return   sand storm got that we could hardly stand up in it   just as we started home we jumped a wolf   had lots of time to shoot but did not realise that it was a wolf until it was to late shoot   Had a tough time getting home   nearly drifted acrost the lake   Raining rest of day

Andrew doesn't make much of this wolf sighting but it was a rare occurence at the time. Several more decades would pass before wolves reestablished a population on the Kenai Peninsula.

Tuesday 24   Alex Lind left us this morning going down Lake somwher'es   August &

*Gunar went up Lake Emma trail looking for bears
I and Ralf went with boat to Woods Island   went
over Christ trail up glaser flats to foot of glaser
saw three rams   got one   was back home at
four with all of the sheep exepting horns*

*Wednesday 25   At home all day   strong southerly
wind on lake   filled 25 jars with sheep meat
cooked for nearly four hours   feeling poor this
evening   have a nasty cold aguing all over   Ralf
was out in foornoon loking for moose   August
brought in about three gallons of crane berries
wind went down towards evening but switched
around to north*

*Thursday 26   Put in a nasty night coughing
having a bad cold   after breckfast I started out
on a bear hunt   the other three boys went down
lake on a moose hunt   I got one black bear   the
boys came home emty handed   this evening I
fleshed the bear hide*

*Friday 27   Have been home all day and put in
the bigest days work cooking cleaning stritching
bear hide patching my shoepacks   lost my knife
& turned tings topsy turvy hunting it   the rest
tok a climb after sheep but came home with out
meat having seen lot of sheep but noting in reach
of rifles   saw no bears or tracks of bears but
then they had no feild glasses   was out far
anough to see Arctic Lake*

*Saturday 28   Started to blow this morning as we
started to put out for our trip down so I cleaned
out the shade   washed som underware and sox
& hankerchifs   brought a hoist down to lake
shore   raining lightly with south easterly volys
August made two trip   came in this evening with
one porcupine*

The Tustumena hills were full of meat hunters from the Kenai Peninsula and Anchorage and trophy hunters from all over the United States. The Alaska Guides, Inc. brought fourteen paying customers to the Tustumena district. A typical client, Dr. William Trice from Waco, Texas, spent three weeks and bagged one moose, two sheep, two brown bears and one black bear.[9] Robert Bragaw, the president of Alaska Guides, spent seven weeks at Birchwood Lodge overseeing operations and enjoying the area with his wife.[10]

Hunting was no longer the only business activity at Birchwood Lodge. Tom Odale and Ed Zettle were raising mink. Odale was granted several permits for capturing live mink from the wild for breeding stock and they also purchased mink from other farmers. On October fourteenth Zettle departed Anchorage with some newly purchased mink on the *M.S. Discoverer*.[11]

Ferrying live mink around Cook Inlet was all in a day's work for Heinie Berger and the *Discoverer*. Berger was known to go beyond the call of duty and provided an extraordinary level of service including personal shopping and caring for unaccompanied children on board.[12]

A group of Alaska Guides' hunters with their trophies, guides, packers and chef. Tom Odale is the second man from the right with his hands on his hips. Photo courtesy of Wanda M. Griffin.

Russell Merrill and his Travel Air 7000 Pegasus, Anchorage Air Transport No. 1, on the shore of Tustumena Lake. On September sixteenth of this year, Merrill made a trip to Tustumena early in the morning, then flew a load to the Alaska Guides' Rainy Pass camp. He headed out on his third trip of the day from Anchorage toward Bethel and was never seen again.[7] Photo courtesy McLane Collection.

Between fox farming, big game hunting, competitive shipping and road building, the western Kenai Peninsula was teetering on the brink of prosperity. Then the stock market crashed in late October. Wall Street probably seemed immeasurably distant at the time but the repercussions would eventually reach Cook Inlet.

Andrew Berg was in Kenai during the market's tumble and didn't deem the event worth mentioning in his journal when he returned to Tustumena.

Thursday 7 November   Started from Kenai this morning trying out my new skiff   got to Kussiloff tok on 30 galons of gazoline   ran up to Pete & Pete   stay night

Friday 8   Waited to Alex Lind came   went up river   stay at Penninsula Cabbin over night

Saturday 9   Came home   had fairly good weather   found four sheep hunters at cabbin just bringing in a mountain sheep

Sunday 10   At home all day   blowing & snowing early this morning   got a nice lot of trout   turned out to be fine day but to late to go anywheres

Monday 11   Had a storm to day   som of the boys was up on the glaser flats but had to come home on acount of rain so we all stay home playing pinokle

---

Anchorage Daily Times
October 15, 1929

Discoverer Sails For Inlet Points; Goes on to Seward

The motorship Discoverer, Captain Heinie Berger, sailed at 2 o'clock Monday morning with a good list of passengers for points on the inlet and Seward. Stops will be made at Old Tyonek, Kenai, Kusilof, Ninilchik, Kalgin Island, Seldovia, Snug Harbor, Illiamna, Port Chatham and Nuka Bay, after which the voyage will be continued to Seward. Returning to Anchorage, the Discoverer will ply out of this port for points on the inlet until ice precludes further water travel. Included among the passengers leaving Anchorage yesterday on the motorship were the following:

Dr. Kendrick Pierce, for Kusilof and Tustumena lake on an outing and hunt. L.D. Chadwick of Cleveland, O., with his guide, Frank Revelle, for Kusilof and Tustumena for a moose trophy. Henry Gottberg, for his winter camp at Old Tyonek on Nicholai river. Fred Judd, for his fur farm on Kalgin island. E.E. Zettle for Kusilof, with some mink from George Johnson's fur farm for foundation stock of a new fur farm on Tustumena lake established by Zettle and Tom Odale. Mrs. Brown and two children, for Kenai. Allen Peterson for Seldovia, returning home from a guiding trip.

Tuesday 12   Got a fine lot of trout among them a large rainbow   I have made bread   12 large loaves   Pete & Alex was up to foot of glaser saw som rams on smole mts   for the rest we been reading Current History

Wednesday 13   While still dark the boys started up to sheep mountain   I stay home fixing an old evinrude   wether mild   was out gatering moss started to rain towards evening

Thursday 14   Alex Lind & Pete Madson went up mts   Alex came home early having incountered lot of new snow and turned back   Pete came at dark   I try evenrude   Croker came back with stolen garment & lost propeller for 8 h Johnson the rest me included was sleeping & eating all day thru   I started a cold   sick at stomack

Friday 15   Was feeling poor stay home all day Pete Madsen was out five hours came home with two porkies   Nissen Cole & Lind was up on mountains came home without sheep   had a fine day   no wind   sound caring far for hunting

Saturday 16   Sheep hunters left this fornoon Alex Lind to Bear Creek hunting moose   the rest to Big House   so after they left I cleaned up it was near noon   about 3:30 Earling came on his way to Bear Creek   I was then fixing a dogs packsack

Sunday 17   Erling started for Bear Creek   after he left I decided to go for a walk   set a few traps   saw four moose quite handy but have no use for that amount of meat   lake Emma was frozen at north end but east half of lake was oppen   did not see any tracks of fur animal bears or anyting els   heard coyotes yelping on Indian River

Monday 18   Was late getting out of bed this morning   stay home all day tinkering about cabbin   finnis mending pack sack for scott toward evening I heard an outboard motor goin in to Devils Bay   half hour later Lind came here have taken Erling home from Bear Creek weather unsettled

Tuesday 19   Started out this morning against a nasty head wind to go over glaser flats to look for sheep   saw one ram down to the flat   went

up to the sadle but wind was so strong that it was impossible to look into the wind   saw two bull moose comming back home

Wednesday 20   At home all day building bread & sawing some grate bars with hacksaw   Alex Lind was ready to start down this morning but the volys off mountain made traveling by dorey imposible so he had to stay over   just two weeks since I left & noting acomplished

Thursday 21   I heard Alex moving long befor day breck but I did not turn out to 6:30   he had the fire started   I cooked breckfast and helped him to get the boat off the beach   I could hear the machine for two hours after he left   the sound carying far in quite atmosphere   I drew the fire in range & put in five fire bars for fire back & front   now is heating water to have a bath   weather cloudy   feeling for snow or rain

Friday 22   Have been at home all day   weather have been treatining all fornoon   I was out in midle of day caulking my skiff   this evening it started to rain with southeasterly wind   I was feeling of rain storm comming that I could hardly keep awake   anyway I slept half the time I was trying to read

Saturday 23   Got out of bed early this morning but after breckfast when it got light anough to se I found it cloudy and raining wich it kept up nearly all day   I was making a new fire dore for my stove at Lick House & washing clotches

Sunday 24   An other day of rest   got up late was hearing the wind howling so I stay in bed to I got tired of rolling from side to side   house just shaking in the storm   about noon it stopped rain   I spaded a bed for garden patch   no frost

Monday 25   Raining hard this morning with som wind wich swung to west in fornoon and changed to snow and by noon the ground was covered thermometer is at frezing point   most of the snow melted out of the trees but the ground remain covered   had a walk up creek bed & to mouth of Indian River   saw no signs of any game   have not acomplished anyting   Lizaplsudski (the cat) is sick and I dont know wath to do so I just put her out for the night

Tuesday 26   Fine weather   I started pulled up to flats   went along the hogback   set out a few traps   came in at dusk   set out the net   I try to make up my mind to kill the cat but I will see if she gets any better by morning

Wednesday 27   Cloudy but otherwise fine weather   cat was dead   I cant but miss the poor ting   som sort of indigestion   got only one trout so I did not set the net out and hauled hom four logs fire wood   sawed up a few blocks   just starting to repair my pack sack

Thursday 28   Had a snowstorm all day   I stay in reading current History of wich I brought in fourteen montly issures that I have not redd and have a fine time to digest it on days like we got to day   was out trying to set the net but brok my fish pole

Friday 29   Found everyting white this morning snow that fell yesterday and during the night mad tings look like a winter in the old country   my first act this morning was to clear away snow from door step & shed   was out launched sciff set net   calked lower seems on house   sawed couple blocks of wood   windy to night turning mild

Saturday 30   Lay this morning listening to the storm screaming thru the tree's so I stay in bed as long as I could   was out midnight to tie up my boat   this morning all the snow is gone and warm but raining with wind   found my net blown in all in a tangle but full of fine trout   calming this evening

Sunday 1 December   Stormy but otherwise nice warm as a summer day   Erling Frostad came about noon going down to Bear Creek and probbably as far as Birch Wood   expecting som mail   when he gets back we starts sawmill

Monday 2   Started about ten o clock acrost the lake   set out 17 traps for lynx   drizly rain all time   got back here about four   Erling have just came up from Bear Creek   had the fire going made supper   play three games of pinocle snowing to beat the band

Tuesday 3   Waited to about midle of day went to Erlins place   walked to Clif House loking for saw log that will make boat lumber

Wednesday 4   Cut down log from side hill   had a time of getting it to where we wanted it   buildt a saw pit   got the log up ready to start the mill by hand power

A saw pit was a structure designed to allow two men to cut boards out of logs. The logs to be cut had to be elevated, parallel to the ground, high enough for one man to stand underneath. The partner would stand on top of the log. The team would push and pull a two-man saw lengthwise through the wood. It took a tremendous amount of effort to cut a single plank.

Thursday 5   Daylight comes so late that by the time we pulled over to the pit it is ten o clock so we have hardly any time to work   got all the cuts up and shifted   saw is dull and not running good

Friday 6   Sawed four cuts thru   not used to working together   making hard work of it   I am short winded from cold

Saturday 7   Finis sawing to day   got som fine lumber   packed it in to Clif House to dry   got thru early

Sunday 8   Coldest morning we had   8 abov zero   waited to after ten got in to boat ran down south shore   I put Erling ashore at black spruce he walking back loking after traps   I came acrost lake home

Monday 9   10 abov this morning   I pulled up to flats and up along hog back I walked folowing my trap line   crepening thru alders that was bending low with new snow   saw lot of tracks of fox and coyotes   one sheep track & cyotes tracks following that   2 moose

Tuesday 10   Have been home all day thermometer at fifteen   calm   snow still hanging on bushes making traveling in timber nasty heated water   had a bath and scrubbed the floor   cooking & eating (days a waste)

Wednesday 11   Thermometer was down to 13 abov this morning   I stay home all day reading any old book I find on the shelf   towards evening Erling came on his way to Bear Creek   he told of finding a place on the sand dunes where

Cutting lumber out of a log in the saw pit. A picture may be worth a thousand words but what you cannot see in this photo is the sweat pouring off the men or the delicate balance needed between the partners to maintain a straight cut and prevent the saw from binding. Photo courtesy of Carpenter Collection, No. 147, Library of Congress Prints and Photographs Division.

coyotes have worked at a killed sheep   foggy over lake   16 this evening

Thursday 12   15 abov this morning   waited until 10:30 started up Emma Trail   found fine traveling   moose have tramped the trail   I saw four of them although snow is making lot of noys Erling came from Bear Creek just as I got fire going   had a couple of games of pinocle then after super we turned it to reading room

Friday 13   Erling started home this morning   I waited to sun came over the hill then I tok a trip with boat to glaser flats   set out a few traps for fox & coyotes   weather clear until this evening it clouded up and now it is warmer   was at fifteen this morning

Saturday 14   Have had a heavy fogg all day until this evening when it tinned out so I can see the mon quite plainly but still in a smal fram thermometer have stod at 20 all day   now at 15 abov   not a breath of wind   no ice making on the lake   the water are still to warm   was up Indian a ways cleaning up trail but to mych snow in trees to do much so I came back in

Sunday 15   Very foggy this morning   about noon it lifted som and I tok skiff and pulled to flats   had a walk on hogback and thru alders to I came to oppen flats then it got tick again   I crossed over to islands   saw two moose and tracks of fox and coyotes   came on ice acrost creek first island   12 this morning & 13 this evening

Monday 16   The thermometer is creeping down from day to day   this morning it was eleven abov   the coolest I have seen it here this far fog very thick   I was up to Dirty Cannon   jumped several moose and saw tracks of diffrent animals lynx fox wolferine & sheep but to thick to see them   absolutely flat calm lake is unruffled   still making no ice

Tuesday 17   At home trying to make bread   tok in som flour chilled my batter so it was a long time rising   it is seven o clock and I just got the last baking in pans   making sixteen loaves   I got it tropicle in here   ran up to 104 but now that I got door oppen it is down to ninty two   it

was 13 outside this morning but I think we got a change   18 now

Wednesday 18   I got up late was reading to two o clock last night   intended to go to glaser but by the time I had breckfast cleaned the cabbin it was to late to go so I continued reading   weather cloudy   24 afternoon   I launched skiff   set out net   pulled up to flats where I have som traps got two magpies

Thursday 19   Blowing up lake this morning pulled in the net got five trouts   tok skiff up to glaser flats   set out som traps on woods islands for coyotes and fox   saw no game   crossed woods island met Erling Frostad   blowing to hard coming home so I had to leve the boat this side Indian River   mild

Friday 20   At home   weather fine calm thermometer up to 24 this morning   clearing up in afternoon   getting cooler so that now it is down to 13   went up creek to find out wath it is making that much noys about   river is rising on anchor ice   starting to climb the banks unles we get som snow   was out and brought the boat home   made a set of turksheads on the oars and sawed up a few sticks of wood (thats all)

Saturday 21   Clouded up and turned milder   24 this mor   som new snow fell during night making a fine track snow but noting here making tracks and frost hanging in trees making it nasty in timber   so I cut and hauled home som logs for fire wood   tok a walk up Indian walking on ice up to Nicanorka Trail (no game)

Sunday 22   Cleaned the snow off the skiff lauched it   after setting my net I pulled up to glaser flats   going up by way of islands to Rays Mine and Dirty Cannon looking for sheep   fog drifted against mountain side that it was no use of climbing up   no sheep have been down for couple of days to the flats   comming back home saw a lot of moose but that is to much meat for me I dont need that much and hate to destroy an animal I cant use   shot four parmigans   saw track of coyotes fox and one lynx

Monday 23   Was late getting out of bed   my side hurting when I take a long breth or coughin Erling came about eleven o clock on his way to

Bear Creek   stay for lunch   showed him how to tie a turkhead   got eleven trout this morning mostly makinaw   fixing tings and sawing som heat wood   made a new handle on meat cutter 20 abov this morning   clearing up getting colder just started heating water for bath and befor time to go to bed I will have my swim   my take a run down lake if weather is warm after x mass

Tuesday 24   12 abov this morning   got a bad stich in my side   felt as if somting tore oppen and have been smarting bad ever since   it make it bad far me as I cant bend down   Erling came from Bear Creek   stay over   he hurt his foot to day so that he got hard to walk   thermometer down to 8 this evening

Wednesday 25   Snowing lightly   14 abov loking dark & drery   I put in a better night then I expected   got up at three a.m. buildt a fire in stove made a cup of coffe   after I wandered around the floor to I got tired turned out light and sleept to daylight   after breckfast hobbled off to traps set for porcupine   got 3   have been in cabbin all day reading and trying remember wath nice time childrens used to have in old country (Jule Tide)   Erling is just having his forty naps

Thursday 26   14 this morning with noyse of surf som where out on the lake or other shore about seven miles away   after breckfast Erling split up som wood for me then started over to his place I went out got a porky   skinned it and give half of it to the dog   heated water washed lot of hankerchifs & slips   30 during day   going down again this evening

Friday 27   Strong wind this morning   loking like snow towards glaser   stay around home until noon then wanted to see if I was able to walk so I moved along slowly to the flats and

into hidden lake   set out two traps coming back I walked up Indian coming back looking after porky traps

Saturday 28   Intended to go up on flats this morning but it started to snow so I decided to stay home and mend & wash clotches   The snow quit early but a heavy southery wind sprung up and the lake was foaming white with brecks   was out & brought in two porcupines   thermometer have stod abouth 24 abov zero all day

Sunday 29   Snowing and high wind this morning lasted to dark   calmed down   turning colder was out and sawed a thick of wood   down to 8 this evening   can still hear the surf brecking in on beach

Monday 30   2 below zero this morning   waited to eleven o clock went up on flats   the new snow makes walking rather heavy   saw track of fox & coyotes one track of lynx   was to stream in upper island   loked at the few traps I have out & set two more   came back thru alders and along hog back   getting cold   a wind coming up from south west   surf is making lot of noys it is now 10 p.m.   thermometer registers 10 below zero

Tuesday 31   At six below this morning and a fog painting everyting white with frost wich indicate moistur in atmosphere and a change   have been in all day   was trying to split som wood but my side smart when I swing the ax that I had to quit lay down a while and when I went out   it was snowing and thermometer have rised to six a bov but if it is only fog comming down it turn cold

CHAPTER 15

1930

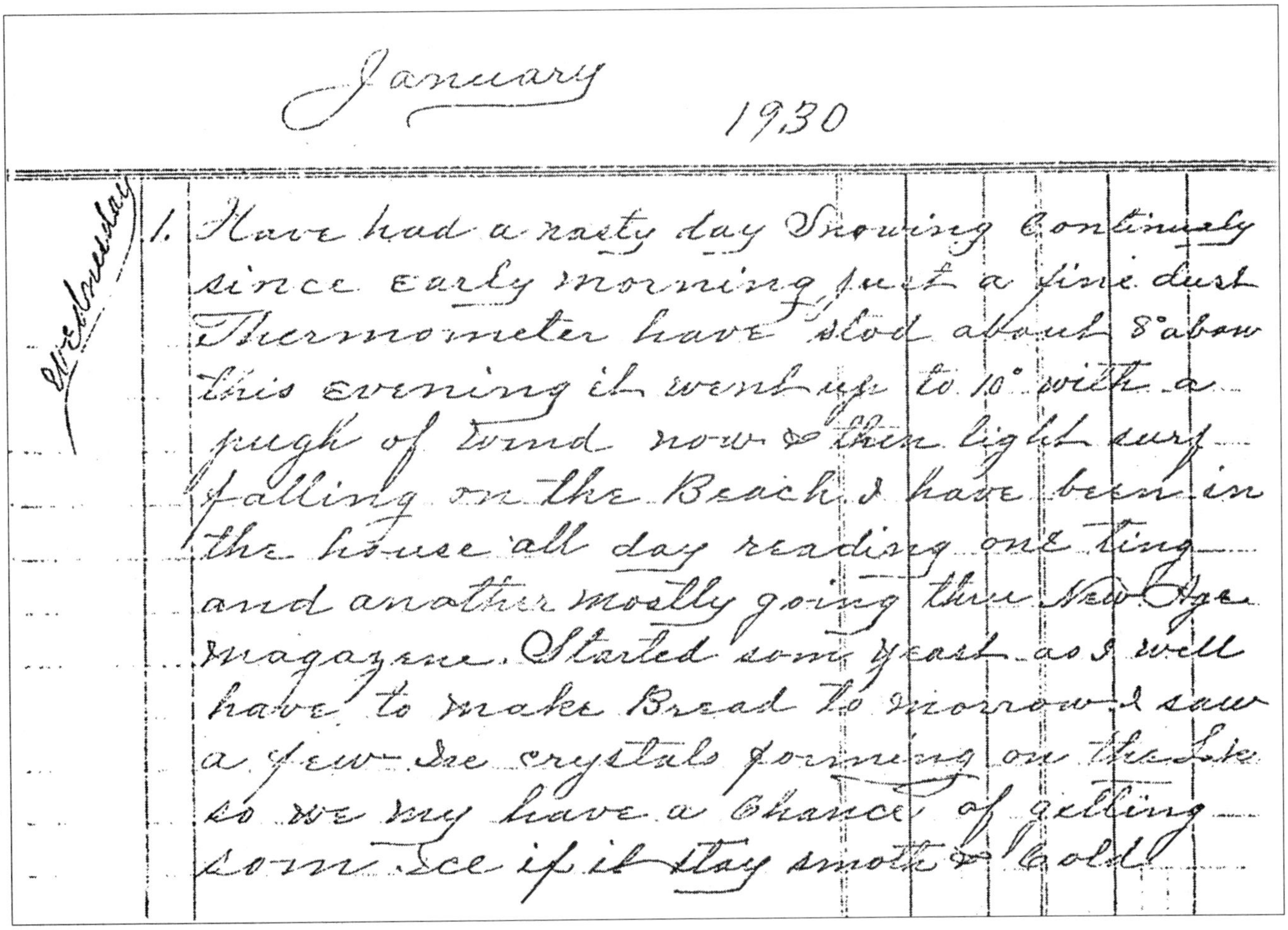

January 1930

Wednesday

1. Have had a nasty day Snowing Continuly since early morning just a fine dust Thermometer have stod about 8° abov this evening it went up to 10° with a pugh of wind now & then light surf falling on the Beach I have been in the house all day reading one ting and another mostly going thru New Age magazine. Started som yeast as I will have to make Bread to morrow I saw a few Ice crystals forming on the Lake so we my have a Chance of getting som Ice if it stay smoth & Cold

Thursday 2   Have been home all day watching bread   it was 2 abov this morning and getting up so that this evening it is at eleven abov at eight p.m.   try to split som wood to day but my side hurt that I had to quit   have been reading while waiting for bread to rise that my eyes is tired   heard som racket of ice brecking som where   no ice in sight from here yet but water getting cold

Friday 3   Waited to after sun got over this mountain then it was after eleven I went up the Nikanorka Trail to Lake Emma   saw several fox tracks on Indian a short distance abov the house waded thru the new snow without snowshoes saw som old tracks of lynx and moose tracks everywhere but no living animal or dead did I see   came back just as the sun started down (almost in south)

Saturday 4   Got out of bed just it was making day about 8 o clock   after brecfast I decided to take a trip to mouth of Dirty Cannon but found heavy walking   did not take any snowshoes ran acrost Erlings track   he wrote in snow that he will be here on the 5th   saw both moose & mountain sheep   got tired before I got home set traps for porkies

Sunday 5   Mild thermometer at 18   still   the surface of the lake are over run with a thin skin of ice   Erling came over about noon   stoped for lunch and went on for Bear Creek   he have one lynx   have been in cabbin all day   cooked up a kettle of mexican beans   am getting so I wants a mess of trout   afraid of putting out net on acount of ice building

Monday 6   First storm to amount of anyting this winter   I heard the wind squeling in the trees while yet dark and I had my boat turned over on the lake shore but not made fast   so I got out of bed to tie it to a stump and from som volys shaking the cabbin I was glad I had the boat secured   Erling came from Bear Creek   he had to walk thru timber   wind to strong to walk against

Tuesday 7   Weather fine this morning   shoved my dory out to set net and when I got thru I put on machine ran acrost to south shore loking over som traps I had there   lake smoth so I was back here by two o clock   had lunch & went out brought in two porcupine   cleaned them and fed the dog   tok a walk in   lokated a place to cut birch for fire wood   chopped out trail

Wednesday 8   Just amazen   a regular sumer day   thermometer 30   clear and calm and I getting interested in som old yarn and stay in all day reading   I had hardly time to cook and wash dishes

Thursday 9   Was just going to start som work outside when a wind came up from below with rain and it have kept it up all day so had put me in the house   the second time or (two days) without doing anyting worth mentioning

Friday 10   I intended to go look over som traps to day but a lot of new snow have fallen during the night and it was still mild anough to run off the trees during midle of the day   so I was out tramping trail and started to build a sort of ways to stack wood on   walked up creek got one porky

Saturday 11   Stay at home to after sun up   then put the pack sack on scott and tok a trip up glaser flats up on hogback and along thru timber along foot of mountains to the open flats   had to cut lot of brushes that was bent over into the trail loaded with snow   saw only one moose got home at dark

Sunday 12   Have had a lazy spell   was awake early but to early to get up when I had noting to require it so I lighted the lamp and read for two hours   then when my eyes got tired I blow out the lamp and went fast asleep and did not wake to eight o clock   fine weather   abouth frezing point and nice and calm

Monday 13   Have put in most of my time to day at cutting and hauling home drift logs and piling them on the ways for fire wood   not that I need them now but snow is right for sleding   heard a coyote this evening

Tuesday 14   Got up earlier than usual   that is befor day[break]   found it cooler   the thermometer have gone down to 13 so I waited to sun up before I started up Emma Trail   walking rather heavy after I pased the summit   no signs of game exepting moose   saw two buls carying fairly good sets of horns for this time of the year tok home one porky

Wednesday 15   Down to 12 this morning and did not rise much during the day on acount of a heavy fogbank hanging over the lake and the heat of the sun remained aloft   got home a couple of sticks of wood and at dusk tok a walk to lower end of flat just to wast time

Thursday 16   Have turned mild   up to frezing point this morning but not warm anough to melt the snow out of the trees   anyway I cut down bucked up and hauled hom three birch trees just to get a starter on woodpile   can hear easterly wind but it has not got down here yet   couple volys hit this morning

Friday 17   Tok a walk up on flats to day   strong wind off the glaser but I managed to get to islands two of my traps sprung by fox but got noting climded up on island but saw no game   saw one grouse and one rabit   the first I have seen for a long time   got one porkie

Saturday 18   Started fixing wood road this morning   shoveling snow to bare spots   hauled home a few sticks and now an easterly wind is on and thermometer is up to 40 so I can just see where my road fixing is headed for but then I got lots of time befor spring

Sunday 19   Not done a ting worth recording snow is going fast   temperature still about forty strong wind take out spels and the snow that is left are mostly water   tok a walk out to where I was cutting birch   try to get down a hanging one only partly stuck   clouded up this afternoon but no rain so far

Monday 20   Weather beutiful this morning so I decided to start cutting som birch   after working for an hour I had to come home for som wedges and loking out over lake I spied Erling comming in his new skiff   stay for lunch on his way to Birch Wood   I went back to my work

Tuesday 21   Started to haul wath I cut yesterday tok me to two o clock to get it in and the way I feel right now I dont think I care for any physical culture   Erling came back with a lot of reading matter and other news

Wednesday 22   Erling waited here until sun up and as there was no ice he had fine weather   fine traveling   no wind   he helped me set the net before he went   I was out chopping som birch came in after twelf   had lunch and it tok me the rest of the day to haul in wath I had chopped

Thursday 23   Just a little cools   not anough to make ice   have been in all day watching bread made twelf loavs and fine bread   the yeast just right   got done early so I was out cut couple of birch

Friday 24   Tok a walk up glaser flats   walking good   slipery in plases   foggy   could not see

---

My Pioneer Days   Marion Cole

(continued)

The latter part of May [1929] we went to Anchorage by boat to await the birth of our baby which happened about two weeks early because of the rough trip on Cook Inlet. The captain, Heinie Berger was afraid the baby would be born before we got to Anchorage. When we reached the dock the tide was out and the dock was at least two stories above the boat, I started to cry and asked how I could get up there. Milt said "Don't worry Sweetie, you just have to climb the ladder and I will be right behind you."

We boarded with Mr. and Mrs. Axe and Milt worked on the Alaska Railroad to pay our expenses. When our daughter, Ramona, was a month old we went back to Kasilof on another boat, the Princess Pat. It was a beautiful trip on a calm Inlet.

In October of that year I had to take our baby to the hospital in Anchorage to have a blood tumor removed from her head which was caused at birth. We went on the last mail boat of the season and planned to return on it. The weather turned very cold and the boat was icing up so they had to leave without us. Ramona had steel stitches in her head incision and had to stay there until they were removed. We were stranded at the Anchorage Hotel with very little money.

After Christmas some friends asked us to stay with them and help take care of their baby son who I furnished mother's milk to save his life, when he was a month old and recovering from surgery on his stomach. The doctor said the only thing that could save his life would be mother's milk and I was the only mother in the hospital at that time. Even after I left the hospital the nurse came to our friend's house to get my milk. They nicknamed me the Kasilof Dairy.

It was the last of January [1930] before Milton could drive our dog team out to the railroad to meet us. We went down to Lawing by train then rode across Kenai Lake in an open boat to where Milt left the dogs. Doc Pollard, who I had met in Anchorage, was on the train and sat with us most of the way and showed me points of interest.

Some nice Alaskans asked us to spend the night with them before starting out on the trail. It took us four days and three nights to make the trip in about thirty degree below [zero] weather. We spent the night in the cabins which were built for the mail carriers by dog teams to stay in and they were the only buildings along the way. They were made of logs with bunks made of poles with hay on them and an oil drum stove to cook on and heat water which I needed for baby milk bottles. The floor was the good earth. Because the cabins were small they heated up fast. Before our last night's stay the dogs got loose and ate our bacon and butter so our rations were pretty low. There were no roads, only a blazed trail through the woods, over frozen lakes, rivers and streams. The scenery was beautiful and I was too cold to be scared.

far but saw four moose   walked right up to them befor they heard me   found a pair of sheep horns   brought them in   weather cloudy   about 20   making som ice

Saturday 25   Stay home all day reading som cheap trash Erling Frostad brought from Toms at Birchwood   hauled in few sticks of birch this evening   the weather is dead still and the lake on point of closing but the temperature is abov 20   not cold anough

Sunday 26   Had a walk up trail today   lots of moose tracks   found one wolferine track but had no snowshoe so I did not follow him to find wath buisnes he had thru timber   calm and mild about 26 at night while it is much higher day time

Monday 27   Could not sleep so I lay reading to four o clock this morning then I slept to daylight a big ice field was forming up nice and smoth landed about noon filling the whole head of lake now this evening a storm is on and naturaly beating ice to pices   thermometer at 24   still it apear cold   hauling water to have a bath

Tuesday 28 January   [illegible] northery storm all the ice have drifted to Devils Bay so it is no ice in sight from here   lake have been feather white in spels all day   have been reading som cheap periodicals all day   this evening I gathered anough corage to wash clotches

Wednesday 29   The wind have [illegible] just a light breez from south and a litle cooler   no ice to amount of anyting   som smole crystals drifting been in all day   had som berries that started to spoil had to preserve them

Thursday 30   Thermometer was at 6 this morning and a young ice was forming as far as I could see   but later in the day a northerly wind cam up and all the skim ice disapeared   wind was cold to do anyting outside   anyway I got noting particular to do just to take up a few traps and fill my wood shade for next winter   I am still reading som books   have put in the whole day at it exepting cooking and eating and feeding the dog   got one porkepine for the dog

Friday 31   This is the first day I atended to do anyting this month   I got thinking if I figured on given myself credit for a months work it was time to start   in the first place I got up late that the sun came peeking over the mountains befor I had breckfast   then when I loked out it was feeling sort of cold and I have got used to look for som excuse so I com in got to reading som more westerns stuf   anyway I was out   rigged up and planed a couple of scantlins

Saturday 1 February   Wind kept on until early morning so there was no ice in sight this morning was getting cold this afternoon and is down to ten abov at nine o clock and everyting dead calm that I expect to see som ice in the morning

Dead calm and frosty, the lake is just about to freeze. Photo by Terry Rude.

Sunday 2 The weather turned mild 16 this morning still there was som ice just a thin crystal but and it was cracking up but it held to this evening anyway a little dust of snow is falling and that will keep it from freeze anyway I cleaned up a pair of scates Erling came and went to Bear Creek to start taking in traps

Monday 3 12 abov this morning but the ice still lay but hardly strong anough to carry a man weight finnished my pole tok it out to mouth of Indian River and set out my net Erling came up from Bear Creek brought som mail and other news I also got som mail

Tuesday 4 Cold wind blowing from glaser this morning thermometer at 14 after we got fire started at daybreck we walked to mouth of Indian River fished the net got two nice makinaw trout boiled them with potatoes served with butter sauce I say they were good rather cold to walk up again the strong wind so we had two games of pinocle then we went up flats saw a coyote and directly another fell in step disapeared in willows I brought in the first load of traps walked on ice but it is weak it grone crack and complains when it take my weight

Wednesday 5 February Everyting apears quite the lake is finely closed to stay the snow that fell was not anough to prevent the ice from growing I walked off from shore could hardly hear it crack this morning when I went to fish my net got two trout was out and collicted another dog pack of traps thermometer at 13 this morning

Thursday 6 Thermometer down to 1 abov this morning wich is the coldest we had for quite a time got only one trout this morning and in setting the net I thought I had it foul so about noon I went back there to clear it when the sun was high got two more trout sun went down at four o clock and the western sky a smoth hasy orange color indicating cold and the thermometer started down fast with the ice having a war by it self on acount of explansion of ice in quick change made quite bombardment

Friday 7 At 5 below this morning and stay at that point until sun up I stay in to about eleven fixing up a set of old bob sleds harnes the dog

and drove out to fish net got one white fish two dolyvardens and four large makinaw trouth calm and still

Saturday 8 0 below this morning so I waited to it got warmer hooked up the dog got on my skates ran acrost the lake gatered all my traps and tok them hom saw tracks of wolferine and som coyotes got a porke nasty wind about zero nearly froze my hands this evening fishing & cleaning the net

Sunday 9 10 below zero this morning and it stay at that point until eight thirdy when sun got up later a wind came up the lake wich made me think I rather stay in where it is warm went out and tok home the net it froze that hard in bringing it home it tok long to taw

Monday 10 Not feeling good have the cabin good & warm still I am filing cold thermometer was 2 below this morning with a westerly wind blowing mad it feel cold was out and shifted som porky traps to day as I am in nead of dog feed nice clear moonlight

Tuesday 11 2 below this calm and nice weather after sun got high anough to warm up tings I got my hevy hokyskcates out for a run over to see why Erling hadnt come he was soposed to have been here two days ago found him at his cabbin busy sewing at a pair of moccasins the cold spell have kept him from coming over

Wednesday 12 Scot had somting in his troat I saw he was sick and filing up and down his troat I found a lump had to handle it rough but I got it to move and he looks better to day had a good long walk and after coming home I skinned a porkypine and fed him to scot he was eating but apearently he was sore for his eating was very slow it was 20 abov this morning but got cold in afternoon I went to set the net about sunset and I could hardly keep my face from frezing a strong wind blowing at about zero

Thursday 13 9 below zero this morning got up early buildt fire went back to bed waiting for cabbin to warm fell a sleep and did not get up to daylight then got busey to set batter for making bread made an unusual lot of bread it well last to I go down or nearly so when I got the first batch in oven I tok a walk to mouth of Indian   fished the net   got four trout one doyvarden

Friday 14   9 below again this morning but it feeling cooler on acount of moisture in the air it is fixing to change   Erling came over to day when I was out fishing   got six trout cooked three and we had a fine meal   days are getting long   I was reading this evening to five by daylight   have not done anyting wort while to day

Saturday 15   Clouded up last night as if it was turning warmer   but this morning it was as clear as a bell but only 3 below   fine during sun up not a breath of wind   chopped som croks for my bob sled that is to be   as I probbably will have to haul my boat out over ice

Sunday 16   [illegible] daylight and found clouds have gathered during the night and temperature climbed to 5 abov   but did not go up only few degrees during the day on acount of the thin clouds shutting off the heat of the sun   also we had a light dust of snow comming down   feeling cold so I kept company with the stove nearly all day but is getting short of reading matter   5 abov to night

Monday 17   5 abov this morning and a thin cloud drifting acrost the sky from the east   after brecfast over I went to fish the net   found four inches of ice on the net right at mouth of Indian River   got two trout   hunted & found a log for saw horse   hauled it home got the logs under it but my three inch auger works slow so I did not get finnis   got only three sets of pins

Tuesday 18   The first ting after breckfast I finished the sawhorse   had to go to woods to hunt a sapling to get anough pins   put in sixteen of them   when I got thru it was nearly lunch time when I had lunch nearly redy Erling came along on his way to Kenai   had lunch with me and started down to Birchwood   expected to stay over night with Tom Odale   I hauled in a load of wood   sawed a few chunks of heating blocks tok a walk up Indian   it is turning warmer and she is froze up at the mouth   I expect her to bust out

Wednesday 19   6 abov zero this morning so I waited to sun got stronger   went out and packed home a load of trap   got home about two o clock then I went out fishing the net   got three trout   lay down and slept to six o clock   after awhile Emil came in   he have been over to Fox River and came all the way from his cabbin betwin Fox River and Sheep Creek   it is three abov zero now   clear and calm

Thursday 20   Emil started down this morning by way of the big house where he left his house keys then on to Hugos for night   I filed a saw this morning   after that I went to look at my trout net and as I expected it was just on point getting lost the Indian River was over flowing and making glaser over the net   set the net close home   had a job getting it set ice being about sixteen inches thick

Friday 21   I tok a good long walk up Emma Trail to see how tings look on the hill   found lot of moose tracks but only one moose did I see but the snow was making lot of noys   after I got home I fished the net   got only one trout but anough for a meal   and then I found that my perculator was not working good   so I put a handle on a fine sewing nidle and for two hours I was punching the screen

Saturday 22   Washingtons birthday   temperature up to 20   after breckfast and cleaning up I got on my scates and ran down to Birch Wood and can you beat it here I found men ignoring a national holyday   they were pecking away at a log wall and not wanting to delay people who wanted to work that bad I came back home   had a fine scate   ice was fairly good off from shore extending to glaser tours camp   havy north east wind at Birchwood   stopped in at Bear Creek Camp   everyting lookes neat & clean there walked all the way back from there on acount of hour frost making skating hard

Sunday 23   A gale of wind this morning and mild northeaster   had to stay home anyway and mild anough that I did not nead a fire so I undertok to fix the stove   it tok to after noon before I could cook lunch   and in afternoon between spels at reading I started to file a saw snowing thru later part of day

Monday 24   Som snow have came during the night and a thin film are still hanging over the lake   I finis filing the saw   tried it out   tok a walk out thru timber did not se a track of any kind   weather is warm   betwen 20 & 30 at night

Tuesday 25   Strong wind this morning so I undertok to clean the atik and I sure dumped a lot of trash   mild tawing   the ice are clearing on the lake   that is the snow is wearing away by the wind   cut a couple of birch and hauled home that be all I bring hom this winter   got the wood shade nearly empty

Wednesday 26   Rainstorm on this morning so I tok chance   I been waiting for warm so I could scrub floor and clean the cabbin   thermometer at 40 to night but no rainfall since noon   after I got thru cleaning I started to rebuild stairway that tok me the rest of the day

Thursday 27   Mild   everyting melting   snow is gone off lowlands   strong wind carying water over ice   extended a pair of bobsleds to move the boat if the ice frezes clear   tok in the net got two trout   first for several days

Friday 28   Here we are at end of February with a roaring storm   ice are cryialized and heaving under presure of the wind coming down the moutains   if this wind last a day or two longer the ice will go   shifted the last wood from woodshade to cabbin   otherwise reading the three muskateers

Saturday 1 March   This have sure been a day of rest   raining with strong wind   later in day it came down in form of snow but melted as soon as it hit the ground   this evening the wind quit cloudy at 35

Sunday 2   Did not sleep good last night   got up befor six   had breckfast then waited to it got nice and warm   went out to try if hard labor would not help to bring sleep so I sawed and split wood to about 3 p.m.   then I tok a walk up Indian to Box Cannon   when I got back if was getting dark and the way my back feels I have done a day work

Monday 3   Tok a walk over to Erling Frostads place to get som reading matter & som potatoes got back after noon had lunch and tok a rest sawed one stick of birch to wood   now I am heating water for a bath   lake clear but to rough to skate   clouding up to night

Tuesday 4   Put my boat on the old bobsleds and started down the lake   ice rough crytalized and bad foting but sled runs easy   got to Peninsula after five hours   feeling stif and lame   had a head wind that kept me back som but ice got good so I used the skates the last four miles   stay all night at penninsula cabin

Wednesday 5   Heard the wind this morning befor I got out of bed   looking out I found light snow with strong northerly wind so I could quarter befor in but the snow drifting so bad I did not dare use the scates   anyway after fighting thru

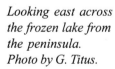

Looking east across the frozen lake from the peninsula. Photo by G. Titus.

it half the way it got better so I rode most of the way the rest   got home about 2:30 p.m. and enjoyed the intitled rest after twenty miles of travel for this cloudy day

Thursday 6   Have been in the house all day weather warm with a fine dust of snow falling have been reading and resting up after my trip down the lake   the dog have been taking tings easy to   guess tender feet is the real cause with him running barefoot on sharp crytalized ice   the only labor exepting cooking & eating   washing som underwear

Friday 7   A nice little blizard laying to day anough snow falling to cover the ground and make it look like real winter   was out and fished got four nice trout two makinow one dolly varden & one golden trout   cooked one for dinner and sure was nice   reading trash

Saturday 8   A new winter   cleared off and turned cold so that my windows was icy this morning to cold to saw wood   that birch when frozen saws hard and I got time anough to wait until weather is favorable

Sunday 9   This have been as cold a day as any we had all winter   not by thermometer but strong westerly wind with moist atmosphere making it cutting   but as I got nice warm cabin and som books I can get along   just preparing yeast as I have to make bread on the tomorow

Monday 10   Have been at home all day making bread and just the right sort of beans 8 abov this morning   about nine o clock a southwesterly wind sprung up and blow strong   the wind vired around to northwest   temperature dropped to 5 long before sundown 7 p.m. at 3   while baking bread stove pipe started to burn creosote and I had bread in oven so I could not put out fire in the stove   got stove pipe so hot that I had fire both in seling and roof

Tuesday 11   Here is another day past along with noting acomplished   am in a vortex of wind com clean around at all points of the compass and light snow falling and wind strong anough to pick up the snow and made it apear like a scein in a flour mill   this evening it quited down som and turned milder

Wednesday 12   Snowing and thick clouds this morning and by nine o clock quit   starting to clear up at noon   sun came out and gave us a bright afternon   was out fishing got five trout went out and brought in a dry spruce as I see that my suply from last year about burnt everyting nice and white   a new winter

Thursday 13   Snowing again this morning but unlike yesterday after it quit snowing it did not clear but remained cloudy   tok a walk up Indian snow getting so deep that it makes hevy walking cleaned snow away from saw hors   have to get to work

Friday 14   Lay reading last night to late then when I wanted to go to sleep I was wide awake and could not get any sleep   so I lighted the lamp again and kept on reading to nearly six o clock   finaly slept to eight   after breckfast I started to saw and split wood and put in a good days work to

Saturday 15   Light drisly rain all day and the day have been extra long   staying in the house digesting som old books that I know befor I start reading   the snow is melting som   the lake turning blue but temperature is about frezing point

Sunday 16   Storm again this morning and rather cold   any way I mastered anough curyge to roll a stick on the saw horse and after I got started it did not go bad at all so I kept on to I finished one rick and started on a new one   but it is getting to cold so that the wood is frezing and saws hard so I quit

Monday 17   Dust devils have been dansing a regular ragtime fandango over the lake to day temperature at zero and with a storm again make it feel nasty cold so I have been home trying to find somting to read that I have overlooked but no

Tuesday 18   5 below this morning and som wind but not a storm but it apeared cold   in getting a buket of water from the well my mustash was icy and that about ten minuts   calmed down in afternoon   clouded som but getting cold again this evening   got two trout hauling the net

Wednesday 19 Was up early this morning but it was cold anough out to make me stay by the stove to sun got high anough to warm up tings   by ten o clock it was getting cloudy and a lot warmer so I started saw and split wood (cut good lot)

Thursday 20 Som snow have [illegible] during the night   everyting quite   after it got warmer towards midle of day I sawed and split som wood finished the rick and started on the last one   had to go haul home a stick of dry wood as last years wood are nearly gone

Friday 21 The birchwood are still frozen but I want to get finis with sawing wood   have been working at it nearly all day but did not git as done as I wanted to   still with one more good day at it I come near being thru   clouding this evning so it my get a little warmer   got only one trout   net foul

Saturday 22 To cold this morning to work at the wood pile so I stay in until the afternoon   then I worked for a couple of hours but did not finis weather rather cold   not so cold by thermometer but moist penetrating cold that cut

Sunday 23 Finished cutting wood to day   had to bring home one stick to finish the last rick   som wath warmer to day   hevy bunchy clouds gathering in south west   apear very much like a storm a brewing

Monday 24 Had a rely nice day to day   warm anough when sun was high to melt snow   was over to the mill   stripped som wire webbin off an old skeleton frame also som old lumber   fished the net and got five nice trout   thre makinaw 2 to 5 lb one white fish & one doly varden

Tuesday 25 Fine weather again to day   had a trip up Indian River to get a load of hydrylic pipe the lower part of river was fairly good but upper part rough   rest of day storing tings for the summer an start to pack up tings to take down with me to Kenai

Wednesday 26 Hevy storm   easterly storm ragin warm   snow melting fast   been in cabbin all day cleaning and sorting out tings to take out with me   the ice are clear as far as I can see and aucto make fine traveling when it frezs up again

and I am getting so I just as soon get to som new sights and get news   besides I have to move or provision get short

Thursday 27   Have been busy washing clotches scrubbin floors washing windows so as to leve the place clean wen I leve it for the summer   tok in trout net got only one dolyvarden about 2 lb weather warm   som pufs of wind off & on during day   cloudy all fornoon but cut up towards evening   getting chylly

Friday 28 Started home or to Kenai

Berg's entry on March twenty-sixth is unusual in his expression of a desire to get back to the sights and news of town life. Judging by his journal entries, there were fewer Lake residents this winter. The companionship of card games and shared hikes was missing and Berg went back to town early in the spring.

The federal census enumerator was counting Kenai and Kasilof around this time. The census data showed a decrease in Kenai's population from 332 in 1920 to 286 in 1930.

Kasilof and Ninilchik had grown a bit. Kasilof's official count was up to 45 and Ninilchik's was 124. In contrast, the communities on the railbelt were growing significantly.

An example of the old rivetted mining pipe which Berg and others recycled into chimneys, stoves and well casings. This piece is around 10" in diameter. Photo by G. Titus

ANCHORAGE DAILY TIMES

June 13, 1930

Anchorage Hub of Greatest Big Game Belt in Alaska

A circle having a radius of 150 miles, with Anchorage in the center, takes in the Rainy Pass region of the Alaska range, the Kodiak bear districts on the west shore of Cook Inlet, the famous Kenai peninsula, the Chugach range, sheep and goat country, the Chickaloon, Nelchina, Matanuska glacier belt and Talkeetna mountains.

It is estimated that on the Kenai peninsula alone, there are more than 8,000 moose. To estimate the number of bear, Kodiak, brown, grizzly, glacier and blacks, within this circle, would be a difficult matter. That they are plentiful is proven by the number taken each season by visiting sportsmen. Sheep, the beautiful white ovis dalli, goats and caribou in countless numbers are also found.

Anchorage is headquarters for Alaska's largest hunting organization. Many independent guides also operate from the railroad metropolis. Non-resident hunters can travel to the hunting country either by boat, railroad, horses or plane. About fifty residents of the railbelt devote most of their time to big game hunting.

Big game hunting has taken its place as one of the leading industries of the district. It is estimated that about $100,000 was distributed in this region by hunters during the year 1929. The 1930 season promises to surpass that of 1929, not only in the amount of expenditures but also by the number of sportsmen....

With judicious conservation of the big game resources of the Anchorage district there is no reason whatever why the hunting industry should not disburse $250,000 annually. There is room in this region for hundreds of non-resident hunters....Big game hunters are not looking for meat — they are after trophies. Only the oldest of each specie are taken. In most cases the animals killed in sport would not live much longer were they left alone. This is game conservation, as the old bulls by being removed give the younger ones their chance to carry on. Some residents of Alaska are under the impression that hunters are depleting the game. One wolf will do more harm than 20 sportsmen. The wolves pick on the young and females and so do many of our own residents, but not so the sportsman....

California sportsmen are just discovering the Anchorage big game paradise.... [They] have been doing most of their hunting in Canada, a foreign country. They would help Alaska come into its own and help a part of the United States of America with their expenditures were they to spend their vacations in this magnificent primitive playground.

Perhaps an Alaskan hunt may cost a little more, but what of it? The hunter will be compensated in finding more and better trophies, more hunting country, and better hunting crews. The Alaskan white guides and crews are far superior to the Indian guides and crews of Canada. Sportsmen who have hunted in both places will testify to this.

Alaska is still a frontier country with frontier conditions prevailing; there is no pauper labor and there are no paupers. The very highest type of men follow the big game hunting profession. They are not only appreciated for their ability but also for their companionship.

A hunting trip in the Anchorage region will be a revelation. The scenery alone with the majestic peaks of the Alaska range in view, make a background for a hunt that cannot be equalled anywhere.

And then the fishing. Almost any stream in the hunting country teems with fish.

There are no poisonous plants nor snakes in the country. There are no polluted streams — you may take a drink of water anywhere without risking your health. The cool fall days, when the flies are gone, make hunting or fishing a real outing — the kind that most sportsmen plan and look forward to but rarely have. Why risk chances of failure when your can have a hunt under the most favorable conditions out of Anchorage? You are invited to hunt here. Will you?

[The growing world-wide depression was shrinking the pool of potential trophy hunters. Anchorages's hunting interests were participating in the competition for customers with no holds barred. This article was also targeted toward a visiting delegation from the Los Angeles Chamber of Commerce.]

Seward's 1930 census count was 835 and Anchorage's was 2,277.

Anchorage offered most of the urban amenities one could expect at that time. Kenai had a roadhouse, two merchants, three teachers, two shoemakers, a U.S. Deputy, a midwife, a priest and three salmon canneries.[1]

Andrew Berg was in Anchorage in May when he witnessed Alex Lind's petition for U.S. citizenship. In the naturalization papers, both men listed their occupation as fisherman, although this summer they were employed as stream guards.[2] The Bureau of Fisheries Report for 1930 mentioned that gill nets operating in Redoubt Bay, Trading Bay and other areas on Cook inlet's west side were monitored by Berg and Lind who were "operating from a dory propelled by outboard motor."[3] The two men were also working on the east side of Cook Inlet. On June sixth, near Point Possession, they discovered nine set gill nets fishing during the weekly closed period. The owners of the nets were fined $500.00.

In July Berg made a quick trip to Tustumena Lake. In his journal entry it appears that he was conducting stream surveys although July is too early for definitive counts. Counting salmon may have been an excuse for him to visit the lake:

Friday 25 July   Left Pete & Pete fox ranch 7:45 this morning   had engine truble but got good ways from the starting point   just the same had lunch at lower end of penninsula at 1:30   ran to Nicolai Creek   walked up aways to examin the seeding   very few fish there yet but lot of them in the lake   folowing south shore to Muddy and Clear Creek then came acrost here   got here after 7 p.m.   cut grass around cabbin and trails   now ready for bed   Andrew Berg USBF [U. S. Bureau of Fisheries]

Andrew next surfaces on August sixth in the "Personal" column of the *Anchorage Daily Times* as a guest at the Hotel Anchorage. It is interesting to picture him in the metropolis. Berg was no rube but he was a 60 year old man who had been living in remote Alaska since long before anyone dreamed of Anchorage. Surely he would have scorned a taxi ride from the ship docks up to town but did he indulge in Chinese food at the Chop Suey and Noodle House or take in a movie? *The Woman Racket*, an "all talking" feature, was playing at the Empress Theatre.

Meanwhile, back at Tustumena Lake, some Kasilof fox farmers were enjoying a bear hunt from the comfort of Andrew's cabin:

August 10th   Ed Lovdahl Pete Madsen and Myself arrived here August 7th for a bear hunt we had fairly good weather but rather to much rain for hunting   the evening of the 7th we got the dady of all brown bears over on glacier flat packed him out the next day and then took in other hunt and got another good size brown bear on glacier flat   packed him out the 9th and this ends our hunting in glorious [illegible] for this trip here   making record time as both starboard and port engine is working perfectly   one running time from Kusilof to Birchwood 3 hours and five minutes   from Birchwood to Bear Creek 26 minute   from Bear Creek to Andrews 20 minutes   from Andrews to Clear Creek 32 minutes leaving Andrews cabin in ship shape to day Aug 10   we all thank you very much for the use of the cabin   John Sandwick Peter Madsen Ed Lovdahl

Hunters and pack horses on the Moose Horn Trail between Tustumena Lake and Funny River. The shrubby growth in evidence here is ideal moose forage. Photo courtesy of Art Frisbee.

Famous trophy hunter Prentiss N. Gray and his two children hunted with the Alaska Guides this season. They were guided by Hank Lucas and H.A. Anderson. Gray's account of the trip mentioned that they spent six hours motoring up the Kasilof while much of their gear went to the lake on pack horses. They took another pack train over the Moose Horn Trail toward Funny River to hunt moose.[7]

Left to right are Duncan Little (cook), Prentiss Gray, Hank Lucas, Barbara Gray, Sherman Gray, H.A. Anderson and Henry McKinnon (wrangler). Photo courtesy of W. M. Griffin.

An Alaska Guides' pack train loading up at the Kasilof cannery. Including preparation time, it would be a two day trip from here to Birchwood. Photo courtesy of Wanda M. Griffin.

Ed Lovdahl was Abe Erickson's 30 year old nephew who had emigrated from Finland in 1921.[4] Ed and Pete Madsen had been on a hunt on the west side of Cook Inlet the previous month. Pete was mauled by a brown bear on that trip but apparently wasn't discouraged from further hunting. The meat from the bears they killed at Tustumena wound up in cold storage at Erickson's.[5]

Berg was back on Tustumena Lake counting salmon from August sixteenth through twenty-first. The Bureau of Fisheries Report stated that Berg performed the escapement counts for Kasilof and Tustumena in August as he had "for the past six years." [6] Young Ralph Petterson accompanied Andrew as an assistant on the stream surveys.

Tuesday 19 August   Came here this evening after being two days on the lake examining seeding on salmon streams   saw only one bear   tell it go as it did not seem to desire to give us any troble Ralp Petterson is with me for the trip   Andrew Berg

Bureau of Fisheries payroll records show that Berg worked eleven days in May and every day in June, July and August. His rate of pay was seven dollars per day making his total compensation $721. This was good money as wages for cannery work averaged ninety dollars a month.[8]

Andrew had enough income to cover his basic needs and provide some luxuries. He could buy books and magazines and he is remembered as a reliable source of peppermint candies for the children in Kenai.[9] Berg was also known for storing his candy and sugar in human skulls; a practice considered very disrespectful by some Kenai residents whose ancestors' remains were being treated as household objects.[10]

Pot-hunting, or collecting artifacts and remains, was pervasive among Euro-Americans. Academic researchers and collectors had been mining Alaska's archaeological resources for many decades, gathering artifacts from residents and historic sites. A short article in the *Anchorage Daily Times* in September of 1930 described 100 exhumed skeletons of Alaska Indians arriving in Seattle on their way to the Smithsonian Institute.[11] An archaeologist from the University of Pennsylvania, Frederica de Laguna, passed through Kenai this summer and acquired three skulls and a stone lamp from Andrew Berg.[12]

The acquisition of wildlife trophies was still drawing plenty of people to the Kenai Peninsula this year. Berg was not at Tustumena during September but many hunters enjoyed the use of his Home cabin and wrote in his journal:

Saturday Aug 30   Came up today from Birchwood to pick up Chas Madsen and party from the yacht "Westward" who are up south fork will take them to Birchwood to hunt moose when they come down   TM Odale

Sept 2   Our party stopped overnight Aug 24 and enjoyed the comfort of this cabin on our way up the south fork of the Indian River   We hope to accept your hospitality again in the future and should Mr Berg ever visit Virginia it would be a pleasure to have him call upon any all of us   A. C. Barrow [illegible] Va   C Dolare   F. M. Hill   F. C. Scruggs Jr Denver Colo   J. R. Duprest Denver Co 1630 Lawrence St

Sept 2nd   We returned here last night with some of our party and stayed in our tent near this cabin Mr Barrow and his friends names are written on privious days but our crew are as follows   Chas Madsen Head Guide Kodiak   JM Walker Guide W John Harris Guide   Fred Kvasnikoff Packer Kodiak   Nick Bleskie Packer Jasper Canada AB Webb Packer Jasper Canada   The writer would be pleased to meet you personally and hope you may drop into Kodiak some day Respectfully yours   Chas Madsen   Field Manager Kodiak Guide Assn

Sept 5th   Stopped here over night with Pete Matson and Ed Lodell   enjoyed your cabin for the night and are having a fine trip   on way to moose country   Ray Shurgeon   Buckley Wis   Al Jones Guide

This same day, back in Kasilof, Al Hardy and Ed Zettle were motoring up the river with a load of supplies for a hunting party. They stopped to kill a porcupine and when they set out from shore their skiff struck a partly submerged tree and overturned. Zettle made it back to the riverbank but Hardy did not.

Two days later, after much searching, Pete Jensen and John Sandwick found their neighbor's body downstream. The *Discoverer* transported the body, Alice Hardy and a sad retinue of friends to Anchorage for the funeral and burial. The newspaper reported:

Al Hardy was highly esteemed by his neighbors of the little fur farming community of which he had long been a resident. 'We all mourn the loss of a true friend and neighbor at Kusilof,' one of them writes. 'There will never be a more loyal and sincere friend than Al has been to us. He was always first to aid in sickness of any kind, having several times rushed patients to the railroad with his dog team. He was always seeking to better the community in every way.[13]

The tragic of loss of Hardy was probably keenly felt by Perry Cole who needed all the help he could get in his own efforts to better the community. He was in Anchorage at the time of Hardy's death, generating another newspaper article extolling Kasilof's bright future. Cole praised the seven miles of newly completed highway and predicted that the road would soon be extended to Tustumena Lake which was, in his opinion, not only a big game hunting paradise but also an ideal place for a tourist resort.[14] Perry Cole's dream for his own homestead included creating a dude ranch frequented by movie stars and collecting a covey of investors who would pay him to manage the operation. He was successful in selling shares to a few businessmen in Anchorage, including a dentist, Clayton "Doc" Pollard.[15]

At this time, popular opinion decreed that the U.S. economy would be back to normal by the following spring. The Alaska Guides' business increased to twenty-six clients in 1930 and they had plans for further expansion.[16] Prospects were considered good for fur farming, fur prices were still holding at a high level for the farmers and trappers.

Andrew Berg headed out from Kenai in late October:

Thursday 23 October   Left Kenai came down to Kussiloff but found that Charly Sands who was to go with me was away stay over night at Koleys

"Koleys" would have been the home of Odman Kooley, a Norwegian immigrant. This year he, his wife Marva and their three young children were living in Kasilof.[17] Kenai was normally

their home but Odman spent some time as watchman at the old Kasilof cannery.[18]

Friday 24   Ran up to Pete Madsens   stay over night   saw Emil Gust Ness and the boys at Abrams Farm

Saturday 25   Went down to Kusilof   stay at Sands over night   Emil Berg Gust Ness went to Kenai

Sunday 26   Started early   rafted three dorys togather and came up thru to smoth water abov Moose Horn rapids and back to Kussilof

Monday 27   Stay at Kussiloff (snow storm)

Tuesday 28   Started up with suplies   got to Silver Rapids broke oil lead on outboard motor walked to Petes Fox Ranch   got fixed up   stay all night

Wednesday 29   Walked back to Silver Rapids ran the rest of rapids   hoked on to the two dorys at Moose Horn and came up to Hugos

Thursday 30   Started from Hugos at one   got here 3:30   found Erling who have just come from his place   been busy putting tings to order and finding lots of tings missing   so much that if it continus I will have to lock the cabin   it is

Crossing the Coal Creek bridge on Kasilof's new "highway." Progress is always relative. Photo courtesy of McLane Collection.

rotten when people get so low that they cant respect an open door ofering shelter to any one who may happen along   Andrew Berg   Kenai

Friday 31   Had breckfast late   was reading got sleepy tok a nap   Earling was at the mill working at the log house   afternoon I started to build a window case

Saturday 1 November   Was up early   after breckfast I started to work at finis window casing hew down logs and put in new windows   had no level and got it in croked   Erling starting timbering new log house at the mill

Sunday 2   At home making bread and chinking around windows and putting up new facing keeping busy all day   cold 14 abov this evening walked up creek a way this evening trying to find porcupine for dog feed   got dark   saw lot of tracks of porcupine coyotes rabits squirrels and ermine   set net this evening   that is Erling did

Monday 3   Mild this morning with som rain & snow coming   Erling was going home but weather to bad   he stay to about one o clock then left for home   I have been working all day

shifting one window to north east wall   finis in time to take a walk before evening

Tuesday 4   Raining hard when I awok this morning   as the rain quit I begin diggin down som fence posts and put up som wire webb around a garden patch east of the house   started to breck ground to   did not do much on acount of squalls

Wednesday 5   Got up drousy for som reason   I could not sleep last night   lay reading to nearly morning   a nasty rainy weather out so I stay in tok a bath   washes som clotches   painted window cases   managed to keep busy all day just the same   mild   snow melted very high on mountain side

Thursday 6   Raining and blowing so I stay home tok one window case and fixed it   reputtying tryed to row toward glaser flats for fens rails but wind to strong   a bunch of sheep hunters came this evening

Friday 7   Working in new garden patch rolling out old logs   went out to get som fenc rails Erling came over   Pete Madson & Elmer Stohl

Erling never finished the log house he started building at the old mill site. The cabin was eventually finished by Joe Secora, pictured here, who came to Tustumena in 1938 to mine gold. Joe was from New Jersey and prospected in California before coming to Alaska with his brother John.[19] Photo courtesy of Dolly Cole Christl.

Andrew is in the stern of this dory parked by Woods Island. The "boys" and dogs are unidentified, but they all appear to be enjoying a calm, sunny day on the lake. Photo courtesy of Joan McLane Lahndt.

was out got som mountain sheep   I finis garden fence

Saturday 8   Spading garden and put in big days work   Erling went to Bear Creek   Crist cutting wood   the other boys was out packing sheep got home late   had a contest at penokle

Sunday 9   All hands got in dory went to islands I tok a run over island trying to lokate a bear den   the rest packing meat   got back early (no bear)   got a grous

Monday 10   Pete Madsen & Elmer Stall started about 8 a.m. for overhanging trail   Christ Jensen & I left to wash breckfast dishes untangle trout net and clean the cabbin   then we also decided to take a walk over glaser flats   went up old indian trail   got one ram   brought it in all of it even head & hide   got in early   saw one fine moose going out

Tuesday 11   Pete Madsen & Christ Jensen went up Nikanorka Mts   Elmer Stolh to foot of glaser to pack in a ram   he got in early and helped me set nets for trout   the boys from Nikanorka also came in at dark with a ram   I been at home all day   rendered som lard   cooked a kettle of dog

feed & a stew of mts sheep bricket   tok my old evinrude to peases and soldered up leak in tank

Wednesday 12   Stay home all day   I putting ting up to take along with me to Kenai   boys have been cutting som fire wood to replace wath they have burnt during stay   this evening they tok a walk to look for porky pine   a coyote was yelping at them   I could hear him from here

Thursday 13   Everybody was getting ready to start down lake except Erling who intended to go to Nyman Coast   but wind sprung up and we all had to stay at home   tok a walk up Indian River to hydrylik working   crossing on ice for the first time one mile up   was zero this morning but turning mild with high wind from several points during the day

Friday 14   Was out early this morning intending to start down but found it snowing so I went back to sleep and did not get up until Earling was down making fire about 7 a.m.   tok our time about breckfast and everybody decided it too nasty to travel   had a couple of games of penoukcle about noon now   let up som and we had lunch and the boys all went   Erling to his place   Christ Pete & Elmer to Big House   I cleaned snow out

ANCHORAGE DAILY TIMES

November 12, 1930

Cole Is Enlarging Kusilof Fur Farm

According to word brought to Anchorage on the Princess Pat, Perry Cole, of the Cole-Black Fur Farm, is branching out in his operations. He has under lease a tract adjoining his own property and in addition to adding to his fur-bearing animals, will increase his herd of wool bearing goats.

Mr. and Mrs. J. Jones, son-in-law and daughter of Mr. Cole, have recently arrived at Kusilof from New York and Mr. Jones will assist in the work of the Cole-Black projects.

My Pioneer Days   Marion Cole
(continued)

On November 22nd, 1930 our son [Lyle] was born. We were having a terrible snowstorm and the nearest doctor was 100 miles away with no phone to get him if we needed him. My Mother-in-law kept reading a pamphlet entitled "What to do until the doctor comes." Our neighbor, Mrs. McLane, was soaking her hands in Lysol water when Lyle arrived safe and sound. Neither lady had ever seen a baby being born but were willing to do their best to help me.

of my boat   heated water and scrubbed floor had a bath   that kept me busy all afternoon

Saturday 15   Started for Kenai 10 a.m.   ran down north shore of lake to Hugos   landed som tings   Ed Jarvel [Zarwell] came home as I was living   ran on to Moose Horn Rapids   pulled the rest of way   got in ice jam at Kussiloff Post office   landed   walked back to Abs ranch stay all night

Ed Zarwell was listed in Kasilof's 1930 census as a forty-eight year old single man originally from Wisconsin. He described his occupation as "trapper."

Sunday 16   Put my tings in old post office   tok up the boat   had a box of trout Erling was sending to Kenai   no chance of getting them any farther so I told the people to help them selfs lot of new snow

Monday 17   Started about eight waiding thru new snow   started to blow strong northerly wind so I was climbing thru rolling hills for shelter came to Ed Zarwels 2 p.m. in snow storm

Tuesday 18   Stay at Zarwels on acount of storm & snow

Thursday 20   Still storming but I got tired of laying still   started about eleven o clock   off shore wind at times I nearly blow out on lake   at one place I tok dory painter [bow line] and walked on lake shore but had to quit on acount of line

getting caught in boulders   finaly reched Friman about as tired as I ever been

Friday 21   Stay at Friman Cabbin all day   snow to wet to go out so I cleaned up   put tings to order and chopped som wood   cleared up one net   set it

Saturday 22   Cloudy again this morning so I decided to come home   put on machine it worked all right but tank leaking so bad that I ran out of gas and had to pull in   caut 3 makinaw trout at Friman   cooked one after I got home Thermometer at frezing point

Sunday 23   Thermometer have stod at 36 abov all day so it been to wet to go anywhere   I been in all day   first I made a new draw for the tols in seat of dory   after I found one ting after another that needed repair so I kept busy all day   still trying to boil carbon out of som generator for gas lamp   raining to night

Monday 24   At home   rather wet to go any place so I tok tank loose from evinrude to repair it   got leaking so bad that I lost as much gas as I burned coming home the other day   got six nice trouts this morning   getting cooler so this evening I tok a few steel traps set out six along beach to glaser flats   dug into exposed bank of sand it not frozen   saw som salmon at mouth of Indian River   making yeast will have to build som bread to morrow

Tuesday 25   Have been busy making bread made anough to last me to Christmass   made 6 loves used four pound of raisins and anough sugar that it will keep   towards evening I heated water & tok a bath   it was hot anough to use for a bath house having big range hot anough to bake   clouded up during day   starting to snow to night   shot three squirrels to day   they comence to do mischif   cut up two all wool union underwear & this morning they have destroied a whole roll of toilet paper for wich three of them payed the supream penalty

Wednesday 26   Did not get out of bed to daylight and then weather looking murky and it been falling a light dust of snow off & on since morning   I filed a saw this fornoon and after noon washing som clotches   tok my long fish pole down   drag it to lake shore and set out net with it   just befor dusk I walked up to glaser flats got a squirrel & shot one close to cabbin

Thursday 27   Last thursday in November Thanksgiven day and I have been out setting traps   it is the first day I been out for the purpos of setting traps and I put in a good day   set out 26 traps 20 for lynx & woferine and six for mink & ermine   had to wear snowshoes all day climbing hill to Lake Emma   had a fine day calm and not to cold

Friday 28   Was up befor six this morning   eat a havy brecfast one larg mackinow trout with potatoes   after I had cleaned dishes it was still rather early to go out so I lay down reading   fell to sleep & sleep to nine o clock   tok a few smole traps went to glaser flat but set only three   had no snow shoes and snow to deep   got a grouse and ermine   Erling was in about noon on his way to Bear Creek   did not state when coming back

Saturday 29   Went up on glaser flats to set traps set out sixteen and had a hard day of it   lot of loose snow hanging on grass no sign of game but I set out traps anyway to have somting to keep me busy   Earling just arived from Bear Creek as I got home   temperature at 26 abov

Sunday 30   Here we are at end of November & not even got traps set   fine weather this morning Erling pulled acrost to his place about ten o clock

I tok the foot webb out of my old snowshoes and fixed the frames   by then it was noon and I fixed som lunch   to night thermometer at 36 above zero

Monday 1 December   Stay home all day   easterly wind blowing with temperature up to 40   snow is almost gone or will be befor morning   had noting that I could do to advantage   grined a couple of axes & mixed som gasoline   in taking in trout net this morning I got thirteen fine trout

Tuesday 2   Snow did not entirely go but lake shore & open places are naked   dry loose gravel along beach   to day have been like a sumer day no wind   stay in nearly all day   not feeling good   tok a walk to edge of flats   got one ermine (not prime)

Wednesday 3   Got up at five this morning   loked out find it windy & raining went to bed again and slept to daylight   to wet to go any place so I stay in   tok a walk toward evening to Woods Islands and barely escaped a bad wetting   tok a bath befor going to sleep   thermometer have stod about 38 to 40 abov all day

Thursday 4   Here is another day pased with noting acomplished   weather warm with a wet fog hanging low and tretning to blow   and did com off the glaser a few strong cats paws   tok in net got 4 nice makinow trout   been reading Currant History betwin naps   thermometer 40 abov zero

Friday 5   A little new snow   just anough to hang in grass   I started to go up to Lake Emma before tryed it without snowshoes but found that I could not so I came back home and started to do somting else   about 3 o clock Erling came up from Bear Creek   had lunch and playing penouchle until evening   Temperature 30 abov

Saturday 6   Awoke this morning at 4:30   then hear wind & rain making a racket went back to bed but only lay rolling for one hour   made fire & cooked breckfast   have been hunting tings to do   made a swivel for a steel trap & repaired som other tings   playing card with Erling   set the net

Sunday 7   Out of bed at a quarter to six   Erling got up and went to fish the net   wen he came in I had coffe ready   he got four trout all makinaw and two of them went to furnich us with breckfast after we was thru with brecfast & dishes washed & cabbin swept it was 8:30 o clock   Erling started right off for his place   I went half hour later up to Lake Emma   got one lynx   lost one mink trap clog & all but snow have covered everyting   cant tell wath tok it   still warm starting to blow again this evening

Monday 8   Got up early   started for glaser flats at daybreck   ran into big bunch of grouse on the beach getting gravel but to dark to see them befor they fly   went up over hogback   no game   went up to Dirty Cannon   saw two rams shot at one but missed   came back by island jumped many moose   saw only one   try to locate the grous on my way home   could not   a regular sumer day about 40   snowing to night

Tuesday 9   Had one inch of new snow this morning with snow hanging on grass & trees make it look wintery   tok a walk down lake shore   set five smole trap for ermine   no tracks in new snow   set net   tok a walk up Indian saw tracks of cyoties   colder   24 abov this evening

Wednesday 10   After breckfast I put my tings in the sciff started the evenrude and in one hour four minutes I was on south shore   snowshoed to King Lake found cabbin in good shape   lot of moose   no fur bearing animals cyotes

Thursday 11   Went down outlet half a mile set som traps   crossed over to Rat Lake Creek set a few more traps   turned back   noting to go on to Rat Lake for this trip   walking heavy   lot of snow

Friday 12   Stay in little cabbin all day   snow rain and blow all day   set a few lynx sets this evening

Saturday 13   Wet snow   havy snowshoing but I plowed thru got to Tustumina Lake at eleven a.m. set som traps   got in hury to cross looked likely to blow   got caught half ways and had a nasty time getting home   taking sprays over in great style   just after I got home Erling pulled in by

hanging close under weather shore   helped me set net

Sunday 14   Erling Frostad pulled out for Bear Creek this morning   I started to repair my snowshoes finis at one o clock   tok a walk and kept on to I was three miles out on glaser flats only tracks I saw is moose & cyotes   came in at dark   wind changed to day   blowing up the lake   35 abov

Monday 15   4 abov this morning   apear cold to me   not feeling good so I stay home nearly all day   got reading som rot of cheap story books early morning when I saw window frosted   tok in net got four trout two makinaw & two dolyvarden   tok a walk down lake shore   fixed cellar

Tuesday 16   28 abov this morning   I started at ten for Lake Emma   heavy walking   snowshoe most of the way   got back here about three   jus in time to set net by daylight

Wednesday 17   30 abov   intended to go to mountains   did not on acount of loking cloudy an thick with fog   about noon I walked to old indian trail to look for grouse   foun only one and a porkupine   hauled the porkupine to Indian River & cleaned him there   set out som traps for cyotes   was getting dark when I got back

Thursday 18   Was huring to get my tings to the boat for a start to Friman   tok a few minutes over two hours to run down   after I got my tings in cabbin I started out to set som traps where I used to set   found that Tom Odale had traps in the old sets

Friday 19   Walked down to Olson Creek   set out nearly all my old sets   saw tracks of Zarwell

Saturday 20   Mild   to wet to go anywhere on snowshores   sawed down som sticks and packed home for fire wood   tok a walk to Toms to send a letter out   Tom thinks he was fooling me

Sunday 21   Breaking trail acrost Cow Cannon setting traps   no sign of furbearers   saw som moose

Monday 22   Started up trail I broke yesterday went on to Lick House   window smashed stove *pipe gone and squirrils have taken all the cotton out of my bed quilts and cut covers full of holes*

Tuesday 23   Tok a long hike down south fork of Funny River   crossed over to midle fork setting traps   did not get to Lick House to after dark set about 20 traps

Wednesday 24   Clear this morning   started early got down to lake shore about noon   had lunch   piled my tings in boat   started for home one o clock   got here about 3   put tings landed boat over turned   set net and it was dark

Thursday 25   Thermometer at 28 abov zero this morning with volys of wind making noys befor I got out of bed   hauled in net got two large makinow trout   after I had chores done cleared the net and started to make yeast when Erling came up from Bear Creek   had a squirrel shoot and after we got back set net again and fixed diner

Friday 26   At home watching bread   got up and had fire going befor six this morning   set batter for bread   pulled the net and got two good size trout one makinaw one dolvarden   Erling started home after breckfast   I stay tending to bread making   getting out at times shooting squirrels repaired sight on my 22 calibre pistol   hauled in one log for heating wood   tok walk down lake shore at dusk   thermometer at 28 abov zero calm

Saturday 27   Was intending to go up on glaser flats this morning but it got loking stormy so I decided to wait   weather warm   thermometer at 33 abov zero   about ten o clock it started to blow   lake was white foam in few minutes and trees bending like whip stocks   its a wonder that no more of them breck   repaired a pair of

slipovers and towards evening I heated water and had a bath   just making ready to wash clotches

Sunday 28   Woke at four this morning   lighted the gas lamp   lay reading to 5:30   turned out lamp tok som time befor I fell to sleep   finaly I got to sleep and slept to seven   got up and had breckfast   tok a walk onto glaser flats   regular spring day   got back by one   had lunch   started right in to mend net   when I finished set it out fishing   fixed up som bedding to take to Lick House   thermometer 32 abov zero

Monday 29   36 abov zero and nice in fornoon so I tok stem pice off the boat   recaulked forward part of boat to stop leak I had somwhere and made new stem peace   afternoon started to rain and blow making nasty weather   I have not acomplished much my back is on the prod   feel as if it is going to breck as I bend   got eight large makinaw trout this morning   wind is just howling and every can & pan in the shed is ratling to beat the band

Tuesday 30   38 abov this morning   was awake early but heard the wind whistling thru trees   so I lay tumbling and finaly got som more sleep and it was after seven when I got up just making day tok a walk down beach and sawed som sticks of wood   gravel on beach is tawed out so that a man sinks in like sumertime   quite this evening

Wednesday 31   28 abov zero this morning and weather looks like it my snow   I went up Lake Emma trail   found nearly all traps as I left them but wolverine have upset one and sprung another and som squirrels caught but noting that I wanted Saw several moose and snow making lot of noys that I run off a good many that I did not see

CHAPTER 16

1931

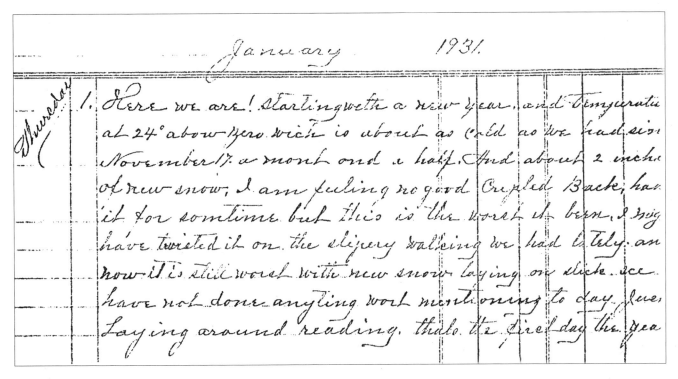

January   1931.

Thursday 1. Here we are! Starting weth a new year, and Temperatur at 24° abov zero wich is about as cold as we had sin November 17. a month and a half. And about 2 inchs of new snow, I am feeling no good Cripled Back, hav it for somtime but this is the worst it been. I mig have twisted it on the slipery walking we had lately. an now it is still worst with new snow laying on slick ice have not done anyting wort mentioning to day. Jue Laying around reading. thats the firsl day the yea

Friday 2 Had frost on the windows this morning thermometer down to 20 abov zero   have been hom all day   my back to lame to move aroun much   got only one trout this morning   using only smole piece of net   lake laying smoth all day but no sign of ice yet   but expect it getting colder this evening   down to 18 all ready at six o clock   I am getting short of reading matter so I have been overhauling the old book shelf trying to locate somting I my have overlook but with very little succes and for a time the afternoon I was mendin som wearing aperal

Saturday 3 Foggy fog coming over from Skilak Lake and completely blanketing the whole upper end of this lake   also making it warmer that I found thermometer higher this morning than last night   Had quite a quake last night but the shake was sharper then ordinary   more like an explosion so it was likely coused by som rock slide in the mountains near by   feeling som better to day   my back have not hurt very much so I was out this afternoon and cut and hauled in a spruce for heating wood   got only one makinaw

Sunday 4 Thermometer down to 12 abov zero this morning being the coldest we had since November 17th   put tings in the boat and ran acrost lake and snowshoed acrost sumit to King Lake   tracks of animals scarce   saw only one track of lynx one of otter & one wolferine

Monday 5 Apear quite cold this morning but no way of telling how cold   came back to big lake and started machine   running along shore to Devils Bay trying to find Erling as I have not seen him since Christmas but could not land on acount of drift ice   ran back around drift and thru a choppy sea and home   just befor I landed I saw Erling coming up from Bear Creek   he is hear now   have been down to Birchwood for his mail

Tuesday 6   Was up at four this morning   Erling set down to do som letter writing   after building fire I went to lake shore   fishing the net got six fine makinaw   after brecfast I filed a saw   cut a few sticks of wood   tok a walk up creek bed set two traps for cyotes   Erling went home about noon   thermometer at 20 abov zero this morning is up to 40 this evening   just had a bath and feel almost like new

Wednesday 7   Raining and blowing this morning thermometer at 38 and rised to 40   clearing up in afternoon so this evening it is 34   as I saw it was no chance of going anywhere I tok my evinrude apart   tank was coming loose   that I repaired and besides that she was developing a knock   found it in loose bearing on conecting rod   washed a suit of underwear som towels scrubbed the floor and set the trout net

Thursday 8   Started for Friman camp after eleven o clock   ran down to Tom Odales place at Birchwood   walked down beach to my cabbin met on the way Mr Hanson & Mr Hirshey the later who was with USBF last summer cleaning streams

Friday 9   Went on up to Lick House   turning milder   cut up a lot of wood and fixing tings in cabbin

Saturday 10   Walked down South Fork of Funy River about three miles   caught two mink crossed to Midle Fork but no sign of game   had big long dry walking

Sunday 11   Came on back to Friman   soft snow falling all the time   wetting like rain   set a blanket set for cyotes on the beach

Monday 12   Went down lake shore to Olson Creek   found no game or tracks   came back to Friman   had lunch & came on to Tom's   stay all night   had fine reception over radio

Tuesday 13   Waited around until ten o clock so as to let sun get up and came home   fine weather

find more snow have fallen at this place   tramped wood trail   set my net   house warming

Wednesday 14   Stay home all day   had to water prove my shoes pack tops as we got about six inches of new snow that is working thru leather and then I have two minks on stritchers   washed them and wet fur dry very slowly   got a fine lot of trout this morning   weather fine   thermometer at 30 abov zero   got a lot of reading matter from Tom that I been loking thru

Thursday 15   Was up early this morning and as soon as it got light anough I started up Lake Emma trail   as we got lot of new snow I expected to have a tough time brecking thru   made it alright but there is more than a foot of loose snow in my old snowshoe trail no game   warm thermometer at 30 abov zero

Friday 16   Raining with strong south easterly wind   thermometer at 38 abov zero   snow setling fast   noting much thu I can do   got a few copys of American Magazene with dates of thre years ago and rainy weather makes me sleepy so I had a nap in midle of the day   filed a wood saw intended to start getting home wood if it cleared up anough to let me at it

Saturday 17   Still warm with heavy squals of wind from south east   had to keep indoors until noon when it quit raining   so I went out cutting birch trees for firewood for next winter or to fill woodshed and let it dry   worked for three hours then tok a walk to glaser flats to get porcupine for dog feed   thermometer at 40 abov zero snow nearly all disapered   wind blowing hard

Sunday 18   43 abov zero this evening with heavy rain squalls   during forenoon the wind was not so very strong   Erling came along at eleven but had to walk on shore and tow the sciff for fear of getting blown to sea   after lunch he went on to Bear Creek   I tok a walk up on glaser flats saw lots of tracks of cyotes and a bunch of moose

Monday 19   Raining & blowing strong   walked down lake shore had to come back thru woods account of wind   Erling came up after dark   I had a bath and cleaned som clotches   36 abov

Tuesday 20   Fine day   lake as smole as a mill pond   34 abov   plased Erlings skiff acrost mine   ran to his place   stay all night thermometer ran down to 17 this evening

Wednesday 21   Up to 22 this morning   ran to King Lake trail while it was still dark   had to cut my way thru alders the heavy snow have bedded them down acrost my trail at all angles got to cabin and left som of the tings out of my pack and went down cannon as far as I had traps set   coming back I had lunch at cabbin and on to Frostad

Thursday 22   I got a crate of potatoes 50 lb whole wheat flour and som onions from Erling as he was over suplied and I my stay late this spring   got a lot to do if I only get to it   down to 20 abov zero this evening with a little wind up lake

Friday 23   Wide awake at four but being to early to get up and since I saw frost on windows I made up my mind to stay home   so I lit the gas lamp and finished an article in Country Gentleman turned out light and sleept to nearly daylight made fire   fished net and got three big makinaw trout   probably not as large as the one Jonah Swalowed but anyway one is as much as I can do to a meal so I did not set net this evening   18 abov zero this morning

Saturday 24   Thermometer at 22 this morning rised to 28 during day & back again to 22 this evening   been at home making bread   try using entire wheat and white flour mixed for the first time   weather fine   calm as a milk pan   I saw som nidles of ice crystals when I was setting net this evening   walked up to flats

Sunday 25   Was up early this morning and found my dog missing   hauled the net and got only one makinaw   it was large so I had anough for breckfast and to spare   dog came in at nine   I tok him along on glaser flats   climbed thru Dirty cannon to Lake   saw where som animal have killed sheep   found a steel trap   saw about fifty moose but only four rams (Mts sheep) thermometer at 20   got home at four

Monday 26   15 abov this morning   everyting quite   lake still   if it was only a few degrees

colder the lake would shorely freeze   got only one trout again this morning   stay in nearly all day   was out hunting porcupine for dog feed did not find any   sawed few sticks of wood

Tuesday 27   Thermometer at 22 abov   a little snow fell during the night   hauled the net and did not get a trout   went up on Lake Emma trail tok in all traps 28 in all   four at head of Lake eleven at cach point thirteen at sumit   got back at 3:30   just had time set net do the house work and it was time to light the lamp   comenci to show signs of ice on the lake

Wednesday 28   At home all day   when I got up this morning my back felt like it have been bent at right angles three difrent ways   buildt fire and fished net   got four nice makinaw trouts after breckfast it started in to snow   snowed heavy for half hour   then it got so mild it turned to rain   42 abov   wind sprung up blowing in squlls all day   had a severe earth quake night befor last   have just had a bath and getting drosey

Sunday 1 February   I and Erling started down lake shore   Erling to Bear Creek and I on my way to Friman   stopped at Tom Odales place for lunch   met Mr Hanson below Birch Wood with his dog team

Monday 2   Was down to Olson Creek   tok in all traps and brought home most of them   living the upper ones in place

Tuesday 3   Went in to Lick House   lot of new snow   saw lot of ptarmigans   got a toe of a lynx but no more

Wednesday 4   Went down in Funny River Basin baiting mink sets   lost one mink   wet snow falling all day   had five hours of the heavyest kind of snowshoing

Thursday 5   Left Lick House early   coming down my trail   full drifting & falling new snow saw lot of moose and tracks of a bunch of cyotes I think five in that bunch   went on to Toms place stay all night   just at dark game warden from Kenai came

Friday 6   This morning I and game warden came up lake shore   crossing lake point to shore south of point found no snow   left sled & load   walked to this place with dog team   got in my boat and ran back to the sled   tok load and sled in boat got home at dusk   just light anough to set net warm   a regular summer day   thermometer at 34 abov zero

Saturday 7   This morning we loaded all of game wardens tings in my boat   lashed the sled acrost the top of load and I started machine   taking load to Erlings place south shore of lake   game warden walking over flats with dogs   started to rain   fixed his sled   two broken uprights   stay all night at Erlings place   Erling was home fixing roof when I came (cooking cake)

Sunday 8   Fine weather this morning 32   calm Erling and I loaded game wardens junk in boat I ran beyond thirth clif   came back and picked him up with his dog team   tramped trail to Fox River   loose snow over summit   got back to Erling at five tired & swetty

Monday 9   Came home   fine weather   ice melting off trail   rest of ground bare   got a nasty hitch of rheumatism   storm on   been laying down since I got home two p.m.   storm broke out after that   feeling better   cooked a meal   set out net   could hardly stand up in wind thermometer at 42   cloudy making evening dark

Tuesday 10   Stay home all day   warm thermometer at 48 during day making icy places almost imposibly to stand up   wanted to go up to flats   afraid of falling   tok a bath   scrubbed the floor   cleaning tings generaly   got two makinaw trout   set net again tonight   snow all gone   no chance of hauling home wood unles we get som snow fall again

Wednesday 11   As I looked out this morning I saw snowflakes comming down as big as duck feathers but to warm to lay   later it turned to rain and been at it all day   still got a few traps out but no chance of any ting getting in   showers still hitting windows   my garden patch looks ready for planting   Have had merganser ducks all winter and som other ducks   today fish loon apeared

Thursday 12   Fine sumerlike day   tok a walk up flats   sprung all traps exept three sets for cyotes   did not bring in traps on acount of slippery walking   just now I had quite occashia played by a lot of cyotes   warm   not raining thermometer at 32 to night   looks like change

Friday 13   Have had a rainy fine day   about 35 abov   calm but I did not yet started to do anyting have been expecting Erling to com over   was graining up som tools making ready to start cutting & hauling timber for firewood but I have to wait to get som snow as here is none

Saturday 14   Here is another day gone and practicle noting acomplished   was trying to make yeast but afraid I let it get to hot in that case I certainly spoiled it   was out & cut som birch to start haul home for filling wood shade   som rain falling   thermometer at 35 abov zero   got three mackanaw this morning

Sunday 15   Was up befor six this morning cooked breckfast and set batter for making bread everyting working fine   yeast strong   had first batch in oven by noon   just fixing lunch Erling came   walked on to Bear Creek and here again by night   was out this evening loking for porkies no got   set out two nets   thermometer at 35

Monday 16   Have been putting in a big day hauling home green birch for fire wood and it is heavy to handle   got home about a cord weather at 35 so it is wet during midle of the day Erling working at new house put in two logs to day   was out and got a porcupine   cyotes scriming to night   had out two nets   got two makinaw in one of them

Tuesday 17   Thermometer down to 20 this morning   clear & calm   had our trout for breckfast as usual   after cleaning up after breckfast sweping floor and making tings ship shape Erling went to work at his cabbin and I got busy with hauling green birch   by noon I had home wath I had cut   in afternoon I cut and hauled and this evening I started cutting

Wednesday 18   Thermometer down to [illegible] abov zero   lake making a shim of ice under hand when no wind hit it but on shore water washes against gravel just like summer   no sign of ice   hauled home several loads of green birch and I think I got anough for next winter   still got about 1/4 of my wood that I cut a year ago turning mild   29 this evening

Thursday 19   Temperature 32   north east storm starting blowing hard   tok a walk up on flats cyote got one of my traps   heard a rumbling noys stopped and diretly saw water splash along creek   it was an earth quake   snowing som in afternoon   dogs barking at cyotes   just making ready to have a bath   wind quit   getting cooler down to 29 this evening   just saw new moon Erling say it be nasty weather from the looks of the moon

Friday 20   Working like a washer women to day as a result I got the clotches line full   weather just fine   about 30 abov   calm   Erling worked at his building to noon then after lunch started acrost flats to his place   said he expected to put in a day skinning cyotes

Saturday 21   Foggy this morning   was intending to cross the lake on way to King Lake but on acount of fogg I did not go   in stead I went out and cut slim spruce sprouts and made spring for my bed   Erling came back about noon and went to work at his building   he reported seeing a moose criple or broken hind leg   anyway it did not use the member   thermometer at 24 this morning   fine in afternoon

Sunday 22   Thermometer at 24   I started acrost lake late   crossing ridge to King Lake had very heavy walking   deep snow and loose   no sign of my old trail   saw som tracks of cyotes and moose   moose having tough time swiming thru snow but lots of feed   gray wilow

Monday 23   Intended to go to Rat Lake but heavy walking with strong north wester and snow drifting bad   so I turned round & came back to cabin   stay in rest of day   had lots of reading matter & with such weathre out side it was easy to stay home

Tuesday 24   Started in good time   facing a nasty head wind coming to big lake   found it choppy   warmed up machine   after I got away from shore and machine started I came along fine wind changed and by the time I got here it was fairly smoot   Erling saw me coming and had

lunch ready by the time I got in   thermometer at 20 this morning

Wednesday 25   Got up early and had breckfast befor daylight   Erling went hauling net but got only one makinaw   it was large   thermometer at 21   I split a few blocks birch wood then I sharpened an ax and filed a saw then had lunch after lunch a little nap   went to try saw   running fine and sawed and split nearly half rick for wood shade   wind blowing   thermometer down to 16 this evening   still going down

Thursday 26   Thermometer down to 14 this morning   came nearly losing one net as it was making ice   a big field about 1/4 inch started to pile ashore taking one net in with it   I was on flats   tok in all traps exepting five that is froze in ice   at noon it looked like winter   thin ice as far as you could see   toward evening wind came up cleaned off all ice   sawed wood for two hours temperature at 12 now

Friday 27   Down to seven 7 abov   after brecfast we went to Indian River set out net   I worked at som sheep bone for knif handle   mended som clotches had a bath and washed the [illegible] Erling been cutting & hauling home logs   getting milder   thermometer registering 22 abov zero

Saturday 28   20 this morning   Erling went to his place after breckfast   I started to Birchwood met Tom and Slim Crocker coming up with dog team   hauling sled over dry rocks & gravel   I stoped in at Toms and saw Mr Larson

Sunday 1 March   Stay at Friman all day   a gail of wind blowing   young Hanson came thru the blizard on his way to Kussiloff   I was busy reading and hearin surf & wind

Monday 2   Fine morning   went up to Lick House fine going   had lots of time to cut wood & hunt porcupine

Tuesday 3   Another fine day   went in to Funny River basin   snowshoed for 4 hours befor I got back to Lick House   hiking along bare headed at Lick House I put tings in order and walked on to Friman having been on snowshoes seven hours getting anough of it

Wednesday 4   Came up from Friman   slipery in plases   saw Tom at his place   strong head wind had to walk thru timber al the way to Bear Creek tok me over four hours to get home   found Erling working at his house   warm   raining

Thursday 5   Erling was up making breckfast when I awoke up   he went to lake shore and brought in a couple of fine makinaw trout   after we had cleaned up our dishes I under tok to set som saws but found the saws set was tampered with so I would not use it   Erling went to his building work   I started saw som wood but quit and came in   filed saw and then cut wood for two hours then stopped to make lunch   after lunch I tok a walk up creek   caming back I stopped at Erling building   started to split wood worked until dark   making yeast for bread

Friday 6   Have been home all day making bread had to have the door open and then it was too hot in cabbin with stove hot and temperature at 40 outside   wath little ice are there is going fast made a good batch of bread & made me a summer cap   Erling walked acrost to his place & came back with his dinky [dinghy]   bringing nails for erecting scafolding

Saturday 7   Was up in good time   Erling went up on creek and got som pipe   I was black smitting   beating a chisel point on a steel bar to cut ice   intending to try for beaver   when that was done I tok foot webbing out of my snowshoes hunted up som old lace and reafilled the shoes repairing smole webbing   tok a walk in along Indian River   shot one grouse but came home again without porkypin   sumer weather

Sunday 8   Stay home until eleven o clock and sun got nice and warm   put my junk in boat started evinrude ran acrost to south shore packed acrost ridge to King Lake   cut som wood and hunted up a porcupine to feed the dog

Monday 9   Waited until sun up   tok shovel ax and bar went to Rat Lake where it used to be som beaver but opon examination I find that they are taken or moved and as I did not see any indication of any being there I packed my tols back to King Lake Cabin thermometer down to 20 abov zero

Tuesday 10   Started this morning by setting traps for a outlaw beaver who have been there since 1923   shifting from one house to another   this is the first time I ever set traps for beaver and ice was three feet deep   came acrost to Tustimina found young ice as far as I could see   put machine on ran half mile   wire broke   had to pull with ores   tok me four hours   temperature 18 abov

Wednesday 11   Thermometer down to 15 abov this morning   som skin of ice in sight but not amount of anyting   had trout net out   hauled it but got only one trout   I was sowing splitting and stacking stove wood in wood shad but did not get much done as my arms was lame from the pull I had yesterday   Erling finished work on log wall today at least as far as he will go this spring

Thursday 12   12 degrees abov zero this morning Erling was out fishing and came in without fish a wind from the north and it feels right cold Erling went to his place and I started to fix a high tension wire in my old evinrude and found a stud broken and the point left in the hole   had quite a job drilling thru point and trying to turn it with left handed remer but rusted to tight reamed it down to the tread and finaly worked it out   tok me nearly all day   just heating water for bath

Friday 13   7 abov zero this morning   saw a film of cloud rising in west   might mean change but to night it is all clear   coolest evening so far   at half past seven down to 14   falling fast   will problbly be cooldest in morning   have been home nearly all day only out cutting & hauling home few sticks of fire wood   most of my day labor was at washing clotches   I did set out net this evening but I fear that if it calms down I will have trouble with ice

Saturday 14   Change in weather   was out at three o clock this morning and thermometer was at 8 abov and this morning it have gone up to 10 started sawing wood but it was a light breeze and started to nip at my ears so I quit   was in reading Erling came over flats to put his tings away   had lunch and started back   I started sawing splitting and could have finished second rick but as in no hurry and want somting to pass the time

Sunday 15   At 5 abov this morning   waited until 9:30 when sun got warm tok my skates along and tings I neded for two days including snowshoes provision gun ax etc   walked acrost flats to Erlings place   here I could use skates for about three miles   Earling was to have started for Kussiloff this morning but I found him stil here   went acrost to King Lake   got there in good time   cut som wood & hunted up a porcupine for dog feed

Monday 16   Not so cold this morning   foling with two beaver traps and about ten o clock started on my way back home   when I got to Lake Tustemina I found sled track of Erling   he have started down this morning   I came over ice to glaser flats   ice fine and smoth but full of large openings   got home at 2 p.m.   28 abov

Tuesday 17   At 5 abov again this morning   calm lake   still open but ice floting all over   ice building all day   try to walk along shore on ice but it only carried me at som places   was out cut a dry spruce   my dry birch will be running low befor long   not feeling good

Wednesday 18   Coolest morning so far this winter thermometer down to 3 abov zero   I can not se the ice field moving any to day   weather fine   absolutely calm   ther is strips of oppen water at difrent places and ice are building very slowly   close along shore it is perhaps a little over on inch thick but not anough to make it safe skating   it was feeling cold this morning   stay in until sun warmed tings up som   tok a walk to mouth of Indian to look after net   did not get any trout   sawed and split a few sticks of birch wood   tok a walk looking for porkies   foun on in a standing holow cotton wood   had a job cutting holes to get him

Thursday 19   3 abov zero   clear and calm and I can not see any open water so it is conclusive that the lake is frozen   althoug it is that big there can be lots of open water out of sight   have been in reading som trash and put in the whole day at it   this evening I saw a cloud rising in the west so there is probbly a chang in weathre

Friday 20   At 0 abov zero this morning everyting clear   fine morning   started to cut som wood and done good at it   I be out cutting for about an hour then sit in reading and repeat about noon a cloud came up over the mountain and more followd that this evening the sky is covered   a regular makrill sky   lake been whistling quite a lot indicating ice shrinking

Saturday 21   Just because ice ofered me a skate I ran along head of lake acrost to south side   I kept close to shore as the ice was weak   where I crossed cracks ice was heaving badly   22 abov in the morning   got acrost in good time over to King Lake

Sunday 22   Mild   came home to day   lucky I did not try to cross on ice   I felowed the shore clean in to Devils Bay then it started to rain & blow easterly wind   in fifteen minutes no ice in sight so our winter just lasted two days   42 abov when I got here

This relatively warm winter described by Berg may have contributed to another tragedy in Kasilof. Three young children drowned after falling through the ice on a lake at the Cole's homestead. Perry and Posey Cole's youngest child, Burton, and John and Jenny Sandwick's daughter and son, Shirley and John, Jr., were playing near the house when the accident occurred. More than

My Pioneer Days   Marion Cole

(continued)

One day in late winter of 1931, John and Jenny Sandwick and their two children came to visit us. While they and Mr. and Mrs. Cole played cards for a short time the children went out to play in the snow. A short time later when they were called to go home they couldn't be found. Milton followed their tracks on the lake which led to an edge by the beaver house and they had fallen through the melted ice. He got them out right away and said their bodies were still warm. The ice water was too much for their lungs and they were all dead. We all worked on them for a long time trying to save their lives but had to give up. Burton Cole was 6 years old. The Sandwick's girl was 5 years old and their son was 4. I think that was the saddest thing we ever experienced.

at any other time, the isolation of their community must have weighed heavily on the families in the hours following the disaster.

Monday 23   Loking out of window this morning I found it snowing heavy and keept on to nearly noon   but it was so warm that snow was melting in fact it was half rain as it fell   half hour after it quit the trees was clean of snow but in low places water stands like lakes   was down to Indian River   hauled my trout net got one white fish   stay in all day until evening   as it cooled down a bit I went out and sawed down a big dry spruce   as my dry birch is soon all burnt I will have to cut wath wood I need   just got about enough dry birch to bake bread to morow

Tuesday 24   Have been home all day making bread   fine weather out   only the snow that fell is still on the ground   lake is lying as smoth as a mill pond   walked out to fish net while I had the last pan in oven   got only one makinaw thermometer at 35 abov in the morning

Wednesday 25   At 24 abov zero this morning had a tuch of reumatism this morning so I stay home   have not don a ting all day   had som wind up the lake this fornoon but changed to south east and had few heavy squalls

Thursday 26   Wind from the north this morning with few snow flakes falling   finaly it got warmer wind in vortex   one puf coming up lake the next off mountains   thermometer at 30 abov zero am but snow tawing in afternoon   sawed a few blocks of birch   towards evening walked out to mouth of Indian River   fished the net got one dolvarden

Friday 27   Way up at 40 with moistur in the air just to wet to go anywhere   was out to look at my net it was gone   came back home put out the boat   riged a drag found net   no fish   net torn split som wood but most of my work have been reading Saturday Evening Post

Saturday 28   Was feeling peppy this morning so I went at sawing wood and did a good days work to   filled the last rick   that is as much as I had last year or perhaps more and now I got several sticks left so I will have to put in another rick cloudy and som wind   sumer day

Sunday 29   Weathre unsettled   a fine rain falling almost like heavy dew   not feeling good and to top tings I lost an inlay   now I got an exposed nerve and a most perfect tooth ague   have not don anyting wort mentioning so I call it a lazy day

Monday 30   Stay home all day   raining weathre extra ordinary warm   I cleaned out the well heated water & had a bath   walked out to mouth of Indian River   hauled net   got two nice trout one makinaw and one dollvarden

Tuesday 31   Got cooler during the night and this morning I had an inch of new snow but most of it was gone by noon   climbed on to the hill to look over lake but saw no ice anywhere   cleared up and sun shining brightly all afternoon

Wednesday 1 April   Hauled home a large dry spruce and sawed most of it to blocks firewood lengts   clear this morning but started to cloud up early   by night whole sky covered   got four fish today one dolvarden one makinaw & two white fish

Thursday 2   I intended to go acrost the lake to King Cabin that need the roof fixed   have waited for the snow to melt befor I go but to day I have been feeling out of sort   sleepy   muscles sore and aguing so I been in all day

Friday 3   I was slow getting ready this morning finaly got my ting togather started machine and ran acrost lake and on to King Lake   got working at fixing roof of cabbin and nearly finis when it got to dark to hit a nail

Saturday 4   When I looked out this morning I was in the midle of a snow storm   after I had breckfast I cleaned the roof and had to finis temporary on acount of snow   then I started on home and bad traveling   new snow sticking to my snowshoes and the lake rough with snow fall making it hard to see   got home one o clock wet & cold

Sunday 5   Was out hauling my trout net this morning thinking I would get a trout for breckfast but no such luck   a lot of ice have drifted up the lake during the night   that my have som ting to do with it   sawing som firewood   thats about all

Monday 6   A little cooler this morning so I split the few blocks of wood I had sawed   then tok dog with pack sadle went up on glaser flats where I had som traps frozen down   got them home cut som more wood   got one makinaw trout

Tuesday 7   Have been busy all day and noting to show I don anyting   was out to net first ting got two trout wich I transformed to breckfast then split som wood & sawed and split som more and found that I did not have anough home to fill the extra ricks   so I went out cut down a birch and packed home pice at the time until it got dark

Wednesday 8   Finis cutting wood this forenoon & got more wood put up than I had at anytime tok home som grate bars for new fire place in stove   tok up the net this morning to dry it   got only one makinaw   just anough

Thursday 9   Have been working all day that I feel realy tired and got noting to show for wath I did   just changing tings about and putting away to another year   among other ting I scaffolded up a heavy cutting wood   under cut & sawed it to it is ready to drop   waiting for easterly wind

A front view of Andrew's "little house out back." Photo by G. Titus.

to tow it   a beutiful day   my garden patch is getting soft   if I had carrot seed I would plant befor I go down

Friday 10   Having a most beutiful weathre   realy like california only so much nicer   my work to day was building a gate for my garden patch and making a hood for the stove pipe and cleaning up around the place   comence to feel like going away

Saturday 11   Got a sort of kink in my back and not feeling good   I stay in most of the day reading and tinkering about the place   not liking one rail on my garden fence I tok it down   launched the boat and pulled up lake shore and brought home new rail and put it up

Sunday 12   Tok a walk up Indian River to find out if any bears have comensed to move but no sign of any tracks   everyting seemes quite hunted up som old lumber and put new floor in the little house out back   noting much that I can do here   expect to be making ready to start down river with the boat

Monday 13   Not feeling good   had a dizzy spell this afternoon and I have not done a ting that I can give myself credit for   was out to net and did not even get a trout   have been reading most of time   cloudy but no wind   fine weathre   55 in midle of the day

Tuesday 14   Have been home all day making bread anough to last until I get down to Kusilof getting tired of doing noting   had quite of wind up the lake but no ice drifting so I think I can get with the boat as far as Penninsula   just heating water to have a bath

Wednesday 15   Been feeling lazy and slippy all day   expect probbably som change in the weathre som wind blowing up the lake this afternoon but quit by to night

Thursday 16   I have been home all day not doing much of anyting   did wash som clotches but got som ting wrong with my back   it is posible from the kidneys   have been on my back in bed reading   a very strong south or perhaps a point westerly wind sprung up during the day and the heavy surf cut down the beach that could not get my net this evening

Friday 17   The first ting I did this morning was putting out the boat and pulled to mouth of Indian River to try to get my trout net   but to much gravel was washed on it so I got only the lines the webb stripping as I pulled it in   after I got water warm I scrubed the floor   cleaned shed mixed oil and trying to live tings ship shape for the summer

Saturday 18   Set my little net last night and got two fine makinaws this morning   have been in all day   a nasty cold wind blowing up the lake and I got a sleepy spell   cant seem to get anough sleep

Sunday 19   Went down to Penninsula

After such a poor trapping season, Berg was probably happy to get back to work on Cook Inlet. The Bureau of Fisheries Report for 1931 stated that Special Warden Andrew Berg operated a Bureau speed boat and patrolled the fishing grounds on the west side of Cook Inlet north of West Foreland during the season.[1]

The Bureau of Fisheries also worked on predator control. Their big issue at this time was reducing populations of trout and Dolly Varden which were considered predators of salmon.[2] On the Kenai Peninsula, residents and tourists enjoyed fishing for trout and were strongly opposed to the government's efforts to eliminate the fish. The author of the 1931 BOF Report complains that residents in the vicinity of Tustumena Lake were unwilling to participate in eradication programs. But Perry Cole is remembered as a Dolly Varden trapper.[3] He set traps in the creeks around Tustumena Lake and collected a two cent bounty on each Dolly tail. The fish carcasses probably fed his foxes.

Cole was operating a sawmill at his place as another business venture. A newspaper article published in the *Seward Daily Gateway* in July attested to Cole's continued optimism for Kasilof's prospects. He was pushing for road construction between Kenai and Homer. This was an effort to expand local markets and connect the western peninsula communities with an ice-free winter port.

The Alaska Guides Inc. was also using the newspaper for promotion and marketing. Articles began appearing

---

SEWARD DAILY GATEWAY
July 10, 1931

Kasilof Fur Farmer Works for 50 Mile Road, Kenai-Homer

Perry L. Cole, Kasilof fur farmer was a recent visitor in Seldovia and was brimful of enthusiasm about the expansive possibilities of the Kenai country, especially the section touching the east shore of Cook Inlet between Kenai and Homer.   Cole announced it as his plan to promote in every way possible the advantages of this district from both an agricultural and fur farming viewpoint. Mr. Cole was en-route to Anchorage when in Seldovia for the purpose of concluding formalities effecting ownership of his homestead holding. As a traveling representative of the Fur Breeders Association of New York, Mr. Cole for four years covered every fur bearing state in the union and Alaska. Out of all territory traversed the Cook inlet district offered the strongest appeal so much so that he gave up his eastern connections came west, took up a 167 acre homestead at Kasilof and has a neighboring tract under lease...

---

in the *Anchorage Daily Times* in August touting the names and credentials of clients arriving in Alaska to hunt with the Alaska Guides. The names of the guides were also published, promoting their celebrity status. The guides working on the Kenai Peninsula included Hank Lucas, Slim Crocker, Theodore Van Bibber, Carl Anderson, Luke Elwell and H. A. Anderson.

Andrew Berg, meanwhile, was quietly earning his wages from the Bureau of Fisheries. The Report for this year mentioned that Berg made a preliminary survey of the lower Kenai River and Skilak Lake in early August and another survey of the Kenai River system from August twenty-third to thirty-first.[4] Between those trips he was at Tustumena Lake:

Monday 17 August   left Kusiloff 4 o clock this morning   was at Nikolai Creek in 3 hours after wasting lot of time on the river   walked up Nicloai about five miles   came from Nicolai to here in one hour six minutes against strong head wind & stopped to fill tank

Tuesday 18   Started machine this morning going to Clear Creek   past woods Penninsula in seven minutes   got to Clear Creek in seventeen minutes

Hank Lucas and trophy moose. Photo courtesy of Wanda M. Griffin.

was up this stream only clearing out two or three obstructions   ran down to muddy   saw only few salmon here   ran to Nyman Coast   few salmon   landed south of woods island no water creek gone dry   came home for luncheon   went to salmon stream on glaser flats   good awrige [average]   met Pete Madsen Milton Cole & Ed Lovedall who was at upper island loking for fox feed   Ed reported seeing three cyotes   went to mouth of stream saw quite lot of salmon half mile up   came home for the big feed   it was good

Wednesday 19 Went down to Bear Creek this morning   tok us eleven minutes   found Mr & Mrs Bragaw camping at Bear Creek out fishing Mr Charles Smith was with them   ran down to Birch Wood to bring up a motor   was up creek to heavy breck   no salmon   got abov it saw two black bears   fox farmers came in here this evening

Berg mentions seeing the Bragaws camping at Bear Creek. This, and other references, make it clear that the Alaska Guides were no longer operating their Tustumena base camp at Birchwood Lodge. Tom Odale was running an independent guide business from the lodge. This year Odale obtained a homestead patent on forty-nine acres at Birchwood. The patent map showed the lodge, two other buildings and mink pens all surrounded by a fence.

It is a curious fact that Andrew Berg never acquired a homestead patent on his place at the lake. Nor has evidence been found to indicate that he secured ownership of property in Kenai. Many Kenai residents were traditionally communal in their attitude toward property but Berg's friends in Kasilof generally owned homesteads. Perhaps his lack of descendants made him unconcerned about the future of his assets.

September was the height of the hunting season with parties coming and going by boat and by airplane. Anchorage had two airlines at this time. Pacific International Airways pilot Frank Dorbandt took care of most of the Alaska Guides' business. The pilot plucked Hank Lucas from the Tustumena hunting grounds on September fourth and flew him to Anchorage for an emergency appendectomy. Slim Crocker was with Hank when he became ill. Slim made a 24 hour run to Anchorage by skiff to arrange for the airplane and a doctor.[5]

Other news this month included an article in the Seward Gateway about Heinie Berger building a new dock at Kasilof.[6] While wintering in Seattle, Heinie had married Al Hardy's widow Alice. The new dock was constructed at Alice's homestead on the Kasilof River.

Newspaper articles in October related details of successful hunts and included references to the depression. English banker Sir John Mullens enjoyed his second trip to Alaska this season and opined that

---

SEWARD GATEWAY

September 21, 1931

Berger Erecting Fine Dock At Kasilof

Due to development of business attendant upon big game hunting and fur farming, Capt. Heinie Berger of the MS Discoverer, plying Cook Inlet between Anchorage and Seward, is erecting a dock at Kasilof. When completed the dock will have a length of 30 feet for berthing the ship and 50 feet to shore. Piling has been driven and workmen are now flooring the structure.

It is Captain Berger's plan to erect a large storehouse and commodious quarters for big game hunters and other visitors to the famous Tustumena Lake country. On his next trip out of Anchorage Captain Berger will tow a scow loaded with 50 tons of coal consigned to upper Cook Inlet ports.

"things will work out all right in due course and that the world again will find itself moving along on an even keel almost before people realize it."[7] Finishing his seventh hunt in Alaska, Gunn Buckingham of Memphis was quoted saying: "There is no evidence anywhere...that the depression had made itself felt among the Kenai game."[8]

Guided trophy hunters were finding plenty of moose but residents were perceiving an overall decline in the population on the Kenai. The concept of a moose preserve was resurrected by the Alaska Game Commission. The visions of Dall DeWeese and William Langille were finally achieving official recognition. The commission formally recommended that the federal government establish a moose sanctuary encompassing some 1,230 square miles of the peninsula.[9] Their recommendation began a slow journey toward the goal of executive proclamation. In the meantime, the Game Commission closed the area north of the Kenai River and west of the Chickaloon River to moose hunting.

The game commission also decided that protecting the moose required a better understanding of the conditions which had allowed them to thrive on the Kenai. Hank Lucas was hired to conduct a study and then contributions were solicited from private sources to fund his work in the following year.

Like most locals, Andrew Berg may have had an opinion about moose preserves, but he was primarily occupied with the tasks of daily life:

Friday 9 October   Came up from Penninsula after running down to Hugos leaving my schiff and engine   had fine weather   got here shortly after 2 o clock been busy since storing my supplies and checking up tings for winter garden truck fine   not had time yet to take it in

Saturday 10   Stay home all day taking in garden truck   about ten o clock Pete Madsen & Luis Fransen came up from Birch Wood   tok a hike upon Indian River saw lot of silver salmon   came home fixed trout net   set it   boys came off mountain   saw no sheep but sighted three black bears   mild but to night it is clearing

Sunday 11   Everybody out this morning exept I the boys went to Nikanorka Mountain after sheep but weather was bad   they only got one   I was up Indian River   saw eighty four sheep two

moose & one brown bear   shot at bear two shots but to long range   raining & snowing with heavy wind   I was up to Guids camp   saw sheep at both sides of Indian river   most of them close to north fork junction

Monday 12   Stay home all day cutting wood & started digging garden   the rest was up on sheep mountain   weather fine but no sheep came home the hunters got in way after dark

Tuesday 13 Stormy early this morning but moderated later   two went up Indian   others fishing   I and Pete Madson was out constructing Madsens Bolevard   doing several days work in one day   the boys out of cannon reported seeing a bear and from its action I decided that it was a brown bear

Wednesday 14   Tok a walk over home trail   saw lot of sign of bears but no bear   had heavy climbing thru long grass & alders   crain berries & blue berries in plenty   the boys all came in after long sheep hunt   got three sheep among them   came in after dark tired & quarelsom

Thursday 15   Stay home all day   filing a saw this morning but before I got after som wood it started raining   the boys went up to get som sheep meat that left there day before   got in early about four o clock good and wet

This group was from Anchorage and was outfitted by Tom Odale:

Oct 22 12:30 p.m.   Hello Andrew: H. J. Gaillsema Anchorge W. H. Smith Fred Judd — S. Beners   On way to sheep hills had trouble with motor and stopped on beach to repair same visited your cabin   like it a lot   even figured out how to work the latch in door   Best & luck

[Andrew writes:] *Sunday 15 November   Georg Cook & myself left Kenai at noon   walked to Kussiloff   stoped in at Erik Isackson   I pay'd him for gasoline I barowed on acount of USBF $500   on way to Alex Lind saw Emil stuck in ice with sciff   he reported that he killed two brown bears   one extra larg   had coffe at Alexs   stay all night at Abrahams fox ranch*

Monday 16   Weathre nice & crisp down to 4 started walking to Tustemina Lake   stopped in at Coles had coffe   fine walking   got to lake in two hours forty six minutes   stay at Ed Zarwels all night

Tuesday 17   Waited at Zarwels until weathre got warmer about ten   ran little evenrude to Bear

Tom Odale at the tiller of his skiff coming up the Kasilof River. Photo courtesy of McLane Collection.

Creek on one gallon of gasoline   had lunch with Pete Kalning & his partner   got home in good time   found cabbin the dirtiest I have seem it in many years   had to wash every dish pot pan before they was fit for use   foggy with som wind from south west   Andrew Berg

Wednesday 18   Was up early this morning to make breckfast start yeast and fix tings ship shape but found it to late for our contemplated sheep hunt   but tok a walk to mouth of Dirty Cannon just to see condition of water in creeks saw two larg headed bull moose on flats at close range   lot of cyotes tracks   set net   12 abov

Thursday 19   Stay at home making bread and it did not turn out as good as I wanted and I dont know the reason for it   Cook was up on sheep mts got two sheep   brought the sadle of one started near ten o clock and got in after dark   I just set net   thermometer up to 15 abov zero

Friday 20   Storm started during the night   I got out at three to take in net   lighted lamp lay reading couple of hours   after breckfast sewed at a canvas pack sack for the big dog   washed clotches and again this eve I was working at pack sack   we are having a nasty south easterly storm trees swaying like hemp stalks   lake fether white as far as you can see

Saturday 21   Started to go to mountains to bring in the sheep Cook killed but wind was to strong   we was unable to get the boat to glaser flats so we try walking but Indian River have shot   could not cross it   came back home finis pack sack   was out got a grouse   set net caught two red salmon just spawning one 17 inch the other 19 inch long

Sunday 22   Was up befor six o clock fished net got one trout & one salmon intended to go to mountains but wind still to strong   worked all fornoon on a bucket after tea I went up Lake Emma trail and did a lot of work clearing wind falls out of trail leading up hill   got one grouse two porkies   still som wind otherwise a regular summer day   ground tawing out

Monday 23   Was sleeping late this morning huried breckfast   started motor trying to get to glaser flats but wind whiped the boat around and drove us in shore   was unable to get machine started again and came on home   filed & fixed a saw   started to rain to wards evening   that killed the wind

Tuesday 24   Up early this morning in order to have lot of time to bring in sheep meat   just as we was making ready to go Earling Frostad & Pete Kalning partner came up from Bear Creek that destroyed us about one hour   however we was up packed in 1 1/2 sheep and was home just as it was getting dark

Erling Frostad was married to Louise Darien in Kenai on June fifteenth of this year. On June twentieth he filed his citizenship naturalization petition in Anchorage. His brother Ole had married a Kenai woman in 1929.[10] While marriage appeared to have kept Ole closer to home, Erling still maintained his Tustumena trap lines.

Wednesday 25   A heavy south easterly storm broke loose during the night   I awok at one twenty hurried out to secure the boat   during fornoon it carried water in sheets but quit befor night   thermometer at fourty abov   I been working on a stove for Friman   did not finnis got so dark during rain squall that I had to quit working

Thursday 26   Storm still ragin so I continued to work at stove   finished it about noon   weathre quite warm just now   after being thru super for about one hour the fire out and door wide open we have it 82 farenhest   this afternoon I was hoeing the garden   there is frost under the soil

Friday 27   A drisely rain all day   to wet to go out   stay at home   the only ting I can give myself credit for as leveling trail to lake shore grinding an ax and putting up provisions for a trip to Friman

Saturday 28   Started late taking Cook to lower end of lake   but when we got to Camp Friman saw it getting late so we stay over night   put in new stove & set trout net

Sunday 29   Caught ten nice trouth nine makenaw one dolvarden and it took somtime before we had

brecfast & rested from labor so we started late a dust of new snow have fallen during the night getting cold   stay only couple of minutes   I came back to Friman alone   nasty cold wind

Monday 30   Cold wind blowing   stay at camp all day to evening   tok a walk to Toms place he was not at home so I came back to Friman after dark   saw Toms tracks on beach   he have been down to set out his trouth net

Tuesday 1 December   Tok a walk to Olson Creek (no game)   set nine traps for mink and lynx nasty north cold wind blowing

Wednesday 2   Stay in camp all day   to cold north wind to even think of crossing sumit to Funny River   was out hunting porkies for dog feed   buildt a new saw horse & sawed up som wood

Thursday 3   Fine this morning   went to Lick House found everyting fine   killed a porky & som grouse   just a little snow on ground not anough to interfere with walking   I was loaded with a new stove   dogs with provisions for the trip

Friday 4   Went down in Funny River basin to my last Cabbin north where I am bringing stove to got there early and good ting I did   found the place broken into by bears   window smashed door broken bedding destroyed everyting smashed   put up new stove   stay all night

Saturday 5   Came back to Lick House setting out traps on three streams   set out 25 traps in all got in late feeling tired   my feet sore   not used to such hard play

Sunday 6   Chopped trail from Lick House thru timber   dogs turned back   I expected them to come so I went on to Friman Camp

Monday 7   No dogs yet this morning so I went back to Lick House   found them there and they was glad to see me   tok there packs off while I made myself a cup of tea   sadled up again & came down to Friman

Tuesday 8   Blowing havy from the south so no chance to go out with the boat so I made it a day of rest   walked over to Toms   stay all night listening to radio

Wednesday 9   Still stormy   Tom & I went along beach to his net   it was snaged   continued on to Friman   got my boat out   had a rough time getting to net   landed boat   packed net to Toms   I got boat this evening as far as Toms place (som more radio)

Thursday 10   To havy wind yet this morning   Tom went to Pipe Creek   about noon it moderated   I had truble with engine   met Erling at Bear Creek come here in company   wrecked my motor   Erling went home

Friday 11   Heard a heavy wind early morning got out at six   quit blowing   started to snow that by daylight we had three inches of snow & wet anough that it hangs to trees   has worked at the motor all day and think I got it so it will run   fixed yeast had a bath changed clotches had a shave & feel better

Saturday 12   Have been busy all day   set batter for bread this morning & this evening I got a fine lot of bread & betwin time I have been at the work bench fixing tings   first a stove door then saw handle   then at the motor again adjusting proppeller at proper pitch   now I got water warm to wash clotches   turned warm this evening snow melting   35 abov zero

Sunday 13   Did not sleep well last night so I did not get out of bed to after seven   changed from rain to snow so that this morning we again had new snow & continued off & on during the day have not acomplished much   just altered and fixed som bedding

Monday 14   Intended to go up to Lake Emma started rather late   after walking a while I know I did not have time anough to get up & back on acount of snow & I tok no snowshoes so I came back in   saw no tracks of game   clearing up & getting cooler   hauled down my fish pole & set out the net   reading som cheap trash

Tuesday 15   Had five trout & one salmon this morning & put the salmon in kettle for the dogs then at ten forty I went up Lake Emma trail overlooked my cache of traps going up   saw no

sign of game so I came back without setting a trap   went without snowshoes & snow got to over my knees upon the ridg & at the lake I found water on the ice covered with loos snow so I did not cross   started to snow befor I got home

Wednesday 16   Still snowing continualy all night & all day   not a heavy fall but a very thin drizle somwhat cooler with strong breeze from the north to nasty for me to go anywheres   stay in cleaning house reading & sleeping

Thursday 17   Had ice on windows this morning with northerly wind blowing but wind not strong anough to shake snow out of trees & bushes they are padded ful and dont want to go creeping thru them to they clear as I dont see anyting to be gained by it

Friday 18   Turned cold & I have a slight cold in my troat so I have not feelt like going anywhere been putting in my time reading   set out net   did not notice how cold in was this morning but this evening it is 2 below zero & clear so it my down a lot more before morning   wanted to go on the glaser flats to try and get a moose

Saturday 19   Turned milder during the night   up to 12 abov this morning and back to drizling snow so that gives me an other excuse to stay in the house   hauled the net get several nice trout & one steelhead   its cloudy & turned dark that I had to light the gas lamp at half past three

Sunday 20   Was early this morning intending to take a walk out on the glaser flats but it started snowing & looked so nasty I did not venture out until about noon   I cleaned my guns   tok a tramp to edge of flats   no tracks exepting cyotes & rabbits   they seemed to be on increas   heard my dog growling looked out two moose right at door   this was about midnight   moose did not scare

Monday 21   Snowing in great style this morning and I was sleeping late   did not get up to nearly eight and as just I was having breckfast Erling Frostad came   he was on his way to Kenai to celebrate x mas   weathre warm but more snow than I seen in years

Tuesday 22   Fine day   5 abov zero this morning after I had my breckfast I got my snowshoes and started out to see wath it was like   plowed along for couple of hours but snow is to soft to go anywhere and timbre just loaded with snow came back   set out net but is afraid of losing it som skim ice is making   2 abov at six this evening but sinking slow

Wednesday 23   Thermometer was up to twelf this morning   dealty still   young ice floting nearly drove my net in but I got the net out   had one dolyvarden one makinaw one steelhead two salmon   tawing ice out of net   went out got wilow bark boiled tan and just tanning the net cloudy   if it clear during night we will have ice

Thursday 24   Had eartquak last night that made the cabin groan in all the joints   movement from south east to north west   thermometer climbed to fifteen abov zero   started snowing   kept on nearly all day   towards evening it quit   I got on my snowshoes and tramped trails so I could get wood & that is the first time I remember of having to do so in all the time I have been here

Friday 25   Just a few flofy clouds in sight thermometer at 8 abov   I sleept to 7:30 o clock had a bath befor I went to bed   sleept untill three   lighted the lamp & read to my eyes got tired   turned out the light & proceaded to finish my sleep   som ice starts to make noyes down lake but noting have shown here exepting young crystals building and drifting down the lake by wind from mountain   it is now 2 abov at 7 p.m.

Saturday 26   Clouded up during the night and temperature was 8 abov   calm that ice built during night is still in sight this evening & as it is zero this evening & I hear no noys of moving ice it is a fair chance that it will close   had trip on snowshoes for three hours   did not se any sign of furbearers but several moose   started in to build a sled after I came back   it look like overland travel from now on

Sunday 27   4 below zero this morning and very little water to be seen   tok a walk on ice to day along the beach but it was so weak that I was forsed up on beach wher it was to thin   just befor dark I thought I heard air plane motor raising & slowing as it warming up   thermometer at 3 abov this evening   som clouds apeards just about dusk

Monday 28   12 abov zero this morning   about noon I got on my scates ran down to Bear Creek found Pete at home & Erling who have just come up from Kenai   had my hair cut & Erling came with me here   went out on ice fell & cut my scalp nearly on top of my head   lost consosnes   now my neck feels sore anoug to be broken

Tuesday 29   Erling went over flats this morning I went along to see that he got to the flats as the ice are still very pore   after I came back tok a walk looking for ptarmigan   saw som tracks but did not rise a bird   then I started to hunt for a axe I got missing   did not find it

Wednesday 30   Thermometer at 1 abov this morning   clear calm   feling to sore to move around much   stay home reading June copy of Current History   about 2:30 Pete Kalning came up from Bear Creek to get som books   after he left I went & put out net at mout of Indian River walked clean thru woods island   saw six or seven cyotes in one bunch   got a moose this evening

Thursday 31   Put a bunch of traps in the sled hitched up & went to set traps for cyotes   set out 19   coming back home stopped at mouth of Indian River   fished the net got four nice big trout   getting home just as it was getting dark temperature this morning was 5 below zero   the lake have been covered with fog   2 below at seven this evening

Chapter 17

1932

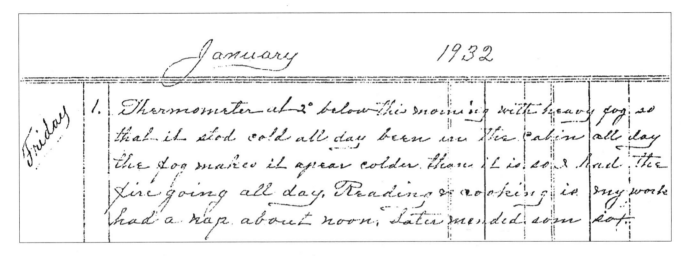

Saturday 2   Was milder this morning   clouded from the east but no wind   tok a few more traps went along lake shore towards Erlings   set them for cyotes   saw an object moving way out on ice apeared like a man scating but so far off that it might just as well been wolferine or cyote   got seven big trout coming in out of the net

Sunday 3   3 below this morning   everyting clear   looks like cold weathre is starting   was ready to go down lake but as I know there is noting to go for I rather wait to tings are right tok in my net & have everyting so that I can live any time

Monday 4   At zero this morning   cloudy with a drizly snow falling although last night thermometer went down to six below   not feeling good ever since my fall   feeling sore all thru have been afraid to start anywhere

Tuesday 5   Cold is right   14 below zero this morning & stay low all day & to night it is at 9 below   seeing it be to cold to travel I started yeast to night   just as well make a batch of bread as I stay in anyway

Wednesday 6   14 below this morning and eight o clock this evening it is 19 below zero   have been making bread this day & lots of it so I dont epect to have to bake again this month   have a pain in right side low   afraid it is apendix   any whay it apear trublesom   sharp pain when I straigten up after sitting down for a while

Thursday 7   At 10:30 last night the thermometer was at 22 below   the lowest I have seen it is good many years & this morning it was at 20 below zero   rised to 10 below at noon   I went out traveled for two hours   turning milder   I can hear diferent sound in the cracking of ice

Friday 8   Snowing to beat the band this morning & kept on to noon   I went to set my net and waided in loose new snow   knee deep temperature 10 abov zero   cant do anyting now out so I will continue as I have for a whole mouth

Saturday 9   Started to blow about midnight but not anough to clean the trees although the loose snow on the lake was running   tok a walk out on ice   found ice sinking   the snow is to heavy and water coming thru   had to use snow shoes *again to day to tramp trails about the place   have been about zero all day   now at 10 below*

Sunday 10   8 below this morning with fog or thin clouds driftening from north east & a very thin dust of snow coming down   about noon a sort of hase apeared forming a sundog east & west of the sun   started clearing at the same time thermometer started to sinking   it is now 7 o clock temperature at 24 below & aparently still going down   tok a walk to Indian River to fish the net   got only two trouts but they was large lot of loose snow with water on the ice   by the time I got home my shoepacks was loaded with ice

Monday 11   A fine excuse for staying in today 29 below zero this morning and I am not going any place in that chill unles nessesary   did not rise much all day   toward evening she started to rise   it up to eleven below now after dark   have not done anyting exepting made three meals & enjoyed them   also feed my two dogs   (Readin)

Tuesday 12   8 below this morning & stay below zero all day until evening   then it clouded up & by nine o clock it rised to 7 abov   Erling Frostad came here over flats   fished net got only one sub speices of dolvarden

Wednesday 13   Up to 10 abov this morning Erling was out fishing net got two trout so we had real frish trout for breckfast   Erling went over flatts home   I mended dogs harneses and snowshoed out to look at cyote sets   one steped on the jaw of a trap   at another place just tuched the trap   snowshoing heavy   tok me 3 hours

Thursday 14   16 below   som fog over the lake clear overhead   have put in all day repairing som old snowshoes   at midle of day she was up to 8 below but from that point started to desend was 10 o clock   saw a man walking along lake shore   I presume it was Pete Kalning who got som traps set for cyotes there

Friday 15   29 below this morning and it feel good to be in a warm cabin   waited to noon for it to get warmer but a thermometer started to go down   it was then 22 below   I went to mouth of Indian River fished net   got two trouts and set the net again   after I got back I went out to feed

my dogs   glansing up I saw two cyotes about 200 yds in front of landing   done noting   just keeping stove going & reading   31 below tonight

Saturday 16   38 below this morning   stay low all day   I have been in all day keeping fire going & just rising the duce with my wood pile unles this lets up I will have to get home more wood before winter is over   banked around the cabbin with snow to day   my dogs although they are black loked iron gray when they came out of thier house (frosty)   36 below this eve at 8

Sunday 17   22 below this morning but clouding up   light wind from north   thermometer risin slowly   by night it is six below   I was out to bring in som pickled salt pork   found it frozen solid had to bring barrel in & then no chance to get any without the use of dynamite   been in all day as usual

Monday 18   14 below this morning with high flying clouds rising from the south   about noon I hoked up the dogs & loked over cyote traps noting been near them   coming back I saw a cyotie out on ice   he was playing out there for an hour while I came by   tramped wood trail & put new lace in snowshoe after I got home

Tuesday 19   Abov zero this morning & about 8:30 it started snowing big flakes   about noon clearing up   I got on my snow shoes tramped down to Bear Creek with som periodicals   found both men at the cabbin   only stay few minutes as I had hardly time to get home befor dark

Wednesday 20   Warm to day   snowing a fine dust until towards evening when som over grown flakes comensed   was out to Indian River choped thru ice fished the net   got five nice trout   this evening I hear noys of wind   the first for a long time as the snow that fell on December 10th is still on the trees

Thursday 21   A lot more new snow have fallin during the night   thermometer at 20 abov   rising slowly in afternoon   I hear the roaring of the wind and snow starts to shake out of trees   have not been away from cabbin all day

Friday 22   An other day past & noting acomplished   warm snow   melting som snow on ice wetting thru   about six inches deep   went out tramping wood trail   to wet to go any place started to go fishing net   squall of sleet mad me turn back

Saturday 23   Was snowing again this morning with strong southeasty wind   was out to Indian River tok in the net   nearly lost it   snow drifting into opening at mouth of stream & settling down forming mush ice clean to bottom   got thre trout

Sunday 24   Foggy and calm this morning   about 12 abov   late afternoon cleared and thermometer started to go down   at present it is 15 below and icing the windows Nicily   was out on snowshoes nearly imposible to go anywhere   snow laying that soft you are sinking away down

Monday 25   18 below zero this morning   awoke at five by a ratling earthquake   to cold to do anyting out   stay in to afternoon   tok a trip up on the flats   saw two moose and lots of cyotee tracks my   traps are all covered with drift snow will have to go clear them if it get milder

Tuesday 26   It got down to 20 below befor I went to bed last night but this morning it was back up to 12 below   stay about two abov all afternoon   this evening after dark it rised another degree   I started wittling at som runners for bob sleds   days are getting long   I did not light the lamp to 4:30 this evening

Wednesday 27   12 below this morning   fog al over the lake and feeling coole   been below zero all day   been in all day   tok in the grindstone   after it got the frost out of it sharpened a two faced ax & som plain bits worked som at carpentering   not acomplished much

Thursday 28   Milder this morning   intended to go look over my cyote sets but had lots of time so I started chipping at sled runner   Erling came cut his hair and got a patch of skin of his neck went out to traps   one cyote pulled out   Erling went on home

Friday 29   Foggy this morning with thermometer registering 20 abov   a thin dust of snow started and kept up nearly all day   I am not feeling just right   try to work at som tings but did not seem

to do any good so I just quit   tried to make a spoke shave from a trap spring but did not get the temper right so I will have to do it over

Saturday 30   Have been in nearly all day weathre mild   it have rained during the night that it formed a noysy crost   I can hear moose crunching in timbre close to cabin   I saw som animals out on the lake ice but it was so foggy that it was dificult to determine just wath they were   was out fishing got only one trout but that is quite anough for my breckfast   the trout is large   this evening I went up the creek a way set som traps for porcys as I am getting short of dog feed   after I got back I cooked & had my super & now I am just finins filing two of my hand saws

Sunday 31   A wet snow coming down this morning thick that it darkened the day   been doing som carpenter work but dont get anyting finished   everyting awkward timber tools & place to work   walked out to look at my porky traps one have been in but it got loose   also hauled the net but no fish   snow is getting that heavy that water is coming up   in going to mouth of Indian to fish the net I waded thru snow & water all the way

Monday 1 February   Stay home all day   still snowing   tok a walk loking over som cyotee traps but got so bad I could not get to the last

Tuesday 2   Working at my sleds som during the day   had a bad night hardly any sleep   bothered with wath I think are apendisilis   afternoon Pete Jensen & two other men came up   I fished the net & got one makenaw trout

Wednesday 3   Got up at six made brecfast   after wards I set bread   Pete tok a walk by old wagon road to Indian River folowed the stream down to the mouth   when they came back we had coffe the boys hitched the team of eleven dog started for Erlings   I was busy with bread & washing clotches   weather turned mild this morning towards evening I heard roar of som wind from the glaser   I think it quit

The "boys" were probably Comer Cole and Ed Jackinsky. Ninilchik resident Ed Jackinsky remembers making a trip to Tustumena around this time. Comer was one of Perry

Cole's sons. The two young men were friends and went to the lake with Comer's dog team for fun.

Thursday 4   Weathre mild   almost thawing   stay in all fornoon   about noon the boys came back from Erlings   I talked them in to stay all night   tok a walk up Indian   after we got back we caught several games of penolke and then we had quite of music by coyotee band answered by a bunch of malamutes

Friday 5   Got about one inch new snow this morning   the boys hitched up thier big team & started down the lake   going fast   all three men riding   they where going to Tom Odales to day   I finis one of the sleds I been working on to day   walked out to fish my net and the cyotee gave me a fine serenade   they was yelping & howling from three different directions   som was up Indian River   som towards Bear Creek but the main band was up glaser flats   I got only one trout again to day

Saturday 6   A fine drisly snow coming down this morning and continued all day   was expecting Erling thru on his way to Toms   was up creek got a porkupine   also take a walk on glaser flats to find out why the cyotes are keeping the consert in just that place but the snowshoing got too heavy I had to quitt   this evening I started to

This picture was labeled "Andrew Berg and Ed Jackinsky." They are on the lake ice checking the net for trout. Photo courtesy of McLane Collection.

whittle out uprights for the hand sled that I got in the making   (mild)

Sunday 7   Snowing all night and still som dust coming down but it does not amount to anyting on the ground   perhaps a couple of inches   I heard quite som consert this fornoon from a big congregation of cyotes   done som carpentering walked out to fish the net got only one trout again the new snow makes walking very por   lot of water on the ice   som places water was ancle deep

Monday 8   The weathre still the same   heavy fog hanging over the lake & just cold anough to make snow coming down steady   I got on my snowshoes to go look over my cyotie sets but had to give it up as there was that much snow water on the ice that I was getting my snowshoes all iced up   they got so heavy I had a hard time getting back   it apear like a change in the weathre   I am expecting a storm   had none this winter

Tuesday 9   Did have som northerly voleys of wind but being sheltered from that quarter it did not shake things as it may have   about ten o clock in loking thru the window it was given a fine imitation of a flour mill as seen on movie picture screen   windows iced up & look quite wintery   cleared up towards evening temperature ran down to 10 below stay right home   mended wearing apearls

Wednesday 10   I was down to 30 below this morning and feeling snapy to a sort of damp cold building frost   my windows have a beutiful design   put you in mind of the song the great big sugar mountain   all I been out to day is getting in wood & water & feeding the dogs   have been putering with one ting and another   sharpening axes and tools

Thursday 11   Mercury was frozen this morning & it was down to 34 abov in the cabin wen I got up this morning   no chance of going anywher so I put in day at dressing down a pair of bobsled runners   went out to porky traps   got one   the dogs ran in & got their faces ful of quills   it was then about 25 below & I had a beast of a job pulling quills beating out a knife blade along side the stove it is now 7:30 -30 below outside   70 abov inside rather stay in

Friday 12   Last night at bed time it was 32 below this morning when I got out it have rised to ten below with snow and light breze up the lake   kept rising   at dusk this evening it was six abov   wind rising all time   tok in my clotches off the line put then in shade & little good it did   from the noys the storm is making its a real storm   the house is shaking at the voleys   fixing & tempering knife   put it on the handle   ground it & exept for a [illegible] I would have the cutest sharpest little knife in four kingdoms   tramped my wood trail   jumped several grouse but had no gun along

Saturday 13   The storm did not last long but it certainly rised cain while it was at it   the dog houses drifted full & drove the dogs out & I had snow over everyting in the shed and up in the atik clean to the ridge pole   tok me all fornoon to clean out snow   went out & shoveled open wood trail but not doing much good as it keept snowing all day and is still at it   filed a short saw to fall with   18 abov zero

Sunday 14   I awoke about four this morning and lay wake for long time   finaly I fell to sleep and sleept to daylight   it have been snowing during the night but have quit   clouds flying from south by west at high speed   quite warm snow started tawing on trees during midle of the day   tok a walk to som porky traps but no catch set one more trap on Indian River   moos was close to cabbin during the night

Monday 15   Raining & blowing this morning snow was wet & sticky   tok out the bob with the dogs thinking of making a sled track   put on one green birch but it was to heavy   ran into a tree & nearly bursted my new bob sled   unloaded & rode in snow   sinking fast but no sign of wetting thru on the lake   try to fix my net but had to give it up   it was tore from line to line & I had not sufecient twine   got a porky

Tuesday 16   At four this morning I heard my big dog barking so far I could hardly hear him thinking that he had a porky I got to sleep again got up at seven started making breckfast   steping out I again heard him   it being unusual for him to bark I know somting was wrong   started right a way found him in one of my trap   now this evening he apears sick   filing a saw fixed a pair of pliers   tok a walk up Indian got one porky

Wednesday 17   Fine weathre this morning   got busy setting bread as soon as I got up   about eleven Pete Kalning came up from Bear Creek had lunch   just then bread was ready to be kneded & put in pans   after getting set for first baking I retempered ax for Pete and helped him grind it   my apendix started to give truble so I have given it a treatment with ice pack   at least I think it is the apendix it is in that vincity

Tuesday 23   32 below zero this morning and it tok a long time after sun up before it warmed up that you could notice it   to cold to be out befor two P.M.   I was out sawing som green birch just then a bunch of cyotes gave me a selection from thier latest band music   it sounded so close that I got my rifle thinking I get a chance to join in   tok a walk to look over my porky traps   got one old boy

Wednesday 24   33 below this morning   ice on the windows was much more indicating moistur in atmosphere so we are due for a change changed underwhere this morning intending to do som washing but it was to cold to play with water   so I went out & cut few sticks of birch hauled it home & sawed som for imediate use feelt som pain in the side this morning but keept a tin of ice again it 45 minutes   after that it been better

Thursday 25   20 below this morning   waited until it got warmer than I hoked up my dogs went to take in trap   got all in   found a dead moose partly frozen in ice   saw several life moose   just as I was ready to start this morning I saw two cyotes towards Bear Creek   not very far but rather to far for rifle shots   had a bad time of it last night the apendisitus caused acute indigestion   finaly I got my bowels to operate with that and frezing the apendix it keept me in som pickle   if I could get word to som air plane I go to town

Friday 26   8 abov this morning   snowing just anough to spoil the trails   one of my dogs was busy during the night trying to keep moose from the house   they came right to the dog house I could see by the tracks this morning   about noon I went and cut som birch and hauled it in but I am so weak I cant do much   I have not eat to amount of anyting   trying to starv out my stomak truble   not so good this evening

Saturday 27   At zero this morning but clear so it is likely to go cold again   my old alarm clock went on strike and I tok it down as far is you can go without using cold chisel & hamer   had no oil fit for such work so I got it running by lying face down   was out cut som birch   hauled in three loads   this evening tok a walk to porky traps   did not get any   bad walking   moose brecking up my trails and as snow is deep they live holes like smole wells   seeing moose all day out on lake & every where   they got a bad time getting thru   expect to see good many of them die this spring   one of my dogs was out last night   he shore found dead carcas somwhere the way he stunk

Sunday 28   23 below this morning   I did not think it was that cold until I read the thermometer loffed around awhile this morning then hapened to notice my old rikely grind stone bench   I have been putting off fixing the bolts   all sleck & rusted solid   I had to hack saw nuts & bolts rost them in fire to get nuts clean & put together again & I got it rigid to & good as new after it been here over thirty years   then I found another smole black smiting job that neaded tending to finaly I had to make that alarm clock go upright that was then two o clock & she is still chiping away   it is now 8 o clock in the evening   ice on windows

Monday 29   30 below zero this morning with dry cold that it dont even make ice on windows that I genaraly have at ten below   I just keept the stove going all day with chunks of sour birch that it take a long time to consume   towards evening went to Dawson Slough & set out couple

of traps for porky pine   tok a walk out my wood trail saw a porkee up a spruce   had no gun cold again to night

Tuesday 1 March   25 below this morning but shortly after sun up I som mare tail clouds rising about south by west and coming fast   but the weather keept cool all day   at 3 p.m. I went and got in couple porkies and my mustach froze to you could have knocked it off with a stick   just at dusk I heard a roar of the wind in the mountains and temperature rising so it now is 12 abov

Wednesday 2   A storm on this morning & getting mild   was out and cut several birches but by time I got in it was getting to mild to haul any home   so just pasing time by reading som periodicals of 1929   wind gone down som this evening   not feeling right

Thursday 3   A duster of a snow storm this morning but in afternoon it got so warm that snow quit drifting   I hooked up the dogs to go over trail to keep it open   it did not pull hard so I keept on until I got home   all I had cut was to traps & got a porkie   wath with washing clotches & house keeping I put in a fair day

Friday 4   Mild   realy to wet to go anywhere was out to get a dry tree just then Ed Lovdal & Emil cam up   fixed trout net & set it out   saw two cyotes

Saturday 5   Was out to net early this morning but no fish   cam back and built breckfast jus the same   about ten Emil & Ed left   had a team of eight dogs strung single along towline loking like an endles string   I was out cut a few trees for firewood but it was to wet to atempt to haule it in and it got so mild that my trail would hardly stand up to walk on and a big job tramp down snow for new trail   heard cyoties yelping this morning to be answered by malamutes

Sunday 6   Have had a real fine day   went out & fished the net first ting this morning and came home without fish so it looks like trout have gone to unknown regions   anyway I got home wath birch I had cut and cut anough to haul to morow getting colder

Monday 7 *Feeling drowsey & out of sort just like at begining of storm got up early had brecfast picked up an old Saturday Evening Post and read the [illegible] trough then harnesed the dogs & hauld four loads of birch cyotes have been serenading me all day from out on ice I saw either two of them twice or two difrent pair*

Tuesday 8 *Had som ice on the windows this morning but temperature was only one below zero my dogs was away but came back shortly with noses full of porkie quills the been looking after som traps I had set & did make a mess of cleaning that porkie I got three trout in hauling the net one extra larg 23 inch long with 15 inch curcumfrence started yeast to make bread sawed up som wood*

Wednesday 9 *Six below zero this morning got out of bed at six made brecfast & set batter for bread sky as clear blue as it can be although last night just after sunset a cloud rose over the mountain colored like forest smoke the lower edge deep lead color and under the cloud to the mountain a deep purple this apeared east north east western sky orange color baked to day firing with green birch worked fine a moose came after me in to the shade I jumped in closed door*

Thursday 10 *Snowing just a dust I got afraid that it my spoil my trail so I went out & choped five birch trees & hauled them home I think I got anough but if hauling be good I my cut couple more trees fell quit a lot of snow this evening still at it*

Friday 11 *Anough new snow to make it wet and nasty out and I being far from well it is easy to keep in was out & got home a wind falen spruce to help out with my dry wood tok walk out to porkee traps two cyotes was almost in rifle range this morning I was tempted to shoot but left it to better chance*

Saturday 12 *Mild so that the new snow got wet in sun during mid day was out cut two more large birch wich be all I wont for sumer drying for next winter but to wet to haul them in was out to mouth of Indian to fish the net but got no fish*

Sunday 13 *Have had a realy fine day was out hauling the last of the wood stock home got it in easy as it was a light frost this morning making trail strong have not seen any ting moving or heard a noys not even howl of a cyotie*

Monday 14 *Not feeling so good to day been to bed half the time tok a walk out fished the net no trout again so I tok the net home saw three cyotes way out on ice heading for Windy Point clouding up feeling like I my expect snowstorm*

Tuesday 15 *Started storming after I got up this morning snow was drifing in cycling clouds at first but it soon got too warm I hitched my sled and dogs took my rifle & went to where I know a moose calf was frozen in ice thought that I my get a shot at cyotes but I found it partly devoued by eagles and such but no cyotie track anywhere near it my ink is getting so lumpy by having been frozen so often that it is hard to smear it out*

Wednesday 16 *Mild snow melting on the roof been in fixed a change of clotches had a bath scrubbed the floor and this evening I went & set out the net altoug it is mild the snow is not disapearing very fast*

Thursday 17 *An other warm wet day snow melting the lake are turning blue towards the glaser flats wetting thru snow on ice I was to the net befor breckfast got one trout the truble is my net got to big mesh stay in reading getting short of reading mater*

Friday 18 *After I been out fishing the net I tok a walk to Bear Creek to visit my neibors but they was out som place so I came bak home walking still heavy sinking to the ancles in wet snow at times also it is more snow down that way*

Saturday 19 *At home all day snow to wet to go anywhere tryed it with snowshoes but sank right thru Indian River started an over flow on to the lake ice a storm started this evening and blow the water along it traveled a mile befor dark can hear wind roaring*

Sunday 20 *Still dripping of the roof another day and the snow will be off the roof that been there since December 10 took a walk after*

*breckfast   brought in all the porkie traps and is
my sawhorse have come out of snow that I can
use it   I rolled a log to get started on my wood
pile   a cyotie came by out on ice   I shot   could
not see if I hit it   went out to his track found him
bleeding on one front foot   the distance was
from 3 to 4 hundred yards   had on snowshoes
when I was out but it dont make much diffrent as
I sank thru the wet snow to bottom   got one
makinaw when hauling net*

*Monday 21   Snow is still melting with wind from
north east   just a bright warm day until toward
evening when it clouded up and the wind filt cold
just sawed a couple of logs of birch   to night I
thought I smelted tobako smoke   dont seemes
posible   heard a cyotie barking   feeling lacy*

*Tuesday 22   Roof of cabin was clean of snow
first time since December 10 and still got snow
on the north east eve   was sawing up a lot of
birch to day but my side got hurting so I could
not split the wood with out a sharp pain so I quit
have not got a fish for two days   my have to
shift the net*

*Wednesday 23   The first ting after I got out of
bed I went haul the net   another blank   after
breakfast hitched the dogs went all the way to
Erlings place but no sign of anybody have been
there since he left   brought som meat I chaped
out of ice for dog feed   sawed couple of logs*

*Thursday 24 Still warm   started sawing at som
wood after I had breckfast and been out fishing
the net   just before noon Gust Ness came up
from Birchwood with dog team   he brought his
trout net and we went & set it out   tok a walk to
glaser flats*

*Friday 25   Got out of bed at 5 this morning to
make brecfast   heard a lot of cyotes howling
called Gust Ness but befor he got out they quit
just dressed & went to fish nets   came back with
only one trout   I had breckfast ready when he
got back   we tok a walk along lakeshore   I
started to saw up some wood   had target practis
with pistols   make tea for lunch   Gust hooked
up his team & started for lower end of lake on
his way to Kussilof   apendix bothered som when
I split wood*

*Saturday 26   Yesterday afternoon about 3 o clock
I had a eartquake and again nine at night
somtime yesterday I heard a noys as exposion
to day been warm   clearing up   I stay in sleeping
most of the time either not feeling good or lacy*

*Sunday 27   Fine crost to travel this morning but
I had made ready to make bread so I stay and
tend to bread making   was out and hauled in
both trout nets   spread them on dry gravel to
dry*

*Monday 28   I walked down lake on my way to
Friman   saw no sighn of any one at Bear Creek
stopped with Tom Odale for lunch and on to
Friman*

*Tuesday 29   Started early this morning to take
advantage of crost   got up to Lick House after
eleven   stay only few minutes   went acrost
Funny River basin   snow getting soft   getting
tired   got to Castle Inn late   broke snowshoe
fraim just befor riching cabin*

*Wednesday 30   Snowing and snow sticking to
snowshoes right from start   foggy and murky
that I had to watch my navigation to keep my
course   stopped for lunch at Lick House   stay
1 1/2 hours and came on to Friman   saw lot of
moose and couple of calfs this trip*

*Thursday 31   Went on down to Olson Creek this
morning   sloppy wet in coming out   abandoned
my snow shoes   getting tired rested at Friman
and towards evening came as far as Toms   stay
over night   feeling sick   trying to doctor up*

*Friday 1 April Stay at Toms watching his afforts
to burn up a larg stack of frozen chips covered
with two foot of new snow (made it)   had a nice
reception of Anchorage Program & news idhems
[items] & some wiggles of ice worms*

*Saturday 2   Snowing & wet   stay all day as it
was to nasty to wade thru unles a person had to
started taking sotapathica   tok three doses after
that I started to go from place to place   had fine
news ithem & heard outside*

*Sunday 3   Came home   hard walking loose
snow   stopped at Bear Creek got som moose
meat that was spoiling and left to rot   500 lb or*

more tok along about sixty pounds started snowing after I got home

Monday 4 Froze som last night the windows was icy this morning tok cold coming home yesterday so I have been in all day besides everyting covered with new snow started som wind from south east been quite warm during the midle of the day trees clear of snow this evening

Tuesday 5 At home cut up som wood snow melt som at mid day but still we have som new snow left that fell while I was at Toms set out trout nets this afternoon had a musical program by cyotes this eve

Wednesday 6 Chiping at the wood pile saw split & rick wood for couple hours then I get som book & read for an hour just pasing the time hauled the nets but got no fish so I set only one saw som cyotes toward evening cloudy but no rain or snow clear over the inlet

Thursday 7 Working at the wood got more than a half rick to day and in cabbin half the time readin or sleeping was to net this morning but the trout seems to have left

Friday 8 Was out to mouth of Indian River to fish trout net got one large makinow trout after I got back I hicht the dogs up went to Bear Creek for a load of meat sawed a few sticks of wood this evening found my axe that been missing since first snow fall

Saturday 9 Not feeling so good split some wood this mornin while it was frozen sawed up anough to fill the thirth rick cloudy with a few snow flakes falling during the day did not look after net until evening got 2 trout cyoties yelping all around this evening

Sunday 10 Had a warm day south easterly wind from the glaser the ice on the lake is turning blue that is the snow on the ice are disapearing I shoveled snow from around my dory turned up snow is still & foot deep on the beach sawed som wood

Monday 11 Finished cutting wood to day weathre fine heard sea guls this morning soon as I went out & going to my net they came over

to investigate started to put tings away for summer & clean up

Tuesday 12 Tok a walk to mout of Indian River did not get any trout riged up the bobsled for to haul my dory to the house snow soft hurt my side lifting heated water washed the dory & put it in attic had quite job getting it up then I under tok to clean the well it was getting royly at bottom got it fairly clean got no pump overhauling tings to take out when I go made yeast

Wednesday 13 At home building bread to last until I go below have in mean time been cleaning up around the place putting tings away for summer

Thursday 14 Tok in my net hauled home my fishing gear exept one net was icy so I trew it on dry gravel to taw out at high noon washed lot of clotches and scrubbed the floor was out and got a set of runners for a makeshift sled to take me to Kusilof

Friday 15 Have put in a big day putting tings in shape for leaving I built a sled that tok up most time hitched dogs up hauled it on gravel beach to scaur rust off of the shoes got every ting lined up ready to go in morning weathre permitting

While Berg was getting ready to go back to town, Hank Lucas was preparing to go to the Tustumena hunting area to study moose for the summer. The Alaska Game Commission had received funding from some eastern conservationists for the investigation. Lucas and an assistant surveyed the drainages of Funny River and Killey River counting a total of five hundred twenty-one moose. Lucas reported that neither market hunting nor bears posed a significant risk to the animals. He speculated about other threats but ultimately recommended that further studies be conducted to conclusively determine what factors influenced the moose population.[1]

The moose sanctuary proposal had been taken on by the U.S. Bureau of Biological Survey and was percolating through the territorial and federal hierarchies. Local residents were mixed in their reception of the idea. Petitions supporting a preserve came out of Ninilchik and Kasilof. Opposition came from some Kenai residents who feared for the future of trophy hunting. Dena'ina on the Peninsula and in Tyonek were concerned about losing access to traditional hunting grounds. Boundaries were a contentious issue as most people appeared to support the concept as long as it did not encompass their personal hunting area. Territorial Governor George Parks insisted that homesteading and other development not be impeded. The General Land Office argued that allowances for development negated the purpose of the refuge. Some members of Congress had their own opinions about the location of the boundaries. The proposal was shelved amidst the general discord.[2]

Monday June 27   Pete Matson and I arrived here Saturday from Tom O'Dells   We found Mr Mytle here who is sizing up the country as a trapping and mining prospect   He hadn't figured out your safety latch   Pete planted in your garden and mowed down some of the grass around the cabin   We have been hunting for porkies and black bear but so far have not been very lucky   We are leaving this morning for Erlings Cabin   We have enjoyed our stay at your cabin very much   Pete Matson Kasiloff   Mr Mytle Kasiloff   Arnold Granville Ninilchik

Mr. Mytle was not mentioned again in the journal. Perhaps he learned from the other men that the trapping areas around the lake were customarily used by the established residents. Unlike staked and recorded mining claims, traplines were not formalized but individuals' trapping territories were common knowledge for locals. Fifty years later, Kenai resident Peter Kalifornsky could remember who was trapping certain creeks in the Kenai and Kasilof drainages.[3] A young man or outsider could join up with an established trapper to acquire experience and local knowledge. But even the expansive Kenai Peninsula could support only a limited number of trappers.

As we know from Berg's journal, traplines had to cover a lot of ground to be productive. Andrew's experience demonstrated that a good territory was still no guarantee of success as animal populations cycled, prices fluctuated and trapping pressure reduced harvests. This year fur prices dropped by almost fifty percent.

The depression had arrived in Alaska. The value of Kasilof's farmed silver foxes had declined even more than wild pelts. The number of salmon canneries operating in the territory dropped from one hundred fifty-seven in 1929 to eighty-seven this year. Over eighty-five hundred cannery jobs were lost. The average value of a case of canned salmon had declined from $12.57 in 1930 to $5.61.[4]

Fortunately, canneries still operated in Kenai, Anchorage, Ninilchik, Seldovia and Seward.[5] The Bureau of Fisheries also continued to provide seasonal work. According to the Bureau of Fisheries Report for 1932, "Andrew Berg Special Warden was in charge of Bureau Speed boat and patrolled the west shore of Cook Inlet from May 24 to August 8."[6]

Though he was finished with his enforcement patrolling on August eighth, Berg apparently missed the boat when his friend Roy Cole went to Tustumena on August fifteenth and left this note in Andrew's journal:

Alex Lind and the writer arrived here to enjoy the comforts of your cabin at 6:00 P.M. Aug 15 1932   Came up river from Jensen and Madsen fur ranch   Stopped at Nikolai River and went up stream about one mile   the water in stream

AVERAGE FUR VALUES IN ALASKA 1926 -1932							
	1926	1927	1928	1929	1930	1931	1932
Lynx	$20.00	$29.47	$45.25	$61.10	$57.00	$43.50	$23.29
Mink	$12.00	$14.52	$15.87	$20.70	$8.50	$9.60	$5.69
Weasel	$1.60	$1.85	$2.04	$1.74	$1.15	$1.15	$.44
Silver Fox	$100.00	$111.66	$121.00	$125.00	$100.00	$90.00	$44.00

Alaska Game Commission Reports to the Governor of Alaska, 1927 - 1933; General Correspondence of the Governor of the Territorial Government of Alaska, 1909-1958; Archives and Manuscripts Department, Consortium Library, University of Alaska Anchorage *was running bank full muddy brown hence very few salmon could be observed   Making headquarters at your cabin   we investigated all of the streams at head of lake   showing only fair   Endeavored to thin out your turnips but concluded the tops would be more valuable for greens   This is the writers first trip to Tustumena Lake without you   your cabin home has been much enjoyed but still there seems to be some one missing   it must be Andrew Berg   We are leaving for Bear Creek 8:00 a.m. Aug 18   R. L. Cole US Bureau of Fisheries*

In spite of commercial salmon's overall decline in the territory, it was still the backbone of the rural economy in Cook Inlet. Perry Cole's Alaskan dream had not included salmon fishing. When fox farming's profitability evaporated, Perry packed up his family and headed back to New York. According to Marion Cole's account, her pioneer adventure ended in September as she, Milton and their babies joined the exodus.

Similar scenarios of dreams sought and lost played out everywhere, especially during the Depression. The stories seem more poignant in this primitive little corner of the world where the climate and the physical isolation increased the time and effort required for every small accomplishment. Those who stayed were possessed by fatalism, stubbornness or dreams which incorporated the qualities inherent in a secluded, subarctic wilderness.

Comer Cole remained in Kasilof and took up salmon fishing. Clayton "Doc" Pollard ended up with Perry Cole's homestead. The Pollard family spent summers in Kasilof but maintained their home and Doc's dental practice in Anchorage. They loved the homestead but chose the amenities provided by an urban dental practice and established schools.

School became an issue for Kasilof this year. Mary and Gust Ness had seven children and Enid and Archie McLane's three children were reaching school age. Funding for teachers and school supplies for rural communities was provided by the territorial government. Abe Erickson donated a small log building located on the south side of the Kasilof River near the Ness home. Enid McLane was hired as the teacher.

Like most endeavors here, education required extra effort. The McLane's homestead was a few miles from the schoolhouse. This distance, combined with the

ANCHORAGE DAILY TIMES
August 5, 1932

Record Pack Of Salmon Is Put Up Here

Modern Plant of Emard Packing Co. Makes Fine Showing For Season

With a pack of approximately 40,000 cases of the choicest Cook Inlet Salmon, the Anchorage plant of the Emard Packing company has just completed a record season for both quantity and quality, the pack consisting almost entirely of the choicest species of salmon. The operations were started with a hand-packing crew putting up king salmon in half pound tins and when the choice red salmon began making their appearance in the inlet, the hand-packing was discontinued and the tall can line set in motion and speeded up to handle 144 cans per minute. When the season ended this week the cannery had a pack of 14,000 kings, 14,000 reds, 10,000 silvers and approximately 1,000 each of pinks and humpies.

The operations of the cannery put a large amount of money in circulation in Anchorage and along the inlet, the expenditures for labor and fish being roughly estimated by Mr. Emard at $100,000 for the season. And all of the labor was employed locally.

Seven hand traps were operated during the season but it is estimated that seventy-five per cent of the fish were caught by the gill netters, fishing on both sides of the upper inlet. On the average, the fishermen had a very good season, with an income of from $1,000 to $2,000 per boat, and most of them were in Anchorage this week for settlement....

Discoverer Will Leave On Sunday

The mail boat Discoverer, Captain Heinie Berger, which arrived from the lower inlet yesterday, will sail for Iliamna and Seward Sunday morning at 7 o'clock.

The vessel brought in mail and several passengers, the list including Mr. And Mrs. Joe Bell and family, Stanley Parsons and Earl Olmstead. Mrs. Berger also was a passenger on the boat from the Berger homestead at Kasilof.

The Discoverer moved 20 horses from Kasilof to Beluga, from which point they will start overland for the Rainy Pass district, where they will be used for packing by the Alaska Guides during the fall hunting season...

necessity of crossing the river, was enough to prevent Enid and her children from making the trip daily. They lived in the back room of the school during the week and returned home on the weekends. Enid spent her days off performing a week's worth of baking, washing and ironing.[7] This was their routine for six years, crossing the river by boat or on the ice as the season dictated. Enid always remembered a particular crossing: "One spring when the river was full of broken ice chunks and it was time for us to come home, ropes were tied to each of us and with the use of a plank we hopped from one bobbing chunk of ice to the other, the entire width of the river." [8]

The permanent residents accepted conditions as they were. Even after Andrew Berg's appendicitis scare the previous winter he returned to Tustumena for the winter, still without any means of contacting civilization.

Tuesday 18 October   Left Kenai on Prince Pat for Kasilof   landed my tings & walked up to Alex Linds   had coffe and walked up to Eriksons Ranch   stay all night

Wednesday 19   Walked back to Charle Sands to get som potetes   waited all day for Ed Lovdal

Comer Cole and Ed Lovdahl. Photo courtesy of Dolly Cole Christl.

he & I ran down to Cape Kasilof to get som steel traps   got tings in boat at Kasilof   went to Eriksons place   got there at dark

Thursday 20   Was at Eriksons Ranch lending a hand with leveling fox corralls   got most of them done as I & Dr Rising with the men on the ranch made it five of us shoveling

Friday 21   Dr Rising started out first walking taking my big dog on acount of our heavy load he walked up to Cape Horn where we picked him up   ran up to new cabin   had coffe & on to big house where we stay all night

Saturday 22   Ran up to clif house where we left som provision for boys stopping there   had coffe & visit at Erlings place with Frency & John Edleman   came home & found cabbin in nasty shape

Sunday 23   Stay home   making yeast cleaning tings and puting them in there proper place   Ed Lovedal   Harpham &   Dr Rising went up on sheep mountains   two of them came in after dark but Dr is still out   it is now 9:30   weather fine after fog lifted   I have been busy all day and noting to show just wath I have been doing

Monday 24   Dr Rising who got late & had to camp out came in just as we were having breckfast   the other two went out to get a load of meat they left yesterday   I stay home making bread   at dark Pete Madson & Tom Odale arived

Tuesday 25   Was up befor six o clock   every one making ready to go on mountain   when ready a shower of hail struck delayin trip for an hour   four went toward glaser   I left last at nine   I went up to bridge on Indian River hunters came home at dark with one sheep among the lot   reported seeing black bear with cubs   I just noticed som fool have used a green spruce for target   I am nursing spruce for wind breck and a stump aucto serve just as well to hang a target on

Wednesday 26   The hunters went out full forse this morning   I intended to go for a walk my self but we had a lot of meat exposed and if no one

John Sandwick and Comer Cole are pictured here in hunting camp. Photo courtesy of Dolly Cole Christl.

stay at home the birds would have rised cane with the meat   boys came in again with one ram

Thursday 27   The hunters was all making ready to go back   a strong wind sprung up so they decided to post pone the trip   I Ed & Pete ran to Island   tok a trip on to mountain looking for bear   found none   machine was stuck in insulator when we got home   it tok to midnight to get it fixed and then did not finish

Friday 28   Hunters left to day   I have been busy all day cleaning out my dory & painting tok me to 6:30 to finis painting inside   weathre mild   clearing from inlet

Saturday 29   Stay in bed until eight o clock this morning   then after cleaning the dishes and started fix to turn over the boat   John Edelman Frency Cannon Tony Johanson & young Ring Bolt came   stopped for coffe   helped me turn over my sciff   left for Bear Creek   cleaning of the sciff   smoting it with sand paper   here came Lee Vadell a married couple & Mr haris   som more coffe   just got dory painted at dusk

There were quite the crowds at the lake this hunting season. John Edelman was a half-Finn from Kenai

in his mid-twenties. Tony Johansen was Mary Ness's son from her previous marriage. Frency was twenty-five year old John "Frenchy" Cannon. Notwithstanding his nickname, Frenchy had immigrated from County Donegal, Ireland.[9] He became a regular at the lake.

Sunday 30   Had a sleepy spell went to bed early and woke up at four in the morning   being to early to get up I -the read until my eyes got tired fell to sleep & slept to seven o clock   did noting useful in fornoon   reading and hunting up tings that been shifted in my absens   in afternon I had a bath & scrubbed the floor   weathre fine warm   clearing over the inlet   light breeze up lake

Monday 31   Lay dreaming this morning & finaly woke up it was nearly seven o clock   got up tok a look at the weathre and found it promising for any hunt   coked breckfast and decided to go up glaser flats take a creep thru dirty cannon   half way up I saw a bunch of sheep   only one ram with a lot of ewes & lams but I started out to look for bears so I did not try to get near the sheep saw one fresh track of bear   when I got out of cannon I saw about two hundred sheep   showing

Berg's view from his Home cabin looking southeast to the glacier flats and the mountains. This picture was taken in late summer before the fall snows started.   Photo by C. Cassidy.

of starting to mate   saw an extra large ram shot several long range shots him but to far   did not hit him   came crost from cannon lake to Maddsens but leward   met the new Indian agent but he did give his name Cook & one tyonek native   stopped at thier camp   no one hom

Tuesday 1 November   Had som frost last night I did not look at thermometer until after sun was high then it was 18 abov   stay in all day not feeling good   calm weathre   lake lay smole as a loking glass   heard noting from sheep hunters shot at target to try out my rifle   made nearly a perfect shot   cut half of nail in centre of target at about seventy yards

Wednesday 2   Rather cold to go after sheep so I just hunted for som ting to do   firs I made a new handle on a butcher knife then I tok my outboard motor apart   cut & spliced the conecting rod to mak it longer   turned my dory over & hauled it to lake shore   tok a walk to sheep hunters camp met Albert the Havian from 3 mile

Thursday 3   Started this morning at eight o clock to Nicanorka mountain   got to sheep at eleven o clock   saw ewes & three rams & it would have been easy to get a ram but I would have had to bring the meat up hill a long way & I still had a chance to find them nearer home so I did not shoot   saw about twenty sheep   two moose tracks of one bear   several cyotes & foxes   got in early

Friday 4   Clouding up   thermometer down to 8 this morning   stay in starting to make yeast   was repairing a pair of slipers loking out I saw snow starting   went out and turned my dory over   in afternoon three mile Albert came in after an unsucessful moose hunt   som wind up the lake Albert reported that Mr Cook Indian Agent of Magwake Reservation ["Moquawkie" Reservation at Tyonek] did not arive in camp last night nor yet this morning when he started on his days hunt a nasty night out   snow & wind   not much snow but pentrating driven by wind

Saturday 5   Mr Cook of Tyonic Reservation came this morning to get som gasoline   I gave him couple gallons although I can ill aford it   at noon I saw the reservation party going down lake I have been baking & made a lot of bread   the biggest lot I made so far   themometer at 2 abov zero

Sunday 6   Cloudy this morning with temperature at 12 abov   stay low all day to evening when it rised to 30   hunting for som pains of glass that I know I have som place   did not find it so I cut som to take to Castle inn   tok a walk to glaser flats   saw lots of salmon at Indian and lake shore   saw som I tok to be red salmon

Monday 7   It looked so much like snow this morning & indeed som snow sprincled that I decided to stay in and take care of my wardrobe and I was at that deligently until dusk and not being nearly thru   so I see where I got work cut out for me when snow storms gets to working overtime

Tuesday 8   Here I am on election day when all good men should register thier ideas   hovever it would make me take a walk of 80 miles wich is rather far to tramp if you can do without   3 abov this morning with som moisture in the air as there was hoar frost   tok a walk up glaser flats to mouth of dirty cannon to see if any sheep was handy but did not see any   ice is strong on upper part of glaser stream to enable you to cross anywhere   was into Rays drift it looks much as usual   saw wath I tok to be a fairly frish track of sheep on flat abreast of mine

Wednesday 9 Was up early   tok a trip up Indian River for the purpos of fixing a foot bridge crossing cannon   insidentaly surveying country for game espricialy bear   did not see any tracks of bear but saw wath my posible be a den or cave   saw lots of sheep   fixed bridge so it is posible   tok sick had a dizzy spell tipped over had to hang on to keep from falling off

Thursday 10   Did not sleep good was up several times during the night   had a good sleep this morning   have been home all day mending som tings & doing od jobs am feeling better but not good   heated water and just about to take a bath   weathre milder with light south west wind

Friday 11 At home all day not feeling good   som wind up the lake & a couple of times a cats paw came off mountain & glaser   doing noting untill towards evening I heated water & cheated the washer woman so I got som clean clotches coming up

Saturday 12   Left here at eight walked up glaser flats   climbed up to sheep hils   only few was saw anough that I would take them out & they were all ewes & lams so I came acrost mountain saw no sign of bears   som tracks of cyotes & so far I seen two young sheep apearintly killed by cyotes but les tracks of cyotes

Sunday 13 Went up south fork to bridge   crossed saw a ram on granit cliff   climed up but did not locate the animal   saw lots of ewes & lams' but

no other ram that is close anough for a shot   lost one of my beaver mittens   saw two moose

Monday 14 Was intending to go to mountain to look for my mitten and probably get a sheep   but looking out thru the window it was snowing to beat the band so I rolled over & had a good long sleep   snow keep falling all day so everyting is covered   have been in all day   mad new hook for removing stove plates   thats all for to day

Tuesday 15   Loked cold & dreary out early morning so I lay in bed just as long as I had a chance of still felling to sleep   by seven twenty I got up had breckfast read som articles in Curent History then started mending my trout net wich tok me nearly all day   hauled my fish pole out set the net   cooked a kittle full of dog feed of two large silver salmon

Wednesday 16   Hauled the net this morning and got only one lake trout and one silver salmon but the trout was larg so the catch was sufcint for my domestic need   have not been just right all day   sleepy and feeling chilly as if I had a change of weathre coming & being fortold by reumatism

Thursday 17   Weathre a little warmer   cloudy with light wind from south east trelining all day and towards evening it started to snow   just a dust coming down   have been in all day exept setting out the net   have not done a ting   my back apear disconected

Friday 18   Was awake bigest part of the night laying and reading   lost my sleep som how   did not get up before daylight   went out hauled the net got one silver salmon two red salmon one arctic king and three lake trout   got started to sew a part of fur mits   heating water for a bath mild calm

Saturday 19   Have been the mildest day for sometime the snow started to melt on sunny side of the spruce   thermometer went up to 28 at noon   I been in all day washing som clolches and this evening I finished one of my fur mitts had a slight tremor of eartquake at 12:30 noon

Sunday 20   A drisly snow all day   stay in the cabbin finis my fur mitts   had the net out   tok it in about noon   got a can full of fish two salmon & nine trout extra large   they must have average 18 inch in lengt   I get 3 inch mesh net so I only get the large ones   finished my last copy of Currant History   the october number

Monday 21   Got out of bed late this morning as I heard a strong wind pelting snow again the cabbin   after I had breckfast & about ten o clock Tony & his partner came up from Bear Creek   stay the rest of day   was out cutting trail to Indian Creek   walked out to glaser flats   after getting back filing my saw that somone ruined by filing   just got news that democrats was in office

Tuesday 22   Snowing this morning   had breckfast late   at daylight Tony & Hun left for clifhouse   I undertoke to mend my trout net   tok me until 2 o clock to finish   set out net   sawed & split a few blocks of birch   started to clear wood trail   it got dark   still snowing but do not stack up much

Wednesday 23   A heavy wind this morning   snow drifting   surf making loud noys so I did not want to take in the net   calmed down later in the day   I went for the net found it blown ashore but not frozen down badly   rolled   tok me two hours to untangle   have to comence use snowshoes

Thursday 24   Thanksgiven day   shortly after breckfast Erling Frostad came up from Bear Creek   tok motor in for overhauling   went on to his place   weathre mild   som cats paw of wind off the hill   tok a walk this evening but snow shaken out of trees by the wind made it (no very pleasant)

Friday 25   Had a lot of new snow this morning and my net was in on the beach   trown in by heavy swells but still I had two trouts   net not hurt on acount of new snow   a foot of new snow fell during day & night   put on my snowshoes for the first time tramping up my most necesary trails   20 abov   still snowing

Saturday 26   Quit snowing this morning but trees are loaded with Christmas decorations & brush wood look like ostrige plums   realy to dirty to go into   trying to set my net towards evening

got it snaged half way out   left it to I can dig my boat out of snow drift   warm & calm

Sunday 27   Lake smote this morning   I waited to about noon dig my boat out   got the net out without much truble   after I got there with the boat caught one nice steelhead   tok net home for clearing & mending   tramped down snow around my wood yard   Sawed up a couple sticks   was out in garden dug out som curly kale   a mess of greens

Monday 28   Was cold during the night but clouded later so that when I got up at day it is ten abov   but from the ice on the windows I know it have been cold   was out on snowshoes to glaser flats   hard walking   snow hanging in trees   saw no tracks of game that is fur bearers   after I got back I set out the trout net   snowed a little in the afternoon   to night it was up to 18

Tuesday 29   Did not sleep good   it was late before I fell to sleep   awoke lit the light and was reading for couple hours   toward morning got to sleep   got up late with a headache   heavy surf up lake   pulled net got lot of fish one steelhead 30 inch long   had a sleep this evening getting cold to night   5 below at 7:30   still going down

Wednesday 30   Windows looking icy this morning so I went out looking at thermometer found it at 10 below zero   stay cold all day 3 abov   about four it started to go down went to 4 below changed at six o clock & started to rise   at zero by 8 o clock   sleded in couple of sticks of green birch in case I nead heating wood   sawed & splitt

Thursday 1 December   Snow coming in style as I looked thru the window at breck of day so I rolled over & tryed for more sleep   but evidently I have used up my alowance so I got up   stay in most all day   tok a walk up glaser flats to first islands   tok me to dark befor I got back

Friday 2   Snowing all day but not acumulating much on the ground   thermometer up to 30 this evening and I hear noys of wind from mountains have been sleepy all day & stay in exepting when I was out setting the net   hunting old periodicals for reading

Saturday 3   Snowing again to day   got a nice bunch of trout this morning when I tok in my net after I cleared the net cooked & eaten breckfast I tok down traps that been hanging in the shed looked them over asorted & counted found I had 72 in all   tok a walk to Indian river   set out 3 traps so I have started traping   no sign of game

Sunday 4   Got up late this morning as have been getting the usual ting lately   after breckfast cleaning up the cabbin   had a shave and then a little nap and here it was noon   started after twelf o clock went upon glaser flats   snowshoing rather hard   loose snow and bushes full   saw a big bull moose at 2 p.m.   killed it   tok me an hour to skin & butcher   got back home just after four   getting dark   thermometer down to zero this evening

Monday 5   Thermometer up to ten abov zero this morning   about eleven o clock I went up on flats with axe to cut up meat & cash it   so that birds would not get it   found lot of birds about but no animal tracks exepting ermine   got back about 2:30   sawed up som green birch for heating wood   getting cold towards evening with south westerly drift in upper clouds

This night the *M.S. Discoverer* was making a late trip, heading south from Kenai. Captain Heinie Berger and three crew members were running between Kasilof and Ninilchik around midnight when disaster struck. Berger told the story several days later for the newspaper:

It was the greatest good fortune...that we got out of that bad mess alive. The night was inky black, and we were eight miles offshore, and the sea was running high. We had plowed for many hours between Kenai and Kasilof, bucking a sheet of solid ice an inch or two thick, and had emerged into the open sea and we were going along nicely until the salt sea waters, then free of ice, began to thaw the ice out of the seams of the ship and the holes where she had been cut by the icesheets. The ice had cut a rim all about the hull and you might say she had been cut in two. As the thawing around that rim set in she began taking water, and finally had several feet of water in the hold. Several tons of coal which we were carrying helped to make the conditions worse. Finally the water got up to the engines, and they

stopped and we realized the ship was doomed. Nothing remained for us to do but to take to the life boat. We hurriedly got a few things together, and put them in the boat and shoved off.

We were careful to take along a compass, and but for that fact we never would have been able to make shore. It was so dark we could see nothing ashore, but as the sea had broken up the float ice, we could handle the oars to advantage, and after three and a half hours, made land.

We had taken along a can of coal oil and some blankets, and axe and some grub. When we struck the shore we had to leap from the life boat, but we carried with us the axe, the coal oil and blankets, but the food was lost with the boat as she swamped, and we struggled out waist deep in the chilly waters. The coal oil and the axe were our salvation. We never could have made a fire without the oil and the axe, and we even saturated the blankets and threw them in for fuel.

We probably would not have had a dry match but for the fact that we corked them tight in a bottle before leaving the ship. The continuous spray from the sea during those three and a half hours in the open boat blew over us, and formed a coating of icy mail, and we were in a shell of ice when we struck shore — and too cold to even light a match for some time. To set up our circulation we ran up and down the beach like wild men for a time and finally were able to cut a little dry wood and strike a match and get the blaze going with aid of the oil.

At day break we set off along the shore for Kasilof, 25 miles over the rough shore. It was a grueling test, I am happy we all made it, and are safe.[10]

Cook Inlet is a truly inhospitable place in the winter. The group's amazing survival was undoubtedly aided by Tuesday's warm spell which was noted by Andrew back at the lake:

Tuesday 6   Just wath I have been expecting hapened during the night   wind came from south east turned mild   snow is melting fast   water dripping of roof   snow was out of trees allready this morning   stay in   made yeast   preparing to do som baking   strong wind in puffs   to wet to go out

Wednesday 7   Stay home all day making bread and I got real nice bread & twenty loaves of it strong southeastern   mild   snow be intirely gone in another day   my roof had foot & half snow yesterday morning   now it is gone   was out to beach set out net   lake feathre white

Thursday 8   Storming harder then ever to day som voly shake the cabin like an eartquake hauled in the net   got a lot of fine trout & one steelhead salmon or trout   the wind is to strong to stand up in   It carries water in sprays on the lake as far as I can see

Friday 9   Storm still on but not quite as hard but still carrying water on the lake   tok a tramp thru the timbre this afternoon   snow is gone where wind hits but in som places it go over my shoepack tops   have not done anyting to mention for to day

Saturday 10   Intended to go up on flats this morning but by the time I was ready to go it was to high wind to go any place exepting in timber built a fire and cleaned out som drift wood at my boat landing   tok a walk by mouth of Indian set out net   still blowing

Sunday 11   Heard the wind early morning got up at 5:40 to look at weathre   decided that it was no place to be early so I went back to bed sleept to 8   got up found the wind have slacked up & som clouds over head blod red that everyting you looked on apeared like looking thru orange colored glass   got four trouts   tok a walk on glaser flats for load of meat

Monday 12   Raining all night and wind just making the cabin sqeeck in the joints   the preasure was so strong that it cracked a pan of glass   have been in all day   sleepy and drowsy just reading a while & back to sleep   towards evening the rain let up but I can still hear the wind whistling in the trees   snow gone   nice greens in garden   just had a mess

Tuesday 13   A regular sumer day   warm   a drizly rain continued all day   the ground is tawing that its getting soft underfoot   I tok my

evinrude motor out this afternoon   had it running for a while but the tank is leaking so I my have to make a few shots with a solder iron befor I make any longer trips   if ever I go anywhere wind quit interely   a deathly calm prevails

Wednesday 14   Loking out this morning I loked into a brand new winter   it have fallen about four inches of snow during the night   just wet anough to stick to bushes nicely   talk about your xmas trees   tok my evinrude apart playing at soldering tank & think that I got it fixed to do for the season   30 abov to night

Thursday 15   Rather murky looking this morning but not snowing or raining   I wanted to walk out somwhere so I went up glaser flats nearly to the glaser   walking not bad   saw tracks of moose and cyoties   not a life animal of any kind did I see   light breeze up the lake   water in the lake rising   so are all the streams

Friday 16   Snow melted out of trees to day   been as quite as a grave all day but to night I hear wind coming of mountains   thermometer at 35 water driping of eves of the roof   have been in all day mending clotches and reading

Saturday 17   Mild   tok a walk after breckfast to look at my trap line consisting of three traps saw Tony Johansen coming over glaser flats to visit   set out net after I got back   now we just had a contest at cribbage   cloudy & dark drizly rain

Sunday 18   Tony Johanson started home this morning   I gave him a few pounds of sugar as he was getting out   drizly rain all fornoon temperature at 35   hauled in my trouth net got only three makinaw trout   net was getting foul slimy so I went out hunted up a willow   peeled som bark and tanned the net   heated water had a bath   wind is down intirely   everyting quite look like the weathre is about to take a change this was one of the longest taws I remember for mid winter

Monday 19   Lay in bed untill day light this morning   everyting quite   a low hanging fog making it apear dark even at midle of the day   I have got a sleepy spell   all I have done is washing som clotches & cooking   I did go into the garden and gather a mess of greens thermometer still abov freezing so it is wet out

Tuesday 20   Just lay reading after breckfast   a light fog out over the lake otherwise a fine day about noon I went out my wood trail   cut & piled up a few loads of birch   then befor dark I came home to set out my trout net   then I tok the matock went out a level of wood trail as the moss is not frozen   went fine

Wednesday 21   A very thin dust of snow falling continuing all day   I expected Erling or som one from devils bay to start down for x mass but none came   was out cutting som birch for wood timber

Thursday 22   Had som fixing to do this morning befor I went out to hitch my dog to bob sleds to try them out at hauling in wood   there is not anough snow for sledding   just tok home couple sticks then I went out and cut down four birch trees   cut them to lengts for hauling   piled just had time to get net set befor dark   have expected to hear motor of Erling bound for Kenai

Friday 23   Just rosling aroun the cabin up to noon   then while I was out hauling my net I saw a man coming in a sciff and I waited   it was Emil coming over from Big House   got four nice large makinaw trout   weathre just the finest   about ten abov in the morning   a snow dust hanging in trees making it dirty to go into

Saturday 24   Got up about seven had breckfast afterwards tok a walk up glaser flats   saw a sheep below dirty cannon   Emil went up over the hill   I waited on the flats one hour   finaly an other sheep came along   it saw me   the sheep got a way

Sunday 25   We had a dispute about som distances at dirty cannon so I went out this morning to measure   I found that I was right   fine day   clear but brush are full of frost from yesterdays fogg I slipt & fell   buised my right kne & left elbow expect to go quite lame   have been in bed since I cam in

Monday 26   Emil was out to day & brought in hide of a ram   got it just over sand mounds south of glaser   came in after dark   I stay in had a bath   dust of snow falling making hard to

ANCHORAGE DAILY TIMES
December 22, 1932

Berger Sails For South to Get New Boat
Cook Inlet Mail Carrier Will Try To Find Suitable Craft For Work

Capt. And Mrs. Heine Berger left Anchorage on a freight train this morning for Seward, where they will spend a day or two before catching the steamer Northwestern for the south.

The skipper is going out to get a new boat to replace the motorship Discoverer, recently lost in Cook Inlet. Despite his heavy reverse, the stout-hearted old salt is full of resolution and determination to go ahead with his work, and did not hesitate a minute in making his plan for a 1,500 or 2,000 mile trip down the coast to pick out the new kind of ship he wants, and to arrange some matters of finance.

"I'll be back here all right in good time," said the indomitable Heine this morning, while breakfasting at the Anchorage Grill, "and I'll bring back a ship that will be a credit to this port and the north coast, even if it takes dynamite to get it. I hope to be on the run again by the end of March, if not sooner, and will not wait for all the flowers to bloom in the spring. If I cannot buy a good ship already built in some coast port I may build a new one. We will sail north in our new ship, and hope in the meantime to have a good visit outside. We will spend Christmas day on the Northwestern on the way south."

see any distance   scrubbed cabin floor this afternoon

Tuesday 27   Emil went up the flats to bring out the meat he left yesterday and coming back started on to Bear Creek but head wind sprung up & he came back   I stay in   I notice mice was starting to cut my vegatables so I cleaned out cellar put in mice proof platform   mended my trout net & it was night   set it just at dusk

Wednesday 28   Light wind up lake   Emil pulled down towards Bear Creek   later I saw him heading out towards Big House or perhaps to penninsula   he hauled in the net befor he went but got no fish   the first time that acured this winter   I got hurt in a fall and been putting in my time reading & trying to patch my self up from the efects of bumps

Thursday 29   Mild fine weathre   was up befor day looking around   thermometer at 32 abov zero although it was long time before sun up   a little new snow fell yester eve so I tok the bob sleds into my wood stack   hauled in one stick just to deep the road brokin & finished in case it would freze   tok a walk up the flats to mouth of dirty cannon

Friday 30   Not feeling the best to day   got an old stone bruse on my heel   was fixing that up after breckfast and about noon Erling came up from Kenai   brought me som reading matter and a cliping reporting the sinking of motor boat Discoverer and other news conserning Kenai &

Alaska   hooked up my dog & trying to have him go a head of me out my wood trail he decided again me and we had quite a fight   any way we got home several sticks   getting cool   close to zero

Saturday 31   Five below zero this morning   stay in to noon   tok a walk up Indian River to old diggins   looked over som old sluce box lumber but it is getting to old for any use   traveling fine when I got back home I saw tracks of some one going south   I supose it was Tony on home trail after christ mass   have been busy reading new suply

Andrew wasn't the only one hauling his wood with a dog sled. These young men in Kenai were using at least a 2 dog-power rig. Photo by Slim Crocker courtesy of Betty A. Crocker.

CHAPTER 18

1933

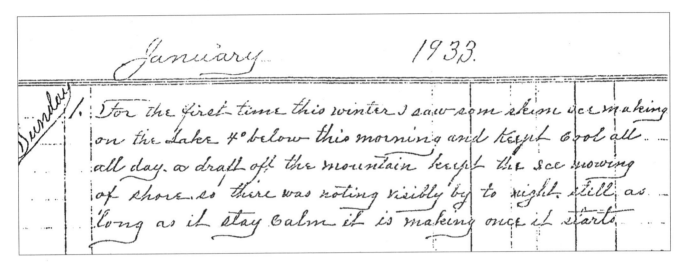

January   *1933.*

Sunday 1. For the first time this winter I saw som skim ice making on the Lake 4° below this morning and kept cool all all day. a draft off the mountain kept the ice mowing of shore. so there was noting visibly by to night. still. as long as it stay Calm it is making once it starts

Monday 2   below zero this morning and everyting a dead calm   ice as far as I can see   stay about zero all day to about three o clock   the thermometer dropped to 7 below but started to rise again shortly   a thin skim of cloud drifting over the skys   I sawed up a stick of wood   started the yeast and doing house keeping acts

Tuesday 3   At zero this morning   was up at five buildt the fire   just as cabbin got warm I set batter for bred   it worked fine   got done early look like good bread   harnesed the dog hauled in three loads of green birch   sawed up one stick for heating wood   it got dark   6 p.m. one of the strongest earth quakes in long time

Wednesday 4   Eight below zero this morning   got up late   skys clear as a silver bell not a speck of moisture anywhere   stay in to after noon   it was then three below   hoked up the dog went up to flats to get a peace of meat   had it covered with moose hide   just got one peace   frozen down just about spoiling

Thursday 5   Thermometer at 14 below zero this morning and the cabin have cooled to 35 abov

inside   I been in all day exepting from 1:30 p.m. to it got dark   I tok a walk out on ice then I hauled in couple of sticks of wood and sawed & split anough to keep fire going for night & morning   (15 below at eight p.m.)

Friday 6   Stay in bed to late   12 below zero just as I was having breckfast Erling Frostad & Olof Horn came in   Horn was on his way to Kenai   Erling to Bear Creek   I went with him to Bear Creek   try scates but frost & snow to thick set out our net at mouth of Indian   still cold

Saturday 7   Did not sleep good last night   keept the light burning to two o clock   got up about eight   8 below zero but 42 abow zero inside the cabbin   was out to Indian fished net   got three trout & one duck   turned the duck loose   Erling went home   I hauled in som wood

Sunday 8   Stay in all day going thru som reading matter Erling brought me   was out to fish the net got six nice trout   the duck we turned loose was doing a lot of diving but did not apear fritened thin cloud and not so cold

Monday 9   Stay in bed until day light   was slow at making breckfast   after I had brecfast I hooked up the dog to bobsleds went up creek to deserted mine   found 8 boards 8x1 1/2 inch 12 feet long   came down Indian River to the mouth stopped to fish   got the largest trout I ever caught   a makinaw 27 3/8 inch long 16 1/4 circumference wight perhaps 16-20

Tuesday 10   Heard the wind singing in the trees befor I got up so I stay to daylight   when I got up I found that it have been snowing during the night but turned to rain when I got out   40 abov wind driving water up from mouth of Indian flooding the ice   started cleaning up stairs & shed   tok nearly all day so by the time I cooked super & had a bath it was night

Wednesday 11   Have been busy all day   heated water to wash clotches and as I lifted the tub of the stove the handle broke and dumped the water over the floor   heated more water washed clotches   tok ten traps went to flats   set them for lynx   fished net coming back   got five trout strong wind southerly   lake on point of brecking loose from shore

Thursday 12   A snowstorm started just after I got up this morning   keept coming down all day not amount of much   wind southerly all day towards evening switched to north west   blow strong for a spell

Friday 13   A lot of new snow this morning and turning cold   was in all forenoon   in afternoon I went out wood trail cut a birch   hitched the dog hauled it home just to keep the trail oppen went to fish trout net   got nine large trout   tok in net

Saturday 14   Nine below zero when I got up this morning and no place where I perticulary wanted to go so I stay in to middle of day   then I went out intending to cut som wood but trees are hanging full with snow so I just hauled in wath I had ready cut

Sunday 15   A real nasty cut this being Sunday and turned out to be the menest weather we had about zero this morning   started blowing up lake with snow drifting in clouds untill it cut to naked ice in patches   about two p.m. the wind

whipped around & came of the mountains with equal force   just shaking cabin when volys hits so I realy hade a day of rest

Monday 16   Not feeling as good this morning just had som breckfast and lay down to read and that continued to about 10 a.m.   I went out   warm as a summer day but wet   the new snow was melting   just hauled in on birch to keep the wood trail oppen

Tuesday 17   Tok a notion to climb up on the hill of lake Emma trail to see if posibly there was a lynx in the country and as it soon be time for them to travel I set out a dozen traps   saw no tracks of lynx   som of moose & cyotes   5 below this eve

Wednesday 18   At zero this morning with fog hanging low   I undertok to fix my trout net   got it in shape to set out   tok it to mouth of Indian got it out & tok a walk to mountain side looking after few traps I got set   coming back I heard a rumbling sound on the mountain   now the storm is on

Thursday 19   A baby snowfall continuing all day   I had a pain in my left lung I under tok to relieve by painting with iodine   it feel like one spot in the lung is congested but after scorching with iodine of potasium I felt it loosen up   walked out to fish net   fell & hit my elbow in ice that was still sore from a previus bump   got my tenders got four trout

Friday 20   Stay in bed until day light and after breckfast tok a walk down to Bear Creek   there I met Olaf Hone who just came up from Kenai after spending Russion Christmas at Kenai   so we came here in company   was out hauled the net   got only three trout   just as I was eating super I got one of the dizzy spells   lay down on floor to save a fall

Saturday 21   After the spell I had last night I have been feeling poorly all day   putting in most of the time in bed reading som cheap periodicals   weathre foggy but not cold

Sunday 22   Weathre cloudy   temperature about zero with fog   stay home until midle of the day hitched up the dog went up on glaser flats to get

The beautiful Russian Orthodox Church in Kenai, built in 1895. Father Paul Shadura was the rector from 1906 to 1952. Photo courtesy of Ella and John Secora.

in som meat   had a job getting it loose   frozen in one solid mass   finaly got loose a shoulder & ham frozen in one lump   dog hauled it home allright   stopped at the net got only two trout

Monday 23   It have been snowing during the night about one inch and kept at it most all day just anough to make it to nasty to cut wood timbre I cut a smole cotton wood close to my well   it got interfering with the whip droping snow in my neck it twisted on the stump fell sidewais broke my bobsled   dug a mess of curly kale from under snow in my garden   just as good as summer time

Tuesday 24   25 below this morning   I had a bath last night just at bed time   just as I got thru

I had a fainting spell   just managed to lay down when my heart comence to race at high speed   I thought that my time have com   finaly got over but I am like a drunken man yet to day   had to stop writing and lay down couple of times to write this

Wednesday 25   Weathre moderated som 10 below this morning   at about zero all day   I feeling a little better but weak walked out to look at net   that all I did tired anough for bed when I got in   net clear of ice   a frost been comming down all day so it my go cold again

Thursday 26   Got up at day breck   24 below zero   tok in the bobsled that I broke a couple days ago   worked on it to about noon had it all fixed   about two o clock I went to fish the net got eight trout   froze a patch on my cheek coming back   head wind with 18 below at dark this evening it was 22 below   had another spell of pelpitalion this eve

Friday 27   30 below   clear blue sky   hardly a draft of wind   this is the coldest so far this winter I tok in the sign board from the place where James G Chase of Rob Morris Lodge AT & AM drowned in 1902   the year I buildt this cabbin   got the sign board repainted in white ready to letter   24 below at seven P.M.

Saturday 28   Mercury frozen this morning and I found that my thermometer register wrong   it

The Chase monument sign board today. In the late 1950s Phil Ames found it washed up on the beach of the lake and preserved it. On the lower left corner you can see just a little of the lettering Andrew mentioned adding. Photo by C. Cassidy.

was 1 1/2 lower than 40   been trying to make som bread and must have got it too cold as it tok nearly all day to make it come right   worked in new lettering on Chases munument and taking som shots with a solder iron and sawed up a peace of green birch to burn slow & keep heat in the stove

Sunday 29   Got up this morning at day breck and found it cloudy with temperatur at 10 below after I had breckfast I harnessed the dog tok Chase marker and went down to erect it from whence I tok it   continuing on to Bear Creek and dizzy all the way and when I got there I could hardly stand up   stay far an hour   got feeling better came hom & tok som physick   at four below   dark cloudy or fogg

Monday 30   16 below this morning   I had a fine sleep toward morning so I stay in bed to quite late   just as I was preparing breckfast Pete Kalning came up from Bear Creek to look after me while I was feeling bum   had two spels of pelpitation of the heart during the day   was out fished the net got six nice trout   at other times we was working at making a knife and handle

Tuesday 31   26 below zero this morning weathre clear & calm   have been in all day not doing anyting just trying to fight of dizzy spells have a dull head aque but think I am improving have had a couple of fairly good meals to day and sleept some

Wednesday 1 February   28 below zero this morning but with this difrence   there is a thin streaks of clouds high in the skye indicating change and during the day it was getting warmer so that by sun set it was only 8 below & by nine o clock up to zero   labor cook & eat

Thursday 2   Mild with wind roaring on the mountains and snow shaking out of trees making it look like the flour mill   working overtime   was washing som clotches and in afternoon went out to fish the net   got five trout and tok with an atack of the heart that shook me up badly & lasted long leaving a dull head aque   23 abov this evening

Friday 3   Warm & fine weathre but been in the house all day feeling weak as a cat with a dull

head aque   I have comenced to fast   just eat very little this morning and noting since   Pete Kalning has been doing the chores cutting a stick of wood and for the rest of the day reading & sleeping

Saturday 4   Warm fine weathre   stay in all day John came up from Bear Creek   he and Pete was out fishing the net got only three trout   John Canon went back to Bear Creek   Gust Ness came up late   left for Cliff House   he brought a lot of news papers & other news

Sunday 5   John Canon came to get thier dog that ran away   turning mild with wind starting Erling came to wards evening   stay over night he was out fishing got one big trout   was busy playing Pinocle all evening   I am feeling som better but not good

Monday 6   Erling got up this morning making a storm a brewing   after we had breckfast and Erling was ready to start the storm was that strong that it would be hard to stand up against so he stay to this evening   just before dusk he left cut a couple of birch trees   hauled home a stick to breck trail

Tuesday 7   Was laying reading last night untill late & slept until daylight   tok a long time at making breckfast them we set out grind stone sharpened som axes   stay in to about two o clock   went out wood trail cut about a cord of birch   got two large makinaw this morning

Wednesday 8   Soon after breckfast I hiched up my dog   starting to haul in birch logs for firewood & hauled in about a cord   Pete Kalning was cutting som but road got to soft to haul any longer   I got only one trout this morning   40 abov zero

Thursday 9   Snow nearly all gone   no chance of hauling wood to som new snow comes   feeling rather poorly to day   dizzy and smoky before my eyes   tok a walk to hog back   tok in my traps   Pete came along to the net   got one steelhead & one trout

Friday 10   A beutiful day   bright & clear   just cold anough to dry up water on the ice   I have put in the day baking bread and put tings to

*gather ready to start out in the morning   Pete
tok in the net   John Canon was up from Bear
Creek   I made arangements with him to go with
me to Kasilof*

Andrew's illness apparently sent him back to town. His
friends could be counted on to help him and take care of
his business when he was gone. When Erling was
heading to town around the end of trapping season he
stopped on his way to spring the traps closed on Andrew's
trapline. Erling left the following entry in Andrew's
journal:

*March 1   Got here at noon   went up lake Emma
trail & sprung your traps   twelv it was   guess
that was all   tok the flags home   lot a squirrel
I know you are supposed to be here tomorrow
but as Im on my way to Kenai and dont know in
what contision you be if you came here at all so*

*I thought I better spring them and nobody has to
worry over them   Hope I did the right thing
E Frostad*

Berg did not get back the next day. As far as we know
he worked for the Bureau of Fisheries again during
salmon season. In deference to his health, this year he
may have switched from his usual patrol job to a less
rigorous position of monitoring a particular stream.

The federal government began providing additional jobs
this year on the Kenai Peninsula. The "Emergency
Conservation Act" of 1933 established an employment
program which would later be renamed the Civilian
Conservation Corps. In the states the program was
administered by the Army for unmarried men between
the ages of 18 and 25. In Alaska it was conducted under
the auspices of the U.S. Forest Service and was open to
men of any age or marital status.[1]   Most of the work

ANCHORAGE DAILY TIMES

July 5, 1933

Tells Of Forest Work Under Way In Kenai Area

District Ranger Sherman Reports Progress Under National Program

W.M. Sherman, district ranger in charge of the Kenai
division of the Chugach National Forest, with headquarters
at Anchorage, had been busy for the season at Kenai lake,
and was in town over the fourth. He has had charge of the
federal forestry work in the district. Referring to the work
Mr. Sherman said today:

"The emergency conservation work act as applied to
the Kenai division of the Chugach National Forest, which
comprises approximately 1,319,000 acres on the Kenai
Peninsula, has given employment to 30 additional men,
above the regular work force employed during the summer
months.

Formerly a trail plan was developed based on geological
data for the construction of trails into isolated localities to
encourage prospecting, and included in this plan were
trails known as protection trails to facilitate quick action in
case of forest fires. This program has been carried out
gradually from year to year until at present there are
approximately 200 miles of completed trails. But to cover
the vast area in a practical way it will take approximately
350 miles of trail, at which these E.C.W. are employed.

The first crew of 10 men were put to work May 27,
building a trail from Cooper Landing on lower Kenai lake
to mile 9 on the Moose Pass highway. This trail, somewhat

different from the rest, serves approximately 60 settlers
who have located at lower Kenai. This is the only means
of ingress or egress for these people for about six months
of the year, and means a lot to them in getting supplies and
getting medical attention during the winter....

In Alaska the Forest Service enlists these men, and
after they pass the required physical exam in either
Anchorage or Seward, they are given very good
serviceable work clothes and sent to these trail camps.
Each camp is in charge of a civilian foreman, formerly of
the regular Forest Service crews, and who is experienced
in these construction projects.

These men are required to work 40 hours per week...
They have very comfortable camps with the best of food,
and about the only restriction outside of the regular camp
requirements is that they cannot leave camp without
permission of the foreman.

On their time off they fish and wash clothes, and the
younger, inexperienced ones are sometimes taken out by
the foreman, or older men who understand prospecting
and show how it is done. So far these camps have been a
big success, just as much labor per man day worked has
been performed by these men as in civilian crews. They
are apparently well satisfied, healthy and in good spirits.

The new M.S.
Discoverer *at anchor in
the Kasilof River.
Photo courtesy of
McLane Collection.*

was conducted in the Chugach National Forest. Tasks included construction of trails, roads, bridges, stream-gauging stations and other structures.[2] While the employment opportunity was a boon, no road building projects connected the eastern and western sides of the Peninsula.

Boats remained the transportation link for the western Peninsula. The fleet this season included Heinie Berger's new vessel. Built at Berg Shipyards in Ballard, Washington, the new motorship was christened the *Discoverer* when she was launched in February. At seventy-six feet long, she was significantly larger than her predecessor.[3]

The Alaska Game Commission and the Bureau of Biological Survey continued studying Kenai Peninsula moose this summer. Hank Lucas was joined by Frank Dufresne and L.J. Palmer, a senior Bureau biologist. They examined the moose population between Tustumena Lake and Skilak Lake during June and July. Their aim was to compare the creatures' summer habits against the springtime observations Lucas had made the previous year. They also were looking for explanations for the population's gradual decline but again concluded only that more research was needed.[4]

Berg returned to Tustumena in August. His activities, as recorded in his journal, make him appear fit and strong.

Wednesday 16 August   Started from Kenai in afternoon   got to Pete Jensens   stay over night met Ed Setter who was in charge of the place

*L.J. Palmer, Hank
Lucas and Frank
Dufresne in moose
country conducting
field work. Palmer
would be back in
1938 for more
research. Photo
courtesy of U.S. Fish
and Wildlife Service.*

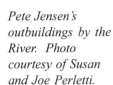

Pete Jensen's outbuildings by the River. Photo courtesy of Susan and Joe Perletti.

Thursday 17   Left Jensens early   came thru fine   had lunch at Abs shak at moose horn   came acrost penninsula ran into a rain squall   went in to big house   stay over night

Friday 18   Left big house at six a.m.   got here in one and a half hour   mowing hay out of roads   put tings to order   done som prospecting cutting wood

Saturday 19   Started early cuting out trail over sadle and up Indian River to bridge   crost

cannon prospected som but found no pay   saw no game of any kind   strong wind of mountain this evening

Sunday 20   Tok the boat out of slough to set John & Alfred Wik acrost Indian River   saw smoke at edge of glaser flats   pulled over and found Emil Berg building a cabin   John & Alfred went out & got som sheep meat

Monday 21   Started out early cutting out alders from Pete Madsens boulevard   missed J & Wik

One of Emil Berg's two cabins at the lake. This may be the one Andrew refers to on August 20, the photo appears to have been taken around this time. Andrew is on the right, Bob Huttle is to his left. Note the dead eagle hanging on the far left. Photo courtesy of Lorraine and Ray Blake.

I went up to foot of sugar loaf   I then found tracks of them so I know they started down   I overtok them just befor I came to our dory   both packing sheep   I saw lot of ptarmigan but no bear but lot of red salmon

Tuesday 22   Was up early to make ready for a day at home   set bread the first ting   cooked breckfast   John & Alfred washing the dishes & shortly started up Lake Emma trail as it was to windy to take the boat out & Indian river to deep to ford so they go up this side to my bridg   I cleaned meat & canned 23 pint presto jars   one broken   tok me to five o clock to get thru baking & canning

Wednesday 23   Was up before six   had brecfast raked up som hay and making som changes about the place   started raining and I lay down to read   fell to sleep and shortly I heard John & Alfred Wik com of Indian   it was then after eight all tackled my wood pile and finis in time to make a prospecting rigg

Thursday 24   Was up early   went up on the creek prospecting but found the gravel would go only $100 to the yard   about noon Harpham came over   him & Doctor Rising came from Clif House this morning   Emil Berg & Dr Rising went for a sheep hunt   I had a bath changed & made ready for the trip to Kenai

The resurgence of prospecting was likely a consequence of the Great Depression. The Alaska Guides, Inc. was still operating in spite of the economy. Newspaper articles about the comings and goings of their notable clients were noticeably absent from the *Anchorage Daily Times* in 1932 and 1933. Perhaps publicizing personal wealth became impolitic as economic conditions worsened.

The *Times* did run a piece about a group of six Anchorage men who spent a week hunting on Tustumena with Tom Odale.[5] The article mentioned several other parties of hunters and tourists at the lake. It was a busy place in September and October. Berg returned to his Home cabin in late October to find his hospitality had been abused again.

Tuesday 24 October   Left Kenai got to Kussiloff mixed oil   stopped at Pete Madsens got potatoes & vegetables   ran on up river got to Jensens

Fox Ranch   stay all night   two strangers also was there

Wednesday 25   Started from Petes Ranch ran thru river   was at Abbe's shack 12:15   met Charles Sands   had no time to give him a tow got here just before five   fine weather   good trip

Thursday 26   A light new snow   Emil went up on the flat   John Wik took mining tools & was upon Indian but reported no strike   I been home trying to locate tings but finds lot of tings missing Holigan & Robinson came from Clif House reported lamp chimney broken at my cabin Camp Friman   I gave them a chimney to replace the broken one   Andrew Berg

Friday 27   Started to make yeast but got it to hot so I had to begin over again   John was up to cannon looking for som quartz   Emil was up looking for som sheep   I tok my boat down from upstairs   hauled it to lake shore

Saturday 28   My yeast failed again   yeast cakes no good   Emil and John Wik left this morning for Hugos   after they was gone I got my little motor ran down to Bear Creek   got a package of yeast and started all over again   but it apear that it was unnecesary as my yeast from this morning are going strong   I just did not give it time to go   at Bear Creek Pete Kalning & John Canon have buildt a dory & dug a garden patch

Sunday 29   Made twelf loaves of nice bread cooked up a kettle of dog feed   put out the boat to set the net   just heating water to take a bath fine day   turning cold   thermometer at 21 early this evening   a cyoty was close to cabbin last night

Monday 30   cloudy this morning   temperature at 18 abov   hauled in the net got no trout but six hooknosed silver salmon & one red salmon just spawning   its a smal varity that come up during winter   not doing much   putting tings to order cleaning up cabbin scrubbed the floor

Tuesday 31   Stay in all day a light snow was falling I think just from vapor cloud arising of the lake   have not atemted to do any work exept hitch dog to my bobsled & haul in couple of sticks

ANCHORAGE DAILY TIMES

October 3, 1933

Great Trip In Wilds By Party From Anchorage

Sextette Ventures Forth On Memorable Voyage – Bring Home Bacon

Participants -- Tony Wendler, chief and chef; Bill Boudreau, affected with sleeping sickness on the deep; Chris Eckmann, sport and sportsman; "Buck" Haynesk who pots his game at the camp-fire; Frank Bayer, who got tired feet, and Coleman Cohen, who gets his game with brush and palette. This sextette embarked on Tuesday evening, September 19, aboard the "Agta," Frank F. Smith skipper, bound for Tustumena lake in pursuit of game, large and small.

The first night out was spent on the bounding billows of Cook inlet with Bill and Buck holding down their berths and dinners; all the rest proving good sailors.

The ship dropped anchor in Kasiloff river on Wednesday afternoon, and all rested after the voyage. Wednesday greeted the party with four inches of snow.

The party left Kasiloff aboard Tom O'Dale's motorboat for the trip through the river rapids to "Slackwater," about four miles from Tustumena lake, encamping at Erickson's cabin.

The hunters took to the game trails, but the first moose was put on the spot by the marksmanship of Bold Bill Boudreau.

Autumn's golden tones adorned the woodland, the dark, rich green of the spruce enhancing the warmer colors of alders and birch. First day's trophies were one moose, three grouse and one porcupine, stilled with an axe.

Friday saw all hunters early to the field except the brush wielder, who tried to express on canvas the beauty of the river and its forest environs.

Al Jones and his party of hunters visited the camp with their spoils and helped the party kill a case of "Blue Ribbon."

The total kill at Slackwater was: Seven grouse, one moose, two porkies, three cases of beer, and one canvas.

Leaving Slackwater for Tustumena lake and stopping at O'Dale's hunting lodge, the party was made very welcome. All hit for the wilds but failed to hit anything else the first day at the lake, which failed to dampen the spirits of the party....

Visitors at the lodge were: Jim Delaney and party, Harry Becker and George Johnson, who were shooting wildlife with their cameras....

Buck Haynes, Wayne Cook and Jackie, with Cohen and Frank Smith, left the party for a trip to Tustumena glacier to garner a crop of mountain sheep, and Cohen to try to snatch off a color memento, in oils, of the glacier. Rain failed to daunt them. After two days their trophies totalled a fine specimen of ptomaine poisoning, acquired by Haynes, a pair of wet feet and experience as a wet-nurse by Smith, nothing to Cook; four grouse by Jackie Cook, aged 12 (Jackie, not the grouse), and a view of the glacier by Cohen.

On return of the main party at O'Dale's, the gun of Frank Bayer stopped two brown bear; but moose were conspicuous by their absence.

L'esprit de corp was cheerful despite the fact that game was elusive. The compensating factors were the enjoyment of the beauty of the woodland, stream and the lake, the resplendent sunsets at Tustumena Lake in its setting of snow-clad mountains and the primeval forest, the cheerful gathering around camp-fires and the gustatory pleasure of inhaling the cookery of Tony Wendler.

The party left the lake Friday morning and after a pleasant, but rough, voyage through Cook inlet arrived at Anchorage at 4 a. m., on Sunday, full of good fellowship, good cooking, tired feet and pleasant memories.

of birch   walked out to Indian River saw frish tracks of cyotes   weathre mild

Wednesday 1 November   Feeling lazy this morning & expected a storm   had my outfit put up ready to go   waited to noon & as the wind have not started by three it was safe to go stopped at Toms place on Birchwood   meet a man by the name of Huttle but had no time to go in   just got tings in shore when quite of breeze

sprung up   just managed to get net out and it was night

Thursday 2   Stay in camp all day cleaning up the place   took out half ton of spruce bows and trash   towards night I walked up to see Huttle wind so strong it was hard to walk against it   got to Tom Odales at dark   about six inches of snow

Friday 3   Not feeling good   started back to my cabin about 10 a.m.   after I got to Freman and tok som medicine I got ok   cut down a birch cut it up to stove wood   got a salmon   a chum   the first I ever seen on the lake   it was not quite ready to spawn   I ate trout cooked chum for my dog

Saturday 4   Stay around camp   to wet to go any place   snow all gone   tok a walk along beach jumped a lot of grouse   set the net towards evening   heard cyotes yelping after it got dark   weathre clearing

Sunday 5   Was sort of afraid climbing the hills to Lick House but being a fine morning I ventured out & made it fine   saw sixty moose   cabin door broke oppen and tings trown about inside two pane of glass broken out of window   noting else destroyed

Monday 6   Fine weathre for hiking   long hike but down hill most of the way   left my rifle to easy up pack   bringing in window to Castle saw about twenty moose & two bulls fighting cabin in bad shape   bear taken bedding out thru window   packed it to riverbank & torn it to ribbons   stove turned over   stove pipe tramped flatt

Tuesday 7   Snowing during night & continued all day   a wet drizly slush   tok me six hours to Lick house   saw two moose calfs   among 150 moose I seen on trip this was the only calfs   saw one cyotie

Wednesday 8   Came from Lick House to Camp Freman   saw a lot of moose   a strong north

wind did not bother as I was going the same direction   set net

Thursday 9   Intended to cruise the country but seeing lot of mare tails in the sky I decided to go home   saw Huttle at Birchwood & Pete Kalning at Bear Creek   fine run home   som fair head wind   a fine dust of snow on the ground here

Friday 10   Had a bath befor going to bed last night and to day I have been busy washing clotches and still boiling white goods   pulled to mout of Indian to get my fish pole   set out trout net after I got back   not feeling so good this evening   stomak seems gone wrong with heart playing pranks sympatic   foggy at the mountains

Saturday 11   Was intending to go looking for sheep but did not like the looks of som low hanging clouds   just after wards John Canon came from Bear Creek going to Lake Emma for som miners tools a snow storm and a nasty one broke loose   I was out on creek but got in before storm broke   been washing tings and mending five pair of sox   now was not I doing fine

Sunday 12   After breckfast John Canon started for Bear Creek   I have set bread   at noon Emil & Ole Matson came in from Bear Creek   the last leg from Kenai   pulling a schif   I made eighteen loaves of bread & good bread at that   it have keept me busy all day   tok my rifle a part cleaned & shot it three times

Monday 13   I was waiting this morning to ten o clock for John Canon   we was going to look

The hunters from Anchorage described in the October third Daily Times *article couldn't seem to find any moose but Andrew could hardly keep count of the number he saw a month later. Photo taken in the late 1920s by Slim Crocker, courtesy of Betty A. Crocker.*

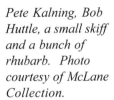

Pete Kalning, Bob Huttle, a small skiff and a bunch of rhubarb. Photo courtesy of McLane Collection.

for sheep   he did not com   I put my boat in water & pulled to Emils place   he & Ole have gone on the mountain   I cut som sticks of dry wood   brought them home   cut down two green spruce to make easier landing the boat

Tuesday 14   Stay in bed to I comenced to see day thru the window   after I had breckfast and dishes cleaned cabin sweeped out it was nine o clock   looking for my big auger an hour & not finding it   finaly I got working at my boat slip but didn't finish untill it started to snow   set out net & cooked dog feed   after super I cut som snow shoe strings

Wednesday 15   Had about one inch of snow this morning so after I got cleaned up after breckfast I riged up my bobsleds   hitched up the dog and hauled home about half cord of birchwood that I left out last spring   after I got thru I tok matlock and leveled trail to som frish birch to cut & haul in when snow & weathre gits right   weathre fine all day   no frost in ground

Thursday 16   Mild   strong wind during night   I could hear the wind & surf on lake shore so I stay in bed to it was full daylight and that about eight o clock   tok a walk to Emils camp talked to Ole   Emil was cutting som trees to saw for sheeting   I cut a dry spruce at mouth of Indian but surf to heavy to take the boat on the beach so I been cutting som birch along wood trail

Friday 17   Got out of bed at 4:30   had breckfast befor six   was going after sheep but I lay down tok a sleep as it was to dark to tell wath weathre was doing   just at day breck I walked up on glaser flats but ice was melting in creek & I could not cross   a wind sprung up after noon   cut som birch for wood   feeling heart pelpitation

Saturday 18   Left befor daybrick   puled dory 20 minuts   walked thru island to foot of glaser saw two sheep   fired 3 shots   missed   went up tunel pas   killed two sheep one shot   pulled loose rocks to cover one sheep   tok one home got in at 4

Sunday 19   Lay in bed to seven o clock   when I looked out it was snowing the ground intirely covered so I made a huried start   had to git my other sheep home   tok machine & ran to Island got up to sheep   skinned it   made up packs for my self & dog   ready to start back ten to one got home three thirty   shortly after John Canon came from Emils place   he is up for a sheep hunt   expect to go after them to morrow

Monday 20   John Canon went to sheep hills just after day breck   I stay home put up 32 glass jars of mountain sheep   fished trout net got a tub full of trout   all makinaw trout   cooked up a kettle of dog feed   John came in this evening had killed one big ram   got it down to foot of glaser   freezing som to night

Tuesday 21   Was up early   cooked & had breckfast then waited for daylight   John tok my dory   pulled to islands to go for his ram   I shot a couple of spruce hens close to cabin   hooked up dog to bob sleds & hauled in eleven sticks of green birch but quit at ten o clock as I had to haul over naked ground most of the way   John came back at two o clock   I was then thru rendering talow & fixed lunch   John walked to Bear Creek   barowed my mining pick   he is digging a well   I killed two more grouse   cut som kindling wood

Wednesday 22   Just as I turned out the lamp at ten o clock Ole Matson came in   Emil moved camp with insuficient instruction   Ole got lost three this morning   Kiser Bill & Ed lovedall came from Kasilof to se me   left shortly after daybreck   Ole started at same time   again he could not find Emils new camp   was back here again at one o clock   I made a map for him   Pete Kalning & John Canon came up from Bear Creek to get there ram   I hauled in three birch sticks   hunted & found grouse that I lost yesterday   sawed som wood

Thursday 23   Got up late this morning and found couple inches of new snow   but just the same I went up the first hill   walking good so I continued to Lake Emma   saw som tracks of wolferine on trip out   was to determine if to set out that line of trap   I conkluded to set them   a great lot of moose tracks   som rabit tracks cyotes wolferine & I think one lynx track   it continue to snow a little all day   to night it is coming strong

Friday 24   New snow not amount to much   after brecfast and tings cleaned & put away I went along my wood trail patchin up places where snow have not fallen under trees & such places new snow is about two inches but try to sweep it up it falls down to noting   hauled in six loads with the dog   two sticks at the time   got it all home that I had cut   mild   32 abov   south wind

Saturday 25   Not feeling so good this morning heart is on the jump or mis so I stay in all day exepting toward evening was out for one hour choping som birch trees and setting out the net thermometer down to 13 abov to night

Sunday 26   Was up at day light   weathre mild 28   stod at that all day   was out choping a few birch sticks   hitched up the dog & hauled in everyting I had chopped   was thru by noon then it started snowing but hardly fell anough to make track snow   snow is sticky & puts heavy I am not feeling good   tings are not just right

Monday 27   A dull sort of forenoon   smol clouds covering the whole skye   looked for a general snow fall but it did not com yet   this evening a gale of wind from north west   heavy surf brecking in from down the lake   have been in all day getting tings in shape so as to be ready to start setting traps at beginning of season   Greb werdna

Tuesday 28   Last night befor going to bed I had an atack of heart pelpitation rather three of them & have been feeling shaky all day   however I was out with the boat to mout of Indian River & brought in a dry spruce   it have been snowing som all morning but let up just long anough to get started then it came down heavy   so I got the boat foul with snow befor I got home   warmed som water had a sponge bath   heated water for washing clotches but been afraid to atemt it but I am thru with half of it   just writing while I am resting to be able to finis

Wednesday 29   Had a fine day   cloudy this fornoon but cleared up and this evening have a fine moonlight naight   moon nearly full anyway he apears quite round   cleaned away snow the first ting this morning   fixed som pins in the saw hors   sawed first som dry spruce for kindling wood   got started at sawing green birch keept on until five o clock so I finis splitting by moonlight   I just had an atack of the heart   did not fall I was so near to bed that I could rich to grab it as it come by

Thursday 30   A cold wind coming up lake to day & this morning as the sun came up coloring the top of redout it had a pecular color   a pink orange wich geneal indicate cold and the thermometer is starting to drop this evening   I have not been good   feeling that a atack my come anytime   I was starting to put tings up for a trip to Friman but quit not knowing when I well dare to go so I been laying around reading som trash of old periodicals

Friday 1 December The coldest morning so far this year down to 4 ferenheit and getting cooler but during the day it have been fine about 22 exepting a wind from northwest cut five birch logs to stovewood set out net & cooked two silver salmon for dog feed thermometer dropping fast down to 2 at 5:40

Saturday 2 2 when I got up this morning and dropped to 0 at sunrise was rather cold out all forenoon staing in reading not feeling any to good was out in midle of day cut a couple of birch but pulling hard on this snow

Sunday 3 Tempeature at 7 this morning with stringer red clouds in upper strata indicating a storm up there a swell coming up the lake with light breeze from west went out chopped a few trees & hauled them home loking over my bread suply I found that I be short for extended trip so started making yeast to night

Monday 4 2 below this morning stay about 10 all day down to 2 abow at five this evening but started rising it is 11 now at nine o clock made 12 loaves of bread at noon Emil & Ole Matson came by on thier way for Kenai just tuched shore & started on

Tuesday 5 Thermometer at zero this morning but very slow rising waited until eleven o clock befor I thaut it nice anough to go out to chop down a few birch hauled home five loads have nearly anough for an other year one more day of it and I got anough one below at 7 p.m.

Wednesday 6 Started out this morning on my way to Freman temperatur at zero when I got up dropped to 2 below at sunrise just before I got to Bear Creek machine broke stay all night bad atack of heart Pete Kalning was away witnes in jury trial

Thursday 7 8 below at Bear Creek started with dog & sled along lake shore but loose snow on gravel made going to havy had to quit went down with boat to get sled back was 12 below at seven then came up

Friday 8 At 4 below this morning started down pulling below Birch Wood I saw Tom Odale & Mr Huttle got ashore at Friman ice making fast

Saturday 9 Waited until noon befor I got my boat out of ice pulled up to umka point set the net & five mink sets ice in the making shot som grous

Sunday 10 Not feeling good stay at Friman cutting som wood untill after two then walked over to Toms place found Mr Huttle & John Canon have started for my place on a sheep hunt

Monday 11 Tom walked down with me to my boat had to take in the net on acount of ice got no fish had a falling spell on the beach stay in the rest of day trying to doctor myself up

Tuesday 12 Feeling som better went crost cow canon cutting alders & fallen trees out of trail set a five traps stod trip fine even though I tok quite a high climb for weak heart

Wednesday 13 Started early went to Olson Creek set out twenty traps made a big day of it

Thursday 14 Went to Toms to find news about the sheep hunters no one at home so I sawed up som wood after I got back & hauled in few dry sticks

Friday 15 Went acrost ridge to Lick House on Funny River was there in good time killed a porkey pine for dog feed cut a dry spruce & sawed it up to fire wood turning cold

Saturday 16 Went over ridge against a dirty cold north wind it must have been ten below zero at times I though I would have to turn back but in Funny River it was not so bad cut trail down South fork of Funny river set seven traps for mink

Sunday 17 Still colder but wind moderate went along trail I cut yesterday crossed to Prince Creek went down it to it joined swamp creek set out seven traps for mink sighns very few

Monday 18 Started down to Freman blowing to cold to go down Funny it was bitterly cold even going with the wind set couple of traps

for lynx   caught one mink the first this season
came up to Toms stay all night   Mr Huttle just
got in from sheep hunt   radio

Tuesday 19   Came home from Toms   stoped in
at Bear Creek saw John Canon   he was busy
skinning som ermine   got here at noon found
my thermometer register 5 below   found
everyting right   vegetabels in cellar not frozen
allthough it was cold down there   made fire
while waiting for cabin to warm up shifted my
fishing out fit to Indian River & set the net   it is
now six p.m.   thermometer register 12 below
zero

Wednesday 20   17 below this morning   to cold
to go anyplace   been fixing difrent tings   was
to Indian fished net   got three larg makinaw
trout two sub species of dollys   went & got a
porky   cooked it for dog   temperatur nearly 15
below at 7 p.m.

Thursday 21   17 below zero this morning and
stay cold all day so I did not ventur out anywhere
besides having trouble in my left breast heart is
giving me trouble   ben at mending up som tings
was intending to go to Lake Emma but it was afer
eleven o clock befor it warmed up to amount of
any   sixteen below zero at 7:30 this evening

Friday 22   It was 15 below this morning & is 13
below this evening at 8:30 o clock   was out to
lake Emma this cold day   at uper end of lake
got into draght from off mountain and it was sharp
as knifs   caught one ermine & lost two wolferines
traps & all   after I got home I tok in the net   got
one salmon & three trout

Saturday 23   A little better then 15 below with
penetrating cold wich is cause generaly by
moisture in the atmosphere   waited until noon
got on my scates ran down to Bear Creek to se
Frency about going to Birchwood for christmas
tok my evinrude and tings with me home & reding
mater

Sunday 24   Left here at 1 o clock going to Tom
Odales to celebrate Christmass   John Canon
joined me at Bear Creek   got to Birchwood just
at dusk   had a nice evening listening to radio
programs & hearing Christmass carrols from
every where   18 below

Monday 25   Stay in bed to daylight   from then
on we just injoyed every minute the whole blessed
day with all good tings to eat and drink   a stuffed
roast turky for christmas diner   musick donated
by the best band obtainably by toning in on the
radio to say noting of Tom & Jerry and other
refreshments   worked som picture pusles   finaly
finished with a game of penocle   16 below this
morning

Tuesday 26   Mr Huttle got up early to go on a
hunt & we all heard him getting up and did
likewise & at around to daylight I went to Friman
landed my suplies   went to Olson & Philip Creek
got one mink two ermine

Wednesday 27   Went up to Lick House   traveling
fine   a strong wind blowing acrost the ridge but
surprising anough the wind was actualy warm
after leaving frozty morning at Friman   caught
one mink

Thursday 28   Went down south fork of Funy
River crossed to Prince De Gika creek & on back
to Lick House   got two mink & three ermine
got in at dark

Friday 29   Came off of the hill ran into a nasty
cold streak crossing the lower cannon   got to
Friman early   cut up som wood & hauled in som

Saturday 30   Had som traps on Olson Creek
that I was afraid would ice under so I went down
to find out   changed couple   got two ermine
when I got back to Friman Mr Huttle was paying
me a visit   he was afraid somting my be wrong
as he know that I am trouble with weak heart

Sunday 31   Apeared cold this morning   awok
early made fire at 5 o clock   lay reading by
lamp light   finaly my eyes got tired   blow out
lamplight and had an hour of sleep   got up had
breckfast cleaned up everyting   put my ting up
for travel   went to Amberil Point   loaded my
boat on and brought it home   had no time to
stop in any place   got in early   14 below with
wind of mountain   nearly froze   18 below at 7
p.m.

CHAPTER 19

1934

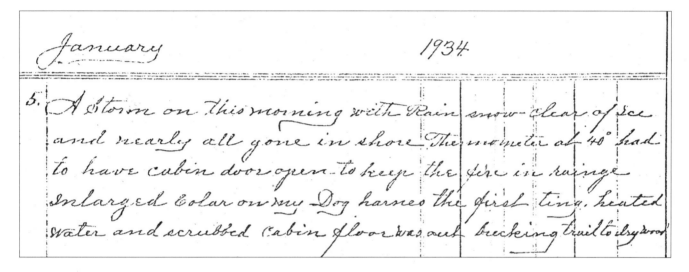

January   1934

5. A Storm on this morning with Rain snow clear of Ice and nearly all gone in shore Thermometer at 40° had to have cabin door open to keep the fire in rainge Inlarged Colar on my Dog harnes the first ting. heated water and scrubbed Cabin floor was out brecking trail to dry wood

Saturday 6   Raining and blowing with anough water on the ice to make it apear like the lake was free of ice   noting that can be done outside I did go out with matlok and leveled the wood trail   sawed one tree ready to haul & sawed up som dry spruce to stovewood

Sunday 7   Everyting white this morning   covered by several inches of new snow and snow continued falling nearly all day but so fine it didnt amount to much   went to Lake Emma warm so I went light dressed   without snowshoes hill trail   rain glased it with a cover of new snow   cam back thru timber   caught one mink

Monday 8   Was up early but did not go to woods to about ten o clock   cut down a good size dry spruce   hanged it in a spreading birch and had a time getting it down   hauled in three loads pulled heavy   too warm but if it freezes will make good trail   saw mink track by Emils Slough set out four traps   cut up two logs of dry timbre to stove wood   strong wind south west thermometer 24 up & getting cooler

Tuesday 9   Started for Friman eleven o clock walked steady to I got to Birchwood   stopped at Toms place stay for an hour   went to my cabin got one ermine on the way   keept me busy getting tings in shape & cabin warmed up

Wednesday 10   Cold morning   going to Olson Creek against the wind   mighty cold going   ran trapline   got one mink & two ermine

Thursday 11   Went up to Lick house and a beuty of head wind meating me coming over sumit   got one mink and one ermine on the way   cut up a lot of fire wood   hunted up a porky for the dog filed up the saw

Friday 12   Went down south fork of funny crossing to Prince creek   jumped many hundreds ptarmigan   a long snow shoing   tok me over five hours   got two mink & three ermine

Saturday 13   Came down to Friman in a bitterly cold wind   got an ermine on No 2 creek   set out one trap   broke a chunk out of my hunting axe used reminder of day to cutting wood

Sunday 14   Went down to Olson & Philip Creek got som traps frozen in   fixed som traps but did not get frozen ones as I struck water in trying chop them out   coming back continued on to Birchwood   stay all night   not much news as it was Sunday

Monday 15   I & Mr Huttle left toms at twenty to eleven   cold head wind   had to stop to put on my parke   getting to Bear Creek found Kalning at home   his thermometer register this morning 21 below   at leaving Bear Creek I noticed losing the dogs pack sack som place in route   got home made fire   walked to Emils slough   got one mink two ermine   was 18 below at 7

Tuesday 16   Befor going to bed last night thermometer went down to 19 below then started to rise   it was 12 below this morning   skinned som furs   went out sawed som wood   tok a walk to Emils slough   no game   was cleaning & stritching 5 mink & 10 ermine   18 below now at 11 p.m.

Wednesday 17   Got up late   ten below zero at eleven o clock   I & Mr Huttle decided to take a walk to Cliff House   shot at cyote was up in Clear Creek   no game exepting cyotes   looked over Clif House   called at Erlings   found place in good shape   18 below at quarter to ten

Thursday 18   Stay about home all day   weathre rather cold & jumpy to go any place   I have been fixing yeast preparing for a batch of bread saw two cyotes on the lake   Mr Huttle started after them but they ran away   had a quake but I think it caused by rock slide   16 below & going down steady   went to 18 below at 10:30

Friday 19   Was up at five built fire to warm cabin for building bread as this is the baking day thermometer registered 20 below zero the lowest I notised so far this winter   Mr Huttle was out and shot a cyote   brought it in at one o clock   I got 12 -2 lb loaves of very nice bread   12 below this evening

Saturday 20   20 below zero this morning stay in until noon   Mr Huttle was out looking for cyotes when he got back we had lunch   we went to Bear Creek to see if John Canon have com back from Kenai   I came back hom Mr Huttle continued on to Birchwood   I made a new bowl for the lamp at Lick House   21 below at 10

Sunday 21   26 below this morning   waited to sun got high   cut a birch log for heating wood went out felled a dry spruce but my frost bitten nose is tender so I did not haul it in   walked to Emils slough this evening

Monday 22   28 below zero the lowest I have found it at this place this winter   waited untill 10:30 went out cut a birch & got the dog in harnes hauled in both birch & spruce I cut yesterday got a porky cooked it for the dog Mr Huttle

Bob Huttle and coyote skins at Birchwood. Photo by Tom Odale, courtesy of Simonson Collection, Accession no. B91.9.101A, Anchorage Museum of History and Art.

came bringing my lost dog pack sack   4 abov at 7 p.m.

Tuesday 23   22 below this morning with a blue hase over inlet   was now getting milder but towards noon it clouded up and a fine dust started to com down   Mr Huttle scoured his rifle carefully & started down the lake   I was grinding som Axes   chopped green birch   sawed up som tok a walk to glaser flats

Wednesday 24   A tiny dust of snow falling started for Lake Emma 9:15   no sighn of game got one mink   reset several traps   tok me to two o clock befor I got back   fixed my sled   tok a walk to glaser spit   saw tracks of several cyotes been nice out to day but for snow dust   clearing turning cold   7 below at 6 p.m.

Thursday 25   Started for Camp Friman at ten o clock   stopped in at Bear Creek saw both Pete & John   continued on to birchwood   stopped in had a cup of postam and went down to Friman loose snow mad it heavy walking   feeling tired several cyoty tracks seen

Friday 26   Went down to Ohlson Creek & Philip Creek   only got one ermine   saw one mink track

Saturday 27   Went up to Lick House   tok in lumber for a table top   cold over the sumit   shot a porky about one mile befor riching cabin   after I had cabin warm I went back to get it & it was night

Thursday 1 February   Came down from Lick House to Friman   was out early   found nearly all snow gone of off the lake   cut & hauled in larg spruce

Friday 2   Was down to Philip and Ohlson creek started early   cought one larg mink   started on my way home   got as far as Toms   stay all night listened in at radio   got to bed at eleven

Saturday 3   Com home to day   had good going to bear creek the just before turning in started to snow hard   by time I got in I was all white stay to it quit   came on bad walking loose snow on slick ice every ting and glear ice around here

Sunday 4   Was up at daybreck built fire   started turning furs on stritchers   since ten last night a

wet snow coming down   after breckfast I mended som clotches   built a fire outside to cook for the dog   heated water had a bath   just thru puting in a foot webb in one of my snow shoes

Monday 5   Larg flaks of snow coming down this morning but it was too warm so it did not show on the ground   by noon it comenced to take off the old snow   been in all day trying to wash clotches but have not acomplished very much

Tuesday 6   It froze up a little during the night that the snow stuck to the slick ice so it is posible to walk now without smashing one self flatt by doing som fancy high kicks   I rinsed & hanged out my washing then filed a saw   sawed and split a dry spruce   saw two cyotes out on ice toward Bear Creek

Wednesday 7   Left here nine o clock going up lake Emma trail   icy hillroad but last snow was wet anough to stick   that made it better   got noting but saw the first shore anough lynx track got in early had a rest   was out all evening hauling snow repairing wood trail as I need a few more sticks of wood

Thursday 8   was out during fornoon   cut down six large birch   got in after twelf had lunch then I reliced that I have been taking to strong exersize my heart felt jumpy   lay down to rest   just then Gust Ness & his boy Icky came in from Cliff House hauled in my birch logs   tok me to six o clock & dark

"Icky" was Ike Johansen, Gust's stepson.

Friday 9   Turned out early   set bread   Russian Pete Kalning was hamering at old mill   I went over to see wath was going on   he was getting som scrap lumber out of som old sheds   thru baking by one   went out set both nets   thats all

Saturday 10   Intended to cross the lake this morning but not feeling any to good   I put it off to som futur day   looking at my suply of dry wood I saw I my get short   went in cut one larg spruce   John Canon was to old mill for lumber I went to flats hauled the nets   not a fish

Sunday 11   A peach of a rainstorm to day   all snow gone exepeting ice frozen to the ground stay in nearly all day   made a new cartridge *pouch   towards evening had a light earth quake before dark tok a walk to glaser flats to take care of my nets & just in time   on was made fast to steel bar driven in to shore   it was loose   tok in the other   got 4 trout*

Monday 12   Have not done a ting of any use all day   reading som old cosmopolitan   snow is all gone   just som patches of ice left along trail have not rained much but themperature at 40 with strong wind   cut up ice fast   water everywhere

Tuesday 13   The storm quit during the night but it started snowing so that this morning we have a new perfectly clean winter   I was hoping it would freze without snow just for a chance to use the scates   water on ice last night made the whole lake apear like a mirror   fished the net   got six trout five makinaw one dolvarden

Wednesday 14   Walked acrost the lake & cut acrost the ridge to King Lake cabbin   found tings allright exepting the bear have smashed the window & stove & pipe neads renewiating   saw several cyoty sighns   som mink tracks

Thursday 15   Set out fifteen traps for mink & cyotes before I came home as I will have to go there again to fix window & repair roof   perhaps new stove   got home by one o clock   saw tracks of Gust Ness & his dog team going out was up to flats tok in net   just fixin a bath

Friday 16   Started down to Camp Freman   had to whip rex to get him to go by Bear Creek met Ed Lovedall at lake point   no one home at toms

Saturday 17   Was down to Ohlson Creek   got few ermine   sprung all traps at Philip Creek

Sunday 18   Went to Lick House   was afraid it was to wet to get up there   was heavy the last couple miles

Monday 19   Good traveling this morning started early and was up on north fork before it got soft   got two mink & five ermine squirrels in nearly all traps

Tuesday 20   this the day I put in the long hike   left Castle Inn six thirty five and in four hours and half I was at Lick house   stay

long anough to put tings to order   hiked down to Friman   expecting rain or snow   thats why the rush

Wednesday 21   Saw Ed Lovedall & Tom Odale in the distance on the way to Kussiloff   I stopped at toms saw Mr Huttle & John Canon   John came to bear creek with toms team   called at bear creek got a bunch of books from Pete   when I got home found Mr & Mrs Ness on a visit

Thursday 22   Was up to Lake Emma to day   did not take in traps as I intended   not feeling good saw Gust Ness at glaser flats   I have just came out of an attack of heart just then   He started to Clif House   I hoked up the dog Rex   went to fish net   got four trout   just had an other bad spell nine p.m.

Friday 23   Have been home doing house work got up after six as I did not sleep any to after mid night   after breckfast I cooked som dog feed mad a log fire out side   cooked fifteen jars of mts sheep that have been frozen since December 18 but weathre being to warm now I was afraid it my spoil   filed a saw & sawed up som wood fished net got four trout   picked thru my potatoes

Saturday 24   Left here at eight this morning   tok som frish trout to Mr & Mrs Ness   they was out so I did not see them   went down south shore to my trail   crossed ridge to King Lake   got to my cabbin 12:45   had lunch   ran over traps   got one mink one ermine   got back here at 5:00

Gust and Mary Ness. Photo courtesy of Irene Ness Wilcox and Rocky Johnson.

Sunday 25   Was up early had breckfast & set spong for making bread   lay down reading   just then Mr & Mrs Ness came for a visit & stay to I made lunch   they went to Bear Creek   I started kneading bread molding loafs   the Ness people came back about four o clock   I went along to fish my net at flatts got ten trout   scrubbed floor

Monday 26   Sawed som wood   working on som frames for smole wood saws   making ready for sawing up my next winters wood   tok in traps of glaser flats   a cyotie came by here on ice about noon   was just making lunch had no time to go out to kill it   cloudy   will probbably snow

Tuesday 27   Went up to Lake Emma to take in traps   cashed thirteen at lynx cliffs & ten on sandslide just over the summit   just after I got home John Wik & Andy came in from Emma Creek is out on mining expedition

Wednesday 28   Was up on Indian River to day survaying for som mining location   tok us to noon   had lunch   just then Gust Ness came in he been out fishing the net   after they all have gone I sawed up two birch logs in trying out my new saw outfit   just thru having a bath & it is bed time

Thursday 1 March   Was up early   washed a couple suits of underware   went to glaser flats to take in the net   I saw Mr & Mrs Ness coming from clif house on the way to Kasilof   I was ready to go to Friman so I followed   befor I got to birch wood was overtaken by John & Andy Wik so we was four dog teams at Toms

Friday 2   Went to Ohlson creek sprung the traps and in coming back to Friman found that I had to come home before I dared to go on the ridge and started right home against a nasty blizard snow dust devils dansing all over the lake stoped at Birch & Bear creeks on way   got four nice frish trout at Bear Creek

Saturday 3   Went down to Friman camp   stopped both at Bear creek & Birch wood   had lunch with Mr Huttle   clearing & getting cold   trees snaping this eve

Sunday 4   Waited until sun got high   started to Lick House walking as fast as I dared (on acount

of heart) so as to keep warm without putting on to much clotches   but near summit I had to put parke on & then I nearly froze my cripled hand

That was his first direct reference to his disabled hand. Berg was sixty-four years old, had only one usable hand and a heart condition which caused blackouts. Yet he continued to hike his trap lines in the middle of winter over twenty miles from the nearest help and over eighty miles from the nearest doctor.

Monday 5   Cold but started in good time as I had long walk ahead of me   went to my last cabin   sprung all traps   most of them sprung by squirrels & camp robbers   to cold to do anyting with this cabin roof this trip so I just made shooters [shutters] for windows & baricaded the door to try to keep the bears from smashing thru

Tuesday 6   Left early   weathre still cold but clouds gathering in mountain   make it look like a storm is brewing   got to Lick House early but stay just long anough to rest up & pushed on to Friman

Wednesday 7   Blowing a gale with snow devils whirling over the lake   tok a run down to Ohlson Creek crossing two of the lakes   come out at Fox Point   she was just a blizard coming back

Thursday 8   Started for home   stopped at birch wood   started to rain   stay to it cleared som started on   got cought in a nasty squall   riched Bear Creek ringing wet   stay all night

Friday 9   Left for home   looked dry but there was ancle deep water on the ice between partly frozen snow drifts   warm but not raining   tok my fish pole from glaser flats   set both of my trout nets at mouth of Indian River

Saturday 10   Stay in nearly all day   not feeling right   tok a run out to fish nets   got a tub full of trout   anough that I can cook a lot for the dog while out there I had a dizzy spell then just laying reading

Sunday 11   Went to fish the net this morning   I saw Emil coming along   he went by while I was fishing with out saying hello   cut down a dry spruce brought it hom   cut it up to fire wood

Monday 12   Have put in a good day at cutting wood   cut split and ricked a rick ten feet long six feet high at eighteen inch stove wood clouding up   looking like we my have a storm

Tuesday 13   Started early this morning going to Erling place to look over the roof & have a look at the boat   put few plates of tin on roof & covered boat with spruce   climbed to an old bear hole on island on my way back but found no one home

Wednesday 14   Weathre loking good this morning and I needed som porkypines for dog feed so I went cross the lake   climbed the ridge to King lake to put shooters [shutters] on the cabin window   came right back   found only two porky's

Thursday 15   Stay home all day making bread

Friday 16   Started in good time this morning to saw wood   got the second rick finis and a lot more sawed   forenoon Emil & Ole Matson came up from Bear Creek   Ole came in & had lunch with me

Saturday 17   On the wood pile agan to day   got the thirth rick done and all havy stoff sawed so the reminder dont amount to much   can finis easy in a day but I got other tings to tend to so I will let it go for a time   weathre just the finest

Sunday 18   A very thin dust of snow falling this morning so I went in to woods   chopped a couple of trees dry for wood & hauled it home or rather Rex did   been in most all day   went to fish net   tok a bath

Monday 19   Had a real lacy day of it   couple of inches of new snow covered the ground this morning & hanging to trees making it unfit to do anyting in the woods   I did wash som clotches for the rest just sleeping & reading   Greb werdna

Tuesday 20   Stay in camp   just sawed a few remainding birch sticks but did not finis   snow is melting out off trees but ice on the lake still covered white   was out hauling net but only got one dolvarden

Wednesday 21   Stay in reading som trash story books untill noon   then I went out sawed som

wood   cleaned up around my saw horse & wood ways   was out fishing the net   got seven dollys weathre murky

Thursday 22   Not feeling good this morning so I lay down again after I had breckfast   about ten o clock I got out tok a walk   hunted a porcupine started it cooking on log fire   tok a run to Bear Creek to exchange books   saw Pete & John

Friday 23   Have been in all day   was working grinding down a pece of steel shaping it to a knif   did not even get it finished   hauled the net no fish

Saturday 24   An other day gone & noting acomplished   ground knif to a finis   made a sheep horn handle for it   tok my old evinrude apart to find out wath was broke   found the crank shaft broken fished the net tok a walk up Indian River   new snow each morning for days

Sunday 25   A drizling rain & snow   just anough to make tings wet so there was noting that I could do   so I stripped corkline of a trout net   that tok me couple of hours   fished got only one trout

Monday 26   Was making a new firing pin for my pistol & covering cotage window case   tok a ride to Bear Creek   Ole Matson came over   I got four big trout

Tuesday 27   John Canon came up from Bear Creek this morning   we hitched his dogs & mine to my boat   hauled it up from beach   then we tok walk up Indian but could not pass hells gate so we turned back home   went to visit Emil & Ole Matson they were rigging up a shingle plane came back had lunch   John went back   I was down beach for load of dry wood

Wednesday 28   Have been at home making bread used all my flour so I will have to move soon the bread will problbly last me twenty days   Put my boat up in the atic while waiting on bread feeling not so good this eve

Thursday 29   Have been fixing ods & ends about the place   not anyone ting I could point out as an item   weathre the nicest kind   light morning frost   had an earth quake a little after six this eve   fishing poor   hauled the net no catch

Friday 30   After I had breckfast I lay reading John Canon came up from Bear Creek   I went along with him to help him get som pipe   got three joints   barowed my bobsleds to haul in som logs for building a bath house   been fixing som bedding   not feeling so good   had som dizzy spell

Saturday 31   Stay in bed late this morning so I did have breckfast after seven & then not feeling good anough to do anyting   I lay reading most of the day   Afternoon I went up Indian to get corect measurment of placer location

Sunday 1 April   Volys coming of the mts with snow & rain but to warm for snow   it melts as it hits the ground   been in all day   had several dizzy spells   acording to my way of figuring this aucto be Easter Sunday

Cannon and Kalning built this sauna at their camp at Bear Creek. Photo by G. Titus.

Monday 2   Anough snow fell to day to make the ground white again so I had som excuse for not going anywheres   I think I am feeling a little better   still the heart is beating irregular

Tuesday 3   The weathre still unsettled   fornoon fairly good but towards evening a wind sprung up & acompany by snow squalls   ice are nearly all gone from my garden patch   was over to Indian River to haul net   no fish

Wednesday 4   After I had breckfast I lay down reading a book   after a while John Canon came

bringing my bobsleds that he borowed som day back   he have been sick ever since he was here he lent me a hand at cleaning out the well   was out hunting a dry birch   made a motor handle my heart been cutting som nasty capers to night

Thursday 5   Feeling week   can not do anyting but it starts my old heart a fluttering   walked out to get a porky had a hard time getting home hauled the net while I was out there no trout   net too rotten

Friday 6   Stay in all day   can't move around only slowly without starting disturbans about the heart   weathre still bad   snow fell good at one time to day but it dont lay on naked ground   but ice on lake is all white

Saturday 7   New snow again this morning   try to do som work but found myself unable to acomplish wath I wanted to do so I hooked up the dogs & rode to Bear Creek   saw two cyotes out on ice   saw Pete Kalning   got som salt salmon & frish trout   was howing in garden but tings turned black for eyes [he blacked out]

Sunday 8   Had a bath last night and to day I washed som clothes but tok my time about it   have not had any ataks to day but feeling sick at my stomak   A strong northerly wind during the day with som snow flakes drifting

Monday 9   A beutiful morning   I got working in the garden but frost interfere in patches so I got about half finis   Mr Huttle came up shortly after noon   we had a walk over to Emils place clouded up & a drizle of snow fell this evening

Tuesday 10   Have not done anyting again to day to mention   started to cut a tree for sled runners but did not even get it down befor I found I had to quit   got in som dry wood

Wednesday 11   New snow again this morning so I hunted up an old saw that needed a new handle & worked in part of a sheep horn   later I was getting a pair of sled runners blocked out of a larg spruce   Huttle came back this evening

Thursday 12   Have just put in lazy day   not feeling like doing anyting   reding   weathre my have somting to do with it   nice early this morning clouded with a hasy snowy look

Friday 13   Heavy wind from north east   been looking like rain all day but only few drops fell made som uprights for a sled   hunted up som wilows for bents & finis howing garden

Saturday 14   Drizly rain with voleys of wind all day & evening   stay in all day working at sled as long as I could stand it   then I lay resting & reading   finished sled & out of reading mather

Sunday 15   Blowing hard this morning & very murky south east   tok a run down to Bear Creek started snow squalls   Pete cut my hair   I got som carrot seeds & planted this afternoon   had a few potatoes that started sprout put them in allso   wind is down   raining

Monday 16   Raining steady all day so I heated water & scrub the floor & laying down most of the time   heart bothered me several times   just picking out tings to take with me going down almost ready to go

Tuesday 17   Fine morning   looking at my landing I saw it neaded looking after so I built a crib & rolled the boulders of the beach & filled the crib   so I got a nice clean landing now untill surf pile up more rocks   Ole Matson came over & while we sit talking Ed Lovedall came in   he came thru from Kussilof a foot

Berg mentioned surveying a claim in his entries on February twenty-eighth and March thirty-first. He and John Wik filed the placer claim jointly on May tenth. They named the claim "Last Chance." There is no telling if they meant a last chance for Indian Creek or themselves.

While Berg was in Anchorage in May he received another fifteen minutes of fame, thanks to the *Anchorage Daily Times*. The newspaper published an article about Andrew calling him the "sourdough of sourdoughs" and making much of his longevity in Cook Inlet. [1] (Ironically, the old-timer used packaged yeast to make his bread rather than the famous sourdough of Alaskan lore.) In the article Berg reported that placer miners were once again working the beach sands of Cook Inlet around Anchor Point. This was another probable result of the Depression.

Other effects of the economic situation came to light this year from a new source. Between January and June, someone in Ninilchik was writing regular articles about the town for the *Daily Times*. The reporter described how most of the town members had come together to form the "Organized Citizens of Ninilchik." Reduced fishing income and depressed fur prices had caused hardship. The town's response was to conceive and implement a major community gardening project under the auspices of the "Organized Citizens." The group's Constitution included the following language, "It is our plan and purpose to do all possible to solve the problems of this depression and to act in harmony with the government in promoting the new deal." [3]

Another sign of times was the description in the Ninilchik dispatches of the fishermen's union organizing which occurred over the coarse of the winter. Men were mushing dog sleds between Homer, Ninilchik and Kenai to disseminate information and rally support. By spring,

Berg, Andrew   2806 Last Chance   May 10, 1934   11 R, 382   Indian River

Notice of location of mining claim placer. Notice is hereby given. First that the undersigned Andrew Berg and John Wik are citizens of the United States have discovered a valuable placer deposit of gold and other minerals within the limits of this claim. Second that at the point of discovery have erected a monument and on the first day of March 1934 posted a copy of this notice upon said monument. Third that the name of this lode or claim is LAST CHANCE. Fourth that the number of feet or acres claimed are six hundred and sixty by thirteen hundred and twenty feet.... Sixth, that said claim is located in Seward recording district, situated on Indian river, Kenai Peninsula.... Eight, that in accordance with the laws of the United States and the laws of Alaska hereby claim the above described property as a placer mining claim. Dated March first 1934. Andrew Berg, John Wik, File for record at 7:30 p.m. o'clock May 10, 1934 at the request of John Wik. [2]

ANCHORAGE DAILY TIMES
May 18, 1934

Noted Sourdough Cook Inlet Area Is Visiting City
Andrew Berg, Resident Of 45 Years, Is In From Kenai

Andrew Berg, sourdough of sourdoughs in the Cook Inlet country, who was in these parts long before gold was struck on Turnagain Arm or in the Hope or Sunrise camps is in Anchorage on a short visit. He has resided on Cook Inlet 45 years or since he sailed to the Kasilof River with an outfit which established a cannery there in 1889. Ever since that he has made his home in the vicinity, and now has a fine residence at Kenai and another at Lake Tustumena.

Tall, rugged, and bearing a snowy touch to his looks, Mr. Berg is one of the most enduring of Alaska's pioneers, and is still a very active man. He holds No. 1 license as an authorized Alaska Guide, and has conducted many famous hunting parties seeking the big game of the realm from Kenai Peninsula to Kodiak. He also has devoted years to prospecting, fishing and hunting, and is one of the real men who have helped in a big way to put Alaska on the map.

Years ago, before Anchorage and Seward were dreamed of, Mr. Berg shot himself accidentally in the wrist while near Kenai, and in order to save his life a party of his friends there hastily bound the wounded member, and setting out in face of a storm with him made a wild trip over the waves in a sail boat from Kenai to Kodiak, to get the services of a doctor. With the tides and fierce gale favoring them they covered the approximate 200 miles in a bitter night trip, and got there in time to get surgical attention which resulted in saving his life. He still bears the scar of the wound.

Mr. Berg reports that placer gold was being mined on the beach near Anchor point long before the Turnagain or Sunrise Discoveries were made, and that right now old Anchora point is again yielding gold, and last season quite a little gold was recovered there. Mr. Berg has every confidence the greatest days of the Kenai Peninsula and the Cook Inlet and Alaska as a whole are yet to come, and he gives promise of living long to enjoy the sharing of the new era.

[Although full of minor inaccuracies, the article still must have been gratifying to Andrew.]

most of the Ninilchik fishermen were reported to have signed up with the Cook Inlet Associated Fishermen's and Workers' Union.[4]

The government, via the Alaska Road Commission, was contributing to the town's welfare through funding of some road and bridge building in the locality. Area residents were employed on the project. The manner in which they received their pay provides an interesting view of business in this region where the nearest bank was in Anchorage. An Anchorage merchant, I. Koslosky, flew to Ninilchik with the paychecks and cashed them for the recipients. Mr. Koslosky rounded out his trip by buying some furs.[5]

Apparently no government funding was available for health care. The Ninilchik schools and the Organized Citizens raised enough money to hire Seldovia doctor Isam Burgin to provide dental checkups for the town's children. Doctor Burgin, and his equipment, came in by dogsled from Homer in late January.[6]

Another subject regularly addressed by the Ninilchik reporter was mail delivery. On January third readers learned that: "Lee Hancock, Alaska Guide of this place, is making trips from Ninilchik to Kasilof twice a month, bringing the mail here. Last year the mail came in from Homer once a month."[7] A bit later in the winter came the update that the Kasilof-Ninilchik mail run was temporarily turned over to Brown and Victor Kelly while Lee Hancock mushed to Seward with Ed Jackinsky and Walter Jackinsky, Jr.[8] In late April the *M.S. Discoverer* began service in Cook Inlet and took over mail delivery for the spring, summer and fall.[9]

The trip taken to Seward by Hancock and the Jackinsky brothers was a lark. They made a one-way trip of nine days with two dog teams. After experiencing the bright lights of Seward, the crew, dogs and all, shipped out on

In Kasilof the mail was delivered by Comer Cole, pictured here with his dog team and an unidentified man at Doc Pollard's house. Photo courtesy of Jim Taylor.

the *S.S. Northwestern* for Seldovia. From Seldovia they caught a boat ride to Homer and then finished their journey overland. The most remarkable aspect of their adventure was the exaggerated account provided by the home town reporter:

Three Ninilchik boys, Walter Jackinsky, Edward Jackinsky, his brother, and Lee Hancock make the first continuous trip on record from Ninilchik to Seward which took nine days... With six dogs carrying their provisions and mushing through a virgin country for 150 miles via the Skilak lake region, these northern courier de bois traversed a section but little traveled by other than trappers, explorers, or prospectors. The country they crossed is perhaps the greatest moose and bear country on the American continent.

Leaving the well traveled trail terminus at Kenai, they turned their dogs in the direction of their destination. They were soon lost in the almost interminable solitudes of the Alaskan wilds. To these lads the vast stretches of the Northland hold no fears. They are at home anywhere in that vastness in which, to many another, would be many uncertain omens.

All along the trail, wherever perchance the abode of human beings was found, they were greeted with welcome and the hospitality that only

this great Northland knows. In the evenings came stories of adventures and new thrills, then off again in the early light of the morning ready for the thrills incident to the day.

Past Lakes Skilak, Tustumena, and Caribou Island, bidding good day to the fading sun, and bon jour to the morning light, they pursued their onward way. After a halt at Kenai Lake, they passed the night at Lawing. In sub-zero temperatures, thru nine long, but to them not weary days, these sons of the North held the battle of the day, and the rigors of the night as nothing, snug asleep in their bags as their faithful dogs kept watch through the frosty silence of the night...[10]

One gets the impression that the reporter was a newcomer to the area; an idea reinforced by the boosterism evident throughout the articles. At one point the writer editorialized about the need for roads and the prejudice toward this historic town:

The country around Ninilchik is considered by many to be from an agricultural point of view one of the most promising in Alaska. There are hundreds of square miles of level ground well suited for farming, dairying and ranching. As a grass country this country beats them all. More roads are needed to open this country so that settlers can get into and onto the land. The prospective road from Homer to Kenai would be a boon to this district.

The general impression seems to be that Ninilchik is a backward Indian village in a state of semi-civilization. How that idea got abroad is not sure, but surmised. We find that the people here are entirely civilized with possibly one or two exceptions. Most of us speak the English language, aspire to American ideals, and try to maintain a deferential regard for all the rest of mankind. [11]

Regardless of motive or style, we are indebted to this writer for the vignettes of daily life on the western coast of the Kenai Peninsula. Other news items included holiday masquerade balls, trappers and hunters returning to town with bounty and the perseverance of fox farmers Joe Leman and Walter Jackinsky, Sr.

Most of the fox farmers on the coast had not yet quit the business. Silver fox and mink prices came up slightly this year to average around $46 and $9 respectively.[12] Other fur prices hadn't changed much since they crashed in 1932. Having any source of cash was consequential during these hard times.

Come fall, Andrew headed to Tustumena once again for hunting and trapping.

Monday 8 October   Came from Kenai to Kasilof with Alex Lind   Left Kenai at four p.m. got to Kasilof at dark

Tuesday 9   Walked to Abrams fox ranch teleponed to Christ Jenson   he came down   we ran down to cannery to get som provision stopped at Alexs place for lunch   got more provision at Abs & up to Pete Jensens fox ranch stay all night

Berg and Alex Lind had witnessed Christ Jensen's citizenship petition in Seldovia on June eighth. In the paperwork, Andrew described his occupation as "Guide" and Alex described his occupation as "Fisherman." [13]

Wednesday 10   A drizly rain all morning   got under way at 9:30 after drifting down to Sandwicks befor we got machine started   came up to flat water at 2 o clock   found Muligan there   stay all night

Thursday 11   Frosty this morning   waited to nine o clock   came on thru home   called at Birch wood   tok Mr Cannon to Bear Creek with a lot of provision   got home at two and tings put away & cabin warmed up

Friday 12   Started to blow this morning with rainsquals so I decided to do the baking stunt but had to make yeast and proces of rising was very slow so I just got bread in pan   anyway I have been busy mowing hay out of trails and around cabbin   Christ busy at salvacing a new trout net

Saturday 13   Christ have put line on two trout nets so we are fixed nisely with trout gear   I was putting tings down in cellar   tok my evinrude to parts   put in new crank shaft   got it asembled at dark   rainy

Sunday 14   Blowing a southerly wind   to rough to cross the lake so we had a stay home   I try the machine & it was making noise anough for a good motor   spaded part of my garden patch quit blowing this eve

Monday 15   started on a trip this morning   first to Bear Creek then crossed over to Alex Linds place   Alex was repairing his cellar   stepped in hurt his leg   from there we went to Big House & crossed the lake to Friman

Tuesday 16   Went to Ohlson Creek   walked in to lakes   started blowing so we huried back tok a walk in Cow Cannon   set the trout net got som fine makinaw

Wednesday 17   I went out picked about four gallons of craneberrys   evening tok a walk out loking for bear   did not find any

Thursday 18   Started for home early   stopped at Birchwood   had som refreshments at Toms & getting warmed up   came to Bear Creek   Canon give us som frish trouts got home at noon   swans are migrating this afternoon

Friday 19   Started in good time this morning to look for sheep   ran down to island lake   show coming thru wood to fish creek   jumped a cyote unexpected   he got away   went up over foot of glaser found lots of sheep   I shot one shot at two rams in a string of young sheep   got them

Christian Jensen on the beach on the west side of the peninsula at Tustumena Lake. Photo courtesy of Susan and Joe Perletti

milling so I could not shoot again   saw about 200   the bunch I shot at 60

Saturday 20   stay home all day keeping busy at doing noting   after breckfast I cleand   found put in new mantels and genrator for gas lamp looked thru stock of gasoline   changed to new containers   soldered up tank on gas engine spaded a garden patch

Sunday 21   Was up early to go up for sheep about 6:30   just as we was ready to go it started to snow   keept on to everyting was covered   tok a walk up Indian   set yeast for making bread looks snowy yet this evening

Monday 22   Got up early   set the bread & had it baked by ten o clock   tok in my garden truck & spaded the last bed   cut down a tree for a new dog house   Emil came in to find out when Christ was going down to Kasilof

Tuesday 23   Got up at 4:30 started to sheep hills saw seven cyotes   Christ shot at them   scared a brown bear   it ran thru smole mts scaring the sheep   we saw lots of sheep but only one that we could have shot and that at long range

Wednesday 24   Just as we was ready to start for Kasilof Emil came in a canoe   we tok him canoe and all to slack water   saw Sands there   Emil jumped ashore at big edie   I stay at Petes

Thursday 25   I and Christ went to Abes fox ranch I stay   Christ went to visit Heeny Berger and take a load of moss to his new location   in coming back brought a load of provision to the fox farm from Abs

Friday 26   I walked to Kenai in a northerly gale

Saturday 27   Came back from Kenai walking up to Abes fox farm   stay all night   was up late watchin a game of penocle

Sunday 28   Was on my way early walking acrost country to Tustemina   rough   got in my schif got motor started ran only short of three miles motor quit   pulled to Friman   stay over night

Monday 29   raining hard all day   stay in taking motor apart   noting I could do to fix it   set it up again   got som nice makinaw

Tuesday 30   Pulled homeward but at Birchwood wind got to strong   landed   walked to Tom Odales place   stay all night   found som pieces to fit motor   Tom got request over radio to be at Kasilof tomorow

Wednesday 31   Helped Tom roll out his boat   I walked to my boat   pulled up to Toms place Tom started before I got there   I had to make a new key for flywheel   got it fixed   started out in starting machine I got it a fire and had a lively blaze but finely floded the ting with water   filled *tank with water   pulled to shore   emtying water out off tank & bailed out the boat   pulled to lake point   wind sprung up   try motor again got it started   ran to Bear Creek   stay all night*

Thursday 1 November   came up from Bear Creek this morning   fine weathre   Alex Lind came of mountain with a ram   been busy overhauling motor & doing house work & bringing dayry [diary] to time

Friday 2   Started this morning befor day light wen over Nikanor mountain down into north fork got the only ram I saw   packed it in   that is I & Rex did   Rex got tired so I must have been generous in deviding the meat   got in before dark Ed Lovedahl started down to day

Saturday 3   Was up early   I found that I have contracted a peach of a cold   Alex Lind went over to Emils place to build a saw hors   I was busy washing jars & cleaning meat   put up 21 jar of nice frish sheep meat   weathre fine

Sunday 4   Alex Lind & Emil had a date for a sheep hunt   Alex left befor daybreck so he did not see to start his motor   he was back here by noon with a sheep   I put up 23 jars of meat to day   that is all I got out of the sheep exept leg I sent to Pete Jensen   I have a bad cold the worst ever   weathre fine   Alex left here at two on way to Kasilof

Monday 5   Had som nasty spels at coffing   flem sticking in my troat to I choke as in whoping cough   cut a spruce   cut it to five feet lengts started building a dog house   put up nine logs started afternoon   weathre fine

Tuesday 6   Working at the dog house   got it nearly done   tok old ones apart using wath I can of then   cleaning up ground where they stod   burning up wath is of no use   mild look like we will have snow

An *Anchorage Daily Times* article this month reported that coyotes were decimating mountain sheep on the lower Peninsula.[14] Sheep populations were not noticeably affected around Tustumena, but coyotes were clearly increasing. A coyote pelt was only worth five to six dollars. Over the next few years the Alaska Game

This may have been Rex with Andrew. His big dogs did their share of the work and obviously provided companionship. Photo courtesy of Lorraine and Ray Blake.

Commission would increase the bounty on coyotes to twenty dollars.

Wednesday 7   Was just making day when I got out   mild   finis dog house   gatherd moss calked it   leveled of a patch of ground where I burned rubish   soldered tank & put in som missing bolts in evinrude   washed out boat mixed oil

Thursday 8   Have not acomplished a ting to day feeling out of sort   a snowy look over mountain and a very little sprincle apeard this morning pulled to mouth of Indian River loking for salmon for dog feed   water to deep

Friday 9   raining all fornoon   early morning had a quake   I think caused by land slide   later in the day a similar acurence   been busy making bread   had a bath   still at work mending trout net   warm

Saturday 10   Continued with mending net   tok to noon befor I finis   I am just all in with the bad cold   I get tired trying to do anyting   been washing this afternoon   still boiling som white goods

Sunday 11   Had a tough night   a bad atack of indigestion   after taking anema got relief so I slept two hours   after that I lay turning all night fixed a mast step in my dorey   tok a walk up Indian river   ice just making

Monday 12   Getting over the cold som but I am weak   I cant undertake any work and get away with it   scrubbed the floor to day & had to lay down after I was thru   heard a motor down lake

this evening just befor dark   my have been a plane   little frozty

Tuesday 13   still fightin the cold   was out for a while to day cutting up som hydrylik pipe to make repair parts for stoves in out laying cabins   a flury of snow fell this evening

Wednesday 14   Built a fire out side to aneal som 14 gage steel plate in order to be able to turn it into six inch stove pipe   made a good work out of it   tok nearly all day drilling for rivets walked to Indian   saw mans track have not heard any noys for several days weathre good

Thursday 15   Put tings in dory   hoked up motor   crossing lake   walked acrost ridge to King Lake   found tracks of Emil being there day befor   repaired stove & pipe so as to put it in servis

Friday 16   Was out gathering som moss & cutting up som wood   found a tree that split good so I made it into roof on wood shade at end of cabin Emil came by at noon on way in

Saturday 17   Started on my way home but such of fine walking swamps frozen & no snow so I left trail   wandering over hills   finely it was getting late   got to boat   wind sprung up could hardly get of shor   finely made it   motor busted I drifted back in   had to walk back to King Cabin   got there at dark

Sunday 18   Left in good time as I know I had to pull acrost lake   struck a light head breeze the first hour   the later part was just fine   got here in good time   warm   just a summer day

Monday 19   Was up early had breckfast befor day   had to wait to daylight befor I undertok take my motor a part & everting worked badly all day   finely when I got it asembled I found tank leaking by then it was dark   "weathre mild"

Tuesday 20   After fixing tank got it reasembled set it up to try   heard right away I had loose flywheel causing heavy vibration   found a bolt with stripped tread   a crack in lynite of armature got in new Key seat & key   exchanged bolts waiting for liquid solder to dry

Wednesday 21   Got machine ready but have not tryed it out   mixed oil   put up provision for a trip if weathre is favorable & I get motor to do its bit   noting sure about that   foggie

Thursday 22 Went to Freman   just after I got tings ashore I heard a motor   thinking it to be Tom Odale   finely the boat got abreast   came in it was Ed Lovedal   he has som mail for me & Tom Odale   a box of freight for Tom   informing me that Tom was in Anchorage

Friday 23   Went to Ohlson Creek   made ready mink sets   befor snowfall put traps in place ready to set   after I got back I fell & hurt my hand badly

Saturday 24   Stay in camp nursing my hand swolen badly

Sunday 25   Ventured up over hill to Lick house saw a lot of moose but no sign of game animals

Monday 26   Hurying on to Castle In so is to find out condition it was in befor snow fell   thinking this was 28   just found myself two days out

Tuesday 27   Was up north fork to open valey saw noting to indicate fur bearer exept cyotes

Wednesday 28   Started snowing during the night so I had to get busy getting out as I had no snow shoes   wet & sticky   Found it hard finding way

Thursday 29   Came over sumit to Friman   found a dead cow moose at sumit

Friday 30   Went to Ohlson Creek   set som traps lost my hand ax   walked back to Friman

Saturday 1 December Put my tings in dory   went to Ohlson to hunt my ax   did not find it   found signs of mink   started snowing so I came on home   no sign of anyone at Birch wood or Bear Creek

Sunday 2   Had a busy day of it mending tings from gum boots to steel traps & making twelf loafs of bread   a south easter was on for a spell   tok nearly all snow   wath little we had   fine this eve   mild

Monday 3   The hardest storm so far this winter trees falling fast   I feelt the ground tremble when

som heavy cotton wood came down   cleaned out my cellar   raining   warm   ground tawed up three inches   still blowing

Tuesday 4   Calm but with a fog hanging high wich means moistur abow   about mid day a storm broke thru of mountain   started raining & been at it ever since   had a bath   washing som clotches   truble with gas lamp

Wednesday 5   Still storming   been in all day had to take my gas lamp apart to try to get it to work   broke four mantles & one generator finaly got it working but not good   strong wind no rain

Thursday 6   Waking this morning I heard a tremendos raket   a heavy rain squall hit the cabin   tok a walk out to Indian River   it running bank ful the bigest I ever seen it   blown down trees everywhere

Friday 7   Raining & blowing with apearently smole chans for chang   been putting new webbin in my snow shoes   tok in my trout net and it was full of salmon trout & steelhead

Saturday 8   Storm ended towards morning   I made ready   ran acrost to south side   set a few traps   got to King cabin in good time   a regular sumer day snow all gone   water high   no game

Sunday 9   Went out to Rat Lake drainage   set out som traps   cutting oppen the trail saw signs of som mink   got back to cabin after dark

Monday 10   A drizly wet snow falling so I huried to leave as I had no snowshoes   came in fine snow changed to rain so I got wet crossing lake this evning I cut som wind falls out of my wood trail and did som grading   warm   foggy

Tuesday 11   Tok a run to glaser flats   set a few mink trap   chopped out som wind falls   a drizly fog coming down got everyting wet   coming in had an atack of acute indigestion   just managed to get hom   had a bad time of it

Wednesday 12   Stay in all day recuperating   had to bring motor in to taw it up   turn boat over trying to get it free of snow   had a bath   look like snow   warm

Thursday 13   Went down to Freman   saw John Canon at Bear Creek   stoped in at Toms   left a box in the old house   got to Freeman in good time

Friday 14   was to Ohlson Creek   found hand ax I lost   creek on rampage flooding

Saturday 15   Went up to Lick House   no snow to speak of   wearing gumboots   no snowshoes

Sunday 16   Crossing country to north fork of Funy River   sure neaded gumboats   had foot deep water for hundred yards at places   heard plane

Monday 17   Was up north fork   it had been frozen shot and piled up ice floes in great style   lost good many traps that I have left at old sets

Tuesday 18   Came back to Lick House   freesing up som

Wednesday 19   Came down to Tustumina Lake   tok a walk to Toms place   found Tom John Canon & Stanly Pearson at playing penocle   after getting all the news listened to radio   had an other game of cards   retired at 12 mn

Thursday 20   I & Stanley started down the beach at day breck   he to look over som cyotie sets   I to Freeman   clear of ice   I loaded boat started for home   got mine & Emils Xm precents   a bear skin & books from Bear Creek   saw Pete Kalning   got a aplecation blank from gam warden Jack O Connor   after filling in one very similar exepting it was white   this is orang   it was in October this in December

Friday 21   One below zero this morning   feeling cold to go out   had a lot of tings to do so I stay in all day and am not thru yet   just fixing to take a bath   got net set after I blustoned it first   two abow this evening   calm   clear

Saturday 22   Two abow this morning but keeping cool all day   been in nearly all day   had a walk over to Emils camp with a roaster sent by Mr Huttle   Indian River is overflowing with ice   no ice in lake   clear

Monday 24   Have been in making bread   Ole Matson came over from Emils camp   stay to

afternoon   went home   I walked with him to Indian River   temperature up over twenty   cloudy   north west wind

Tuesday 25   At home and busy all day   had a bath last night & the change of underware had to be laundried   weathre being mild so there is no time like precent so I did it   walked over to see Ole Matson   he came over spent the evening   he just left for his quarters   look very much like it is going to snow   thermometer at twenty five abow at eight this evening   dark as a stack of black cats   hear cyotes on flats

Wednesday 26   Was up early this morning planning to go get a moose befor season closes but was not feeling good so I just tok a short walk down lakeshore   shot at a grouse & missed it   got in at dark   warm

Thursday 27   Tok a walk on glaser flats   got right close to a moose   Old Bull in good condition but I let it go   At Rays mine saw a ram peached four shots at it   missed it clean   came home as I had only six shots along   Matson here this evening

Friday 28   Started to blow when I was ready to start acrost the lake so I lay down to wait & see wath it was going to be   after ten it looked better so I went   got rough so I had a tough time landing   fine walking acrost country   made to cabin allright

Saturday 29   Cold   left after ten oclock   tok ax along to cleanout trail but bushes to full of hoar frost   it running like flour   just after I got on way a cyote picked up two traps with light clogs   I tok his track   he lost both clogs   had chains twisted so I out ran him   (He Hobbled)

Sunday 30   Snowing this morning with wind   I being anxius to get home started out   built a fire to taw up motor   got of shore & motor going bad   sea running   snowing thick   was out of sight of land soon as started

Monday 31   Been in all day   cold with new snow in bushes out be nasty to travel   skinned & tended to five ermine & one cyotie   make pattern for cutting a pair of slip overs from a bear skin now 3 below at nine p.m.

CHAPTER 20

1935

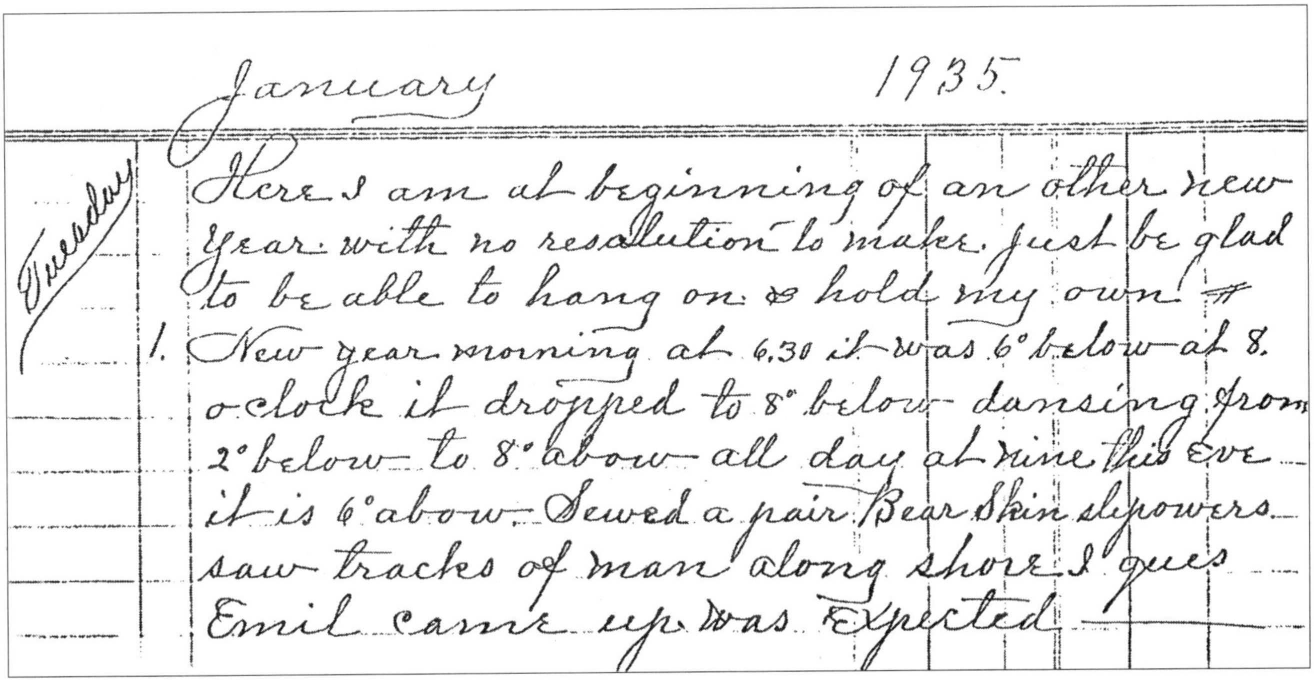

January   *1935.*

Tuesday

Here I am at beginning of an other new Year with no resolution to make. Just be glad to be able to hang on & hold my own #

1. New year morning at 6.30 it was 6° below at 8 oclock it dropped to 8° below dansing from 2° below to 8° abow all day at nine this eve it is 6° abow. Sewed a pair Bear Skin slipowers. saw tracks of man along shore I gues Emil came up was Expected ——

Wednesday 2   was busy all day mending old clotches   about ten o clock John Canon came up from Bear Creek   going on the hill after som blankets but I talked him into stay over till tomorrow

Thursday 3   I went with John Canon up Indian to show him the beginning of my Hogback Trail he was back here at one o clock with his blankets and belongings   had lunch & started for home I was overhauling motor & fixing tings for a trip

Friday 4   Intended to go down lake but a heavy swell came up   lake to rough to get of shore without getting wet   so I cut a couple trees out of wood trail that fell in   hauled them home light snowfall   warm

Saturday 5   Ran down to birchwood   landed boat   put my tings on sled & went down to Friman not snow anough the shoes cutting gravel   no rim ice or icewall

Sunday 6   went down to Ohlson creek   som loos snow but walking fair   hardly any tracks of game

Monday 7   went up to Lick House   foggy   drizly snow   mild anough to make it wet   no snow on ridge

Tuesday 8   went acrost country to north fork of Funny river   wet snow falling all day   went up stream to look over traps to be ready to start back in morning   no snowshoes   snow getting deep

Wednesday 9   A foot of new snow and 8 miles to next cabin   got there allright but mighty tired just manage to get fire in stove   tumbled in to sleep an hour

Thursday 10   Came down to freeman   had lunch & went to Toms   stay all night playing penocle

Friday 11   Started this morning by making a bushing into a nut for fly wheel of my motor   got it on it   worked like a new machine   called at Bear Creek with word to John Canon from Tom Odale   met John at landing

Saturday 12   At home tending to housekeeping mending tings   had a bath   washed clotches anyway I have kept fairly busy all day   weathre warm

Sunday 13   Intended crossing the lake to day but know it could not be did even befor I got out of bed   hearing a south easter howling in timber so I set yeast   heated water   scrubbed floor tok a walk to Emils place   talked to Ole

Monday 14   At home all day making bread warm   thermometer at 30 abow

Tuesday 15   Was out on glaser flatts   saw a lot of cyotie tracks   Stanley Pearson came up from Bear Creek   Ole Matson came over this evening ice making

Wednesday 16   Stanly left this morning for Bear Creek & Birchwood   I went out starting chopping trail   took me to sunset to get one mile out   mostly new trail   came to first bench Emma Trail

Thursday 17   Stay in to noon my back being stif got a kink at lifting a tree out of the trail yesterday went out continue with trail   got to summit sawed out lot of fallen trees   changed trail at times when it was croked or easier to cut a new foggy   18 abow

Friday 18   I saw two men on scates going down lake   presumable Emil & Ollie   I went up on flats set out twelf traps for cyotie   had one before that   make thirteen   hope its unlucky for cyotes

Saturday 19   Cleared my net   coiled it ready to set   hauled pole & outfit to glaser stream   set the net   after I came home I tok my scates started for Bear Creek   Ice bad from Chase monument got a lot of books   (mild)

Sunday 20   was ill this morning after breckfast I lay down was reading to noon   got up putered around to one o clock   got on my scates ran to island   crossed to flats   came back by traps & net   two fish one ermine

Monday 21   was going to Lake Emma this morning but not feeling good anough to venture that long walk with climb trown in   so I been home doctoring   was out fishing got two makinaw 16 inch   2 below 7 a.m.

Tuesday 22   At home   rather cold to travel & I am not feeling good   tok a walk to flats   fished the net   got one splendid steelhead   was out got a dry birch pevy stock   (zero in morning)

Wednesday 23   was up early to go across to King Lake but looking at thermometer I changed my mind   it is 6 below and I am not well   if I tok a spell had to lay still a spell I be frozen   got one steelhead & on trout

Thursday 24   Still at home & as tings looks likely to remain   probably for som days   everyting indicate a cold spell   8 below zero this morning & 7 below at 8 p.m.

Friday 25   8 below again this morning   I have been in all day doing som tailoring   cold all day toward evening a cloud came up from south but disapeared at dusk   but traveling fast for cold weathre

Saturday 26   Snowing lightly more like a fogg coming down forming snow   4 abow   started acrost lake at 10:30   in ten minutes I lost sight of land   thick as a wall   got acrost found tracks of party

Sunday 27   was up to end of line using snowshoes the first time this season   started blowing from north   snow drifting   catch one mink six ermine

Monday 28   Mild   starting home   choping som windfalls along the trail   coming in towards here ran into water on ice   40 abow at 2 p.m.

Tuesday 29   After breckfast I tok fur of stritchers turned them   as a little new snow fell during night I hooked up Rex to bobsleds   hauled in two sticks just to keep road oppen   John Canon came   him & I tok a walk on glaser flats looking for cyotes   looked at few traps   I got two mink coming home fished net   Gust Ness & Ikey came on way to Clif House

Wednesday 30   A wet snow fell this morning but tined out about nine o clock   so I went up to lake Emma   thick fog all time   lot of tracks of cyotes   set 17 traps   6 mink & ermine sets the rest for lynx cyotes & wolferine   mild

Thursday 31   Have been in all day & busy but to describe any outstanding ting I find it hard to find that I have acomplished   making ready for a trip down lake to run my traps   mild & windy

Friday 1 February   went down lake   stopped at Bear Creek & at Birchwood   meet Emil on his way up acompanyd by Ed Lovedall   Ed just was on a trip acrost lake   I got to Friman early

Saturday 2   was down to Ohlson Creek without snowshoes   snow rather deep   made heavy day of it

Sunday 3   went up to Lick house   fine day broke trail snowshoing thru loose snow   not very deep

Monday 4   Put in a extra heavy day   turned mild   snow got sticky   had to make last three miles on foot   fourteen inch loose snow

Tuesday 5   waded up north fork Funy River two miles   wet   a drizly rain fog   I started cavin in

Wednesday 6   Stay at cabin   mild   rainy   cut down spruce split it scooped out halfs to build a new roof   made twelf scoops foot wide   so I put in fair day even I had to dodge in when rain squals hit

Thursday 7   Snowshoed back to Lick House fine going   made trip in four & one half hour

Friday 8   Came down to Friman   stoped for lunch & put tings in order   came on to toms place   stay all night getting news   listen to Radio   came in fine exept anchorage

Saturday 9   Colder this morning   Tom Odale hooked up his dog team coming along to Bear Creek   ice broken along shore making it dangerus   meet Lovedahl starting for Kussilof mended my net   my fish pole blown away making yeast   weather still mild   foggee

Sunday 10   Started early to make bread & turned out a nice large batch   betwin time I tended to my catch of fur   lost a steelhead in hauling net tok a bath the last ting befor going to bed

Monday 11   Tok a run out to glaser flats climbed up on gull pininsula   found the ice broken clean acrost to south shore   por chance of getting over now unles we get a cold spell caught no trout again

Tuesday 12   Tok me to ten o clock befor I had the chores done then I went to Lake Emma   I got thirteen traps set   only seven traps was in order

Tom Odale and his dog team on the north shore of Tustumena by Fox Point. Photo courtesy of McLane Collection.

got two ermine one lynx two porcupine   one mink pulled out

Wednesday 13   Started cutting birch for my wood suply   worked to about two   got a cord or more ready to haul when we get som snow   was out fishing   coming in fell off the sled   hurt my shoulder   afraid I be crippled for a spell   still mild   not tawing   22 abow 7 a.m.

Thursday 21   Clouding up south west   look like more snow   cut birch this am   hauled it in afternoon   I think I got anough   lake bad water on ice in places

Friday 22   Started in good time this morning as I saw it ready to snow and lot of new snow befor to breck thru   it caut me   snowed all time   got wet   heavy tramp   got one mink

Saturday 23   Rain & snow coming down heavy turned to rain 38   up repairing two pairs of slipovers   saw Emil on my way to fish

Sunday 24   Been in to day not feeling good fixing som wearing apearal   still wet out   cleared towards evening   started yeast for bread

Monday 25   Made a smole batch of bread heated water   had a bath and got into clean clotches   fished net got two makinaw

Tuesday 26   Cold this morning so I ventured to cross the lake   at that I went way towards windy point   found lots of oppen holes but generaly stonger ice then I expected   tok in traps along lake shore   crossed ridge to King Lake   after lunch went & tok in traps at rat lake creek (clouding up)

Wednesday 27   Snowing and looking nasty out yes I am sure glad I went and tok in traps   last night came a cross ridge snow   getting wet   a dog team have gone down south shore   snow so thick that it took me 3 hours fifteen minuts to cross lake   dropped ink well   got ink splattered over whole page

Thursday 28   went down Lake   stopped in at Bear Creek had lunch with Pete Kalning   loose snow getting deeper   was all tired when I got to Toms birchwood   stay all night

Friday 1 March   went down to Friman   walking bad   snowshoed all way   ice sinking   got snowshoes icy

Saturday 2   went to Ohlson creek   fairly good traveling   creek filled with flow ice   lost a number of traps

Sunday 3   Snowshoed to Lick House   weathre rather cold   saw several moose & great number of ptarmigans

Monday 4   went to Castle Inn   hard day   sinking bad in loos snow   Prince creek & north fork frozen

Tuesday 5   Put in a big day splitting schoops for roof & to cold to be lacy so I had to work fast to keep warm

Wednesday 6   Again a big day   made a snow shovel   cleaned of snow   stripped off old roof put on new one

Thursday 7   On my way home ward   got to Lick Hous in good time   hunted a porcy for dog feed & fixed tings in order for sumer lay over

Friday 8   Came to Friman & on to Tom Odales stay all night playing penocle & listen to radio John Canon was there chopping wood   we got lot of news about air ship getting lost & revolution in grece politicks and ice worms

Saturday 9   Coming home from Birch wood using snowshoes to Bear Creek   at caribou point a cyotie came out on ice & had nerve anough to come with in range of my 22 stevens pistol   I hit him in the hind part and he put up som dance stopped at Bear Creek   put a new mainspring in my watch & now got stove full of kettles

Sunday 10   Snowing this morning with foggy thicknes   at noon it quit   was up to glaser stream   set out trout net   saw tracks of cyotes made during snow

Monday 11   Was up on glaser flats   tok in som cyotie traps   killed a cyotie with 22 pistol   tok in trout net   no trout   weathre fine   below frizing in morning

Tuesday 12 Three abow zero this morning at 6:30 stay in to noon filing a saw went down to Bear Creek with trout net

Wednesday 13 was up to Lake Emma to put away som traps left aroun when snowstorm caught me Feb 22 cyotes made a rawe this morning tok big rifle got no shot

Thursday 14 Got up early heated water washed som clotches later scrubbed the floor just then Ole Matson came in stopped for tea Hershey went by started snowing I tok a walk to Bear Creek

George Hirshey was back at the lake mining gold. In 1934 he filed on two new placer claims about four miles up Indian Creek.[1]

Friday 15 Foggy this morning about ten am John Cannon came from Bear Creek we tok a walk on glaser flats loking for a shot at cyotes did not see any

Saturday 16 got up early had brecfast set bread John Canon started down my bread dough working fast work it to loaves had it baked befor noon rised to high nearly colapsed started raining snow disapearing

Sunday 17 At home all day and noting acomplished had to go thru my watch again it keept stopping it has run twelf hours now since I fixed it weather mild snow melted of the roof

with south east wind lake commence to look blue as snow disapears Hershey team went down to Birchwood

Monday 18 Dried up during the night was out cut som birch hauled in three loads got all I wants Ole Matson was in to see me this morning saw 2 cyotes

Tuesday 19 Tok a walk to glaser flat found my net pole in ice saw tracks of cyotes but did not see any after I got back I tok som tools went out chopped my pole out off ice ice very slick fell and hurt my shoulder (weathre fine)

Wednesday 20 Not feeling good this morning lay down after eating it started to snow about two hours later cleared up tok a run to Bear Creek had Pete Doctor my shoulder fished net got four trout

Thursday 21 Stay in all day my shoulder to sore to do any work and I got a new book from Bear Creek that was itching to be read warm clouded up snow flurry this eve

Friday 22 Strong westerly wind and mild anough to make it wet been in all day and done noting (reading)

Saturday 23 Blowing hard from north tok a run on glaser flats loking for cyotes got into a voley of wind nearly froze before I got to timber have not been feeling good (24 abow)

An example of a gold sluice set up on Indian Creek, circa 1939. Work does not get much harder than this. Photo by Joe Secora, courtesy of Ella and John Secora.

> ***ANCHORAGE DAILY TIMES***
> March 22, 1935
>
> ### Navigation On Cook Inlet For Season Opening
>
> ### Arrivals Of Discoverer And Kasilof Sunday Marks Opening For 1935
>
> The motorships Discoverer and Kasilof left Seward last evening for Seldovia, Kenai, Kasilof and Anchorage. They were scheduled to be at Seldovia at 10 o'clock today and to arrive at Kenai and Kasilof early tomorrow morning, remain there during the day and will arrive at Anchorage at 7 o'clock Sunday morning to unload cargo. They will be the first ships to arrive in Anchorage this year. Their arrival marks the opening of the 1935 season of navigation on Cook Inlet.
>
> [Heinie Berger added the *M.S. Kasilof* to his fleet this year. He had it built as a replica of the original *Discoverer*, but on a smaller scale.[2]]

Sunday 24   2 abow zero this morning and a gale of wind brewing   it feel as cold as any time this winter   getting short of wood   sawed one stick of birch   first this winter   (calm to night)

Monday 25   2 below zero this morning   stay in to noon   John Canon came to see me about ten o clock   stay to one   then I went out and got som dry timber to repenish my wood

Tuesday 26   2 abow   was out cut a dry spruce hauled it in   weathre fine   clear   turning warmer

Wednesday 27   10 abow   waited to eleven o clock   tok a run to islands loking for a shot at cyotes   did not see any   got back at two rested a while   went to Bear Creek   got a trout and som old moose meat for dog feed

Thursday 28   Have been sawing up som sticks for firewood but my shoulder bother me   milder about 28 this morning

Friday 29   Started to make bread this morning but my yeast was slow so I done wait to in after noon   however I got it in the oven & it looks good   weathre mild

Saturday 30   I broke the spring in my watch again   drilled a new hole   put it in but somting is wrong   wont run   started to saw up som wood to fill shed for next winter

Sunday 31   warm and wet out so I stay in   had a bath washed som clotches   lay around reading som cheap periodicals   at dusk I sawed couple sticks of wood

Monday 1 April   was up to glaser flats this morning   saw tracks of cyotes but did not see one   cut up som wood   ice are getting bad open holes comence to apear

Heinie Berger's new motorship Kasilof *at Berger's dock on the Kasilof River. Photo courtesy of George Pollard.*

ANCHORAGE DAILY TIMES

April 3, 1935

Augustine Isle At Mouth Cook Inlet Is Now Roaring Volcano

Long Silent Volcanic Cone Breaks Into Action — Pilot Roy Dickson And George L. Johnson Of Anchorage Fly Around Place And View Magnificent Spectacle

Augustine Island, long slumbering beautiful pine cone rising sheer from green waters of the sea off the mouth of Cook Inlet is a roaring volcano, hurling a mighty volume of smoke into the heavens, pounding thousands of tons of lava down the sides into the sea and hurling dust over the areas for a radius of seventy miles.

News to this effect was brought yesterday by Pilot Roy Dickson of the Star Air Service, returning here from that vicinity, after flying over and around the roaring inferno, accompanied by George L. Johnson of this city. Mr. Johnson took a moving picture of the volcano in action.

Dickson and Johnson describe Augustine as one of the most awe-inspiring and magnificent sights they ever witnessed. Huge clouds of vapor are rising from the high cone, oozing from a main rupture in the center of the peak, and from cracks at various places about the top. The cone has an altitude of 3900 feet above the sea.

The Augustine rises cone shaped sheer from the waters of the sea, For many years it has been dormant, and has presented the aspect of a reddish cone, having only a narrow border of land about the bottom, where for a long time wild strawberries have thrived. Now they are buried under the flood of lava and deposit of ash, and the material pouring down the steep sides pours into the sea at many places. Huge pieces of black material, lava or other light substance from the cone float on the waters.

The smoke seems to be blowing chiefly toward Bristol Bay. Dickson and Johnson visited the volcano several days ago, flew over and around it several times, and attempted to return, but cloudy weather prevented the return. They flew there from Illiamna.

Tuesday 2   Have put in a good day on the woodpile   got first rick finis   9 feet long 6 feet high   snow going fast   (cloudy)

Wednesday 3   went down to Friman   stoped at Bear Creek to see P.K.   toward eve John Canon came up from Ohlson place where he is cutting house log   I started cutting.

Cannon started building a cabin on the lake shore west of Friman, near Ohlson Creek. Berg also began cutting logs for a new cabin for himself at Friman.

Thursday 4   I worked hard hauling in logs & cutting more   hard sleding as snow is intirely gone   went to toms place to get news of the radio

Friday 5   mild but still I got the logs to place cut & hauled som more   sharpened saw & ax cut logs below place

Saturday 6   under tok to haul logs up hill   to heavy had to quit   started cut up hill   went with John to Tom Odals place

Andrew's new cabin was about twelve feet wide by fourteen feet long. The logs he was hauling were at least that long and averaged over eight inches in diameter.

Sunday 7   Raining to day   cleared after nine came to camp   started to rain heavy   kept it up all day   John came back wet

Monday 8   Cold   everyting icy   fine sledding finis hauling   went to toms place on my way home   ice getting soft near shore

Tuesday 9   John Canon & I came up from Birch wood to Bear Creek   stay there a half hour Emil Berg & Charles Sands came from Sands place going to Emils   (snow dust)

Wednesday 10   Frosty this morning   stay home sawing wood   cut & split half a rick   busy hunting sqirrels   (cloudy)

Thursday 11   was up to glaser flats to bring in a bunch of traps that I left to I got better   going tok a walk to Emils place   saw Emil and Charles

Sands   ice are getting rotten holes in places of snow drifts

Friday 12   Have sawed a lot of wood to day started the last rick this evening   Charles Sands came this fornoon stay about an hour   started snowing & keept it up all day so the smole ground are covered   (North wind)

Saturday 13   Taking advantage of the new snow I went and cut a house log   hauled it hom   faced and peeled it as I got a bad log to replace   dont know if I be able to get it done this spring as I have piled up work   probably more than I have time to acomplish

Sunday 14   Sawing wood   finis all birch   got a couple of spruce sticks left   making yeast making bread to morow

Monday 15   Making bread   drew temper in one of my knifs & worked it into a sheep horn handle (blowing)

Tuesday 16   An easterly wind blowing with squalls of rain so I stay in nearly all day   main feild of ice moving

Wednesday 17   Snowing all day   just cold anough so that ground is still white this evening but turnin to water fast   (calm cloudy)

Thursday 18   Cut a dry spruce the first ting this morning   hauled it in on remains of new snow   Charles Sands & Kalning from Emils where they been cutting shingles started to move

Friday 19   A fine day been putting tings away hanged up a bunch of traps   kinked my back (mosquitos plenty)

Saturday 20   went down lake over ice   stoped at Bear Creek   got three nice trout from Pete got to Freeman early

Sunday 21   working at building new cabbin   got the foundation squared   walked up & got a pece of net

Monday 22   Keept me busy all day to get down four logs and at that I did not get the fourth finis

Tuesday 23   Had net in a crack of from shore got four nice trout   working with logs

Andrew was joining the logs at the corners with a dovetail notch. He also scribed the logs lengthwise so they would fit together with no gaps.

Wednesday 24   There was frish bear tracks when I got to Freman on the 20th   raining all day

Thursday 25   Raining on morning   cyotes serenaded me all night

Friday 26   working hard put in a full round   tok a walk this evening saw som moose but no bears

Saturday 27   A little new snow this morning but turned out fine later   put in a good day   have the wals up halfways

Sunday 28   Came home to day   was sure surprised to find lake free of ice this side of lake point   saw Pete

Monday 29   Tok a walk up Indian river to day trying to find som quartz but to much ice & it my be covered with gravel   saw lots of sheep tracks one family of bears   crossed lake Emma on ice Pete Kalning have been up from Bear Creek   left a note that Frency was back up from Kenai   no other news

Tuesday 30   At home making bread   tok nearly all day   finis the flour so I will be moving as I finish this lot of twelf loaves   getting cloud fixing to rain   (mosquitoes)

May Wednesday 1   was up early and started work rightaway   first put a round of logs on cribb at landing   was to old millsite for drift bolts   gathered all larger rocks   filled the crib and smotin beach for boats   sawed up a larg spruce to finis last rick of wood   tok vegetables up from cellar   sorted seed potatoes

Thursday 2   Have been busy all day and noting perticular that I could mention to show for it blowing quite hard this evening   loking like it my rain

Friday 3   went down to Friman   came back ninth and hurry planting potatoes & garden truck

Friday 10   Just ready to start down   have to stop at Toms   Pete are planting toms garden

ANCHORAGE DAILY TIMES   May 21, 1935

Kenai Highway Would Benefit Vast District

In accordance with assurances given weeks ago, Jack Lean, mail carrier between Cooper's Landing and Kenai the past winter, is circulating petitions praying for the construction of a highway between the two communities.

This embraces a distance of 70 miles, and the petition points out that the completion of such a road would connect Kenai, and Cook Inlet generally, with the rail belt, and besides being of permanent benefit to the peninsula the work of construction would furnish employment to "many needy individuals."

The petition, which is addressed to Anthony J. Dimond, delegate from Alaska to Congress, is being generously signed, residents of the district directly involved, and of Seward, realizing the vast importance of getting such a road, and the instant benefits to be realized with its completion.

The 125 names now attached to the petition represent only a portion of the bona-fide residents, people who have long desired such a road, and who propose to follow up the present appeal with other and stronger ones should doubts arise as to granting the request.

In speaking of the proposed road, Mr. Lean said: "Our petition is in line with the petitions that are now going in for the building of a highway between Homer and Kenai. The importance of such a road becomes at once apparent to anyone who has visited the areas involved."

"Besides opening a vast stretch of the country for settlement at a time when the government is selecting districts to carry out vast colonization plans that have been programmed, the road would connect Seward, creating heavy overland traffic from Cook Inlet to take advantage of such facilities...."

[The last paragraph refers to a relocation program established by the Federal Emergency Relief Administration and the Territory of Alaska. This year, one hundred and fifty-nine destitute farmers from Michigan, Minnesota and Wisconsin were moved to the Matanuska Valley northeast of Anchorage and provided with land, building assistance, schools, a hospital and a guaranteed market for whatever they could grow.[3] The guaranteed market was essential. Agricultural projects in Alaska which overcame obstacles related to climate typically foundered due to the lack of local markets and the prohibitive cost of shipping products to larger population centers.]

Gardens, fish and game for victuals plus a little cash from trapping – these men were well set to weather a depression. The price they paid was unremitting hard work. Berg must have been feeling strong this year to start his new cabin at Friman.

Other area residents were pushing for government intervention. Roads connecting the communities of the Peninsula were a hot topic. They were sought for purposes of long term economic development and providing short term employment. The Civilian Conservation Corps continued to provide some jobs but the trails they were building in the National Forest were of no immediate benefit to the struggling citizenry.

Andrew made no entries in his journal over the summer, presumably he was working for the Bureau of Fisheries again. He never mentioned spending time at the gold claim he filed the previous year. Andrew was back briefly at his Home cabin in September with his claim partner, John Wik and others. They may have been mining or hunting.

Tuesday 10 September   Left Kenai 11:07 a.m. got here 9:15 p.m.   fastest trip I ever made   from Kenai that is   I John Wik Alfred Wik & Mike Juliusson all of Kenai stopped at Kasilof Abrams place & Bear Creek

Andrew returned in November with lumber for the new cabin in addition to his usual winter supplies.

Friday 1 November   Came up from Kasilof yesterday   to havy [too heavy] load   had to relay at Silver Salmon   met Harpham at slack water   peel off [unloaded] four hundred feet of flooring at Friman   got here at seven   Ed Lovedahl went back to Kasilof this morning   been busy putting away my suplies

Saturday 2   Slipy all day   cooked & canned a lot of fruits   Tony & Cedar came in about mid day from where they are working at plaser mining making som net corks this evening   weathre rainy mild & calm

SEWARD GATEWAY

September 24, 1935

Bureau Surveys Spawning Areas Kenai Regions

Concluding a three-weeks survey of Tustumena lake, adjacent spawning grounds and the Kenai river, W. B. Berry, Bureau of Fisheries warden of Cook inlet, was in town Friday to make his annual trip to Seattle.

Mr. Berry reports that Dolly Varden trout have been reduced by 300,000 by the activity of trout fishermen employed by the bureau in the Kenai region this year, that many fish having been caught and turned over to fox farmers to be reduced to fox food.

The fish, said Mr. Berry, are fearful destroyers of salmon spawn and fry, 415 salmon eggs being found in one fish alone. A trap device is used in catching the fish, from which rainbows and other sporting fish are released unharmed.

The matter of clearing streams and lakes of the destructive dollies has proved a problem to the bureau, and renewed effort is being put forth to do the work....

Sunday 3   Have been busey all day making net corks & got them on the net   wind sprung up from south east with rain   mild as sumer

Monday 4   Blowing a gale all day   stay in doing noting wort mentioning   not feeling good

Tuesday 5   Stay in nearly all day fixing sinkers on the net   towards evening was out to get vilow bark   cooked up a tub of tan   tanned the net & got it ready for fishing   set som yeast making ready for making bread   weathre fine

Wednesday 6   At home making bread   at noon Tony & Ceder came of their claim stating it was getting to cold to work as tings are frezing up for them

Thursday 7   Tok the old alto apart   cleaned out oil leads & tank   did not try it   spliced my net rail & set out the net   first time   clear

Friday 8   Got a lot of trout & two salmon this morning   try out motor   not doing good fixed botom schiff   found I lost gazoline   cut windfalls out of trail

Saturday 9   not feeling to good   stay in all day had a bath   wash som clotches   scrubbed floor clear

Sunday 10   At home   put in most of day at mending net that I tore badly while setting it the first time   just cant get started at anyting

Monday 11   Had an other rasle with that old motor   tok it apart   cleaned tank & oil line   set the net   put in som new panes in window reputied   clouding up

Tuesday 12   Clouded up during the night starting to snow   Tony & Cedar came by on way to Kenai   Emil went later

Wednesday 13   At last I think I found the truble with the elto   had it running fairly smoot to day tok in net and repaird & retempered ax so I been busey all day   new snow on ground   clear

Thursday 14   Cold this morning   have been busey puting up provisions & making ready for a extended trip to my cabins at Friman & funy river   it my be rather cold to go

Friday 15   Sleept until late this morning & yet it was down to eight   rather cold to set in the boat tok a walk out   saw tracks of several difrent furbearers

Saturday 16   Shoved the boat out   loaded started motor   it ran fine to I got into a sloppy head sea   it quit   had to pull back   looked thru machine   carburator pluged

Sunday 17   Started again to day but only got motor running a few miles   it quit   pulled to birchwood   stay all night

Monday 18   Pulled down to friman   put ting to order in old cabin

Tuesday 19   was to Ohlson Creek   tok in all traps to lick house trail

Wednesday 20   Chopped up trail out of Cow cannon

Thursday 21   was up to trail lake locating som traps I lost

Friday 22   looked up som posibly cyote sets

Saturday 23   Cold   windy   chopped som wood   stay in

Sunday 24   Went up to lick House   stormy   fine walking

Monday 25   Crost country running to Castle In

Tuesday 26   Snow falling   fixing cabin chopping wood

Wednesday 27   afraid to stay longer   no snowshoes   start back

Thursday 28   Came from Lick House to Friman

Friday 29   Snowing   was out grubbing trail stay at Friman

Saturday 30   Ab Erikson   Ed Lovedahl   Ed Zettles came by up for a sheep hunt

Sunday 1 December   Snowing & blowing when I left Friman   stopped at Toms returning mattoc pulled on to Bear Creek   got som pototoes & rutabaga from Pete   got here at dark   Abraham Erikson came over late   stay all night   left at day breck for sheep hunt   cold

Monday 2   Stay home all day making bread   set the net   Abram came in late after getting a ram

Tuesday 3   Been home all day repairing tings in fishing the net I broke the setting rail so I fixed that   fastned the handle on ax   ground it mended som clotches   got four trouts & one steelhead   weathre fine   14 abow   Abram came over this evening   he is leaving tomorrow

Wednesday 4   Got up this morning at five o clock made breckfast as Abraham Erikson was leaving for Kasilof   they left at ten   I got fixing my snowshoes   intended to tramp trail   went thru to lake Emma   saw one cyote   set out eleven traps   started blowing

Thursday 5   A heavy wind to day & cold   tok in net   six larg makinaw trout   cleaned motor tok a walk trying for a shot at cyotes   (down to zero)

Friday 6   2 below this morning   about noon Ed Lovdahl came over   burod four steel traps   I set six mink traps on indian this evening

Saturday 7   9 below this morning   waited to after ten went out Emma trail   set eleven traps combined cyotie & lynx sets   wind cold strong

Sunday 8   5 below this morning & keept below all day to this evening   moisture in air make it feel cold   in all day reading

Monday 9   5 down   waited to nearly midday to get warmer   pulled out with sciff   wind sprung up   hard pull to get in   wind quit   to late to go

Tuesday 10   Looked like cloud this morning but it was only fog   a storm sprung up shaked som snow dust out and left it clear as a bell   went out in boat   caught in blow   cut up a trail   set few traps on flatts

Wednesday 11   5 down   to cold with strong wind blowing & noting particular to tend to so I stay in mending clotches   set out net   had a bath   calm this evening at about zero

Thursday 12   A fog hanging high & a dust of snow falling   thermometer at 8 below   I waited

---

ANCHORAGE DAILY TIMES

December 7, 1935

First Flights of Air Mail to Kenai, Kasilof Attract Stamp Collectors in States

Another barrier in "America's Last Frontier" was torn down last week when pilot Chet McLean made the initial flight of the new mail route from Anchorage to Kenai and Kasilof.

Two flights have already been made from Anchorage to the Kenai district. Pilot McLean left last Wednesday and Pilot Oscar Winchell left yesterday.

Stamp collectors from all over the country mailed letters to the postmasters at Anchorage, Kenai and Kasilof for cancellations from this initial flight...

Formerly mail was taken by train to Moose Pass and from there by dog sled to neighboring towns. Time of mail arrival depended largely upon the weather.

Under the present arrangement mail is carried by plane to Kenai and Kasilof and then distributed by dog sled to neighboring communities. Two planes a month are scheduled to carry freight and passengers besides the mail over the route.

to noon went to Lake Emma   set all traps exepting two smole   nearly froze handling traps

Friday 13   3 up   stay in to day   put new foot web in snowshoes   fished net got anough trout tok in net   washing clotches   tending furs   got one ermine this evening & mink last night

Saturday 14   warm this morning   tok a walk to flats to look over mink sets   saw one track   met Ed Lovedahl   he got a cyotee

Sunday 15   went down lake   called at Bear Creek   pulled all the way to Birch wood   met Cuningham who is visiting Tom & John

Monday 16   Pulled thru rain to Friman   just time   dry then dark

Tuesday 17   was to Trail Lake   set net   raining & blowing

Wednesday 18   To nasty & wet to go   cut wood between rain squalls

Thursday 19   Tok in net   got eighteen trouts went up to Lick House   tough tramping   lot of snow on the ridge   to wet to use snowshoes

Friday 20   Went acrost to Castle on north of Funy river   2 mink

Saturday 21   Came back to Lick House   lot of water in streams

Sunday 22   Came out   Tony went to Kenai Christmass

Monday 23   John Canon went to Hugos   I to Ohlson Creek

Tuesday 24   pulled up to toms   John got back had a fine time celerating   getting news over radio   a game at cards   even som highland fling

Wednesday 25   Tom & Mr Cuningham came with me to Bear creek using Toms motor   I got here at two o clock running Toms machine   warm temperature   32 abow

Thursday 26   I pulled up to glaserflats   crossed on to fish creek   loking over a few mink traps no sighn of any game   slipery   started to rain havy as I got back   stritched som furs

Friday 27   Stay in making bread & cutting snowshoelace   warm

Saturday 28   went up to Lake Emma   going in I saw Emil in timber aways of   shouted helo   he did not answer   most traps foul   saw cyotee got a lynx

Sunday 29   waited to nearly noon before fur on lynx was dry to stritch it   Tony & Ike came up got my mail

Monday 30   was up to mtn   saw 2 rams in alders   climbed up   alders thick   just saw one got a smole one   22 abow

Tuesday 31   Had a lazy spell   stay all day reading som western story trash & sleeping by spells   a little coler   down to thirteen up this morning

CHAPTER 21

1936

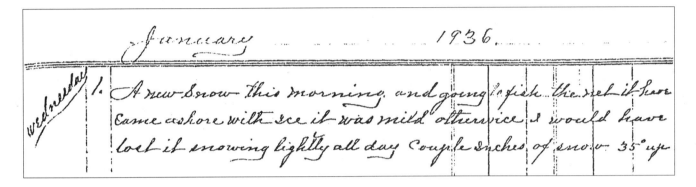

January   *1936.*

Wednesday 1. A new snow this morning and going to fish the net it have came ashore with ice it was mild otherwice I would have lost it snowing lightly all day couple inches of snow 35° up

Thursday 2   *Stay in to noon*   *did not like to go wallowing in new snow but decided to take a look at som traps at islands*   *no game*   *walking bad with loos snow over icy ground*   *22 up*

Friday 3   *at home*   *awake at two*   *ligted lamp got a book lay reading to nearly morning then slept to nine o clock*   *befor I had time to start day was gone & noting acomplished*

Saturday 4   *Have put in all day mending my trout net that got caught in ice*   *not feeling so good*   *had a spell of tings going black for my eyes*   *som snow fluries but clearing*   *turning cold*

Sunday 5   *Snowing & coming down good*   *all of six inches this evening*   *I was debating wath I better do this morning*   *finaly tok motor a part & reasembled*   *found one loose bolt*   *tok me all daylight*   *set the net*   *18 up*

Monday 6   *Cloudy dull day*   *tok a walk along Indian*   *no game tracks exepting cyotes*   *loose snow makes hard walking with slick ice under weathre at about 20 up*

Tuesday 7   *Put up 16 jars of preserves to day intended cross the lake but got up late*   *not feeling so good*   *thick fogg over lake*   *no ice this morning 13 up*

Wednesday 8   *Up in good time this morning intending to cross the lake but found young ice making so I went over hill to lake Emma*   *from top I could see ice making in larg fields*   *Devils Bay is froze over for som time as the ice are covered with snow or frost*   *cought noting*   *saw track of lynx*   *this morning 9 up*

Thursday 9   *Started to snow this morning & later a wind sprung up*   *I thinking it be a fine chance to get a shot at cyotes went up on flats*   *wandering around all day & never saw a ting alife*   *met Mr Cedar*   *18 up*

Friday 10   *Raining with voleys of wind off glaser stay in all day*   *mended & washed six pair of sox*   *cleaned snow of boat*   *set net*   *trying to run motor*   *fixed sled*   *loaded with traps & bait to set for cyotes if weathre permit*   *42 up*

Saturday 11   *was out by day put loded sled in boat*   *pulled to glaser flats*   *harnes dog*   *sleded to Rays mines*   *got som meat*   *started at uper island set 23 traps for cyotes*   *cut trail*   *30 up*

Sunday 12   *Loaded tings in boat*   *started toms motor*   *ran into ice before I got to Guides camp*

put tings on sled   left motor at toms   no one home   sleded along beach to Friman

Monday 13   went to Ohlson creek   met John Canon   went to toms   stay all night listening in to radio news

Tuesday 14   walked back to Friman & up to Trail lake looking over traps

Wednesday 15   went up to Lick house on funy cold head wind crossing sumit

Thursday 16   acrost coutry to north funny   cold but fair going   10 down

Friday 17   about ten inches of new snow   poor snowshoes   tok me five hours twenty minutes to rich Lick House   mild

Saturday 18   Came from Friman to Toms late after I came from Lick House   ice sinking making bad travel

Sunday 19   Came home from toms   stoped in at Bear Creek   going poor   folowin cracks watered thru   30 up

Monday 20   Raining to flood everyting   larg pools of water on top of ice   snow on ice intirely gone   set out net at Indian   saw oppen water to wards head of lake   this eve I hear ice grinding with storm my open   it is at 38 up yet

Tuesday 21   was up to Lake Emma to day   tok snowshoes up to first bench   decided it to wet to use snowshoes so I left them   cyote got one of my traps & clog befor last snow   have to mak an other trip to try to find it   40 up

Wednesday 22   was up trying to find my lost trap & cyote but to much snow have fallen   could not find it   located several places where it been tangled & biting brushes   30 up

Thursday 23   Loked rainy but as it apear ice is going so I huried to cross   saved som walk but got into a rain storm   got in at 2 p.m. wet   ice still hold   storm   40 up

Friday 24   Ice disapeard during night   blowing & raining hard   no ice as far as I can see   ice tok my net but I found it with two makinaw one

fine steelhead   made big batch of bread & doing other culinary work   45 up   snow gone

Saturday 25   Still raining steady all day but wind quit   only a cats paw ones in a while   stars out this evenng   was fixing up som bedding   had a tutch of indigestion so I keept to bed bigest part of the day   38 up

Sunday 26   Started late going to look for missing cyotee   met tony & ceder going to my place they came along with me   tok a look at Lake Emma   came on here got home about 1:30 found Icky Ness & young holden here having came up with my boat from Birchwood   stay all night so we had a set of Penocle & one man over 42 up

Monday 27   All visitors left me after we got thru with target shoot   I went into clean up trail for hauling in wood   cut couple loads of green birch snow all gone   frost leving the ground   tretening to rain   windy   42 up

Tuesday 28   Blowing hard last night and continued moderatly all morning   been out cutting timber for wood & leveling trails to stack frozt leaving ground   raining som this evening 40 up

Wednesday 29   not feeling so good this morning had but very little sleep during night   Cedar came from Clif House with my schif   preserved seventeen jars of fruit   cut som wood

Thursday 30   Had another hunt for the lost cyotie snow all gone   no chance of finding him again ran the line of traps on Lake Emma   a porcupine have got in one set   cyotie tearing it to pieces no other signs of any fur animals   foggy   mild 34 up

Friday 31   Had a bad fall yesterday & this morning I feelt all sore raw bruised & even my intestines seems pulled out of place   been in bed nearly all day   towared evening I went to mouth of Indian river & set the trout net that blow in during storm   had to splice the pole in two places   drisling rain out of fog   38 up

Saturday 1 February   Still favoring som bruises was out couple hours cutting birch   later sawed up couple of spruce blown acrost my trail   lot of ice drifted in   calm   foggy   still warm   34 up

Sunday 2 Sleeping late had breckfast at nine lay reading waiting for hot water to wash clotches Cedar & Ike came   Ike going to Clif House   I went up on flats showing my trail   as we started saw emil coming up in dorey   foggy   30 up

Monday 3 Got up again late this morning everyting quite   temperature 28   ice building on lake   looks oily   scrubbed out cabin   20 up this eve

Tuesday 4 A wind sprung up broke up the ice that was forming   just got there in time to save my net   to cold with storm to be out so I stay in sewing a pair mule slippers   this evening 9 up

Wednesday 5 Put in a lazy day not feeling good stay in reading   Boys came from clifhouse on way to Kasilof   13 up

Thursday 6 Snow fall six inches during night & day   got busy haul in birch   I had cut about half I need   snowing   14 up

Friday 7 was up early this morning to have breckfast for boys on way to Kusilof   set yeast hauled in seven sticks of wood & cut eight more dropped my mit & pulover in Indian river   had to force my boat thru skim ice to get it   still boating   warm

Saturday 8 Started making bread this morning was out got four rabits   22 up this morning strong wind up lake   no ice in sight   hauled in eight sticks of wood   3 up this eve

Sunday 9 Thermometer showing temperatur going up & down all day   morning 14 up   10 a.m. 8 up   1 p.m. 18 up   8 p.m. 4 down   a thin skim of ice showing this morning   in after noon intirely gone   cut three birch trees   thats all for to day

Monday 10 Snowing this morning   8 up   was out hauling few sticks of wood this afternoon so as to keep trail oppen   this cornor of lake is closed but can see oppen water southwest   12 up

Tuesday 11 went out late to lake Emma   loos snow   looked heavy but after I got on way it went good   no game exept moose   22 up this eve

Wednesday 12 was on my way to flats this morning but ice did hold so I came back   set net at Indian   fixed web in snowshoes   28 up

Thursday 13 went to glaser flats about eleven o clock   walked on young ice along lakeshore   it was that weak that it saged as I stept on it   cyotes tramped over three sets   just missed the traps loose snow makes tramping hard   got back four thirty   27 up   tawing at noon

Friday 14 Stay in to nearly noon   Pete Kalning came in on his way to Bear Creek   I went along aways to find out about ice   its very thin as far as I went   it was crecking avery step   cut down couple of birches   to warm to haul   44 up mid day

Saturday 15 was up in good time   hauled in the wood I had cut   stoped for lunch   went to fish net got one larg lake trout   cut three more birch trees   waited until four o clock then hould in wat be anough for next year   I belive I have biger wood pile then I ever had   starting to blow   27 up

Sunday 16 Snow dust during night   tok sled & dog try to cross to island   ice to poor   left sled walked along shore   waded creek   saw a snipe & two golden eye ducks   fished the net coming home got two nice trout   20 up

Monday 17 At home   had a bath & a real clean up after mending som clotches   feel like it mean to snow   cloudy   26 up

Tuesday 18 started for Friman camp   ice poor traveled on it right close to beach   stopped at bear creek for haircut   called at Tom Odale had lunch   went on thru to Friman   broken ice here

Wednesday 19 not feeling good   stay in camp all day   cut som wood

Thursday 20 Tony Johanson came along on his way to Kenai   I went with him as far as ohlson creek   sprung & tok in som traps   no sign of game exept cyoties

Friday 21   walked rather much yesterday   lay off today all day

Saturday 22   Started to upper cabins using snowshoes most of the way   found lot more snow over sumit

Sunday 23   went up to last cabin   sprung traps on three branches of funny river   caught one mink one cyote

Monday 24   Boarded up window   put tings in shape for summer   stepped in my snowshoes started back forgetting my pack sack fur mits parka speticles   walked 1 1/2 hours befor I thought of it   to late to return   continued clean to lake stormy

Tuesday 25   was to old lake trail & came to Toms   stay all night   meet one Thomas from Fairbanks   play Penocle

Wednesday 26   John Canon & Thomas started for Kasilof   I started home   stopped at Bear Creek   saw cyotie   got here early   12 down

Thursday 27   stay in to noon   went around islands up flats to upper noll   came down trap line   tok in all mink traps zero an   12 up eve

Friday 28   turned over slop bucket this morning the first ting & as tings started that way I decided to stay in and snowing out made it easy to decide Tony came up this evening from Kenai bringing mail & news   12 up

Saturday 29   Snow have fallen during night started blow   snow flying a regular blizard Tony went to see his parner   sewed pair of fur slip overs   cut som Birchwood   first this winter 4 up this eve

Sunday 1 March   snow drifting all day   stay in all day reading & sleeping   it was 4 up this morning   12 up to night

Monday 2   Making bread & it tok all day   made anough to last to later part of mont   look like in a flour mill outside   storm on   snow shaking out of trees   driftin all directions   30 up

Tuesday 3   walked to Indian river this morning found mout forzen where I used to have my net set   snow drifted in yesterdays blizard & froz tok a run to Bear Creek   ice sinking along lake shore   12 up

Wednesday 4   A fine day   14 up this morning feeling bum   stay in bed most of time

Thursday 5   was up to lake Emma   it started to snow as I went & falling faster I got back   made it tough going   sprung traps   to wet to take them in

Friday 6   Everyting covered with loose new snow to nasty in timber to do anyting so late this afternoon I kleaned up around the saw horse & cut thre logs   begining of next winter wood   13 up

Saturday 7   On the wood pile all day exepting when I had a little nap midle of the day   got quite a lot of wood for a start   just nice weathre 30 up

Sunday 8   Thote aque kept me a wake till towards morning   then I sleept to after seven a.m.   snowing all day   was out to indian River cutting ice to set net but to dirty to put out the net 28 up

Monday 9   Lot of new snow   I worked an hour cleaning snow away from wood pile & sawhors got nearly half my wood cut   was out to set the net this eve   getting cleare   22 up

Tuesday 10   Sleepy & drowsy not feeling right was in bed to seven this morning   did not do anyting to after noon then I worked at the wood pile couple of hours   hauled the net but not a trout   13 abow zero

Wednesday 11   At the wood pile   finis two ricks about 2/3 of the lot   started blowing in for noon in afternoon snow started falling   at five this evening started to go to net   had to turn back

Thursday 12   Had a sick spell to day   stay in bed most of time   in the afternoon I went to clear my net   in evening Ed Lovdall came up went to Emils for the night

Friday 13   Drizly snow coming down   went to glaser flatts saw four cyoties   it just hapened to be a thick spell   they looked to be to far   later I saw it was in range   did not shoot

Saturday 14   At hom feeling lacy   warm snow wet midle of day   tramped trail to som dry trees as my dry wood is running low   sawed few blocks of green birch   that all

Sunday 15   Hauled in a log of dry spruce this morning   started to snow   keept it up to nearly evening   sawed & split the log to wood   its the first wood for imeadit use I cut this year   lot of snow

Monday 16   9 up this morning so I huried to split up som wood I had sawed   tok me couple hours then I saw I was short of fruit so I cooked four gallon   put up 30 pint jars   snow this evening

Tuesday 17   On the wood pile   sawed few sticks found two next to imposible to split so I did not get much acomplished

Wednesday 18   Have a gale of wind from south with snow early in the day   finis the third rick to day   nearly thru   just about one days work to complete wood for next winter   from 20 to 30 up

Thursday 19   Still same kinds of weathre   cats paws of wind with fluris of snow   drowsy sleeping in spels   reading & sleeping   Ed Lovdall came in towards evening after a walk up Indian river   red sunset   18 up

Friday 20   I & Ed Lovdahl tok a walk on glaser flats loking for cyotoes   had a bunch stiring but saw none until I went home   Ed my have found them later   plane made several trips to day   28 up

Saturday 21   New snow again this morning   fine day to stay in but that is just wath I did   tired feeling   snow melting of roof at noon

Sunday 22   Just not feeling good   scrubbed floor   fished net got one makinaw   14 up

Monday 23   Still doing noting   looked like a mild spell to day   blowing toward evening but wind was from south by west   cloudy   32 up

Tuesday 24   was up to Lake Emma gathering traps   found 29   got back 1 p.m.   fished net got three trout   finis sawing birch   have to haul in more

Wednesday 25   4 abow zero this morning   split wath wood I had sawed   cut & hauled in couple of dry spruce logs   cut one into fire wood

Thursday 26   3 below zero this morning   waited to about eleve o clock when sun have warmed tings up   cut a few sticks of birch   hauled it in Ed came up from a visit to Toms

Andrew wasn't the only one "on the wood pile" at this time of year. This is Paul Wilson junior helping with chores in Kenai. Paul was likely one of the kids who enjoyed peppermint candy treats when Andrew was in Kenai. Photo courtesy of Ella and John Secora.

Friday 27   2 up this morning   made big batch of bread   busy all day

Saturday 28   Fine day   sawed up anough wood to have as much as I ever had & still lots of time to cut more   cloudy   14 up this a.m.

Sunday 29   In bed nearly all day   lay down after breckfast reading sleept & so on   snow is setting fast   40 up

Monday 30   was out on flats   tok in a load of traps   snow settling fast to day   so is ice   water getting up under snow

Tuesday 31   Had truble with my heart this morning wich was signal to lay low so I been in bed nearly all day   no work

Wednesday 1 April   hauled in a windfall for sumer firewood   had a bath washed som clothes   snow is nearly all melted of roof that been there mont   snow on roof longest I seen

Thursday 2   went down to freeman   stoped in at Bear Creek & toms at Birchwood   snow in drifts   traveling none to good

Friday 3   Cut som logs   hauled in one   not feeling good

Saturday 4   Cut & hauled in wath logs I neaded   rested up   went to Birch wood   Ed Lovedall here on way out   stay all night

Sunday 5   Ed started for Kasilof   I came home stoped at Bear Creek helped Pete haul out a timber   set my net after I got home   hunted rabits for dog feed   foggee   14 up

Monday 6   was up early   had breckfast   tok a nap   at eleven went out cut a larg spruce   cut two blocks   split shakes   worked steady to six

Tuesday 7   New snow this morning   waited expecting it to melt   no chance so after noon I went to split shakes   yesterday I cut a birch for two young moose   they was back to day   hearing me knocking at shakes   had a time chasing them to get a chance to fall tree & not hit them

Wednesday 8   Snowing all day & lot of snow for this time of year   trees full

Thursday 9   went to woods to get som dry spruce for firewood but it was to nasty   everyting full of loose snow   cut som on hand

Friday 10   Set my big saw first ting this morning at ten o clock as frost was geting out of wood I sawed three lengts & split shakes

Saturday 11   windows was icy this morning   after I had breckfast I lay reading   Tony came of the creek   had lunch   tok a walk aways up Indian after I got back sawed four blocks   split two to shakes   coming in my ears hurt from cold

Sunday 12   Easter Sunday   started to blow from north east   I expected it to turn mild   hauled out two loads of shakes & split couple of blocks   wind swing back to north west   cold

Monday 13   Started out late   cut a block & split few shaks   tony & ray came they are tawing ground prospecting   got one trout   (clouding)

Tuesday 14   Hauled out a load of shakes   tok home a load of wast cut & split   nearly two hundred square feet of shakes

Wednesday 15   Hauled wath I cut yesterday & finis the second tree   did not get anough as wath I cut to day was full of knots   warm

Thursday 16   Brought all shakes out I had cut & waste slabs & tools   later cruised timber   found a tree that split straight   felled it cut but block & split it to shakes   this tree gives me anough

Friday 17   Finis cutting shingles this morning   John Canon came up with mail for Emil & brought a dog for Tony   raining to day

Saturday 18   Brought out the last slack of shingles & waste for wood   sawed up a log for fire wood   snow melting fast   cloudy

Sunday 19   Tok in net this morning got one trout   hunted up som vilows   made the new bents in my old sled

Monday 20   was up early to make bread   yeast no good   warming it got it parlty scalded   started a new   put up 27 jars of fruit   set bread 4 p.m. soon ready to bake

Tuesday 21   was up on flats   started six got back at nine   had a bath   thought I heard sea guls yesterday but to day I heard them plane extraordinary late spring   frezing every morning

Wednesday 22   going down to Friman

Wednesday 29   Have been at Friman since 22 working at new cabin   came from Birchwood to day   meet Emil going out   ice just a floating skim   walked the beach all way

Thursday 30   Have been caulkin my schif   calm all fornoon   a cold wind sprung up & I quit   to night ice started to move

Friday 1 May   Finished caulkin this morning had a job scraping pitch of bottom   found som white paint   got boat ready when dry   ice are moving up and down but hardly any wind

Saturday 2   calm all fornoon   south east wind sprung up in afternoon   ice disapearing rapidly to night   oppen out of sight to windy point

Sunday 3   At home all day blowing & raining started yeast but no go   got som dead yeast cakes   the last I have   been here long

Monday 4   My yeast got sour   try to make new raining   sewed a pair of slippers   cant get anyting done

Tuesday 5   Stay in   washed a lot of clotches & made a dozen loves of bread   Ole Matson came in about noon   windy

Wednesday 6   Scrubed the cabin floor   walked down brought up boats   tok one to shake pile this evening   wind set one back before I finis burning grass   nearly destroyed cabin

Thursday 7   got tings in boats ready to go but wind rather strong

Friday 8   went to Camp Freeman   working at new cabin   finely finis   got back to day May 26 busy spading garden this eve

Wednesday 27   finished spadin & planted 112 stands   made a heavy maul & wedges   lifted one corner of cabin

Thursday 28   Making bread   rain storm prevented me doing anyting out

Wednesday 29   A storm on   fixed som lumber for combing to house   tok som moss

Andrew finished his new "Homestead" cabin at Freeman on May eighth. It still looks brand new in this picture taken in 1938 by L.J. Palmer, Bureau of Biological Survey biologist. Photo courtesy of Smithsonian Fish and Wildlife Service Records Group, Box 16, Folder 3.

ANCHORAGE DAILY TIMES

September 17, 1936

California Sportsmen Back From Kenai
Peninsula With 67-Inch Antlers From Moose

Three California Sportsmen were in Anchorage
today after a successful two weeks big game hunt during
which each bagged a sheep and a moose.

The men, Maxmilion von Romberg, a German baron
who established residence in the United States in 1928,
and Edmund C. and Roger Converse, brothers, came to
Alaska the last of August and flew immediately to
Tustamena Lake.

From their base camp they moved to a sheep camp
on the south fork of Indian Creek, where each bagged a
sheep. The party then moved to the south fork of Funny
River and each brought down a moose.

Roger Converse bagged the prize moose of the hunt,
with antlers that had 13 points on each side and a 67
inch spread, members of the party said.

Baron von Romberg and a guide, Earl Olmstead,
returned by plane last night and the Converse brothers,
with their guides, Harry Boyden and Tom O'Dale, came
in this morning. Pilot Al Horning brought the party in...

November 16, 1936

Berger To Take 22 To States On Two Boats
Discoverer and Kasilof To Sail On High Tide
Tomorrow Eve

Twenty-two persons have booked passage on the
motorships Discoverer and Kasilof, which are scheduled
to leave Anchorage tomorrow evening on the tide. It
will be the last trip of the season for the Berger boats.
Both will be overhauled at Seattle during the winter.

Passengers for the Discoverer include:

Mr. and Mrs. Guy Waddell of Homer, who are going
on a trip to the states. They will board the boat at
Homer in its outward journey.

Bonnie Bell, Daughter of U.S. Marshal and Mrs. Joe
Bell of Kenai, leaving for school Outside. She will be
picked up at Kenai.

Mrs. Alice Berger, wife of Captain Heinie Berger.
Mrs. Berger has been spending the summer at their
ranch at Kasilof and is going to Seattle for the winter....

*Thursday 30   working all day   tok a log out of
wall   fitted in new one*

*Friday 31   started to put ting in shape to travel
going out*

The Bureau of Fisheries report for this year showed Berg
as an employee. He worked as a stream guard at Fish
Creek from July 1 through August 15. At a daily rate of
five dollars, he earned a total of $230.[1] Tom Odale was
also listed in the report. He was hired to captain the
U.S.F.S. Teal at the lofty wage of $7 per day. (Another
sign of the times – stream guards were paid $7 per day
in 1930.) Tom later escorted another Bureau man on a
salmon escapement inspection and they left an entry in
Andrew's journal:

*August 22nd Saturday   Tom Odale & W. R.
Newcomb stopped in after looking over the
spawning grounds   fine country & plenty of red
Would buy you a drink but as how you are off
hard liquor well do the courtesy   Fine weather
W. R. N.*

Odale finished his work with the Bureau in time to guide
a trophy hunt which was written up in the *Anchorage
Daily Times*. The three hunters were from California
and included a former German Baron, an actor and the
actor's brother who was "connected with the national
Republican campaign."[2] Another party hunted the Kenai
Peninsula and Cook Inlet area collecting specimens for
the American Museum of Natural History at New York
City. The big game guiding business was still providing
employment opportunity.

Andrew was occupied in Kenai until early November.

*Friday November 6   Just put in a big day   left
moose horn 8:30 this morning   ran into head
wind wich lasted to Fox Point   stopped in at
Toms   saw John Canon   had tea   continued
home with toms machine making good time   got
here early   got all my suplyes packed up and
put away   everyting looks ship shape   Andrew*

*Saturday 7   Been fussing about with one thing
and an other but more aspeicialy digging
potatoes   spading at the same time   started
blowing from glaser this after noon   warm*

*Sunday 8   Started making bread this morning
after I got it going went & washed out my boat
tok in motor & repaired broken part   Ole Matson*

came in to weigh som gold dust   Emil not up yet   raining

Monday 9   was up Lake Emma trail cleaning out wind falls & looking country over   no game saw som grouse tracks of coyots & bears   frosty this afternoon   Emil came up but he was all alone   cleaned up carburator on toms motor cleaned boat

Tuesday 10   was out in good time   crossed lake by nine o clock   had nasty head wind   Packed new stove to King Lake Cabin   bears have smashed window   got back here after dark   put in big day   rain & snow in spels

Wednesday 11   To much of a day yesterday been in bed nearly all day   not realy sick just all in   clearing   getting cooler

Thursday 12   At home all day trying make ready to move to homestead   not feeling good   som snow fell this afternoon   cloudy

Friday 13   South west wind just strong anough to keep me from going down lake   got a little snow   just anough to light up the evening although it hardly cover the ground

Saturday 14   Started down to Friman   got blowing had to put in at Bear Creek   started snowing   fell eleven inches   had stay all next day   came home for snowshoes and got to Birch wood Monday   finaly to Friman tuesday weathre tough for ten days   turned mild   snow disapear

The tough weather Andrew mentioned almost capsized the *M.S. Discoverer.* On her way from Seldovia to Seward on November 21, the vessel encountered a storm which swept one man and some lifeboats overboard. Both the *Discoverer* and the *Kasilof* made it through the storm and into port at Seward.

At this time there was a national longshoreman strike and freight was not getting to Alaska. Thanksgiving turkeys and produce were coming in on small airplanes from Canada.[3] The federally owned Alaska Railroad

---

ANCHORAGE DAILY TIMES   November 27, 1936

Tells of Furious Storm Which Cost Life of Smith On Discoverer Last Sunday

The motorships Discoverer and Kasilof left Seward early this morning in their voyage to Seattle, according to word received by the Berger distributing office in Anchorage.

The Kasilof reached Seward at 6 a.m. yesterday morning, ending widespread anxiety for the safety of the boat and passengers. According to word received in Anchorage, the Kasilof hugged the shelter of Nuka Bay during the storm which battered the Discoverer and took the life of Barney Smith, second mate on the Discoverer. Reports in Anchorage said the Kasilof was undamaged.

Two passengers of the Discoverer, Lee Hartley of Anchorage and R.F. Alexander, returned to Anchorage Wednesday evening by train from Seward.

Details of the Discoverer's harrowing voyage were revealed in Anchorage today by Mr. Hartley:

The giant wave which claimed the life of Mr. Smith, struck the Discoverer sideways and knocked the boat clear over on her side, Mr. Hartley said. Passengers claimed the keel of the boat was higher than the masts before the ship righted herself. The ship took in water through the exhaust funnel.

Smith was on deck at the time and was swept overboard along with a lifeboat and davits.

Mr. Hartley said he did not see Smith go over, or while he was in the water, but another passenger claimed he went under immediately and did not have a chance to grasp wreckage or save himself.

To turn about in the giant seas in which the boat was wallowing would have meant certain disaster, and the Discoverer continued to Nuka Passage and spent the night offshore near the cabin of Pete Sather.

The storm struck Sunday during the forenoon. The drowning occurred about an hour after the gale began. The storm continued for several hours. While the Discoverer encountered heavy weather during much of her trip, the gale Sunday was the worst of the voyage.

Monday morning after the storm the vessel returned to the place off Point Gore where the mate was lost, but an extensive search failed to reveal a trace of the man. Another storm coming up forced the boat to again run to Nuka Passage for safety, where she spent the next night. On Tuesday the ship continued to Seward, arriving in the afternoon....

had a near monopoly on freight once it reached the territory. Colonel Otto Ohlson, general manager of the Railway, was trying to finagle ways of getting ships to Seward with goods. While Heinie Berger was in Seward checking and repairing his ships he publicly sent a radiogram to Ohlson offering his vessels and crew to assist in the transportation emergency.[4] Berger probably delighted in the irony of his offer. Over the years Ohlson had repeatedly and openly tried to put Heinie out of business to eliminate the competition. Ohlson's usual strategy was to prevent Berger from docking his ships at Anchorage or blocking the route from the dock to town so freight could not be moved.[5] Heinie inevitably prevailed.

Mail was interrupted by the strike, but otherwise, residents in more isolated parts of the territory had already stocked their larders and hardly noticed the disruption.

27   John Canon came up from Kasilof   I stay that night at toms   the stormy days I put in at digging cellar under new cabin put in floor & windows   covered celing with moss

28   went acrost country to cabins of Funy River   just returned from that trip   saw tom & Pete Kalning on way up

Thursday 3 December   The day I returned from my trip to Funy River

Friday 4   Found new covering ground this morning   found my zite [scythe] returned   cut red top away along trails not been away from house all day   snow falling   26 up

Saturday 5   A drizle of snow falling nearly all day   lost my glass case   looking for them most of the day   cut up seal skin for pack sack   making ready to have a bath

Sunday 6   Have put in day at making bread washing clotches and doing other chores   cooked big kettle of stew   20 up

Monday 7   working at making a pack sack of a seal skin and had not time to finis it lot of sewing   10 up this morn

Tuesday 8   Finis pack sack   was out got three rabbits for Tub & Jerry   heavy north westerly storm   had to move boat acount of swell

Wednesday 9   Raining   40 up   made a new handle for sledge hammer   cut a spruce   sawed up som blocks   set out net   nearly all snow gone   rotabaga tops in garden still green

Thursday 10   Strong wind from south   no chance of fishing net   fixed som slabs   squared stove body from pipe   32 up

One of the buildings at Funny River on the Moosehorn Trail is this Alaska Guides' cache. Hank Lucas is on the left, Duncan Little on the right. Photo courtesy of G. Titus.

Friday 11   Calm cooler   went to lake Emma set twenty odd traps for lynx & mink   saw two coyotes   no sighn of any fur so I left seven smole traps on a snag on lake shore

Saturday 12   At home all day   put in rather hard day yesterday   feeling all in to day   cold wind up lake   heard air plane below   12 up

Sunday 13   Coolest morning   thermometer going down to nine o clock   3 up   fished net got 17 trout   one bright steelhead   got two rabbits cutting steel platte with dull hacksaw   working at stove

Monday 14   A westerly wind with fluries of snow no weathre to go out fiddling with stove   got everyting redy exepting pipe conection   12 up

Tuesday 15   Got finis with stove   had to drill thirty holes to fit colar for pipe   clouding up six degree abow

Wednesday 16   was up early   waited to day breck   not lookin good   windy   went to islands made foot bridge   got icy coming back

Thursday 17   Snowing all day   tok apart alot of gasoline cases to get lumber for shelfing at homestead cabin   scrubbed the floor   cold this eve   at ten down to zero   lowest so far this winter

Friday 18   Cold   feeling cooler than it realy is at five below zero this morning   stay cold all day   at six o clock this eve 7 down

Saturday 19   Turned milder during the night   7 up this morning but stay at about ten all day an other day I have not acomplished a ting

Sunday 20   Tok a walk to Lake Emma   saw no tracks exepting porky cyote rabbit   cold anough to ice mustash   five abow when I got back

Monday 21   Had a tramp up glaser flats intended to get a moose but in alders it was hard to tell if it was cows or buls so I came home without meat   saw one sheep   it was a ewe   1 down

Tuesday 22   Stay in to day   cold this morning had to put out boat to take in net   got lot of fish trout steelhead & sokeye   6 below

Wednesday 23   went up glaser flats   jumped two moose   saw four sheep   one ram in shooting distance   fired three shots but have been facing cold wind   sights blur   missed   2 below

Thursday 24   walked to Bear Creek had Pete to cut my hair   float of ice drifted in at Bear Creek first ice I seen this winter   John Canon have been to Petes no game   2 up

John "Frenchy" Cannon's cabin, sixty years later. The building was fifteen feet wide by seventeen feet long. Photo by G. Titus.

Friday 25   At home   warm   up to 28 abow with fine mist coming down in form of light snow cooking eating & sleeping   fed Jerry the cat to it got sick & I am not much better   26 up

Saturday 26   went to mountain   saw one ram to far to shoot   went to islands   jumped five moose   one old bull   one shot got it   got back at dark   butchered covered meat   10 up

Sunday 27   went up on the flats to set som coyotie traps   a light snow falling   whirl winds came of mts   warm   changed to rain   swong around compas now north west   Mr Nilsen was just leving as I came   called him back to stay all night   30 up

Monday 28   About 7 inch of new snow this morning   fixed up a pair of old snowshoes for young Nielsen   I stay in   hanged out som washing   put a new buckle in packsack   clear 20 up

Tuesday 29   At home trying to make som bread my yeast was slow that I did not set my batter until noon   still working slow   cut down tubs pack sack   tok me bigest part of day   warm 30 up

Wednesday 30   A lot of new snow   was out shoveling snow from my boat   tramped trail mixed oil   making redy to take som stuff down weathre permitting   after noon John Canon & Pete Kalning came up   got me ten lb box of peaches   radio for Emil & sheep hunt   34 up

Thursday 31   Had a tramp on glaser flats to look at som coyote sets   cut trail thru last patch of alders bringing open trail from lake shore to glaser thru island   clouding up turning milder som noys of wind   just heating water for a bath to be clean to start new year   42

Andrew Berg with Polly Teresin and her sister Mary Ness. Photo courtesy of Joan McLane Lahndt.

CHAPTER 22

1937

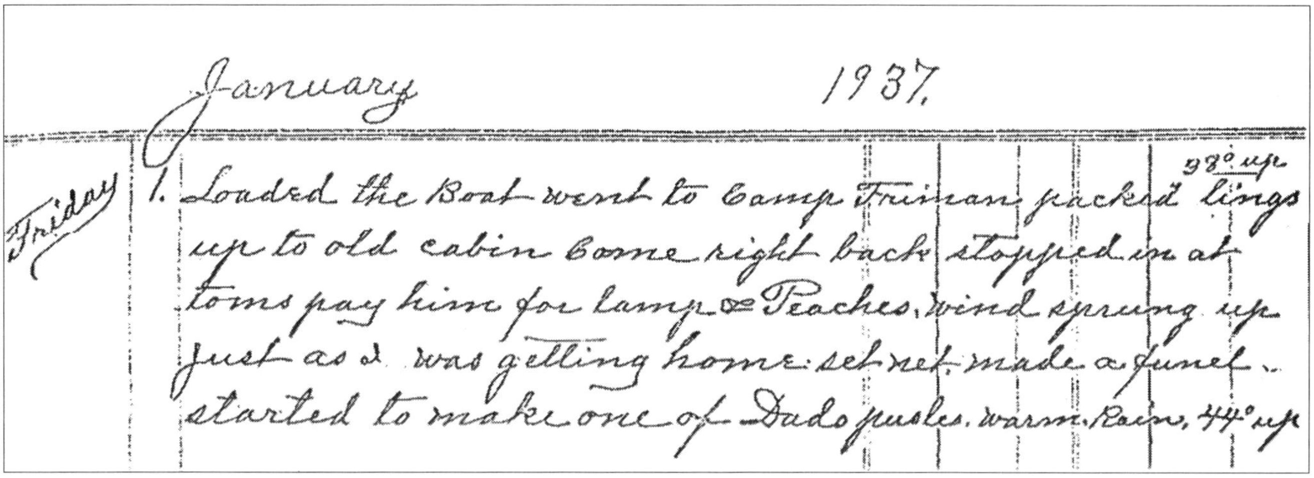

January   *1937.*

Friday 1. Loaded the Boat went to Camp Truman packed tings up to old cabin come right back stopped in at toms pay him for lamp & Peaches. wind sprung up just as I was getting home set net made a funel. started to make one of Dads pusles. warm. Rain. 38° up 44° up

Saturday 2   Started to go up to Lake Emma but decided it be too wet so I set out eight traps for coyotie   heavy southerly wind with rain squals this evening got cool anough to snow   had a nap after I got home   solved a pusle

Sunday 3   Climbed to Lake Emma   no game lost one trap mink set   coyote or fox got it   clog light   no way of tracking   got away during rain & light new snow over tracks   15 up

Monday 4   At home   did not get out of bed to breck of   had to cook up som dog feed   busy doing noting   22 up

Tuesday 5   Raining havy all day   wethre warm 45 abow with havy wind easterly   feeling lacy mended som slipovers   wanted to fish net   to rough to put out boat   38 up

Wednesday 6   A heavy swell came in from Devils Bay this morning with a rainy looking skye   busy at one ting & another   got smoot about noon put out boat   fished net got 12 trout   to late to cross lake after it smotened   38 up

Thursday 7   Raining & blowing all day   heavy swell from south   38 to 42 up

Friday 8   Ran acrost the lake to trail crossing ridge to King lake   tok me 52 minutes   light head wind   32 up

Saturday 9   Mild snowshowing   set out few traps no tracks of game   came backe here Sunday 10 in thick fogg   was here by one o clock   saw coyote   32 up

Monday 11   Started out to glaser flats at ten o clock   was thinking of coming back as it was starting to rain but keept on going   looked over som coyote sets   got one   raining heavy when I was skinning but I had a nice place under a spruce so I just came thru fine   ice over flats slipery   44 up

Tuesday 12   At home   stritched pelt   heated water had a bath   keept busy all day   cant see I done anyting   30 up

*Friday 22   Left here the 13th went to Freman &
crost country to Funny river   rest of time working
at new cabin at Friman   had my boat at Tom
Odalls place   raining & tawing all time   no
snow in lowlands   48 abow when I came here to
day   no indication of game any place*

*Saturday 23   A new snow on this morning   fogg
hanging low   I started late for a walk on the
flats   found a beastly walking   half inch new
snow on slick ice   tok a nasty fall   left arm feels
heavy as lead   no broken bones   30 up*

*Sunday 24   At home   intended to go to Lake
Emma but my left side to sore to go slipping
around the hills   fine weathre   cooler   28 up
so I been busi making a batch of one handed
bread   the left hurting sumpatic of using the
right   getting along*

*Monday 25   Loafing at home   got lots to do but
fine excuse now to put everyting off   sleeping
reading   cookin   eating   18 up*

*Tuesday 26   Stay in to after sun up then went to
Lake Emma   most traps out of order   got two
porkies one squirrel one coyote one mink   came
down thru caribou pass   saw lots of rabits   11 up*

*Wednesday 27   A drizly snow falling this morning
I tok a walk up on glaser flats   set out two traps
for coyotes   walked down new cut trail to look
over som mink traps   tok in som meat   Jerry
sick   28 up*

*Thursday 28   Jerry (the cat) bad sick this morning
simes to go paralyzed   I got it to eat a pill of
physic and that nearly killed him   Pete Kalning
& Ole Matson came up from Bear Creek to saw
som boat lumber at Emils   calm   macrill sky
34 up*

*Friday 29   Went acrost lake   started after ten
tok up boat   looked over som coyotie traps   one
sprung   set couple more   fine going acrost
country   was down King Lake Creek   mink
trap sprung*

*Saturday 30   Started to go home but after I got
out saw that wind would be too strong on
Tustumina so I cruised country all day*

*Sunday 31   Came thru to day   som Ice making
at Devils Bay*

*Monday 1 February   A skim of ice forming this
morning   8 abow zero   tok a walk to Lake
Emma   saw Emil Ole Pete of my trail where
they had a saw pit   fine walking   got a big
buck lynx*

*Tuesday 2   Got myself blody packing in lynx
had to wash clotches the first ting this morning
then my net was frozen two inch of ice   got it out
by noon then a four hours walk on glaser flats
got one coyote   had late super   9 up this morning*

*Wednesday 3   Tok two traps from here went to
flats   got two more   came thru island trail   set
traps on lake shore for coyotes   still open water
but closing fast   7 up*

*Thursday 4   was up early   after breckfast I got
cleaning & sharpening my scates   skated down
lakeshore couple of miles   set out 3 traps for
coyote   8 up*

*Friday 5   went to Friman & down beach to Philip
Creek   lost a wolferine*

*Saturday 6   up on Lick house trail to sumit   tok
8 traps off trail lake*

*Sunday 7   to Olson Creek & back to Toms   stay
all night   got radio news*

*Monday 8   Came here   stopped at Bear Creek
got can of coffe I lent them when they was sawing
lumber   Ole Matson must have been here as I
found his mittens here   about 7 up*

*Tuesday 9   Started out to the glaser flats   in
putting on my scates I broke a strap   stay home
restrapping scates & altered dog harnes to fit
Tub my new dog   temperature jumping from 5 to
30 up & back*

*Wednesday 10   A light snow fall   I went to lake
Emma no game or sign of game a real nasty day
to be out but better then using snowshoes   5 up*

*Thursday 11   waited to after ten o clock for the
day to warm up then tok dog & sled acrost to
islands & on to glaser flats   intending to bring
in som meat but pulled to heavy in new snow   so*

Andrew's view of Mt. Redoubt, about seventy-five miles away across Cook Inlet. Photo by C. Cassidy.

I just got in som bones for dog feed   Frency been here & left sled & dogs   gone to Emils turning cold   12 up this morning   5 below 7:30 this eve   no catch any game

Friday 12   22 down this morning   set yeast last night and it started slow so I set bread late   so it be probably ten o clock befor I be thru   Frency came from Emils near noon   started for Birch Creek

Saturday 13   Temperature down to 16 down 10 p.m.   but this morning it was up to 12 below rised to 3 abow stay there all day   staying in all day exepting cooking a kettle of dog feed   not done a ting

Sunday 14   4 up this morning   started blowing from south   shaking som snow out of trees at the same time a fine dust of snow was falling alltogather no time to be out

Monday 15   4 up this evening   was down to Bear Creek   a south wind sprung up   had a cold time coming home for drifting snow

Tuesday 16   10 below this morning   stay in to 12:30   went up on glaser flats   clouding up & feeling cold

Wednesday 17   10 below this morning & feeling snappy all day   I stay in I dont seem to stand cold   getting chilled thru after I walked to I get swetty   probably som change   saw cloud cap on redoubt this eve

Thursday 18   16 below   Ole Matson came in got his bearskin slip overs   shortly after he went I saw four coyotes   shot at one   just cut som furs this evening   Mr Neilsen came   have walked from Fox River

Friday 19   a storm brewing   wind is whipping around from point to point   wind probably is N. E. or N. N. E   Karl Nielsen stay to noon fixing his snowshoes & gun belt   temperature about 32 up

Saturday 20   went acrost to King   Lost a trap with coyote   also a mink   fine traveling   snow trovn up in drifts   mild

Sunday 21   Started snowing during night   mild got foggy   coming over got turned around found my own track   John Canon came up from Birch wood   twenty six abov zero

Monday 22   Not feeling good   John Canon went to Emils   I went to glaser flats to get som meat   when I got back found note from Icky Ness that John Canon killed coyote in my trap on his way to Birchwood   I went & got it   it on stritcher 8 p.m.   zero 10 p.m.

Tuesday 23   Alex Ness came over this morning stay to noon   I went to look for coyotie set coght one   it got away from clog   Emil tok after it   I went to his place   got trap back   14 below 7:30

Wednesday 24   Alex Ness was here during day he said he was starting down on to morrow but I think I saw his track going towards Big Eds   Ole Matson came in this evening

Thursday 25   tok a walk to Lake Emma   Emil & Ole was at the saw pit cutting lumber   lynx have sprung one trap   to much snow to take in traps 5 up a.m.

Friday 26   walked down to Friman   stopped at Bear Creek & Birchwood   10 abow

Saturday 27   was down to Olson Creek   sprung & tok in traps   missed one set   two traps short

Sunday 28   Skinned coyotie   went over hill to Lick House   sprung all traps in route

Monday 1 March   went thru Funy River   lost one trap by coyotie at Castle Cabin

Tuesday 2   came back to Friman pasing Lick House   7 1/2 hours snow shoeing

Wednesday 3   went down lakeshore   found traps tok in all   stay at toms all night   20 down

Thursday 4   waited to after ten   came here stoped at Bear Creek   getting cold   16 down

Friday 5   20 below zero this morning   moisture rising sort of fogg   in all day   had som work to atend to & feeling change of whitre   reumatic aque sleepy & lacy   cellar was cool   noting frozen

Saturday 6   waited to after ten for it to warm up went up to glaser flats   sprung traps exepting som snowed under   that is som coyotie sets   lot of new snow fell during night   14 below this morning

Sunday 7   was to go to Lake Emma to day but snowing to beat a flush this morning so I stay in was out on snowshoes tramping wood trail   not feeling good   muscles sore from reumatism about 20 up this morning

Monday 8   At lake Emma & sumit packing traps to caches   got in about four   Frency been in left me som salt salmon

Tuesday 9   At home this fornoon   Charles Sands came from Emils on his way to Hugos   about noon Tony Johanson came of the creek where he examined his old cabin   Ole Matson came in before Tony left & stay to evening

Wednesday 10   warm to day   stay in making bread & cooking a kettle full of head cheese som rain fell at one time to day   snow still in spruce

Thursday 11   Stay in to afternoon   tok a walk to Bear Creek   got a hair cut & trout netline told that Game Warden Jolovas & Jack Lean was there to day

Friday 12   Not feeling good   stay in all day to evening   went out cut a birch   first cutting towards replenishing wood in wood shed   Ole Matson came over stay couple hours   snow melting

Sunday 13   was at outs with sleep last night   did not get any sleep to after 3 a.m.   cut som birch logs   not feeling good   did acomplish much

Monday 14   Trying to haul som wood logs this morning but to wet snow   melting fast   lake turning blue this evening   hauled in three sticks waded thru wet snow & pools of water to mouth of Indian   raining

Tuesday 15   was up early shovling snow onto wood trail   hauled in about a cord of birch logs tok me to noon   was afraid that all snow would melt & leve me without filling wood shed clouded up & started snowing   got two inches of new snow 6 p.m.

Wednesday 16   Lot of new snow this morning tok a tramp with snowshoes to tramp trail for hauling wood but did noting as trees hanging full of snow & that snow wet   blowing

Thursday 17   As I got out this morning at 5:30 three coyotes had thier opera out on the ice about 300 yards out   I started to go to flats but to much water on ice   cut & necked in two loads birch

Friday 18   Started to go to flats for som meat but got in to wind   had my pack sacks laying loos on sled   wind got the sacks   when I got to islands notised sacks gone   came back

Saturday 19   Cold anough to haul in som wood got in six sticks   started to pull hard as snow warmed up   rested one hour   went to get in som meat   cut two larg birch

Sunday 20   Frosty this morning   hauled in six loads of birch   Emil was going down lake toward Bear Creek   Tub tok after him with bob sleds Tub got whipped

Monday 21   Hauled in four loads   called it anough birch   have to cut som heavy spruce aroun cabin   that will give me lots

Tuesday 22   At home   had a bath   washed clotches   scrubbed floor   fished net got only one larg makinaw   Emil came from Bear Creek

Wednesday 23   went acrost to King Lake to cover window cashe traps & store tings for summer foun cyotie & trap I though I lost   I missed it midle of February   som one kill it   it hangd it up

Thursday 24   On my way here I remember of not emtying water 6 a.m.   tough going   used snowshoes on part of the lake

Friday 25   at home not feeling good   put in two heavy days & generaly feel over work for days after   cooked a batch of dog feed   8 up

Saturday 26   Cold this morning   5 up   stay in to noon   went out choped few loads of birch to make shore I had anough

Sunday 27   A dust of snow falling all day   not amount of much   tok bobsleds hauled in on slick   intended to haul more but snow to wet was out this eve   sawed a log out of old trail sleeping   reading

Monday 28   was out early   had home 7 log of firewood by 1 o clock   fished the net   walked to Bear Creek   dug som traps out of snow

Tuesday 29   Stay in filing a saw & cutting down saw frame getting it ready   I sawed couple logs trying out saw   5 up

Wednesday 30   was having a rest after breckfast Ole Matson came in visiting   stay till after noon some flurrys of snow coming down   shifted old wood to the house   sawed & split birch to start a rick

Wednesday Thursday 31   Started sawing wood this morning but working couple hours at a time then lay reading   got along good so far

Thursday 1 April   A storm started this morning expected it to taw but did not   yet that mild   to stormy to do much out   just sawed few sticks finis one rick

Friday 2   Tok a trip to glaser flats   brought in most of the meat   just left couple of ribs   still lots of snow   stormy afternoon

Saturday 3   Sawed a few sticks of wood   about half rick   fished net got one makinaw   saw Emil go towards Bear Creek   started yeast

Sunday 4   At home making bread   got a batch of nice bread   Ole was down to Bear Creek with som lumber   stoped in on way back

ANCHORAGE DAILY TIMES

April 26, 1937

First Of Big Game Hunters Are Due Soon

New York, Michigan Party To Hunt With Jim Simpson On Inlet

Mr. and Mrs. A. E. Ellinger of Buffalo, N.Y., and Frank Mostellar of Kalamazoo, Mich, will come to Alaska soon for big game hunts, according to Jim Simpson, who is making arrangements for the party.

The party will take the steamer Curacao, either at Cordova or Seward and meet Mr. Simpson at Seldovia. The hunt will be for Kodiak bear somewhere along Cook Inlet or perhaps Kodiak.

Mr. Simpson will leave here about Wednesday in the Vigilante, now undergoing an overhaul at Anchorage, with Ed Lovedall, skipper of the Vigilante; Tom O'Dale, guide for Mr. Mostellar; F.W. Rising and Ward Gay, who will comprise the camp party for the hunters.

Mr. Mostellar will leave the main party and hunt alone with his guide, Mr. O'Dale. Mr. Mostellar plans to spend the summer in Alaska, and has several more hunts in prospect.

Mr. and Mrs. Ellinger, who plan to take the month of May for their expedition, have hunted in Wyoming, Montana, Idaho and British Columbia. They are bringing Elmer Keith of North Fork, Ida., with them on this trip. Mr. Keith is a guide and is author of many articles in sporting and outdoor magazines.

The party will return from its hunt by way of Anchorage in the Vigilante, which had been chartered for the hunt.

Monday 5   was on the wood pile all day   found a mean stick to split first ting   tok lot of pounding to get it to stove wood   finis second rick and a lot sawed for last rick

Tuesday 6   sawing & splitting wood all day   that is between rests   I work couple hour then rest a like period

Wednesday 7   Finis wood pile & cut out som alders thats trowing shadow over my garden patch   look like change of weathre

Thursday 8   Not feeling so good   lay in bed to noon readin & slumbering   in afternoon I cut down a couple of large spruce for wood

Friday 9   Cut an old dry spruce   sawed & split fire wood   the first cut for immediat use   snow melting fast   I think I heard seagulls to day first this spring

Saturday 10   Tok a run to Bear Creek   no one there   ice getting soft   run trout net no catch   light southe east wind

Sunday 11   a fogg on this morning   started a drizly rain in fornoon   stay in mending old clotches   kept me busy all day   feeling bum

Monday 12   Burning spruce brush & cleaning up about the place   fixed up a piece of root to bend sledrunners

Tuesday 13   Froze a little this morning so I tok a run to woods islands & up on glaser flats to get in som dry moose ribs   started at five so as to be back befor it got to warm

Wednesday 14   Started this morning heating water & had a bath   lay down for a rest   fell to sleep   scrubbed floor after I came to   Emil Pete & John came up   saw them by

Thursday 15   Started early for Camp Friman was at Birchwood 8 a.m.   have been down there clearing land & finishing cabin

Friday 30   Came home to day walking along lake shore & thru timber   stopped at Bear Creek where Emil & Pete Kalning was building a dory trying to start yeast   night cold

Saturday 1 May   My cat Jerry is out hunting   I was out looking for him   tok a walk over to Emils   no one home exept a little cat and that looking slender   loking like it might rain

Sunday 2   Lost sleepe about three this morning   got up had breckfast   set bread   made a big batch   thru by noon   caulked bottom of my schiff   southeaster sprung up   ice moving down

Monday 3   waited to it got warm   started painting my boat   rough under bottom making it hard to paint   Ole Matson came with his new dory   going to Bear Creek for seeds

Tuesday 4   Splitting & dressing a pair of sled runners & not got anywhere for it was raining *early morning & started to blow an easterly wind its likely the end of ice was out & put a second coat of paint on dory bottom*

Wednesday 5 Still playing with sled runners & building a frame to bend them on no ice in sight rain during night rain this evening

Thursday 6 Raining all night & all fornoon then wind got hard stay in mending som clotches saw a boat down towards Bear Creek I guess Emil & Ole going out

Friday 7 Got tings ready to bend sled runners steam box & all but it started sprinkling again to night tok a look a round for cat

Saturday 8 Try out steambox tings worked just right steamed & bend runners rest of day worked at som hydralic pipe for smoke stack to homestead location at Friman put out boat set net fine day

Sunday 9 The first ting this morning I turned the boat over in order to stop a leak ran the net no fish had a bath putting tings up to take down to Friman mixing oil & such (cloudy)

Thursday 20 Have been at Freeman working at my homestead brecking new ground for garden plot tough brecking frost still under leaf mold & moss my battery ran down had to pull east wind

Friday 21 Have been busy all day spading & planting pototoe garden heared motor of Big

Ed coming from Devils Bay going to Bear Creek to pick up Pete Kalning I got my tings packed ready to go in morning if tings look good

Berg's reference to his homestead is intriguing. Was "homestead" just an expression or was he intending to file for a homestead patent on the property? A news item in the *Anchorage Daily Times* in April described seven recent homestead applications on the Kenai Peninsula so it appears to have been a recent trend. The government was providing surveys of homestead land for free.[1]

The federal government increased the number of Civilian Conservation Corps jobs in Alaska this year. They raised the number of workers from 325 to 600 with the stated purpose of providing opportunity to Alaska Natives. The work performed by the CCC was also expanded to include the building of roads and airfields outside of National Forest boundaries.[2] The roads sought by the Kenai Peninsula residents were not among the new projects.

Salmon prices were in the news this spring. The fishermen's union negotiated prices with the three Anchorage canneries. Fishermen using their own gear were paid ninety-three and a third cents for each king salmon, twenty-one cents for each red or silver salmon and five and a third cents for each pink or chum salmon. The king, red and silver prices were a few cents higher than they were the previous year. The pink and chum price had come up a penny.[3] Prices at other canneries around the inlet would have been comparable.

Emil Berg's big house at Tustumena. Photo by Joe Secora, courtesy of Ella and John Secora.

During salmon season many western Peninsula residents stayed at fish camps along the beach. A community picnic was traditionally held on July 4th at the old Kasilof cannery. (Heinie Berger supplied barrels of wieners.) This year the picnic ended in disaster when Gust Ness had a heart attack on the way home in his skiff and died.[4] Gust was only in his late fifties.

Roy Cole was back in Cook Inlet this season with the Bureau of Fisheries. After salmon fishing ended he went to Tustumena Lake with Alex Lind and made two entries in Andrew's journal.

Sunday August 22   Alex Lind and R. L. Cole came up from Tom Odales place 4:30 p.m.   got good wetting from -wester was held up at Odale for day and half on account of wind   Good escapement salmon noted at Birchwood   the only stream visited so far in Tustumena Lake

Monday August 23   Cole and Lind left here at 7:00 a.m. for the streams in the vicinity of the Cliff House   called at salmon stream on glacier flats   this stream running muddy water   only few salmon observed   Slim Crocker and party camped at Cliff House   Tom O'dale and his hunter came up to Cliff House where they intended to make camp before starting into the hills for sheep   Returned here at 11:30 p.m. The weather and wind has moderated so that traveling will be good   Hope to cover Bear Creek and return to O'dales place for the night   Thanks Andrew for the use of your home   only wish you had been here with us   Sincerely R L Cole USBF

Crocker and Odale may have been guiding European hunters. An *Anchorage Daily Times* article reported

that Francois Edmond Blanc of Paris and Count Jaroslaw Potocki of Warsaw were at Tustumena Lake at this time. With special permits the two men were hunting and collecting specimens for museums. In November they were to report on Alaskan hunting conditions to the Conseil Internationale de la Chasse at their annual meeting in Berlin.[5]

Andrew Berg would have enjoyed that meeting as it was held in conjunction with "the largest international exhibition of [hunting] trophies held since the war."[6] But in November he was attending to the business of hunting, trapping and his increasingly poor health. Gust's death may have increased Andrew's sensitivity to his own heart problems.

Friday 5 November   Left Kenai for Kasilof in a rainy chop

Saturday 6   got tings from cannery to Madsen place   stay all night

Sunday 7   started early for lake   picked up Carl Croker at Jensens   towed my schif to Victors cabin   rest of way I ran a head of Madsen who caried most of my load   got to Abs in good time

Monday 8   Cold   left late   landed som tings at Friman   dug potatoes   came to toms saw Frency Emil & PK   got here befor dark fine

Tuesday 9   went up home trail   saw lot of sheep boys shot but missed

Wednesday 10   I stay home   Madsen & Croker went Nica Norka mt   got one sheep

Slim Crocker took this picture of a small group of Dall sheep. Photo courtesy of Betty A. Crocker

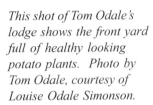

This shot of Tom Odale's lodge shows the front yard full of healthy looking potato plants. Photo by Tom Odale, courtesy of Louise Odale Simonson.

Thursday 11   Boys up Nika Norka   got another ram   came in good time

Friday 12   Boys left for Kasilof   I over hauled & repaired my motor

Saturday 13   was up to woods islands   cut trail inside swamp

Sunday 14   stay home not feeling good   got lot of trout   doing chores   boiled out net

Monday 15   at home washing clotches doctoring my self   weathre fine

Tuesday 16   was on glaser flats   set 14 traps for coyotes   saw Emil at distanse

Wednesday 17   at home not feeling good   a dust of snow falling   weathre warm

Thursday 18   at hom doctoring   no suckuss abow frezing all day   fine weathre

Friday 19   was up to flats   brought in a crow bar   feeling no good

Saturday 20   set out a few traps for coyotes   cold this morning   10 up

Sunday 21   was up to Lake Emma   packed in 20 large traps   20 up

This winter a strike of steamship workers cut off supplies to Alaska again. At issue was the union's desire to rotate available jobs through the membership in order to alleviate unemployment. On November twenty-second the *Anchorage Daily Times* headline read "Hope For Timely Delivery Of Christmas Mail Dim." The strike ended two days later, but it was another reminder of Alaska's dependence on a vulnerable line of supply.

22th   was out towards Bear Creek   set out 12 coyotie sets   1 trap each

23 At home on the bum   forgat new daiys [diaries] *have to make each line*

There were only nine pages left in Andrew's journal at this time. The previous entry appears to mean that he forgot to bring a new diary to the lake and he had to make each line count. His handwriting became smaller and tighter and his entries rarely exceeded one line.

24   was out on glaser flats   saw coyotie tracks no game

25   at home   snowing all day   no chance doing any ting out

Friday 26   in all day to late   tok a walk   snow anough to make walking heavy

Saturday 27   Stay in   started to build bearskin mits   brecking trail   used snowshoes (8 up this a.m.)

Sunday 28   was out on snowshoes   saw first moose track   mild   snow sticking

Monday 29   Snowing all day a thin drizle   still on the sick list   mild   sewed on mitt   33 up

Tuesday 30   finis mits   snow shoed roads   fished net got 36 trout   put foot webb in snowshoe

Wednesday 1 December   mended web in snowshoes   run line toward Ber Creek   not a track of coyotie

Thursday 2   5 up this morning   ice on windows cleaned som clolches   cold all day

Friday 3   at 6 last night colest so far   2 up stay in   am no good   tok a walk this eve   8 up a.m.

Saturday 4   Laid up yet   was out in after noon clened snow of boat   20 up noon

Sunday 5   pulled to wath we call icelands snowshoed thu heavy   got coyotie   bad spell

Monday 6   Heart gave me truble last night skinned & stritched coyotie   feeling bum   38 up

Tuesday 7   tok a run to Bear Creek   Emil came as I was leaving   heart bad   set net   35 up

Wednesday 8   In all day   Emil came up from Bear Creek   foggy   slighlty coler

Thursday 9   started out for a walk   got notice from the heart to quit   plane went by   9 up this eve

Friday 10   6 up a.m.   snowshoed out this afternoon   coyotie missed trap   2 sets   I no good

Saturday 11   Snow   bigest snowfall for years used snowshoes to get wood from shed

Sunday 12   snowing yet this morning   turned warm   38 up   tramped up trails   set yeast

Monday 13   made bread   Emil was to Bear Creek   fine weathre   mild

Tuesday 14   had a bath   raining all day shoveled snow from boat   cooked dog feed   40 up

Wednesday 15   warm   snow melting   still lot of snow   scrubbed floor   washing clotchs

Thursday 16   not acomplished anyting   had a sleepy spell   cleaned 4 sets   20 up

Friday 17   pulled along lake shore   found nine out of 12 traps   swell on deep snow

Saturday 18   heavy southeast winds   rain galore sleeping nearly all day   40 up

Sunday 19   mild   light rain   tok a walk to five coyotie sets   no tracks   sleepy   40 up

Monday 20   heavy south wind   was out found three traps I missed friday   windy   34 up

Tuesday 21   got up to late to go to flats   sleeping & reading   windy   16 up

Wednesday 22   was up to flats   traps froze down solid   lot of tracks of moose   20 up

Thursday 23   had a lazy day   stay in bed to day light   oild motor   12 up

Friday 24   sleept to day light   tok a walk up Indian   got a coyotie   cold   8 up

Saturday 25   in all day   skinned & tended coyote   reading & sleeping   4 up a.m.

Sunday 26   tok a walk   looking at som traps towards Bear Creek coming back

Monday 27   cleaned & stritched pelts   tok in net got 13 trouts   north wind   2 up a.m.   zero p.m.

Tuesday 28   stay in   strong northerly wind tended furs   cold   4 down this morning   stod about zero all day   started down at 3 p.m.   at 6 9 down

Wednesday 29   4 up   strong wind   fine in house   10 down 8 p.m.

Thursday 30   Tok a walk down the trapline   no sign of coyotes   4 down below all day

Friday 31   was up to flats   atack of heart   nearly blind getting in   4 down a.m.

CHAPTER 23

1938 - 1939

January   1938.

Saturday   Started to go up Indian to som traps had to comeback acount of heart Lake aperently closing Calm not very cold 4 ups. a.m.

Sunday 2   had a bad attack of heart   going like a machine gun two hours   made bread   5 up

Monday 3   tok a walk down lake shore   heart gave truble   came back   mild   15 up a.m.

Tuesday 4   strong wind   ice feild broken   see open water two miles out   had a bath   22 up

Wednesday 5   warm   SE   no ice visible   stay in heart bother least exertion   40 up

Thursday 6   Had bad time with heart 4 hours shot coyote 200 yards out   unable bring it in

Friday 7   sleept to nine   got in coyotie on stritcher   feeling weak but gaining   fine warm day

Saturday 8   Intended to go to flats   to sick to ventur   rain n e & se   feeling bum   40 up

Sunday 9   Lay down after breckfast   went along beach   met tony   got mail   23 up

Monday 10   set out net   was going to flats   had to quit not feeling good   stay in   windy   10 up

Tuesday 11   felt better this morning   was up on glaser flats   all icy   no catch   5 up a.m.

Wednesday 12   walked down to Bear Creek   tony went yesterday   fine day   14 up

Thursday 13   Made bread   hauled net got 18 trout   ice making   calm   22 up

Friday 14   Stay in   tok a walk up Indian   dog ran away   freezing   hear ice grinding   10 up

Saturday 15   This a m all ice   this evening no ice snowing strong during day   32 up

Sunday 16   Raining in squalls all day   snow going fast   rised som traps   had a bath   40 up

Monday 17   try to walk out but everyting like a glass bottles   washed clotches   rain   35 up

Tuesday 18   tok a walk down lakeshore   snowing & raining   tracks of one coyotie   33 up

Wednesday 19   was on flats   coyotie sprung two traps stepped on two more   no catch   22 up

Thursday 20   had a tired sort of day   sleeping to 2 p.m.   tok a walk up Indian   stay to dark 20 up

Friday 21   Hauled in one log firewood   had to quit   heart truble   cooler tonight   14 up

Saturday 22   Sawed up a few blocks of wood making ice to night   south wind   5 down

Sunday 23   was to islands   got two coyotes hungd them under spruce   no time to skin   cold lake closing   5 up

Monday 24   see no open water   made bread down lake   shore ice poor   got one coyotie 2 up

Tuesday 25   skinned coyotie   fixed dog harnes no wind   lake aperently froze   2 down

Wednesday 26   hocked dog to sled started thru islands   dog broke loos   I puled sled   2 coyotes 2 down

Thursday 27   put a lot of traps on sled   went towards Clif House   no tracks   set two on flats 10 up

Friday 28   stay home all day not feeling good bad spot on left lung   8 up

Saturday 29   Coyghnin [coughing]   stay in to noon   hauled in log of wood   walked to coyotie traps   got one   1 down

Sunday 30   went down to Friman   called at Bear Creek   stay all night at Birch   set cabin in shape   set twenty traps   came back fift day Frency came to lake point   got back here February 3 th   cold   north west blow brewing   5 up

Friday [February] 4   cold strong wind from northwest   5 below at 7:45 this morning

Saturday 5   tok a run to glaser flats   strong wind blowing   cold   9 below 8 a.m.

Sunday 6   Coolest morning this winter   11 below zero a.m.   sawed wood   cooked dog feed   p.m. 5 down

Monday 7   Made a batch of bread   cold   11 below zero again this morning   clouding to night

Tuesday 8   tok a walk up Indian   coyotie got away with no 3 newhouse   followd half hour struck track of an other dragging trap back tracked it to next set from first one   it got a no 4 newhouse   rather cold   stay in washing clotches 17 below

Wednesday 9   was out tracking coyotes   they got fast crosted snow   was close to one   6 below

Thursday 10   tok a run on scates   ice fine   set ten trap at windy pt   came in by bear   3 up

Friday 11   Ran to glaser flats   no coyotie   after I got back set two traps on Indian   4 down

Saturday 12   Ran to Birch wood & to traps to Olson creek & back to Birch   no game   two

boys from Nilchik came from Emils   got mail   stay over Sunday   got radio

Monday 14   Came from Birch by way of Wind Point   tok a walk up Indian   no game

Tuesday 15   had notice of heart to take it easy been in bed nearly all day   10 up

Wednesday 16   was up Lake Emma trail   found tracks of missing traps & coyotes   lot of snow 12 up

Thursday 17   was on flats   one trap sprung one pan down   no catch   cut spruce dry   18 up

Friday 18   making bread   tramped wood trail cut & hauled in one birch   2 up

Saturday 19   hauled in two loads dry spruce lost one coyot & trap   was toward BC   8 up

Sunday 20   was up Indian   set six traps replasing 3 lost   set net   cut wood   12 up

Monday 21   started crost   plane came   south east wind sprung up   rain   plane still here

Tuesday 22   Rained all night   Air Plane left at noon for Homer   caught coyotie   40 up

Wednesday 23   went to Windy pt to Linds Cabin to Friman   back to Birch   got coyote for John stormy

Thursday 24   came here   stopped at Bear   was up Indian   fished net   mild   ice wet   40 up

Friday 25   Saw Emil sail dory   went to flats saw coyotie close   no catch   north east   rainy

Saturday 26   Sleeping all fornoon   filed saw cut cople blocks   washed clotches   40 up

Sunday 27   Raining & blowing heavy south east thermometer up to 48   ice lose

Monday 28   Rain & storm to afternoon   Indian river running full stop ice   lost net   45 up

Tuesday 1 March   was to Indian   net buried in gravel   got lines 8 trout   was down lake & up Indian   50 up

Wednesday 2   went to hogback   set 3 snares one trap   rain   got boots full crossing Indian 48 up

Thursday 3   At home making bread   set net scrubbed floor   sawed four blocks   30 up

Friday 4   was on flats   bridge gone on slough fine day   tok in net no fish   26 up

Saturday 5   went to traps at Ohlson   run back to Birch   stay all night   16 up

Sunday 6   came in by windy point   no coyotis put new handle on ax   10

Monday 7   had a lacy day   sleeping most of time   change of weathre   16 up

Tuesday 8   was up Indian to canon   it is open mile   I follow hill to hogback   windy   40 up

Wednesday 9   another sleepy day   dull cloudy a snow flurry in afternoon   34 up a.m.

Thursday 10   stay in   not feeling good   som snow falling   warm   wet   40 up

Friday 11   dust of snow falling   filing saws   cut a spreading spruce   3 inch snow   27 up

Saturday 12   Cut som Birch for firewood   snow in trees   dirty   fine day   16 up

Sunday 13   hauled wood   was up Indian & to hogback   broke thru ice   hurt leg   start yeast 27 up

Monday 14   Snowing all day   light dust   made bread   leg sore   still 27 up

Tuesday 15   hauled in som wood   walked down lake   had bath   snowing   22 up

Wednesday 16   lot of new snow this morning washed clotches   tramped trail to wood   27 up

Thursday 17   heavy going   snow shoed eight mile   saw one coyotie track   loos snow   8 up

Friday 18   Snowing   was out in afternoon sawed down large spruce for firewood   at 16 up

Saturday 19   hauled in a stick   worked it to wood   still snowing   trees is full   22 up

Sunday 20   Lay down after breckfast reading rather cold out   cooked feed   3 up

Monday 21   Colest day this winter   iced bobsled runners   hauled in som birch   18 down

Tuesday 22   hauled in few sticks of birch   calm cut som more birch   5 up

Wednesday 23   got home som wood   Sands came from Emils at noon   mild   20 up

Thursday 24   hauled in a few more sticks of Birch   sawed wood   fished net   12 up

Friday 25   Snowstorm from north   let up afternoon   was up Indian   1 coyotie   16 up

Saturday 26   hauled in two loads of dry wood windy   snow flurrys   tended fur   18 up

Sunday 27   A lasy day sleeping & reading   sawed wood   cleaned stove pipe   8 below

Monday 28   was up Indian crossed to hog back saw wood   cooked dog feed   2 up

Tuesday 29   Snowshoed to flats   ice sinking water seeping thru   heavy going   22 up

Wednesday 30   Snow disapearing fast   south east   mild   making bread   reading   45 up

Thursday 31   Blowing   snow all gone of lake all blue   had a bath washed clothes   45 up

Friday 1 April   was to Bear Creek   wet snow on ice makes traveling bad   lost coyotie   heart acting bad all day   44 up

Saturday 2   Raining & blowing this morning   still blowing   not feeling good   42 up

Sunday 3   went to windy point   tok in traps went to Birch   meet g men   43 up

The "g men" were Bureau of Biological Survey biologists L.J. Palmer and Jack Warwick who had come to Tustumena for more moose research. The Bureau was still working on designating a moose refuge on the Peninsula. When Andrew met the men on April 3 he gave them permission to stay at his Homestead cabin. In his report, Palmer gave an overview of their time in the field:

...We left Anchorage by airplane on March 20th and arrived that same day at the Odale Hunting Lodge on Tustumena Lake, where we established field headquarters. We began field work the next day and continued until May 16th.

On April 4th and 5th we moved field quarters down the Lake about four miles to the Andrew Berg cabin (Camp Freeman) near the mouth of Phillip Wilson Creek, in order to reach more conveniently the lower winter and spring range. On April 29th and 30th we moved back to the Odale quarters. John Canon was employed as guide on April 12th and 13th to show us the various trails leading into the country between Tustumena and Skilak Lakes, In addition, Mr. Canon and Mr. Andrew Berg voluntarily assisted us in observing and reporting the number of moose on areas near Kasilof and at the upper end of the Lake which we did not reach ourselves. On May 8th we employed Peter Kalning and his outboard motor boat to take us to the head of the Lake where we examined the range between Indian Creek and Bear Creek. On May 16th we secured transportation by boat to Kasilof and thence to Kenai, where we embarked via the motorship "Princess Pat" for Anchorage, arriving there May 21st. I returned to Juneau on May 30th...[1]

Andrew does not mention counting moose for them, but he apparently did so on his routine tramps around home.

Monday April 4   Came here   set traps from lake point up   got lot of trout from Pete   30 up

Tuesday 5   fixed saw horse   sawed up a dry log cleaning up around cabin   40 up

Wednesday 6   was up Indian   altered door step sawed up som birch   warm

Thursday 7   Started to go acrost lake to islands ice to poor   sawed wood   set net

Friday 8   went early to glaser flats   noting in traps   came back by hog back

Saturday 9   Sawing wood & ricking   dog was away   fished net got a trout

Sunday 10   The wood pile   put in big day   finis one rick   sawed up more

Monday 11   Split wath I had sawed   cooking dog feed   caught one trout

Tuesday 12   finished second rick   this evening ice brecking slowly

Wednesday 13   was up Indian river   tok in som traps & snares   hauld net

Thursday 14   filed saw   cut a couple of sticks so twisted that it is no good

Friday 15   making bread   had a bath   washing clotches   ice field moved

Monday 18   Back from three day hike to Philip & back   ice brecking to lake point

Tuesday 19   Sleeping & reading all day   had a bum spell in morning

Wednesday 20   sawing up som wood   walked out to som traps

Thursday 21   Overhauld motor   going to flats got to foggy   walked to hogback

Friday 22   saw first motor run on lake this spring think it Kalning   cloudy

Saturday 23   was running motor to glaser flats got back at 12 m   fine

Sunday 24   Sleeping nearly all day   tok walk up Indian   bear track

Monday 25   Sawed up one birch   finis wood for this year   strong easterly wind

Tuesday 26   not feeling good   had to do som doctoring   cloudy   warm   55 up

Wednesday 27   for the third time I made poor bread   heavy gale easterly

Thursday 28   still blowing   have not done anyting that I can mention

Friday 29   Cooked up the last of coyotie for dog feed   snow squall of the hill

Saturday 30   Ran down to Freeman & back   got one coyotie   fine day

Sunday 1 May   was out on flats   saw several bands of sheep & three moose   buildt a foot bridge   striched coyote skin   had a sleep

Monday 2   Lacy   sleeping   tok a walk up Indian reading   windy

Tuesday 3   was up to hog back   tok in som traps started sled work

Wednesday 4   not feeling so good   doing som carpentering   wind

Thursday 5   making som uprights for sled hunting vilows   got one

Friday 6   Busy all day working at sled   cloudy dismal day

Saturday 7   out hunting vilows   hard to find   set yeast   windy

Sunday 8   Lary Palmer   Jack Warick & Pete Kalning came up from Birch   former go by Lake Emma to Bear Creek

Palmer and Warwick interviewed Berg and the other Tustumena Lake old-timers to record their local knowledge of the moose and other animal populations. Regarding the wildlife in the area at the time Palmer wrote:

Rabbits are now scarce. They started to come back two to three years ago, but were soon cleaned out by coyotes. These animals are much in evidence. Last year Mr. Berg trapped eight coyotes and Mr. Canon also got eight. This year Mr. Berg secured twelve coyotes and Mr. Canon took ten. We noted much sign of coyotes and frequently heard them howl in the hills. On May 2nd we saw three in one group on a gravel bar of Birch Creek. We observed very little sign of rabbits (seven actually encountered) or grouse (eight seen). Emil Berg reported seeing twelve spruce hens between Kasilof and the Lake on May 4th. Grouse and ptarmigan were abundant two years ago, according to Mr. Sands, but now are scarce, as we have noted. Mr. Sands believes they will be abundant again three to four years hence. He claims about a six or seven year cycle for rabbits, grouse, and ptarmigan; Mr. Berg about a ten or eleven year cycle. Red squirrels

are abundant, but furbearers generally are scarce or wanting. The death blow to furbearers in this section, it is claimed, took place some years ago when fur farming was at a boom stage. Even the porcupine were largely killed out, but we have noted that now they are beginning to come back. On the high upper ranges mountain sheep are reported to be abundant, in good condition, and on the increase. Bears, both black and brown, are said to be tremendously increased. This is emphatically the opinion of Messrs. Berg, Canon, Sands, Kalning, and Odale. Berg figures there are twenty times more bear than when he first came to the country in 1890.[2]

Monday 9   tok in som traps   try to spade garden still frost in places

Tuesday 10   fixed steam box   put vilow bents on sleds   ice this morning

Sunday 15   Came up from Bear Creek after several days at Friman

Monday 16   was to flats   got into Sandstorm coming back   cold

Tuesday 17   feeling lacy   stay in nearly all day nasty cold wind SE

Wednesday 18   Planted carrots   working at sled heart give truble   tok digitalis

Thursday 19   Busy doing noting   was to flats spaded garden   cold

Friday 20   still tinkering with sled   storming as usual

Saturday 21   One of my lacy days   lay reading stormy

Sunday 22   finis sled and not so good job raining & storming

Monday 23   Planted potatoes   set yeast   strong wind south east

Tuesday 24   At making bread   had a bath storming

Wednesday 25   busy all day doing ods & ends cleaned well

Thursday 26   was up on flats   tok in traps   saw biggest black bear ever

Friday 27   Chopped trail to Indian   cold nasty wind

Saturday 28   Ready to go down lak   weathre bad   mending old trash net

June 8   4:30 a.m. starting for Kasilof

L.J. Palmer wrote up his findings from the moose study in June. The team had counted moose again, analyzed their seasonal ranges and forage, examined carcasses and feces of moose and their predators and determined threats to the population. Palmer's conclusions supported the Bureau of Biological Survey's aim of creating a moose refuge. His arguments echoed those of William Langille in 1904 and Dall DeWeese in 1902.

Palmer wrote that the Kenai Peninsula moose herd was a resource of "local and national importance."[3] The animals provided economic benefit and recreational opportunity to the area through meat hunting, trophy hunting and tourism. Anecdotal evidence and the research team's observations this spring strongly suggested that moose numbers were in decline. Primary threats to the population included legal and illegal hunting by the growing number of humans living in the Cook Inlet basin and the kill of calves by predators. The report noted that the best hunting grounds, the benches and ridges between Tustumena and Skilak Lakes, were easily accessed by airplane or boat and therefore heavily targeted by hunters.

Palmer recommended that the Tustumena-Skilak Lakes area and a range between Tustumena and Kachemak Bay be set aside as moose and mountain sheep reserves. His vision was to allow hunting and trapping, within limits, but exclude homesteading or other land location.

Data collection was another strong recommendation in the report. Maintaining the herd required knowing at least the basics of how many animals there were, the rate of successful reproduction and the numbers killed by hunters. Palmer suggested that the Alaska Game Commission begin collecting moose harvest numbers from hunters on the Peninsula. In his study he started looking at calf crops and survival based on the number of yearlings observed, but his field period ended before the cows began calving. The biologist concluded that further investigation was needed in that subject as well

ANCHORAGE DAILY TIMES
November 8, 1938

Moose Horns Crowd Pedestrians From Sidewalks; They're Largest

The largest moose horns ever seen anywhere in the world were placed on display in the window of George Kennedy's Hardware store this morning after Game Warden Jack O'Connor completed the official measurements of the unique specimen.

Tom O'Dale who found the horns on the Kenai peninsula, carried them to the store and excited widespread attention as he went down the street. The horns extended the width of the walk and O'Dale had to hold them length-wise to avoid crowding pedestrians into the street. The official measurements placed the spread at 78 ¾ inches. The spread of the horns that held the world's record for spread until O'Dale made his find, is 76 ½ inches. They were found in 1901 by Andrew Anderson on the Kenai Peninsula and the horns are now at the Field Museum of Natural History in Chicago. The length of the right palm of O'Dale's specimen 43 ½ and the left palm 45 ¾ inches. The circumference above the right burr is 8 5/8 inches and above the left burr 8 ½ inches....

O'Dale said the horns were found on a dead moose. The carcass was under water and one antler was protruding. "Moose usually die in the water," O'Dale said "they fight and after getting scarred up and feverish they go into the water to cool off. This one must have had a terrific battle before he died. There was one point of the other moose's horns in this one's skull. With such wide antlers the moose was not well protected in the center."

[Overall moose numbers on the Kenai Peninsula may have been in decline, but the animals were still growing to record size.]

as forage production and moose diseases. He further recommended that a field headquarters station be established in Anchorage as a base for the ongoing research which could be expanded to include bears and mountain sheep. Regarding the location of the field station he wrote: "I visited both Kasilof and Kenai and do not recommend either one as a suitable station site because of isolation and general inconvenience."[4] The headquarters station was not established but Palmer was sent back to continue his research in the fall and the following spring.

A main street in Kenai. Geography isolated and protected this historic town. Photo courtesy of Ella and John Secora.

Andrew Berg considered Kenai a fine headquarters site for his summer work. The Bureau of Fisheries report for this salmon season described a daily enforcement patrol carried out "...from a base at Kenai. This patrol was carried on by Andrew Berg a resident of Kenai Village and Tustumena Lake who furnished his own dory and motor for the work. In addition to this patrol Mr. Berg also collected scale samples taken from Red Salmon in the Kasilof and Kenai Rivers."[5] Andrew was employed from July 1 to August 25 and earned $336.

While Andrew was finishing up his work, a hunting party was heading to his Home cabin and recorded their adventure in his journal.

Aug 26 1938   Pete and Grace Madsen Ralph and Dorothy Waggoner arrived here at about 4:00 P.M. having had perfect weather and smooth water on the lake

27th   The men left early hunting for sheep but a fog drove them back to camp   Pete brought a turnip home

This lake dory is equipped with an outboard motor, three sets of oarlocks and the sail.
Photo by Tom Odale, courtesy of Simonson Collection, Accession no. B91.0.101C.

The Madsens are pictured here along with some Kenai and Kasilof friends. Left to right are Ed Roth, Ted Johansen, Mike Juliussen, Grace Cole Madsen, Ella Hermansen Secora, Margaret Juliussen, Pete Madsen and Julius Juliussen. Photo courtesy of Ella and John Secora.

28th   All the campers decided to try a long hike so started up "Nikonorka" about 5:30 A.M.   It was a beautiful day   the view from the top making the long hike worthwhile althouth we saw only ewes and lambs   We think we got some fine pictures

29th   Men went up the over hanging trail came back disgusted with themselves for having missed some sure shots at rams   Were all getting hungry for meat

30th   Thinking it might change our luck we all went over to Wood Island glacier stream and got about 30 fine trout   Stopped to see Emil Bergs cabin

31th   Men left at 4:00 a.m.   women had just cleaned the cabin when the men arrived with one ram and broad grins   They had shot two rams from the foot of the "old overhanging trail" and they ablighinly rolled to the mens feet   We all walked over the glacier flat to get the second one   It was a perfect day for pictures

Sept 1   Spent the day canning sheep   Pete fixed one head for mounting   Got 112 cans from the two rams

Sept 2   Broke camp about 10:00 a.m.   leaving for Friman to try to get a moose   We had a

A view of Tustumena Glacier from the Overhanging Trail. Photo by Slim Crocker, courtesy of Betty A. Crocker.

wonderful time here and apprieciate having the use of the cabin more then we can say [signed] *DW*

These entries filled up the last pages of Berg's final journal. Andrew returned to Tustumena but his diary ended. He may have forgotten, again, to bring a new journal with him. He may have started a new one which was lost. Sadly, we are missing the record of his last few months of life.

On February 20, 1939, the *Anchorage Daily Times* reported that Andrew had been flown from Tustumena to Anchorage the previous day and was admitted to the hospital. He remained in the hospital for nine days until his death on March first.

How remarkable that he died, not packing a sheep down the Overhanging Trail, but in a hospital bed. Andrew spent his life pushing against limits in his dogged, determined way. As a young man he sought and found the outer bounds of America's frontier. In his maturity he coped with injury and illness, never allowing either to change his chosen lifestyle.

From his journals we get a sense of both his persistence and patience. He may have been born with those qualities or he may have been shaped by his environment. Even the most impetuous person would learn to wait for Cook

> ### ANCHORAGE DAILY TIMES
> February 20, 1939
>
> ### Radio Summons Plane For Sick Man
>
> Andrew Berg, oldtimer at Tustumena, was rushed to Anchorage by airplane yesterday for medical treatment after a radio call for help was received by Star Air Lines. Pilot Jack Elliott made a special flight to Tustumena for Mr. Berg. He was reported in critical condition today at the Anchorage Hospital.
>
> The oldtimer, who has resided at Tustumena since 1914, had been ill several days before a radio call for aid could be dispatched.

Inlet's mighty tide to flow in the desired direction before undertaking a journey. In Andrew's world survival depended absolutely on knowing when to accommodate overpowering forces of nature.

The utilitarian endurance he achieved in his relationship to the natural world was wonderfully depicted in his writing. The quality was not unique to Berg but only he left us the gift of journals as a window into that time and place.

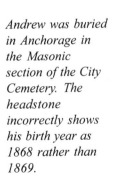

Andrew was buried in Anchorage in the Masonic section of the City Cemetery. The headstone incorrectly shows his birth year as 1868 rather than 1869.

ANCHORAGE DAILY TIMES

Wednesday, March 1 1939

Andrew Berg, Veteran Guide, Passes Away
Heart Illness Fatal To Alaskan Once Known As Most Powerful Of Kenai

Andrew Berg, 71 dean of guides in Alaska and one of the first white men to go into the Tustumena country, died at the Anchorage Hospital this morning following a lingering illness of heart trouble. Mr. Berg was brought to the hospital last week by airplane after lying ill in an isolated trapper's cabin at Tustumena several weeks. Funeral arrangements are being made by John Wik, longtime friend of the veteran guide. Mr. Berg went into the Tustumena country 49 years ago when that section was a great caribou and wolf country. There were no moose or coyotes when he first arrived.

During the years of his residence there, Mr. Berg saw the section develop into the greatest moose pasture of the world. Caribou and deer disappeared and were replaced by moose and coyotes. Mr. Berg served as guide for many parties and hunted for museums. His trophies are on display at the Smithsonian Institute, Field Museum of Natural History at Chicago, Berkeley University in California and other institutions as well as museums in England and European nations. Mr. Berg's name appears often in the Remington tabulations of record trophies, both as hunter and guide it is said that many of his record trophies can never be beaten because the game has disappeared. The veteran Tustumena resident was the first game warden of that district and also served as fish warden for some time. He trapped each winter and was responsible for the naming of many lakes and creeks of the Kenai, Skilak and Tustumena sections. He maintained a home at Kenai but spent most of his time in the hills. His guiding activities were confined largely to the Kenai and Alaska Peninsula but he sometimes took parties as far as the Talkeetna mountains. For the last 10 years he did no guiding because of his heart ailment which caused fainting spells. Of Finnish extraction, Mr. Berg was known in his heyday as the most powerful man of the Kenai country. He was six feet two inches tall and weighed 235 pounds. He out-traveled all others in speed and distance. As a trapper, he built 14 cabins, many of them which are now in ruins. Four were in use by him until he came to Anchorage recently.

Mr. Berg was a great reader, maintaining a fine library on his trapline. He wrote with a fine hand and kept a meticulous diary of his movements from day to day. He never married. Surviving is a half-brother, Emil Berg, a guide in the Kenai country. Despite warnings from physicians that he must rest due to his heart condition, Mr. Berg led an active life to the end. After leaving the hospital here following treatments last year he went to Kasilof and spent a week traveling by open dory to his cabin on Tustumena Lake. He went 11 miles on the lake by breaking out a path for the boat in ice one and one-half inches thick. While burial arrangements are pending the body is at the Carlquist and Menzel funeral Parlors.

[A fine obituary, notwithstanding a few inaccuracies. Andrew was only sixty-nine years old at his death, and Emil was his full brother.]

CHAPTER 24

AFTERWORD

Change would eventually come to the western Kenai Peninsula but not to Andrew Berg's winter stomping grounds on Tustumena Lake. Conservation efforts which began in the 1890s would finally coalesce in time to spare the central Peninsula from the bulldozer of progress. Berg would be hard pressed to recognize the city of Kenai today but his Home cabin still sits serenely at the beginning of the trail to Emma Lake and Nikanorka Mountain.

In late 1939 Larry Palmer finished his final report on his eight months of moose field research. The report argued strongly for a preserve for the Kenai Peninsula's outstanding populations of moose and sheep. Palmer pointed out that most of the western peninsula was composed of either wetlands or "shallow soiled, glacial deposit."[1] These conditions were not suited for cultivation but were proven in their ability to support moose. Homesteaders were steadily trickling into the area and would eventually get their roads. Palmer saw that as a twofold threat. More residents would put more hunting pressure on the herds. Homesteads would occupy the lower country, important winter and calving range for moose. Palmer drew a parallel with the disastrous consequences of fencing off winter elk range in the western United States.

He went on to argue:

If we let this [Kenai moose] *herd become depleted now, it will be the old story over again of squandering a resource and them spending a lot more money in the future in an effort to replace it.*

Andrew's Home cabin today. The land subsided from the 1964 earthquake. When the water level in the lake is high, such as in this picture taken in late summer, the cabin is much closer to the water than Berg ever anticipated. Photo by C. Cassidy.

We have established National Parks to conserve outstanding scenic and recreational features and to annually harvest the crop in regulated use of this resource by tourists. Likewise, we have established National Forests for the conservation of the timber resource through regulated use. Why not similarly establish preserves for the conservation of outstanding wildlife features and to harvest the annual crop under regulated use? In the case of the Kenai moose, the purpose sought in reserving a definite area for this animal is to conserve an outstanding wildlife feature, to regulate its use through a safe harvesting of the annual crop and most essential of all to prevent undue encroachment in the establishment of homesteads on the range in question. I feel that any homesteads that might be located on the area proposed for reservation would be chiefly of speculative nature or with the deliberate intention of living off the country, i.e. in this case, the moose and mountain sheep.[2]

The proposal for the game preserve at this time included roughly the central and western portions of the Peninsula except for a six mile strip along the Cook Inlet and Kachemak Bay coasts. This strip was already inhabited to an extent and was the most suitable land for agriculture.

Between 1939 and 1940 the Bureau of Biological Survey and the Bureau of Fisheries were merged into the Fish and Wildlife Service and moved from the Department of Agriculture to the Department of the Interior. The proposed game refuge not only survived the reorganization but found a champion in the Director of the new Fish and Wildlife Service, Ira Gabrielson. In 1940 the army was requesting part of the Kenai Peninsula for use as a bombing range and another federal department was proposing to resettle European refugees there. The resettlement issue died in Congress and Gabrielson fended off the army. The bureaucratic cogs moved slowly but an executive order establishing the Kenai National Moose Range was signed by President Franklin D. Roosevelt on December 16, 1941.[3]

Hunting and trapping in the 2,000,000 acres of newly designated Range were not affected. These activities were still regulated by the Alaska Game Commission. Prohibited within the Moose Range were settlement, lease, grazing, or sale. Through recognition of the intrinsic

and economic value of the Kenai moose herds, both they and the other wildlife that shared their range were given sanctuary from the impending population boom on the Peninsula.

World War II slowed development for the duration but accelerated growth later. Alaska's importance in national defense was recognized by the federal government. Settlement was encouraged and assisted. Veterans were given a break on homesteading requirements. The Alaska-Canadian Highway was improved. Roads were constructed within the territory and the government surveyed large parcels of land into ready-made homesteads.

The long-awaited road connecting all the communities of the Kenai Peninsula finally was built between 1947 and 1949. A road from the Peninsula to Anchorage was opened to traffic in 1951. People came, some speculators, some hardy homesteaders, but the economic realities of this distant, sparsely populated territory hadn't changed.

Fox farming was finished. The McLanes were the last to give it up, pelting their last fox in 1943.[4] The McLanes successfully turned to growing potatoes. Farming was feasible in a few areas, but there was a limit to the number of potatoes the Alaskan market could absorb. The market could be finicky as Doc Pollard learned in the late 1940s. He started raising short-horned Herefords in Kasilof and discovered that people buying meat preferred the imported corn-fed beef with white colored fat to his grass-fed beef with yellow fat.[5] Another problem for Alaskan growers was that retailers had year-round contracts with their suppliers outside the territory and couldn't accommodate the local seasonal products. Many homesteaders who came to the Peninsula intending to farm ended up working in the salmon industry.[6] Fishing was the old standby but jobs and income were limited. Men often sought jobs in Anchorage or elsewhere leaving their families behind in primitive conditions to meet homestead residency requirements.

Life on Tustumena Lake didn't change appreciably. Joe Secora became a year-round resident occupying himself primarily with placer mining. John Cannon is remembered, in the early 1950s, for walking from Kasilof to his Tustumena cabin to hill his potatoes. During fishing season he would go up and back in the same day. Emil Berg frequently stopped by Pollard's for a supply of fresh milk which he drank for his ulcer.[7] For a time he kept

Joe Secora's dory headed downstream in the Kasilof River. The water level is so low in the spring that outboard motors cannot be used. Photo by Joe Secora, courtesy of Ella and John Secora.

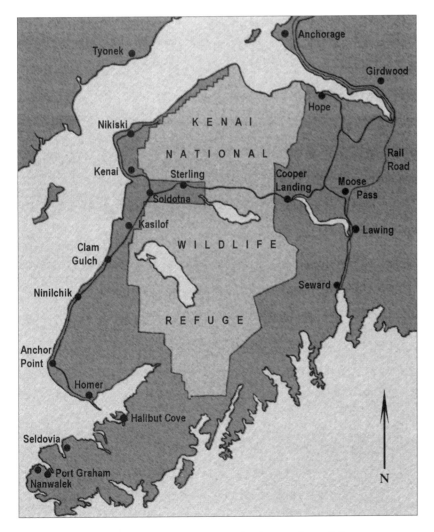

The long-awaited highways on the Peninsula and the current boundaries of the Kenai National Wildlife Refuge.

his own milk cow, taking her back and forth to Tustumena in his dory. Emil died in 1953 at the age of seventy-four.

Emil, Joe Secora and Tom Odale were the only people to have acquired deeds to land on Tustumena Lake before the designation of the Moose Range prevented further private ownership in the area. Frenchy Cannon and others who had cabins continued to use them and even sold or transferred deeds to the buildings. The McLane family bought a deed to Andrew's Home cabin in the 1950s.

The post-war homestead push came and went. Many settlers arrived with enthusiasm and left in disappointment. The roads which had been so long anticipated made life easier but they couldn't overcome the territory's general isolation. The natural resources available at that time provided sustenance but not riches. The next economic boom was approaching and it would bring unimaginable change to southcentral Alaska.

In July of 1957 the first major oil strike in the territory occurred on the Kenai Peninsula. The first successful well happened to be located within the Kenai National Moose Range. Development of the oil industry and the ensuing influx of people put the Moose Range to a severe test. Between 1959 and 1961 the Peninsula's moose population was calculated to have dropped from 4,736 to 2,719 animals as a direct result of all of the new oil workers becoming moose hunters.[8]

Human population increased dramatically. The census counts for the town of Kenai went from 321 in 1950, to 778 in 1960, and to 3,533 in 1970. The Moose Range was besieged by demands for oil and gas development and private development. Around 300,000 acres were withdrawn from the Range as a result. The Fish and Wildlife Service and other advocates managed to retain over 1,700,000 acres to fulfill the original mission of safeguarding the wildlife resources and their essential habitat.[9]

The Moose Range evolved into the "Kenai National Wildlife Refuge." In the late 1970s 1.35 million acres of the Refuge was designated a wilderness area. Tustumena Lake is largely contained within the wilderness area and thereby preserved in a state which would be quite recognizable to Andrew Berg.

Around 50,000 people now live on the Kenai Peninsula. The moose population is in decline today. A combination of natural forest succession and fire suppression has resulted in extensive stands of mature spruce trees which do not provide moose forage. Careful management of hunting harvests, prescribed burning in the Refuge and

other strategies work to ensure the perpetuation of the Kenai moose.

Over the years most of the old cabins dotted throughout the Refuge disappeared through neglect or fire. Andrew Berg's Home cabin received enough maintenance for preservation. Members of the McLane family and others continue to use it as a base for hunting and trapping. Berg's Homestead cabin, although thirty-six years younger, suffered a collapsed roof and was deteriorating rapidly when it was moved in 2001 to the Kenai National Wildlife Refuge Visitor's Center in Soldotna, Alaska. It has since been restored and now serves as a museum documenting Andrew Berg's life on Tustumena Lake.

Andrew Berg's Homestead cabin in its new location at the Kenai National Wildlife Refuge Visitor's Center in Soldotna, Alaska. The job of moving and restoring the building in 2001 was planned and supervised by Gary Titus. Many community volunteers helped with all phases of the project. Photos by Candace Ward, courtesy of the Kenai National Wildlife Refuge.

Chapter 1 - Introduction

1 Näs, Lars, personal communication, Jan. 18, 2002.
2 Näs, 2002.
3 "Noted Sourdough Cook Inlet Area Is Visiting City," *Anchorage Daily Times*, May 18, 1934.
4 Boraas, Alan, "Native Life," *Alaska's Kenai Peninsula, The Road We've Traveled* (Hope, AK: Kenai Peninsula Historical Association, 2002) 5-7.
5 Rollins, Aden M., "Census Alaska: Numbers of Inhabitants, 1792-1970," 1978, Archives and Manuscripts Department, Consortium Library, University of Alaska Anchorage

Chapter 2 - 1890-1899

1 Springer, Susan W., *Seldovia, Alaska* (Littleton, CO: Blue Willow, 1997) 99.
2 Bayou, Katherine, "Brownie in the Dark," *The Alaska Sportsman Magazine*, Jan. 1946: 12.
3 Townsend, Joan B., "Journals of Nineteenth Century Russian Priests to the Tanaina: Cook Inlet, Alaska," *Arctic Anthropology*, IX-1, 1974: 14-17.
4 Moser, Jefferson F., Commander, U.S. Navy, "The Salmon and Salmon Fisheries of Alaska," Report of the Operations of the United States Fish Commission Steamer Albatross for the Year Ending June 30, 1898 (Washington:Government Printing Office, 1899) 140-143.
5 Naske, Claus M., "The Kenai National Moose Range," National Wildlife Refuges of Alaska, A Historical Perspective, Part 1, U.S. Fish and Wildlife Service, 1979: 120-121.
6 DeWeese, Dall, "A Red Letter Day With Alaska Big Game," *Forest and Stream*, Feb. 2, 1898.
7 DeWeese, 1898.
8 Lloyd, Steve K., *Farallon* (Seattle: Univ. of Washington Press, 2000) 1;12.
9 Boraas, Alan, "Turning Point," *Peninsula Clarion*, Nov. 21, 1996.
10 Moser, 1899: 142.
11 DeWeese, 1898.
12 Kalifornsky, Peter, *A Dena'ina Legacy: K'tl'egh'i Sukdu: The Collected Writings of Peter Kalifornsky*, ed. James Kari and Alan Boraas (Fairbanks: Alaska Native Language Center, 1991)
13 DeWeese, Dall, "Hunting Alaskan White Sheep With Rifle & Camera," *Outing Magazine*, July, 1899: 247-253.
14 DeWeese, Dall, "Hunting Bull Moose in Alaska," *Outdoor Life*, March, 1899.
15 DeWeese, Dall, "Alaska Game Doomed," *The Alaskan Sitka*, December 3, 1898.
16 Twelfth Census of the United States, U.S. Dept. of Commerce, Bureau of Census, 1900.
17 "Noted Sourdough Cook Inlet Area Is Visiting City," *Anchorage Daily Times*, May 18, 1934.
18 Gerberg, Harry, interview Sept. 27, 1980, transcript in author file.
19 Parrish, Morris L., *Hunting on the Kenai Peninsula*, (Philadelphia, 1913) 22; 89
   Tweedy, Mary Nissen, interview by Mona Painter, Jan.10, 1981, transcript in author file.
20 DeWeese, Dall, "A Sportswoman In Alaska," *Outdoor Life*, October,1899.
21 Bayou, 1946: 12

Chapter 3 - 1900-1909

1 Records of Office of United States Commissioner and Ex-Officio Recorder at Valdez, Alaska, Volume A, book 59, Mortgages, Seward Recording Office, Seward, AK.
2 Cane, Col. Claude, *Summer and Fall in Western Alaska*, (London: Horace Cox, 1903) 86.
3 "Game Law in Alaska", 57th Congress, 1st Session, House of Representatives, Report No. 951 accompanying H.R. 11535, March 14, 1902: 1-8, E.E. Rasmuson Library, University of Alaska Fairbanks.
4 Cane, 1903: appendix.
5 *Alaska Prospector*, June 26, 1902: 4.
6 *Alaska Prospector*, July 17, 1902: 4.
7 *Alaska Prospector*, July 31, 1902: 3.
8 *Alaska Prospector*, Sept. 4, 1902: 3.
9 Cane, 1903: 86.
10 Cane, 1903: 86.
11 *Alaska Prospector*, Nov. 6, 1902: 3.
12 *Alaska Prospector*, May 21, 1903: 5.
13 *Alaska Prospector*, May 28, 1903: 4.
14 *Alaska Prospector*, June 25, 1903: 5.
15 *Alaska Prospector*, July 2, 1903: 5.
16 *Alaska Prospector*, July 30, 1903: 3.
17 *Alaska Prospector*, Sept. 10, 1903: 4.
18 *Alaska Prospector,* March 19, 1903: 5.
19 *Alaska Prospector*, Oct. 1, 1903: 3.
20 *Alaska Prospector*, Nov. 12, 1903: 3.
21 Mason, J.T., Secretary of the Board, Colorado Museum of Natural History, letter to T.S. Palmer, Assistant in Charge of Game Preservation, Dept. of Agriculture, Wash. D.C., March 17, 1904, Denver Museum of Natural History Archives.
22 Radclyffe, Captain C.R.E., *Big Game Shooting in Alaska* (London: Rowland Ward Ltd: 1904) 176.
23 Radclyffe, 1904: 223.
24 Radclyffe, 1904: 228-229
25 Affidavits of annual labor. No. 1. Cook Inlet Recording District, Third Division. Alaska: 25, Seward Recording Office, Seward, AK.
26 *Alaska Prospector*, June 2, 1904: 3.
27 *Alaska Prospector*, June 30, 1904: 3.
28 *Alaska Prospector*, Nov. 3, 1904: 3.
29 *Alaska Prospector*, June 22, 1905: 2.
30 Naske, 1979: 122.
31 Kenai Historical Society, *Once Upon the Kenai*, (Kenai: Kenai Historical Society,1985) 408.
32 Archives, Museum of Vertebrate Zoology, University of California at Berkeley.
33 Rakestraw, Lawrence W., *A History of the United States Forest Service in Alaska*, (Anchorage, 1981) 44.
34 Naske, 1979: 122.
35 Palmer, L.J., "Management of Moose Herd on Kenai Peninsula, Alaska," June 1, 1938, Report, Kenai National Wildlife Refuge Headquarters Library.
36 "The Alaska Game Law and Regulations of the Department of Agriculture, 1908," United States Department of Agriculture, Bureau of Biological Survey Circular No. 66, General Correspondence of the Governor of the Territorial Government of Alaska, 1909-1958; Archives and Manuscripts Department, Consortium Library, University of Alaska Anchorage (G.C.G., Archives, UAA).

Chapter 4 - 1910-1919

1 "Rules and Regulations Governing Licensed Guides, July 9, 1910," G.C.G., Archives, UAA.
2 Berg, Andrew letter to Gov. Clark, Feb.24, 1910, G.C.G., Archives, UAA.
3 Painter, Mona, "The Kenai Lake/Kenai River Transportation Corridor," Dec. 1, 1984, paper in author file.
4 Berg, Andrew letter to Gov. Clark, March 1, 1910, G.C.G., Archives, UAA.
5 Hunter, William letter to Gov. Clark, Oct. 10, 1910, G.C.G., Archives, UAA.
6 Berg, Andrew letter to Gov. Clark, Dec. 28, 1910, G.C.G., Archives, UAA.

7 Berg, Andrew sworn statement, December 28, 1910, G.C.G., Archives, UAA.

8 Berg, Andrew letter to P. Vian, Dec. 28, 1910, G.C.G., Archives, UAA.

9 Bayou, 1946: 12.

10 Bayou, 1946: 12.

11 Berg, Andrew letter to Gov. Clark, Jan. 30, 1911, G.C.G., Archives, UAA.

12 Berg, Andrew letter to Gov. Clark, Jan. 30, 1911, G.C.G., Archives, UAA.

13 Seward Recording District, Cook Inlet Precinct, Third Division, Alaska, Book 2-A, 1911-1921, Seward Recording Office, Seward, AK.

14 Vian, P.F. letter to Gov. Clark, May 1, 1912, G.C.G., Archives, UAA.

15 McCullagh, Keith, diary, April 1, 1913, U.S.F.S. Chugach National Forest, Anchorage, AK, Daily Diaries 1908-1965, Record Group 95, Box 11, National Archives - Pacific Alaska Region, Anchorage, AK.

16 Berg, Andrew letter to Gov. Clark, July 28, 1912, G.C.G., Archives, UAA.

17 Bennett, Hugh H., *Report on a Reconnaissance of the Soils, Agriculture, and other Resources of the Kenai Peninsula Region of Alaska*, (Wash. D.C.: USDA, 1918) 119-120.

18 Berg, Andrew letter to Gov. Strong, Jan. 29, 1914, G.C.G., Archives, UAA.

19 Strong, J.F., Gov., letter to Andrew Berg, March 11, 1914, G.C.G., Archives, UAA.

20 Phelps, Mason, letter to Gov. Strong, July 21, 1914, G.C.G., Archives, UAA.

21 Baughman, J.A., game warden report to Gov. Strong, Nov. 11, 1914, G.C.G., Archives, UAA.

22 Baughman, J.A., game warden report to Gov. Strong, March 31, 1915, G.C.G., Archives, UAA.

23 Berg, Andrew letter to Gov. Strong, Nov. 22, 1915, G.C.G., Archives, UAA.

24 Boraas, Alan, "Native Life," 2002: 11

25 Baughman, J.A. game warden report to Gov. Riggs, Jan. 31, 1919, G.C.G., Archives, UAA.

26 Baughman, J.A., game warden report to Gov. Riggs, Jan. 31, 1919, G.C.G., Archives, UAA.

27 Riggs, Thomas, Gov., letter to J.A. Baughman, May 14, 1919, G.C.G., Archives, UAA.

28 Baughman, J.A., game warden report to Gov. Riggs, July 8, 1919, G.C.G., Archives, UAA.

29 Bayou, Katherine, "The Starving Moose of Kasilof Lake," *Alaska Sportsman*, Nov. 1945: 20.

30 Baughman, J.A., game warden report to Gov. Riggs, Nov. 6, 1919, G.C.G., Archives, UAA.

Chapter 5 - 1920

1 Riggs, Thomas, Gov., telegram to J.A. Baughman, June 17, 1920, G.C.G., Archives, UAA.

2 Baughman, J.A., letter to Gov. Riggs, June 30, 1920, G.C.G., Archives, UAA.

3 Baughman, J.A., game warden report to Gov. Riggs, July 1, 1920, G.C.G., Archives, UAA.

4 Baughman, J.A., game warden report to Gov. Riggs, Sept. 1, 1920, G.C.G., Archives, UAA.

5 Berg, Andrew, game warden report to Gov. Riggs, Sept. 30, 1920, G.C.G., Archives, UAA.

6 Baughman, J.A., game warden report to Gov. Riggs, Sept. 30, 1920, G.C.G., Archives, UAA.

7 Berg, Andrew, letter to Gov. Riggs, Oct. 30, 1920, G.C.G., Archives, UAA.

8 Bureau of Fisheries Annual Report 1934, Cook Inlet District: 30, Fish and Wildlife Service Annual Reports, Cook Inlet District,

1930 -1941, Alaska Department of Fish and Game Library, Soldotna, Alaska.

9 Berg, Andrew, game warden report to Gov. Rigg, Nov. 30, 1920, G.C.G., Archives, UAA.

10 Riggs, Thomas, Gov., letter to Andrew Berg, Dec. 1, 1920, G.C.G., Archives, UAA.

11 Folta, G., Sec. to the Gov., letter to Andrew Ber, Dec. 1, 1920, G.C.G., Archives, UAA.

12 Berg, Andrew, letter to G. Folta, Jan. 8, 1921, G.C.G., Archives, UAA.

13 Bayou, 1945: 20-22.

Chapter 6 - 1921

1 Berg, Andrew, game warden report to Gov. Riggs, Jan. 2, 1921, G.C.G., Archives, UAA.

2 Berg, Andrew, game warden report to Gov. Riggs, Feb. 1, 1921, G.C.G., Archives, UAA.

3 Berg, Andrew, game warden report to Gov. Riggs, March 6, 1921, G.C.G., Archives, UAA.

4 Riggs, Thomas, Gov., letter to Andrew Berg, March 23, 1921, G.C.G., Archives, UAA.

5 Folta, G., Sec. to the Gov., letter to Andrew Berg, March 23, 1921, G.C.G., Archives, UAA.

6 Berg, Andrew, game warden report to Gov. Riggs, April 2, 1921, G.C.G., Archives, UAA.

7 Berg, Andrew, letter to G. Folta, May 14, 1921, G.C.G., Archives, UAA.

8 Berg, Andrew, game warden report to Gov. Riggs, May 14, 1921, G.C.G., Archives, UAA.

9 Berg, Andrew, game warden report to Governor, June 30, 1921, G.C.G., Archives, UAA.

10 Berg, Andrew, game warden report to Governor, July 8, 1921, G.C.G., Archives, UAA.

11 Cadle, W.W., letter to Gov. Bone, July 13, 1921, G.C.G., Archives, UAA.

12 Bone, S.C., Gov., telegram to Andrew Berg, July 16, 1921, G.C.G., Archives, UAA.

13 Berg, Andrew, game warden report to Gov. Bone, July 31, 1921, G.C.G., Archives, UAA.

14 Secretary to the Gov., letter to Andrew Berg, August 15, 1921, G.C.G., Archives, UAA.

15 Culver, Walter G., "Miscellaneous Observations Kenai Peninsula and Vicinity, February 22 - March 15, 1923": 6, Report, Kenai National Wildlife Refuge Headquarters Library.

16 Nylander, Jonas Alexander, Naturalization Records of the U.S. District Court for the District, Territory and State of Alaska (Third Division) (1903-1991); Petitions 420-A630, 1930-1938, File: 418-A442, 1930-1931; Record Group 21; National Archives - Pacific Alaska Region, Anchorage, AK.

17 "Coyotes Get Mountain Sheep Kenai Peninsula," *Anchorage Daily Times*, Nov. 8, 1934.

18 Kenai Historical Society, 1985: 271.

19 Kenai Historical Society, 1985: 265.

Chapter 7 - 1922

1 Cotter, George, Game Warden, letter to L.L. Harding, Sec. to the Gov., July 13, 1922, G.C.G., Archives, UAA.

2 Culver, Walter G., "Report of Moose on Kenai Peninsula, February and March 1923": 16. Report, Kenai National Wildlife Refuge Headquarters Library.

3 Cotter, George, Game Warden, letter to L.L. Harding, Sec. to the Gov., July 13, 1922, G.C.G., Archives, UAA.

4 Dunning and Faulks, letter to Gov. Riggs, Nov. 3, 1919, G.C.G., Archives, UAA.

5 Baughman, J.A., Game Warden, letter to Gov. Riggs, Sept. 2, 1919, G.C.G., Archives, UAA.

6 Cotter, George, Game Warden, letter to Sec. L.L. Harding, Aug. 12, 1922, G.C.G., Archives, UAA.

7 Cotter, George, letter to Andrew Berg, Sept. 7, 1922, G.C.G., Archives, UAA.

8 Berg, Andrew, letter to George Cotter, Sept. 12, 1922, G.C.G., Archives, UAA.

9 Harding, L.L., letter to George Cotter, Oct. 5, 1922, G.C.G., Archives, UAA.

10 Cotter, George, letter to L.L. Harding, Oct. 12, 1922, G.C.G., Archives, UAA.

11 Jensen, Christian and Hans Peter, Naturalization Records of the U.S. District Court for the District, Territory and State of Alaska (Third Division) (1903-1991); Petitions 420-A630, 1930-1938, File: 418-A442, 1930-1931; Record Group 21; National Archives - Pacific Alaska Region, Anchorage, AK

12 Fifteenth Census of the United States, U.S. Dept. of Commerce, Bureau of Census, 1930.

13 Tolman, Game Warden, letter to Shorthill, Sec. to the Gov., Sept. 13, 1912, G.C.G., Archives, UAA.

Chapter 8 - 1923

1 Fifteenth Census of the United States, U.S. Dept. of Commerce, Bureau of Census, 1930.

2 "Shipment of Furs Reported from Alaska - from December 1, 1922 to November 30, 1923, USDA, Bureau of Biological Survey, G.C.G., Archives, UAA.

3 Culver, Walter G., "Report of Moose on Kenai Peninsula, February and March, 1923" and "Miscellaneous Observations, Kenai Peninsula and Vicinity, February 22 - March 15, 1923".

4 Fishery & Fur Seal Report for Fiscal Year 1923, Bureau of Fisheries, Alaska, U.S. Dept. of Commerce, National Marine Fisheries Annual Reports 1925-1966, Record Group 370, National Archives - Pacific Alaska Region, Anchorage, AK.

5 Cotter, George, game warden report to Governor, Oct. 1, 1923, G.C.G., Archives, UAA.

6 Cotter, George, game warden report to Governor, Jan. 1, 1924, G.C.G., Archives, UAA.

7 Barry, Mary J.P., *Seward, Alaska: A History. Vol. III: 1924 to 1994*, (Anchorage: M.J.P. Barry, 1995) 120.

Chapter 9 - 1924

1 Jackinsky, Ed, personal communication May 31, 2002.

2 Näs, Lars, personal communication, March 29, 2002.

3 "Report From Kenai", *Alaskan Prospector,* March 19, 1903: 5.

4 Shadura, Zeke, personal communication, August 15, 2002.

5 Bureau of Fisheries Report for 1930, Cook Inlet District: 8, Fish & Wildlife Service Annual Reports 1930 -1941, Soldotna Fish & Game Library.

6 Fifteenth Census of the United States, U.S. Dept. of Commerce, Bureau of Census, 1930.

Chapter 10 - 1925

1 Crocker, Betty, personal communication, Aug. 12, 2002.

2 Shipment of Furs Reported from Alaska — from December 1, 1924 to November 30, 1925. USDA, Bureau of Biological Survey, G.C.G., Archives, UAA.

3 Bureau of Fisheries Report for 1930, Cook Inlet District: 8, Fish & Wildlife Service Annual Reports 1930 -1941, Soldotna Fish & Game Library.

4 Naske, 1979: 123.

5 MacLean, Robert Merrill and Rossiter, Sean, *Flying Cold The Adventures of Russel Merrill, Pioneer Alaskan Aviator*, (Fairbanks: Epicenter Press, 1994) 33-38

6 Olthuis, Diane, "Seward," *Alaska's Kenai Peninsula, The Road We've Traveled* (Hope, AK: Kenai Peninsula Historical Association, 2002) 30.

7 "Proposed Kenai Peninsula Road Connecting Westward Districts With Seward, Tremendous Asset", *Seward Phoenix Log* Prosperity Edition, Dec 5, 1925: 22.

Chapter 11 - 1926

1 "Furs Shipped From Alaska During the Year 1926," Compiled by the Alaska Game Commission, USDA, Bureau of Biological Survey,G.C.G., Archives, UAA.

2 "Birchwood Camp To Be Improved For Next Season," *Anchorage Daily Times (ADT)*, Sept. 28, 1926.

3 "Hunters Pleased With Experience Gained On Trip," *ADT*, Sept. 24, 1926.

4 "Hunters Pleased With Experience Gained On Trip," *ADT*, Sept. 24, 1926.

5 "Another Party on Way to Make Big Game Hunt," *ADT*, Sept. 3, 1926.

6 "Birchwood Camp To Be Improved For Next Season," *ADT*, Sept. 28, 1926   "Birchwood Camp To Be Improved," *ADT*, Oct. 25, 1926.

7 Eastman,Thomas, "Alaska Hunt," *Outdoor Life*, November, 1928: 30

Chapter 12 -1927

1 "Furs Shipped From Alaska During the Year 1927," Compiled by the Alaska Game Commission, USDA, Bureau of Biological Survey,G.C.G., Archives, UAA.

2 Letter to H.W. Terhune, Exec. Officer, AK Game Commission, July 7, 1927, G.C.G., Archives, UAA.

3 "Fawcett and Heilner Coin New Name for Subsidiary Company," *Seward Daily Gateway*, Sept. 24, 1927.

4 Thirteenth Census of the United States, U.S. Dept. of Commerce, Bureau of Census, 1910.

Chapter 13 -1928

1 Ramsell, Ann, "History of Fox Farming in Kasilof Area," paper submitted to Kenai Peninsula Historical Assoc. Oct. 6, 1979.

2 "New Yorkers To Start Fur Farm On Large Scale," *ADT*, July 16, 1928.

3 Pollard, George, personal communication, Aug. 2, 2002.

4 "Fox Farmers in Kasilof Section Install Storage," *ADT*, Sept. 15, 1928.

5 *"Al Hardy is Establishing Power Plant on Fox Farm,"* *ADT*, Sept. 15, 1928.

6 "Kasilof Boasts of Telephone System," *ADT*, Sept. 13, 1928.

7 "Sportsman Author Seeking Moose On Kenai Peninsula," *ADT*, Sept. 17, 1928.

8 "Guides Here To Make Plans For Hunting Season," *ADT*, July 23, 1928.

9 Barry, 1995: 97.

10 Springer, Susan W., *Seldovia, Alaska,* (Littleton, CO: Blue Willow, 1997) 118.

11 Fifteenth Census of the United States, U.S. Dept. of Commerce, Bureau of Census, 1930.

12 Crocker, Betty, personal communication, Aug. 12, 2002.

Chapter 14 - 1929

1 "Furs Shipped From Alaska During the Year 1929," Compiled by the Alaska Game Commission, USDA, Bureau of Biological Survey, G.C.G., Archives, UAA.

2 Boraas, Alan, "Cannery Row on Cook Inlet," *Peninsula Clarion*, May 8, 1987.

3 "Fishery & Fur Seal Report for Fiscal Year 1930: 224, Bureau of Fisheries, Alaska, U.S. Dept. of Commerce, National Marine Fisheries Annual Reports 1925- 1966, National Archives Building, Anchorage, AK.

4 Jackinsky, Ed, personal interview May 31, 2002.
5 "Fishery & Fur Seal Report for Fiscal Year 1930: 272, Bureau of Fisheries, Alaska, U.S. Dept. of Commerce, National Marine Fisheries Annual Reports 1925- 1966, Record Group 370, National Archives - Pacific Alaska Region, Anchorage, AK.
6 Barry, 1995: 37.
7 MacLean, Robert Merrill and Rossiter, Sean, *Flying Cold The Adventures of Russel Merrill, Pioneer Alaskan Aviator*, (   ) 163.
8 Kenai Historical Society, 1985: 272.
9 "Waco Doctor Has Enjoyable Outing Big Game Region," *ADT*, Oct. 12, 1929.
10 "Kenai Peninsula Game Increasing; Hunting Popular," *ADT*, Oct. 10, 1929.
11 "Discoverer Sails For Inlet Points Goes On To Seward," *ADT*, Oct. 15, 1929.
12 Barry, 1995: 97-98.

Chapter 15 - 1930

1 Fifteenth Census of the United States, U.S. Dept. of Commerce, Bureau of Census, 1930.
   "Chronological History of Salmon Canneries in Central Alaska," compiled by Lewis G. MacDonald, 1951 Annual Report: 71, Alaska Fisheries Board and Alaska Department of Fisheries Report No. 3, Juneau, AK.
2 Nylander, Jonas Alexander, Naturalization Records of the U.S. District Court for the District, Territory and State of Alaska (Third Division) (1903-1991); Petitions 420-A630, 1930-1938, File: 418-A442, 1930-1931; Record Group 21; National Archives - Pacific Alaska Region, Anchorage, AK.
3 Bureau of Fisheries Annual Report 1930, Cook Inlet District: 2, Fish and Wildlife Service Annual Reports, Cook Inlet District, 1930 -1941, Alaska Department of Fish and Game Library, Soldotna, Alaska.
4 Fifteenth Census of the United States, U.S. Dept. of Commerce, Bureau of Census, 1930.
5 "New Road will Benefit Farms in Inlet Area," *ADT*, Sept. 6, 1930.
6 Bureau of Fisheries Annual Report 1930, Cook Inlet District: 8, Fish and Wildlife Service Annual Reports, Cook Inlet District, 1930 -1941, Alaska Department of Fish and Game Library, Soldotna, Alaska.
7 Gray, Prentiss, *From the Peace to the Fraser*, (Missoula, MT: Boone & Crockett Club, 1994) 333-359.
8 Kenai Historical Society, 1985: 436-444
9 Secora, Ella Hermansen, personal communication, Feb. 14, 2003.
10 Swan, Clare, personal communication, Aug. 3, 1996.
11 "Bones of Alaskan Indians Arrive at Seattle on Tupper," *ADT*, Sept. 8, 1930.
12 De Laguna, Frederica, *The Archaeology of Cook Inlet, Alaska*, 2nd ed. (Anchorage: Alaska Historical Society, 1975) 133.
13 "Body is Found Held by Snags Near Accident," *ADT*, Sept. 9, 1930.
14 "New Road Will Benefit Farms in Inlet Area," *ADT*, Sept. 6, 1930.
15 Pollard, George, personal communication, Aug. 28, 2002.
16 "Alaska Guides are Expanding Hunting Area," *ADT*, Sept. 18, 1930.
   "Bob Bragaw Tells Gateway of Alaska Guides Activity," Nov. 14, 1930.
17 Fifteenth Census of the United States, U.S. Dept. of Commerce, Bureau of Census, 1930.
18 Ramsell, Archie, personal communication, June 16, 1994.
19 Secora, Ella Hermansen, personal communication, Feb. 14, 2003.

Chapter 16 - 1931

1 Bureau of Fisheries Annual Report 1931, Cook Inlet District: 8, Fish and Wildlife Service Annual Reports, Cook Inlet District, 1930 -1941, Alaska Department of Fish and Game Library, Soldotna, Alaska.
2 Bureau of Fisheries Annual Report 1931, Cook Inlet District: 9.
3 Pollard, George, personal communication, Aug. 28, 2002.
4 "Fishery & Fur Seal Report for Fiscal Year 1931: 7, Bureau of Fisheries, Alaska, U.S. Dept. of Commerce, National Marine Fisheries Annual Reports 1925- 1966, Record Group 370, National Archives - Pacific Alaska Region, Anchorage, AK.
5 "Plane Carries Anchorage Aid To Sick Guide", *ADT*, Sept. 4, 1931.
   "Dorbandt Back With Sick Man; Condition Bad," *ADT*, Sept. 5, 1931.
6 "Berger Erecting Fine Dock At Kasilof", *ADT*, Sept. 21, 1931.
7 "Sir John Gets Camera Record Big Game Hunt," *ADT*, Oct. 13, 1931.
8 "Buckingham Has Busy Summer In Big Game Areas," *ADT*, Oct. 12, 1931.
9 Naske, 1979: 124.
10 Frostad, Erling and Frostad, Ole, Naturalization Records of the U.S. District Court for the District, Territory and State of Alaska (Third Division) (1903-1991); Petitions 420-A630, 1930-1938, File: 418-A442, 1930-1931; Record Group 21; National Archives - Pacific Alaska Region, Anchorage, AK.

Chapter 17 - 1932

1 Naske, 1979: 124.
2 Naske, 1979: 124-126.
3 Kenai Historical Society, 1985: 177.
4 Fishery & Fur Seal Report for Fiscal Years 1929-1932, Bureau of Fisheries, Alaska, U.S. Dept. of Commerce, National Marine Fisheries Annual Reports 1925-1966, Record Group 370, National Archives - Pacific Alaska Region, Anchorage, AK.
5 "Chronological History of Salmon Canneries in Central Alaska," compiled by Lewis G. MacDonald, 1951 Annual Report: 71-77, Alaska Fisheries Board and Alaska Department of Fisheries Report No. 3, Juneau, AK.
6 Bureau of Fisheries Annual Report 1932, Cook Inlet District: 8, Fish and Wildlife Service Annual Reports, Cook Inlet District, 1930 -1941, Alaska Department of Fish and Game Library, Soldotna, Alaska.
7 Kenai Historical Society, 1985: 216.
8 Kenai Historical Society, 1985: 216.
9 Cannon, John, Naturalization Records of the U.S. District Court for the District, Territory and State of Alaska (Third Division) (1903-1991); Petitions 420-A630, 1930-1938, File: 418-A442, 1930-1931; Record Group 21; National Archives - . Pacific Alaska Region, Anchorage, AK.
10 "Berger Plans Put New Ship On Inlet Run," *ADT*, Dec. 12, 1932.

Chapter 18 - 1933

1 "Tells Of Forest Work Under Way In Kenai Area," *ADT*, July 5, 1933.
2 Rakestraw, Lawrence W., *A History of the United States Forest Service in Alaska*, (Anchorage, 1981) 95.
3 Barry, 1995: 98.
4 Naske, 1979: 127.
5 "Great Trip In Wilds By Party From Anchorage," *ADT*, Oct. 3, 1933.

Chapter 19 - 1934

1 "Noted Sourdough Cook Inlet Area Is Visiting City," *ADT*, May 18, 1934.
2 Records of Office of United States Commissioner and Ex-officio Recorder at Valdez Alaska. Book 3, 1922-1952. Book 11 R: 382.
3 "Ninilchik Works Out Detail Plan For New Scheme," *ADT*, Feb. 13, 1934.
4 "Latest News Of Ninilchik," *ADT*, April 23, 1934.
5 "Ninilchik Organizes For Experiment In Local Living Plan," *ADT*, Jan. 3, 1934.
6 "Ninilchik Musher Rescued On Trail - Beginning Freeze," *ADT*, Feb. 10, 1934.
7 "Ninilchik Organizes For Experiment In Local Living Plan," *ADT*, Jan. 3, 1934.
8 "Ninilchik Musher Rescued On Trail - Beginning Freeze," *ADT*, Feb. 10, 1934.
9 "Latest News Of Ninilchik," *ADT*, April 23, 1934.
10 "Fishermen of Kenai, Homer And Seldovia Are Forming Unions," *ADT*, Feb. 26, 1934.
11 "Ninilchik Organizes For Experiment In Local Living Plan," *ADT*, Jan. 3, 1934.
12 "Furs Shipped From Alaska During the Year 1934," Compiled by the Alaska Game Commission, USDA, Bureau of Biological Survey, G.C.G., Archives, UAA.
13 Jensen, Christian, Naturalization Records of the U.S. District Court for the District, Territory and State of Alaska (Third Division) (1903-1991); Petitions 420-A630, 1930-1938, File: 418-A442, 1930-1931; Record Group 21; National Archives - Pacific Alaska Region, Anchorage, AK.
14 "Coyotes Get Mountain Sheep Kenai Peninsula," *ADT*, November 8, 1934

Chapter 20 - 1935

1 Cook Inlet Recording District, Third Division, Alaska, Book 3, 1922-1952, Book 11 R: 355 and Book 12 R: 66, Seward Recording Office, Seward, AK.
2 Barry, 1995: 98.
3 "Colony Well Stocked For Winter," *ADT*, Nov. 27, 1935.

Chapter 21 - 1936

1 Bureau of Fisheries Annual Report for 1936, Cook Inlet District: 14, Fish and Wildlife Service Annual Reports, Cook Inlet District, 1930 -1941, Alaska Department of Fish and Game Library, Soldotna, Alaska.
2 "Three Sportsmen Leave For Tustumena Lake on Big Game Hunt," *ADT*, Aug. 28, 1936.
3 "Plane Takes Turkeys To Fairbanks," *ADT*, Nov. 25, 1936.
4 "Berger Offers Ship, Crew To Aid Emergency," *ADT*, Nov. 27, 1936.
5 Barry, 1998: 98.

Chapter 22 - 1937

1 "Homestead And Timber Tracts Taken," *ADT*, April 27, 1937.
2 "Alaska CCC Is Doubled This Year," *ADT*, April 28, 1937.
3 "Fishermen To Get Higher Pay For Salmon," *ADT*, April 28, 1937.
4 Lahnt, Joan McLane, personal communication, March 20, 1998.
5 "Hunter-Scientist Will Tell Of Alaska Game Before Famous International Sportsmen Group," *ADT*, Aug. 24, 1937.
6 "Hunter-Scientist Will Tell Of Alaska Game Before Famous International Sportsmen Group," *ADT*, Aug. 24, 1937.

Chapter 23 - 1938-1939

1 Palmer, L.J., "Management of Moose Herd on Kenai Peninsula, Alaska," June 1, 1938: 1-2, Report, Kenai National Wildlife Refuge Headquarters Library.
2 Palmer, 1938: 5-6.
3 Palmer, L.J., 1938: 30.
4 Palmer, L.J., 1938: 36.
5 Fishery & Fur Seal Report for Fiscal Year 1938, Bureau of Fisheries, Alaska, U.S. Dept. of Commerce, National Marine Fisheries Annual Reports 1925-1966, Record Group 370, National Archives - Pacific Alaska Region, Anchorage, AK.

Chapter 24 - Afterword

1 Palmer, L.J., "Kenai Peninsula Moose, Alaska", Research Project Report, May, June, July, 1939: 30, Kenai National Wildlife Refuge Headquarters Library.
2 Palmer, 1939: 31.
3 Naske, 1979: 126.
4 Kenai Historical Society, 1985: 216.
5 Pollard, George, personal communication, Aug. 28, 2002.
6 Ramsell, Archie, personal communication, June 16, 1994.
7 Pollard, 2002
8 Naske, 1979: 133.
9 Naske, 1979: 133.

Indian Creek. Photo by Gary Titus

Bathing in Tustumena. Photo courtesy of McLane Collection.

AUTHORS

Catherine Cassidy moved to Alaska from the east coast in 1987. For many years she worked at a fishing dock on the site of the first salmon cannery on the Kasilof River. Her experience of unloading fishing boats in that place, working around the same immutable forces of tide, weather and wild salmon runs which existed a hundred years earlier, forged her interest in the Kenai Peninsula's history. This connection to the past was strengthened when she and her husband purchased and began renovating Tom Odale's old hunting lodge on Tustumena Lake where Andrew Berg was a frequent visitor. Catherine teamed up with Gary to transform piles of sources into a book. She has previously written about the environment and commercial fishing.

Catherine and her husband, Erik Huebsch, on the front porch of Tom Odale's lodge on Tustumena Lake.

Gary Titus is a ranger and historian for the Kenai National Wildlife Refuge. Driven by curiosity about the big game hunting era of the Kenai Peninsula, over the last twenty years he accumulated most of the sources used in this book. He also spent countless hours painstakingly transcribing Andrew Berg's journal. Gary's interest goes well beyond locating paper documents. He has retraced the steps of the old-timers and searched out the remains of many of their hunting and trapping cabins. Gary enjoys restoring and building cabins as well as finding them. In his job he directs the restoration of historic cabins within the Wildlife Refuge, including Andrew Berg's cabins. In addition, he has built his dream cabin in a remote location on the Alaska Peninsula (see this at www.windsongwildernessretreat.com). Gary recently joined the exclusive club of those who have been chewed on by a grizzly bear. He has since recovered sufficiently to resume hiking, happily, in bear country.

Gary enjoying a hike in the upper reaches of the Kenai Mountains.